W9-DEV-814

INTERPRETING
CANADA'S PAST

INTERPRETING CANADA'S PAST

ℰ A PRE-CONFEDERATION READER

FOURTH EDITION

Edited by:
J.M. Bumsted, Len Kuffert, and Michel Ducharme

OXFORD

UNIVERSITY PRESS

OXFORD
UNIVERSITY PRESS

8 Sampson Mews, Suite 204, Don Mills, Ontario M3C 0H5
www.oupcanada.com

Oxford University Press is a department of the University of Oxford.
It furthers the University's objective of excellence in research, scholarship,
and education by publishing worldwide in

Oxford   New York

Auckland   Cape Town   Dar es Salaam   Hong Kong   Karachi
Kuala Lumpur   Madrid   Melbourne   Mexico City   Nairobi
New Delhi   Shanghai   Taipei   Toronto

With offices in

Argentina   Austria   Brazil   Chile   Czech Republic   France   Greece
Guatemala   Hungary   Italy   Japan   Poland   Portugal   Singapore
South Korea   Switzerland   Thailand   Turkey   Ukraine   Vietnam

Oxford is a trade mark of Oxford University Press
in the UK and in certain other countries

Published in Canada
by Oxford University Press

Copyright © Oxford University Press Canada 2011

The moral rights of the author have been asserted

Database right Oxford University Press (maker)

First Published 2011

All rights reserved. No part of this publication may be reproduced,
stored in a retrieval system, or transmitted, in any form or by any means,
without the prior permission in writing of Oxford University Press,
or as expressly permitted by law, or under terms agreed with the appropriate
reprographics rights organization. Enquiries concerning reproduction
outside the scope of the above should be sent to the Permissions Department
at the address above or through the following url:
www.oupcanada.com/permission/permission_request.php

You must not circulate this book in any other binding or cover
and you must impose this same condition on any acquirer.

Every effort has been made to determine and contact copyright holders. In the case of any
omissions, the publisher will be pleased to make suitable acknowledgement in future editions.

Previous editions copyright © 1986, 1993, 2004 Oxford University Press Canada

Library and Archives Canada Cataloguing in Publication
Interpreting Canada's past / edited by J.M. Bumsted, Len Kuffert and Michel Ducharme. — 4th ed.

Includes bibliographical references.

Contents: [v. 1]. A pre-Confederation reader.

ISBN 978-0-19-542779-0 (v. 1)

1. Canada—History—Textbooks. 2. Canada—History—Sources.

I. Bumsted, J. M., 1938– II. Kuffert, L. B. (Leonard B.) III. Ducharme, Michel, 1975–

FC170.I57 2011   971   C2011-900505-0

Cover image: © The Trustees of the British Museum

Oxford University Press is committed to our environment. This book is printed on permanent (acid-free) paper ∞.

Printed and bound in Canada

1 2 3 4 — 14 13 12 11

Contents

Preface   xi

One | Origins   1

Introduction   1

PRIMARY DOCUMENTS

1   'Where the First People Came From', in *Cree Legends from the West Coast of James Bay*   3

2   From *Historia Natural y Moral de las Indias*
      JOSÉ DE ACOSTA   5

HISTORICAL INTERPRETATIONS

3   From 'The First Colonization of North America'
      E. JAMES DIXON   6

4   From 'What Do You Do When No One's Been There Before?'
      DAVID J. MELTZER   21

Two | Missionaries and First Nations   35

Introduction   35

PRIMARY DOCUMENTS

1   From *Word from New France: The Selected Letters of Marie de l'Incarnation*
      JOYCE MARSHALL   37

2   From *The Jesuit Relations and Allied Documents: Travels and Explorations of the Jesuit Missionaries in New France, 1610–1791*
      REUBEN GOLD THWAITES   40

HISTORICAL INTERPRETATIONS

3   From *Harvest of Souls: The Jesuit Missions and Colonialism in North America, 1632–1650*
      CAROLE BLACKBURN   44

4   From *Bitter Feast: Amerindians and Europeans in Northeastern North America, 1600–1664*
      DENYS DELÂGE   55

Three | Seigneurial Regime in New France   65

Introduction   65

PRIMARY DOCUMENTS

1   From *Edicts, Ordinances, Declarations and Decrees relative to the Seignorial Tenure*   67

2   From *Travels into North America: Containing Its Natural History and a Circumstantial Account of Its Plantations and Agriculture in General . . .*
      PETER KALM   68

HISTORICAL INTERPRETATIONS

3   From 'Seigneurial Landscapes', in *The Metamorphoses of Landscape and Community in Early Quebec*
      COLIN M. COATES   70

4   From 'The Feudal Burden', in *Peasant, Lord & Merchant: Rural Society in Three Quebec Parishes 1740–1840*
      ALLAN GREER   84

Four | Expulsion of the Acadians   97

Introduction   97

PRIMARY DOCUMENTS

1   From 1755 Council Minutes, in *Acadia and Nova Scotia: Documents Relating to the Acadian French and the First British Colonization of the Province, 1714–1758*
      THOMAS B. AKINS   99

2   From 'Extracts from Col. John Winslow's Journal' in *Report Concerning Canadian Archives for the Year 1905*   105

HISTORICAL INTERPRETATIONS

3   From 'Ile Royale, New England, Scotland, and Nova Scotia, 1744–1748', in *An Unsettled Conquest: The British Campaign Against the Peoples of Acadia*
      GEOFFREY PLANK   106

4   From 'The Decision to Deport', in *From Migrant to Acadian: A North American Border People, 1604–1755*
      N.E.S. GRIFFITHS   118

Five | Representing Acadia and Canada   134

Introduction   134

PRIMARY DOCUMENTS

1   *The Death of General Wolfe, 1770*
      BENJAMIN WEST   136

2   *The Death of Montcalm, 1783*
      FRANÇOIS-LOUIS-JOSEPH WATTEAU   137

3   *The Death of the Marquis de Montcalm, 1783*
      JUSTE CHEVILLET   138

4   *Sketches for the Death of Montcalm, 1902*
      MARC-AURÈLE DE FOY SUZOR-COTÉ   139

5   *A View of the Launching Place Above the Town of Quebec, 1763*
      FRANCIS SWAINE   140

HISTORICAL INTERPRETATIONS

6   'An Empire on Paper: The Founding of Halifax and Conceptions of Imperial Space, 1744–55'
      JEFFERS LENNOX   141

7   '"Taken on the Spot": The Visual Appropriation of New France for the Global British Landscape'
    JOHN E. CROWLEY   162

Six | Loyalists 178

Introduction   178

PRIMARY DOCUMENTS

1   From 'The Diary of Sarah Frost, 1783', in *Kingston and the Loyalists of the 'Spring Fleet' of 1783*
    WALTER BATES   180

2   'The Petition of 55 Loyalists', 22 July 1783 and 'A Memorial of Samuel Hakes and 600 Others', 15 August 1783 in *Vindication of Governor Parr and his Council*   182

HISTORICAL INTERPRETATIONS

3   From 'Patriarchy and Paternalism: The Case of the Eastern Ontario Loyalist Women'
    JANICE POTTER   184

4   From 'An Ancestry of which Any People Might Be Proud: Official History, the Vernacular Past, and the Shaping of the Loyalist Tradition at Mid-Century', in *Inventing the Loyalists: The Ontario Loyalist Tradition and the Creation of Usable Pasts*
    NORMAN KNOWLES   198

Seven | The Fur Trade in the Northwest 212

Introduction   212

PRIMARY DOCUMENTS

1   From *The English River Book: A North West Company Journal and Account Book of 1786*
    HARRY W. DUCKWORTH   214

2   From *A Sketch of the British Fur Trade* (1815)
    LORD SELKIRK   216

HISTORICAL INTERPRETATIONS

3   From *'Many Tender Ties': Women in Fur Trade Society in Western Canada, 1670–1870*
    SYLVIA VAN KIRK   222

4   From *Making the Voyageur World: Travelers and Traders in the North American Fur Trade*
    CAROLYN PODRUCHNY   227

Eight | Immigration in the Early Nineteenth Century 243

Introduction   243

PRIMARY DOCUMENTS

1   From 'Testimony of Alexander Buchanan', *Third Report of the Select Committee on Emigration from the United Kingdom*   245

2   From *Statistical Sketches of Upper Canada, for the Use of Emigrants: by a Backwoodsman*
    WILLIAM DUNLOP   250

HISTORICAL INTERPRETATIONS

3   From 'Transatlantic Webs of Kin and Community', in *Emigrant Worlds and Transatlantic
    Communities: Migration to Upper Canada in the First Half of the Nineteenth Century*
    ELIZABETH JANE ERRINGTON   252

4   From 'Irish Immigration and Settlement in a Catholic City: Quebec, 1842–61'
    ROBERT J. GRACE   267

Nine | Rebellions in Lower Canada   281

Introduction   281

PRIMARY DOCUMENTS

1   From Ninety-Two Resolutions, in *Journals of the House of Assembly of Lower Canada*, 4th
    session of the 14th Provincial Parliament (January 7–March 18, 1834)   283

2   From Lord Durham to Lord Glenelg, 9 August 1838, in *The Report and Despatches of the
    Earl of Durham Her Majesty's High Commissioner and Governor-General of British
    North America*   286

HISTORICAL INTERPRETATIONS

3   From 'The Failure of the Insurrectionary Movement, 1837–1839', in *Economic and Social
    History of Quebec, 1760–1850: Structures and Conjunctures*
    FERNAND OUELLET   288

4   From *The Patriots and the People: The Rebellion of 1837 in Rural Lower Canada*
    ALLAN GREER   303

Ten | Women in British North America   314

Introduction   314

PRIMARY DOCUMENTS

1   'To the Electors of Quebec County', *Le Canadien,* 21 May 1808   316

2   From *The Proper Sphere and Influence of Woman in Christian Society: Being a Lecture
    Delivered by Rev. Robert Sedgewick before the Young Men's Christian Association,
    Halifax, N.S., November 1856*
    ROBERT SEDGEWICK   317

HISTORICAL INTERPRETATIONS

3   From 'The Riddle of Peggy Mountain: Regulation of Irish Women's Sexuality on the Southern
    Avalon, 1750–1860'
    WILLEEN KEOUGH   321

4   From 'Disenfranchised but Not Quiescent: Women Petitioners in New Brunswick in the Mid-
    19th Century'
    GAIL CAMPBELL   333

Eleven | Aboriginal People in British North America   346

Introduction   346

PRIMARY DOCUMENTS

1   From 'Report on the Affairs of the Indians in Canada', (1842–44) in *Appendix to the Fourth Volume of the Journals of the Legislative Assembly of the Province of Canada 1844–45*   348

2   'The Robinson-Superior Treaty', in *The Treaties of Canada with the Indians of Manitoba and the North-West Territories, Including the Negotiations on which They Were Based, and Other Information Relating Thereto*
    ALEXANDER MORRIS   351

HISTORICAL INTERPRETATIONS

3   From 'Empire, the Maritime Colonies, and the Supplanting of Mi'kma'ki/Wulstukwik, 1780–1820'
    JOHN G. REID   353

4   From 'Seeking Honest Justice in a Land of Strangers: Nahnebahwequa's Struggle for Land'
    CELIA HAIG-BROWN   368

Twelve | 'Rushing' the Empire Westward   385

Introduction   385

PRIMARY DOCUMENTS

1   'Letter of Charles Major, 20 September 1859', in *Daily Globe*, Toronto, 2 January 1860   387

2   From *Journals, Detailed Reports and Observations Relative to the Exploration, by Captain Palliser*
    JOHN PALLISER   389

HISTORICAL INTERPRETATIONS

3   From '"A Delicate Game": The Meaning of Law on Grouse Creek'
    TINA LOO   390

4   From 'Mapping the New El Dorado: The Fraser River Gold Rush and the Appropriation of Native Space'
    DANIEL MARSHALL   406

Thirteen | Métis   422

Introduction   422

PRIMARY DOCUMENTS

1   'La chanson de la grenouillère' (1816) in *Textes poétiques du Canada français*
    PIERRE FALCON   424

2   From J. Halkett to Earl Bathurst, 3 June 1818, in *Correspondence in the Years 1817, 1818, and 1819, between Earl Bathurst and J. Halkett, Esq. on the Subject of Lord Selkirk's Settlement at the Red River, in North America*   426

HISTORICAL INTERPRETATIONS

3   From *The Ermatingers: A 19th Century Ojibwa-Canadian Family*
     W. BRIAN STEWART   428

4   From 'Prologue to the Red River Resistance: Pre-liminal Politics and the Triumph of Riel'
     GERHARD ENS   435

Fourteen | Confederation and Anti-Confederation   445

Introduction   445

PRIMARY DOCUMENTS

1   From a speech by Joseph Howe at Dartmouth, Nova Scotia, 22 May 1867   447

2   From *Parliamentary Debates on the Subject of the Confederation of the British North American Provinces*
     A.A. DORION   449

HISTORICAL INTERPRETATIONS

3   From 'The Case Against Canadian Confederation', in *The Causes of Confederation*
     GED MARTIN   455

4   From 'Who's Afraid of the Fenians? The Fenian Scare on Prince Edward Island, 1865–1867'
     EDWARD MACDONALD   468

Permission Credits   485

Preface

As with the Third Edition of *Interpreting Canada's Past*, it remains our intention to provide students of Canadian history with a collection of primary and secondary sources, a collection that represents the material historians use daily. Paying attention to current scholarship is essential, and bearing in mind the not-so-current interpretations of a particular theme is likewise part of the historian's job. The privilege of setting aside the work of historians and encountering voices from the eras we are studying is another perk not usually available to students in lecture courses. We wanted once again to give those using the readers an opportunity to see how our understanding of the past is built upon evidence, carefully sifted and handled, and how sometimes these bits of evidence can lead historians to offer conclusions that prompt still more questions.

Accordingly, even though the volumes have been streamlined considerably based on student and instructor feedback, the emphasis is again on interpretation. The primary documents have been chosen so that students will take those first steps toward generating the kind of questions that are useful even outside the discipline of history: What does this document mean? Why did its creator want to express the ideas it contains? How reliable is it? What does it tell us about change? The secondary source selections have been simplified in this edition, with the assumption that students can dig deeper into each article or excerpt, dealing with less in terms of who-did-what-when, but discovering more in terms of connections with the primary sources and the overall theme of each section. On the basis of user comments and classroom experience, we have retained some of the more popular selections and added more that are entirely new, also altering our lists of topics.

We thank the staff at Oxford, and Jack Bumsted, for his vision for the readers and commitment through three editions.

Michel Ducharme, University of British Columbia
Len Kuffert, University of Manitoba

Chapter One

Origins

READINGS

Primary Documents

1   'Where the First People Came From', in *Cree Legends from the West Coast of James Bay*

2   From *Historia Natural y Moral de las Indias*, José de Acosta

Historical Interpretations

3   From E. James Dixon, 'The First Colonization of North America', in *Bones, Boats, and Bison: Archeology and the First Colonization of Western North America* (Albuquerque: The University of New Mexico Press, 1999), 19-43.

4   From David J. Meltzer, 'What Do You Do When No One's Been There Before?' in *First Peoples in a New World: Colonizing Ice Age America* (Berkeley: University of California Press, 2009), 209-38.

Introduction

It is safe, but not entirely satisfying, to say that before Aboriginal peoples and Europeans met, traded, fought, made peace, co-operated, intermarried, and lived the colonial dream/nightmare, First Nations had occupied vast areas in the Americas for thousands of years. Knowing how Aboriginal people lived before contact with newcomers and how long they lived that way, as well as trying to reconstruct and understand their daily routines and perhaps even their beliefs, using the often faint traces of their settlements and travels, are desirable goals. For the purposes of our look into the history of what is now called Canada, understanding contact and the period afterward requires an acknowledgement that the two sets of people in each contact zone viewed the world and approached knowledge in different ways.

One way to appreciate this is to look at accounts of origin. Whether they emerge from Aboriginal or European traditions, these stories were important enough to both groups to be preserved. The primary sources here consist of a Cree explanation for the presence of first peoples in the Americas, and an early European attempt to explain the same reality. The Cree narrative, like the biblical story of Adam and Eve, suggests a world with few people in it—a world in which people could communicate with powerful beings who directed or advised them, and who could help them find different places to live. Although this story might seem rather mystical to readers operating in the Western intellectual tradition, it does what it needs to do: it accounts for the peopling of North America. It also suggests that after this rather dramatic installation on the continent, the first people there had to contend with the problem of surviving, just like those who heard the story and passed it on through the generations. The European account, from a Spanish clergyman called José de Acosta, reflects the assumptions of his background. Within a framework that placed Christian belief above other sorts and privileged evidence known to European scholars at the time, Acosta pieced together his own story. Its translation by London's Hakluyt Society, one of the foremost chroniclers of Christian nations' encounters with exotic places, gave it more weight. Aboriginal peoples emerge in his account as a group reacting to environmental pressures and opportunities, more instinctive than rational.

Neither origin story holds the key to understanding how or why a great variety of First Nations came to be where they were when, via contact events spread widely in time and location, everything changed. At first glance, the secondary material for this topic looks to answer the same questions that the primary sources do: How did humans get to the Americas? How did they live? The answers provided, however, differ from both the Cree narrative and Acosta's account. James Dixon's explanation considers the sum of the movements that brought people to the continents to be 'colonization', interpreting that term (more broadly than historians usually do) to include migrations of occupation that happened over several hundred years—migrations that would lead eventually to a stage called 'settlement'. Climate and resources determined migrants' ability to survive and form communities that could leave behind traces for archaeologists to find. Dixon does not (probably wisely) leave much room for Aboriginal people to do anything more than seek resources or flee unsuitable circumstances. Writing ten years later, David Meltzer extends this idea of colonization to include the act of gaining knowledge about the environment, seasonal patterns, food, and so on, in local areas and over wider regions of the continent.

Thanks to the secondary sources, we see that we cannot be absolutely sure how First Nations came to occupy the continent because we should not assume that their arrival and occupation happened according to any sort of orderly pattern. The ideas of waves of settlement or of one point of entry (the 'land bridge') are convenient, but, like most historical theories, they obscure a past marked by an increasing diversity. The variety of First Nations that made and maintained contact with Europeans from the late fifteenth century onward was matched by the variety of methods and motives that the Europeans brought with them.

QUESTIONS FOR CONSIDERATION

1. Does the Cree narrative portray the new place to live as a reward, a punishment, or neither? What leads you to this conclusion?
2. Acosta expresses disbelief that Aboriginal peoples came to be in the Americas on purpose or that they came by boat. What would prompt him to make these assumptions?
3. Which of the theories about migration to the Americas is the most plausible? Why?
4. Why is the question of how long Aboriginal peoples occupied the land before contact an important one for scholars and society at large?
5. Where does archaeology end and history begin?

SUGGESTIONS FOR FURTHER READING

Dewar, Elaine, Bones: Discovering the First Americans (Toronto: Random House Canada, 2001)

Dixon, E. James, Bones, Boats & Bison: Archaeology and the First Colonization of Western North America (Albuquerque: University of New Mexico Press, 1999)

Fagan, Brian M., *Ancient North America: The Archaeology of a Continent, 3rd ed.* (New York: Thames & Hudson, 2000)

Haynes, Gary, *The Early Settlement of North America: The Clovis Era* (Cambridge: Cambridge University Press, 2002)

Jablonski, Nina G., ed., *The First Americans: The Pleistocene Colonization of the New World* (San Francisco: California Academy of Sciences, Distributed by University of California Press, 2002)

Meltzer, David J., *First Peoples in a New World: Colonizing Ice Age America* (Berkeley: University of California Press, 2009)

PRIMARY DOCUMENTS

1   'Where the First People Came From', in C. Douglas Ellis, ed., *Cree Legends from the West Coast of James Bay* (Winnipeg: University of Manitoba Press, 1995), 2–5.

So then, I shall tell another legend. I'll tell a story, the legend about ourselves, the people, as we are called. Also I shall tell the legend about where we came from and why we came . . . why we who are living now came to inhabit this land.

Now then, first I shall begin.

The other land was above, it is said. It was like this land which we dwell in, except that the life seems different; also it is different on account of its being cold and mild [here]. So then, this land where we are invariably tends to be cold.

So that is the land above which is talked about from which there came two people, one woman and one man . . . they dwelt in that land which was above. But it was certainly known that this world where we live was there.

Now then at one time someone spoke to them, while they were in that land of theirs where they were brought up. He said to them, 'Do you want to go see yonder land which is below?'

The very one about which they were spoken to is this one where we dwell.

'Yes', they said, 'we will go there.'

'The land', they were told, 'is different, appears different from this one where we dwell in, which you dwell in now during your lifetime. But you will find it different there, should you go to see that land. It is cold yonder. And sometimes it is hot.'

'It fluctuates considerably. If you wish to go there, however, you must go see the spider at the end of this land where you are. That is where he lives.'

The spider, as he is called, that is the one who is the net-maker, who never exhausts his twine—so they went to see him, who is called the spider.

Then he asked them, 'Where do you want to go? Do you want to go and see yonder land, the other one which is below?'

'Yes', they said.

'Very well', said the spider. 'I shall make a line so that I may lower you.'

So then, he made a line up to—working it around up to, up to the top.

'Not yet, not yet even half done', he said.

Then he spoke to them, telling them, better for him to let them down even before he finished it the length it should be.

Then he told them, 'That land which you want to go and see is cold and sometimes mild. But there will certainly be someone there who will teach you, where you will find a living once you have reached it. He, he will tell you every thing so you will get along well.'

So he made a place for them to sit as he lowered them, the man and the woman.

They got in together, into that thing which looked like a bag.

Then he instructed them what to do during their trip. 'Only one must look', he said to them. 'But one must not look until you have made contact with the earth. You may both look then.'

So, meanwhile they went along, one looked. At last he caught sight of the land.

The one told the other, 'Now the land is in sight.'

The one told the other, 'Now the rivers are in sight.'

They had been told however, that 'if one . . . if they both look together, before they come to the land, they will go into the great eagle-nest and they will never be able to get out and climb down from there.'

That's where they will be. That's what they were told.

Then the one told the other, 'Now the lakes are in sight. Now the grass.'

Then they both looked before they arrived, as they were right at the top of the trees. Then they went sideways for a short while, then they went into the great eagle-nest. That's where they went in, having violated their instructions. . . .

Then the bear arrived.

So he said to them . . . and they said to him, 'Come and help us.'

The bear didn't listen for long; but then he started to get up on his hind legs to go and see them. Also another one, the wolverine as he is called. They made one trip each as they brought them down.

But the bear was followed by those people.

That was the very thing which had been said to them, 'You will have someone there who will teach you to survive.'

This bear, he taught them everything about how to keep alive there.

It was there that these people began to multiply from one couple, the persons who had come from another land. They lived giving birth to their children generation after generation. That is us right up until today. That is why we are in this country.

And by-and-by the White People began to arrive as they began to reach us people, who live in this country.

That is as much as I shall tell.

2   From José de Acosta, *Historia Natural y Moral de las Indias*, vol. 1 (London: The Hakluyt Society, 1880 [1590]), 45–80.

CHAP XVI—By what meanes the first men might come to the Indies, the which was not willingly, nor of set purpose

Now it is time to make answer to such as say there are no Antipodes, and that this region where we live cannot bee inhabited. The huge greatnes of the Ocean did so amaze St. Augustine as he could not conceive how mankind could passe to this new-found world. But seeing on the one side wee know for certaine that many yeares agoe there were men inhabiting in these parts, so likewise we cannot deny but the scripture doth teaching us cleerely that all men are come from the first man, without doubt we shall be forced to belieeve and confesse that men have passed hither from Europe, Asia, or Affricke, yet must wee discover by what meanes they could passe. It is not likely that there was another Noes Arke by the which men might be transported into the Indies, and much lesse any Angell to carie the first man to this new world, holding him by the haire of the head, like to the Prophet Abacus; for we intrest not of the mightie power of God, but only of that which is conformable unto reason, and the order and disposition of humane things. Wherefore these two things ought to be held for wonderfull and worthie of admiration, yea, to bee numbred among the secrets of god. The one is, how men could passe so huge a passage by Sea and Lande; the other is, that there beeing such multitudes of people they have yet beene unknowne so many ages. For this cause I demaund, by what resolution, force or industrie, the Indians could passe so large a Sea, and who might be the Investor of so strange a passage? Truely I have often times considered thereof with my selfe, as many others have done, but never could I finde any thing to satisfie mee. Yet will I say what I have conceived, and what comes presently into my minde, seeing that testimonies faile men whom I might follow, suffering myselfe to be guided by the rule of reason, although it be very subtill. It is most certaine that the first men came to this land of Peru by one of these two meanes, either by land or by sea. If they came by sea, it was casually, and by chance, or willingly, and of purpose. I understand by chance being cast by force of some storme or tempest, as it happens in tempestuous times. I meane done of purpose, when they prepared fleetes to discover new lands. Besides these two meanes I see it is not possible to find out any other, if wee will follow the course of humane things and not devise fabulous and poetical fictions; for no man may thinke to fine another Eagle as that of Ganimede, or a flying Horse like unto Perseus, that should carie the Indians through the aire; or that peradventure these first men have used fishes, as Mirmaids, or the fish called a Nicholas, to pass them thither. But laying aside these imaginations and fopperies, let us examine these two meanes, the which will bee both pleasant and profitable. First, in my judgement, it were not farre from reason to say that the first and auncient people of these Indies have discovered and peopled after the same sort as wee do at this day, that is, by the Arts of Navigation and aide of Pilots, the which guide themselves by the height and knowledge of the heavens, and by their industrie in handling and changing of their sailes according to the season. Why might not this well be? Must we belieeve that we alone, and in this our age, have onely the Arts and knowledge to saile through the Ocean? Wee see even now that they cut through the Ocean to discover new lands, as not long since Alvaro Mendaria and his companions did, who parting from the Port of Lima came alongst the West to discover the land which lieth Eastward from Peru; and at the end of three moneths they discovered the Ilands which they call the Ilands of Salomon, which are many and very great, and by all likelehood they lie adioyning to new Guinnie, or else are very neere to some other firme land. . . . Seeing it is thus, why may we not suppose that the Ancients had the courage and resolution to travell by sea, with the same intent to discover the land, which they call Antiethon, opposite to theirs, and that, according to the discourse of their Philosophie, it should be with an intent not to rest untill they came in view of the landes they sought? . . . But to say the truth, I am of a contrary opinion, neither can I perswade my selfe that the first Indians came to this new world of purpose, by a determined voiage, neither will I yeeld, that the Ancients had knowledge in the Art of Navigation. . . . I conclude then, that it is likely the first that came to the Indies was by shipwracks and tempest of wether, but heereupon groweth a difficultie which troubleth me much. For, suppose wee grant that the first men came from farr Countries, and that the nations which we now see are issued from them and multiplied, yet can I not coniecture by what meanes brute beastes, whereof there is great aboundance, could come there, not being likely they should have bin imbarked and carried by sea. . . . I coniecture then, by the discourse I have made, that the new world, which we call Indies, is not altogether severed and disioyned from the other world; and to speake my opinion, I have long beleeved that the one and the other world are ioyned and continued one with another in some part, or at least are very neere . . . And I beleeve it is not many thousand yeeres past since men first inhabited this new world and West Infies, and that the first men that entred, were rather savage men and hunters; then bredde up in civil and well governed Common-weales; and that they came to this new world, having lost their owne land, or being in too great numbers, they were forced of necessitie to seeke some other habitations. . . .

HISTORICAL INTERPRETATIONS

3   From E. James Dixon, 'The First Colonization of North America', in *Bones, Boats, and Bison: Archeology and the First Colonization of Western North America* (Albuquerque: The University of New Mexico Press, 1999), 19–43.

ORIGINS

The human colonization of the Americas was the final continental dispersal of the human species on earth. This epic in human history required specific types of adaptation to enable humans to move through the high-latitude environments of northeastern Asia into North America. Social and ecological factors were involved that influenced the character and timing of this great event.

Humans evolved in the Old World beginning in Africa, and subsequently colonized Asia and Europe. Many archeologists believe that the first humans to enter the Americas came from northeastern Asia about 12,000 years ago.

However, this is not the only possible time for humans to have reached the New World. Some archeologists (Carter 1952, 1957; Irving et al. 1986; Jopling et al. 1981; Simpson et al. 1986; and others) believe humans may have come to the Americas 150,000–200,000 years ago. Still others (Griffin 1979; Haynes 1969; Hrdlička 1928; and others) are of the opinion that humans first arrived in the Americas within the last 50,000 years or more likely within the last 14,000 years. At least one linguist (Nichols 1990) suggests that the Americas may have been inhabited possibly as early as 35,000 years ago.

[. . .]

THE BERING LAND BRIDGE

The concept of a land connection between Asia and North America is deeply rooted in American science. In 1589, Fray de Acosta (1604) first suggested a land connection as an explanation of how humans and some plants and animals may have first entered North America from Asia. He suggested that there was, or had been at some time in the past, a land bridge between Asia and North America in the high northern latitudes. The reason he held this premise was that he believed that the human species had originated in the Old World based on the teachings of the Bible. He fully accepted that all humans had descended from Adam and Eve and that they had been created in the Old World. He reasoned further that early humans and many of the animals found in the New World were not capable of crossing the vast expanses of oceans. Consequently, humans and some types of animals could have only reached the Americas via a land connection with the Old World. He lacked firm scientific evidence for his hypothesis and relied on the Judeo-Christian doctrine of his time as the foundation for this interpretation.

Although subsequent scientific discoveries have demonstrated that the human species did originate in the Old World and developed over a period of almost four million years, this evidence was not available to de Acosta. Since de Acosta's time, the concept of the Bering Land Bridge has been invoked repeatedly over hundreds of years to explain the human migration route to the Americas. It has become deeply imbedded in New World scholarship and has been bolstered by a vast amount of scientific research.

[. . .]

Direct evidence that proves the existence of the former land bridge has been discovered in recent years. The remains of extinct animals have been dredged from the ocean floor (Dixon 1983). In addition, ancient river channels that could only have formed by water flowing across the surface of the land have been documented on the sea floor (McManus et al. 1983). Cores taken from the sediments beneath the Bering and Chukchi Seas contain deposits, such as peat, that could only have been formed when the continental shelf was exposed as dry land (Elias et al. 1992; Hopkins 1967; McManus et al. 1983). Radiocarbon dating of beetles that had to have lived in a subaerial environment were recovered from sediment cores from the Bering Land Bridge. [. . .] Hopkins demonstrated that the land bridge was not flooded until sometime shortly after 10,000 years ago (Elias et al. 1996). [. . .]

The broad land connection between Alaska and Asia came into existence and disappeared during the Ice Age, or Pleistocene. During the Pleistocene, vast amounts of snow fell on the continents. The snow was derived from water evaporating from the oceans. This caused the sea level around the world to drop almost 200 metres (650 feet). The snow gradually became glacial ice in the northern regions of the northern hemisphere and at high elevations in the southern hemisphere. When the continental glaciers melted due to the warmer climate at the end of the Ice Age, the water was transported back to the oceans by the earth's rivers and calving glaciers. This caused the sea level to rise.

For some people, the thought of the Bering Land Bridge conjures up a vision of a narrow strip of land connecting Alaska and Siberia in the area that is now the Bering Strait. However, the Bering Land Bridge was a vast region of low topography stretching between North America and Asia. At the height of the last Ice Age, it was more than 1,000 kilometres (620 miles) wide from north to south. A few mountains, which are today islands in the Bering Sea, were widely spaced across the land and rose abruptly above the flat landscape.

The land bridge and adjacent areas of North America and Asia form a geographic area called Beringia. [. . .]

Approximately 18,000 years ago, most of the continental shelf was exposed as dry land.

This occurred during the height of the last major glaciation, called the Wisconsin, after the state where it was first clearly identified and described. At the close of the Wisconsin, beginning about 14,000 years ago, sea level began to rise and the configuration and size of the Bering Land Bridge began to change dramatically. [. . .] The most recent evidence from sediment cores from the Bering continental shelf indicates the land connection between Alaska and Siberia was severed for the last time by approximately 10,000 B.P. (Bobrowsky et al. 1990; Elias et al. 1992).

[. . .]

HUMAN MIGRATION ROUTES

Knut Fladmark (1983) has provided what is probably the most comprehensive review of the possible routes by which humans may have first entered the Americas. Careful review of the paleoenvironmental literature and glacial geology led him to conclude that the two most plausible routes are: (1) the Beringian midcontinental route, and (2) the Beringian northwestern coastal route.

Midcontinental Route

During the last glaciation (the Wisconsin), an enormous glacier called the Laurentide ice sheet formed in eastern Canada. Concurrently, glaciers in the Canadian Rockies began to flow out of the mountains; they coalesced and spread eastward, forming another massive ice sheet called the Cordillera. These massive Laurentide and Cordilleran glaciers expanded until they met in the areas that are today Alberta and northern British Columbia, Canada.

The merged Cordilleran and Laurentide ice would have formed an impenetrable barrier stretching from the Atlantic Ocean to the Pacific Ocean and more than 800 kilometres (500 miles) from eastern Beringia to southern Alberta. For human groups who survived on an economy based on hunting, gathering, and fishing, the massive continental glacier would have presented a lifeless, dangerous, and seemingly endless icescape. Archeologists agree that the merged continental glaciers would have formed a barrier so severe that it would have been impossible for humans to cross it during the late Pleistocene.

The Beringian midcontinental route proposes that people moved south from eastern Beringia through central Canada east of the western mountains. There exist two versions of the midcontinental route. The first and more accepted concept suggests that southward migration could not have begun until the continental glaciers had melted enough to permit people to move southward, sometime between 11,000–12,000 years ago. The other theory suggests an earlier migration through a hypothetical ice-free corridor that some scientists believe may have existed sometime during the last Ice Age. Although little evidence supports this theory, it is popular among some archeologists because of some archeological sites in North America that may be more than 12,000 years old.

The concept of an ice-free corridor stretching between eastern Beringia and the unglaciated southern areas of North America was suggested by W.A. Johnston in 1933 and reinforced by geologist Ernst Antevs (1937) and others. The archeological need for such a theory arose because some scholars felt it was necessary to explain the possible evidence for the presence of humans south of the continental ice before the melting of the continental glaciers. The term *ice-free corridor* is applied to a hypothetical, relatively narrow strip of unglaciated land that was thought to exist between the Laurentide and Cordilleran ice sheets. For many years, researchers agreed that these two ice sheets joined in western Canada; however, some believed that this may have been a very brief event and that the ice soon melted, leaving a relatively narrow strip of unglaciated land between these huge glaciers. It was further theorized that this narrow corridor would have provided an avenue through which plants, animals, and humans could have passed from Beringia into other unglaciated regions of North America. Other species could have moved from south to north through the corridor.

Belief in an ice-free corridor began to crumble when Canadian paleoecologist Glen MacDonald (1987a) demonstrated that some of the most important radiocarbon dates used to support the existence of an ice-free corridor were incorrect. He persuasively argued that an ice-free corridor did not exist until the very end of the Wisconsin glaciation, when the continental ice began its final retreat (MacDonald

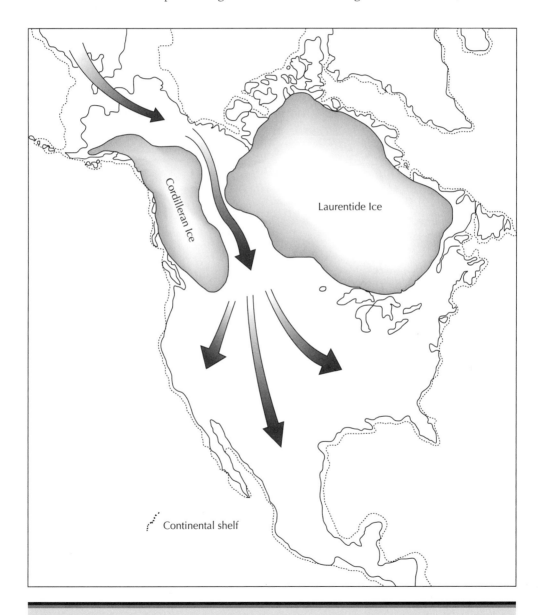

Cordilleran Ice

Laurentide Ice

Continental shelf

Figure 1   The hypothetical interior, or midcontinental, migration route. Graphic by Eric Parrish.

1987a, 1987b). Other evidence suggests that even if an ice-free corridor did exist, it would have been inhospitable for human colonization (Burns 1990, 1996; Mandryk 1990).

Geologic research (Jackson et al. 1996, 1997; Leboe 1995) appears to have finally resolved the issue of existence and timing of an ice-free corridor. Passage between Beringia and the unglaciated areas of North America remained blocked until sometime shortly after 11,000 B.P. (Jackson and Duk-Rodkin 1996; Jackson et al. 1996, 1997). Because the earliest

Clovis sites are dated between 11,500–11,000 B.P., this late date for the establishment of a deglaciation corridor suggests that Clovis people were south of the continental glaciers prior to the melting of the midcontinental ice.

[. . .]

The dating of a deglaciation corridor at the end of the last Ice Age is supported by a series of radiocarbon dates on the bones of large mammals found throughout Alberta, Canada. These dates range from about 40,000 years ago (the approximate reliable limit of 14C dating)

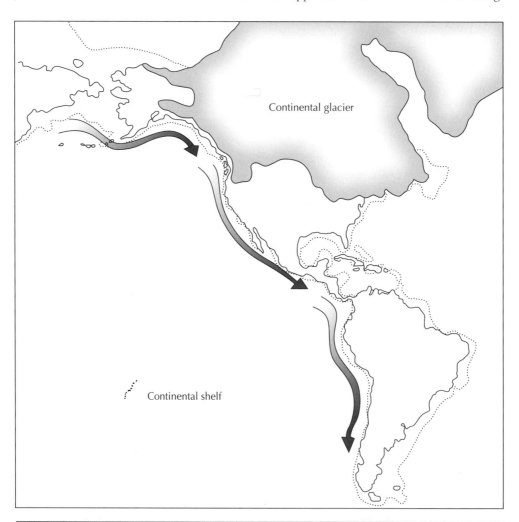

Figure 2 The hypothetical coastal migration route. Graphic by Eric Parrish.

to about 21,000 B.P. There is a significant gap between 21,000 B.P. and about 11,500 B.P. This gap in the radiocarbon dates indicates that the region was covered by glacial ice during that time. It wasn't until sometime around 11,500–11,000 B.P. that the ice had melted sufficiently to enable animals to reoccupy the region (Burns 1996).

By about 11,000 B.P., the glaciers had melted enough to form what might be called a deglaciation corridor between the ice sheets. This would have enabled people to move from eastern Beringia southward into the more southern areas of North America (Clague et al. 1989; Jackson et al. 1996, 1997; Rutter 1984). Conversely, if humans were already south of the continental glaciers, the melting of the ice would have enabled humans to move northward into the region that is now northwestern Canada and Alaska. Scientists agree that as the ice melted, plants, animals, and humans soon colonized the new land. Many archeologists believe that humans first entered the southern areas of North America by gradually moving into and settling the new environment created by the melting ice. This process would have enabled people to move gradually southward to places south of the continental ice.

If this scenario were correct, the North American continent south of eastern Beringia would not have been colonized by humans until sometime after the glaciers had melted enough to permit people and animals to pass between the melting ice sheets, sometime about 11,000 years ago (Figure 1). The interior migration route requires an economy based on hunting terrestrial mammals, gathering limited plant products, and probably on freshwater fishing. This type of subsistence adaptation, characteristic of high-latitude environments, would have been an essential factor for colonizing recently deglaciated lands.

Northwest Coast Route

Support is growing for the theory that people using watercraft, possibly skin boats, may have moved southward from Beringia along the Gulf of Alaska and then southward along the Northwest Coast of North America possibly as early as 16,000 years ago. This route would have enabled humans to enter southern areas of the Americas prior to the melting of the continental glaciers.

Until the early 1970s, most archeologists did not consider the coast a possible migration route into the Americas because geologists (Antevs 1929; Coulter et al. 1965; Johnston 1933; Nasmith 1970; Prest 1969) originally believed that during the last Ice Age the entire Northwest Coast was covered by glacial ice. It had been assumed that the ice extended westward from the Alaskan/Canadian mountains to the edge of the continental shelf. This would have created a barrier of ice extending from the Alaskan Peninsula, through the Gulf of Alaska and southward along the Northwest Coast of North America to the area that is today the state of Washington.

The most influential proponent of the coastal migration route has been Canadian archeologist Knut Fladmark (1979, 1986). He theorized that with the use of watercraft, people gradually colonized unglaciated refugia and areas along the continental shelf exposed by the lower sea level. Fladmark's hypothesis received additional support from Ruth Gruhn (1988) and R.A. Rogers (1985) who pointed out that the greatest diversity in Native American languages occurs along the west coast of the Americas suggesting that this region has been settled the longest.

More recent geologic and paleoecologic studies (Blaise et al. 1990; Bobrowsky et al. 1990; Josenhans et al. 1995, 1997) documented deglaciation and the existence of ice-free areas throughout major coastal areas of British Columbia by 13,000 B.P. Research now indicates that sizable areas of southeastern Alaska along the inner continental shelf were not covered by ice toward the end of the last Ice Age (Dixon et al. 1997; Heaton 1995, 1996; Heaton and Grady 1993; Heaton et al. 1996). Mann and Peteet (1994) suggest that except for a 400-kilometre (250-mile) coastal area between southwestern British Columbia and Washington state, the Northwest Coast of North America was largely free of ice by approximately 16,000 years ago. Vast areas along the coast may have been deglaciated beginning about 16,000 B.P. possibly providing a coastal corridor for the movement of plants, animals, and humans sometime between 14,000–13,000 B.P. (Josenhans et al. 1997).

The coastal hypothesis has gained increased support in recent years because the remains of large land animals, such as caribou and brown bears, have been found in southeastern Alaska dating between 10,000–12,500 years ago (Heaton and Grady 1993; Heaton et al. 1996). This is the time period that most scientists formerly believed the area to be inhospitable for humans. It has been suggested that if the environment were capable of supporting breeding populations of bears, there would have been enough food resources to support humans (Dixon 1995). Fladmark (1979, 1983) and others (Dixon 1993; Easton 1992; Gruhn 1988, 1994) believe that the first human colonization of America occurred by boat along the Northwest Coast during the very late Ice Age, possibly as early as 14,000 years ago (Figure 2). The most recent geological evidence indicates that it may have been possible for people to colonize ice-free regions along the continental shelf that were still exposed by the lower sea level between 13,000–14,000 years ago.

The coastal hypothesis suggests an economy based on marine mammal hunting, saltwater fishing, shellfish gathering, and the use of watercraft. Because of the barrier of ice to the east, the Pacific Ocean to the west, and populated areas to the north, there may have been a greater impetus for people to move in a southerly direction.

Transoceanic voyages across the Atlantic or the Pacific also have been considered as a possible means by which humans may have first colonized the Americas. However, [. . .] it has not been demonstrated that humans were capable of making transoceanic crossings while carrying enough people and provisions to make colonization of the Americas possible. While New World archeologists keep their minds open to the possibilities of transoceanic voyages across both the Pacific and Atlantic, currently there is not adequate archeological evidence for watercraft capable of crossing the broad expanses of the oceans during the Pleistocene.

COLONIZATION

During the past few decades, knowledge of world colonization by modern humans has increased at a phenomenal rate. Major advances in paleoenvironmental studies are expanding our understanding and interpretation of paleogeography and past environmental conditions. This new knowledge enables archeologists to view colonization as a larger cultural and biological phenomenon. Identifying and understanding the processes of colonization are important to the disciplines of anthropology and the natural sciences in general. By focusing on the earliest human colonization of the New World, archeologists can provide significant insight into the nature of humans as colonizers, their impact on pristine environments, and the influence of different environments on cultural development.

[. . .] Currently very few models for the peopling of the Americas exist. [. . .]

J.E. Mossimann and Paul S. Martin (1975) theorized that humans could have colonized both North America and South America in approximately 1,000 years [. . .] (Figure 3). However, Wormington (1983:192) believed that human colonization of the Americas took much longer than the model proposed by Mossimann and Martin. In her view, early hunters and gathers needed more time to develop familiarity with their environment and its resources, and once they had gained this knowledge, they were reluctant to move.

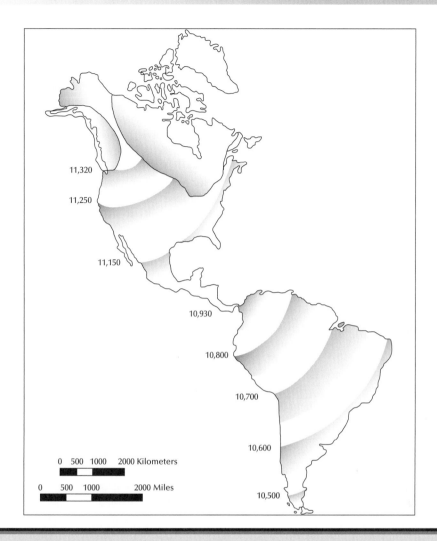

Figure 3   The hypothetical 'Bow Wave' model for the human colonization of the Americas from North to South (modified from Mossimann and Martin 1975). Graphic by Eric Parrish.

She regarded environmental change and population pressure as the mechanisms causing human groups to move. This type of model requires a much longer time for humans to colonize the American continents than that advocated by Mossimann and Martin.

Robert L. Kelly and Lawrence C. Todd (Kelly 1996; Kelly and Todd 1988) have advanced a variation of Martin's model. They suggest that the first Paleoindians were technologically based foragers. Unlike modern foragers who are geographically based and generally confined by neighbouring foraging groups, they suggest that the earliest human groups in North America may have relied more on knowledge of animal behaviour and technology rather than knowledge of geography. This may have enabled them to move from region to region exploiting various species, some of which may have been preferred over others. According to Kelly and Todd, such a foraging strategy could result in comparatively rapid human migration and the extinction of select species.

[. . .]

The problem of explaining New World colonization is continental in proportion, so it must be approached with a large scale of analysis. For example, it is clear from the archeological record that the first Americans must have been hunters and gathers because at the end of the last Ice Age, the earth's human population relied on hunting and gathering as its economic mainstay. Since that time, hunting and gathering has declined, until only a few isolated human groups continue this life style in marginal habitats unsuitable for other economic pursuits. Based on our knowledge of available migration routes, genetics, and language, the first immigrants to the Americas most likely came over the Bering Land Bridge or along its southern coastal margin using some form of watercraft. Hence, knowledge of relatively contemporary northern hunter-gather settlement patterns may provide important insight essential to understand factors that might lead to migration.

[. . .]

A universal aspect of hunters and gatherers is that these societies must maintain a territory, or range, from which the essential resources to sustain life are derived. Frans Boas, the founder of American anthropology, clearly recognized the important role of natural resources in determining human settlement patterns during his field research among the Inuit in the central Canadian Arctic in 1883–4. He wrote:

> All depends upon the distribution of food at the different seasons. The migrations or accessibility of the game compels the natives to move their habitations from time to time, and hence the distribution of villages depends, to a great extent, upon that of the animals that supply them with food. [Boas 1964:11]

Within each territory, resources are not distributed uniformly. Certain resource concentrations play a more important role in subsistence activities than others. Because the harvest of these resources is essential for human survival, their distribution and the timing of harvesting them result in concentrations of human populations. Furthermore, collective efforts enable hunter-gatherers to maximize their harvests. For example, Robert McKennan (1969) analyzed the ecological basis for Northern Athapaskan band composition and identified two major technological devices that required collective effort to harvest large numbers of animals: the fish weir and the caribou fence. As a result of these co-operative activities, an economic surplus was generated that facilitated human settlement for extended periods of time. These types of subsistence activities led to predictable settlement locales that were restricted to specific geographic locations for a specific duration of time.

Although each group, or band, maintains a geographical range, or territory, there is 'communication between groups, including reciprocal visiting and marriage alliances, so that the basic hunting society consisted of a series of local "bands" that were part of a larger breeding and linguistic community' (Lee and DeVore 1968:11). The major limiting factor on band size is how many people can be supported, or carried, by the harvest of the resources within their territory. The maximum number of people that can be supported by the environment is called the carrying capacity, which is a general ecological term referring to the number of living things an environment can sustain (Odum 1975). Human carrying capacity is determined by the resources that can be harvested within the territorial range given a group's level of technology.

There are many controls on carrying capacity. For example, a technological innovation, such as a shift from simple spear fishing to using fish weirs to concentrate the fish and force them to swim past one spot or into a trap, could greatly increase a harvest and the number of people that might be supported. It is not only the total amount of resources within a given environment that is important, but also the ability of the people to perceive and harvest them. This is called the effective environment and is limited to the resources conceptualized and utilized by the band (Kaplan and Manners 1972:79). The band's potential to harvest resources is dependent to a large degree on their specific level of technology and their knowledge of their territory's resources. Environmental factors also affect carrying capacity, such as unusually cool summers that might alter the migration routes of caribou or high water that might reduce salmon harvests. Gradual and more efficient adaptation to the effective environment could conceivably take hundreds of years or more following colonization before the carrying capacity of a specific territory is reached.

Considerable ethnographic evidence shows that social conflict, frequently over resources, causes groups of people to break away from the larger group and relocate. Anthropologists call this phenomenon fissioning. Given our knowledge of hunter-gatherers, a hypothetical colonization model for the Americas can be constructed. Very simply stated, as a group approached or exceeded the carrying capacity of their territory, fission occurred. Although adjacent bands might be able to absorb some of the splinter population, this would also create increased competition for resources. To successfully colonize and settle adjacent unoccupied territory, the splinter group separating from the parent band would have to be a viable breeding population containing at a minimum adult males, young adult females, and possibly children.

This model is based primarily on environmental criteria and views colonization as a process characterized by a series of stages. The first stage is exploration by humans of unoccupied regions adjacent to a settled area. Exploration provides knowledge of the adjacent region's geography and resources, but the area remains unsettled by humans. Fission is the second stage: it requires that a viable breeding group break away from an existing parent population.

The third stage, migration, is the actual process of the splinter group moving from the parent settlement to the known, but unoccupied, region to be colonized. The fourth stage is colonization. Colonization is the establishment of residential locales, or frontier settlements, in a territorial range that provides the resources essential to sustain life. The final stage is settlement, the process by which the colonizing population expands to fully exploit and occupy the effective environment of the new territory. As the splinter group adapts to and settles new territory, they would be expected to extend their exploration to adjacent unoccupied territory. Exploration may have been undertaken primarily by young adult males able to travel long distances unencumbered by children, pregnant females, and the elderly.

As adaptation to the new territory becomes increasingly effective, a greater number of people are supported by the available resources. Over time the population would eventually approach or exceed carrying capacity and fission would occur again. A subsequent migration would take place and an adjacent explored but unoccupied territory would be colonized. The absence of competition would tend to promote colonization of unoccupied territory.

This model favours colonization within the same general type of environment, or megapatch, such as coastal margins, or high-latitude/high-altitude tundra, or forests. Once adapted to a major environmental type, such as coastal margins, a group would have the technology and knowledge essential to harvest specific types of resources already familiar to them. This type of colonization would be safer and more predictable than colonizing new environments when establishing frontier settlements, because it requires less risk. Furthermore, it maintains a linguistic, cultural, and genetic bond to the parent bands still occupying adjacent territory. This bond would tend to enhance the survival of the frontier settlement because it would establish opportunities for trade, various types of alliances, and exchange of marriage partners. In

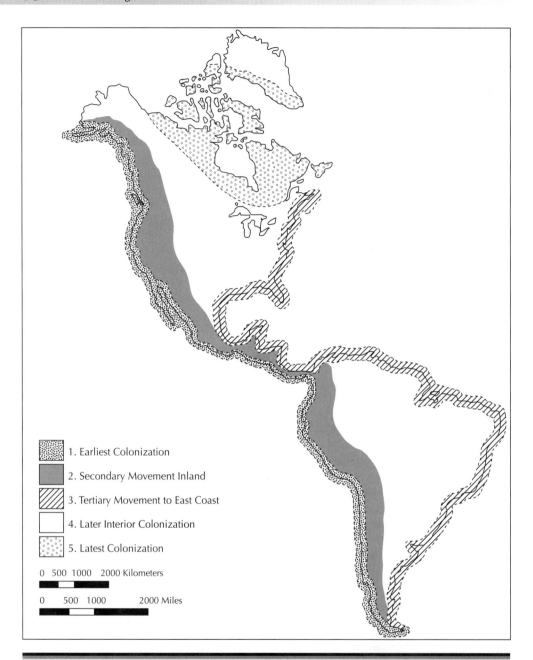

Figure 4   Hypothetical sequence for the colonization of the Americas by macroenvironmental zones.
Graphic by Eric Parrish.

many respects this conceptual model is similar to the modified concept of stem groups discussed by Dillehay (1997:810) and Beaton (1991), whereby the splinter group maintains contact and possibly shares overlapping territory with the parent band.

The 'bow wave' model illustrated in Figure 3 is characterized by bow shaped horizontal lines, or waves, symbolizing the sequential advance of the human population at approximately the same latitude (Mossimann and Martin 1975). By comparison, the macroenvironmental zone model illustrated in Figure 4 is characterized by vertical (north to south) lines along major environmental zones, such as the coasts and the western Cordillera. When observing the major physiographic and ecological regions of the Americas, they tend to be oriented vertically from north to south. For example, the western Cordillera of North America is a huge mountainous spine extending from Alaska to Arizona, the plains extend from Canada to northern Mexico, and the western coastal coniferous forest stretches from Alaska to California. Figure 4 presents the abstract concept for colonization of the Americas and is not a map depicting human New World colonization.

North to south colonization also could have occurred along ecotones, which are zones of transition between two or more biomes. These transitional environments may have been the megapatch of choice, possibly being more productive than either of the adjacent biomes and possibly permitting people access to resources in adjacent biomes. On a very large (continental) level of analysis, the coastal zone, the interface of the plains and mountains, and other analogous environmental zones could be regarded as ecotones.

It is difficult to estimate how long the first colonization of the Americas may have taken. If an ecological model similar to the one suggested here is applicable to the Americas, the length of time it takes to approach or exceed carrying capacity and the distance moved to establish a new territory or range would have to be known. In relatively linear environmental zones, such as river systems or coastal margins, colonization might be expected to be rapid, possibly resulting in high-velocity migration in conjunction with the use of watercraft. In other types of ecological settings, colonization may have happened at a much slower rate. With colonization occurring along major environmental zones, it may be reasonable to assume that different environmental regions of the Americas were colonized at different times and possibly at different rates of speed. Some territories may have been occupied for hundreds of years before fissioning occurred. For example, coastal zones may have been inhabited long before the interior plains or deserts. Given the current level of knowledge regarding the very early archeology of the Americans, attempts to mathematically model this process would be extremely speculative.

[. . .]

Although the archeological evidence for the actual processes of New World colonization remains poorly understood, the peopling of the Americas was one of the great colonizing achievements of humanity. It stands as an important event in human history and poses fascinating questions. For example, what are the earliest reliable archeological 'signatures' documenting initial colonization of the Americas? Can this evidence be used to define the timing and geographic sequence of colonization? What characterized the cultures of the first colonists, and are these characteristics shared across geographic and temporal boundaries? What were the environmental impacts of human colonization on the pristine New World environments, and can they be documented archeologically? What was the impact of new environments on cultural development? These are some of the intriguing questions that may only be answered by evidence from America's oldest archeological sites.

REFERENCES

Acosta, J. de. (1604). *The Naturall and Morall Historie of the East and West Indies*. Reprinted by Bart Franklin, New York, by permission of the Haakluyt Society.

Antevs, E. (1929). Maps of the Pleistocene Glaciation., *Bulletin of the Geological Society of America* 40:631–720.

———. (1937). Climate and Early Man in North America. In *Early Man*, edited by G.G. MacCurdy, pp. 125–32. J.D. Lippincott, Philadelphia.

Beaton, J.M. (1991). Colonizing Continents: Some Problems for Australia and the Americas. In *The First Americans: Search and Research*, edited by Tom D. Dillehay and David J. Meltzer, pp. 209–30. CRC Press, Boca Raton, Florida.

Blaise, B., J.J. Clague, and R.W. Mathewes. (1990). Time of Maximum Late Wisconsin Glaciation, West Coast of Canada. *Quaternary Research* 34:282–95.

Boas, F. (1964). *The Central Eskimo*. University of Nebraska Press, Lincoln, Nebraska.

Bobrowsky, P.T., N.R. Catto, J.W. Brink, B.E. Spurling, T.H. Gibson, and N.W. Rutter. (1990). *Archaeological Geology of Sites in Western and Northwestern Canada*. Centennial Special Vol. 4, Chapter 5, pp. 87–522. Geological Society of America, Boulder.

Burns, J.A. (1990). Paleontological Perspectives on the Ice-free Corridor. In *Megafauna and Man: Discovery of America's Heartland*, edited by Larry D. Agenbroad, Jim I. Mead, and Lisa W. Nelson, pp. 61–6. Scientific Papers, Vol. 1. The Mammoth Site of Hot Springs, Hot Springs, South Dakota; and Northern Arizona University, Flagstaff.

———. (1996). Vertebrate Paleontology and the Alleged Ice-free Corridor: The Meat of the Matter. *Quaternary International* 32:107–12. Great Britain.

Carter, G.F. (1952). Interglacial Artifacts from the San Diego Area. *Southwest Journal of Anthropology* 8(4):444–56.

———. (1957). *Pleistocene Man at San Diego*. Johns Hopkins Press, Baltimore.

Clague, J.J., J.M. Ryder, W.H. Mathews, O.L. Hughes, N.W. Rutter, and C.M. MacDonald. (1989). Quaternary Geology of the Canadian Cordillera. In *Quaternary Geology of Canada and Greenland*, edited by R.J. Fulton, Chapter 1, pp. 17–96. Geological Society of Canada, Geology of Canada, No. 1. Ottawa.

Coulter, H.W., D.M. Hopkins, T.N.V. Karlstrom, T.L. Pewe, C. Wahrhaftig, and J.R. Williams. (1965). Map showing extent of glaciations in Alaska. U.S. Geological Survey Miscellaneous Geologic Investigations Map, 1-415, scale 1:2,500,00.

Dillehay, T.D. (1997). *Monte Verde: A Late Pleistocene Settlement in Chile*. Smithsonian Series in Archaeological Inquiry, Washington, D.C.

Dixon, E.J. (1983). Pleistocene Proboscidean Fossils from the Alaskan Continental Shelf. *Quaternary Research* 20:113–19.

———. (1993). *Quest for the Origins of the First Americans*. University of New Mexico Press, Albuquerque.

———. (1995). The Fabulous Baker Family. *Museum Quarterly* 4(1). Denver Museum of Natural History.

Dixon, E.J., T.H. Heaton, T.E. Fifield, T.D. Hamilton, D.E. Putnam, and F. Grady. (1997). Late Quaternary Regional Geoarchaeology of Southeast Alaska Karst: A Progress Report. *Geoarchaeology: An International Journal* 12(6):689–712.

Easton, N.A. (1992). Mal de Mer above Terra Incognita, or 'What Ails the Coastal Migration Theory'. *Arctic Anthropology* 29:28–42.

Elias, S.A., S.K. Short, C.H. Nelson, and H.H. Birks. (1996). Life and Times of the Bering Land Bridge. *Nature* 382:60–3.

Elias, S.A., S.K. Short, and R.L. Phillips. (1992). Paleoecology of Late Glacial Peats from the Bering Land Bridge, Chukchi Sea Shelf Region, Northwestern Alaska. *Quaternary Research* 38:371–8.

Fladmark, K.R. (1979). Routes: Alternative Migration Corridors for Early Man in North America. *American Antiquity* 44:55–69.

————. (1983). Times and Places: Environmental Correlates of Mid-to-Late Wisconsin Human Population Expansion in North America. In *Early Man in the New World*, edited by Richard Shutler, pp. 13–42. Sage Publications, Beverly Hills.

————. (1986). Getting One's Berings. *Natural History* 95(11):8–19.

Griffin, J.B. (1979). The Origin and Dispersion of American Indians in North America. In *The First Americans: Origins, Affinities, and Adaptations*, edited by William S. Laughlin and Albert B. Harper, pp. 43–56. Gustav Fischer, New York.

Gruhn, R. (1988). Linguistic Evidence in Support of the Coastal Route of Earliest Entry into the New World. *Man* 23:77–100.

————. (1994). The Pacific Coast Route of Initial Entry: An Overview. In *Methods and Theory for Investigating the Peopling of the Americas*, edited by Robson Bonnichsen and D. Gentry Steele, pp. 249–56. Center for the Study of the First Americans, Oregon State University, Corvallis.

Haynes, C.V., Jr. (1969). The Earliest Americans. *Science* 166:709–15.

Heaton, T.H. (1995). Middle Wisconsin Bear and Rodent Remains Discovered on Prince of Wales Island, Alaska. *Current Research in the Pleistocene* 12:92–5.

————. (1996). The Late Wisconsin Vertebrae Fauna of On Your Knees Cave, Northern Prince of Wales Island, Alaska. *Journal of Paleontology* 16:40A–41A.

Heaton, T.H. and P. Grady. (1993). Fossil Grizzly-Bears from Prince of Wales Island, Alaska, Offer New Insights into Animal Dispersal, Interspecific Competition, and Age of Deglaciation. *Current Research in the Pleistocene* 10:98–100.

Heaton, T.H., S.L. Talbot, and G.F. Shield. (1996). An Ice Age Refugium for Large Mammals in the Alexander Archipelago, Southeastern Alaska. *Quaternary Research* 46:186–92.

Hopkins, D.M. (1967). *The Bering Land Bridge*. Stanford University Press, Stanford.

Hrdlička, A. (1928). The Origin and Antiquity of Man in America. *New York Academy of Medicine Bulletin* 4(7):802–16.

Irving, W.N., A.V. Jopling, and B.F. Beebe. (1986). Indications of Pre-Sangamon Humans near Old Crow, Yukon, Canada. In *New Evidence for the Pleistocene Peopling of the Americas*, edited by Alan Lyle Bryan, pp. 49–63. Center for the Study of Early Man, University of Maine at Orono.

Jackson, L.E., Jr., and A. Duk-Rodkin. (1996). Quaternary Geology of the Ice-free Corridor: Glacial Controls on the Peopling of the New World. In *Prehistoric Mongoloid Dispersals*, edited by Takeru Akazawa and Emöke J.E. Szathmáry, pp. 214–27. Oxford University Press, New York.

Jackson, L.E., Jr., E.C. Little, E.R. Loboe, and P.J. Holme. (1996). A Re-evaluation of the Paleoglaciology of the Maximum Continental and Montane Advances, Southwestern Alberta. In *Current Research* 1996-A; *Geological Survey of Canada*, pp. 165–73.

Jackson, L.E., Jr., F.M. Phillips, K. Shimamura, and E.C. Little. (1997). Cosmogenic 36Cl Dating of the Foothills Erratics Train, Alberta, Canada. Geology 25(3):195–98.

Johnston, W.A. (1933). Quaternary Geology of North America in Relation to the Migration of Man. In *The American Aborigines, Their Origins and Antiquity*, edited by Diamond Jenness, pp. 9–46. A Collection of Papers by Ten Authors Assembled and Edited by Diamond Jenness. Published for presentation at the Fifth Pacific Science Congress. Canada. Cooper Square Publishers, New York, 1973. University of Toronto Press, Toronto.

Jopling, A.V., W.N. Irving, and B.F. Beebe. (1981). Stratigraphic, Sedimentological and Faunal Evidence for the Occurrence of Pre-Sangamonian Artifacts in Northern Yukon. *Arctic* 34(1):3–33.

Josenhans, H.W., D.W. Fedje, K.W. Conway, and J.E. Barrie. (1995). Post Glacial Sea-Levels on the Western Canadian Continental Shelf: Evidence for Rapid Change, Extensive Subaerial Exposure, and Early Human Habitation. *Marine Geology* 125:73–94.

Josenhans, H.W., D.W. Fedje, R. Pienitz, and J. Southon. (1997). Early Humans and Rapidly

Changing Holocene Sea Levels in the Queen Charlotte Islands-Hecate Strait, British Columbia, Canada. *Science* 277:71–4.

Kaplan, D. and R.A. Manners. (1972). *Culture Theory.* Prentice-Hall, Englewood Cliffs, New Jersey.

Kelly, R.L. (1996). Ethnographic Analogy and Migration to the Western Hemisphere. In *Prehistoric Mongoloid Dispersals*, edited by Takeru Akazawa and Emőke J.E. Szathmáry, pp. 228–40. Oxford University Press, New York.

Kelly, R.L. and L.C. Todd. (1988). Coming into the Country: Early Paleoindian Hunting and Mobility. *American Antiquity* 53:231–44.

Leboe, E.R. (1995). Quaternary Geology and Terrain Inventory, Eastern Cordillera NATMAP Project. Report 2: Surficial Geology and Quaternary Stratigraphy, Pincher Creek and Brocket Map Areas, Alberta. In *Current Research 1995-A; Geological Survey of Canada*, pp. 167–75.

Lee, R.B. and I. DeVore. (1968). Problems in the Study of Hunters and Gatherers. In *Man the Hunter*, edited by R.B. Lee and I. DeVore, pp. 3–12. Aldine, Chicago.

MacDonald, G.M. (1987a). Postglacial Development of the Subalpine-Boreal Transition Forest of Western Canada. *Journal of Ecology* 75:303–20.

———. (1987b). Postglacial Vegetation History of the Mackenzie River Basin. *Quaternary Research* 28:245–62.

Mandryk, C.A. (1990). Could Humans Survive the Ice-free Corridor?: Late-Glacial Vegetation and Climate in West Central Alberta. In *Megafauna and Man: Discovery of America's Heartland*, edited by Larry D. Agenbroad, Jim I. Mead, and Lisa W. Nelson, pp. 67–79. The Mammoth Site of Hot Springs, South Dakota, Inc. Scientific Papers, Vol. 1, Hot Springs, South Dakota.

Mann, D.H. and D.M. Peteet. (1994). Extent and Timing of the Last Glacial Maximum in Southwestern Alaska. *Quaternary Research* 42:136–48.

McKennan, R.A. (1969). Athapaskan Groupings and Social Organization in Central Alaska. Anthropological Series 84. *National Museum of Canada Bulletin* 228:93–115.

McManus, D.A., J.S. Creager, R.J. Echols, and M.L. Holmes. (1983). The Holocene Transgression of the Arctic Flank of Beringia: Chukchi Valley to Chukchi Estuary to Chukchi Sea. In *Quaternary Coastlines and Marine Archeology*, edited by P.M. Masters and M.C. Flemming, pp. 365–88. Academic Press, New York.

Mossimann, J.E. and P.S. Martin. (1975). Simulating Overkill by Paleoindians. *American Scientists* 63:304–13.

Nasmith, H.W. (1970). Pleistocene Geology of the Queen Charlotte Islands and Southern British Columbia. In *Early Man and Environments in Northwestern North America*, edited by R.A. Smith and I. Smith, pp. 5–9. University of Calgary, Calgary.

Nichols, J. (1990). Linguistic Diversity and the First Settlement of the New World. *Language* 66(3):475–521.

Odum, E.P. (1975). *Ecology: The Link Between the Natural and the Social Sciences*, 2nd edition. Holt, Rinehart, and Winston, New York.

Prest, V.K. (1969). *Retreat of Wisconsin and Recent Ice in North America*. Geological Survey of Canada Map 1257A.

Rogers, R.A. (1985). Glacial Geography and Native North American Languages. *Quaternary Research* 23:130–37.

Rutter, N.W. (1984). Pleistocene History of the Western Canadian Ice-free Corridor. In *Quaternary Stratigraphy of Canada—A Canadian Contribution to IGCP Project 24*, edited by R.J. Fulton, pp. 49–56. Geological Survey of Canada, Paper 84–10.

Simpson, R.D., L.W. Patterson, and C.A. Singer. (1986). Lithic Technology of the Calico Mountains Site, Southern California. In *New Evidence for the Pleistocene Peopling of the Americas*, edited by Alan Lyle Bryan, pp. 89–105. Center for the Study of Early Man, University of Maine at Orono.

Wormington, H.M. (1983). Early Man in the New World: 1970–1980. In *Early Man in the New World*, edited by Richard Shutler, Jr., pp. 191–5. Sage Publications, Beverly Hills.

4 From David J. Meltzer, 'What Do You Do When No One's Been There Before?' in *First Peoples in a New World: Colonizing Ice Age America* (Berkeley: University of California Press, 2009), 209–38.

[. . .] What must it have been like more than 12,000 years ago for those Ice Age peoples who first colonized the Americas? Although adept and well adapted to hunter-gatherer life, they were armed with little more than wooden or bone spears tipped with stone projectile points. They were assuredly predators; occasionally, they could be prey. More challenging still, they were colonizing a landscape far different and in many ways far more complex, diverse, and dynamic than at present. Although they were seasoned veterans of life in Siberia, as these wide-ranging peoples made their way across to Alaska and turned south into what was truly a New World, the land and its resources became increasingly unfamiliar. More than that, they were facing those adaptive challenges alone. It must have been a strange sensation to look around and realize it had been months, years, decades, or even longer since they had last encountered people outside their band, or seen telltale human signs like smoke on the distant horizon, or evidence of a freshly killed and butchered animal.

[. . .]

PEOPLE WITHOUT NEIGHBOURS

We're about to venture farther into unknown territory and explore questions about why people may have left Asia for America, what kinds of adaptive challenges they faced, and how they may have met those challenges and colonized a continent, possibly at record speeds. We won't have much help: although there is a rich body of anthropological knowledge about modern hunter-gatherer adaptations and processes of migration and colonization, much of it is irrelevant.

The reason? Our world filled up long ago. Nowadays, migration mostly involves moving relatively short distances over brief periods of time into already-occupied landscapes—hardly the scale or circumstances of the colonization of America, which played out much longer and over a much larger area. Moreover, all anthropologically known hunter-gatherers have neighbours, near or distant, on whom they can rely for information, resources, and potential mates (the latter are especially important, since one can always gain information and resources on one's own), or against whom they may compete. Either way, having neighbours fundamentally changes the decision-making calculus of landscape use. Finally, our anthropologically known hunter-gatherers possess deep knowledge of their landscape: not complete knowledge (no group ever has that), but knowledge sufficient that it has reduced much of the uncertainty in their lives. The process of hunter-gatherers learning a wholly new landscape has rarely, if ever, been recorded.[1] By the time anthropologists arrived on a scene, most indigenous peoples were already long resident on their landscape, had mapped its major features, knew what resources were available and where to find them, and were efficient foragers.

All that said, we can still use anthropological knowledge of the processes of human migration and adaptation observable in the present as a key to explaining the past: it's the uniformitarian principle, borrowed from geology and applied to archaeology. That doesn't mean the present and past are identical, but rather that ideas and explanations about the past should begin with (and must not violate) what we know of, say, general principles of human adaptation, or the limits of mobility or demography. The discussion below aims to do that. And, of course, we can supplement the anthropological record with what has been learned archaeologically of other cases in the near and distant past of hunter-gatherers colonizing new lands.

[. . .]

WHY MOVE?

Let's start with motivation. What would prompt a band of hunter-gatherers to leave Siberia for the New World, or once here, expand the length and breadth of the continent? Studies of modern peoples who migrate find they routinely know something about what the destination has to offer, and decide to move or not accordingly. Indeed, it is an anthropological truism that people are unlikely to migrate into areas about which they have no prior knowledge. Yet, at a certain point in the peopling of the Americas, there was little choice in the matter. *Someone* had to be the first to set foot on this continent.

History records many reasons why groups venture from their homeland, and these can be divided into two broad categories: negative factors in the home region that *push* a people out, and positive attractions in a distant area that *pull* them in. The push side of the ledger includes a decline in resources, environmental or climatic stress (such as drought), overpopulation, exile, strife, or warfare. Groups might be pulled from their homeland by the lure of preferred resources (such as in the example of the Thule whale hunters); by the seeking of new economic or trade opportunities or adaptive 'insurance' (ascertaining where to go when current circumstances deteriorate); or by motives as intangible as curiosity, a sense of adventure or wanderlust, the joy of discovery, or the journey to gain prestige or mates.[2]

Of the peopling of the Americas, we cannot say which push and/or pull forces were motives, but perhaps we can identify which were not. First and foremost, it seems highly unlikely that siphoning off overpopulation in their Beringian homeland—one of the most common forces pushing historic population out-migration (think of the post-sixteenth-century desire to escape crowded Europe and make a new life in America)—was a factor in the colonization of the Americas. There is no archaeological evidence of population crowding in Siberia or Alaska: quite the contrary, in fact. And the first Americans travelled much farther and much faster than they had to if they were merely looking for uninhabited land to settle.[3]

Likewise, we have no reason to believe exile, strife, or warfare played a role. Conflict that creates refugees is a much-later phenomenon in prehistory, initially occurring when village-based farmers arc past the tipping point when populations have expanded to the degree they must compete against others for food or the arable land to grow it.

Still, there are push factors that might be relevant to the peopling of the Americas. Northeast Asia and Siberia in the late Pleistocene were not easy places to live, and harsh glacial climates may have driven human foragers out of the region. They appear to have fled during the LGM,* but toward the south, and not evidently toward the east and the Americas. Other climate changes at later times may have played a role. But caution is in order here: throughout prehistory, major changes in climate have occurred without flinging colonizers outward, and many colonization events had no environmental trigger.[4] We must be mindful of the fact that people can be agents of their own actions.

Another potentially important impetus was economics, though this is not to be thought of in modern market terms, such as setting up shop in a nearby town to make and sell widgets because the home widget market is saturated.

---

* LGM: Last Glacial Maximum

* the first large scale occupation of North America

Rather, it is akin to cases where, for example, only the first-born child inherits family land. Later-born children who receive nothing must seek new territory where they can found their own house and lineage, and assure their off-spring access to quality resources. Polynesian oral traditions of ancient exploration of the Pacific abound with stories of younger brothers who left to colonize new islands.[5]

In terms of pull variables, groups headed toward the New World might have hoped—but could not have known—they would find prestige or prized resources or trading partners here. Obviously, for the first Americans, there were no trading partners to find. But perhaps the unknowing hope there were such partners might have been motivation enough. People setting off for new lands did not have to be right about what they might find in order for it to be a reason to go looking for it.

For that matter, one should never down-play curiosity, wanderlust, the joy of discovery, and the like, even though such motivations are impossible to see in the archaeological record. Over the tens and hundreds of thousands of years modern humans spread around the globe, surely some were motivated by little more than wanting to see what was over the next hill.[6]

Curiosity, in fact, has an adaptive under-pinning. Hunter-gatherers live off the land, but conditions change over the course of a year, several years, and longer. Plant and animal density and distributions fluctuate, particularly as a consequence of human predation or exploitation. Knowing this, hunter-gatherers routinely scout out places they can go when local conditions begin to sour (such as when the firewood supply is exhausted, the animals are hunted out, or the plants are no longer in season).

[. . .]

So how do groups move across empty and unfamiliar landscapes? Clovis* poses a challenging case, since its spread occurred quickly across a wide geographic area, possibly in a matter of centuries and certainly no more than a millennium—or so it appears, judging from its narrow range of radiocarbon ages and the continent-wide similarity of Clovis and related toolkits.

As a very rough measure of Clovis move-ment, dividing their maximum geographic range (in kilometres) against the duration of the Clovis period puts their expansion at a net 10–20 kilometres per *year*.[7] That's not much by our measures: many of us have longer daily commutes. But it's extraordinarily fast by hunter-gatherer standards, and furthers the suspicion Clovis people encountered few (if any) others along the way. Yet, the question of how fast they moved is not nearly as interesting as how or why they moved so far, so fast, in a new (or at least people-free) landscape.

[. . .]

Robert Kelly and Lawrence Todd argued in a very influential paper that Clovis groups moved quickly into and across the Americas by following the big-game animals of late Pleistocene North America. It's an argument since elaborated by others, and it has obvious appeal. Preying on large animals, and espe-cially targeting the Pleistocene megafauna, would have made it possible—even obligatory, they say—for the first Americans to move rapidly across long distances and through the continent, and it would have enabled them to easily hurdle any ecological boundaries. The journey from open plains into closed forest would not have required a change in adapta-tion. Just take aim at mastodons, now that their distant elephant cousins (the mammoths) had been left behind.[8] This idea, taken to its extreme, roots Paul Martin's belief Clovis groups hunted the several dozen genera of Pleistocene megafauna to extinction.

Could the colonization of the Americas have been that straightforward? Unfortunately for them (and us), probably not. Not all animals, let alone all elephants (or mam-moth and mastodon, in our North American Pleistocene case) are alike in their behaviour. Wildlife biologists and skilled hunters alike know that finding animal prey requires knowledge of how they behave on the landscape, and that varies by the animals' age and sex; the size and composition of the herd (and where they fit in the herd hierarchy); whether animals are breeding, pregnant, or lactating; the season; the availability of forage and water; the topography; exposure to predation; and so on.[9] As archaeologist (and lifelong hunter) George Frison observes: 'To successfully match wits with wild animals with the intent to kill them requires a thorough knowledge of the hunting territory and the behavioral patterns of the species residing within it.'[10]

[. . .]

But let's not stop the pursuit of big game just yet, for mammoth and mastodon were occasionally taken by Clovis groups, and there's reason to suppose hunting big game was important, even if it did not serve to propel Paleoindians across the continent. The reasoning goes like this: colonizers newly arrived in North America were 'pre-adapted to hunting', most often large game.[11] [. . .]

When the first Americans arrived south of the ice sheets in unglaciated North America, they would have found an environment teeming with animals, and a far richer supply of carbohydrate-yielding plants, allowing a wider range of food choices. Even better, the animals had never before peered down the shaft of a spear, and initially were surely naïve about the danger humans presented. Faced with a full menu of possible entrées, the first Americans likely did what hunters the anthropological world over do: they ranked their targets based on their expected return rate. High-ranked resources, the ones worth pursuing, are those that provide the greatest payoff for the effort expended.

As a general rule, resource ranking of animals roughly correlates with body size: large game tends to be a high-ranked resource, smaller game lower ranked. [. . .]

Given a choice between pursuing a high-ranked resource and a low-ranked one, hunter-gatherers will pursue the higher-ranked one. They do so even if the lower-ranked resources are more abundant, simply because the costs of going after lower-ranked resources—capturing, killing, and butchering all those prairie dogs—tilt the cost-benefit equation in favour of the one-stop shopping offered by a bison. The number of lower-ranked resources in the diet is thus not a consequence of their abundance, but instead of the abundance and availability of higher-ranked resources (a good thing, too, else we humans would have spent an inordinate amount of our evolutionary history eating beetles).

[. . .]

What of our newly arrived American colonizers? The diet breadth model, as Kelly shows, predicts that hunter-gatherers will decide on which food to take based on a knowledge of the quality of different foods, and on a knowledge of resource densities (and hence search costs) and processing costs (return rates). The hunting of the naïve prey was likely good at first, probably so good that the high-ranked resources in an area would soon decline in the face of hunting pressure, and once the prey realized this new predator was something to be avoided (this is called *resource depression*).[12] Faced with diminishing returns, colonists could choose to move to unoccupied areas where familiar game animals were present, or stay in place and expand their diet by working their way down the food chain.

But when to stay and when to leave? *Patch choice* models hold that foragers will stay in a place as long as the expected return rate is above the average return rate for the environment. Once it appears better return rates can be had elsewhere—when the grass, it's realized, really is greener on the other side—and after factoring in the cost in time and energy of moving, the original place will be left behind. But whether moving or staying, the forager needs information: What other resources are available in other patches? What other, possibly less-familiar and lower-ranked animal and plant resources are available? Where are they?

LEARNING LANDSCAPES

These models assume a forager knows something about resource availability across a wide area, and can make informed decisions about what to pursue, how long to stay, and when to leave. Gaining that knowledge requires extended periods observing how the animal behaves over the seasons and in different settings and circumstances: the more time that's invested, the more reliable the chances of success.[13] Colonizers new to a landscape haven't had the luxury of long experience learning their prey, and early on would not have the

TABLE 1 Components of Landscape Learning			
	Geography	**Climate**	**Resources**
What humans bring:	sense of direction	generic climatic knowledge (seasonal changes, etc.)	generic knowledge of geology, hydrology, plants, and animals
	ability to store information		
	ability to integrate time, motion, and position while moving	ability to store or capture information human generation time	ability to store information
			ability to relocate resource occurrences
	generic navigation knowledge (celestial markers, etc.)		
What humans look for:	prominent landmarks	scale of climate change relative to generation or residence time (detectability)	relative movement of the resource (fixed/not fixed)
	geographic features (rivers, mountain chains, etc.)		relative stability and availability of resource (reliability)
	spatial patterning to natural features	duration, periodicity, and amplitude of climate changes (predictability)	
		variability of climate (stability)	abundance, behaviour, and/or distribution of resources (predictability)
How humans learn across space and through time:	begins at the most general landscape features, then becomes more spatially specific and refined over time ('megapatch' to 'patch')	begins with specific features (local weather), then becomes more general and cumulative over time (climate)	early, redundant use of fixed, permanent resources (stone) learning begins at general level (animals of same size class; plants of same family or general), and becomes more specific knowledge increases with residence time but may also require experimentation
	begins on landscapes easiest to traverse and navigate, then later on landscapes that impede travel or wayfindingmay involve artificial signage/ waypoints (caches)	predictability increases with residence time, depending on periodicity and stability of climate	
		learning may have upper limits, depending on detectability, residence time, and capture capacity (one cannot 'see' a glacial period)	may have gender correlates depending on relative labour investment in hunting vs. gathering

knowledge to anticipate when and where their prey would be found. Nor can they ask the locals for help: there aren't any. Each new habitat colonizers entered would, for a time, have been unpredictable and perhaps unreliable.

[. . .]

Though they were entering new habitats as they moved across the continent, as pedestrian hunter-gatherers, they would have done so (literally) step by step: they could see in the distance, for example, periglacial environments give way to northern grasslands, and thus would have had time to scout what was ahead and anticipate some of its adaptive challenges. Few colonizers (and the first Americans were not among them) are suddenly thrust into utterly unfamiliar environments poles apart from where they've been. The English in the late sixteenth and early seventeenth centuries in America came close, and nearly perished as a result (it hardly helped that the Roanoke Island and Jamestown colonies both had the monumental bad luck of arriving and trying to establish themselves during the worst years of an extraordinary drought).[14]

What America's first peoples therefore needed to build on their prior knowledge so as to maximize their chances of success were 'maps' of near and increasingly distant lands to know *where* to move; an understanding of the seasons and climate to know *when* to move; and a familiarity with a region's animals and plants as well as the location of other necessities like water and stone to know *how* to move. To be a successful colonizer of the Americas meant using the neural hardware and cognitive software with which all humans come equipped, taking cues from the environment, and above all, paying attention and learning (see Table 1).

FINDING THE WAY

[. . .]

In times past and on unknown landscapes, the penalty for geographic inattention may have been more severe, as when hunting parties

became lost and failed to retrace their steps, or ocean-going colonists were not as prudent as they needed to be. Being lost on land was not always fatal, of course, nor would it carry the same costs as being lost at sea. Still, even in places like the lush tropics, becoming lost can be fatal if one fails to recognize the potential foods in that setting; the Spanish Conquistador Gonzalo Pizarro nearly met his demise in the upper Amazon in 1540–2 for just that reason. In the unforgiving desert or high Arctic, the danger is much greater. Hunter-gatherers there take great measures to avoid getting lost and rarely do, save when ill or overtaken by bad weather.[15]

[. . .]

Within these respective areas, the landscape was known and named with remarkable detail, all without benefit of maps or instruments. [. . .] In their absence and in the face of utterly unknown terrain, colonizers could use a variety of topographic markers, environmental cues, generic knowledge, and the cognitive 'software' we humans have developed over evolutionary time: a sense of direction; the capacity to store information; and the ability to integrate time, motion, and relative position as one moves. Wayfinding, our universal ability to 'determine a route, learn it, and retrace or reverse it from memory', enables us to travel across a landscape without getting (too) lost, while constantly maintaining an awareness of a position relative to a starting point, and do so despite the well-documented tendency of humans in featureless environments to veer (by an average of about 18°).[16]

Studies of wayfinding suggest that initial colonizers on an unknown landscape would likely be guided by features that are large, readily visible, or otherwise distinctive: prominent landmarks, or major topographic and geographic features (mountains ranges, rivers, coastlines). This, of course, varies by landscape. [. . .]

The less familiar the forager is with an area and the greater its size, the coarser the resolution of the cognitive 'map' of the landscape.

Over time, however, knowledge of the region will come to include highly specific references to particular places, their characteristics, their use, and their identity (social, geographic, historic, ritual, and so on), for the events of a place give it meaning.

Human behaviour being what it is, mapping a new landscape was likely a staged process, initially involving scouts or hunters pursuing game while probing into unfamiliar terrain. The oldest archaeological site in an area may not represent the first settler, but instead the first person to scout around.

[. . .]

In addition to the many and often highly visible or prominent natural features humans may have used as landmarks for their emerging cognitive maps of the landscape, colonizers likely also created artificial markers to help find their way. These would be especially important on geographically monotonous landscapes like flat, featureless grasslands. [. . .]

WHAT FEEDS AND WHAT CURES, WHAT HURTS AND WHAT KILLS

Having made it this far, the first Americans had already figured out fire, shelter, and clothing. Once here, they needed to find the materials (stone, wood, bone) suitable to make or maintain those items, as well as meet their daily requirements of food and water. Learning where, what, and how to locate those critical resources could be relatively fast and easy, or not.

Outcrops of stone suitable for tool manufacture, for example, don't move, and once found become known and predictable points on an emerging map of a landscape. [. . .] And those can be relatively easy to find: the famous Alibates agatized dolomite outcrop near Amarillo, Texas, prized for its high-quality stone by hunter-gatherers since Clovis times, is bisected by the Canadian River, which carries cobbles of the stone as much as 600 kilometres

downstream of the outcrop. Anyone seeing those cobbles in the river gravels would know it was merely a matter of following the stone trail back to the outcrop source. It's no surprise Clovis-age sites often occur near where major rivers and streams (which we presume were Pleistocene travel corridors) intersect geological outcrops of high-quality stone.[17]

Locating water can be relatively easy as well, even in dry environments: there, one follows game trails or the flights of birds. Finding it in the same spot again is hardly guaranteed, however, at least not in semi-arid and arid lands where water is neither permanent nor reliable, or during drought when springs and lakes disappear from the surface, and stream flow diminishes. Still, where water might be found beneath the surface or will return after heavy rains generally does not move, and that can be predicted, too. Surely the first Americans possessed the knowledge of geology and hydrology to enable them to find water—there's even tantalizing but unconfirmed evidence of well digging in Clovis times. [. . .]

Neither water nor stone were resources that required new knowledge to be exploited. Once found, stone could be flaked into useable tools, and water collected in skin pouches and transported. There wasn't much to learn.

Plants and animals, of course, are far more ephemeral and less predictable on the landscape: game-rich areas may lack edible plants; plants may not be edible all times of the year; and animals (especially larger ones) can wander away from a previously grazed habitat, or change their range altogether. Some resources might also require considerable study to ascertain their use(s).

This was particularly true of plants. In North America alone, there are an estimated 30,000 species and varieties of plants, and those in temperate and near-tropical areas were surely unfamiliar to bygone Siberians. The process of learning about specific plants, whether they had food, medicinal, or other value, or possibly were poisonous, must have entailed *observation* (watch to see if other animals eat them), and possibly considerable *experimentation* (try it . . . and see what happens).

Yet, daunting as the overall task surely was, the process of botanical learning was ultimately accomplished in prehistory with astonishing success: as Daniel Moermann observes, 'No one has ever found a plant native to North America with any medicinal value not known to and used by American Indians.'[18] In Moermann's view, intense periods of plant research ('research' being an appropriate term here) would likely occur under two conditions: when new diseases appeared, and when there was a substantial environmental transformation. Colonizing the Americas met the first condition and possibly the second, with medicinal plants perhaps being needed when the tropics were entered for the first time.[19]

[. . .]

As knowledge of a plant's properties was built through observation and experimentation, there would have been considerable advantage to maintaining it. Otherwise, each subsequent generation would have to scan the plants anew. That seems unlikely, given the vast number of plants to scan. One supposes, instead, that once broad classes were identified—recognizing it's an oak, say, and not a pine—and their general properties learned—oaks produce acorns that can be palatable when leached of tannic acid—this knowledge was broadly shared. Then it was merely a matter of correctly spotting different species of oak in new settings. So it was, for example, that in 1492 Columbus's crew saw few trees on Hispaniola known to them, but they did recognize some pine and palm trees; however, they readily noticed 'the palms were extraordinarily high, very hard, slender, and straight [and] Even the fruits they produce in abundance were unknown.'[20]

Having knowledge at a more general level would be easier to retain (there are only about 290 families of plants in North America, as opposed to its 30,000 species and varieties) and transmit to subsequent generations, especially if the plant in question was a long-lived perennial. Knowledge at this level would give

colonists an entrée into new habitats in which the species might be novel, but where they would at least recognize the plant as familiar. [. . .]

Learning about the New World's unfamiliar animals was perhaps less of a challenge (there were far fewer of them), but there was still the task of understanding each species' habits and habitats, and seasonal and longer-term patterns in abundance and distribution. Certainly, clues about animal movements can abound on a landscape, and surely these colonizers were adept trackers—otherwise, they would have perished somewhere in Beringia!

They likely could also count on four-footed help. DNA evidence indicates dogs were domesticated from wolves some 15,000 years ago. Although the clues are faint, it appears dogs accompanied the first peoples in their trek to the New World, since dog remains have been found in several Paleoindian sites. Dogs have held various jobs for humans in the past, besides being our best friends: they helped in the hunt to bring animals to bay, served as beasts of burden, were food sources (regularly in some places, only as an emergency backup in others), and indeed, may have been vital in the exploration of new lands. Dogs figure prominently in many American Indian origin stories, acting as helpmates in ritual passages.[21]

As hunters and their dogs shifted into novel settings, there were animals never before seen or encountered, [. . .] making humans just as naïve as their prey, though not as disadvantaged for being so. [. . .]

A generalized knowledge of animal behavior could be extrapolated from one area to another, and hunting skills and weaponry were (to varying degrees) transferable from one target to another. Kelly and Todd rightly argued it is 'easier to locate, procure, and process the faunal as opposed to floral resources of a region.'[22] That said, it is also true the location of animals is fleeting and unpredictable (while groves of plants, once found, can be readily relocated). Exploiting a new, high-ranked prey species required (as earlier noted) studying its behaviour, learning where and when it might be found (its preferred grazing or browsing areas), and how best to approach it.

Animal prey can be highly mobile, moving seasonally as forage conditions change, especially in response to the arrival of hunters on the scene. Prey quickly get over any initial naïveté they might have once the spears start flying. They either change their behaviour or move out of reach. Finding fewer targets, the hunters themselves need to range more widely in search of game.

It's a volatile market for hunter-gatherers, and one they monitor by moving: insurance for hunter-gatherers is knowing where to go next, when return rates diminish where they are. Colonists entering a new region, Bird and O'Connell suggest, 'should occupy the highest-ranked patch first', all other things being equal (and assuming they can find it).[23] Whether, when, and where to move is decided after solving a complicated equation incorporating knowledge about climate, plants, and animals. Long-time residents of a landscape have relatively complete information about resources on which to base decisions about how long to stay and when to leave.[24]

[. . .]

TRUST ANYONE OVER THIRTY

[. . .]

One individual or group can only cover so much ground. By talking to others and tapping their knowledge about resources available in other areas, a person can learn about places they've never been, animals they've never hunted, and plants they've never tasted, not to mention draw maps of areas far larger than they had ever seen. Not surprisingly, as Silberbauer observed, when calculating moves on the landscape, all adults in the foraging group participated in the decision-making process.[25]

Colonizers new to a landscape haven't got elders, relatives, or neighbours who can pass along what they have learned over their lifetimes (though it perhaps goes without saying, they haven't got written records either). But they have descendants. As groups moved into the new landscape, knowledge was gained by observation and experience, and 'recorded' in folklore, storytelling, and ritual. But how quickly would colonizers learn the routes, climates, and resources of a landscape, particularly a landscape the size of, say, North America? We have no answers. Most studies agree detailed landscape learning is a prolonged process, with estimates ranging from 200–1,000 years. Even the early English colonists in America, with all the relative technological advantages they possessed, took more than a century before they had accurate maps of their region.

[. . .]

Knowledge grows exponentially, since it can be transmitted by the telling (genetic adaptations take longer to pass along) and thus shared widely within and between generations, thereby rapidly spreading information about areas, events, and conditions otherwise experienced by only a few. To be sure, lessons learned in one area may be irrelevant in different settings, but one never knows.

Landscape learning likely begins at the broadest geographic scale, in what John Beaton calls *megapatches*, which are ecological features on the order of coasts, plains, mountains, deserts, or forests.[26] The first occupants of the Great Plains (a possible megapatch) would have seen large-game animals on a vast grassland. It likely all looked the same to them, for they would not have known and would have to learn there was surprising variability in the grasses on which those animals grazed, and thus differences in their abundance and distribution across the region. Over time, those came into better focus as colonists saw more of the details within the plains.

In effect, landscape learning of routes and resources probably took place from the *general to the specific in terms of space*, but from the *specific to the general in terms of time*, particularly in the case of climate (which is initially observed as the daily weather).

Landscape learning has costs in terms of time and energy. But those costs are offset by the benefits of acquiring information that reduces uncertainty and increases one's odds of surviving and thriving.[27] People can still get lost, can still starve, and can still run out of food or water. But they are less likely to do so the more they know.

It's fair to surmise that the greatest effort in information acquisition would occur in patchy and unpredictable environments, the very situation in which the first Americans initially found themselves. Accordingly, early on in the colonization process, there was a great advantage to learning the local geography, climate, and resources of these unfamiliar landscapes. Under the circumstances, there was good reason to see what was over the next hill . . . and the hill after that.

[. . .]

CONTINENTAL COLONIZERS

How, then, might a colonizing band move into an unoccupied land, maintain their demographic viability, and thereby minimize their risk of extinction? John Beaton envisions two strategies that mark the opposite ends of a continuum of possibilities: Estate Settlers and Transient Explorers. We'll call them the Cautious and the Bold.[28]

Cautious is the band that moves slowly and over relatively shorter distances. They settle into a valley, and explore it and the surrounding region; over time, their numbers build. As this happens, some of the younger members see the area becoming crowded, minor spats become more frequent, and once-plentiful game declines. On their increasingly more-distant hunting forays, hunters spot rich and unoccupied lands down the valley and beyond the edge of the home 'estate'. A decision is made, and soon a part of the group splinters off, but they don't venture too far. Instead, they stay close enough to maintain contact with kin,

keep to an environment with which they are familiar and in which they have become successful, and a place from which—if things go badly—they can always retreat and find relatives who will help. It's a low-risk strategy. Over time, the process of population growth followed by budding repeats itself, and the descendants of the estate ultimately expand to cover the continent. This process does not happen at a terribly fast pace. Beaton envisions groups that 'moved only slowly across the latitudes and longitudes, each daughter colony being spawned by the overflow of a saturated estate.' Since colonization is ultimately fuelled by population growth, to speed it along would require higher population growth rates, sometimes unnaturally high rates.[29]

Bold is the band that moves independent of population size. They come into the country and occupy a habitat, but the moment return rates begin to decline, they move on, without waiting until crowding forces their hand. And so they move often. In rich and unoccupied Pleistocene North America, when hunting returns declined, there was little incentive or need to stay put, not when there was a better living to be had several valleys over, down the coast, or over the mountains. This strategy favours rapid dispersal over a large area, with much of the continent ultimately passed over lightly, as colonizers leapfrogged from one high-ranked patch to another. They can make a good living, these transient explorers, but it's not without risk: small groups that go too far too fast soon find themselves geographically isolated, alone on a vast landscape. That can put a severe strain on their ability to maintain long-distance contacts and an accessible source of mates for their children, raising the specter of inbreeding and drift (cultural and genetic), and making the group as a whole vulnerable to disappearing altogether in the face of drought, blizzard, disease, or accident.[30] Calamities happen.

Thus, colonizers on a landscape with few other people—and this applies to both the Cautious and the Bold, but especially the latter—not only had to be able to find distant mates and marriage partners (and incidentally exchange information and resources), but they also had to be able to get along with any groups they encountered, kin or no. Having large and open social networks, flexible kin relations, and the ability to move easily between and integrate new individuals and groups, as well as maintain long-distance exchange and alliance networks, all combine to diminish differences among peoples who need to stick together under geographic circumstances that might otherwise keep them far apart for years at a time.[31] Strongly territorial behaviour, or hostility toward strangers, would be decidedly disadvantageous to people at this place and time.

On a diverse and unfamiliar landscape, the risk of extinctions is greatest soon after dispersal, when population numbers and growth rates tend to be low. The Cautious hedge their bets and stay close enough to readily maintain overall numbers, but the price is slow colonizing progress. The Bold run greater demographic risks, but the rewards are higher: 'with a generalized tool kit, a naïve fauna, an unconstrained social/political environment, and a bit of luck, a lineage might see the Northern Lights, note the transit of the Equatorial sun, and feel the chill winds of the southern oceans in the space of ten or fewer generations. This is its own form of success.'[32]

Arguably, then, colonization of a new landscape likely involved trade-offs between a series of competing demands, including

1. *maintaining resource returns*, or keeping food on the table, particularly as preferred or high-ranked resources declined, and in the face of limited knowledge of the landscape;

2. *maximizing mobility*, in order to learn as much as possible, as quickly as possible about the landscape and its resources (in order to reduce environmental uncertainty in space and time);

3. *maximizing residence time in resource-rich habitats*, in order to enhance knowledge of specific changes in resource abundance and distribution (you learn more by staying longer);

4. *minimizing group size*, in order to buffer environmental uncertainty or risk on an unknown landscape; and, finally and perhaps most critically,

5. *maintaining contact between dispersed groups*, in order to exchange information, resources, and especially mates.

Colonizers had to balance the equation between *moving to explore* and *staying to observe*.

So were the first peoples Cautious or Bold? It's a trick question, since these are just the extreme possibilities, and there are many variants in between. But I lean toward the Bold and for a very simple reason. The archaeological record we have, whether of Clovis of pre-Clovis, is not dense enough to match what we would expect to see of Cautious estate settlers. [. . .] That does not rule out a role for population growth in the New World colonization; it only means this was not the apparent driving force. [. . .]

NOTES

1. Making it rather odd that some colleagues complain about models for colonization of the Americas that lack ethnographic examples (G. Haynes 2002). Of course they do. That's hardly a fault of the model—just a reflection of reality.

2. Anthony 1990; Irwin 1992:211–2; Keegan and Diamond 1987:69; Kirch 1997:64–5.

3. Expansion beyond what's needed to settle an expanding population seems true of Oceania as well, as noted by Kirch 1997:64; Irwin 1992:212–5.

4. Gamble 1994:94.

5. Kirch 1997:65.

6. Irwin 1992:214; also Gamble 1994:182, 241–2, 245.

7. For example, Barton et al. 2004:149.

8. Kelly and Todd 1988; also Kelly 1996. Kelly and Todd expressly disavowed the exploitation of Pleistocene megafauna, but their model essentially demands it—and most others accept the notion that these were the prey in question (see Meltzer 2004 for a fuller discussion).

9. Van Dyne et al. 1980:285–98; also Frison 1991:41; Johnson et al. 1992; Winterhalder et al. 1988.

10. Frison 2004:226.

11. Much of the discussion that follows comes from Meltzer 2002 and 2004, and references therein.

12. Resource depression, as more formally defined, is 'the situation in which the activities of a predator lead to reduced capture rates of prey by that predator' (Charnov, Orians, and Hyatt 1976). As Donald Grayson explains, 'These reduced capture rates may result from "behavioral depression", in which prey adopt behaviors—for instance, increased vigilance or altered periods of activity—that decrease the likelihood that they will be preyed upon. They may also result from "microhabitat depression", in which prey decrease their vulnerability by moving out of geographic reach of their predators, or from "exploitation depression", in which numbers of prey individuals decrease because harvest rates exceed both reproductive rates and rates of in-migration. From the point of view of the predator, all have the same impact—reduced prey availability' (Grayson 2001:5).

13. Van Dyne et al. 1980:286, 320.

14. Stahle et al. 1998.

15. See R. Nelson (1969:99–104) on being lost in the Arctic; Silberbauer (1981) on desert foragers.

16. Golledge 2003.

17. Wyckoff 1993; Anderson and Faught 2000.

18. Moermann, personal communication, 2000. Also Berlin and Berlin 1996:53. Moermann estimates the number of medicinal plants among the North American flora at approximately 2700 species.

19. Dillehay (1991) examines the role of disease in the colonization of America.

20. MacNutt 1912, letter of November 1493.

21. Snyder and Leonard 2006.

22. Kelly and Todd 1988:234.

23. Bird and O'Connell 2006:155.

24. Kaplan and Hill 1992:186; Kelly 1995:96–8; Stephens and Krebs 1986:75.

25. Silberbauer 1981:249.

26. Beaton 1991:220–1.

27. Binford 1983:34; Kelly 1995:150–1.

28. Beaton 1991.

29. Beaton 1991:223; see also Martin 1973; Szathmary 1993.

30. Borgerhoff Mulder 1992:341–2; MacArthur and Wilson 1967:78, 80, 88; Meltzer 1995, 1999; Whallon 1989:434–5.

31. Anderson 1995; Meltzer 2002; Lourandos 1997:28.

32. Beaton 1991:224.

REFERENCES

Anderson, D. (1995). Paleoindian interaction networks in the eastern woodlands. In *Native American interaction: multiscalar analyses and interpretations in the eastern woodlands*, edited by M. Nassaney and K. Sassaman, pp. 1–26. University of Tennessee Press, Knoxville.

Anderson, G. and M. Faught. (2000). Paleoindian artefact distribution: evidence and implications. *Antiquity* 74: 507–13.

Anthony, D.W. (1990). Migration in archaeology: the baby and the bathwater. *American Anthropologist* 92: 895–914.

Barton, M., S. Schmich, and S. James. (2004). The ecology of human colonization in pristine landscapes. In *The settlement of the American continents: a multidisciplinary approach to human biogeography*, edited by C.M. Barton, G.A. Clark, D.R. Yesner, and G.A. Pearson, pp. 138–61. University of Arizona Press, Tucson.

Beaton, J. (1991). Colonizing continents: some problems from Australia and the Americas. In *The first Americans: search and research*, edited by T.D. Dillehay and D.J. Meltzer, pp. 209–30. CRC Press, Baton Rouge, LA.

Berlin, E. and B. Berlin. (1996). *Medical ethnobiology of the Highland Maya of Chiapas, Mexico: the gastrointestinal diseases*. Princeton University Press, Princeton, NJ.

Binford, L.R. (1983). Long term land use patterns: some implications for archaeology. In *Lulu linear punctuated: essays in honor of George Irving Quimby*, edited by R.C. Dunnell and D.K. Grayson. *University of Michigan Anthropological Papers* 72: 27–53.

Bird, D. and J.F. O'Connell. (2006). Behavioral ecology and archaeology. *Journal of Archaeological Research* 14: 143–88.

Borgerhoff Mulder, M. (1992). Reproductive decisions. In *Evolutionary ecology and human behaviour*, edited by E. Smith and B. Winterhalder, pp. 339–74. Aldine de Gruyter, New York.

Charnov, R., G. Orians, and K. Hyatt. (1976). The ecological implications of resource depression. *American Naturalist* 110: 247–59.

Dillehay. T.D. (1991). Disease ecology and human migration. In *The first Americans: search and research*, edited by T. Dillehay and D. Meltzer, pp. 231–64. CRC Press, Boca Raton, FL.

Frison, G.C. (1991). *Prehistoric hunters of the high plains*, 2nd ed. Academic Press, New York.

———. (2004). *Survival by hunting: Prehistoric human predators and animal prey*. University of California Press, Berkeley.

Gamble, C. (1994). *Timewalkers: the prehistory of global colonization*. Harvard University Press, Cambridge, MA.

Golledge, R. (2003). Human wayfinding and cognitive maps. In *Colonization of unfamiliar landscapes: the archaeology of adaptation*, edited by M. Rockman and J. Steele, pp. 25–43. Routledge, London.

Grayson, D.K. (2001). The archaeology record of human impacts on animal populations. *Journal of World Prehistory* 15: 1–68.

Haynes, G. (2002). *The early Settlement of North America: the Clovis Era*. Cambridge University Press, Cambridge.

Irwin, G. (1992). The prehistoric exploration and colonization of the pacific. Cambridge University Press, Cambridge.

Johnson, A.R., J. Wiens, B. Milne, and T. Crist. (1992). Animal movements and population dynamics in heterogeneous landscapes. *Landscape Ecology* 7: 63–75.

Kaplan, H. and K. Hill. (1992). The evolutionary ecology of food acquisition. In *Evolutionary ecology and human behaviour*, edited by E. Smith and B. Winterhalder, pp. 167–201. Aldine de Gruyter, New York.

Keegan, W. and J. Diamond. (1987). Colonization of islands by humans: a biogeographic perspective. *Advances in Archaeological Method and Theory* 10: 49–92.

Kelly, R.L. (1995). *The foraging spectrum: diversity in hunter-gatherer lifeways*. Smithsonian Institution Press, Washington, D.C.

———. (1996). Ethnographic analogy and migration to the western hemisphere. In *Prehistoric Mongoloid dispersals*, edited by T. Akazawa and E. Szathmary, pp. 228–40. Oxford University Press, Oxford.

Kelly, R.L. and L. Todd. (1988). Coming into the country: early Paleoindian hunting and mobility. *American Antiquity* 53: 231–44.

Kirch, P.V. (1997). The Lapita peoples: ancestors of the Oceanic World. Blackwell, New York.

Lourandos, H. (1997). *Continent of hunter-gatherers: new perspectives in Australian prehistory*. Cambridge University Press, Cambridge.

MacArthur, R. and E.O. Wilson. (1967). *The theory of island biogeography*. Monographs in Population Biology 1. Princeton University Press, Princeton.

MacNutt, F.A. (1912). *De orbe novo, the eight decades of Peter Martyr d'Anghera*. Translated from the Latin with notes and introduction. G.P. Putnam's Sons, New York.

Martin, P.S. (1973). The discovery of America. *Science* 179: 969–74.

Meltzer, D.J. (1995). Clocking the first Americans. *Annual Review of Anthropology* 24: 21–45.

———. (2002). What do you do when no one's been there before? Thoughts on the exploration and colonization of nev lands. In *First Americans: the Pleistocene colonization of the New World*, edited by N. Jablonski. Memoirs of the California Academy of Sciences 27: 25–56.

———. (2004). Modeling the initial colonization of the Americas: issues of scale, demography, and landscape learning. In *The settlement of the American continents: a multidisciplinary approach to human biogeogaphy*, edited by C.M. Barton, G.A. Clark, D.R. Yesner, and G.A. Pearson, pp. 123–37. University of Arizona Press, Tucson.

Nelson, R. (1969). *Hunters of the northern ice*. University of Chicago Press, Chicago.

Silberbauer, G. (1981). *Hunter & habitat in the central Kahalari Desert*. Cambridge University Press, Cambridge.

Snyder, L.M. and J. Leonard. (2006). Dog. *Handbook of North American Indians, Vol. 3, environment, origins, and population*, edited by D. Ubelaker, pp. 452–62. Smithsonian Institution Press, Washington, D.C.

Stahle, D., M. Cleaveland, D. Blanton, M. Therrell, and D. Gray. (1998). The Lost Colony and Jamestown droughts. *Science* 280: 564–7.

Stephens, D. and J. Krebs. (1986). *Foraging theory*. Princeton University Press, Princeton.

Szathmary, E.J. (1993). Genetics of aboriginal North Americans. *Evolutionary Anthropology* 1: 202–20.

Van Dyne, G.M., N. Brockington, Z. Szocs, J. Duek, and C. Ribic. (1980). Large herbivore system. In *Grasslands, systems analysis, and man*, edited by A.I. Breymeyer and G.M. Van Dyne, pp. 269–537.

Whallon, R. (1989). Elements of culture change in the Later Paleolithic. In *The human revolution: behavioural and biological perspectives on the origins of modern humans*, edited by P. Mellars and C. Stringer, pp. 433–54.

Winterhalder, B., W. Baillargeon, F. Cappalleto. R. Daniel, and C. Prescott. (1988). The population dynamics of hunter-gatherers and their prey. *Journal of Anthropological Archaeology* 7: 289–328.

Wyckoff, D. (1993). Gravel sources of knappable Alibates silicified dolomite. *Geoarchaeology* 8: 35–58.

Chapter Two

Missionaries and First Nations

READINGS

Primary Documents

1 From *Word from New France: The Selected Letters of Marie de l'Incarnation*, Joyce Marshall

2 From *The Jesuit Relations and Allied Documents: Travels and Explorations of the Jesuit Missionaries in New France, 1610–1791*, Reuben Gold Thwaites

Historical Interpretations

3 From *Harvest of Souls: The Jesuit Missions and Colonialism in North America, 1632–1650*, Carole Blackburn

4 From *Bitter Feast: Amerindians and Europeans in Northeastern North America, 1600–1664*, Denys Delâge

Introduction

With the French determination to stay and colonize a corner of North America came a determination to make the indigenous people living in what came to be called New France into faithful Christians. The belief system that had conquered Europe and had also led its faithful into battle during the Middle Ages was, by the mid-sixteenth century, undergoing its own crisis in the form of the Protestant Reformation. The Jesuit order that emerged as one of Catholicism's weapons during the struggle was well-suited (at least in the eyes of church leaders) to undertake missionary work in the new world. After their arrival in the early 1610s, the Jesuits and other orders took some time to set their missionary work in motion, not really becoming effective until the 1630s. Part of the problem for them was that the French colonial claim to the region was not yet at its strongest.

We include one primary source, the *Jesuit Relations*, which has been the richest account of the Jesuits' work. In the *Relations*, essentially a massive collection of reports, the missionaries reflect upon the successes and failures in their work, and try to describe some of the characteristics of life among a wide variety of Aboriginal peoples. Their contact with the Huron, or Wendat, people was especially significant, as disease and the Wendat alliance with the French and Jesuits would result in the nation's destruction and dispersal by 1650.

The other primary source comes from the same era, but from a member of a female order, the Ursulines. The Ursulines arrived in Quebec in 1639. Their initial objectives were to convert and educate Aboriginal girls. In order to do so, they opened the first learning institution in New France shortly after landing in the colony. Their convent soon afterward began to provide education to the daughters of the French colonists. The Ursulines eventually also provided care for the sick. As Roman Catholic nuns, the Ursulines took great pleasure in the news of religious conversions among indigenous people.

We have scant evidence of suspicion among these missionaries that their work may have been harming its targets. Why would they doubt the faith when having faith in its eternal truth was part of their 'job description'? Secondary sources, looking into the records of these missionary groups, cast a different light on the interaction between missionaries and Aboriginal peoples, interpreting the presence of missionaries as a disruption to the livelihoods and long-term physical and psychological or spiritual health of these societies. In her article, Carole Blackburn focuses on the resistance offered by the Hurons to the missionaries. For his part, Denis Delâge explains the reasons that led some Hurons to convert.

As you read the secondary work included here, try to hold these two perspectives in mind: the missionaries' eagerness to deliver salvation and the often tragic results of that effort. It is a theme that would be repeated much closer to our own time.

QUESTIONS FOR CONSIDERATION

1. The simplest and most obvious answer to the question 'What motivated the missionaries?' is probably 'faith'. Is there a better answer—one that addresses missionaries' earthly goals for the First Nations people they lived with?

2. What aspects of Aboriginal life did those who compiled the *Jesuit Relations* consider worthy of their attention? Why?

3. Why do you think missionaries needed to live for extended periods among Aboriginal people? Could they just have visited once in a while?

4. What might have led the Huron/Wendat to distrust the missionaries among them?

5. What might have led the Huron/Wendat to believe that a higher power favoured the missionaries?

SUGGESTIONS FOR FURTHER READING

Blackburn, Carole, *Harvest of Souls: The Jesuit Missions and Colonialism in North America, 1632–1650* (Montreal and Kingston: McGill-Queen's University Press, 2000)

Greer, Allan, *Mohawk Saint: Catherine Tekakwitha and the Jesuits* (New York: Oxford University Press, 2005)

Kennedy, J.H., *Jesuit and Savage in New France* (New Haven: Yale University Press, 1950)

Parkman, Francis, *The Jesuits in North America in the Seventeenth Century* (many editions)

Thwaites, Reuben Gold, ed., *The Jesuit Relations and Allied Documents: Travels and Explorations of the Jesuit Missionaries in New France, 1610–1791* (73 vol. in 35) (New York: Pageant Books, 1959)

Trigger, Bruce, *The Children of Aataentsic: A History of the Huron People to 1660* (Montreal and Kingston: McGill-Queen's University Press, 1976)

PRIMARY DOCUMENTS

1 From Marie de l'Incarnation to her son, 30 September 1643, in Joyce Marshall, ed., *Word from New France: The Selected Letters of Marie de l'Incarnation* (Toronto: Oxford University Press, 1967), 122–6, 387–8.

17. NEWS OF JOGUES

TO HER SON.

Quebec, 30 SEPTEMBER 1643

My very dear and well-loved son:

May the love and life of the King of nations consume your heart with the ardour with which he transports the hearts of our converts.

You ought now to have received the letters I wrote to you in the month of July last and in which I gave you a brief account of what happened last year in New France and in the new Church of Jesus Christ. [. . .]

But I must not waste time; let us begin to speak of our converts. The first foundations of the Church have been laid this year at Miscou,[1] which is a French settlement solely for traffic in furs. Ten leagues beyond the settlement, a chapel has been built and a large mission established for the Savages to the north, who have been drawn to the Faith by the conversation of our Montagnais Savages from Tadoussac. This mission promises great fruit, for the material is ready. It is about a hundred and fifty leagues from here, going in your direction.

A hundred leagues to this side of it is the Tadoussac mission, where marvels have been seen this year, a great many Savages, who live more than twenty days' journey by land away, having come there to be instructed and then baptized. They have such religious sentiments and perform such Christian acts that they make us ashamed and surpass us in piety. This is the fruit of the zeal of our good settled Christians, for they go in one direction and the other expressly to win souls to Jesus Christ. All these nations are from the regions to the north; and Tadoussac, where they assemble, is forty leagues or thereabouts from here, going towards Miscou.

Sillery is one league above Quebec and we are midway.[2] Some of our settled Savages are at Sillery and the others at Quebec, where trade is carried on.

Last year the Attikamegue nation came here to be instructed and more than half of them were baptized. The first baptism was held in our church, and the first marriage also, for when a man and woman are baptized they are at the same time united before the Church. Several others were afterwards baptized and married. I must confess that the joy my heart feels when I see a soul washed with the blood of Jesus Christ cannot be expressed.

These good people were instructed every day in our chapel. After Mass we made them a feast of peas or sagamite—Indian corn with dried plums—after which they spent almost all the day at our grille, to receive some instruction or learn some prayer. It was a prodigy to see with what promptness and facility they learned everything they were taught.

One poor woman, who had a slightly duller mind than the others, grew angry with herself and said as she prostrated herself, 'I shall not get up, from this day, unless I know my prayers.' She kept her mouth pressed against the ground all day and God so blessed her fervour that, when she arose, she knew everything she had wished to learn. Fervour is universal and we are overjoyed to see great men coming eagerly to see us so that we may teach them to make interior acts and jaculatory orisons, which they employ when required.

The chief of this nation was a great sorcerer and the most superstitious man alive. I listened to him uphold the virtue of his charms and superstitions, and soon afterwards he came to see the Father with whom he had disputed, bringing his charms and the drum he had used in his enchantments, and declared that he intended never to use them again. I am sending the drum to you so you may see how the devil beguiles and seduces this poor people with a child's device, for you will know that it is used to cure sickness, to predict things to come, and for similar extraordinary things. After this change of heart, we had the consolation of seeing all the drums of this nation sacrificed to God in a single day.

Later they all went back, hunting, to their own county [the upper St Maurice valley], so as to arrive there in the spring. And because they are newly instructed, one of our new Christian women of Sillery went with them in terrible snowy cold to make them repeat their prayers each day for fear they might forget them. We have learned that they are leading an admirable life.

It is a marvel to see the fervour of our good converts. They are not satisfied with believing in Jesus Christ, but their zeal so carries them away that they are not content and think they only half believe if all do not believe as they do. The chief of the Abnakiouois [Abenakis] left his country and his people to come to settle here so he could be instructed and afterwards win his people to the Faith of Jesus Christ. He was baptized yesterday and married to one of our seminarians, named Angèle, of whom the *Relations* spoke last year with great praise. His zeal will carry him even further for he is resolved to carry the Gospel into many other nations. 'I shall not be content', he told me, 'to bring my people and my young men to faith and prayer, but as I have been in several other nations and know their tongues, I shall make use of this advantage to go to visit them and bring them to believe in God.'

It is not only the men that are on fire with this zeal. A Christian woman went to a very distant nation expressly to catechize those that live there and succeeded so well in this that she brought them all here, where they were baptized. She needed an apostolic courage to face the dangers to which she exposed herself in order to render this service to Our Lord. We often see like fervour in our good converts who, to be quite truthful, put those that were born of Christian parents to shame.

There is no prominent person among the Hurons that does not wish to be a Christian. Four chapels have been built in their country this year and hitherto they would scarcely suffer one. The Iroquois, nevertheless, persecute this poor nation greatly. They captured and killed a great number of them two years ago and but a fortnight since they defeated their fleet again.[3]

You know that last year they captured the Reverend Father Jogues, some Frenchmen, and one of our seminarians. They killed the old men[4] and made captives of the others. The Reverend Father was beaten into insensibility and stripped naked upon his arrival in their country. His thumb was cut off and his index finger gnawed to the joint. The ends of his other fingers were burned and then he was made to suffer a thousand ignominies. As much was done to a Frenchman

[Guillaume Couture], his domestic, and another [René Goupil], who was also in his service, had his head split by the blow of a hatchet.[5] The poor Father, believing that the same would be done to him, go down on his knees to receive the blow and offer his sacrifice, but nothing further was done to him. The same was done to the greater number of the captives as to the Father, and then all their lives were spared. Our seminarian, Thérèse, has suffered no injury and has courageously continued to profess the Holy Gospel and to pray in public. The Reverend Father is at present preaching the Gospel among the Iroquois; he is the first to have that honour, and God has so blessed his labour that he has baptized more than sixty persons in his captivity.[6]

I must speak a little of our seminarians, who give us all possible satisfaction.

One said to me a little while ago, 'I often speak to God in my heart. I get great pleasure from naming Jesus and Mary. Ah, what beautiful names they are!'

We sometimes hear them conversing together about God and making spiritual colloquies. One day among others they were asking one another for what they believed the were most greatly obliged to God.

One said, 'It is because he made himself a man for me and suffered death to deliver me from hell.'

Another replied, 'It is because he made me a Christian and placed me, by baptism, in the number of his children.'

A little girl, who is but nine years old and has been receiving communion for a year and a half, raised her voice and said, 'It is because Jesus gives himself to us as meat at the Blessed Sacrament of the altar.'

Is this not delightful in girls born in barbarism?

They never fail to make their examination of conscience or to accuse one another of their offences, which they do with matchless simplicity. They sometimes ask to be punished so they can pay the penalty to God for their sins while they are still in this world. When one of them had been punished, we asked her what she thought of the chastisement she had been given.

'I thought', she said, 'that you must love me, since you punished me to bring me to my senses, for I have no sense yet. I, who have been instructed, am much much more guilty than my companion, who was not.'

You see our employments. I beg you to be very mindful of the kingdom of Jesus Christ. Pray for the conversion of the Iroquois, who hinder it greatly and close the passages lest the more distant nations come here to be instructed. The Iroquet nation was not allowed to pass through the lands of these barbarians, who fired more than a hundred shots at them, but God so well protected them that there was not a single one of them wounded.[7]

I am writing to you at night because of the pressure of letters and the imminent departure of the vessels. My hand is so weary that I can scarcely govern it—it is this that makes me finish by begging you to excuse me if I do not reread my letter.

NOTES

1. The Jesuits had maintained two priests at Miscou—an island off the northeast coast of New Brunswick at the entrance to the Baie des Chaleurs—since 1634 for the benefit of the Frenchmen who came there in connection with the fur trade. Marie de l'Incarnation's use of the words 'first foundations of the Church' refers to the building of the chapel and a mission devoted exclusively to the Indians.

2. The Ursulines had occupied their new monastery in the upper town of Quebec since 21 November 1642. It was situated just west of the fort and was the first building encountered by the Indians of

Sillery as they came along rue Saint-Louis (Grande Allée). This is undoubtedly Marie de l'Incarnation's meaning, though her use of the word 'milieu', middle, is somewhat ambiguous. At the time there was no direct access to Sillery from the lower town except by boat.

3.   As the result of this most recent capture, of a fleet that was attempting to carry supplies to the Huron missions, the Jesuits in Huronia were deprived for the second year in a row of the necessities of food and clothing that they were accustomed to receive annually from Quebec.

4.   According to Jogues's own account, only one old man had been killed.

5.   Goupil was killed 29 September 1642 at Ossernenon (now Auriesville, New York), on the order of an old man, who was angered because Goupil had made the sign of the cross over a child. Couture was adopted by a Mohawk family to replace a dead relative, according to a common Indian custom.

6.   News of these things had been brought to Quebec by Thérèse's uncle, Joseph Teondechoren, who had escaped with some of the other prisoners. Jogues himself had managed to send a letter to France and to have others delivered to Quebec. Within weeks of his capture, Arendt van Corlaer, the Dutch commandant of Fort Orange (Albany, New York), had tried without success to ransom him from the Mohawks.

7.   The *Relation* (JR XXIV) tells a different story. A group of Algonkian Iroquets, who had sought refuge at Montreal, was sent out to parley with some Iroquois that had approached the settlement. The Iroquois then fired upon them, though none of the Iroquets was injured. The Iroquets, who lived above Montreal between the St. Lawrence and the Ottawa Rivers, had no occasion to traverse the Iroquois country.

---

2   From 'Of the Huron Who Wintered at Québec and Sillery', in Reuben Gold Thwaites, ed., *The Jesuit Relations and Allied Documents: Travels and Explorations of the Jesuit Missionaries in New France, 1610–1791* (Cleveland: Burrows, 1898), 103–21.

CHAPTER VII.
OF THE HURONS WHO WINTERED AT QUEBEC AND SILLERY.

The Seminary of the Hurons, which had been established at nostre-Dame des Anges some Years ago, in order to educate children of that nation, was interrupted for good reasons, and especially because no notable fruit was seen among the Savages; our experience in beginning the instruction of a people with the children, has made us recognize this fact. Here is an occasion which has obliged us to reëstablish a Seminary in a new fashion, as it were,—but easier, and in behalf of persons, older, and more capable of instruction. God grant that the incursions of the Hiroquois may not hinder us from continuing.

[104] A young man, of those who had formerly been at the first Seminary of the Hurons at Nostre Dame des Anges, happening to be in a great storm, in the midst of their great lake, made a vow to God, if he escaped, to lead a more regular and orderly life. His vow is heard,—he is delivered, contrary to every human probability; he goes to find our Fathers who were with the Hurons, and imparts to them his vow and his resolution. They think thereon; they deliberate; they finally resolve to take him out of his own country, where he was in greater danger, and to send him down here, so that he should be better aided, and that he might see the example of the French and of the Algonquins of Sillery. They gave him for companion another Huron young man, who desired to become a Christian; both these arrived at Sillery last year, in the month of September. It

was on that occasion that I again detained Father Jean de Brebeuf, who had wintered here in the preceding year, and who had not yet gone up again, in order to instruct them and to take charge of them. Several other Huron young men, who had come down to trade, presented themselves [105] also to us, in order to be received and instructed; but, the scanty provisions that we have not permitting us to admit any more, part of them were constrained to return to their own country, and the others, to join the Algonquins in order to go during the winter to the hunt or to the war with them.

Nevertheless, the charity of Monsieur the Governor and of the Hospital Mothers has given us means to add three to the first two, and to baptize those with us who were not baptized. With the help that I have mentioned, we have lodged and maintained four of them, and toward the Spring, a sixth, who came unexpectedly. Generally speaking, all have greatly edified us; they were always among the first at Mass and at prayers, and were the last to leave, both at evening and in the morning. They failed not to say their prayers, quite long, on both knees, whether they were at home or hunting in the woods. Several times in the day they went to the Chapel, to pray to God and salute the blessed Sacrament; they would take care not to begin anything [106] without having first made the sign of the Cross. All, since their baptism, have not failed to Confess themselves and receive Communion at least every Sunday; and several of them went to Confess themselves as soon as they thought they had committed any notable fault. Throughout the winter, they went every Sunday to Quebec, in order to attend high Mass, from which they have not been absent, whatever the state of the weather,—although the distance is about two leagues, and though they were usually obliged to start before daylight, during the rigor of the winter; but the desire of pleasing God, and the satisfaction that they received in seeing the devotion of our French, assembled in the Church, caused them to find nothing difficult. Moreover, the peace and unity in which they have lived together, and with our French and the Algonquin Savages, and the services which they willingly rendered, showed well enough what the power of faith and of the divine grace can do when it has gained possession of even Savage hearts. The foregoing is what was common to all; here follows what is individual. The one who [107] gave occasion for the whole enterprise is a certain Armant Andewaraken, who has aided not a little, by his deeds and his words, in the instruction of the others, and in encouraging them to do well. Our Lord has imparted to him, at intervals, great desires for his salvation,—and sometimes even to forsake the world and to enter into Religion, which he knows very well, and separates from the common life; but it requires a long probation,—to be a Savage and to be a Religious are things which seem very repugnant; nevertheless, the grace of God, and time, will avail to compass everything. This young man came one day of last Winter to find Father Brebeuf, at the end of his Mass, and spoke to him as follows: 'My Father, I have great desire to do right and to save myself; I have wholly resolved that, for I fear those fires which burn incessantly beneath the earth, and which are never extinguished. In order to attain what I desire, I would like to live always with you, and not return to the Hurons, where there is great difficulty in saving oneself,—the opportunities for sin are frequent in our villages, [108] and the liberty in them is great. I am nevertheless determined to obey, and to do everything which the Father Superior shall order. If he commanded me to go to the Hyroquois, I would go very willingly, without any escort; and even if he commanded me to cast myself, at the loss of life, into this river which passes yonder before us, I would do so at once.' Thus he spoke, not looking at the thing which in itself is illicit, but simply at the command. 'Moreover,' he said, 'let the Father Superior tell me what I ought to do; I am sure that it will be the will of God, and therefore I shall acquiesce therein. Archiendassé'—that is to say, Father Hierosme l'Allemant, who is Superior among the Hurons—'has addressed me to him. I know well that you have still other Superiors in France; but it is he who here takes the place of God, and who will tell me what I must do.' The Father Superior sent him word that he greatly praised his design and his devotion; that he should persevere courageously; that we would always have a most special care for him; that, with reference to living down there with us, we would think of it, [109] and we would recommend the matter to God, and that he, on his part, should do the same. There was a consultation after prayers were done, and it was found best that he should return again to his own country,—that God-fearing, as he is, and assisted by our Fathers, this would be the best for him and for his fellow Countrymen. He has mightily applied himself to the mortification of his impulses and inclinations; often he felt himself prone to dispute, and sometimes he would grow angry at certain words; but straightway he would return to himself, and stop short in silence, remembering that he had resolved to do right. One day, having had some difference with one of our Frenchmen, he not only went straightway to Confess, but he went to ask pardon of the one whom he had offended, embracing him tenderly; and since then he has rendered him all the services in his power.

The first to profit by these examples has been a young man named Saouaretchi, who had come down with him; he is of an excellent disposition,—gentle, peaceable, obedient, industrious,—and endowed with a good mind, by means of which he has quickly [110] learned all the prayers. He was baptized on Christmas eve, in the Chapel of the Ursuline Mothers, and named Ignace, by Monsieur Martial Piraube. On the very night of that great Feast, he received his first Communion; and since that time he has always continued to confess himself and receive Communion every Sunday, with much devotion: his desire to be instructed has notably appeared in this point. His comrades, toward the beginning of Lent, having taken the resolution to go hunting for the Moose, he said that, for his part, he would not go; and that he had not come from so far in order to go hunting, but in order to know God, and learn to serve him, and that he made account of no other thing than that; that it was this which he aspired to carry away at his return, and not skins of Moose, or other things. His particular devotion has been to fast every Saturday, in order to prepare himself for Sunday Communion, and for the prompt performance of all that was commanded him. The Baptism of this young man causes us to hope for the Conversion of many others; [111] for, besides that he is very exemplary and very zealous, he belongs to one of the largest and most numerous families of the Hurons, which already is thoroughly attached to the faith, and which awaits, it seems, only the Baptism of this young man in order to plunge after him into those blessed waters.

About the middle of January, one of the other Hurons, who had gone to live among the Algonquins of the Island, and who until then had remained with them near the fort of Richelieu, came down to Sillery, expressly to be instructed in the faith. The village of which he is native is named Arrente,[1] and he is nephew to one of the Captains; but what commends him still more, is his extreme gentleness and docility in every respect. He has very good wit and judgment; mild and thoroughly obedient.

The Hospital Mothers have lodged and fed him, with a charity which embraces all sorts of nations. It is remarkable how much satisfaction he has given them in all the services which have been desired of him; these he has rendered with a cheerfulness, promptness, and constancy that [112] would cause shame to many Frenchmen. His affection toward the faith has made itself noteworthy,—not only in that he constantly came, evening and morning, to find the Father, in order to be instructed; but also in that, having been instructed in some new prayer or lesson, he would repeat and meditate upon it, and that so much and so long, that he knew it before going away. Hence there was no need of telling him the same thing twice over. He failed not to go into the Chapel of the Hospital every evening and every morning, in order to say his prayers there; and stayed there a good space of time. He was baptized at the Hospital, the 8th of March, and was named Pierre by Monsieur de Repentigny, who since then has ever shown him much affection.

About the middle of February, two other Huron young men—natives of the same village as the preceding, and impelled by the same desire to have themselves enrolled in the number of the Christians—also abandoned the Algonquins at the fort of Richelieu, in order to come in quest of Father de Brebeuf, so as to be instructed by him. [113] We received them, moreover, at our abode; for want of room we were constrained to lodge them with our workmen; one was named Atarohiat, and the other, Atokouchiouani. The longing to be baptized as soon as possible, so greatly kindled in them the desire to be instructed, that they had learned all the prayers and the Catechism in a very little while; and one of them, moved with this vehement desire to learn, was not willing to divert himself by going to the hunt with his Comrades, saying: 'The time that we have for staying here is too short: I desire to employ it in obtaining instruction; and then, besides, I have not the happiest memory in the world. I have not come down here to go hunting; and, as for eating meat, if I had cared to eat any, I had only to stay with the Algonquins up there at Richelieu, where the hunt is much better than here.' Seeing that they knew the prayers well, they requested Baptism so ardently,—saying, among other things, that they feared lest, going often into the woods, upon the waters, and into other dangerous places, there might happen to them some misfortune,—[114] that finally it was granted them. It was in the Church of Quebec where they were baptized, very solemnly, the day of the Annunciation of our Lady, when they also received Communion for the first time, according to the custom of the Church. Monsieur de saint Sauveur[2] gave the name of Joseph to Atarohiat; and Monsieur de la Vallée, that of René to Atokouchiouani.

I have said that they had been baptized as solemnly as possible,—and this designedly, because that has much effect upon the minds of the Savages, and is to them, not a slight incentive to belief. To this end, after the baptism of these two latter, Father de Brebeuf—having led all the Hurons before Monsieur the Governor, in order to thank him for so much kindness and honor as he did them—asked them in his presence, all in succession, what that is which touched them the most, and most inclined them to embrace the faith. The first said, that what struck him chiefly was, to consider the omnipotence of God, with whom nothing is impossible; and to think of the [115] marvelous works which he has done, from the beginning of the world,—as, to have drawn so many creatures out of nothing; to have caused the children of Israel to pass through the red sea with dry feet; to have fed them with the Manna for the space of forty years; to have satisfied several thousand persons with five loaves and two fishes; to have raised Lazarus from the dead, four days after death; and countless other like wonders.

Another said that what touched him very strongly was, to see men and Religious maids leave their own country, where they were much at their ease, and without danger, in order to come to places where there is nothing but dangers and incredible inconveniences,—and all that in order to instruct them, and win them to God.

But the most part answered that what mainly attracted their attention was, to see all that was done to honor God. 'When we see,' said they, 'every one assemble here on Sundays and Feasts, in order to hear the Mass and to pray to God; when we see Confessions and frequent Communions, [116] observed with so much devotion; when we consider what is done for the Savages,—how fields are prepared for them, how houses are built for them, how they are assisted in body and soul,—that is what makes us say that faith is something important, and that what you teach is true.' Toward Spring there arrived a sixth, who had been baptized in passing through Montreal, together with some Algonquins. He lodged, as a rule, at the Hospital, with Pierre, his Comrade, and tried to compensate with his fervor for the little time that he should have, and to become instructed before his Baptism. He has given every sort of contentment to Father Brebeuf, in the short time that he could have him for his Teacher. Such has been the status of our five or six Huron boarders, who no doubt would be more numerous if the means were greater. Howbeit, one thing has caused them fear and given them pain,—to wit, the return to their country; 'For,' they said, 'while we shall be here among you, it [117] is hardly possible for us to offend God, seeing so many good examples of virtue, and no vices: but in our own country, it is quite the contrary,—one knows not what it is to do right; it is a chaos of confusion and of disorder.' 'And then,' said the one last baptized, 'there is as yet scarcely any one in our village, or in those round about, who has solidly embraced the faith. We are the first and the only ones.' Thus they spoke, and represented the danger wherein they believed themselves to be, of offending the divine Majesty. In fact, they have just cause to fear, and we also; and if, indeed, some one of them should happen to stumble, we must not be surprised. Nevertheless, we hope in the divine goodness that it will preserve them, and that it will perfect what it has begun. They all went away toward the middle of June, in order to return to their own country, in the company of about six-score other Hurons, who had come for trade. This plan of Seminary is easy, and can be realized at small expense, and is excellent,—choosing a number of young men, of twenty [118] or twenty-five years, of good will and good intelligence, and training them one Autumn and one Winter among our French and our Algonquin Christians; causing them to see and to taste the profession of Christianity among us, and among people of their very country; and then sending them away, under the Guard and the guidance of our Fathers who are with the Hurons. But I know not whether the rage of the Hiroquois will not deprive us of this consolation; and them, of so great a good fortune. If the Hurons were won over, the nation of the Neutrals, and others neighboring, would hardly be slow to follow. The Hurons who have come for trade have told us that these who are being instructed are, at present, the principal men of the country.

NOTES

1. For location of Arent (Aronte), vol. x, *note* 23.
2. Jean le Sueur, a secular priest, came to Canada in 1634, with Giffard (vol. vi, *note* 8); his other title was derived from a parish in Normandy, which he had served, Saint Sauver de Thurry. In 1645–46, he was missionary at Côte de Beaupré, and later officiated in the chapel at Côteau Ste. Genevieve. In March 1646, he became joint proprietor, with Jean Bourdon, of the fief St. Francis (vol. xi, *note* 11). *The Jounr. des Jesuits* frequently mentions him, up to 1660. One of the suburbs of Quebec is named St. Sauveur, for this priest.

HISTORICAL INTERPRETATIONS

3   From Carole Blackburn, *Harvest of Souls: The Jesuit Missions and Colonialism in North America, 1632–1650* (Montreal and Kingston: McGill-Queen's University Press, 2000), 105–28, 153–5.

CONVERSION AND CONQUEST

The Jesuits hoped to promote the obedience and submission that was a necessary attribute of Christian life by reconfiguring Aboriginal social and political relationships. Conversion itself, however, and the Jesuits' ability to gain compliance most frequently occurred after a process of chastisement and humiliation that had been brought about by disease or the consequences of warfare. The Jesuits described the misfortunes that were increasingly experienced by Native people during the 1630s and 1640s as afflictions and crosses, and they wrote that these afflictions had an especially beneficial effect in inducing conversion and generating the humility and obedience that were appropriate to Christian behaviour. Le Jeune, for example, wrote that affliction 'opens the eyes of the understanding' (14:183). He and other Jesuits argued that suffering was necessary in order to reduce the pride and independence that kept people from recognizing the necessity of submission and their obligations to God and the Jesuits. This understanding was pointedly expressed in the *Relation* for the years 1642 and 1643, which stated: 'Humiliations are the harbingers that mark the dwellings of the great God; and tribulation attracts us more strongly and with much more certainty than does comfort. It is necessary to abase the pride and the haughtiness of these people, in order to give admission to the faith' (25:39).

THE HAND THAT SMITES THEM

Shortly after the Jesuits arrived in Huron country, many of the villages were stricken with a disease of European origin. This was the first of a series of epidemics that further reduced the Huron population by almost half over a period of six years (Trigger 1987, 499). Although the Jesuits and other French also became ill during the initial epidemic, they recovered and remained relatively unaffected as the outbreaks of disease recurred. This was in sharp contrast to the inability of large numbers of Huron to withstand the diseases, and it suggested to many of them that the French had some effective means of prevention and cure. The Jesuits were accordingly asked to help stop the sickness—at which point, they took the opportunity to insist that all Huron pray and believe in God, presenting this as 'the true and only means of turning away this scourge of heaven' (13:159). While many people were initially prepared to adopt the

Jesuits' terms, most did not realize the exclusive nature of the priests' demands, and they continued to seek other remedies, leaving the Jesuits to accuse them of hypocrisy and backsliding (13:165, 177).

As the diseases continued unabated, the Jesuits' proposed cures were soon discredited, though most Huron continued to believe that the priests had the power to protect themselves from the illnesses—a belief that was reinforced when the Huron observed the Jesuits spending so much time with the sick yet remaining 'full of life and health' (19:93). For the Huron, withholding assistance from someone who was ill violated community reciprocity, and as a sign of disregard for the welfare of others it could only be motivated by hostile intentions. Such behaviour was easily interpreted as a sign of complicity in a disease that had been caused by witchcraft, which was believed to be the most common cause of incurable illnesses and the most frequent expression of antisocial, hostile sentiments (Trigger 1987, 66–7). Although the residents of most Huron villages first sought to identify and eliminate possible witches among themselves, the majority came to the conclusion that the French, and particularly the Jesuits, were causing the diseases through sorcery.

This interpretation of the Jesuits as witches was encouraged by the priests' reputation as successful and potentially powerful supernatural practitioners. Evidence that the Jesuits possessed power had already been apparent in their success in praying for rain and their ability to predict lunar eclipses (15:139, 175), as well as by a number of the technologies they had brought from Europe. Brébeuf had been involved in a successful bid for rain during his first years with the Huron, before the English defeat of the French and the removal of the missionaries to France (10:43–9). This was not forgotten by those Huron who knew Brébeuf, and during the very dry spring and summer of 1635 they asked the Jesuits to pray for an end to the drought. The efforts of Huron *arendiwane* to do the same had been unsuccessful. One shaman in particular blamed the Jesuits for his failure and demanded, much to the chagrin of the priests, that they take down the cross they had erected in front of their cabin in Ihonatiria (10:37–43). The Jesuits not only refused to remove the cross but they twice enjoyed seeing their prayers and processions followed by a significant amount of rain, as well as by the admiration and respect of many people.

Suspicion about the Jesuits' involvement in the diseases also stemmed from the fact that most Huron did not completely understand the priests' intentions in wanting to live among them (17:125). While it was accepted that traders and warriors had occasion to live with allies or trading partners, the missionaries' evangelical purpose, based as it was on a universalist belief, had no precedent and consequently was open to local interpretation (Trigger 1987, 534). As the diseases spread, the Jesuits' teaching and habits were easily shaped into indisputable proof of hostile intentions and sinister activities, whose ultimate objective was the destruction of the Huron people.

This was particularly the case with behaviour that was culturally alien and either oddly inappropriate or more directly suggestive of the stinginess and uncooperative spirit which the Huron associated with witchcraft. The priests' habit of closing their door at certain times of the day for private meditation, for example, fell within the range of antisocial behaviour, and many Huron believed that the Jesuits needed this privacy in order to practice their sorcery (15:33). Their practice of speaking to those who were sick about death and the afterlife was similarly unusual and inappropriate (15:23, 69). Most people found the priests' continual references to death disturbing and morbid, and they suspected that the Jesuits were concerned not with an individual's recovery but solely with sending him or her to heaven. The Jesuits attempted to aid the sick as much as possible, hoping to advance the cause of Christianity by discrediting the cures offered by the shamans and setting an example of Christian charity (15:69). However, at the same time as they

were diligently attempting to bring people some relief, their stern criticism of Native curing rites and their refusal to participate in them were viewed by most Huron as socially uncooperative behaviour and interpreted as further evidence that the priests actually wanted to prevent people from recovering. In this way, although the priests cast their behaviour in the benevolent idiom of Christian charity and sacrifice, the Huron interpreted it through the divergent idiom of harmful intent and sorcery. Some Huron even suggested that the Jesuits' wish to see them in heaven as soon as possible caused them to shorten the lives of those whom they felt were best prepared for the afterlife (19:241).

The unfamiliar material and technological features of the mission were similarly subject to interpretation by the Huron, who saw in them further evidence of the Jesuits' sorcery. The act of writing, especially, was subject to a variety of appropriations that challenged the Jesuits' own understanding and their expectation of its significance. Writing was the Jesuits' most potent technology, both as the source of their universal truths and because Native people admired their ability to communicate silently through pieces of marked paper. The Jesuits based much of their faith in the truth of Christianity and its universal relevance on the authority of their written tradition. In their attempt to persuade people to convert, they lost no opportunity to assert the value of the Bible as a written document containing the authentic and undistorted Word of God. They argued that while oral traditions were subject to the fallibility of memory and the accumulation of lies and stories invented for the sake of entertainment, the basis of their own faith in the Word, not just spoken but recorded, was indisputable (11:153; 17:135). Le Jeune quickly identified the word used by the Montagnais to speak of the distant past, *nitatohokan*, as meaning 'I relate a fable, I am telling an old story invented for amusement' (6:157). By comparison, when some Huron asked Brébeuf how the Jesuits 'knew there was a Hell, and whence we obtained all that we told about the condition of the damned', he replied 'that we had indubitable proofs of it, that we possessed it through divine revelation; that the Holy Ghost himself had dictated these truths to certain persons, and to our Ancestors, who had left them to us in writing, and that we still carefully preserved the books containing them' (13:51–3).[1]

The Jesuits' faith in the Bible as a written document was deeply embedded in an assumption that all truth and knowledge was textually dependent (Mignolo 1992, 318). The proof of God himself could be 'read' in nature. As one of the priests explained, 'The reality of a God was . . . so clear that it was only necessary to open the eyes to see it written in large characters upon the faces of all creatures' (13:173). I have already noted that the Jesuits' mission in New France depended, in large part, on an oral practice and that the early history of Christianity was itself strongly oral, relying on an oral praxis of preaching and teaching the Word. However, the Jesuits came to North America after the Renaissance, when an ideology of the letter had emerged which emphasized the primacy of writing as well as the physical form of the book itself, both as the essential repository of knowledge and as its principal means of transmission (Mignolo 1992, 311, 318). While Christ himself was originally the Word of God embodied (11:169), the authority of this Word came to be the authority of the Book. Indeed, in an especially interesting gloss on Christ's physical embodiment of textual authority, Le Jeune referred to Christ as 'the living Book' (16:123). Writing, knowledge, and the material form of the book convened in an ideology and philosophy of writing that had considerable effect on interpretations of the New World and its peoples; the absence of a system of alphabetical writing quickly came to be interpreted as a sign of the absence of civilization and as evidence of the inferiority of New World peoples (Mignolo 1992, 317–18).

The priests knew that 'the art of inscribing upon paper matters that are beyond sight' (15:121) visibly impressed the people they were trying to convert. Notes sent between Jesuits from one village to another caused the Native people to think that the priests could predict the future and read minds at a distance, something that only shamans could similarly claim to do (Axtell 1988, 93). In 1635 Brébeuf wrote that the Huron admired the lodestone, prism, and joiner's tools, 'but above all . . . writing, for they could not conceive how, what one of us, being in the village, had said to them, and put down at the same time in writing, another, who meanwhile was in a house far away, could say readily on seeing the writing. I believe they have made a hundred trials of it' (8:113). He added: 'This serves to gain their affections, and to render them more docile when we introduce the admirable and incomprehensible mysteries of our Faith; for the belief they have in our intelligence and capacity causes them to accept without reply what we say to them' (8:113).

However, while the technology of writing contributed to the aura of power and prestige which the Jesuits' were trying to cultivate, they could not control the whole meaning of the relationship between writing and power in the minds of Huron who suspected them of witchcraft. This relationship was quite different from the priests' understanding of the power of writing as a privileged vehicle of knowledge and the permanent repository and record of the Word of God. While it constituted proof that the Jesuits were figures of some unusual skills and power, it was precisely this power that would have enabled the Jesuits to harm people by causing inexplicable diseases through sorcery. That the Jesuits represented themselves as men who had come to North America only for the good of the Huron was irrelevant, since the Huron believed that powerful individuals did not use their power for good or evil exclusively but could put it to use for both purposes.

Thus, although writing initially contributed to the respect with which the priests were treated, as fears of the Jesuits' sorcery grew it also came to be suspected as a means by which the Jesuits targeted people for illness or otherwise spread the contagion. Lalemant explained in 1639 that if the fathers 'asked the name of some one, in order to write it in the register of our baptized ones, and not lose memory of it, it was (they said) that we might pierce him secretly, and afterward, tearing out this written name, cause the death, by this same act, of him or her who bore that name' (19:129). Similarly, when Fathers Antoine Daniel and Simon Le Moyne visited the eastern Arendarhonon villages, some inhabitants of the principal village of Contarea claimed to have seen these fathers in dreams, 'unfolding certain books, whence issued sparks of fire which spread everywhere, and no doubt caused this pestilential disease' (20:33). Dreams were not random occurrences for the Huron; they were prophetic of events, as well as of the innermost desires of the soul, and the Huron paid close attention to them (Sioui 1994, 297). In these instances, the symbolic significance of writing and its associated technologies slipped their moorings in the Jesuits' ideology and received altered significance at the hands of the Huron. Accusations that linked writing to witchcraft subverted the Jesuits' position as benefactors concerned with saving people rather than destroying them. In this way, they displaced the equivalence which the Jesuits were trying to convey between themselves and health and life. These accusations also denied the ideology of the letter that informed the priests' reliance on the book. By contesting the authority of writing, Aboriginal people acknowledged its power but denied its hegemonic function as the embodiment of a universal truth; in this way, if only temporarily, they refused the translation of colonial signifying practices and the authority embedded in them.[2]

In other instances, the ritual and pictorial symbolism of Christianity was appropriated and resisted in ways the Jesuits could neither control nor possibly have predicted. Many Huron had initially interpreted and received baptism as a healing rite; but as the diseases intensified, the Jesuits' sacrament of life came to be viewed as one of the ways in which they perpetrated their witchcraft. Many people refused it on the

grounds that it was certain to kill them or their children. Others incorporated a facsimile of baptism into their own healing rituals, to the great annoyance of the Jesuits. This particular innovation first occurred in 1637, when it was introduced by a shaman who had fasted for ten days in an attempt to acquire insight into the cause and cure of the prevailing disease, and it involved sprinkling water on the sick (13:237–43). It appeared again in 1639, after a Huron man had a vision of Iouskeha, a central Huron deity, in which Iouskeha blamed the Jesuits for the disease and prescribed a healing ritual that involved drinking ritually prepared water from a kettle (20:27–9). The Jesuits roundly condemned the vision as the work of demons who were trying to defend their territory against the Jesuits, and they described the practitioners of the prescribed healing rite as 'masqueraders' and 'physicians from hell' (20:31).

The Jesuits' vigorous condemnation of these acts suggests the degree to which they frustrated their objectives. These acts also show the ambivalence of Huron resistance. The Huron did not wholly reject the content of the Jesuits' practices or the authority linked to them, nor did their actions leave Huron and French cultural meanings and systems of signification intact, within imaginary boundaries, with their contents unimplicated in each other (Bhabba 1994, 110). The Huron men and women who participated in these rites engaged the potential power of baptism as a healing ritual. In doing so, they allowed some of its significance while disallowing the Jesuits' monopoly over the meaning and potentially life-saving effects of the ritual and its water (20:29–31).

This time of illness and death was, understandably, fraught with the search for signs of the cause of disease. The life-size paintings of Christ and the Virgin Mary displayed by the Jesuits in their chapel in Ossossané were believed to possess magical qualities and to be two of the instruments through which the priests were causing illness among Huron who were unfortunate enough to have looked at the pictures (15:19). Paintings of hell, detailing the torments of the damned—intended to inspire fear and to encourage people to convert—were interpreted as literal representations of the sufferings of those whom the Jesuits had afflicted with disease. Le Mercier explained that 'on the day of the baptism of Pierre Tsiouendaentaha', the Jesuits 'exhibited an excellent representation of the judgment, where the damned are depicted,—some with serpents and dragons tearing out their entrails, and the greater part with some kind of instrument of their punishment' (14:103). While 'many obtained some benefit from this spectacle', some 'persuaded themselves that this multitude of men, desperate, and heaped one upon the other, were all those we had caused to die during this Winter; that these flames represented the heats of the pestilential fever, and these dragons and serpents, the venomous beasts that we made use of in order to poison them' (14:103).

In this instance, the Jesuits' teaching about heaven, hell, and punishment was deflected and was returned to the Jesuits with new and contrary meanings. Even the communion wafers became suspect. As a general principle, the priests had been careful to reveal the doctrine of transubstantiation (whereby the wafers became the body of Christ) only to the few Christian Huron whom they felt most trustworthy in the faith (15:33). In spite of this precaution, the host soon featured in a rumour suggesting that the Jesuits were causing the diseases through a corpse they had brought from France and were hiding in their residence (15:33).

Several years later, after the diseases had largely run their course, stories began to circulate among the Huron of dreams and visions through which people had learned that the Jesuits' teachings were not only wrong but were dangerous. In one story, the soul of a recently deceased woman returned, after having journeyed to heaven, to warn the Huron that all who had become Christian were being tortured in heaven as prisoners of war, by the French, just as war captives were tortured by the Huron and their enemies (30:29). This warning was especially subversive because it situated the

Jesuits as enemies whose objective in making converts was to take prisoners, rather than as people who had come to give the secret of eternal life. It also completely overturned the division between heaven and hell, which many Native people found especially problematic. These incidents demonstrate the decentring that can occur when signs that are supposed to stand for the authority of the colonizers— or, in this case, the missionaries—are exposed to interpretation and appropriation by the colonized; they also illustrate competition for control over the interpretation of events and for what passes as the truth. As assertions of Native beliefs that make sense of Christian symbolism and Christian figures in the context of these beliefs, they are also an ideological response in kind to the Jesuits.

However much the Jesuits were required to argue over meaning with the Huron while they were in the Huron villages, their own understanding of the cause of the diseases was forcibly and categorically expressed in the pages of the *Relations*. It revolved around the influence of the devil in inspiring the persecution against them (19:91) and the biblically precedented interpretation of disease as divinely instigated punishment and trial. After the initial accusation of witchcraft in 1636, Le Jeune wrote that the growing hostility toward the Jesuits was a positive sign that the demons—hitherto unchallenged as the masters of the country—had been 'powerfully attacked, since they put themselves vigorously on the defensive' (11:41). A few years later, Father Le Mercier characterized the accusations and general hostility as part of 'the war that the powers of darkness have openly declared against us' (14:109). The Jesuits described their work with the sick and their unflagging attempts to teach and baptize people in the midst of threats as a literal struggle against the forces of evil (17:191; 20:51). In view of the Jesuits' own understanding of their mission, the allegation that it was they who were manipulating supernatural powers for harm could only be understood and represented as a fundamental misinterpretation of their activities and proof of the blindness of their accusers. Jérôme Lalemant responded to the accusations brought against the Jesuits with righteous indignation, writing that the words of their accusers were 'often only blasphemies against God and our mysteries, and insults against us, accompanied with incredible evidences of ingratitude,—hurling at us the reproach that it is our visits and our remedies which cause them to sicken and die, and that our sojourn here is the sole cause of all their troubles' (17:15).

The Jesuits soon came to represent the diseases as punishment sent by God in response to people's initial refusal to heed the Word and to accept their opportunity for salvation.[3] Once spoken in the New World, the Word of God erased the legitimacy of previous religious practices and, significantly, exposed Aboriginal people to their ignorance as well as to the full force of the consequences of their sin. The words spoken by the Jesuits left a permanent mark, inhabiting the spaces where they had been spoken with a kind of ominous finality. To ignore them and the truths they announced was to make the fatal choice between salvation and condemnation to greater punishment in this life and the next. In a letter to Mutio Vitelleschi, general of the Society of Jesus at Rome, Lalemant explained: 'While they were sound in body, they did not hear; it therefore pleased God to pull their ears through a certain kind of pestilence, which spread over the whole country, and adjudged many to the grave' (17:227).

At the beginning of the epidemics, Le Jeune compared the situation in which the priests found themselves with the persecution suffered by the first Christians and, reversing the accusations made against the Jesuits, attributed the diseases to God's justice: 'All the misfortunes, all the pests, wars, and famines which in the early ages of the infant Church afflicted the world, were formerly attributed to the faith of Jesus Christ, and to those who embraced or preached it. What occurred in this regard in the primitive Church can be seen every day in new France, especially in the Huron country. There is no black malice of which we are not accused. Here are the causes of it. As the contagion caused a great many Hurons to die, these people, not recognizing therein the justice of God, who takes vengeance for their crimes, imagined that the French were the cause of their death' (12:85).

While the Jesuits attributed all power over the diseases to God and continually urged the Huron to have recourse to the faith, most Huron abandoned Christianity completely in an attempt to dissociate themselves from the priests' teachings and, by association, from the diseases. The few who had converted and who remained Christian during the epidemics were warned by their relatives of the injustice of the Jesuits' God and his powerlessness to assist them or to preserve their lives (19:211, 235). But while resistance to the Jesuits became more imperative for the majority of Huron men and women, it situated them in a more perilous position according to the Jesuits' understanding of the epidemic and its causes. The Huron's rejection of Christianity as the only possible cure and their continual search for cures among those offered by the shamans and curing societies confirmed the Jesuits' in their belief that the devil influenced these people's behaviour (15:71). According to this view, such behaviour made them more deserving of retribution for denying the opportunity for their salvation. In the same way, the threats and accusations that the Huron made against the priests—who believed themselves to be there as the instruments of the Huron's salvation—compounded the 'measure of their sins' (13:161) and, consequently, the measure of their punishment. The Jesuits met the active resistance of the Huron with an intensification of their threats of punishment, rhetorically moving the Huron's refusal to comply into the realm of the worst blasphemy. While the Jesuits and many Huron apportioned blame for the disease to each other they did so according to divergent cultural and ideological premises that enabled them to find significant, incontrovertible meaning in their respective actions. The result was a duel over signification, in which each became grist for the other's worst accusations as they struggled—if not for life and death itself—at least for the meaning of life and the cause of death.

The first serious outbreak of disease occurred during the autumn of 1636 and lasted through the winter. After this, the Jesuits moved their principal residence from the village of Ihonatiria, where many people had lost their lives to the disease, to the more southern and less afflicted village of Ossossané. The Jesuits had been publicly accused of practising witchcraft in Ihonatiria that winter and were aware that their lives were at risk. Le Mercier, the author of the Huron *Relation* for that year, identified one family as having been most active in these accusations. According to Le Mercier, it was when the priests' lives were most threatened that 'the scourge fell upon that wretched family that had said the most against us. This chastisement had been for a long time due them on account of the contempt they had always shown for our holy mysteries' (13:217). Lalemant later explained that the move from Ihonatiria was necessary because its population was 'nearly all . . . scattered or dead from the malady, which seems to be, not without reason, a punishment from Heaven for the contempt that they showed for the favour of the visit that the divine goodness had procured for them' (17:11). The following autumn, when it appeared that a council of confederacy headmen in Ossossané would sanction the Jesuits' death, Brébeuf reiterated the priests' assumption that their lives would be preserved or disposed of solely as God willed. Their deaths would prevent the salvation of those they were trying to save, and Brébeuf believed that if God allowed the Jesuits to be killed, this in itself would be a form of punishment: 'And yet I fear that divine Justice, seeing the obstinacy of the majority of these Barbarians in their follies, may very justly permit them to come and take away the life of the body from those who with all their hearts desire and procure the life of their souls' (15:63).

Crop failures, the escalation of the war with the Iroquois, and famines were also represented as the punishments of God. When Jérôme Lalemant described the destruction of one of the outlying Huron villages by an Iroquois war party, he associated this disaster with the village's previous rebelliousness: 'It was the most impious of the villages, and that which had been most rebellious against the truths of the faith in all these countries; and its inhabitants had more than once told the Fathers who had gone to teach them that, if there were a God who avenged crimes, they defied him to make them feel his anger, and that, for anything less than that, they refused to acknowledge his power' (26:175). Similarly, Father Dequen explained to the Montagnais residing at Sillery that the capture of a group of Huron traders and the Jesuit father accompanying them, as well as 'so many other misfortunes', were 'the effects of God's anger, who was justly irritated by the wickedness of bad Christians and of the infidels who would not obey his word' (25:149).

Of course, the few who remained or became Christian during the epidemics were equally likely to suffer from the diseases. Similarly, as more people converted to Christianity after the diseases had run their course, they—like the non-Christians—were caught up in the punitive effects of escalating warfare and famine (25:105; 26:217). Inequities in the distribution of suffering are not unaccounted for in the Judeo-Christian tradition, and the Jesuits drew on well-established precedents when they represented these afflictions as having been sent by God for the improvement and redemption of those he had elected to save (26:217). Such was the argument offered to a group of Huron who complained that the Iroquois, who did not pray, were prospering and that since prayer had been introduced among the Huron, they themselves were perishing from warfare and disease. These Huron were told that God was behaving toward them 'like a Father toward his child; if his child will not have sense, he punishes it, in order to give it some; having corrected it, he throws the rods into the fire. A Father does not put himself to so much trouble about his servants as about his children. God regards you as his children: he wishes to give you sense; he uses the Iroquois as a whip, in order to correct you, to give you faith, to make you have recourse to him. When you shall be wise, he will throw the rods into the fire; he will chastise the Iroquois, unless they reform' (25:37).

The Jesuits had precedents for this language and did not have to invent it for use in North America. However, such language assumes particular potency when used in a situation of evolving political and economic inequality, and in conjunction with what was frequently an aggressive rhetoric of political imperialism, which compared the spread of Christianity in the New World to a territorial conquest. These Huron replied that they had enough sense and suggested it might have been better if God had begun with the Iroquois. The Jesuits advised them that their greater misfortunes were due to the greater love God bore them and that, however much the Iroquois appeared to be prospering, it was certain that, as unbelievers, they would not enjoy the rewards of the next life. The Jesuits' representation of suffering reflects an assumption that the appropriate response to it could only be submission and endurance, undertaken with an understanding of the presence of a superior will to which one must be subordinate, and with the hope of rewards to come (Bowker 1970, 54). This complete abnegation of the self, along with submission before a greater will, was a feature of the Jesuits' training. While the Jesuits' interlocutors frequently appeared unmoved by a God who apparently benefited people through their affliction, for the Jesuits suffering reduced neither the possibility of God nor the justice of God. Those who endured with strength and patience would be recognized and potentially rewarded—'for one is approved if, mindful of God, he endures pain while suffering unjustly' (1 Peter 2:19).

When sent as trials, misfortunes were a tool for separating those who were firm in the faith and willing to submit from those who were not (32:189). It is significant that in the *Relations* these trials were frequently represented as a necessary and important step in the establishment of Christianity in North America, just as they had been in Europe and Asia, where the faith of Christians had been tested through political persecution. While describing the hardships suffered by the Montagnais in the vicinity of Quebec, Le Jeune asserted: 'The Faith must propagate itself as it has been planted,—namely, in calamities. And because there are here no Tyrants who massacre our Neophytes, God provides for them otherwise, deriving proof of their constancy from their afflictions, sore indeed' (16:219). The repeated use of this historical reference situates the experiences of Native peoples in the St Lawrence region—for whom the signature events of Christianity were the remote occurrences in the life of an unknown prophet referring to the deity of an unknown people in a remote and alien land—within the frame of a universal, exclusively Christian and ultimately hegemonic vision of global history. In 1643 Barthélemy Vimont described the general condition of the Christians of New France:

> The condition to which this nascent Church is now reduced is such as to bring to the eyes of all who love it tears both of sorrow and of joy. For, on the one hand, it is pitiful to see these poor peoples perish before our eyes as soon as they embrace the Faith; and, on the other, we have reason to console ourselves when we see that the misfortunes which assail them on all sides serve but to arouse a desire for the faith in those who had hitherto despised it, and to strengthen it and make it shine with still greater glory in the hearts of those who had already received it. We see very well that God is the Founder of this Church, as well as of the primitive one; for he has caused the former to be born, like the latter, in travails, and to grow in sufferings, in order to be crowned with her in glory. (25:105)

By the summer of 1649 most Huron villages had been destroyed or significantly depopulated by warfare and the accompanying famine and disease. The priests and surviving Huron took refuge on an island in Georgian Bay, where they were temporarily safe from Iroquois raiding parties but lacked provisions for the coming winter. 'Then it was', according to Paul Ragueneau, that the missionaries 'were compelled to behold dying skeletons eking out a miserable life, feeding even on the excrements and refuse of nature' (35:89). Conditions reached such an extreme that people were reduced to exhuming bodies for food. Ragueneau nevertheless wrote: 'It was in the midst of these desolations that God was pleased to bring forth, from their deepest misfortunes, the wellbeing of this people. Their hearts had become so tractable to the faith that we effected in them, by a single word, more than we had ever been able to accomplish in entire years' (35:91).

The upheavals in Huron society in the final years of the Jesuits' mission among them made them more dependent on the Jesuits and enabled the priests to exact at least an outward compliance with Christianity. Lalemant had foreshadowed this role of affliction in creating subject relations of dependency, when he wrote of the general condition of Christianity in New France in the *Relation* for the years 1643–44: 'We have, however, great reason to praise God because he reaps his glory from the affliction of these poor peoples and makes it serve still more for their conversion. Although there is not in the world a nation poorer than this one, nevertheless there is none prouder than they. When they were prosperous, we could hardly approach them; the French were dogs, and all that we preached them were fables. But since affliction has humiliated them, and necessity has made them more dependent upon the French, and has made them experience the effects of Christian charity, their eyes are opened; and they see more clearly than ever that there is no other Divinity than he whom we preach to them' (25:111). Lalemant's

comment also reveals the strong sense of cultural superiority that characterized Aboriginal people's initial response to Europeans.

The Jesuits also represented affliction as the enactment of a more final and inevitable justice. In the Huron report of 1640 Lalemant explained that many 'villages and cabins were much more populous formerly, but the extraordinary diseases and the wars within some years past, seem to have carried off the best portion; there remaining only very few old men, very few persons of skill and management' (19:127). To this he added, 'It is to be feared that the climax of their sins is approaching, which moves divine justice to exterminate them as well as several other nations' (19:127). People who resisted conversion or actively argued against the Jesuits and who then suffered misfortune or death frequently figured in the *Relations* as examples of God's justice, however far removed this would have been from these people's own interpretation of their death or misfortune. The punishments featured in these incidents are in sharp contrast to the joy and gratitude which the Jesuits generally associated with conversion. In 1634 Paul Le Jeune attributed the miserable death of a 'blasphemer' to the 'just and terrible vengeance of the great God' (7:283). Ten years later Lalemant described the punishment of three Algonkin men who had come down to Trois-Rivières and were 'placing some obstacles against the expansion of the Faith' by openly retaining more than one wife (31:257). Lalemant asserted that these three 'refractory ones' (31:257) were the victims of 'a thunderbolt hurled from Heaven' (31:257), all dying ignoble or miserable deaths.

One of these men, on becoming ill, blamed Christianity and in so doing was said to have revolted 'more than ever against the arm which struck him only to cure him' (31:263). The Jesuits warned him of the punishment that would come in the next life if he did not open his eyes and accept baptism, but he replied unrepentantly 'that a Law which made men die was abominable' (31:261). He died in this refutation of the faith, a resistance that became, under Lalemant's pen, the 'rage' that was 'the Catastrophe of his life' (31:263). Another of these men especially annoyed the Jesuits by his persistence in attributing a recent outbreak of disease to the effects of Christianity, and when he too fell sick Lalemant described this as an attack by God (31:263). Lalemant referred to this man, who bore the name Joseph Oumosotiscouchie, as an apostate who was unusually 'proud and insolent' because he had been given the name used by several former leaders in his country (31:261).

Oumosotiscouchie publicly denied the utility of prayer to heal, blaming his sickness on the faith, and he undertook to cure himself in a healing ceremony that involved the fulfilment of three dream wishes. On completion of the ceremony, he publicly claimed to be cured, at which point, according to Lalemant, 'a violent fever seizes him in the midst of his triumph, prostrates him to the earth, throws him into a wreck and into torments so unusual that he foamed like one possessed. Those of his cabin— frightened, and fearing lest he might beat some one to death—having tied him, threw over him a blanket, so as to conceal his fury and his rage; behold my blusterer much humbled' (31:265). When the Jesuits and the surgeon arrived, they found the man 'stone-dead' and all who had witnessed the event astonished at 'so awful a spectacle' (31:265). This man was later 'flung into a hole like a common sewer, for fear that he might infect the air with his body, as he had polluted it with his vices and his apostasy' (31:275). After this punishment, Lalemant stated with some satisfaction that no one 'dared longer open his lips against the Faith; it was now spoken of only with a dread and respect that altogether pleased us' (31:267).[4]

Those who physically harmed Jesuits could also be situated in the *Relations* as victims of divine punishment. One man, for example, kicked a priest while the latter was baptizing a child, and 'some time after that, he was carried off by a disease as grievous as it was strange' (14:227). The woman who cut off the thumb of Father Jogues while Jogues was a captive in an Iroquois village apparently 'had no long career after that rage' (29:229). Likewise, wrote Lalemant: 'They who gnawed his fingers and those of his companions, and who treated them with most fury, have been killed by the Algonquin in their latest combats' (29:229). The 'same justice' was applied to the Iroquois who tortured Father Bressani when he was held captive among them, although this punishment was in the form of diseases that would 'perhaps . . . give true health to that poor people' (29:229).

NOTES

[Editor's note: Parenthetical references in the text are to volume and page number in Reuben Gold Thwaites, *Jesuits Relations and Allied Documents*, 73 vols. (Cleveland: Burrows Bros. 1896–1901)]

1. In an especially interesting literal play on the Jesuits' insistence that the Bible was the un-mediated, directly transmitted Word of God, Le Jeune reported: 'When I told them that we had a book which contained the words and teachings of God, they were very anxious to know how we could have gotten this book,— some of them believing that it had been let down from the Sky at the end of a rope, and that we had found it thus suspended in the air' (11:209).

2. Indeed, while the smallpox epidemics ultimately passed, Native critiques of writing were not without prescience of the larger ramifications of entering history. One man, upon being told that his people were dying as a result of the overconsumption of the brandy used in the fur trade, retorted: 'It is not these drinks that take away our lives, but your writings; for since you have described our country, our rivers, our lands, and our woods, we are

all dying, which did not happen until you came here' (9:207). The Jesuits denied these deleterious consequences of writing the New World into a history that embraced the inhabitants with alien pathogens at the same time as it was supposed to proffer them the means of salvation, by explaining to this man that they 'described the whole world' without similarly harmful effects (9:207).

3. A recent attribution of these diseases to the Europeans' abandonment of the 'laws of nature' and more general alienation from the natural world (Sioui 1992, 3–7) is as embedded in the assumption of a universally applicable schema of laws, causes, and effects as the attributions of the Jesuits. While it may be meant to refute such statements as the priests

initially made and to represent the real truth, it matches them in the assumption that the cultural and religious dictates of one people—including an understanding of the natural world and the appropriate human relationships with it—are not, in effect, creations but represent reality as a given, and that, as such, they can be universally binding as a yardstick with which to judge and understand the history, behaviour, and beliefs of other peoples.

4. Aboriginal people who reportedly resisted or abused Christianity were not the only victims of God's anger and punishment in the *Relations*. The Jesuits represented the untimely death of French Protestants in a similar manner (5:233; 6:105–7).

REFERENCES

Axtell, James. (1988). *After Columbus: Essays in the Ethnohistory of Colonial North America*. New York and Oxford: Oxford University Press.

Bhabha, Homi. (1994). *The Location of Culture*. London and New York: Routledge.

Mignolo, Walter D. (1992). 'On the colonization of Amerindian Languages and Memories: Renaissance Theories of Writing and the Discontinuity of the

Classical Tradition', *Comparative Studies in Society and History* 34, 4: 301–30.

Sioui, Georges. (1994). *Les Wendats: Une civilisation méconnue*. Sainte-Foy: Presses de l'Université Laval.

Trigger, Bruce. (1987). *The Children of Aataenstic: A History of the Huron People to 1660*, 2 vols. Montreal and Kingston: McGill-Queen's University Press.

---

4 From Denys Delâge, *Bitter Feast: Amerindians and Europeans in Northeastern North America, 1600–1664* (Vancouver: UBC Press, 1993), 178–94, 358–9.

THE PROCESS OF CONVERSION

The faith must propagate itself as it has been planted, namely, in calamities.[1]

So true are those words, Sanguis martyrum semen est Christianorum—

'the blood of the Martyrs', if they may be so named, 'is the seed and germ of Christians.'[2]

The missionaries had begun to baptize the dying as soon as they arrived in Huronia,[3] and, accordingly, the number of baptisms fluctuated with epidemics.[4] In 1638 only one family had converted to Christianity, but by the following year the Jesuits boasted 'fully 300 souls'.[5] Between 1639 and 1640 they baptized about a thousand people, although among them 'there [were] not twenty baptized ones out of danger of death.'[6] The year 1641 marked a turning point, however, for, despite much stricter standards in evaluating the genuine nature of professions of faith, the number of converts grew. The year 1642 saw 620 baptisms, with both men and women filling the chapels each morning.[7] 'The faith finds no distinction between the sexes', noted the missionaries.[8]

Among the 250 Hurons of the bark flotilla that went down to Trois-Rivières in 1648, nearly half (120) were converts. They prayed twice a day and travelled together 'in the presence of the pagans.'[9] Between the *Jesuit Relations* of 1647 and that of 1648, the Jesuits baptized 'nearly thirteen hundred persons'.[10] Then came the final disaster, and conversions increased as Huron villages fell into the hands of the Iroquois. 'More than 1300 persons' were baptized between July 1648 and March 1649, and 'more than fourteen hundred' between March and August 1649.[11] 'Thus the Christian Church was increased by more than two thousand seven hundred souls in thirteen months, without counting those baptized at the Breach [the storming of the Huron villages], and those who were made Christians in other places.'[12]

For a time, the Jesuits had thought they would convert the Hurons by educating the offspring of sachem families and by systematically baptizing all children. However, such baptisms—often surreptitiously practised by means of a handkerchief or finger dipped in holy water—could not provide the foundation for a new, organized church.[13]

The Jesuits would have dearly liked to send a large number of Huron children to a residential school. This would not only win over children who might 'aspire to the highest positions'[14] in their native land; it would provide hostages to consolidate trade and ensure the safety of the French in Huronia. The Huron women always managed to scuttle such a project, however.[15] In 1636, only five of the twelve children destined for instruction at Quebec actually went. The venture was a fiasco: only two children displayed any pliancy, and these later died. The missionaries complained that the other three were incapable of submitting to the discipline of the Jesuits. The young Hurons were taught how to perform 'neat courtesies' and greet 'our Frenchmen' by 'humbly . . . touching their hats when meeting them.'[16] However, the three recalcitrants 'aimed at nothing but the enjoyment of their pleasures and the gratification of their senses.' They secretly got hold of 'a canoe-load of provisions . . . and one fine morning they stole away, taking with them everything they could.'[17]

Efforts to educate Montagnais children were equally ill-fated. In 1636 the French governor reproached the Montagnais for refusing to entrust their children to the French, although they entrusted a certain number to Amerindian allies. [. . .]

By 1639 the Jesuits had virtually given up the idea of converting Huronia by teaching its children, and their seminary in Quebec was of no use in this respect. The Ursuline nuns of Quebec met with about as much success in their attempts to educate young Amerindian girls, although a few Montagnais families found it convenient to leave their daughters at the convent over the winter.[18] Several little girls were sent to France, where they were fashionable curiosities in aristocratic circles. Generally speaking, however, church authorities considered it impossible to 'train' the children.

> The freedom of the children in these countries is so great, and they prove so incapable of government and discipline, that, far from being able to hope for the conversion of the country through the instruction of the children, we must even despair of their instruction without the conversion of the parents. And consequently, all well considered, the

first matter to which we should attend is the stability of the marriages of our Christians, who give us children that may in good time be reared in the fear of God and of their parents. Behold the only means of furnishing the Seminaries with young plants.[19]

Such were the first in a series of repeated attempts at educating Amerindian children by both French and English throughout the seventeenth and eighteenth centuries. The results were always the same, and young Amerindians never adapted to the manners and discipline of European institutions. The reverse process—that is, the integration of young whites into Amerindian society—was usually successful.

The Jesuits' efforts prospered most in Ossossané, the principal village of the Attignawantans. In 1648, it outstripped all other villages in the number and zeal of its Christians,[20] and it therefore offers the best example for observing the process of conversion. [. . .]

After 1639 the Jesuits concentrated their efforts on converting council members, 'some Old Men, and the more prominent heads of families.'[21] The missionaries had remarked that 'one truly Christian Savage, who is zealous for the faith, accomplishes more among his people than do three Jesuits',[22] and therefore felt that converting leaders would have a ripple effect. It is worth noting that the men generally won over the women and children.[23] The arguments given were the need to conform to the new morality and the desire to meet again in the afterlife. Nonetheless, their influence also indicated the growing power of men involved in trade over their wives and the community in general.

With an eye to winning over community leaders, the Jesuits tightened their grip on the sale of weapons and the price of trade goods. After 1642, the desire to own a firearm became a strong inducement to convert to Christianity. This was the year in which one Ahatsistari, reputed to be the bravest warrior of Huronia,

was baptized. He had been asking for baptism for three years, but the Jesuits had hitherto refused because he could not 'make up his mind to abandon some Superstitious practices that are customary among the Infidels.'[24] Now at last he would be able to replace bow and arrow with firepower and confront the Iroquois on an equal footing. That same year, 'some Infidels, who were about to go to war . . . began to think of their Souls as much as, if not more than, of their bodies.'[25] The following year, the missionaries wrote that 'the affairs of our Lord advance in proportion to the adversities which he sends us. Hardly could one find, hitherto, among our Christians two or three warriors; but, since the capture of that worthy Neophyte, named Eustache, the most valiant of all the Hurons, we have counted in a single band as many as twenty-two Believers—all men of courage, and mostly Captains or people of importance. The use of arquebuses, refused to the Infidels by Monsieur the Governor, and granted to the Christian Neophytes, is a powerful attraction to win them.'[26]

It is no surprise to find Jesuits succeeding in their efforts to convert the families and villages most involved in the fur trade, since the trading expeditions were what exposed the Hurons, more than anything else, to Iroquois guns. Ossossané was such a village. [. . .]

Initially, the Jesuits' efforts at conversion had come up against the Hurons' fear of being separated from their relatives and ancestors in the other world. '"For my part, I have no desire to go to heaven", said one. "I have no acquaintances there."'[27] Dead relatives and friends had gone to the hunting and fishing grounds of the afterlife.[28] Once converts were sufficiently numerous, however, the process rapidly snowballed. The argument that had held people back now became an incentive to convert, and for some the fear of separation from their families was actually the prime reason.[29]

The year 1645 marked a watershed in Huronia. The following dialogue demonstrates the confrontation between converted and unconverted Huron chiefs. '"Then", said the Elders, "we must resign ourselves to seeing our Country ruined, since our chief Captains range themselves on the side of the Faith. How can we prevent this disorder?" "You are thinking of it too late", he replies; "you should have opposed the progress of the Faith before it had entered our hearts. Now it will reign there in spite of you; and it will be easier to tear our souls from our bodies than to remove from our minds the fear of Hell-fire, and the desire for the happiness that awaits us in Heaven."'[30]

[. . .]

The process of conversion may in part be accounted for by dependency and the multitude of constraints under which the Hurons lived. A firearm was worth a baptism, certainly, but this does not offer a satisfactory explanation of why a significant number of converts actually interiorized the new religion. Why, in the words of a converted chief to his peers, had the faith entered his heart?[31] What accounted for the proselytizing zeal of many converts?[32] Some of the answers can, it seems, be found by considering the question from two standpoints: one sociological, the other psychoanalytical.

In the first instance, might the blood of martyrs indeed be the seed of Christianity? In other words, might the sense of insecurity created by the accumulated disasters (epidemics and wars), as well as intensified labour, have provided fertile ground for Christian ideology? Since 1634, disease and war had been undermining native societies and endangering the whole of Amerindian civilization. The mechanisms for transmitting tradition had been dislocated and relations between tribes thrown into disarray. Furthermore, war had contributed to the displacement and marginalization of entire populations.[33] A closer look reveals that it was often the people who had lost or suffered most who were the most receptive to the evangelical message. In 1639, the missionaries reported nearly 60 converts in Ossossané, 'of whom many are Wenroronons from among those poor Strangers taking refuge in this country.'[34] This was a reference to a tribe of the Neutral confederacy that had been defeated by

the Iroquois and forced to abandon its territory. Six hundred arrived in pitiable condition to seek refuge among the Hurons, who took them in.[35] Was there a connection between the rate of conversion at Ossossané and the number of refugees? There does seem to be a correlation between their presence and a willingness to welcome the missionaries.

In the same year, fathers Garnier and Jogues made their first journey to the Petuns. At this time all doors were closed to them through fear of witchcraft, except that of a 'stranger', a former captive who had originally been a member of the 'nation which they call Atsistahronons, "Nation of fire".'[36] The fathers met with an equally frosty welcome on their first journey to the Neutrals in 1640–41, except for in one village where several Wenroronon refugees were lodged.[37] It would seem that the refugees, in other words the most deprived members of the community, were the most willing to listen to what the missionaries had to say. In earlier days refugees would have been integrated into the tribe. With the upheaval of traditional Huron values, however, integration was predominantly religious. In 1642, for example, when an Iroquois attack threatened to overthrow the country, even the unconverted Ossossané villagers asked the Jesuits to baptize everyone.[38] The seed of doubt was already sown. It would seem that recurrent epidemics, intensified warfare, and the process of Huronia's gradual strangulation created not only the material conditions, but the ideological base for conversion. In 1644 Father Lalemant wrote of the Hurons, 'As for the new Christians, their number has been much greater this year than in previous ones. Even the Infidels, who are humiliated and made more docile by affliction, seem to us to be less distant from God's Kingdom. Finally, the body of Christians, after heavy trials sent by Heaven, is becoming more considerable, and begins to be in the majority in some of the villages.'[39]

Also in 1644, Father Vimont described the Amerindians' general situation in more or less similar terms. 'Although there is not in the world a nation poorer than this one, nevertheless there is none prouder than they. When they were prosperous, we could hardly approach them; the French were dogs, and all that we preached them were fables. But since affliction has humiliated them, and necessity has made them more dependent upon the French, and has made them experience the effects of Christian charity, their eyes are opened; and they see more clearly than ever that there is no other Divinity than he whom we preach to them.'[40]

Several years later, in 1656, Father Chaumonot met some Hurons who had become Iroquois captives, about whom he had this to say: 'The Hurons of the Village of Contareia, who, because of their strong aversion to the Faith, never allowed themselves to be instructed, are already beginning to yield, lending an attentive ear to the Father's words. So true is it that *afflictio dat intellectum*.'[41]

Considering the degree to which Amerindian societies had become profoundly destabilized, could the traditional religious system have given meaning to the way of life their members were now facing? Dependency, tension, hierarchization, the establishment of a destructive relationship between man and nature, the crumbling of a civilization, dispossession—all these were realities that shook the old explanations of the world, engendering anomie (that is, the weakening of normative standards of conduct and belief) at the heart of Huron society, and what Pierre Bourdieu calls 'the expectation of a systematic message capable of giving a unified meaning to life by offering its chosen recipients a consistent vision of the world and human existence, and by giving them the means to integrate it systematically into their daily behaviour—a message therefore able to provide them with the justification to live as they do, that is, in a defined social position.'[42]

Such an expectation can be divined from the changes taking place in the Hurons' mythical universe. Thus, Aataentsic, the moon-mother goddess, changed herself into a vengeful goddess, sending fatal epidemics to punish the Amerindians who for years had been waging war with increasing frequency.[43] In the main, however, unlike Christianity, the traditional systems of explanation could not, despite alterations, offer a coherent vision of societies where oppression was the dominant factor. The missionary offensive therefore took advantage (at least in the case of the most deprived) of an ideological destabilization caused by the collapse of Amerindian societies. Pierre Bourdieu cites Max Weber on the historical origin of religions, to the effect that all requests for salvation are an expression of a 'need', economic and social oppression being the most important, but not the only instance of such a need.[44] It might be said that, as of 1640, this request for salvation came as much from within, instigated by the oppression to which Amerindians were subjected, as from without, in response to external pressure applied by the missionaries. The missionaries' conversion strategies could not have succeeded without the Amerindians being socially predisposed to join the faith. The evangelical message focused on themes of original sin, sins committed, redemption, resignation (to hell on earth), and hope (for heaven in the afterlife). It conformed to the world view then held by many Amerindians who, as with all those who are 'disinherited by the brutalities of society', had developed an apocalyptic vision of history.[45]

Epidemics and wars marked the overturning of the Amerindian world. The missionaries interpreted all the visible stigmata (disease and suffering) as signs heralding 'divine election' and eternal bliss. In so doing—that is, by promising 'posthumous subversion' of the social order[46]—the missionaries forced the objective recognition that history was irreversible and that European power had been legitimated. The terms in which they spoke symbolically reinforced a world view where subjugation was the norm, linked to 'the ethos of resignation and renunciation instilled by the conditions of life.'[47] This meant legitimation of the dependency of Amerindian societies and of the process whereby these societies were divided into classes. In fact, insofar as Amerindian societies were crumbling from within, the new religion was the answer both to those seeking compensation (the promise of salvation from suffering for the most deprived), and those seeking legitimation of the established order (the inculcation of a sense of dignity and rightful superiority among the dominant forces).[48]

The fur trade had changed the Hurons' manner of acquiring wealth. Sachems possessed the right to grant passage over trade routes and accorded these rights in exchange for gifts, as well as reserving for themselves a relatively large share of the trade goods. As it developed, the fur trade gave rise to an increasingly unequal acquisition of wealth, and fostered the appearance of a distinction between governed and governors, whereas they had previously been mingled in a collective 'we'.

> Formerly only worthy men were Captains, and so they were called *Enondecha*, the same name by which they call the Country, Nation, district,—as if a good Chief and the Country were one and the same thing. But today they do not pay so much attention to the selection of their captains; and so they no longer give them that name, although they still call them *atiwarontas, atiwanens, ondakhienhai*, 'big stones, the elders, the stay-at-homes'. However, those still hold, as I have said, the first rank as well in the special affairs of the Villages as of the whole Country, who are most highly esteemed and intellectually preëminent. Their relatives are like so many Lieutenants and Councilors.[49]

This dichotomy was not merely one of language; it reflected a socioeconomic reality. In 1636, for example, on the occasion of the great feast of the dead, the 'Old Men and the notables of the Country', according to Father Brébeuf, 'took possession secretly of a considerable quantity' of beaver cloaks.[50] In 1644, the missionaries were congratulating themselves

on having converted Barnabé Otsinonannhont, for 'this man has always been one of the leading personages of his tribe, on account of his birth (for they have their nobility here, as well as in France) and are as proud of it.'[51] Although the comparison is obviously exaggerated, it echoes another comment of 1648 about access to and symbolic value of curing rituals. 'When the prescription is given, the Captains of the village hold a council, as in a matter of public importance, and deliberate whether they will exert themselves for the patient. And, if there be a number of sick who are persons of note, it is impossible to conceive the ambition and intrigue displayed by their relatives and friends to obtain the preference for them, because the public cannot pay those honors to all.'[52]

Taken together, these comments are indicative of emerging class relations and clearly show that there was unequal access to material and symbolic goods. Hitherto, social relations within Huron society had been based on redistribution and sharing. With the advent of the fur trade, however, social relations based on redistribution developed at the expense of those based on sharing. We know that redistribution carries with it a specific tension, because it sets unequal acquisition against equal consumption. It is true that the function of many traditional rituals was to counteract unequal acquisition of wealth by guaranteeing redistribution of goods in the community. Should these redistribution mechanisms disappear, unequal consumption would follow, bringing with it new social relations—relations that had been latent from the beginning. The work of the missionaries helped create a framework for this new social relationship.

The missionaries urged the converts not to take part in the feast of the dead, curing rituals, banquets, and exchanges of goods organized in response to dreams.[53] For ideological and moral reasons, the Jesuits also asked the converts to live among themselves, apart from non-Christians. By doing this, the missionaries effectively severed the traditional bonds of solidarity within the community and cut converts off from the redistribution network. As 'the Feasts, which are the chief pleasure of the country, are so many sacrifices to the Devil', all Christians had to shun them. This meant that those who were well off did not share their wealth, while for those without resources 'it requires a very ardent Faith to banish oneself from them.'[54] As can be seen, Christian precepts favoured the haves and penalized the have-nots. Moreover, some Amerindians quickly grasped the fact that Christianity cost them less and accordingly took advantage of it:

'The Demons', said one of them, 'command us to do impossible things. They do not give us what is necessary for a feast, and they require us to make one. Sometimes they compel us, if we would avoid some great misfortune, to offer what we do not possess, and cannot get. Does not this show that they either trifle with us, or that they are pleased to see us miserable? But the God of the Christians commands them to do nothing that is impossible for them; and, if they fail, it is of their own will. It is by this', he said, 'that I recognize that he alone is the Master of our lives, since he desires only our good.'[55]

Despite their special status, Christians could not easily escape the redistribution ceremonies. Any attempt to do so immediately led to charges of witchcraft by the unconverted,[56] charges that became more frequent after 1634.[57]

Christianity offered two concepts that legitimated such opting out. First, it introduced Amerindians to the idea that acts were private property, that is, the private concern of each individual: to each, in the afterlife, according to his or her works.[58] Then, on the symbolic level, it proposed the view of a world divided between the redeemed and the damned—a view expressed in terms of inclusion and exclusion, to which a social content could be easily added.[59] Christianity thus justified 'the big stones' in opting out of redistribution

mechanisms, thereby legitimating inequality and privileged status. In fact, while the fur trade accentuated the relative importance of redistribution compared to reciprocity, the Christian religion effectively restricted redistribution of the social product.

In 1642, Father Jérôme Lalemant wrote that 'the grace of baptism works powerfully in a heart.'[60] Looking at individual behaviour, one is indeed struck by the profound effect of baptism, and the sometimes radical personality change in certain converts. Like the social structure, personality structure was equally affected by Christianity, and this made interiorization of the new religious values all the more effective. The new religion was thrust upon a society already in the process of destructuration—that is, the disintegration of social and cultural patterns of thought. This was aggravated by the society itself, and it touched individuals whose sense of security had been deeply shaken and whose personalities were undergoing a similar process. It was as though this religion were reprogramming and restructuring profoundly traumatized human beings. One cannot help drawing a parallel, hypothetically at least, with the methods of modern religious sects for converting individuals who are either socially marginal or in a (temporary) state of psychological instability. We are familiar with the effects of personality restructuration resulting from membership in an institution that provides the double security of human and dogmatic support.

What stands out primarily is the intensity of religious practice. Huron converts and the Christian Algonkins of Quebec and Miscou displayed an uncommon degree of zeal and fervour.[61] According to Marie de l'Incarnation, it was beyond description.[62] The missionaries noted that there was nothing half-hearted about the Amerindians' faith, and neither cold nor ice nor distance could deter them.[63] The new Christians were proselytizers as well, and despite all opposition worked ardently to win over friends and relations. Often they had greater success than the missionaries.[64]

The more active the converts, the more they opposed tradition; the greater the aggressivity and hatred displayed by their traditionalist compatriots, the greater their own conviction about their role as 'public victims', martyrs to the faith.[65] Their self-image as members of the chosen few was strengthened by the many sufferings they were able to offer God as a passport to heaven.[66] By implication, pleasure was forbidden in this context of suffering. Take the case of the young girl who adopted a melancholy air in public in order to avoid 'the licence which the young men here assume . . . "When I go anywhere" (she said), "I alter my appearance; I keep my eyes cast down, and my forehead wrinkled, and I try to look sad so that no one is encouraged to accost me."'[67]

The new religion involved a highly negative self-image: that of the sinner who must redeem himself or herself. The following reply by an Attikamègue convert to Father Buteux offers convincing evidence of this: '*Question*: "What thoughts hast thou about thyself?" *Answer*: "That I am a dog, and less than a flea before God."'[68] The convert was afraid of himself, afraid of his thoughts and desires.[69]

In these circumstances, it comes as no surprise to find converts flogging themselves to expiate their sins,[70] rolling in the snow to escape the 'infernal flames' of temptation,[71] or scorching themselves with live coals.[72] It is true that traditional Huron civilization had forms of bodily discipline and self-repressive behaviour. Children were trained from a very young age, for example, to withstand the cold by being scantily clad.[73] Hurons (and Amerindians in general) were very hardy in this respect and always dressed less warmly than the French.[74] Boys were trained to hide their emotions. Men were expected to remain impassive in the face of pain or suffering,[75] to endure ritual fasting for a successful hunt, or to harden themselves to pain by applying brands to their bodies.[76] Such practices appear to have been the exception rather than the rule, however, and were intended to develop, rather than break down, bodily strength and resistance. Conversion, on the other hand, established conscious self-repression as a basic form of behaviour, accompanied by the massive introjection of the missionaries' directives.[77]

Guilt and self-conscious repression, combined with the ostentatious and proselytizing practice of their religion, epitomized the converts' behaviour. The evolution of the human animal to the human being (or *animal sapiens*) involves the conscious repression of basic instincts, beginning with a radical transformation of the original value system. According to Herbert Marcuse, this conversion of the pleasure principle to the reality principle can be defined as follows:[78]

FROM	TO
immediate satisfaction	delayed satisfaction
pleasure	restraint of pleasure
joy (play)	toil (work)
receptiveness	productiveness
absence of repression	security

Transformations within Huron society in the first half of the seventeenth century all resulted in the repression of the pleasure principle. Wars, disease, longer and more intensified labour, and finally the social division of labour, were all factors that brought new constraints and prepared the ground for establishing further controls that went beyond those traditionally required by Huron society. Christianity was to catalyze the need for an ideology and institutions to reinforce what Marcuse calls surplus repression. Theoretically, the inhibition of the pleasure principle in response to the imperatives of reality was aimed at guaranteeing greater individual security. The wars and epidemics that led to the disappearance of Huronia were accompanied by an observable inhibition of desire, a rise in surplus repression, and growing insecurity.

It is perhaps needless to add that constraints imposed in adulthood were not truly interiorized, the Huron super-ego having been formed in the context of the permissive upbringing characteristic of Amerindian civilizations.[79] However, the previously accepted instinctive tendencies were becoming increasingly incompatible with an ever more hostile reality. Although most constraints imposed on children were interiorized and belonged to the unconscious, among converts no prohibition imposed in adulthood could become an automatic, unconscious response. It could only give rise to a strong feeling of guilt accompanied by the need to adopt conspicuous forms of religious practice.

The concentration of religious capital in the hands of the missionaries brought about the correlative dispossession of the converted.

The missionaries' conversion strategy aimed at removing the Amerindian's entire identity, so that 'being oneself' gave way to identification with another, to 'being like'.[80] The religious specialist's view of the convert established his or her identity. It was a view that both structured and destructured the personality. Unable to escape the eye of their religious mentors, the most credulous converts lived a life of pretence, mimicking the desired behaviour. They wore a mask and played a part. What the missionaries had once condemned, they now praised. Behaviour previously considered pagan was no longer associated with witchcraft. Thus the application of live brands to the body became a Christian purification practice—an act that, by the same token, embodied the recognition and legitimation of the missionary. Indeed, the influence of spells, associated with the privilege of being Christian, was now publicly recognized.

NOTES

[Editor's note: *JR* refers to Reuben G. Thwaites, ed., *The Jesuit Relations and Allied Documents*, Cleveland: Burrows Brothers 1896–1901, 73 vols.]

1. *JR* (1639), 16:219.
2. *JR* (1648–9), 34:227.
3. *JR* (1639), 16:59–61, 17:61–3.
4. *JR* (1637), 13:167–9.
5. *JR* (1638–9), 15:187–9.
6. *JR* (1640), 19:123.
7. *JR* (1642), 23:23–5, 101–3.
8. *JR* (1645–6), 30:23.
9. *JR* (1647–8), 32:179, 33:69.
10. *JR* 33:69.
11. *JR* (1648–9), 34:227.
12. *JR* See also (1648–9), 33:227, 34:83.
13. *JR* (1637), 12:89–91, 14:7–9, 41–3; (1639), 17:189–91; (1640), 19:219–27; (1662–3), 48:123.
14. *JR* (1636), 9:283–5; (1637), 12:47.
15. *JR* (1636), 9:283; (1637), 12:41.
16. *JR*, 75.
17. *JR* (1638), 14:231–3.
18. Marie de l'Incarnation, Mère. *Lettres historiques de la Vénérable Mère Marie de l'Incarnation sur le Canada*. Edited by B. Sulte. Québec: L'Action sociale, 1927, letter of 3 September 1640, 23–4. Groulx, Lionel. 'Missionnaires de l'Est en Nouvelle-France. Réduction et séminaires indiens.' *Revue d'histoire de l'Amerique française* 3:1 (June 1949): 62–5. See also *JR* (1647–8), 32:213–15.
19. *JR* (1639), 16:251.
20. *JR* (1645–6), 29:257–9; (1647–8), 33:141–3.
21. *JR* (1639), 17:33, 95; (1642–3), 24:237–9.
22. *JR* (1640–1), 20:231, 21:147–9; (1642–3), 24:239–41, 25:25–7.
23. *JR* (1645–6), 29:277–9.
24. *JR* (1642), 23:27.
25. *JR* 199–201.
26. *JR* (1642–3), 25:27. See also 24:233–9, (1644–5), 28:89–91.
27. *JR* (1637), 13:127, 14:15.
28. *JR* (1637), 13:141.
29. *JR* (1645–6), 29:277–9.
30. *JR* (1644–5), 28:87–9.
31. *JR* (1645–6), 28:87.
32. *JR* (1639), 17:53.
33. *JR* (1640), 19:127–9.

34. *JR* (1639), 17:37–9.
35. *JR* 25–7; (1640), 20:51–3.
36. *JR* 57–61.
37. *JR* (1640–1), 21:235.
38. *JR* (1642), 23:105–7.
39. *JR* (1643–4), 27:69; see also 105–9.
40. *JR* 111.
41. *JR* (1655–6), 42:73.
42. Bourdieu, Pierre. 'Une interprétation de la théorie de la religion selon Max Weber.' *Archives européennes de sociologie* 12 (1971): 9.
43. *JR* (1637), 14:9.
44. M. Weber, *Wirtschaft und Gesellschaft*, 1:385, cited by Bourdieu, 'Une interprétation de la théorie de la religion', 9.
45. Bourdieu, Pierre. 'Genèse et structure du champ religieux.' Revue française de sociologie 12: 3 (1971): 313.
46. Bourdieu, 'Une interprétation de la théorie de la religion', 9.
47. Bourdieu, 'Genèse et structure du champ religieux', 315.
48. Bourdieu, 'Une interprétation de la théorie de la religion', 10.
49. *JR* (1636), 10:231–3.
50. *JR* 303.
51. *JR* (1643–4), 26:307.
52. *JR* (1647–8), 33:205.
53. *JR* (1642), 23:125.
54. *JR* 187.
55. *JR* 129.
56. *JR* (1635), 8:95.
57. CA, 424.
58. *JR* (1634), 6:181.
59. Bourdieu, 'Genèse et structure du champ religieux', 298.
60. *JR* (1642), 23:193.
61. *JR* (1647–8), 32:195–219; (1650–1), 37:51–61.
62. Marie de l'Incarnation, *Lettres historiques*, 35, 52, 55.
63. *JR* (1647), 31:155, 32:49–53.
64. *JR* (1639), 17:51. See also Marie de l'Incarnation, *Lettres historiques*, 1 September 1639, 22.
65. *JR* (1645–6), 30:19–21; see also (1643–4), 26:217–57.
66. *JR* (1642), 23:109.
67. *JR* (1642), 23:73; see also (1638), 15:107; (1642), 23:63, 73, 193; (1643–4), 26:229; (1647–8), 32:215–19.
68. *JR* (1650–1), 37:59.
69. *JR* (1647–8), 32:217.
70. *JR* (1645–6), 29:75.
71. *JR* (1645–6), 30:39.
72. *JR*
73. Sagard, Gabriel. *Histoire du Canada et voyages que les Frères mineurs récollets y on faicts pour la conversion des infidèles depuis l'an 1615.* Paris: Edwin Tross, 1866. 4 vols., 318; Sagard, Gabriel. *Le grand voyage du pays des Hurons.* Montréal: Éditions Hurtubise-HMH, 1976, 119 (171).
74. *JR* (1657–8), 44:281.
75. *JR* (1662–3), 48:169; (1645–6), 39:30.
76. *JR* (1637), 12:69–71.
77. Marcuse, Herbert. *Eros and Civilization.* Boston: Beacon Press, 1966, 16.
78. *JR* 12, 38.
79. *JR* 31–5.
80. Olivier, Christiane. *Les enfants de Jocaste, l'empreinte de la mare.* Paris: Denoël-Gonthier, 1980, 67; see also 32, 65–72, 162–5, 176, 181.

Chapter Three

Seigneurial Regime in New France

READINGS

Primary Documents

1   From *Edicts, Ordinances, Declarations and Decrees relative to the Seigniorial Tenure*

2   *Travels into North America: Containing its Natural History and a Circumstantial Account of its Plantations and Agriculture in General . . .*, Peter Kalm

Historical Interpretations

3   From 'Seigneurial Landscapes', in *The Metamorphoses of Landscape and Community in Early Quebec*, Colin M. Coates

4   From 'The Feudal Burden', *in Peasant, Lord & Merchant: Rural Society in Three Quebec Parishes 1740–1840*, Allan Greer

Introduction

The way that people made a living in colonial New France shaped its social life. Actually, insert any place name in the previous sentence and it would explain an appreciable part of historical development in the 'Old World', the 'New World', or anywhere. One defining aspect of colonial experience in New France has been long studied and deserves to keep its prominent focus: the seigneurial system. This was a method of colonizing the land that kept title to the land in the hands of France's king while allowing prominent citizens (favourites of the king or those loyal to him) to collect rents from the land. The people receiving these grants, the *seigneurs*, could become wealthier if they succeeded in attracting tenants (called *censitaires* or, more colloquially, *habitants*) to the land. The idea was that self-interest would guide seigneurs to provide the services necessary for settlement and guide tenants to work hard.

The seigneurial system defined everyone's duties clearly, but it required a great deal of management. Was this seigneur doing his part? Was that tenant using land or resources without permission? The first primary source presents a legal proceeding between two parties trying to gain some advantage within the system, and reflects how highly regulated it was, even though the regulations were not always strictly, uniformly, or formally enforced. In this case, the conflict was between two relatives, but institutions such as the Catholic church or particular religious orders could also hold seigneuries, so deals and disputes did not always involve individuals.

When Peter Kalm travelled through New France in 1749, he noted another effect of the system: the orderly arrangement of tenants' houses that were not in a village, but situated to allow the tenants to exploit their land and the transportation corridors offered by the St Lawrence and its tributaries. He also noted the poverty among tenants, whose happiness was tied directly to how well or poorly their crops fared in a particular year. With tenants living in this fashion, it was almost inevitable that the system would influence social interactions between tenants, between tenants and seigneurs, and between seigneurs. For seigneurs, the priorities were, as Colin Coates demonstrates, enlarging their holdings and establishing themselves as indispensable to the colonial effort. They renamed geographical features in their seigneuries, served in the military (French and British), allocated land to tenants, sued tenants, and played the role of social elite very well, maintaining their positions despite the considerable upheaval that accompanied the Conquest.

In the final selection, Allan Greer studies the importance of the rents due to the landlords, demonstrating that these rents could be quite burdensome to the *censitaires*. He shows that it was difficult for the latter to accumulate wealth in the way that seigneurs could and did. For most colonists, survival was the priority.

QUESTIONS FOR CONSIDERATION

1. What do you find most remarkable or surprising about the way the seigneurial system worked?
2. What was the main advantage of the highly legalistic system of contracts for the seigneurs? For the habitants?
3. It is fairly well known that lands within the seigneuries were laid out in relation to rivers. How might this distribution affect the way people socialized?
4. List some examples of the ways in which the Lanaudière family consolidated its power under the seigneurial system.
5. Why would the authorities object to cutting down a few trees?

SUGGESTIONS FOR FURTHER READING

Dechêne, Louise, *Habitants and Merchants in Seventeenth-Century Montreal* (Montreal and Kingston: McGill-Queen's University Press, 1992)

Greer, Allan, *Peasant, Lord & Merchant: Rural Society in Three Quebec Parishes 1740–1840* (Toronto: University of Toronto Press, 1985)

Greer, Allan, *The People of New France* (Toronto: University of Toronto Press, 1997)

Harris, R. Cole, *The Seigneurial System in Early Canada: A Geographical Study* (Madison, WI: University of Wisconsin Press, 1966)

Munro, William Bennett, ed., *Documents Relating to the Seigniorial Tenure in Canada, 1598–1854* (Toronto: The Champlain Society, 1908)

Trudel, Marcel, *The Seigneurial Regime* (Ottawa: Canadian Historical Association, 1971)

PRIMARY DOCUMENTS

1   'Ordinance disallowing the pretension set up by Jacques Hamelin . . . (1722)', in
     Edicts, Ordinances, Declarations and Decrees relative to the Seigniorial Tenure
     (Québec: E.R. Fréchette, 1852), 85–6.

*Ordinance disallowing the pretension set up by Jacques Hamelin,
seignior of Grondines, of preventing François Hamelin,
from building upon a lot of land near to the banal mill of the said seigniory.*

MICHEL BEGON, &c.

Jacques Hamelin coproprietor of the seigniory of Grondines, having procured the appearance before us of François Hamelin, his uncle, also a proprietor of the said seigniory, requested that we would be pleased to prohibit the said François Hamelin from constructing a house, which he is about to erect upon a lot of ground near to the banal mill of the said seigniory, inasmuch as the building which the said François Hamelin desires to erect, is very prejudicial to the said mill, the *banalité* of which belongs to him the said Jacques Hamelin as heir to his late father Louis Hamelin, according to the ordinance of Mr. Raudot heretofore intendant in this country, and the report of arbitrators rendered between the said late Louis Hamelin, and the said François Hamelin, in consequence of the said ordinance of the 5th August 1710, and 4th March 1711, the said report of experts homologated by the said Monsieur Raudot the first day of April 1711;—the said François Hamelin, acting as well for himself, as for his son François Hamelin, having been heard stated, that being the proprietor of an arpent and a third on the domain of the said seigniory, as appears by the said report of arbitrators, that the pretension of the said Jacques Hamelin that the building he intends to erect upon the said lot of ground will be prejudicial to his banal mill is unfounded; that the reason alleged is not the true one but that his object is to take advantage of the situation of the said lot of ground, which belongs to him the said François Hamelin, and which is convenient to him for that purpose; that moreover the *building* which he intends erecting upon the said lot of land, will not be more injurious to the said mill than the one now used as a residence for the miller, inasmuch as it will be further from the said mill, praying for these reasons that the complaint of the said Jacques Hamelin may be dismissed, and that he may be permitted to build upon that portion of his said lot of ground which has been set apart by him; to all which the said Jacques Hamelin replied that by reason of the said ordinance of Mr. Raudot, and the report of arbitrators aforesaid, attributing to the said late Louis Hamelin his father, whom he represents, the rights assigned by the said Jacques Hamelin and which the late Jacques Aubert, their father in law, had against the said late Louis Hamelin to the extent of one fourth of the said mill, which belonged to him, as also the sight of *banalité* in the said mill forever, against the inhabitants which up to that period had caused their grain to be ground thereat, he could not prevent him from enjoying the said mill; that his attempt to build so near to the said mill as he intends to do would have that effect, inasmuch as the building used as the miller's residence is inconvenient to him and he intends to cause it to be demolished; and the said François Hamelin answered that he persists in what he has already stated, having no intention to injure the said mill, his object being only to take advantage of a lot of ground which belongs to him, and upon which he believes he has a right to build in such way as will be most convenient to him, and that he is strengthened in this belief, by the fact that the said ordinance and the said report of arbitrators do not prohibit his building upon the said lot of ground, and that no *servitude* can exist without a title;—To all which having due regard, and seeing the ordinance of Mr. Raudot, heretofore mentioned, by which, for the reasons therein set forth, it is among other things ordered, that the said François Hamelin shall remain and be the proprietor of that portion of the seigniory of Grondines which belonged to the late Jacques Aubert, save and except, with reference to the said portion of the said seigniory, of one fourth of the mill which belonged to the said Jacques Aubert, which will remain the property of the said François Hamelin forever, with the right of *banalité* against all the inhabitants who cause their grain to be ground thereat; the report of contractors also hereinbefore mentioned, made by Messieurs Delarue, justice of the ordinary jurisdiction of Ste. Anne, François Trotain, royal notary of Batiscan, arbitrators named by the said Louis Hamelin and the said François Hamelin, and Mr. Ignace Dissy, judge of Champlain named as third arbitrator, the original of which report is deposited among the records of the said Mr. Trotain, by which, among other things, it is set forth, that the portion of the said François Hamelin in the manor of the said seigniory shall be of an arpent and a third, as heretofore enjoyed by him, according to the petition mentioned in the said report, and that the mill of the said seigniory shall belong to the said Louis Hamelin, together with the right of *banalité*, as well against the tenants of the said François Hamelin, as against the tenants of the said Louis Hamelin, in all the said seigniory of St. Charles des Roches, forever, conformably to the ordinance of Mr. Raudot; having also seen the ordinance of the said Mr. Raudot, hereinbefore mentioned, following the said report of arbitrators and confirming the same, to be executed according to its tenor and effect.

We have, inasmuch as by the said ordinance and the said report of arbitrators hereinbefore mentioned, it is not prohibited, nor has it been stipulated, that it would not be lawful to the said François Hamelin, to build upon the arpent and a third which belongs to him in the manor of the said seigniory of Grondines, which would be a *servitude* which cannot be established without a title, dismissed and do hereby dismiss the complaint of the said Jacques Hamelin.

Thus ordered, &c.

Done at Quebec, the sixteenth day of January, one thousand seven hundred and twenty-two.

(Signed)   BEGON.

---

2   From Peter Kalm, *Travels into North America: Containing Its Natural History and a Circumstantial Account of Its Plantations and Agriculture in General: . . .* (London: T. Lowndes, 1773), Vol. 2, 242–4;, 330–1.

All the farms in *Canada* stand separate from each other, so that each farmer has his possessions entirely distinct from those of his neighbour. Each church, it is true, has a little village near it; but that consists chiefly of the parsonage, a school for the boys and girls of the place, and of the houses of tradesmen, but rarely of farm-houses; and if that was the case, yet their fields were separated. The farm-houses hereabouts are generally built all along the rising banks of the river, either close to the water or at some distance from it, and about three or four *arpens* from each other. To some farms are annexed small orchards: but they are in general without them; however, almost every farmer has a kitchen-garden.

[. . .]

The farm-houses are generally built of stone, but sometimes of timber, and have three or four rooms. The windows are seldom of glass, but most frequently of paper. They have iron stoves in one of the rooms, and chimnies in the rest. The roofs are covered with boards. The crevices and chinks are filled up with clay. The other buildings are covered with straw.

There are several *Crosses* put up by the road side, which is parallel to the shores of the river. These crosses are very common in *Canada*, and are put up to excite devotion in the traveller. They are made of wood, five or six yards high, and proportionally broad. In that side which looks towards the road is a square hole, in which they place an image of our Saviour, the cross, or of the holy Virgin, with the child in her arms; and before that they put a piece of glass, to prevent its being spoiled by the weather. Those crosses, which are not far from churches, are very much adorned, and they put up about them all the instruments which they think the *Jews* employed in crucifying our Saviour, such as a hammer, tongs, nails, a flask of vinegar, and perhaps many more than were really made use of. A figure of the cock, which crowed when *St. Peter* denied our Lord, is commonly put at the top of the cross.

The country on both sides was very delightful to-day, and the fine state of its cultivation added greatly to the beauty of the scene. It could really be called a village, beginning at *Montreal*, and ending at *Quebec*, which is a distance of more than one hundred and eighty miles; for the farm-houses are never above five arpens, and sometimes but three, asunder, a few places excepted. The prospect is exceedingly beautiful, when the river goes on for some miles together in a strait line, because it then shortens the distances between the houses, and makes them form exactly one continued village.

[. . .]

August 26th. [. . .] The common people in the country seem to be very poor. They have the necessaries of life, and but little else. They are content with meals of dry bread and water, bringing all other provisions, such as butter, cheese, flesh, poultry, eggs, &c. to town, in order to get money for them, for which they buy clothes and brandy for themselves, aud dresses for their women. Notwithstanding their poverty, they are always chearful, and in high spirits.

August 29th. By the desire of the governor-general, marquis *de la Jonquiere*, and of marquis *de la Galissonniere*, I set out, with some *French* gentlemen, to visit the pretended silver-mine, or the lead-mine, near the bay *St. Paul*. I was glad to undertake this journey, as it gave me an opportunity of seeing a much greater part of the country than I should otherwise have done. This morning therefore we set out on our tour in a boat, and went down the river *St. Lawrence*.

The prospect near *Quebec* is very lively from the river. The town lies very high, and all the churches and other buildings appear very conspicuous. The ships in the river below ornament the landscape on that side. The powder magazine, which stands at the summit of the mountain on which the town is built, towers above all the other buildings.

The country we passed by afforded a no less charming sight. The river *St. Lawrence* flows nearly from south to north here; on both sides of it are cultivated fields, but more on the west side than on the east side. The hills on both shores are steep and high. A number of fine hills, separated from each other, large fields, which looked quite white from the corn with which they are covered, and excellent woods of deciduous trees, made the country round us look very pleasant.

HISTORICAL INTERPRETATIONS

3   From Colin M. Coates, 'Seigneurial Landscapes', in *The Metamorphoses of Landscape and Community in Early Quebec* (Montreal and Kingston: McGill-Queen's University Press, 2000), 13–31, 171–6.

> Land was no longer free as air or light,
> A fixed division mark'd each owner's right.
> Ovid, *Metamorphoses*, 12

In the three hundred years following Jacques Cartier's first sighting of the area that became the seigneuries of Batiscan and Sainte-Anne de la Pérade, the landscape underwent irrevocable change. In contrast to the shields of forests that had confronted the early European explorers and settlers, it became possible by the early nineteenth century to compare the land to European landscapes and to use European artistic conventions to capture it on paper. The changes that occurred were long-term ones caused by different perceptions and uses of the land. At least in the areas close to the St. Lawrence, the landscape became essentially European, with a visible hierarchy of land use.

The appropriation of the landscape by French settlers involved the importing of new animal and plant species and obviously a new race of humans. This process entailed the distancing of the native animals, plants, and humans from the new settlements. There was a dual process in the transformation of the landscape. In the first place, the French colonial state and the seigneurs played important roles in an overall restructuring of the land; the respective importance of the seigneurs and the state varied over time. Even more important, the practical labour of generations of habitants irrevocably altered the bases of society.

REDEFINING THE LAND
Naming
One of the most important ways in which the colonial state initially made its presence felt

in Batiscan and Sainte-Anne de la Pérade was through attempts to redefine the land, to draw and redraw borders around the areas.[1] The first act of appropriating the territories in the name of the French king was to name them (or properly speaking, rename them).

The origins of the word 'Batiscan' are obscure, though it doubtless has an Amerindian derivation. Samuel de Champlain first mentioned 'a river called Batiscan' in his account of his 1603 voyage.[2] Among the various geographical phenomena that he saw during his explorations, he found rivers particularly noteworthy. This interest illustrates the bias of the typical explorer, intrigued by geographical phenomena which demarcate journeys as well as those which promise future explorations.[3] However, the ambiguous chronology surrounding its mention in the account leaves open the possibility that the name does not necessarily refer to the same river as today. Indeed, Champlain's 1612 map placed the 'contrée de bastisquan' to the west of the Rivière Saint-Maurice. By contrast, Marc Lescarbot's map of 1609 illustrated and named the 'R. Batescan' in the same area as the present one. Even if, in reporting the earthquake of 1663, the Jesuits alluded to 'the river which the barbarians call Batiscan',[4] it was a French decision whether or not to adopt the name.

The river with the Algonquin name formed the symbolic locus of future French settlement. The title 'Batiscan' was extended to the seigneury, indicating that early French interest in the area lay, not in the land itself, but in the river and the transportation that it provided into the interior and into fur-trading areas. Over time, French settlers populated the territory and placed more importance on the land than the river. They even occasionally domesticated the aboriginal origin of the name. In 1783, for example, the habitants living along the river drew up a petition in which the name was given as 'Baptiste Camp'.[5]

In his account of the 1609 voyage and on his 1612 map, Champlain had named the river to the east of the Batiscan the Sainte-Marie. This name later came to refer to the seigneury on the west bank of the river, and the river itself took on the name of an island at the mouth, Île Sainte-Anne.[6] As in Batiscan, the river's name was extended to both the seigneury on the east bank and the parish, which included settlers on both sides. The names Sainte-Marie and Sainte-Anne, linked as they were to Christian beliefs and particularly to the Marian cult of the Catholic Counter-Reformation, illustrated another imperial aim: the propagation of the faith.

But the region owed its territorial names not only to explorers and their imperial initiatives. Local seigneurs also made their imprint. To distinguish it from the other Sainte-Annes in the colony, the seigneurial patronymic La Pérade gradually replaced *près Batiscan* (near Batiscan) in the eighteenth century. Likewise, in Batiscan the choice of the Jesuit pioneers for the parish names of Saint-François-Xavier and Saint-Stanislas surely reflect the order's ownership. Finally, when the Jesuits' agent sold businessman Thomas Coffin an *arrière-fief* (a fief within a larger seigneury) in Batiscan in 1795, it is not difficult to imagine the inspiration for the name Saint-Thomas. In these ways seigneurs replicated for their own purposes the state's initial process of imposing names on the region.

Distributing Fiefs

Conceded as seigneuries at different times, Batiscan and Sainte-Anne illustrate two important moments in the distribution of fiefs during the seventeenth century. According to its charter, the Compagnie de la Nouvelle France was compelled to establish a French population in the colony. In 1636 it conveyed

ten leagues of land downstream from the Rivière Saint-Maurice to Jacques de La Ferté, the king's confessor. Three years later, La Ferté conceded part of the immense tract in *arrière-fief* to the Jesuits. The shape of Batiscan seigneury resembled other land grants of the period: a long trapezoid with relatively little waterfront.[7]

Jacques de La Ferté 'for the love of God' conveyed the area around the Rivière Batiscan to the Jesuits, the religious order leading the Counter-Reformation and one of the largest landholders in the colony. The Jesuits' deed stipulated the width of the seigneury—from one-quarter league beyond the Batiscan to one-quarter league beyond the Rivière Champlain—but left its depth ill-defined.[8] It may have been Champlain's reference to an Aboriginal population in the Batiscan area that led to the decision to concede it to the Jesuits. According to the deed, the seigneury was intended for Christianized Amerindians, but their lack of interest and hostility delayed settlement for decades. The Jesuits' intention was clearly to create a new France in the New World, preferably with converted Natives. However, agents of the order did not perform the ritual taking symbolic possession of the seigneury until 1662.

Batiscan seigneury represented one of the larger land grants in the colony. Nonetheless, the exact boundaries were not immediately defined. In 1667 the Jesuits claimed, in vague fashion, ownership of 'a space of land between the Rivière Batiscan and the Rivière Champlain'.[9] Ten years later it was acknowledged that the breadth consisted of two leagues of river frontage from the east bank of the Rivière Champlain to a quarter league beyond the Rivière Batiscan.[10] The seigneury extended 20 leagues into the interior, representing some 282,240 arpents (1 arpent equals 0.342 hectares). Batiscan did not appear in the colonial census of 1663, but many settlers received land grants in the following decade.[11] According to the seigneurs, confirmed deeds of settlement had been delayed by two main

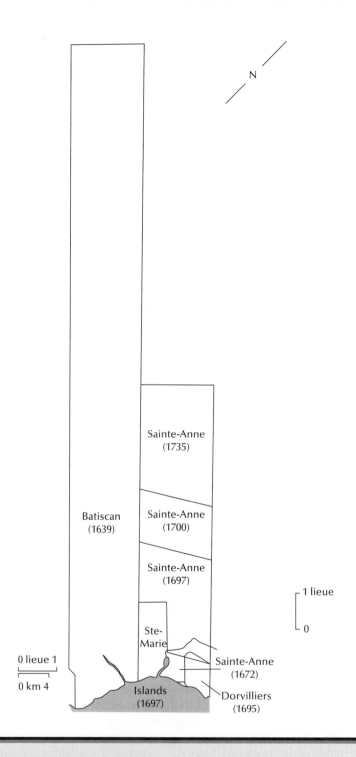

N

Sainte-Anne
(1735)

Batiscan
(1639)

Sainte-Anne
(1700)

Sainte-Anne
(1697)

1 lieue

0

Ste-
Marie

Sainte-Anne
(1672)

0 lieue 1

0 km 4

Islands
(1697)

Dorvilliers
(1695)

Seigneurial boundaries, Sainte-Anne and Batiscan

factors, the Iroquois menace and the absence of established authority—'having no regular or established form of justice in the area'.[12] From the beginning, European settlement required the authority of the colonial state.

Changes in royal policy account for the difference in size of the concessions of Batiscan and Sainte-Anne. After Louis XIV assumed direct control of the colony in the 1660s, he expressed the desire to limit the size of seigneurial grants and to curtail the granting of seigneuries to religious orders. The details of the granting of Île Sainte-Anne to Michel Gamelain, probably in 1666, are not known,[13] but it is clear that the seigneury extended over only a tiny area. Gamelain used this property to establish a fur-trade post, but he nonetheless did concede some land on the island.[14]

Intendant Jean Talon pursued the king's policy more thoroughly, granting smaller seigneuries, many of them to officers of the Carignan regiment.[15] This desire to facilitate the creation of a noble military-seigneurial class led to Talon's approval of the purchase of Gamelain's land by Edmond de Suève and Thomas de Lanouguère. In 1672 the intendant officially recognized the purchase and further conceded land to a depth of one league between the Rivière Sainte-Anne and the seigneury of Grondines to the two noble officers. As he stated, this grant was given 'in consideration of the good, useful, and praiseworthy services that they have rendered to His Majesty in different places, both in Old France and in New France since they passed to the latter on His Majesty's order, as well as in consideration of the services that they intend to render in the future.'[16] The intendant explicitly justified the officers' status as seigneurs by mentioning their service to the monarch. Members of the de Lanouguère family subsequently carved out a long career of service to their king, regardless of the throne on which he sat.

The co-owners of Sainte-Anne divided the seigneury into two distinct sections. In 1695 de Suève willed his half to Edmond Chorel de Champlain, who passed it into the hands of his brother, François Chorel d'Orvilliers. As in the western part of Sainte-Anne, the seigneurial family names over time came to identify the area. However, the seigneurs who owned the eastern section did not reside there. The d'Orvilliers family lived principally in Champlain seigneury during the French regime, and subsequent seigneurs of Sainte-Anne Est in the early nineteenth century were also absentee owners: Moses Hart, a merchant in Trois-Rivières, and Pierre Charest, a merchant at Saint-Joseph de Soulanges.[17]

From time to time boundary disputes set the seigneurial families of the two parts of Sainte-Anne against each other, but by the 1730s it was clear that de Lanouguère's son, Pierre-Thomas Tarieu de La Pérade, enjoyed greater local prominence. He and his mother had successfully petitioned for the extension of the original boundaries in 1697, 1700, and 1735.[18] The two smaller fiefs on either side, Dorvilliers to the east and Sainte-Marie to the west, found themselves bounded on the north by the expanded seigneury. By 1735 Sainte-Anne seigneury encompassed some 60 square leagues. Although the Tarieu de Lanaudière family was by no means always present at its seigneury, it seems to have participated actively in local issues. Like the Jesuits in Batiscan, its members exercised their seigneurial privileges at certain times and provided a link to the world of the colonial state.

Hierarchy in the Landscape

In contrast to the Aboriginal occupation of the territory, the French landholding system entailed a hierarchical view of society. The king, in whom ultimate title rested, distributed tracts of land to seigneurs and preserved certain rights on that land, particularly concerning minerals and timber. The seigneur in turn distributed lots to tenants (*censitaires*) but placed limits on the tenants' control of their property.

When the seigneurs began to distribute land in their seigneuries, it was of course impossible for them to know that immigration would remain negligible over the next century. They could not know that future population growth and the concomitant increase of their seigneurial revenues would depend almost exclusively on natural demographic trends. Therefore in an examination of the way in which seigneurs preferred their landscape to take shape, the earliest years of French settlement are the most revealing.

The seigneurs' attempts to structure their space appear most clearly in their decisions concerning manors, mills, and churches. In both Batiscan and Sainte-Anne the early seigneurs first directed their proprietorial interest towards small islands in the St. Lawrence, perhaps because these were more defensible. In Batiscan the *aveu et dénombrement* (list of landholdings) of 1677 designated Île Saint-Éloi, along with a nearby concession on the mainland, as the 'demesne and seigneurial manor'.[19] The first windmill, constructed in 1668, and the parish church were erected nearby on the mainland. Since this tract of land lay in the middle of the concessions along the St. Lawrence, we can speculate that the Jesuits attempted thereby to provide a symbolic centre for the early seigneury, one dominated by the religious power of the church, the practical economic functions of the windmill, and the legal authority of the seigneur. An early deed of concession referred to this area as 'le village de batiscan', which, given the low density of settlement at that date, represented more a wish than a reality.[20]

In Sainte-Anne, Michel Gamelain first granted concessions on Île Saint-Ignace, at the mouth of the river. He reserved Île des Plaines for himself, and over time, subsequent seigneurs regained most of Île Saint-Ignace for themselves.[21] These islands would remain in the hands of the seigneurs for the next century and a half, but they chose to establish their manor on the mainland. Unlike Batiscan—or for that matter, neighbouring Sainte-Marie and Dorvilliers—none of the habitants' concessions fronted on the St. Lawrence. In Sainte-Anne the seigneurs reserved this privilege to themselves,

establishing their manor a short distance away from the river and only sharing the frontage with a common.[22] Consequently, from the perspectives afforded by the rivers, the seigneurs of Sainte-Anne dominated their landscape: anyone sailing along the north shore of the St. Lawrence or travelling up the Sainte-Anne would first come into view of seigneurial lands. The Lanouguères enjoyed the clearest view of the St. Lawrence from their land, while the principal axis for the habitants' concessions would be the Rivière Sainte-Anne.[23]

The seigneurs of Sainte-Anne also encouraged the founding of a village. Disputing the location of the parish church with the seigneur of adjacent Sainte-Marie, they were ultimately able to establish the church on the east bank of the river.[24] In 1691 de Suève granted to the parish land for a church and a presbytery and permitted the construction of a village on the remaining property, transferring the rents for this land to the church.[25] By the time of James Murray's 1760 map, a rather diffuse village had taken shape, largely to the south of the parish church.[26] It probably owed its existence in part to chance: it served as an important relay post along the royal road, one day's journey from Quebec. In general, the habitants in both Sainte-Anne and Batiscan avoided dense settlement.

Given the fact that Lanouguère, de Suève, and the Jesuits could not have known how slow the rate of settlement would be, we must speculate as to the nature of the ideal landscape that they wanted to establish. It was one in which the seigneurs wished to occupy central and strategic places. From the land that they maintained as a demesne, they could closely watch over the development of their respective seigneuries. The Jesuits' control centred around the church and the mill; that is, it was based on both religion and economy. The lay seigneurs of Sainte-Anne dominated the view of the St. Lawrence and therefore the access to the external world.

After Gamelain's initial, and short-lived, focus on fur-trading activities, subsequent seigneurs turned their attention to a local agrarian economy. But the early attempts to structure the landscape illustrate their desire to assert their ascendancy and reveal the symbolism of land distribution.

SEIGNEURS AND THE STATE
The Lanaudière Family

The local elite ensured the connection of their society to the external world: seigneurs, priests, local state officials (judges, notaries, bailiffs, and militia captains), and military officials all played a role, but in Sainte-Anne the seigneurs enjoyed pre-eminence during the French regime. The colonial state relied on this noble elite to represent it in rural areas and provided privileged access to patronage and favours. For the Tarieu de Lanaudière family, this treatment persisted into the British regime.

For many seigneurial families, military commissions and concomitant fur-trade privileges provided the economic basis of their status. The Lanaudières always remained a military family. All the adult males up to the early nineteenth century held commissions in either the French or the British army, and a couple of the women were famous for their exploits with firearms too.[27] Through the five generations of Lanaudières who owned Sainte-Anne, the family profited from its connections to governing officials to obtain trade licences and other lucrative privileges.

After Sainte-Anne was granted to de Suève and Thomas de Lanouguère, the former managed the seigneury while the latter, with Governor Louis de Buade de Frontenac's support, participated in the fur trade and exercised the military command in Montreal.[28] From an early date the seigneurs defended their rights; in 1673 they appealed to their seigneurial judge to force their tenants to pay their dues.[29] After his death in 1678, Lanouguère's widow, Marguerite-Renée Denys, assumed control of the western half of the seigneury. A 1685 census enumerated 114 residents. In 1704 Denys

abandoned, in exchange for annual payments of 400 livres, ownership to her second son, Pierre-Thomas, under the assumption that his long-absent elder brother was dead.[30]

In the 1720s and 1730s Pierre-Thomas and his wife Madeleine de Verchères initiated a number of court cases as they attempted to enforce their legal rights and ensure their social and economic prominence in the growing seigneury. In 1728, for example, they accused the local priest and several habitants of contravening the requirement to take grain to the seigneur's gristmill. The judgment in this case validated the seigneur's seizure of wheat and required the habitants to take their grain to the seigneurial mill in the future. To add prestige to the economic gain, the intendant ordered that the seigneur should serve as arbiter in any disputes over measurement.[31] In other cases, the family sought confirmation of its exclusive rights over fishing and hunting and for the privilege of first pew in the parish church.[32]

During this time it appealed to the government for other concrete recognitions of its status. In 1731 Madeleine de Verchères requested, through the governor and the intendant, an increase in the royal pension that she received for her youthful heroism in defending her family fort at Verchères from the Iroquois.[33] Although Pierre-Thomas's application in 1729 for the position of chief road officer and his request the following year for a military promotion were not granted,[34] he continued to hold military posts, which he was able to use to profit from trade. Despite his activity outside the seigneury, Pierre-Thomas and in particular his wife were very active in local social relations. Their heirs, however, became less involved in the seigneury.

In the last decades of the French regime, Pierre-Thomas's son, Charles-François de Lanaudière, became even more closely tied to state officials in Quebec. Diarist Élisabeth Bégon described his wife as the intendant's 'princesse'.[35] Charles-François and his younger brother formed part of Intendant François Bigot's retinue, following him on his travels through the colony.[36] Charles-François, while serving as an officer in the colonial troops, earned the cross of the order of Saint-Louis in 1759. He served the governors on a number of occasions in a police capacity: compiling a roll of militiamen and requisitioning provisions from the peasantry for the sustenance of French troops during the Seven Years War.[37] He also participated in the fur trade, establishing lucrative accounts with merchants in La Rochelle, selling seal furs and oil, and importing wine and brandy.[38] In 1750 Lanaudière was granted the seigneury of Lac-Maskinongé, presumably in recognition of the successes of his military career. The official favour that Lanaudière enjoyed in the period before the Conquest confirmed his status in society, but it also drew him away from the seigneury of Sainte-Anne. The estate inventory drawn up after the death of his first wife in 1762 noted that there was no seigneurial manor.[39]

After the Conquest, Sainte-Anne might have passed out of the hands of the Lanaudière family. Charles-François and his only surviving child, Charles-Louis, both sailed to France following the military defeat. However, they did not emigrate definitively. Charles-François, like others in his situation, discovered the difficulties of acquiring a good position in the French army, of maintaining his trade contacts in the newly redefined North America, and of establishing a son who lived more expensively than he could afford. With the direct trade to Canada blocked, Charles-François pursued trading possibilities through the French island of Miquelon off Newfoundland and through Louisiana, dealing in merchandise such as cloths, nails, and sealing lines, but this venture took many years to come to fruition and proved less lucrative than he had foreseen. Charles-François's subsequent correspondence with La Rochelle merchants focused on investing his capital in securities. He hesitated for a while about settling in France, but the news that Canadian officers found it difficult to acquire positions in the French army must have been discouraging.[40]

Charles-François returned to Canada in 1762, after the death of his first wife. Two years later he married Marie-Catherine Le Moyne de Longueuil, with whom he had ten children. Over time, his eldest son, Charles-Louis, developed an interest in Sainte-Anne seigneury, one which appeared to be tied up with noble sentiments and with an assertion of his position among his father's offspring.

[. . .]

Charles-Louis had returned to Canada by 1768, apparently because he was an inveterate gambler and had racked up so many debts that he had to leave France to escape his creditors. During his stopover in London he ran into more troubles and had to make a hasty return to Quebec.[41]

Back at home Charles-Louis de Lanaudière was able to acquire a position as aide-de-camp to General Guy Carleton, a position he relished. As he informed his father in 1770, 'one cannot be happier than I am with my sire the general.'[42] In this position, he returned to England and Europe on many occasions, during which he attempted to enhance his trading activities. [. . .]

According to Charles-Louis, a hunting trip with three English friends awakened his interest in the paternal estate of Sainte-Anne. The English aristocratic predilection for country estates and in particular for hunting privileges is well recognized.[43] Charles-Louis de Lanaudière undoubtedly came to share these tastes. He asked his father for title to the seigneury, which was granted to him less Île des Plaines (or Île Sainte-Marguerite) in an agreement signed in 1772.[44] Nonetheless, he did not establish permanent residency at Sainte-Anne. His activities led him to spend much of his time in Quebec, but the letters that Charles-Louis wrote from Sainte-Anne indicated that his presence at the seigneury was not restricted to any one season.[45] [. . .]

Despite his occasional notable appearances on his seigneury, Lanaudière paid much less day-to-day attention to its administration. He entrusted the management of the seigneury to the Gouin family. By the 1810s he was concentrating his demesne farming on sheep, hay, and wheat.[46] Nonetheless, he still maintained a paternalistic interest in his tenants.

Obviously, Lanaudière would have appreciated the steady, if not elevated, income that the seigneury provided. However, his main projects, such as fur-trading ventures, took place elsewhere.[47] But his principal field of activity was his connection with the new rulers of the colony. He was appointed to the sinecure of surveyor general of forests and rivers in 1771. He demonstrated his loyalty to the British crown in 1775 when he tried to raise militia to fight the American invaders and provided protection for Governor Carleton. Charles-Louis received his share of patronage and social recognition as a result, being appointed to the Legislative Council and to the position of overseer of highways.

Like British grandees of the period,[48] he saw the position of surveyor general as an opportunity to bend rules to his own profit. In 1778, for example, he sent a proposal to his cousin, François Baby, to cut timber from his seigneury and the neighbouring ones for sale in Quebec. Taking advantage of his position and his connections to the government, he suggested supplying the garrison in Quebec with wood: 'As the government must use its authority to cut the wood—I propose this, if I can be given the parishes of Deschambault, Grondines, Sainte-Anne, and all of Batiscan—which never supply wood, with the power to command the men whom I will require for this work.'[49] The government's ability to demand a corvée (required labour) would even release him personally from the necessity of hiring workers to cut the trees. He added in a subsequent letter, 'in conducting government business, I must also do my own.'[50] For Lanaudière, state and personal affairs were not just compatible; they were mutually reinforcing.

He and other members of the family continued to use whatever influence they could muster to support the colonial government. In the 1792 elections for the House of Assembly,

for example, Lanaudière campaigned in favour of William Grant, a candidate who favoured strong British rule.[51] Almost two decades later, his half-brother Xavier-Roch presented himself for election in Sainte-Anne, an act which sister Agathe applauded in trying to convince her other brother Gaspard to do the same: 'it is the duty of all men who are attached to their king to make this effort.'[52]

The Lanaudière family, in particular Charles-Louis, had obviously made an easy transition to the new regime. It is possible that its members counted among the most successful French nobles in this regard.[53] In doing so, Charles-Louis adopted many of the viewpoints of the new rulers, in particular those concerning land tenure. [. . .]

In 1790 Lanaudière submitted his opinions on seigneurial tenure to the Executive Council. After drawing a somewhat exaggerated picture of seigneurial privileges, he concluded, 'The honorary, as well as pecuniary duties and dues are evidently complex, arbitrary, injurious. Can anything further be necessary to induce a benevolent monarch and nation to destroy them, and to grant in their stead that certain and determinate tenure of King Charles the Second, free and common socage, which the other subjects of His Majesty King George the Third enjoy, and with so much reason boast of.'[54] The printing of Lanaudière's petition in 1791 in the *Gazette de Québec* launched a heated public debate with Abbé Thomas-Laurent Bédard over the advantages of free and common socage. Lanaudière reviewed the movement of settlers to other parts of North America and claimed that if he could not alter the tenure on his lands, 'I ran the risk of remaining alone with my family and the few *habitans* who have settled themselves on it; and that the remaining part might lie uncultivated.' Lanaudière continued his appeal by referring to the superiority of English social and economic conditions: 'An english farmer discovers liberty in his very figure and air . . . He consumes more in one month than three fourths of your farmers [i.e., habitants], even of those at their ease, in six.'[55] Of course, Lanaudière's wish was not granted. Nonetheless, he did not give up on his idea of abolishing seigneurial tenure on his lands.

In the meantime he defended his seigneurial privileges, for example, justifying his rights over the Sainte-Anne ferry by exhibiting his titles.[56] But in 1810 he renewed his petition, 'having always ardently wished to hold his land in free and common socage in preference to feudal tenure.'[57] In this light, Lanaudière occupies a rather singular place as an anti-seigneurial Canadian seigneur, preferring English land tenure to French.

A number of visitors to the colony met with Lanaudière and recorded his pro-British sentiments. John Lambert commented that Lanaudière 'is sincerely attached to the British government, and in his conduct, his manners, and his principles, appears to be, in every respect, a complete Englishman.'[58] He certainly was one noble with close connections to the government, and he tried to use these to his best advantage. As it had during the French regime, the Lanaudière family supported the colonial rulers and benefited from its connections. For instance, just as the colonial government and the English elite tried to encourage hemp growing, Lanaudière addressed an appeal to his tenants to grow the plant, offering to purchase all their production at the highest market prices.[59] During his intermittent presences in Sainte-Anne, Charles-Louis worked hard to defend the policies of the British rulers. No French seigneur could have better represented the British colonial state.

The Jesuits

While a noble seigneur's ties to the state are readily apparent, the role of a corporate religious seigneur is more complex. The relationship between tenants and such a seigneur was obviously different from the personal connections that one might have with a powerful family. Nonetheless, the Jesuit owners of Batiscan were no less implicated in the running of the colonial state. In their general relations with the colonial government, they defended a specific elitist and state-oriented view of the social order, one in which religion represented the supreme virtue. Like that of the Lanaudière family, the history of the Jesuits' seigneurial title was linked to their relations with the colonial government.

Historians have shown that ecclesiastical seigneuries were managed with much astuteness and flexibility. This generalization applies to Batiscan also, at least during the French regime. The first concessions there date from 1664, and they multiplied thereafter. The Jesuits had begun to comply with the royal edicts compelling them to see to the settlement of their lands. According to the census of 1685, 261 people lived in the seigneury by that date.

Early riverfront concessions to individuals in the eastern part of the seigneury often accompanied grants of land in the western part. 'The Jesuits', concludes the most detailed analysis of Jesuit policy in Batiscan, 'could thus solidly establish the colonists by assuring them from the beginning a plot on which to settle their sons.' An agent (*procureur général*) for the Jesuits' interests resided in Batiscan during the French regime. By the eighteenth century the order had taken advantage of a larger population base to enforce control over land-granting practices, not conceding land in pioneer zones until some clearing had occurred.[60] The seigneurial court, established definitively at Batiscan after 1726, provided a means for ensuring adherence to the Jesuits' policies. In 1745, for instance, the agent summoned Antoine Trottier to the court in order that he be dispossessed of land that he had worked without proper title for the previous five years.[61]

The Jesuits also constructed mills on their seigneury. A map from about 1726 depicts two windmills along the St. Lawrence and a sawmill situated in the depths of settlement on the Rivière Batiscan. The Murray map of 1760 indicates the existence of a windmill on the St. Lawrence and a watermill on the Batiscan. As shown by their land-granting policy and their construction of mills, the Jesuits' active role in the running of the seigneury continued up to the time of the Conquest.

Although the Conquest did not lead to a fundamental redefinition of land title and obligations in the old seigneuries, when the British abolished seigneurial courts, they destroyed a powerful instrument for enforcing the seigneur's will at the local level. Moreover, the Jesuits suffered more than other seigneurs when Canada was lost.[62] General Jeffery Amherst, the supreme British military commander in North America at the time of the Conquest, refused to grant protection to the property of the Jesuits and the Recollets until the Crown had pronounced on the future status of those orders in the colony. British aversion to the Jesuits in particular was reinforced by the movement in other countries to suppress the order. In 1764 a royal decree dissolved the Jesuits throughout France and its colonies. Nine years later Pope Clement XIV suppressed the entire order. The consequences for Jesuit properties in Canada were complex. In 1775 the British government outlined a policy concerning the Jesuits. Although the order was suppressed, the surviving members would be provided for during their lifetimes. Ultimately, this policy came to mean that they were to enjoy the profits from their properties, but that title would revert to the Crown on the death of the last member of the order.

Meanwhile, General Amherst had requested a grant of the Jesuit lands in recognition of his services to the Crown, and King George III had promised him this recompense. Subsequent attempts to acquire the titles persisted beyond his own lifetime. His nephew and heir, the second Lord Amherst, pressed the claim in the declining years of the last Jesuit, Father Jean-Joseph Casot. Ultimately, the second Lord Amherst received monetary compensation for the king's promise, but he never acquired title to the estates themselves. In 1800, upon Casot's death, the lands previously belonging to the Jesuits reverted to the Crown.

During this period of uncertainty over the disposition of the Jesuit estates (which launched a century-long political debate concerning the use of public funds for education and the relationship between church and state), the Jesuits continued to employ agents to manage their seigneuries. The principal agent for Batiscan, François-Xavier Larue, lived in Pointe-aux-Trembles, near Quebec. In general, the Jesuits now seem to have been less attentive to the management of Batiscan than in the period before the Conquest. However, they were more vigilant than the government itself would be when it ultimately took control.

Judging by the mills, the single most lucrative of the seigneurial privileges, the Jesuits through their agents continued to attend to their property. The 1781 *aveu et dénombrement* made reference to a mill in the process of being built in the seigneury.[63] The windmills along the St. Lawrence were replaced over time by watermills along the Batiscan. A report prepared at the end of the Jesuits' administration noted two mills in operation, one built of stone on the northeast shore of the Rivière Batiscan at Sainte-Geneviève and the other built of wood on the Rivière des Envies.[64] The mills apparently remained functional and at least partially fulfilled the needs of the habitants: a seigneurial agent later reported that the mills 'still worked and were in relatively good order at the time of the last Jesuit.'[65] In providing relatively lucrative banal mills, the Jesuits maintained a traditional seigneurial monopoly, one that offered at least a minimum of required services to their tenants.

However, the Jesuits were much less attentive in their management of land grants in Batiscan seigneury. The numbers of titles conceded provide at least a general overview of their stewardship. From 1763 to 1790 only twenty-two concessions were awarded.[66] The Jesuits' agents were no longer facilitating settlement of the seigneury.

Another measure of the Jesuits' interest in their property is provided by their collection of seigneurial dues. Information concerning the amount collected is available for only a few scattered years. In 1768 the Jesuits acknowledged receiving 1291 *livres tournois* in rents. Thirteen years later, in 1781, different copies of the general recapitulation of the Jesuits' properties indicate between 988 and 1285 *livres tournois* in *cens et rentes*.[67] The reasons for the discrepancies in these figures, which relate to the same document, are not clear. It is possible that land-granting policy limited the amount of seigneurial dues paid up to that point. However, by 1790 the revenues had about doubled, although the population had increased by only about 40 per cent. Batiscan earned about £94 sterling in *cens et rentes*, or 2256 *livres tournois*. The banal mill earned another 1200 livres tournois. Even with this increase, Batiscan was not a particularly lucrative Jesuit seigneury: it provided less than 7 per cent of the total receipts for the estates, much less than other properties such as La Prairie and Sainte-Geneviève near Montreal and Notre-Dame-des-Anges near Quebec.[68]

In the final years of life of the last Jesuit, the land-granting policy changed dramatically. A large portion of the seigneury fell into the hands of English-speaking entrepreneurs. In the 1790s the rhythm of concessions picked up markedly. Between 1795 and 1800, 83 concessions were granted, 53 in 1798 alone. Most of these involved small amounts of land and probably entailed the recognition of land already occupied by tenants. However, among the concessions were huge grants to businessman Thomas Coffin, made under the dubious circumstances surrounding the disposition of the Jesuits' properties. In 1795 Coffin received the *arrière-fief* of Saint-Thomas, comprising all of the seigneury north of the Rivière des Envies, in exchange for 300 sols annual rent. In 1798 he added three ill-defined 'compeaux' of land, 'being the remainders between conceded land, that he [Coffin] is obliged to have surveyed, and pay one "sol" per arpent.'[69]

This vast land grant, with its timber and iron resources, held much promise for profit, since Coffin and his partner, the deputy commissary general John Craigie, were able to establish a new ironworks. Not all colonial officials were pleased with such land grants. In July 1799, before the death of Father Casot, the attorney general, Jonathan Sewell, protested against the land grant, expressing to the agent, Desjardins, 'the disapprobation of Government not only of that Concession but of all others (except perhaps the common Concession en roture to Habitans of small lots at the accustomary cens et rentes).'[70] Likewise, the local agent for the Jesuits' estates protested that Coffin had begun employing men to cut wood in the seigneury without permission.[71] Nonetheless, the owners of this Batiscan land were too well connected to be in danger of losing it.

When Father Casot died in 1800, title to the Jesuit estates reverted to the Crown, which appointed a commission to oversee the management of the property. Coffin and Craigie soon acquired a new partner in the Batiscan ironworks, Thomas Dunn, a former administrator of the colony, who sat on the Board of Commissioners of the Jesuit Estates. Lord Amherst's brother-in-law, John Hale, who anxiously watched over the family's interests in the colony, resigned from the Board of Commissioners when it became apparent that the property was not likely to be turned over to Amherst.[72]

[. . .]

For their part, the Jesuits' role in Batiscan seigneury had changed over time. Following their active involvement in its administration during the French regime, the complicated post-1763 struggle over the order's estates in Canada led to an increasing indifference towards Batiscan. As title shifted from the Jesuits to the Crown, a large section of the seigneury fell into private hands.

CONCLUSION

Seigneurial control over the land was undoubtedly an important aspect of the changes in landscape. It gave the localities their broad outlines, though it did not strictly speaking determine the nature of land use. This responded more to the exigencies of small-scale, family-oriented agricultural production. Superficially, the landscape projected a seigneurial presence, even though this faded the closer and the later one looked.

Since the mid-eighteenth century, commentators have argued over the degree to which seigneurial tenure was incompatible with profitable economic development.[73] But as Françoise Noël has demonstrated, 'seigneurial tenure . . . could be used by large proprietors to monopolize scarce resources.'[74] The

founding of the Batiscan ironworks rested upon seigneurial privileges granted in *arrière-fief* by an increasingly irrelevant seigneur.

Thus the lack of attention that seigneurs showed to their seigneuries could be equally determinant as when they did try to direct matters firmly. The increasing inattention during the British regime gave more rein to local elites to exercise control over social relations. It was during this latter period that the seigneurs had the least impact on the local landscape, marginalized as they increasingly became from local affairs.

NOTES

1. For the importance of naming and drawing boundaries in the appropriation of land, see Paul Carter, *The Road to Botany Bay: An Exploration of Landscape and History*. New York: Alfred A. Knopf, 1988.
2. H.P. Biggar, ed., *Works of Samuel de Champlain*. 6 vols. Toronto: Champlain Society, 1920–36, 1: 132.
3. Carter, *The Road to Botany Bay*, 47–54.
4. Reuben Gold Thwaites, *The Jesuit Relations and Allied Docuements*. 74 vols. Cleveland: Burrows Brothers, 1896–1901, 48: 215.
5. Baby Collection, Université de Montréal (UM-Baby), mf. 2584, Requête des habitants de Baptiste Camp à François Baby, 15 février 1783. John Knox recorded the name as 'Batiste camp' (Arthur G. Doughty, ed., An *Historical Journal of the Campaigns in North American for the Years 1757, 1758, and 1760*. By Captain John Knox. Vol. 2. Toronto: Champlain Society, 1914, 2: 478).
6. Raymond Douville, *Les premiers seigneurs et colons de Sainte-Anne de la Pérade, 1667–1681*. Trois-Rivières: Éditions du Bien Public, 1946, 9–10.
7. Marcel Trudel, *Les débuts du régime seigneurial au Canada*. Montréal: Fides, 1974, 20–1; Richard Colebrook Harris, ed., *Seigneurial System in Early Canada*. 2nd ed. Montreal: McGill-Queen's University Press, 1984, 23–5.
8. Fonds Seigneuries (FS), Archives nationales du Québec à Québec, vol. 3, Batiscan, Acte

de Concession de Messire Jacques de La Ferté aux Pères Jésuites, 3 mars 1639.
9. National Archives of Canada (NA), France, Archives des colonies, Des limites et des postes, Transcriptions, MG 1 série c 11 E (mf. F-409), 14, Estat des Terres que les Reverends Peres Jesuistes Possedent en Canada suivant leurs declarations du 26e novembre 1667.
10. Archives nationales du Québec à Montréal (ANQ-M), Seigneurie Batiscan, P220/1, Aveu et dénombrement, 29 décembre 1677.
11. Philippe Jarnoux, 'La colonisation de la seigneurie de Batiscan aux 17e et 18e siècles: L'espace et les hommes.' *RHAF* 40, no. 2 (1986), 169.
12. 'ayant pas meme sur les Lieux aucune Justice formée ni assurée' (Terres et forêts, Biens des Jésuites (BJ), ANQ-Q, vol. 70, Title Deeds, Jesuits Estates, 82–4, Acte de Monsieur de Bouteroue Intendant pour suppleer au defaut d'insinuation des Donnations des fiefs Batiscan & Champlain, 27 nov. 1668).
13. Douville, *Les premiers seigneurs et colons*, 13–36.
14. C.-M. Boissonault, 'Gamelain de La Fontaine, Michel', *Dictionary of Canadian Biography* (DCB), 1: 320–1.
15. Harris, *Seigneurial System*, 26–31.
16. 'en Considera[ti]on des bons utils et louables services quil[s] ont rendus a sa ma[jes]te en

differents endroicts tant en lancienne France que dans la nouvelle depuis quils y sont passez par ordre de sa ma[jes]te et en veue de ceux quils temoignent encore vouloir rendre cy apres' (FS, vol. 52, Sainte-Anne de la Pérade [Ouest], Acte de concession par Jean Talon, 29 octobre 1672).

17. Ibid., Sainte-Anne de la Pérade (est), Extrait d'un Contrat de vente par Moses Hart à Pierre Charay [sic] et uxor, 26 février 1816.

18. Hale Collection, National Archives of Canada (NA-Hale), vol. 2, Acte de foi et hommage, 23 décembre 1819.

19. ANQ-M, Seigneurie Batiscan, P220/1, Aveu et dénombrement, 1.

20. UM-Baby, mf. 2104–5, Contrat de concession d'une place au village de Batiscan, 13 septembre 1674.

21. Douville, *Les premiers seigneurs et colons.*

22. Carte de Catalogne, 1709, in Marcel Trudel, *Atlas de la Nouvelle-France/Atlas of New France.* Québec: Presses de l'Université Laval, 1968, 169. This map does not, in fact, indicate the presence of a common in Sainte-Anne, though one was established.

23. Loius-Edmond Hamelin, 'Le rang d'arrière-fleuve en Nouvelle-France', *Géographe Canadien/Canadian Geographer* 34, no. 2 (1980), 113–14, notes that the St. Lawrence formed the principal axis for concessions in the majority of cases. Still, according to Catalogne's map of 1709, other seigneurs also assured themselves of the most prominent geographic positions.

24. Douville, *Les premiers seigneurs et colons,* 122–8.

25. NA, Sainte-Anne de la Pérade, Transcriptions, MG 8, F 83, 10–13, Copie du contrat de donation faite par feu messire de Suève, 8 aoust 1691.

26. National Map Collection (NMC), National Archives of Canada, NMC-10842, Murray Map (1760), section FI.

27. For the male Lanaudières' military activity, see P.-G. Roy, *La famille Tarieu de Lanaudière.* Lévis: [n.p.], 1922. As for the women, besides Madeleine de Verchères, Philippe Aubert de Gaspé discussed his aunt, Agathe de Lanaudière, in his Mémoires, 402–4.

28. Raymond Douville, 'Lanouguère, Thomas de', *DCB*, 1: 417–18.

29. Douville, *Les premiers seigneurs et colons,* 56, 62.

30. FS, vol. 52, Sainte-Anne de la Pérade (Est) [*sic*], Acte d'abandon et cession de la seigneurie de Sainte-Anne par Marguerite-Renée Denys à Pierre-Thomas Tarieu de la Pérade (Greffe Genaple), 4 novembre 1704.

31. 'Ordonnance qui déclare bonne et valable la saisie . . . ', in *Pièces et documents relatifs à la tenure seigneuriale.* Québec: E.R. Fréchette, 1852, 120–4.

32. ANQ-M, Conseil supérieur, Registres, M9, (mf. 1197), vol. 28, folio 39r–v, Esmond et Jean Tessier et al. versus Thomas Tarrieu de la Pérade, 18 août 1721; vol. 32, folio 51v–52v, François Chorel Dorvilliers vs Thomas Tarrieu de la Pérade, 12 mars 1725.

33. NA, Nouvelle-France, Correspondance officielle, 3e série, MG 8, A1, vol. 12, 2657–8, Lettre de Beauharnois et Hocquart au ministre, 15 octobre 1731.

34. Ibid., vol. 11, 2427–8, Lettre de Beauharnois et Hocquart au ministre, 25 octobre 1729; NA, France, Archives des colonies, Lettres envoyées, MG 1, série B, vol. 54, folio 423½, Lettre du ministre à Beauharnois, 4 avril 1730.

35. Élisabeth Bégon, *Lettres au cher fils: Correspondance d'Élisabeth Bégon avec som gendre (1748–1753).* Montréal: Hurtubise HMH, 1972, 53.

36. Ibid., 72; Louis Franquet, *Voyages et mémoires sur le Canada.* Montréal: Éditions Elysée, 1974, 129, 141.

37. Baby Collection, National Archives of Canada (NA-Baby), vol. 1, 511a, Beauharnois à Lanaudière, 22 juillet 1744; vol. 3, 1722–3, Marquis de Vaudreuil à Mr de Lanaudière, 23 juillet 1759.

38. Ibid., vol. 30, 18725–61, Inventaire des biens de La communauté entre De La Perrade [Lanaudière] et feue Geneviève de Boishébert, sa première épouse, 5 juillet 1762 (according to this document, Lanaudière held some 63,000 livres in France in the hands of various merchants); Tarien de Lanaudière (TL), ANQ-Q, vol. 1, Accord entre M. de Lanaudière et M. Varin, 16 octobre 1753, and Cession de Gaultier, 4 avril 1754.

39. NA-Baby, vol. 30, 18759, Inventaire des biens de la communauté entre De La Perrade [Lanaudière] et feue Geneviève de Boishébert, sa première épouse, 5 juillet 1762.

40. Ibid., vol. 4, 2139–40, Thouron & Frères à Lanaudière, 22 avril 1764.

41. NA-Baby, vol. 5, 2652–8, Thouron & frères à Lanaudière, 10 mars 1768.

42. 'on ne peux pas être plû heureux que je le sui avec Mr Le generalle' (ibid., 2968, Lanaudiere à son père, 14 septembre 1770).

43. E.P. Thompson, *Whigs and Hunters: The Origins of the Black Art.* Harmondsworth: Penguin, 1977.

44. NA-Baby, vol. 30, 19052, Inventaire et procès-verbal de vente des biens de la succession de Lanaudière, avril 1788.

45. Letters in NA-Baby between 1774 and 1783 were written in March, July, September, October, and December.

46. Hale Family Collection (UT-Hale), Thomas Fisher Rare Book Library, University of Toronto, E.F. Hale to Lord Amherst, 17 September [1819].

47. NA-Baby, vol. 6, 3570–1, Lanaudière fils à Vercher, 24 juillet 1773.

48. Roy Porter, *English Society in the Eighteenth Century.* London: Penguin Books, 1977, 73–8.

49. 'comme nesséscairement il fautdra que le gouvernement fasse, Dotorité faire, faire le bois,—je propose sesi, si lon veux me dormer les paroisses—Déchambaut, grondine, *St anne* & tous batiscand—qui ne fournisse jamais Du bois, avec pouvoir de commender Les hommes Dont jorei besoin pour bucher' (NA-Baby, vol. 8, 4398–9, Lanaudière à M. François Baby, 17 septembre 1778; emphasis in original).

50. 'en fesant l'affaire Du gouvernement il faut que je fasse les miéne' (ibid., vol. 8, 4406, Lanaudière à François Baby, 30 septembre 1778). Evidence that the enterprise was undertaken is shown by a further letter in the same collection (4736–7, Lanaudière à F. Baby, 6 mars 1781).

51. See the criticism of Charles de Lanaudière in the handbill *Commentaire sur le discours de l'honorable Chas. Delanaudiere (qui a paru hier)*, reprinted in John Hare, *Aux origines du parlementarisme québécois 1791–1793.* Sillery: Les Éditions du Septentrion, 1993, 177–9.

52. 'cest le devoir de toutes hommes quis est atachés a son rois de faire c'est [cet] effort' (TL, vol. 2, Agathe de Lanaudière à Gaspard Lanaudière, 2 avril 1810).

53. Roch Legault, 'Les aléas d'une carrière militaire pour les membres de la petite noblesse seigneuriale canadienne de la révolution américaine à la guerre de 1812–1815.' Mémoire de maîtrise, Université de Montréal, 1986, 113–15.

54. 'Answers submitted by Charles de Lanaudière to various Questions relating to the Seigniorial System, October 11, 1790', in W.B. Munro, *Documents Relating to the Seigniorial Tenure in Canada, 1598–1854.* Toronto: Champlain Society, 1908, 273.

55. *Gazette de Québec*, 24 mars 1791; supplément, 28 avril 1791.

56. Archives nationales du Québec à Trois-Rivières (ANQ-TR), Cour de banc du roi (dossiers), T25, Terme de septembre 1808, no. 1, Pierre Bureau vs Jos. Riv[ar]d Lanouette et L'Honorable De Lanaudière.

57. 'ayant toujours ardemment désiré de tenir ses Terres en franc et commun Soccage en préference de Féodalité' (NA, Lower Canada Land Papers, RG 1 L 3 L, vol. 188 [mf. C-2538], 57763–4, Petition de Charles de Lanaudière à Sir James Craig, 21 décembre 1810).

58. John Lambert, *Travels through Canada and the United States of North America in the Years 1806, 1807 & 1808.* 2nd ed. London: C. Cradock and W. Joy, 1814, 461. Lord Selkirk was similarly impressed with Lanaudière: 'a very gentlemanly old Canadian Officer, & a man of reflexion' (NA, Selkirk Papers, MG 19, E 1, Lord Selkirk's Diary, 19749).

59. *Gazette de Quebec*, 22 juillet 1802.

60. Jarnoux, 'La colonisation', 173–5, quotation from 173. See also Raymond Douville, 'Les lents débuts d'une seigneurie des Jésuits.' *Cahiers des dix* 25 (1960): 249–276.

61. BJ, vol. 97, St-Agnian vs. Antoine Trottier, 29 avril 1745. See also Collection des pièces judiciaires et notariales (ANQ-Q), Mesager vs. François Massicot, 6 avril 1748. Lavallée notes that the Jesuit seigneurs of La Prairie became more vigilant in the 1730s, launching a number of court cases for nonpayment of dues in the following decade (*La Prairie*, 100).

62. The following section dealing with the disposition of the Jesuit estates is summarized from Roy J. Dalton, *The Jesuits' Estates Question 1760–1888: A Study of the Background for the*

Agitation of 1889. Toronto: University of Toronto Press, 1968, chaps. 1–6.

63. NA, Executive Council and Land Committee, RG 1, L 7, Jesuit Estates, vol. 38, 11, Extrait de l'aveu & dénombrement des Fiefs & Seigneuries des Jésuites, 12 décembre 1781.

64. BJ, vol. 96, Rapport de l'Etat actuel des Moulins situés en les Seigneuries qui appartenoient ci devant au Jesuites, dans le District des Trois-Rivières . . . (no date; probably July 1800).

65. 'marchoient encore et étoient en assez bon ordre Lors de lextinction des Jesuites' (ibid., vol. 103, Moulin de la Seigneurie, 1824–28, L. Guillet à John Stewart, 2 juin 1826).

66. Ibid., vol. 99, Liste des Concéssions qui ont été faites dans les Seigneuries qui appartenoient ci devant à l'ordre des Jésuites dans le District des Trois Rivieres, en la Province du Bas Canada, depuis la conquête de ce pays, fait par l'agent des ditte Seigneuries dans le dit District en conséquence des ordres des Commissaires pour l'adminstration des dits Biens, Suivant une Lettre du secretaire en date du 18 janvier 1802.

67. NA, Earl Amherst Papers, MG 12, WO 34, packet 47 [mf. C-1215], Compte que rendent les Jesuites du Canada à Mr Guy Carleton, le 7 avril 1768; Executive Council and Land Committee, RG 1, L 7, Jesuit Estates, vol. 35, General Recapitulation . . . ; ibid., vol. 38, Extrait de l'aveu & dénombrement des

Fiefs & Seigneuries des Jésuites, 12 décembre 1781; Haldimand Papers, MG 21 [mf. A-779].

68. UT-Hale, John Hale to Lord Amherst, 6 May 1802.

69. 'étant des restant entre des terres concédées, qu'il est obligé de faire mesurer, à payer un sol par arpent en Superficie' (BJ, vol. 99, Liste des concessions . . . 18 janvier 1802). The government finally was able to ascertain the extent of the three 'grands compeaux' in 1828: 169 arpents behind the falls, 480 arpents behind the ironworks, and 420 arpents near the Rivière à Veillet (ibid., L. Guillet à J. Stewart, 24 septembre 1828).

70. Ibid., vol. 75, Lettres, 1787–1800, Jonathan Sewell to H. Ryland, 27 February 1800.

71. Ibid., vol. 99, Trépagny à Larue, 22 décembre 1799; vol. 257, Larue, 18 juin 1800.

72. UT-Hale, John Hale to Lord Amherst, 5 December 1800.

73. David Milobar, 'The Origins of British-Quebec Merchant Ideology: New France, the British Atlantic and the Constitutional Periphery, 1720–70.' *Journal of Imperial and Commonweath History* 24, 3 (1996): 370.

74. Françoise Noël, *The Christie Seigneuries: Estate Management and Settlement in the Upper Richelieu Valley, 1760–1854.* Montreal and Kingston: McGill-Queen's University press, 1992, 136.

4   From Allan Greer, 'The Feudal Burden', in *Peasant, Lord & Merchant: Rural Society in Three Quebec Parishes 1740–1840* (Toronto: University of Toronto Press, 1985), 122–39.

Were seigneurial and ecclesiastical exactions nothing more than a minor nuisance to the early Canadian peasantry? How exactly was wealth transferred from the agricultural producers to the dominant classes? Was the basis of appropriation fixed or was it at all changeable or arbitrary? Finally, how significant an impact did these feudal dues have on the habitant family economy? In attempting to answer these questions, I shall concentrate on the more problematic seigneurial economy.

SEIGNEURIAL DUES

The most important mechanism of transfer in most Canadian seigneuries was the 'cens et rentes', an annual payment in money, produce, or labour, exacted on all lands in the 'mouvance' at a rate proportional to the size of each lot. The cens alone was a small payment, considered a token of the 'commoners' form of tenure, which carried with it subjection to a number of dues, such as the 'lods et ventes', outlined in the Custom of Paris. Rente was a lucrative charge added to and deliberately confused with the cens in order to subject the inhabitant to the penalties prescribed by law for late payment of the latter.[1] The term 'rent' will be used here in the feudal sense, as it was in the past, to refer to the total of these two charges.

The annual rent on each lot was established at the time of concession and it could not legally be altered, although variations in the value of money and grain had the effect of changing the effective burden of this charge. The edict of 1711 moreover, in ordering seigneurs to make new concessions at the prevailing rates of cens et rentes, implied that a standard rate should apply in each seigneurie, if not throughout the colony, on lands granted at any time after that date. A legalistic bias has led some historians to assume that rents on new concessions therefore remained stable during the French régime and only rose after the Conquest when a French government was replaced by a British one less sympathetic to the habitants. In fact, a clear pattern of ever-increasing rent scales on newly settled sections of the mouvance is evident in seventeenth-century Montreal.[2] Similarly, in St. Ours, new rents rose steadily throughout the French régime, but remained stable after the 1750s, just the opposite of the pattern suggested by the traditional view. Apparently, the development of the region's agricultural productivity led seigneurs to insist on a proper share of the expanding peasant surplus.

But how did the seigneurs of St. Ours manage to defy official policy in this way? An examination of St. Ours concession deeds suggests that the rise was the outcome of a subtle policy of altering the combination of cash, produce, and livestock in the annual rents, substituting pseudo-equivalents so as to change the value of payments while appearing to alter only their form. Cash was substituted for capons, and then wheat was put in the place of the money; also area measurements were substituted for linear frontage. The switch to

payments largely in wheat in the years after 1720 was partly a reflection of the emergence of an agricultural economy in the Lower Richelieu, but it was also a clever hedge against erosion of fixed money rents. The seigneurs' imposition of altered rates made a mockery of legislation intended to protect the peasantry; the eighteenth-century rise in grain prices, joined to biased alterations in the form of payment were such that, at early nineteenth-century wheat prices, a 90-arpent farm conceded in the seventeenth century would owe about 6 livres per year, while one conceded after 1754 (this included the majority of St. Ours farms) would owe 27 livres.[3] The trouble that the French régime seigneurs of St. Ours took to adjust their rent scales suggests that they did not regard these revenues as 'token payments'.

Less is known about the evolution of cens et rentes in Sorel and St. Denis. Towards the end of the French régime, the charge seems to have been a roughly equivalent combination of money and wheat to that exacted in St. Ours, although every lot in Sorel owed an additional levy of one day's corvée labour.[4] (Note that corvée was simply a form of payment, labour rather than money or produce, and not a separate variety of seigneurial exaction, as many have suggested. The corvée in mid-eighteenth-century Sorel seems to have been an element of the cens et rentes, whereas Pierre de St. Ours exacted a day's work from the habitants for use of a common pasture.) However, the seigneurs of Sorel and St. Denis, both of them absentees probably anxious to simplify accounts and collection procedures, converted all charges in labour and kind to a single annual cash exaction. This change occurred around 1770 in Sorel and probably much earlier in St. Denis, with the effect that rents there were greatly devalued by the long-term inflation of the eighteenth century. In the early nineteenth century, a 90-arpent farm was charged about 13.5 livres in St. Denis, 18 livres in Sorel, and between 16 and 32 livres in St. Ours, depending on the price of wheat.[5] The seigneur of St. Ours tended to benefit in the long run by their adherence to rents in kind. The relative advantage of seigneur and habitant in each seigneurie changed, in opposite directions, with fluctuating grain prices. Moreover, the positions of the two parties reverse as one moves from St. Ours to Sorel or St. Denis; that is, a rise in wheat prices favoured St. Ours seigneurs and Sorel habitants, while a price decline tended to favour Sorel seigneurs and St. Ours habitants.

In addition to the cens et rentes, Canadian seigneurs benefited from a variety of lucrative charges, including the lods et ventes, a mutation fine amounting to one-twelfth of the purchase price owed by the buyer of land in the mouvance. In France, and in some Canadian seigneuries, purchasers who paid promptly were charged a third or a quarter less than the legal rate, but this discount was not universal and St. Ours seigneurs invariably demanded the full amount.[6] [. . .] To realize its full value, the right of lods et ventes required that a seigneur be aware of the details of land transactions in his fief and it was therefore closely tied, in its practical application, to the various official and unofficial aspects of his control over people and lands. In addition to his role as the main repository of land title records, the seigneur disposed of the retrait seigneurial to guarantee the proper reporting of prices. Of course the co-operation of the local notary, who officiated at transactions and kept their records, was invaluable, but what notary could risk offending the seigneur, normally his most important client?

Several minor exactions were added to the basic feudal rent and mutation fines. One of these was the annual fee for admission to the common pasture; such 'droit de commune' was demanded of all Sorel habitants until the late eighteenth century and of the residents of the St. Lawrence section of St. Ours until the end of seigneurial tenure. The situation here was not what it was in Old Régime France, where commons were generally controlled by peasant communities whose possession was only partially usurped by aggressive seigneurial offensives.[7] [. . .]

Although they profited through the above-mentioned exactions from habitant grain-growing, livestock raising, and property sales, the seigneurs of the Lower Richelieu were not prepared to let even minor ancillary productions go untaxed. In Sorel, there was a levy on maple sugar-making as well as a fishing fee. In the eighteenth century, choice locations on islands in the St. Lawrence were farmed out to habitants for 78 livres annually, as much as the rents of a dozen farms. A document dated 1809 mentions an exaction of two fish from each netful of shad caught.[8] There was no basis in law for this 'droit de pêche', but this seems to have escaped the seigneurs' notice.

Seigneurs benefited, not only from these direct exactions, but also from various monopolies, above all the 'banalité' (grist mill monopoly), which will be discussed later. These privileges are quite different from the dues mentioned so far in that they were not lucrative in themselves, even though they could be used to enrich the seigneur at the habitants' expense. The banal mill was a protected enterprise with a captive market, but it did provide a service; the milling toll was therefore unlike the almost entirely parasitic cens et rentes as it went partly to defray expenses. Only a portion of this fee was profit for the seigneur and only part of that could be attributed to the effects of protection from competition.[9] Collecting the milling toll was a simple matter of withholding one-fourteenth of the grain processed, whereas seigneurs experienced considerable difficulty in securing payment of annual dues and mutation fines.

PAYMENT

Seigneurial dues were notoriously difficult to collect (frontier or no frontier, Canada was exactly like France in this respect).[10] Most habitants were a few years in arrears on occasion and many fell behind more seriously and were never able to get out of debt. Behind this backlog was probably a combination of

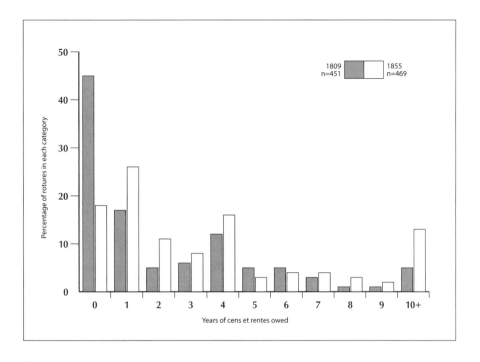

Figure 1   Arrears of Signeurial Rent, Sorel, 1809 and 1855

inability to pay, unwillingness to pay, and a calculated postponement based on the knowledge that it was not worthwhile for the seigneur to take action to recover small debts. Some habitants lived so close to the edge of subsistence that chronic debt to the seigneur must have been almost unavoidable; whereas others, normally able to pay regularly, must have experienced temporary distress that put them slightly in arrears now and then. Most likely, there was also a certain amount of passive resistance to seigneurial exploitation expressed in the failure to pay promptly. Figure 1 shows that only 15 per cent of Sorel's lands had rent arrears of more than four years in 1809. By 1855, however, this figure had risen to 25 per cent, reflecting the general distress of the seigneurie's habitants in the period when fur-trade employment had disappeared.[11] Accumulated arrears seem to have been disproportionately great in recently conceded lands, probably because many of them were not fully cleared and productive for several years. In Sorel, and presumably in other seigneuries, payments of current and overdue rents fluctuated from year to year with the harvests, the general economic situation, and the varying pressure exerted by the seigneur (see Table 1).[12]

Arrears of lods et ventes were more common and of much longer duration than arrears of rents. The former charge usually amounted to a relatively substantial sum due all at once, and many habitants found themselves unable to pay it for years, or even generations, even if they could make the more moderate rent payments year by year. 'Quitte excepté les lods' is a recurrent phrase in the St. Ours estate rolls. From the seigneur's point of view then, the actual revenue in any one year was never even close to the total value of the dues to which he was legally entitled. By about 1840 the

TABLE 1 Seigneurial Rents and Arrears Paid, Sorel 1798–1805			
Year	Annual Rent Due	Rent and Arrears Received	Percentage
1798	2,643	1,817	69
1799	2,787	1,988	71
1800	2,874	2,268	79
1801	2,930	1,523	52
1802	2,942	2,572	87
1803	3,407	3,564	105
1804	3,407	2,213	65
1805	3,407	2,493	73

abandonment—that weeded out undesirables with much less inconvenience. For less serious cases, they were inclined to show a certain amount of patience in the hopes of eventually recovering overdue rents. Paternalistic attitudes may have had something to do with it, but there were also more practical motives for forbearance. Since habitant agriculture was often quite unproductive and short harvests were common, rigid insistence on immediate payment would clearly be unreasonable and self-defeating in many cases. As long as a habitant made a visible effort to make good back dues and as long as his farm was valuable enough to bear the debt, he could usually feel safe. In the end, a seigneur could take advantage of his position as legally privileged creditor to claim arrears from the estate when his debtor died. Prompter payment was certainly preferable, however, and seigneurs used a variety of strategies, threatening, cajoling, setting deadlines, and accepting payments in unusual forms, in order to wring as much as possible out of peasants who had the slimmest of surpluses and who were disinclined to part with them. Always it was the threat, implied or stated, of being deprived of their homes and livelihood that encouraged such marginal cases to turn over what they could.

[. . .]

Documents from St. Ours suggest that seigneurial dues were acquitted in a great variety of forms. There were always a large number of habitants who apparently paid punctually and in the money and wheat specified in their title deeds but, for poorer censitaires, these commodities were only accounting abstractions. Products offered for rents and lods et ventes between the 1790s and the 1840s include oats, barley, peas, lumber, firewood, maple sugar, hay, cattle, and homespun cloth. Labour was also a common means of payment, even though officially there was no corvée in St. Ours after about 1720. The estate rolls show that censitaires received a certain amount of credit for each day spent working on roads and fences or on the construction of a mill. When a gristmill

censitaires of Sorel and St. Ours owed their seigneurs at least 92,000 and 71,158 livres respectively. Of course many of these arrears would never be paid at all. The notaries who drew up the inventory of 1841 following the death of François Roch de St. Ours judged that one-third of the arrears of the seigneurie should simply be written off since they were owed on uncleared lots of very little value.[13]

Extracting payments of arrears from indebted habitants was a delicate task requiring, on the part of the seigneur or his agent, a thorough acquaintance with the individuals and the productive capacities of their lands. If the seigneur was convinced that the debtor would never pay, he would generally take steps to have him removed so that the land could be turned over to a more promising candidate. This sometimes required an expensive and time-consuming lawsuit to obtain a judicial seizure.[14] Seigneurs naturally preferred the various procedures mentioned above—repossession for failure to develop and 'voluntary' on the Yamaska River was planned in 1814, the contract with the seigneur required the builder to employ, as far as possible, St. Ours habitants who would be paid half their wages in cash and the other half in coupons to be applied to their accounts with the seigneur.[15] Once again it seems clear that the form in which feudal dues were officially set down was of no essential importance; what was appropriated was the surplus labour of the peasant, either in its raw form, or as agricultural produce or as produce converted into cash.

SEIGNEURIAL MONOPOLIES

As an outgrowth of seigneurial judicial powers, Canadian landlords enjoyed certain privileges and monopolies over the territories of their estates and the people who lived there; long after they had ceased to act as local judges, the seigneurs of Sorel, St. Ours, and St. Denis continued to insist on the lucrative perquisites of the position. The most important of these was the gristmill monopoly and it was more widespread and more stringent in Canada than it was in most parts of Old Régime France.[16] Here, it was often an important source of seigneurial revenues, and a real inconvenience to habitants. The Custom of Paris only allowed seigneurs to require their vassals to grind the wheat they needed for domestic consumption at the seigneurial watermill and only in cases where the right was sanctioned by written titles or ancient custom. A royal edict of 1686 enlarged the Canadian seigneur's rights in this regard by declaring banal every mill, whether water- or wind-driven, and without any need for stipulation in title deeds.[17]

Nevertheless, every St. Ours deed mentioned the mill monopoly, in order to spell out the habitant's obligations and to specify penalties for infractions. The trend over the course of the eighteenth century was towards more extensive obligations and more stringent penalties. In the seventeenth century, only grain used for home consumption had to be ground

at the seigneur's mill and the fine for processing flour elsewhere was the equivalent of the milling toll on the amount of grain. By the 1790s, the formula in concession deeds subjected all grain grown to the banalité, whether it was consumed at home or sent abroad, and piled penalty on top of penalty: not only would a fine equal to the milling toll be exacted, the illicit flour could also be seized and additional arbitrary fines imposed. This evolution in title deed clauses seems to reflect a wider trend towards a more careful and exacting style of estate management. Note, however, that, right from the beginning, the seigneurs of St. Ours assumed the right to subject all varieties of grain to their monopoly even though the law of the land limited the banalité to wheat alone, and only to the amount needed for domestic consumption.[18]

There is a long-established myth in Canadian historiography to the effect that the law of 1686 giving all seigneurial mills monopoly privileges was as much a burden for the seigneurs as it was for the habitants, since it also forced the former to build mills within a year or forever forfeit their right of banalité.[19] In fact, many seigneurs easily retained their privileges even though they only opened a mill long after that date. Pierre de Sorel had a mill built in 1670, no doubt as much to contribute to the development of his estate as in anticipation of future profits, but Pierre de St. Ours waited until twenty years after the law of 1686 before erecting a windmill, and his banal privileges were never revoked. Worse still, the absentee seigneurs of St. Denis left their peasants with no mill until after the Conquest, noting all the same in concession deeds that granted lands would be, 'sujette au moulin de ladte. seigneurie lorsqu'il y en aura un de construit.'[20] Two small seigneurial mills, one wind-driven and the other water-driven, were eventually built in the late eighteenth century, but the seigneurs of St. Denis found they did not even have to bother investing in milling facilities to profit from their banalité. [. . .]

After a period of severely fragmented ownership around the middle of the eighteenth century, the seigneurs of St. Ours showed a greater willingness than their neighbours to establish their own mills and profit directly from the monopoly. This was partly because the fief was well supplied with good hydraulic sites, but also because the seigneurs generally lived on the estate for at least part of the year and took a personal hand in managing it. In addition to Pierre de St. Ours's old windmill on the St. Lawrence, there was a water-driven mill on the Richelieu, built in 1773 and, following the development of the rear sections of the seigneurie, another watermill was established in 1815, this one on the Yamaska River. This last mill was the largest in St. Ours and it contained three pairs of stones with bolts, as well as a fulling mill; in 1842 the building and machinery were insured for 10,000 livres.[21]

The milling toll in early Quebec was set by law at one-fourteenth of the grain ground but of course expenses claimed a considerable portion of the gross revenue. Mills were always leased out to a miller, either for a set annual rent or, more commonly, for a proportion of the proceeds; in various contracts this amounted to one-half, one-third, or one-quarter of the revenues.[22] The seigneur also had to pay for major repairs and for a portion of the operating expenses. This left, according to one optimistic estimate, about two-thirds of the milling tolls, or 4.8 per cent of all the grain processed, as the seigneur's net profit.[23] In Sorel, badly served by two decrepit windmills, net profits were only 160 minots of wheat (worth 480 livres) in 1782–3, but the big gristmills of St. Ours were worth 1,500 minots of grain (value about 3,000–7,000 livres) annually to their seigneur around 1840.[24]

[. . .]

A source of revenue to the seigneur, the banalité appeared from the habitant's point of view as a double restriction, preventing him both from having his grain ground where he wished and from establishing a gristmill of his own. In practice, it was the latter restriction that was most effectively enforced and economically most important. Although they always insisted

on their right to prevent habitants from taking unground grain outside the fief, seigneurs were unable to police movements of this sort; contraventions seem to have been common.[25] On the other hand, it was impossible for interlopers to build unauthorized gristmills and escape detection. Two St. Denis residents built mills on their own land but the seigneur promptly sued them and, in an out-of-court settlement, imposed the annual tribute mentioned earlier as the price of allowing them to continue operations; a less accommodating seigneur might have had the offending mills razed, with the full backing of the law. The lack of competition did not affect the cost of services to the habitant, since this was set by law at a moderate rate. On the other hand, the quality of flour and the regularity of service may have suffered. More serious was the inconvenience of having to carry grain to seigneurial mills that were, for many users, far from home. In France, only peasants within a certain distance, usually one league, were subject to the mill monopoly but, in Canadian seigneuries, which were generally quite vast, there was no such limit and farmers had to transport their grain many leagues to the banal mill.

[. . .]

FEUDAL EXACTIONS AND THE PEASANT HOUSEHOLD ECONOMY

If we add the ecclesiastical payments to the seigneurial dues enumerated here, it becomes clear that eighteenth-century habitants were subject to a diverse array of rents, tithes, fees, and fines. And yet, according to many historians, these all added up to an aggregate 'feudal burden' that was paltry indeed.[26] The people of the Lower Richelieu, on the other hand, were more inclined to take these matters seriously. We have seen the heated disputes that often arose between priests and parishioners over pew rents and assessments for construction projects. Think also of the great pains that seigneurs took to adjust rent scales and to levy the full mutation fine on every imaginable transaction, and of the risks that many habitants ran in allowing backrents to accumulate even when they were in danger of losing their farms. These exactions mattered both to exploiters and to exploited because the wealth at stake was significant.

What exactly was the material weight of feudalism on the peasantry? This is a question that has bedeviled historians of both Canada and Europe; many have attempted estimates but results have always been controversial and generally unsatisfactory.[27] Source deficiencies—the absence of reliable figures on agricultural production and aristocratic revenues—are only part of the problem. More serious are a number of thorny conceptual issues, many of them connected to the diversity of the forms of feudal exactions. It is very difficult to construct a single index out of the various dues when some were paid in cash, some in kind, and others in labour. Furthermore, some—tithes, pew rents, and seigneurial rents, for example—were due on a regular annual basis, while others—mutation fines and ecclesiastical assessments, for instance—had to be paid only on certain occasions. A further problem has to do with the fact that many payments to priests and seigneurs were at least partially compensation for a genuine service. Mill tolls fall into this category since only part of the fee can be attributed to the seigneur's privileged position. Finally, there is the question of whether the demands of the state—taxes, military service, road work—should be counted as part of the feudal burden. All this makes it next to impossible to measure the feudal economy with any precision or to make meaningful comparisons between different periods or between different countries.

Beyond these methodological dilemmas loom some options more theoretical than technical. Researchers wishing to determine the economic importance of feudalism must consider the questions, important for whom? and according to what criteria? The tendency is often to ignore the distinctions between capitalist and precapitalist economies and treat seigneurs and habitants as though they were landowners and agricultural entrepreneurs. From this point of view it makes sense to divide seigneurial revenues by the area of the censive to find a rate of seigneurial exactions amounting to so many livres per arpent. A similar procedure consists of estimating peasant agricultural income and dividing by the total of seigneurial and ecclesiastical revenues; this gives a percentage figure representing the proportion of habitant harvests absorbed by the feudal classes. This would be fine if the agriculturalists in question were genuine farmers engaged in a profit-making enterprise, selling all or most of what they grew and paying ground-rent as one of the expenses of doing business. Eighteenth-century habitants were of course nothing of the sort; they were peasants and their economy centred on production for domestic consumption. Thus there was a fairly inflexible minimum supply of many crops that habitant families needed to survive and to reproduce themselves. Ignoring this basic characteristic of precapitalist agrarian society allows one to conclude that 'seigneurial dues . . . were very low, representing 10 percent of the produce of their concessions',[28] but it does not tell us much about the realities of the feudal economy since the 'produce' of peasant lands remains an abstract quantity. In fact, the figure of 10 per cent does not seem so low, especially when we realize that it does not include the tithe or other ecclesiastical dues, but that is not the point. The problem with this approach is that we do not know what the loss of 10 per cent of its harvest would mean for an habitant family, whether, for example, this would simply leave it with a little less wheat to sell or whether it would threaten its very survival by cutting into the stock needed for seed and for subsistence.

A better way of evaluating feudal exactions is therefore to consider them in relation to habitant *surpluses*. This requires estimating, not only how much peasants grew annually, but also how much they needed to retain in order to last the year. Because of the methodological and source difficulties mentioned above, I am not in a position to set up a complete 'model' of the habitant economy in the eighteenth century but I do have enough information to make a rough estimate of production, surplus, and exactions for wheat alone. Thus, only one aspect of Lower Richelieu agriculture is covered, although wheat was surely the most important element. Data [from the 1765 census on grain sown] can now be used to estimate the wheat production of all the habitants of St. Ours. Census figures on the population of adults and children, along with information from deeds of gift on flour consumption, allow us then to calculate roughly the amount of wheat needed for home consumption. Taking the difference between production and consumption gives

the estimated wheat surplus of each habitant family in the parish. It is then a simple matter to evaluate the impact on this surplus of the tithe and the wheat portion of seigneurial rents (see Table 2).[29]

According to this model then, almost half (44 per cent) of the wheat grown by the habitants of St. Ours in 1765, beyond what was needed to maintain the growers, would have been owed to the local seigneur and curé just to pay those feudal exactions that were set down in terms of wheat. This of course does not give us a complete picture of the relationship between peasant surpluses and aristocratic exploitation. Habitants raised many products other than wheat, but most of these were exclusively for domestic use and therefore not part of a saleable surplus. On the other hand,

Table 2 Habitant Surpluses and Feudal Exactions, Wheat Only, St. Ours 1765

'habitant' households		99
Production		
(a) grain sown	2098 minots	
(b) wheat sown (2/3a)	1399 minots	
(c) yield per seed	5.8	
(d) wheat harvested (b x c)	8112 minots	8112 minots
Deductions		
(e) wheat seed for next year	−1399 minots	
(f) mill toll (1/14)	−358 minots	
(g) total	−1757 minots	−1757 minots
Domestic consumption		
(h) adult population	238	
(i) boys under 15	158	
(j) 'girls'	134	
(k) adult rations (h+i/2+3j/4)	417.5	
(l) consumption (12k)	5010 minots	−5010 minots
(m) surplus (d − g − l)		1345 minots
Exactions		
(n) wheat portion seign. rent	276 minots	
(o) wheat tithe (d/26)	312 minots	
(p) total	588 minots	588 minots

Feudal exactions = 588/1345 = 44% of habitant wheat surplus

many important feudal dues—mutation fines, pew rents, church assessments, and the cash portion of seigneurial rents, to name a few—do not enter into our calculations. If anything therefore, this partial estimate underestimates the feudal burden.

It should be noted that this is a 'model' and not a detailed description of reality. In fact, harvests varied greatly from year to year, and so therefore did the relative weight of fixed dues; the seed-yield figure of 1: 5.8 is simply one historian's estimate of the 'normal' return. Also, some families no doubt ate more wheat than others and thus the 12-minot ration would not have been strictly uniform. [. . .] But, for the moment it is important to recognize that, imprecise and partial though this aggregate model may be, it does indicate that feudal dues deprived the Lower Richelieu peasantry of a substantial portion—probably more than half—of its agricultural surpluses.

Beyond this 'average' experience, individual returns from the 1765 census make it clear that the production, surplus, and feudal burden varied greatly from one St. Ours household to the next. For half the cases it is impossible to compute the percentage of wheat surpluses drained by tithe and seigneurial rent, since 48 of the families had no surplus at all once the exactions were subtracted. Of these households, 11 grew less than five minots of wheat per 'adult equivalent'; evidently marginal grain-growers, these families may have been artisans or day-labourers. The other 37 who apparently lacked a wheat surplus must have had to scramble to get by, perhaps making do with less bread than their neighbours or earning a little money as hired hands at harvest time. These are no doubt the habitants who let their rents go unpaid for long stretches and who paid the seigneur, when they could, in lumber, cloth, and labour. Feudal dues must have been a serious problem for these families, but also for those, slightly better off, who grew enough in good years to retain a small surplus after they had paid the landlord and the curé. Table 3 shows that the wealthier half of the St.

Table 3 Proportion of Wheat Surplus Devoted to Tithe and Seigneurial Rent (Wheat Only) by Habitant Household, St. Ours 1765		
	Households	Per cent
No surplus left after exactions	48	48
Exactions require 0–10% of surplus	2	2
Exactions require 10–20% of surplus	21	21
Exactions require 20–30% of surplus	11	11
Exactions require 30–50% of surplus	11	11
Exactions require 50–100% of surplus	4	4
Exactions require 100% + of surplus	2	2
TOTAL	99	99

Ours peasantry generally owed a substantial portion of their excess wheat to the aristocrats. Only 2 paid less than 10 per cent, whereas 28 paid more than 30 per cent of their surplus, some losing their entire surplus to feudal dues. For a handful of the richest peasants, on the other hand, tithes and rents were a much less significant drain. The three largest producers had a net wheat surplus after deductions, exactions and consumption of 110, 122, and 122 minots respectively. After them came ten others with 50 to 100 minots surplus. Feudal dues did not exceed 20 per cent of the excess of any of these 13 prosperous families. They normally had substantial quantities of grain to sell and were the section of the community that grain dealers were most interested in.

This 'model' of wheat surpluses by household demonstrates, not only the differing impact of feudal exactions, but also the variety of economic positions within the Lower Richelieu peasantry. As to the economic impact of feudal dues, it seems fair to conclude that they were an obstacle to the accumulation of capital in peasant hands. Certainly tithes, rents and assessments did not absolutely prevent a habitant from amassing wealth, but generally they were a significant drain and particularly so for modest habitants like the Allaires who had a good deal of trouble in keeping above the subsistence line.

If extra-economic exactions and a prevalence of subsistence agriculture are the two primary characteristics of the feudal economy, here then is one connection between them. The first feature tended to reinforce the second by depriving peasants of part of the fruits of their labour. Seigneurial and ecclesiastical dues helped prevent the formation of an agrarian bourgeoisie by working against the accumulation of capital in habitant hands. Instead, a large portion of the agricultural surplus was delivered to priests and landlords who showed little inclination to invest their revenues in the land. Farms therefore remained relatively small and unproductive. Obviously feudal exploitation was not the only factor responsible for this state of affairs. The limited market for agricultural produce in the early years of the Lower Richelieu settlement also discouraged investment and egalitarian inheritance customs counteracted any long-term concentration of property. Moreover, the limitations on peasant ownership inherent in seigneurial tenure could be an obstacle to enterprise in some cases. Thus, although it would be an exaggeration to say that tithes, rents, and so on by themselves prevented the development of agriculture, it is nevertheless clear that they were a real burden for the habitant household, one that added its influence to other factors in making large-scale market-oriented production unlikely.

In other words, many of the basic characteristics of Lower Richelieu social and economic life were mutually reinforcing. The habitant majority lived and worked in family units, with household production organized mainly around the direct satisfaction of household consumption needs. This self-sufficient peasantry found a significant portion of its surplus drained off to support local priests and seigneurs, the latter constituting a local aristocracy whose political ascendancy guaranteed its economic privileges. This combination of peasant self-sufficiency, together with aristocratic appropriation through extra-economic compulsion, is the basically 'feudal' configuration that is essential to an understanding of this rural society.

NOTES

1. Louise Dechêne, 'L'évolution du régime seigneurial au Canada: le cas de Montréal aux XVIIe et XVIIIe siècles', *Recherches sociographiques* 12 (May–August 1971) 152

2. Ibid.; cf. William Bennett Munro, *Documents Relating to the Seigniorial Tenure in Canada, 1598–1854* (Toronto: Champlain Society 1908) 74.

3. The assumption here is that wheat is valued at 10 livres per minot and that the hypothetical farm measures 3 arpents frontage by 30 arpents depth. The earliest concessions were fixed at one sol per arpent of area plus one capon (value 10 sols in 1709) for each arpent of frontage. The rate applied from 1754 on was one sol per arpent plus one-half minot of wheat for each 20 arpents (PAC, St. Ours seigneurie, vol. 1, concession deeds). The evolution of rents in the seigneurie of Longueuil was almost exactly parallel, except that the rise in rates occurred rather earlier. Louis Lemoine, 'Une société seigneuriale: Longueuil: méthode, sources, orientations' (Master's thesis, Université de Montreal 1975) 145.

4. PAC, de Ramezay papers, pp 1532–42, estate roll, Sorel, n.d. (1761–3)

5. ANQM, St. Denis seigneurie, 22RS7, list of arrears, 1840; PAC, Sorel seigneurie, vol. 11, estate roll, 1795

6. PAC, Sorel seigneurie, vol. 12, accounts of the seigneurie of Sorel, 1840–7. Cf. William Bennet Munro, *The Seigniorial System in Canada: A Study in French Colonial Policy* (Cambridge: Harvard University Press 1907) 96; Dechêne, 'L'évolution du régime seigneurial' 157–8.

7. Marc Bloch, *French Rural History: An Essay on Its Basic Characteristics*, trans. J. Sondheimer (Berkeley: University of California Press 1966) 180–9; Régine Robin, *La Société française en 1789: Sémur-en-Auxois* (Paris: Plon 1970) 153–4; Pierre de Saint-Jacob, *Les paysans de la Bourgogne du Nord au dernier siècle de l'ancien régime* (Paris: Université de Dijon 1960) 75–92, 377–80

8. PAC, Haldimand papers, Add. Mss 21885, pt. 2, fols. 217–18; PAC, RG8, C, 278: 196–7, petition of Jean-Baptiste Veilleux, 22 July 1809

9. Louise Dechêne makes this point in 'L'évolution du régime seigneurial' 164. Other historians, on the other hand, include mill tolls, sometimes with operational expenses deducted, in lists of seigneurial revenues. This gives a misleading impression of the weight of seigneurial exactions. Habitants would have had to pay a charge to have their grain ground into flour even if there had been no seigneurial régime and it is difficult to say how much, if any, they would have saved had they not been subject to the banalité. Cf. Marcel Trudel, *The Seigneurial Régime* Canadian Historical Association booklet 6 (Ottawa: CHA 1956), 13; R.C. Harris, *The Seigneurial System in Early Canada: A Geographical Study* (Madison: University of Wisconsin Press 1966) 78.

10. Cf. Jean Bastier, *La féodalité au siècle des lumières dans la région de Toulouse (1730–1790)* (Paris: Bibliothèque nationale 1975) 274–9

11. PAC, Sorel seigneurie, vol. 13, 'Rent Roll of His Majesty's Seigniory of Sorel for the year 1809', 24 March 1810; ibid., 'Sorel Seigniory, abstract of arrears', 31 March 1858

12. PAC, RG8, C, 279: 131, 'Report on the Accounts of Mr Robert Jones Agent of His Majestys Seigniory of Sorel' (amounts shown are in livres)

13. ANQ, A.P.G.–288 PAC, MG11, Q, 240–1: 190–5

14. The disadvantages of this procedure did not stop the seigneur of St Ours from successfully suing ten habitants between 1839 and 1842. *Pièces et Documents relatifs à la tenure seigneurial, demandés par une adresse de l'Assembée legislative, 1851* (Quebec: E.R. Fréchette 1852) 150

15. Ibid., agreement between Charles de St. Ours and Bazile Bourg, 2 November 1815

16. Dechêne, 'L'évolution du régime seigneurial' 164

17. François-Joseph Cugnet, *Traité de la Loi des Fiefs* (Quebec: Guillaume Brown 1775) 36–7

18. Munro, *The Seigniorial System* 117–19

19. Trudel, *The Seigneurial Régime* 15; Harris, *The Seigneurial System* 72

20. ANQM, gr. Deguire, concession par M. de Contrecoeur à Jacques Coder, 8 December 1758

21. Couillard-Desprès, *Histoire de St-Ours* 1: 292–3; PAC, St. Ours seigneurie, vol. 5, agreement between Charles de St Ours and Bazile Bourg dit Canic, 2 November 1815; ibid., vol. 10, Aetna Insurance Company, policy no. 3580, Mme R. de St. Ours, 11 November 1842

22. ANQM, gr. Jehanne, lease by Monsieur de la Bruyère Montarville to Gabriel Chabot, 1 October 1779; ANQM, gr. Michaud, lease by Mr de la Bruère Montarville to Sr Joseph Bourque dit Canique, 21 October 1799; PAC, St Ours seigneurie, vol. 5, agreement between Charles de St. Ours and Bazile Bourg dit Canic, 2 November 1815

23. PAC, Haldimand Papers, Add. Mss 21885, pt. 2, fol. 217–18, 'Etat actuel des rentes et autres revenues de la seigneurie de Sorel, suivant les deux dernières Recettes en 1782 et 1783'

24. Ibid.; ANQ, St. Ours collection, estate inventory of François Roch de St. Ours, 19 June 1841. The seigneur's cash revenues cannot be

estimated with any precision since a variety of grains with different values were ground.

25. *Edits, ordonnances, déclarations et arrêts relatifs à la tenure seigneuriale, demandés par une adresse de l'Assemblée Législative, 1851* (Quebec: E.R. Fréchette, 1852) 139–40; PAC, documents légaux des seigneuries, vol. 971, testimony of Joseph Mignault, 16 June 1860

26. See Fernand Ouellet's critical discussion of this position in two articles: 'Libéré ou exploité! Le paysan québécois d'avant 1850', HS-SH 13 (November 1980) 339–68; 'La formation d'une société dans la vallée du Saint-Laurent: d'une société sans classes à une société de classes', CHR 62 (December 1981) 407–50.

27. Harris, *Seigneurial System* 78; Lise Pilon-Lê, 'L'endettement des cultivateurs québécois: une analyse socio-historique de la rente foncière (1670–1904)' (Ph.D. thesis, Université de Montréal 1978) 168–9; Guy Lemarchand, 'Féodalisme et société rurale dans la France moderne', in *Sur le féodalisme* 86–105 (see also Jacques Dupâquier's comments in ibid. 107); Albert Soboul, 'Sur le prélèvement féodal', in *Problèmes paysans de la révolution (1789–1848):*

études d'histoire révolutionnaire (Paris: François Maspero 1976) 89–115; Bastier, *La féodalité au siècle des lumières* 258–9

28. W.J. Eccles, *France in America* (Vancouver: Fitzhenry and Whiteside 1973) 79

29. Only 99 of the 107 local households are included in this 'model', the remaining 8 being eliminated either because data were evidently missing from their entries or because they had no land and were therefore apparently priests, artisans or labourers. The assumptions underlying this estimate are that two-thirds of the census-recorded grain sown was wheat, that the seed-yield ratio of wheat was 1: 5.8, that the 11,037 arpents held by these 99 families were subject to the prevailing rate of seigneurial rent which included a levy of 'one half minot of wheat for every 20 arpents', that adults required 12 minots of wheat a year (the lowest individual ration commonly found in eighteenth-century pensions alimentaires), while children needed only half that amount and 'girls' (unmarried females not differentiated by age in the census) ate, on the average, three-quarters of an adult ration.

Chapter Four

Expulsion of the Acadians

READINGS

Primary Documents

1   From 1755 Council Minutes, in *Acadia and Nova Scotia: Documents Relating to the Acadian French and the First British Colonization of the Province, 1714–1758*, Thomas B. Akins

2   From 'Extracts from Col. John Winslow's Journal' in *Report Concerning Canadian Archives for the Year 1905*

Historical Interpretations

3   From 'Ile Royale, New England, Scotland, and Nova Scotia, 1744–1748', in *An Unsettled Conquest: The British Campaign Against the Peoples of Acadia*, Geoffrey Plank

4   From 'The Decision to Deport', in *From Migrant to Acadian: A North American Border People, 1604–1755*, N.E.S. Griffiths

Introduction

In today's society, we venerate the ideals of harmony and trust, yet, collectively at least, we frequently fail to embody them. Eighteenth-century colonial North America was one place where similar failures occurred. The early eighteenth century brought significant change to the continent as French-speaking residents of Acadia (today's Nova Scotia and New Brunswick) found themselves under British control, thanks to a peace treaty in which the French 'traded away' this territory. The 1713 Treaty of Utrecht gave the British a region that, a century earlier, had been one site of French colonial hopes. The new owners expected loyalty, but had demonstrated little patience with their Roman Catholic subjects elsewhere and knew little about the local First Nations. As in most conflicts, each side had some merit to its case. Acadians who largely wished to go about their lives unaffected by questions of colonial jurisdiction were urged to swear allegiance to the British monarch. Those who had to govern the region faced a population of Acadians that seemed to be stubbornly refusing to acknowledge British power and hoping for a return to the French fold.

For over 40 years, this was the pattern, an uneasy co-existence. In 1755, it came as a rather rude shock to the Acadians when longstanding suspicions about their disloyalty would be followed up by British action. When the Acadians failed to convince British administrators that they had not been covertly aiding the French, they were handed an expulsion notice. Harmony and trust were impossible in Acadia with the larger conflict between colonial powers affecting the way that governors and governed related to one another.

The Deportation was a process that lasted from 1755 to 1762. The Acadians of Minas Bassin and Beaubassin were the first to be evicted, followed by the ones from Louisbourg and Ile St.-Jean. In total, nearly 12,000 Acadians were deported to the Thirteen Colonies, Britain, and France. The primary sources describe that moment to show us the resolve of Governor Lawrence along with Acadian disbelief and desperation. As for the secondary sources, Geoffrey Plank discusses how the British authorities were reassessing their attitudes toward cultural and religious diversity in Nova Scotia after the Scottish uprising of 1746 and the War of the Austrian Succession. Naomi Griffiths argues, however, that the Deportation was not the result of a long planned program, but of the decision of the local Lieutenant-Governor Charles Lawrence. When the Acadians left, they went or were sent to a variety of places, none of which had agreed to accommodate them.

QUESTIONS FOR CONSIDERATION

1. Do you think that the British gave the Acadians enough warning before carrying out the expulsion?
2. What sort of behaviour did the British seem to expect from the Acadians?
3. What do the Acadians appear not to understand about their situation, and how are British suspicions confirmed later in the summer of 1755?
4. According to Earl Lockerby, what were some of the similarities and differences between the expulsion of 1755 and the expulsion of 1758 from Ile St.-Jean (now known as Prince Edward Island)?
5. How might the question of where the expelled Acadian refugees were to go be resolved today?

SUGGESTIONS FOR FURTHER READING

Daigle, Jean, ed., *The Acadians of the Maritimes: Thematic Studies* (Moncton: Centre d'études acadiennes, 1982)

Faragher, John Mack, *A Great and Noble Scheme: The Tragic Story of the Expulsion of the French Acadians from their American Homeland* (New York: W.W. Norton & Co., 2005)

Griffiths, N.E.S., *From Migrant to Acadian: A North American Border People 1604–1755* (Montreal and Kingston: McGill-Queen's University Press, 2005)

Johnston, A.J.B., *Endgame 1758: The Promise, the Glory and the Despair of Louisbourg's Last Decade* (Sydney: Cape Breton University Press, 2007)

Lockerby, Earl, 'The Deportation of the Acadians from Ile St. Jean, 1758', *Acadiensis*, XXVII (Spring 1998): 45–94

Parmentier, Jon, and Mark Power Robinson, 'The Perils and Possibilities of Wartime Neutrality on the Edges of Empire: Iroquois and Acadians between the French and British in North America, 1744–1760', *Diplomatic History* 31(2) (April 2007): 167–206

Plank, Geoffrey, *An Unsettled Conquest: The British Campaign Against the Peoples of Acadia* (Philadelphia: University of Pennsylvania Press, 2001)

PRIMARY DOCUMENTS

1 From 1755 Council Minutes, in Thomas B. Akins, ed., *Acadia and Nova Scotia: Documents Relating to the Acadian French and the First British Colonization of the Province 1714–1758* (Halifax, 1870), 247–57.

At a Council holden at the Governor's House in Halifax on Thursday the 3rd July 1755.
PRESENT—
The Lieutenant Governor.
Councs.: Benj. Green, Jno. Collier, Willm. Cotterell, Jonn. Belcher.

The Lieutenant Governor laid before the Council the two following Memorials, Signed by the Deputies and a number of the French Inhabitants of Minas and Pisiquid, and delivered to Capt. Murray the Commanding Officer there, by whom they had been transmitted to His Excellency. [Translated from the French.]

'MINES June 10th. 1755.'

'To His Excellency CHARLES LAWRENCE, Governor of the province of Nova Scotia or Acadie, &c. &c.

'Sir,—

'We, the Inhabitants of Mines, Pisiquid, and the river Canard, take the liberty of approaching your Excellency for the purpose of testifying our sense of the care which the government exercises towards us.

'It appears, Sir, that your Excellency doubts the sincerity with which we have promised to be faithful to his Britannic Majesty.

'We most humbly beg your Excellency to consider our past conduct. You will see, that, very far from violating the oath we have taken, we have maintained it in its entirety, in spite of the solicitations and the dreadful threats of another power. We still entertain, Sir, the same pure and sincere disposition to prove under any circumstances, our unshaken fidelity to his Majesty, provided that His Majesty shall allow us the same liberty that he has granted us. We earnestly beg your Excellency to have the goodness to inform us of His Majesty's intentions on this subject, and to give us assurances on his part.

'Permit us, if you please, Sir, to make known the annoying circumstances in which we are placed, to the prejudice of the tranquillity we ought to enjoy. Under pretext that we are transporting our corn or other provisions to Beausejour, and the river St. John, we are no longer permitted to carry the least quantity of corn by water from one place to another. We beg your Excellency to be assured that we have never transported provisions to Beausejour, or to the river St. John. If some refugee inhabitants at the point have been seized, with cattle, we are not on that account, by any means guilty, in as much as the cattle belonged to them as private individuals, and they were driving them to their respective habitations. As to ourselves, Sir, we have never offended in that respect; consequently we ought not, in our opinion, to be punished; on the contrary, we hope that your Excellency will be pleased to restore to us the same liberty that we enjoyed formerly, in giving us the use of our canoes, either to transport our provisions from one river to the other, or for the purpose of fishing; thereby providing for our livelihood. This permission has never been taken from us except at the present time. We hope, Sir, that you will be pleased to restore it, especially in consideration of the number of poor inhabitants who would be very glad to support their families with the fish that they would be able to catch. Moreover, our guns, which we regard as our own personal property, have been taken from us, notwithstanding the fact that they are absolutely necessary to us, either to defend our cattle which are attacked by the wild beasts, or for the protection of our children, and of ourselves.

'Any inhabitant who may have his oxen in the woods, and who may need them for purposes of labour, would not dare to expose himself in going for them without being prepared to defend himself.

'It is certain, Sir, that since the savages have ceased frequenting our parts, the wild beasts have greatly increased, and that our cattle are devoured by them almost every day. Besides, the arms which have been taken from us are but a feeble guarantee of our fidelity. It is not the gun which an inhabitant possesses, that will induce him to revolt, nor the privation of the same gun that will make him more faithful; but his conscience alone must induce him to maintain his oath. An order has appeared in your Excellency's name, given at Fort Edward June 4th, 1755, and in the 28th year of his Majesty's reign, by which we are commanded to carry guns, pistols etc. to Fort Edward. It appears to us, Sir, that it would be dangerous for us to execute that order, before representing to you the danger to which this order exposes us. The savages may come and threaten and plunder us, reproaching us for having furnished arms to kill them. We hope, Sir, that you will be pleased, on the contrary, to order that those taken from us be restored to us. By so doing, you will afford us the means of preserving both ourselves and our cattle. In the last place, we are grieved, Sir, at seeing ourselves declared guilty without being aware of having disobeyed. One of our inhabitants of the river Canard, named Piere Melançon, was seized and arrested in charge of his boat, before having heard any order forbidding that sort of transport. We beg your Excellency, on this subject, to have the goodness to make known to us your good pleasure before confiscating our property and considering us in fault. This is the favour we expect from your Excellency's kindness, and we hope that you will do us the justice to believe that very far from violating our promises, we will maintain them, assuring you that we are very respectfully,

Sir,

Your very humble and obt. servants,'

Signed by twenty-five of the said inhabitants.

'MINES, June 24, 1755.'
'To his Excellency CHARLES LAWRENCE, Esq., Governor of the province of Nova Scotia or Acadie.

'Sir,—

'All the inhabitants of Mines, Pisiquid and the river Canard, beg your Excellency to believe that if, in the petition which they have had the honor to present to your Excellency, there shall be found any error or any want of respect towards the government, it is intirely contrary to their intention; and that in this case, the inhabitants who have signed it, are not more guilty than the others.

'If, sometimes, the inhabitants become embarrassed in your Excellency's presence, they humbly beg you to excuse their timidity; and if, contrary to our expectation, there is anything hard in the said petition, we beg your Excellency to do us the favour of allowing us to explain our intention.

'We hope that your Excellency will be pleased to grant us this favour, begging you to believe that we are very respectfully,

Sir,

Your very humble and very obedient servants,'

Signed by forty-four of the said inhabitants in the name of the whole.

The Lieutenant Governor at the same time acquainted the Council that Capt. Murray had informed him that for some time before the delivery of the first of the said memorials the French Inhabitants in general had behaved with greater Submission and Obedience to the Orders of the Government than usual, and had already delivered into him a considerable number of their Fire Arms, but that at the delivery of the said Memorial they treated him with great Indecency and Insolence, which gave him strong Suspicions, that they had obtained some Intelligence which we were then ignorant of, and which the Lieutenant Governor conceived might most probably be a Report that had been about that time spread amongst them of a French Fleet being then in the Bay of Fundy, it being very notorious that the said French Inhabitants have always discovered an insolent and inimical Disposition towards His Majesty's Government when they have had the least hopes of assistance from France.

The Lieutenant Governor likewise acquainted the Council that upon his receipt of the first Memorial, he had wrote to Captain Murray to order all those who had Signed the same, to repair forthwith to Halifax to attend him and the Council thereon, and that they were accordingly arrived and then in waiting without.

The Council having then taken the Contents of the said Memorials into Consideration, were unanimously of Opinion That the Memorial of the 10th of June is highly arrogant and insidious, an Insult upon His Majesty's Authority and Government, and deserved the highest Resentment, and that if the Memorialists had not submitted themselves by their subsequent Memorial, they ought to have been severely punished for their Presumption.

The Deputies were then called in and the Names of the Subscribers to the Memorial read over, and such of them as were present, ordered to Answer to their Names, which they did to the number of fifteen, the others being Sick, after which the Memorial itself was again read, and they were severely reprimanded for their Audacity in Subscribing and Presenting so impertinent a Paper, but in Compassion to their Weakness and Ignorance of the Nature of our Constitution, especially in Matters of Government, and as the Memorialists had presented a subsequent one, and had shewn an Appearance of Concern for their past behaviour therein, and had then presented themselves before the Council with great Submission and Repentance, The Council informed them they were still ready to treat them with Lenity, and in order to shew them the falsity as well as Impudence of the Contents of their Memorial, it was ordered to be read Paragraph by Paragraph, and the Truth of the several Allegations minutely discussed, and Remarks made by the Lieutenant Governor on each Paragraph, to the following Effect, vizt.

It was observed in Answer to this Paragraph of their Memorial of the 10th of June

'That they were affected with the Proceedings of the Government towards them.'

That they had been always treated by the Goverment with the greatest Lenity and Tenderness. That they had enjoyed more Privileges than English Subjects, and had been indulged in the free Excercise of their Religion. That they had at all times full Liberty to consult their Priests, and had been protected in their Trade and Fishery, and had been for many Years permitted to possess their Lands (part of the best Soil of the Province) tho' they had not complied with the Terms, on which the Lands were granted, by Taking the Oath of Allegiance to the Crown.

They were then asked whether they could produce an Instance that any Privilege was denied to them, or that any hardships, were ever imposed upon them by the Government.

They acknowledged the Justice and Lenity of the Government.

Upon the Paragraph where

'They desire their past Conduct might be considered.'

It was remarked to them that their past Conduct was considered, and that the Government were sorry to have occasion to say that their Conduct had been undutifull and very ungratefull for the Lenity shown to them. That they had no Returns of Loyalty to the Crown, or Respect to His Majesty's Government in the Province. That they had discovered a constant disposition to Assist His Majesty's Enemies, and to distress his Subjects. That they had not only furnished the Enemy with Provisions and Ammunition, but had refused to supply the Inhabitants, or Government, with Provisions, and when they did Supply, they have exacted three times the Price for which they were sold at other Markets. That they had been indolent and Idle on their Lands, had neglected Husbandry, and the Cultivation of the Soil, and had been of no use to the Province either in husbandry, Trade or Fishery, but had been rather an Obstruction to the King's Intentions in the Settlement.

They were then asked whether they could mention a single Instance of Service to the Government. To which they were incapable of making any Reply.

Upon reading this Paragraph,

'It seems that your Excellency is doubtfull of the Sincerity of those who have promised fidelity, That they had been so far from breaking their Oath, that they had kept it in spight of terrifying Menaces from another Power'

They were asked What gave them Occasion to suppose that the Government was doubtfull of their Sincerity? and were told, that it argued a Consciousness in them of insincerity and want of Attachment to the Interests of His Majesty and his Government. That as to taking their Arms, They had often urged that the Indians would annoy them if they did not Assist them, and that by taking their Arms by Act of Government, it was put out of the Power of the Indians to threaten or force them to their Assistance. That they had assisted the King's Enemies, and appeared too ready to Join with another Power, contrary to the Allegiance they were bound by their Oath to yield to His Majesty.

In Answer to this Paragraph,

'We are now in the same disposition, the purest and sincerest, to prove in every Circumstance Fidelity to His Majesty in the same manner as we have done, Provided that His Majesty will leave us the same Liberties which he has granted us'

They were told that it was hoped, they would hereafter give Proofs of more sincere and pure dispositions of Mind, in the Practice of Fidelity to His Majesty, and that they would forbear to Act in the manner they have done, in obstructing the Settlement of the Province, by Assisting the Indians and French to the distress and Annoyance of many of His Majesty's Subjects, and to the Loss of the Lives of several of the English Inhabitants. That it was not the Language of British Subjects to talk of Terms with the Crown, to Capitulate about their Fidelity and Allegiance, and that it was insolent to insert a *Proviso*, that they would prove their Fidelity *Provided* that His Majesty would give them Liberties.

All His Majesty's Subjects are protected in the Enjoyment of every Liberty, while they continue Loyal and faithfull to the Crown, and when they become false and disloyal they forfeit that Protection.

That they in particular, tho they had acted so insincerely on every Opportunity, had been left in the full Enjoyment of their Religion, Liberty and Properties, with an Indulgence beyond what would have been allowed to any British Subject, who could presume, as they have done, to join in the Measures of another Power.

They were told in answer to the Paragraph where,

'They desire their Canoes for carrying their Provisions from one River to another and for their Fishery'

That they wanted their Canoes for carrying Provisions to the Enemy, and not for their own use or the Fishery, That by a Law of this Province, All Persons are restrained from carrying Provisions from one Port to another, and every Vessel, Canoe or Bark found with Provisions is forfeited, and a Penalty is inflicted on the Owners.

They were also told in Answer to the following Paragraph,

'They Petition for their Guns as part of their Goods, that they may be restored to defend their Cattle from the Wild Beasts, and to preserve themselves and their Children, That since the Indians have quitted their Quarters, the Wild Beasts are greatly increased'

That Guns are no part of their Goods, as they have no Right to keep Arms. By the Laws of England, All Roman Catholicks are restrained from having Arms, and they are Subject to Penalties if Arms are found in their Houses.

That upon the Order from Captain Murray many of the Inhabitants voluntarily brought in their Arms, and none of them pretended that they wanted them for defence of their Cattle against Wild Beasts, and that the Wild Beasts had not increased since their Arms were surrendered. That they had some secret Inducement, at that time, for presuming to demand their Arms as part of their Goods and their Right, and that they had flattered themselves of being supported in their Insolence to the Government, on a Report that some french Ships of War were in the Bay of Fundy. That this daring Attempt plainly discovered the falsehood of their Professions of Fidelity to the King, and their readiness has been visible upon every Intimation of force or Assistance from France, to insult His Majesty's Government, and to join with his Enemies, contrary to their Oath of Fidelity.

Upon reading this Paragraph,

'Besides the Arms we carry are a feeble Surety for our Fidelity. It is not the Gun that an Inhabitant possesses, which will lead him to Revolt, nor the depriving him of that Gun that will make him more faithful, but his Conscience alone ought to engage him to maintain his Oath.'

They were asked, what Excuse they could make for their Presumption in this Paragraph, and treating the Government with such Indignity and Contempt as to Expound to them the nature of Fidelity, and to prescribe what would be the Security proper to be relied on by the Government for their Sincerity. That their Consciences ought indeed to engage them to Fidelity from their Oath of Allegiance to the King, and that if they were sincere in their Duty to the Crown, they would not be so anxious for their Arms, when it was the pleasure of the King's Government to demand them for His Majesty's Service. They were then informed that a very fair Opportunity now presented itself to them to Manifest the reality of their Obedience to the

Government by immediately taking the Oath of Allegiance in the Common Form before the Council. Their Reply to this Proposal was, That they were not come prepared to resolve the Council on that head. They were then told that they very well knew these Six Years past, the same thing had been often proposed to them and had been as often evaded under various frivolous pretences, that they had often been informed that sometime or other it would be required of them and must be done, and that the Council did not doubt but they knew the Sentiments of the Inhabitants in general, and had fully considered and determined this point with regard to themselves before now, as they had been already indulged with Six Years to form a Resolution thereon. They then desired they might return home and consult the Body of the People upon this subject as they could not do otherwise than the Generality of the inhabitants should determine, for that they were desirous of either refusing or accepting the Oath in a Body, and could not possibly determine, till they knew the Sentiments of their Constituents.

Upon this so extraordinary a Reply they were informed they would not be permitted to Return for any such purpose, but that it was expected from them to declare on the Spot, for their own particular, as they might very well be expected to do after having had so long a time to consider upon that point. They then desired leave to retire to consult among themselves, which they were permitted to do, when after near an hour's Recess, They returned with the same Answer, That they could not consent to take the Oath as prescribed without consulting the General Body, but that they were ready to take it as they had done before, to which they were answered, That His Majesty had disapproved of the manner of their taking the Oath before, That it was not consistent with his Honour to make any conditions, nor could the Council accept their taking the Oath in any other way than as all other His Majesty's Subjects were obliged by Law to do when called upon, and that it was now expected they should do so, which they still declining, they were allowed till the next Morning at Ten of the Clock to come to a Resolution. To which Time the Council then adjourned. . . .

The Council being met according to Adjournment, the french Deputies who were Yesterday Ordered to Attend the Council, were brought in, and, upon being asked what Resolution they were come to in regard to the Oath, They declared they could not consent to Take the Oath in the Form required without consulting the Body. They were then informed that as they had now for their own particulars, refused to Take the Oath as directed by Law, and thereby sufficiently evinced the Sincerity of their Inclination towards the Government, The Council could no longer look on them as Subjects to His Britannick Majesty, but as Subjects of the King of France, and as such they must hereafter be Treated; and they were Ordered to withdraw.

The Council after Consideration, were of Opinion That directions should be given to Captain Murray to order the French Inhabitants forthwith to Choose and send to Halifax, new Deputies with the General Resolution of the said Inhabitants in regard to taking the Oath, and that none of them should for the future be admitted to Take it after having once refused so to do, but that effectual Measures ought to be taken to remove all such Recusants out of the Province.

The Deputies were then called in again, and having been informed of this Resolution, and finding they could no longer avail themselves of the Disposition of the Government to ingage them to a Dutifull Behaviour by Lenity and perswasion, Offered to take the Oath, but were informed that as there was no reason to hope their proposed Compliance proceeded from an honest Mind, and could be esteemed only the Effect of Compulsion and Force, and is contrary to a clause in an Act of Parliament, I. Geo. 2. c 13. whereby Persons who have once refused to Take the Oaths cannot be afterwards permitted to Take them, but are considered as Popish Recusants; Therefore they would not now be indulged with such Permission; And they were thereupon ordered into Confinement.

2 From 'Extracts from Col. John Winslow's Journal' [1755], in *Report Concerning Canadian Archives for the Year* 1905 (Ottawa: S.E. Dawson, 1906), vol. II, Appendix A, Part III, 19–29.

Septr. 3rd—This Day had a Consultation with the Captains the Result of which was that I Should Give out my Citation to the Inhabitants to morrow Morning.

1755, September the 4th—This Morning Sent for Doctor Rodion and Delivd him a Citation to the Inhabitants with a Strict Charge to See it Executed, which he Promist Should be Faithfully Done.

September 5th—Att Three in the afternoon The French Inhabitants appeard agreable to their Citation at the Church in Grand Pré amounting To 418 of Their Best Men upon which I ordered a Table to be Sett in the Center of the Church and being attended with those of my officers who were off Gaurd Delivered them by Interpretors the King's orders In the Following words:

GENTLEMEN,—I have Received from his Excellency Governor Lawrance, The Kings Commission which I have in my hand and by whose orders you are Convened togather to Manifest to you his Majesty's Final resolution to the French Inhabitants of this his Province of Nova Scotia, who for almost half a Century have had more Indulgence Granted them, then any of his Subjects in any part of his Dominions. what use you have made of them, you your Self Best Know.

The Part of Duty I am now upon is what thoh Necessary is Very Disagreable to my Natural make & Temper as I Know it Must be Grevious to you who are of the Same Specia.

But it is not my Business to annimedvert, but to obey Such orders as I receive and therefore without Hessitation Shall Deliver you his Majesty's orders and Instructions vizt.

That your Lands & Tennements, Cattle of all Kings and Live Stock of all Sortes are Forfitted to the Crown with all other your Effects Saving your Money and Household Goods and you your Selves to be removed from this his Province.

This it is Preremtorily his Majesty's orders That the whole French Inhabitants of these Districts, be removed, and I am Throh his Majesty's Goodness Directed to allow you Liberty to Carry of your money and Household Goods as Many as you Can without Discomemoading the Vessels you Go in. I shall do Every thing in my Power that all Those Goods be Secured to you and that you are Not Molested in Carrying of them of and also that whole Familys Shall go in the Same Vessel, and make this remove which I am Sensable must give you a great Deal of Trouble as Easy as his Majesty's Service will admit and hope that in what Ever part of the world you may Fall you may be Faithful Subjects, a Peasable & happy People.

I Must also inform you That it is his Majesty's Pleasure that you remain in Security under the Inspection & Direction of the Troops that I have the Honr. to Command.

and then declared them the Kings Prisoner's.

And Gave out the following Declaration.

GRAND PRÉ, September 5sh, 1755.

all officers and Soldiers and Sea Men Employed in his Majesty's Service as well as all his Subjects of what Denomination Soever, are hereby Notified That all Cattle vizt. Horsses, Horne Cattle, Sheep, goats, Hoggs and Poultry of Every Kinde, that was this Day Soposed to be Vested in the French Inhabitants of this Province are become Forfeited to his Majesty whose Property they now are and Every Person of what Denomination Soever is to take Care not to Hurt, Kill or Destroy anything of any Kinde nor Rob Orchards or Gardens or to make waste of anything Dead or alive in these Districts without Special order. Given at my Camp the Day and Place abovesd. JOHN WINSLOW.

To be Published Throhout the Camp and at Villages where the Vessels lye.

After Delivering These Things I returned to my Quarters and they the French Inhabitants Soon Moved by their Elders that it was a Great Grief to them that they had Incurred his Majty's Displeasure and that they were Fearfull that the Surprise of their Detention here would Quite over Come their Familys whome they had No Means to apprise of these their Maloncolly Circumstances and Prayd that parte of them might be returned as Hostages for the appearance of the rest and the Biger number admitted to Go home to their Families, and that as some of their Men were absent they would be obliged to Bring them in. I informed them I would Consider of their Motions and reporte.

And Immediately Convened my officers, to advise, who with Me all agreed that it would be well that they them Selves should Chuse Twenty of their Number for whome they would be answerable vizt Ten of the Inhabitants of Grand Pré & Village & other Ten of the River Cannard and Habitant and they to acquaint the Families of their Districts how Maters where and to assure them that the women & children should be in Safety in their absence in their Habitations and that it was Espected the Party Indulged Should take Care to Bring in an Exact Account of their absent Bretheren & their Circumstances on the Morrow.

HISTORICAL INTERPRETATIONS

3 From Geoffrey Plank, 'Ile Royale, New England, Scotland, and Nova Scotia, 1744–1748', in *An Unsettled Conquest: The British Campaign Against the Peoples of Acadia* (Philadelphia: University of Pennsylvania Press, 2001), 106–22.

In 1739, after a series of disputes arising out of Spanish efforts to regulate trade in the Caribbean, Britain went to war with Spain. Sir Robert Walpole had tried to settle his government's differences with Spain peacefully, but domestic opposition to his foreign policy forced his hand. The Walpole ministry's opponents rallied a significant portion of the British public in support of war with Spain in part by associating the interests of British merchants abroad with the political liberties of Britons at home. They cited the government's willingness to negotiate with the Spanish as evidence of Walpole's corruption and an indication that he was willing to sacrifice British liberty and subordinate himself to the Catholic powers to advance his own political ends. At public rallies and in the press, the supporters of war called themselves 'patriots', and by linking domestic liberty with power overseas,

they created a new, broader base of political support for British imperial expansion.[1]

The inhabitants of North America's eastern maritime region followed these events with great interest, assuming that the Anglo-Spanish conflict would broaden into a larger conflagration and that Britain and France would soon be at war. One result was a precipitous decline in the number of New England fishermen visiting Canso. The New Englanders feared a French attack on the island, and many abandoned it after 1739. It turned out that the fishermen were right, though Europe's diplomats staved off war between the British and the French longer than the colonists anticipated. The War of the Austrian Succession, Britain's war with France, began only in 1744, after Walpole had been driven from power. It started far from the coasts of Nova Scotia, but the French on Ile Royal exploited the outbreak of hostilities almost immediately by joining forces with Mi'kmaq allies and attacking the British settlement on Canso after the word arrived from Europe that war had been declared.

In response to the attack on Canso, Massachusetts entered the conflict, first by sending reinforcements to defend the garrison at Annapolis Royal, and then in 1745 (acting alongside forces from elsewhere in New England) by seizing Louisbourg. The New Englanders sent most of the French colonial population of Ile Royale to France, but the French military remained active in the region nonetheless, particularly in the eastern part of peninsular Nova Scotia.

The fighting disrupted the conditions that had allowed for relative peace in Nova Scotia over the previous 18 years by forcing almost all the inhabitants to answer questions that many of them had previously been able to avoid. The Mi'kmaq and the English-speaking colonists, especially on the Atlantic coast, had to define in clearer terms the meaning of Mi'kmaq claims to the land. The Acadians throughout the province had to determine under what circumstances they were obliged to support the British colonial government or resist demands made on them by the government's French and Mi'kmaq opponents. Persons of mixed ancestry, and others whose way of life defied simple categorization as 'French', 'British', or 'Indian', had to decide for official purposes in which community they belonged.

Almost every facet of daily life became politically significant. Growing crops and raising livestock in certain areas served the war efforts of the Mi'kmaq and the French and left the Acadians vulnerable to British reprisals. Other activities such as worshipping alongside Native warriors or French soldiers, dancing with the men or helping Mi'kmaq women care for their children, acquired new importance in the context of the war. And even those who avoided contact with the fighting men or their families had reason to monitor and re-evaluate their habits because the British used behavioural cues to determine whether a person was

Mi'kmaq. From 1744 onward the Massachusetts government offered prizes for the scalps of the Native people.

The New England colonists who participated in military action in and around Nova Scotia in some respects closely resembled those of earlier generations who had fought in the maritime region, and the War of the Austrian Succession only served to intensify existing patterns of interracial violence. But in other respects the mid-eighteenth-century New Englanders were very different from their predecessors. Partly under the influence of the new brand of imperial patriotism, which had spread across the Atlantic since the start of the war with Spain, many New England colonists saw their actions as part of a larger imperial project, one they embraced without the misgivings of the old Puritans. Following their victory at Louisbourg the colonists celebrated in a way they had never done before.[2]

After 1745 political developments in Britain helped recast the terms of the debate surrounding the Acadians. In 1746, in the aftermath of an uprising in Scotland on behalf of the Stuart claimant to the throne, the British government debated a series of measures designed to pacify broad stretches of the Scottish Highlands and culturally assimilate the Highlanders. Ideas originally developed as a solution for perceived problems in Scotland were considered as policy options for the Acadians. Perhaps the most important idea that reached America in this way was a proposal to move suspect populations within the British Empire. Before the pacification of the Highlands, those who had proposed moving the Acadians imagined that they would be expelled altogether from the British colonies (as the New Englanders sent the French colonists from Ile Royale to France in 1745). But from 1746 forward, under the influence of proposals developed in the Scottish context, the debate shifted as policymakers considered forced migrations designed to incorporate the Acadians into the communal life of British North America.

In the years following the outbreak of the War of the Austrian Succession, events far from Nova Scotia had profound effects on the lives of the peoples of the province. This article highlights the influence of groups who came to the colony from elsewhere in the British and French Empires. It begins with the decision of the French colonial administrators on Ile Royale to attack the British fishery at Canso, and proceeds with an analysis of the military response of the New Englanders and the impact of the imperial war on the lives of the Mi'kmaq and the Acadians.

When the French colonial authorities began the large-scale settlement of Ile Royale in 1714, they had hoped that the island colony would attract most, if not all, of the Mi'kmaq and the Acadians. The French succeeded in convincing some Acadian families to move, though fewer than they expected. Similarly, Ile Royale attracted fewer Mi'kmaq than the French would have preferred, and many of those who went only visited. Nonetheless, even without a wholesale migration of Mi'kmaq and Acadians from Nova Scotia, the French colony on Ile Royale prospered. By the early 1740s, Louisbourg alone had nearly 2,000 inhabitants; three-quarters were civilians, including the families of soldiers, fishermen, colonial officials, merchants, artisans, and labourers. The island as a whole had a population approaching 5,000.[3]

Though the French could not entice all the Mi'kmaq or Acadians to move to Ile Royale, various French missionaries and colonial officials remained interested in the affairs of the peoples of Nova Scotia. They continued to think of the Acadians as compatriots, and they thought of the Mi'kmaq as a client people, dependent on the French for pastoral care, trade, and a measure of political direction. As early as 1734, Joseph Saint-Ovide de Brouillan, the governor of Ile Royale, made tentative plans to retake Nova Scotia in the event of a war.[4] His advisors assured him that all of the Acadians and most of the Mi'kmaq would greet the French forces as liberators. Subsequent administrators continued to hold similar views.[5] The outbreak of the War of the Austrian Succession presented the colony's officials with an apparent opportunity to bring the Mi'kmaq and the Acadians back within the borders of the French Empire. Instead of asking them to move, the French would try to shift the boundary and drive Britain's colonial administration away.

The French attack on Canso was intended as a first step toward recapturing all of Nova Scotia. There were several reasons for striking the fishing settlement first. Driving the British from Canso foreclosed any possibility that the island could be used as a base for privateers. The French also hoped to cripple the British fishery in the North Atlantic and thereby acquire a larger share of the world market in fish. Canso seemed vulnerable, and since some of the British settlers there had well-furnished homes, the possibility of plunder made it easier for the French to recruit volunteer troops in Louisbourg. Furthermore, many of the Mi'kmaq continued to resent the British presence on the Atlantic coast, and thus the attack on Canso helped secure a wartime Franco-Mi'kmaq alliance.[6]

The decision to start with an attack on the fishing settlement appears in retrospect to have been a strategic mistake, however, because it had the effect of bringing New Englanders into the conflict from the moment the fighting began.[7] Though they had lost Canso, New England's fishermen and privateers could reach the waters off Nova Scotia from other bases, and the Atlantic fishing banks soon became a battle zone, as New Englanders sought retaliation against the French, and the French responded in kind. In a matter of months hundreds of fishing vessels were taken or destroyed.[8] Within Massachusetts, fishermen supported Governor William Shirley's decision to reinforce the garrison of Annapolis Royal, and fishermen were among the earliest proponents of his project to seize Ile Royale.[9]

More than anyone else it was Shirley who defined and directed New England's response to the renewal of conflict in the maritime region. In many ways he personified an increasingly dominant, cosmopolitan outlook among active members of New England's political elite.[10] He was an English-born lawyer who had trained in London, he had lived in Massachusetts only since 1731, and remained equally at ease on both sides of the Atlantic Ocean. Shirley secured the Massachusetts governorship in 1741 with the help of his patron, Secretary of State Thomas Hollis-Pelham, the duke of Newcastle, and he entered office at a time when Massachusetts was badly divided. Economic disruptions associated with the war with Spain, political struggles over the emission of paper money, and religious upheavals associated with revivalism had combined to divide the colonial population into a complex set of mutually antagonistic groups.[11] Shirley never gained the support of all the colonists, but, as several historians have shown, his military ventures gave him the patronage power he needed to secure political support from the competing factions and govern Massachusetts effectively.[12] Self-interested merchants and office-seekers supported Shirley and his campaign against the French, as did a broad cross-section of the colonial public, including evangelical preachers, conservative Congregationalists and Anglicans, fishermen, and young men eager to advance their prospects through military service and the acquisition of land. The New England churches abandoned their earlier reticence and endorsed Shirley's actions.[13] It helped that the French and the Mi'kmaq appeared to be the aggressors.

The early reports of combat appearing in the Massachusetts newspapers emphasized the participation of Mi'kmaq warriors and presented them in the worst possible light. In June 1744 a correspondent to the *Boston Gazette* indicated that the Mi'kmaq who took part in the attack on Canso had pleaded with the French for permission to slaughter the English-speaking residents of the town and that the French had struggled to restrain them.[14] Similar stories were repeated often during the war and served to convince many New Englanders that the Mi'kmaq were innately irrational and violent.[15]

Such beliefs had long circulated in Massachusetts, and they inspired the New England colonists during the War of the Austrian Succession to adopt a stance toward the Mi'kmaq similar to the one they had adopted in their previous wars. But in 1744 and 1745 the colonists were mobilized for war in the maritime region on an unprecedented scale.

On October 20, 1744 the government of Massachusetts officially declared war on the Mi'kmaq.[16] Five days later the Massachusetts General Court offered a bounty of £100 (provincial currency) for the scalp of any adult male member of the Mi'kmaq nation. For the scalps of women and children, the legislature offered £50.[17] Similar rewards were available for Mi'kmaq prisoners taken alive. Recognizing that it would be difficult to identify scalps by tribe, on November 2 Shirley announced that he would grant a reward for any 'Indian' killed or captured east of the St. Croix River, regardless of his or her language group. By necessity he made an exception for Native warriors serving under the Anglo-American military command.[18]

There is no record of Jean-Baptiste Cope's activities during the war, but the mission near his home on the Shubenacadie River became a centre of Mi'kmaq resistance. The resident missionary at the Shubenacadie mission, Jean-Louis Le Loutre, served as the principal intermediary between the French forces and the Mi'kmaq on peninsular Nova Scotia. It was Le Loutre who informed the Mi'kmaq in the interior of Nova Scotia of the plan to strike at Canso, and, acting on the advice of the governor of Louisbourg, he also sent them directions to lay siege to Annapolis Royal in the weeks immediately after that attack. Le Loutre accompanied Mi'kmaq warriors to the British colonial capital and played an active role as an advisor to the Mi'kmaq in the first three years of the war.[19] Pierre Maillard, another missionary working among the Mi'kmaq, also travelled with the bands on the peninsula of Nova Scotia and at Ile Royale. He provided advice and delivered speeches aimed at strengthening the warriors' discipline and resolve.[20] After disease struck the Mi'kmaq in 1746, the missionaries told them that the British had deliberately infected them by distributing contaminated cloth.[21]

Le Loutre and Maillard may have argued more strenuously than necessary, because the scalp-bounty policy, by itself, was enough to foreclose easy reconciliation between the Mi'kmaq bands and the British. At least among those living within the traditional bands, almost all of the Mi'kmaq supported the war effort. They were fighting not just for land but for survival, and men, women, and children overcame severe hardships to keep the warriors afield. [. . .]

After their seizure of Louisbourg, the New Englanders transported the French-speaking population of Ile Royale to France.[22] That decision inspired a brief debate within the provincial council of Nova Scotia over the possibility of similarly expelling the Acadians, though the option was ultimately rejected as impractical.[23] Proponents of deportation argued that the Acadians had not taken valid oaths of allegiance and that their refusal to contemplate military service undermined the credibility of their professed loyalty to Britain. The councilmen also cited the Acadians' recent behaviour. Those who favoured removing them argued that they had helped supply the French army and Mi'kmaq warriors and refused to sell provisions to the British except at exorbitant prices. The Acadians had seemed slow to inform the British about French and Mi'kmaq military preparations, and the councilmen assumed that they provided the French and the Mi'kmaq useful intelligence. Along with providing information and logistical support, the Acadians behaved in ways that boosted enemy morale. According to a report of the provincial council, when Mi'kmaq warriors and French soldiers first laid siege to Annapolis Royal, Acadian 'men, women and children frequented the enemy's

quarters at their mass, prayers, dancing and all other ordinary occasions.'[24]

As the debate over expelling the Acadians made clear, the outbreak of armed hostilities increased the political ramifications of many aspects of the Acadians' lives. When Acadian merchants and farmers raised the price of food, the men in the garrison interpreted the action as a show of support for the king of France. When Acadian women danced with French soldiers, provincial councilmen took it as evidence of sedition. In part because their daily behaviour came under scrutiny, many Acadians who had formerly worked closely with the provincial government fled Annapolis Royal when the fighting began.[25] [. . .]

Acadian men and women reacted to the pressures of living in wartime in various ways, and it is difficult to generalize about their behaviour. A few young men left their homes and went to fight alongside Mi'kmaq warriors.[26] Others hired themselves out as civilian workers for the British army.[27] At least one merchant who had formerly traded with the British garrisons offered his services to the French military and spent the war ferrying men and equipment to French-controlled regions at the eastern end of the Bay of Fundy.[28] [. . .]

If there was anything 'typical' about the Acadians' pattern of behaviour, it was that almost none of them could hold a consistent political stance. [. . .]

By 1746 the policy debates surrounding the Acadians had changed. Early in the conflict, Shirley and various members of Nova Scotia's provincial council had contemplated mass deportations or large-scale retributive raids, especially against the Acadian villagers at the eastern end of the Bay of Fundy, who seemed to have given the most assistance to the French and their Native allies.[29] In 1745, writing to his commander on Ile Royale, Shirley had wistfully complained, 'It grieves me much that I have it not in my power to send a part of 500 men forthwith to Menis [Minas] and burn Grand Pré, their chief town, and open all their sluices, and lay their country waste.'[30]

But by the winter of 1746 Shirley had shifted his efforts and began to seek ways to gain the Acadians' co-operation and ultimately win their hearts.

Several factors contributed to this change in thinking. In the previous summer a French fleet sent to recapture Louisbourg foundered on the Atlantic coast of Nova Scotia, and from that time forward the British military position seemed more secure, particularly at Annapolis Royal. Disease had swept through the Mi'kmaq community, killing hundreds and weakening the military power of the survivors.[31] Equally important, the New Englanders within the garrison at Annapolis Royal gradually changed their outlook toward the Acadians. Given more time to interact with the villagers outside the context of an immediate military crisis, they began to believe that they could gain the Acadians' friendship. The soldiers depended on Acadian farmers and merchants for food and firewood, and the social environment encouraged the men to seek the company of Acadians outside the context of trade.

In the first year of the war relations between the garrison and the community had deteriorated. Most of the Acadians in Annapolis Royal had shunned the English-speakers in their village when French or Mi'kmaq forces were in the area. In any event there were fewer English-speakers in the French-speaking village; most of the married officers and soldiers at Annapolis Royal had sent their wives and children to Boston for protection, and the departure of their families helped cut the men off from the Acadian community, at least temporarily.[32] Over time new bonds were formed, however, and by the last two years of the war, official British discussions of the Acadians returned repeatedly to the issue of intermarriage between the soldiers and Acadian women.[33]

Overcoming significant cultural obstacles, by 1747 a few New England soldiers managed to court and marry Acadian women in Annapolis Royal.[34] According to reports that reached Shirley, the women who married the New England men were punished with excommunication from the Catholic Church. Shirley complained bitterly about the church's reaction. Though he hoped that the women would leave the church eventually, he knew that church-imposed sanctions would humiliate them and isolate them from their neighbours; excommunication was a strong deterrent to intermarriage. Shirley objected not only for the sake of the soldiers and their spouses, but also because he believed that the church's policy deterred British settlement in Nova Scotia. Almost certainly exaggerating the influence of the policy, he claimed that it 'has had so general an effect as to prevent the settlement of any one English family within the province.'[35]

When Shirley referred to 'English' families, he meant families in which the husband spoke English. This is evident, not only in the context of his concern over the marital fortunes of the soldiers, but also in light of long-term proposals he was developing to promote marriages between Acadian women and English-speaking settlers in Nova Scotia. Intermarriage became a central feature of Shirley's project to transform the Acadians culturally. He wanted to convert them to Protestantism, teach them English, and make them loyal British subjects. As part of that program, he wanted to change the composition of the Acadians' families by encouraging soldiers to settle permanently in Nova Scotia and providing Acadian women with incentives to marry English-speakers and Protestants. He also wanted to force the Acadian women to send their children to English-language schools so that their descendants would become, as he succinctly put it, 'English Protestants'.[36]

Shirley advanced this plan in response to the experiences of the soldiers at Annapolis Royal. Though only a few marriages had taken place between the men of the garrison and Acadian women, he saw those unions as a model for social development in the entire colony. In 1747 Shirley began designing a project to intermingle soldiers and Acadians throughout the eastern Bay of Fundy region, to facilitate integration and gradual assimilation. Annapolis Royal gave him inspiration, but he was also responding to contemporary events in Britain, where the ministry was engaged in a similarly forceful effort at cultural assimilation.

During the winter of 1745, Charles Stuart led an uprising in Scotland in an effort to place his father on the British throne. Though he was ultimately defeated, he received considerable support in certain parts of the Scottish Highlands. Charles was a Catholic and he had counted among his supporters a disproportionate number of Catholics and 'nonjurant' Anglicans, communicants in a conservative wing of British Protestantism. It also seemed from the perspective of British policymakers that his support had been strongest among impoverished Highlanders who came from remote pastoral regions where the clans maintained their own juridical traditions and where a considerable amount of economic activity depended on barter and other forms of nonmonetary exchange. After defeating the Stuart forces, the British government adopted a set of measures designed to 'pacify' the Scottish Highlands by destroying the economic and cultural conditions that they believed underlay support for Charles.[37]

Beginning in 1746, Parliament outlawed Highland dress, made it illegal for the Highlanders to carry weapons, abolished the local court system, and confiscated the property of all those who had fought for the Stuart cause. Missionaries were sent to the Highlands along with land speculators and other investors with the aim of establishing model towns where, through a combination of educational work, economic coercion, and government regulation, the Highlanders could be converted to authorized forms of Protestantism and taught to participate in the market economy. One individual involved in the pacification program summed up the theory as follows: 'Make then the Highlanders as rich and industrious as the people of Manchester and they will be as little apt to rebel.'[38]

In 1746 Admiral Charles Knowles, who had helped guard the sea lanes to Britain during the Stuart uprising, became governor of British-occupied Ile Royale.[39] After he moved to America he continued to participate in the policy debates surrounding the pacification of Scotland, and he brought William Shirley into the debates. Knowles endorsed an idea advanced by William Augustus, duke of Cumberland, that entire Highland clans should be sent to America, and he suggested that space should be cleared for them in Nova Scotia. The Acadians, he argued, could be moved to make room.[40]

When he first learned of this proposal Shirley opposed it, but after a raid against New England troops stationed in Minas in the winter of 1746–7, he entered into an extensive correspondence with Knowles, and the two men worked out a plan to relocate at least part of the Acadian population.[41] They agreed to abandon the idea of replacing the villagers with Highlanders, but endorsed the general theory behind that plan, that shifting peoples within the empire would be an effective way to control them. In a joint letter to the secretary of state they recommended using military force to expel the most 'obnoxious' Acadians and replace them with Protestant immigrants. [. . .] The governors predicted that the introduction of immigrants, and the creation of a cosmopolitan society, would transform the Acadians and turn them into loyal subjects. They did not believe that all of the newcomers had to come from Great Britain. Citing the history of Pennsylvania, they claimed that Swiss and German settlers could serve effectively as promoters of British imperial culture.

In spite of his original misgivings, Shirley soon discovered that he liked the idea of directing the process of migration with the purpose of transforming Acadian society, and he began developing more elaborate plans. In the summer of 1747 he proposed sending 2000 New England troops to the isthmus of Chignecto, to clear the region of its inhabitants and settle on the vacated land. The dispossessed Acadians would be taken to New England and placed in scattered towns in Rhode Island, Connecticut, Massachusetts, and New Hampshire.[42] If everything proceeded as Shirley anticipated, the New England settlers in Nova Scotia would intermingle and intermarry with the Acadians. Similarly, the relocated Acadian families would get absorbed into New England.[43] Shirley was ready to proceed with this experiment, but his superiors in London stopped him. As long as the war with France continued, the ministers opposed the relocation program on the grounds that it would divert scarce resources from other projects, and when the war ended in 1748 the military justification for moving the Acadians lost its force.[44]

The Treaty of Aix-la-Chapelle ending the War of the Austrian Succession ceded Ile Royale back to France.[45] The cession was controversial in Britain and even more so in Massachusetts, where hundreds of families had lost husbands, sons, and fathers in military service on the island.[46] The Massachusetts government had also nearly bankrupted itself and destroyed the value of the provincial currency financing the Louisbourg expedition, an aborted 1746 expedition to Canada, and the reinforcement of Nova Scotia.[47] After the terms of the treaty were announced Shirley tried to soften the blow by getting the ministry to reimburse the Massachusetts government for its expenses. He also asked the imperial authorities to sponsor an effort to resettle and fortify Nova Scotia so that it could be prosperous, secure, and self-sufficient. A central element of Shirley's project was to assimilate the Acadians into a new, cosmopolitan, British colonial society, and he hoped to accomplish this feat by directing a series of large-scale migrations.

In the winter of 1748 Shirley commissioned a survey of the eastern end of the Bay of Fundy. He wanted to identify hills and islands appropriate for forts, and farmland that could be confiscated to support new immigrants.[48] [. . .] Shirley sent his surveyor's report to London in February 1749, along with a proposal to resettle Nova Scotia with farmers from England, Germany, Switzerland, and other parts of Europe. He did not intend to send any of the Acadians out of Nova Scotia to make room for the new settlers. He suggested instead that some of the Acadians should be moved within the colony. Shirley considered short-distance moves necessary, because he wanted to intermingle European immigrants with Acadians. If all the current inhabitants of Nova Scotia were allowed to stay where they were, the province would remain divided, with a geographically separate French-speaking Catholic community.[49]

The proposal to settle Nova Scotia with Protestants from continental Europe helped Shirley politically in Massachusetts. At least since 1747, in serialized publications and newspapers, the governor's opponents in Boston had complained that the Louisbourg expedition and the reinforcement of Annapolis Royal had drained New England's labour supply.[50] Citing treatises on political economy, they had generalized from recent experience and argued that population density was the source of economic and military strength. By scattering the population, any effort to expand the territories of the British Empire in North America risked leaving the existing colonies underpopulated, poor, and vulnerable.[51]

[. . .]

British political elites as well as New Englanders had taken an interest in Ile Royale in the long months of negotiation leading up to the conclusion of the Treaty of Aix-la-Chapelle.[52] It was a measure of the new importance of imperial issues in British politics that the government's opponents in Parliament and in the press hoped to exploit the cession of the island back to France as an embarrassment to the ministry. In an effort to limit political damage at home, alleviate the social ills associated with demobilization, and placate restive New Englanders, in 1749 the Board of Trade appointed Edward Cornwallis, a veteran of the pacification of the Scottish Highlands, as governor of Nova Scotia, and Parliament allocated a large sum of money to encourage Protestant settlement in the colony.[53] The British government offered veterans free transportation, land, tools, and a year's worth of provisions, and asked nothing in return except that they take the trip to Nova Scotia. It offered the same terms to carpenters, bricklayers, and other labourers with economically valuable skills.[54] In 1749 the ministry spent over £40,000 to encourage the settlement of province.[55] In addition to recruiting in England, agents of the government travelled to France, the valley of the Rhine, and Switzerland in search of Protestants willing to move.[56]

The Board of Trade directed Cornwallis to establish a Protestant town at Chebucto Harbor (present-day Halifax) and then disperse some of the new colonists in Acadian-dominated regions around the Bay of Fundy.[57] The board also instructed him to make sure that the new townships included both Protestants and 'French Inhabitants' (Acadians), 'to the End that the said French Inhabitants may be subjected to such Rules and Orders as may hereafter be made for the better ordering and governing the said Townships.'[58] The governor was also told to establish 'Protestant schools', 'to the end that the said French inhabitants may be converted to the Protestant religion and their children brought up in the principles of it.'[59] Following Shirley's advice, the Board of Trade directed Cornwallis to encourage intermarriage between Acadians and Protestants, and to apprehend, try, and punish any Catholic priest who censured his parishioners for marrying out of the faith.[60] If everything had gone

as the ministers wished, within a few generations the Acadians would have converted to Protestantism and joined the new colonists as equals in a single society.

The project of resettling Nova Scotia with a diverse Protestant population, and the articulation of the plan to absorb Acadians into the cultural mix, reflected political developments beyond the shores of the colony. In many parts of the British Empire, public officials were rethinking what it meant to be a British subject and trying to devise new ways to incorporate persons of varying cultural backgrounds into a single political community. The eighteenth-century 'British' nation had always been an aggregation of peoples with distinctive histories and traditions. As Linda Colley has argued, the promoters of British nationalism accommodated themselves to the existence of cultural differences in part by concentrating on a few ideals that Britons were presumed to share, such as opposition to Catholicism and loyalty to the Crown.[61] The opening of the British colonies to Protestant immigrants from continental Europe reflected a growing confidence that such settlers would adopt these minimal necessary attributes of 'Britishness'. Nonetheless, the recent events in the Scottish Highlands served as an object lesson on the dangers that could arise when culturally distinct communities within the realm refused to adhere to the necessary ideals.

NOTES

1. See Kathleen Wilson, 'Empire, Trade and Popular Politics in Mid-Hanoverian Britain: The Case of Admiral Vernon', *Past and Present* 121 (1988): 74–109; Gerald Jordan and Nicholas Rogers, 'Admirals as Heroes: Patriotism and Liberty in Hanoverian England', *Journal of British Studies* 28 (1989): 210–4.

2. See *Boston Evening Post*, July 8, July 15, 1745; *Boston Postboy*, July 8, 1745; Charles Chauncey to William Pepperell, July 4, 1745 in *Collections of the Massachusetts Historical*

Society 1st ser. 1 (1792): 49; Thomas Hubbard to Pepperell, in *Collections of the Massachusetts Historical Society* 6th ser. 10 (1899): 308–9; Daniel Edwards to Roger Wolcott, July 9, 1745, in *Collections of the Connecticut Historical Society* 11 (1907): 334–37.

3. Christopher Moore, 'The Other Louisbourg: Trade and Merchant Enterprise in Ile Royale, 1713–1758', *Histoire sociale/Social History* 12 (1979): 79–96; John Robert McNeill, *Atlantic Empires of France and Spain: Louisbourg and*

Havana, 1700–1760 (Chapel Hill: University of North Carolina Press, 1985), 20–24.

4. McNeill, *Atlantic Empires of France and Spain*, 84.

5. See Rawlyk, *Yankees at Louisbourg* (Orono: University of Maine Press, 1967), 6.

6. Ibid., 2–4.

7. For accounts of the attack, see David B. Flemming, *The Canso Islands: An Eighteenth-Century Fishing Station* (Ottawa: Parks Canada, 1977), 45; William Shirley to Newcastle, July 7, 1744, in Charles Henry Lincoln, ed., *Correspondence of William Shirley* (New York: Macmillan, 1912), 1: 133; J.S. McLennan, *Louisbourg from Its Foundation to Its Fall, 1713–1758* (London: Macmillan, 1918), 111; Mascarene to Philipps, June 9, 1744, Add. Mss. 19,071, doc. 45; *Boston Postboy*, June 11, 1744.

8. For accounts of New England vessels taken, see *Boston Evening Post*, June 11, June 25, 1744; *Boston Newsletter*, September 20, 1744; *South Carolina Gazette*, July 4, 1744. For New England's attacks on the French fishery, see *Boston Evening Post*, September 24, October 22, November 26, 1744; *Boston Gazette*, August 21, 1744; *Boston Newsletter*, August 16, September 20, September 27, October 25, 1744; *Boston Postboy*, September 24, October 22, 1744; *New York Gazette*, October 1, 1744; Douglass, *A Summary, Historical and Political, of the First Planting, Prgressive Improvements, and Present State of the British Settlements in North America* (2 vols. Boston: Evans 6307/6663, 1749/1751), 1:339.

9. See Alexander Hamilton, 'The Itinerarium of Dr. Alexander Hamilton', in *Colonial American Travel Narratives*, ed. Wendy Martin (New York: Penguin, 1994), 261. See also Rawlyk, *Yankees at Louisbourg*, 37, 38; John A. Schutz, *William Shirley: King's Governor of Massachusetts* (Chapel Hill: University of North Carolina Press, 1961), 90. It was a fisherman who first alerted Boston of the attack on Canso, but the printer of the *Boston Evening Post* chose not to publish the story because it was 'looked upon as fishermen's news'. Only after a merchant confirmed the report was it placed in the paper. *Boston Evening Post*, May 28, 1744. For the reaction of the legislature, see *Journals of the House*

of Representatives of Massachusetts 21: 8–11, 29, 42; Boston Postboy, June 4, 1744; *Boston Newsletter*, June 14, 1744.

10. See Schutz, *William Shirley*.

11. Ibid., 23–44; Rosalind Remer, 'Old Lights and New Money; A Note on Religion, Economics, and the Social Order in 1740 Boston', *William and Mary Quarterly* 3d ser. 47 (1990): 566–73.

12. See, for example, Schutz, William Shirley, 80–103; Bernard Bailyn, *The Origins of American Politics* (New York: Vintage, 1967), 116–17; but see William Pencak, *War, Politics, and Revolution in Provincial Massachusetts* (Boston: Northeastern University Press, 1981), 115–47.

13. Hatch, 'Origins of Civil Millennialism in America: New England Clergymen, War with France, and the American Revolution', *William and Mary Quarterly* 3d ser. 31 (1992):492–508.

14. *Boston Gazette*, June 26, 1744.

15. See, for example, *Boston Newsletter*, June 6, 1745; *Boston Evening Post*, July 29, 1745.

16. *Boston Evening Post*, October 22, 1744.

17. *Journals of the House of Representatives of Massachusetts* 21: 99, 106–7; *Boston Evening Post*, November 5, 1744.

18. *Boston Evening Post*, November 11, 1744; using a contemporary term, Shirley called the St. Croix the Passamaquodi River.

19. Rogers, 'Abbé Le Loutre'; Jean-Louis Le Loutre, 'Autobiography', translated by John Clarence Webster, in John Clarence Webster, ed., *The Career of the Abbé Loutre in Nova Scotia* (Shediac: Private printing, 1933), 33–50, 35; See also Rawlyk, *Yankees at Louisbourg*, 7–11.

20. Pierre Maillard, 'Lettre', in Abbé Henri-Raymond Casgrain, ed., *Les Soirées canadiennes* (Quebec: Brousseau, 1863), 289–426, 322–28; Webster, *Career of the Abbé Le Loutre*, 10.

21. 'Motifs des sauvages mickmaques et marichites des continuer la guerre contre les Anglois depuis la dermière paix', in Gaston du Bosq De Beaumont, ed., *Les Derniers jours de l'Acadie* (Geneva: Slatkine-Megariotis, 1975), 248–53, 251.

22. Steele, 'Surrendering Rites: Prisoners on Colonial North American Frontiers', in *Hanoverian Britain and Empire: Essays in*

Memory of Philip Lawson, ed. Stephen Taylor, Richard Connors, and Clyve Jones (Rochester: Boydell Press, 1998) 152–3; *Boston Evening Post*, July 15, July 22, August 5, September 2, October 21, 1745; *Boston Postboy*, July 22, September 9, September 30, 1745; *Boston Newsletter*, September 12, 1745.

23. Mascarene to Shirley, December 7, 1745, CO 217/39, doc. 316, *PRO*; Shirley to Newcastle, December 23, 1745, RG1, vol. 13, doc. 21, *PANS*; Shirley to Newcastle, February 11, 1746, RG1, vol. 13A, doc. 5, *PANS*; see Barry Morris Moody, 'A Just and Disinterested Man: The Nova Scotia Career of Paul Mascarene, 1710–1752' (Ph.D. diss., Queen's University, 1976), 334–42.

24. 'State of the Province of Nova Scotia', November 8, 1745, CO 217/39, doc. 320, *PRO*.

25. For accounts of the general wartime migration to French-controlled territory, see Andrew Hill Clark, *Acadia: The Geography of Early Nova Scotia to 1760* (Madison: University of Wisconsin Press, 1968), 278, 285, 291; Muriel K. Roy, 'Settlement and Population Growth in Acadia' in *The Acadians of the Maritimes: Thematic Studies* ed. Jean Daigle (Moncton: Centre d'Etudes Acadiennes, 1982), 151–52; Jean Daigle, 'Acadia from 1604 to 1763: An Historical Synthesis', in *Acadia of the Maritimes: Thematic Studies from the Beginning to the Present*, ed. Jean Daigle (Moncton: Chaire d'Etudes Acadiennes, 1995), 36.

26. Report of Jean Luc de La Corne, September 28, 1747, RG1, vol. 3, doc 89, *PANS*; Statement of Honore Gautrol, December 13, 1749, in Thomas B. Akins, ed., *Selections from the Public Documents of the Province of Nova Scotia* (Halifax: Charles Annand, 1869), 177; *Boston Evening Post*, January 15, 1750; John Salusbury, *Expeditions of Honour: The Journal of John Salusbury in Halifax, Nova Scotia, 1749–53*, ed. Ronald Rompkey. Newark: University of Delaware PRess, 1980), 76; Edward Cornwallis to Board of Trade, March 19, 1750, CO 217/9, doc. 188, *PRO*.

27. Mascarene to Philipps, June 9, 1744, Add. Mss. 19,071, doc. 45; Mascarene to Secretary of State, June 15, 1748, CO 217/40, doc. 22, *PRO*; Mascarene to Gorham, August 6, 1748, Add. Mss. 19,071, doc. 119; Mascarene to ?, September 29, 1749, Add. Mss. 19,071, doc. 99.

28. Mascarene to Shirley, spring 1745, in Placide Gaudet, 'Acadian Genealogy and Notes', in *Report Concerning Canadian Archives for the Year 1905* (Ottawa: National Archives of Canada, 1906), 38; Council minutes, May 2–4, 1745, in Charles Bruce Fergusson, ed., *Minutes of his Majesty's Council at Annapolis Royal, 1736–1749* (Halifax: Public Archives of Nova Scotia, 1967), 68–70; Council minutes, November 14, 1746, in Fergusson, *Minutes*, 94; Shirley to Newcastle, May 22, 1746, in Lincoln, *Correspondence of William Shirley*, 1: 150; see also E.B. O'Callaghan, ed., *Documents Relative to the Colonial History of the State of New York* (15 vols. Albany: Weed, Parsons, 1850–83), 10: 155; 'Relation d'une expedition faite sur les anglois dans le pays de l'Acadie, le 11 fevrier 1747, par un détachement de canadiens', in Casgrain, *Collection*, 2: 10–16, 15; 'Journal de la compagne du détachement de Canada à l'Acadie et aux mines, en 1746–47' in Abbé Henri-Raymond Casgrain, ed., *Collection des documents inédits sur le Canada et l'Amerique* (3 vols. Quebec: L.-J. Demers and Frère, 1888), 2: 16–75, 47, 51–52. For evidence of the merchant's earlier co-operation with the government, see Mascarene to William Douglass, July 1740 and August 20, 1741, Mascarene Family Papers; Abbé Henri-Raymond Casgrain, *Pèlegrinage au pays d'Evangéline* (Quebec: L.-J. Demers and Frère,1888), 519; Council minutes, August 17, 1736, in Archibald M. MacMechan, *Original Minutes of His Majesty's Council at Annapolis Royal, 1720–1739* (Halifax: Public Archives of Nova Scotia, 1908), 361–62.

29. See Mascarene to Deputies of Mines, Pisiquid and River Canard, October 13, 1744, in Akins, *Selections*, 137; Shirley to Board of Trade, October 16, 1744, in Lincoln, *Correspondence of William Shirley*, 1:150; Shirley to Newcastle, October 16, 1744, RG1, vol. 12, doc 37, *PANS*.

30. Shirley to Pepperell, May 25, 1745, in *Collections of the Massachusetts Historical Society* 6th ser. 10 (1899): 219.

31. 'Journal de la campagne', 1746–47, in Casgrain, *Collection*, 2: 16–75, 44, 48; *Boston Evening Post*, December 1, 1746; see also *Boston Evening Post*, November 3, November 17, 1746; William C. Wicken, 'Encounters with Tall Sails and Tall Tales: Mi'lmaq Society, 1500–1760', Ph.D. diss, McGill University, 1994, 184–205. For a vivid description of the epidemic, see 'Journal', July 25, 1748–September 14, 1748, AC, F3, vol. 50, doc. 447, *NAC*.

32. *Boston Evening Post*, May 28, 1744.

33. See, for example, Shirley to Newcastle, October 20, 1747, RG1, vol. 13A, doc. 32, *PANS*; Shirley to Newcastle, November 21, 1746, RG1, vol. 13, doc. 33, *PANS*; Charles Knowles and Shirley to Newcastle, April 28, 1747, RG1, vol. 13A, doc. 25, *PANS*; Shirley to Newcastle, July 8, 1747, RG1, vol. 13A, doc. 27, *PANS*.

34. See 'Journal de la campagne', 1746–47, in Casgrain, *Collection*, 2: 16–75, 48.

35. Shirley to Newcastle, October 20, 1747, RG1, vol. 13A, doc. 32, *PANS*.

36. Shirley to Newcastle, November 21, 1746, RG1, vol. 13, doc. 33, *PANS*; Knowles and Shirley to Newcastle, April 28, 1747, RG1, vol. 13A, doc. 25, *PANS*; Shirley to Newcastle, July 8, 1747, RG1, vol. 13A, doc. 27, *PANS*.

37. See Allan I. Macinnes, *Clanship, Commerce, and the House of Stuart, 1603–1788* (east Lothian: Tuckwell PRess, 1996), 210–41; Charles W.J. Withers, Gaelic Scotland: The Transformation of a Cultural Region (New York: Routledge, 1988).

38. 'On the subject of civilising the Highlands', 1748, GD248654/1, Scottish Record Office.

39. Laughton, 'Knowles, Sir Charles' (*DCB*), 11: 293; see also Laughton, 'Martin, William'(*DCB*), 12: 1185; Jeremy Black, *Culloden and the '45* (New York: St. Martin's Press, 1997), 89, 124–25.

40. Shirley to Newcastle, November 21, 1746, RG1, vol. 13, doc. 33, *PANS*. See Duncan Forbes, 'Some Considerations on the Present State of the Highlands of Scotland', in Duncan Warrand, ed., *More Culloden Papers* (Vol. 5. Inverness: R. Carruthers and Sons, 1930), 5: 98–103; W.A. Speck, *The Butcher: The Duke of Cumberland and the Suppression of the '45* (Oxford: Blackwell, 1981), 168; John

Prebble, *Culloden* (London: Penguin, 1967), 232.

41. Brenda Dunn, *The Acadians of Minas* (Ottawa: Parks Canada, 1985), 19; *Boston Evening Post*, November 24, 1746, March 2, March 9, September 28, 1747; *Pennsylvania Gazette*, December 16, 1746, March 3, March 10, 1747; Report of Pierre de Chapt, Chevalier de la Corne, September 28, 1747, RG1, vol. 3, doc. 89, *PANS*; Report of Jean Baptiste Le Guardier de Repentigny, November 1, 1747, RG1, vol. 3, doc. 90, *PANS*; *Journals of the House of Representatives of Massachusetts*, 23: 313–15, 319; Knowles and Shirley to Newcastle, April 28, 1747, RG1, vol. 13A, doc. 25, *PANS*; see also Knowles to Shirley, May 24, 1747, HM 9712, Huntington Library.

42. Shirley to Newcastle, July 8, 1747, RG1, vol. 13A, doc. 27, *PANS*.

43. Shirley to Newcastle, July 8, 1747, RG1, vol. 13A, doc. 27, *PANS*.

44. John Russell, duke of Bedford, to Newcastle, September 11, 1747, RG1, vol. 13A, doc. 30, PANS; Newcastle to Shirley, October 3, 1747, RG1, vol. 13A, doc. 31, *PANS*.

45. Jack M. Sosin, 'Louisbourg and the Peace of Aix-la-Chapelle, 1748', *William and Mary Quarterly* 3d ser. 14 (1957): 516–35. The final decision to cede Ile Royale back to France was not made until the end of the negotiations in 1748, but the ministry had considered the island a bargaining chip from the moment it learned of New England's conquest. See Newcastle to ?, August 18, 1745, Add. Mss. 32,705, doc. 65.

46. More than 1,000 New England men died, most of disease after an epidemic struck the New England garrison at Louisbourg after the French surrendered. See George Rawlyk, *Nova Scotia's Massachusetts: A Study of Massachusetts–Nova Scotia Relations, 1630 to 1784* (Montreal: McGill-Queen's University Press, 1973), 177; Gary B. Nash, *The Urban Crucible: Social Change, Political Consciousness, and the Origins of the American Revolution* (Cambridge, MA: Harvard University Press, 1979), 172; William Pencak, *War, Politics, and Revolution in Provincial Massachusetts* (Boston: Northeastern University Press, 1981), 127; Gary B. Nash, 'Failure of Female Factory Labor in Colonial Boston', *Labor History* 20

(1979): 165–88. For London newspaper pieces urging the retention of Ile Royale, see *General Advertiser*, February 21, 1746 (quoted in the *Boston Evening Post*, June 2, 1746); *General Evening Post*, July 26, 1746 (quoted in the *Boston Evening Post*, October 13, 1746); *Daily Gazetteer*, October 16, 1746 (quoted in the *Boston Evening Post*, March 2, 1747); *British Spy*, October 25, 1746 (quoted in the *New York Evening Post*, January 19, 1747); *London Magazine*, December 1746 (quoted in the *Maryland Gazette*, July 28, 1747).

47. The value of the province's notes dropped by one-half. See Douglass, Summary, 1: 357; *Boston Evening Post*, September 25, 1749.

48. Mascarene to Joseph Gorham, August 6, 1748, in Adam Shortt, V.K. Johnston, and Gustave Lactot, eds., *Documents Relating to Currency, Exchange and Finance in Nova Scotia, with Prefatory Documents, 1675–1758* (Ottawa: J.O. Patenaude, 1933), 274–6.

49. 'Report by Captain Morris to Governor Shirley', 1749, in *Report of the Archives Branch for 1912, 79–83*; Shirley to Bedford, February 18, 1749, RG1, vol 13, doc. 45, *PANS*; see also Mascarene to Board of Trade, October 17, 1748, CO 217/32, doc. 103, *PRO*.

50. See especially Douglass, Summary; *Independent Advertiser*.

51. See, for example, *Independent Advertiser*, February 8, 1748; William Douglass, 'To the Publishers of the *Independent Advertiser*', *Independent Advertiser*, July 4, 1748; *Independent Advertiser*, February 13, 1749. Political economists had been advancing this argument against imperial expansion at least since 1670. See Roger Coke, *A Discourse of Trade* (London, 1670. Reprint, New York: Arno Press, 1972), 7; *The Royal Fishery Revived* (London, 1670).

52. See, for example, *London Evening Post*, March 27–29, 1746.

53. James Henretta, *'Salutary Neglect'*: Colonial Administration Under the Duke of Newcastle (Princeton: Princeton University Press, 1972): 287–90. See also *Pennsylvania Gazette*, October 28, 1748; *Boston Evening Post*, May 1, 1749; Instructions for Edward Cornwallis, May 2, 1749, in Gaudet, 'Acadian Genealogy and Notes', 49–51.

54. *Boston Evening Post*, May 1, 1749.

55. *Boston Evening Post*, June 5, 1749; Cornwallis to Bedford, March 9, 1750, CO 217/33, doc. 17, *PRO*.

56. Winthrop Pickard Bell, The 'Foreign Protestants' and the Settlement of Nova Scotia: The History of a Piece of Arrested Colonial Policy in the Eighteenth Century (Toronto: University of Toronto Press, 1961), 284.

57. Instructions for Cornwallis, May 2, 1749, in Gaudet, 'Acadian Genealogy and Notes', 49–51.

58. Ibid., 49.

59. Ibid., 51; see also Board of Trade to the *SPG*, C/Can NS 1, iv, Records of the *SPG*.

60. Instructions for Cornwallis, May 2 1749, in Gaudet, 'Acadian Genealogy and Notes', 51.

61. Linda Colley, *Britons: Forging the Nation, 1707–1837* (New Haven: Yale University Press, 1942).

4   From N.E.S. Griffiths, 'The Decision to Deport', in *From Migrant to Acadian: A North American Border People, 1604–1755* (Montreal and Kingston: McGill-Queen's University Press, 2005), 431–64, 574–81.

One of the earliest historical accounts, as distinguished from the contemporary reports in newspapers, of the events of 1755 was published by Abbé Guillaume Raynal in 1766.[1] In his opinion, the Acadians had been deported because of the prevailing climate of the time, a period of 'national jealousies, and of that greed of government which devours country and man.'[2] But, Raynal concluded, the British had committed a great crime in removing an innocent pastoral people from their lands. Two years later, a work by a certain William Burck appeared in translation in Paris. He believed that, while the deportation was justifiable, in terms of the Franco-British conflict at the time, it involved actions that any 'humaine and generous heart only takes with regret.'[3] These differing opinions, one an explicit condemnation of a crime, the other a regretful verdict that what had taken place had been a cruel necessity, were only the first of many, increasingly bitter, disagreements over how the deportation of the Acadians should be judged.[4] By the middle of the twentieth century, more than 200 articles, books, and pamphlets had been published on the subject and since then a great many more have seen the light of day.[5] As was the case with Raynal and Burck, a significant

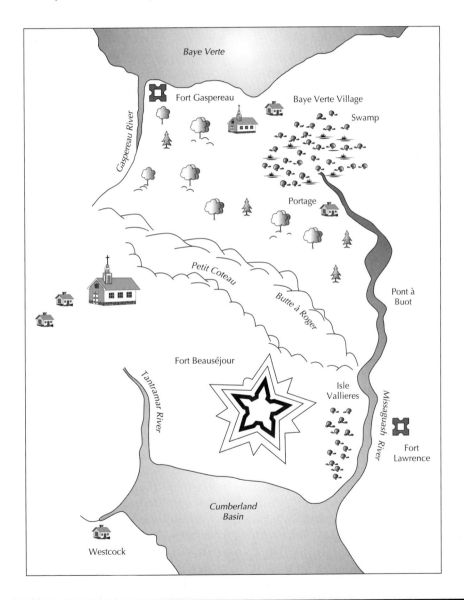

Map 1   The region of Beauséjour, 1755. Redrawn from a map by Louis de Courville (1755), reproduced in Stanley, *New France*.

number of the authors have made their judgment of what happened in 1755 the pivotal question of their work, spending relatively little time on a close analysis of the way in which the decision was reached or the immediate situation in the region at the time when the actual decision was made. The emphasis has been placed less on what is usually the first step of historical inquiry—'How did this happen?'—than on a search to discover the guilty. [. . .]

My approach is different. The focus in what follows is upon the actual experiences of those who lived in Nova Scotia in 1755, whether British administrators, French officials, military officers, or the Acadians themselves. More than anything else, this analysis has sought to present the realities of everyday eighteenth-century life for people of the North Atlantic world. In many ways, the argument I have with a number of colleagues rests as much upon an interpretation of the norms of eighteenth-century life as it does upon questions of ideology. The crucial debate turns upon whether the deportation was the result of a planned policy flowing from ethnic hatred or something that occurred as a consequence of local military action at a time of intense rivalry between competing empires. My interpretation suggests that short-term decision making is central to what happened, the personal convictions of the individuals in question being the framework for their actions but of less immediate significance than the immediate problems that had to be solved.

Of major influence upon the course of events leading to the deportation was the way in which the relationship between Lawrence and the Acadians developed between the late summer of 1754 and the capture of Beauséjour on 16 June 1755. Throughout these months, whenever Lawrence considered the problem of Nova Scotia security, the reliability of the Acadians during an attack by the French was always a major concern for him. The information Lawrence received about the international situation, the knowledge he had of the balance of power between Massachusetts and Île

Royale, Louisbourg and Boston, and his opinion of the reality of Acadian neutrality governed many of his reactions to Acadian matters. The Acadians' response to his internal administration of the colony, towards requests made by his forces for food and labour, as well as the intelligence he received about the strength of the forts at Beauséjour and Gaspereau were major considerations in his thinking. When the steps he took to bolster his command of the colony showed some success, Lawrence was encouraged to continue along the same lines. His organization of the forts, the co-operation of the Acadians with requests for wood for the local garrisons, tentative peace proposals from the Mi'kmaq, and some lessening of the trade between Acadian farmers and Louisbourg and Port Lajoie—all confirmed Lawrence's belief in the wisdom of his tactics. From August 1754 on, one can see Lawrence becoming more and more confident in his office. He began to take decisions without waiting for less than clear-cut directions to reach him from London. This penchant for independent action was strengthened by Governor Shirley's support of his plan to attack Beauséjour as well as by their common interpretation of the freedom of action accorded them by the imperial authorities.

In many ways, of course, Lawrence had no alternative but to act independently, decisively, and with dispatch on matters that were brought either directly to his attention or to his notice through meetings of the Council: [. . .] it usually took five months, and often more, before Lawrence received an answer to his letters to London. But Nova Scotia was ruled by a governor and Council, which he appointed to advise him. Lawrence was charged with the day-to-day administration of a sparsely settled colony, with a minimum of troops and his few councillors. Together, they were responsible for the way in which the civil administration of the colony was carried out and for the security of its settlements. The questions confronting them involved not only the usual difficulties of colonial administrations with matters of local government but also the complex relationship of the British administration with the Mi'kmaq and the Acadians. As well, there was the constant problem of France's strength on the borders of the colony and its influence upon the Acadian population. While clashes with French land forces during the last months of 1754 were rare, two priests, Le Loutre at Beauséjour and Henri Daudin at Pisiquid, did everything in their power to stir up both the Mi'kmaq and the Acadians against the British.[6] [. . .]

Information about events in North America had arrived in London and Paris throughout the spring and summer of 1754. The reaction in London was both stronger and more immediate than that of France. The influence of Governor Dinwiddie of Virginia and Governor Shirley of Massachusetts was far greater upon the course of British politics than that of any French North American colonial official on French policies. As well, at this time, the French were more deeply concerned with European affairs than with matters across the Atlantic, whereas the British saw North American issues of considerable moment. [. . .] The Duke of Newcastle, who had come to power in March 1754, had considerable sympathy with the colonists. [. . .] There is no doubt that there was a general consensus among the political elite that British interests, whether in Europe or in North America, had to be defended. The debate between the different factions centred, of course, upon how, when, and where action should be taken.

Newcastle had chosen Sir Thomas Robinson as secretary of state and leader of the House of Commons.[7] On 5 July 1754 Robinson wrote to both William Shirley and Charles Lawrence. [. . .]

Both Lawrence and Shirley considered that these letters gave them the liberty to mount a joint expedition against the French in the Saint John valley and in the Chignecto isthmus. For Lawrence, Massachusetts co-operation was crucial. Without Shirley's permission to raise volunteers from Massachusetts, without loans from Apthorp and Hancock, Boston merchants and bankers, Lawrence had neither the

manpower nor the money to undertake any major military enterprise, let alone one that would require at least an additional 2,000 men to serve in Nova Scotia. Shirley [. . .] was convinced that war was imminent and [. . .] believed that, should Nova Scotia be lost, 'the Eastern parts of the Province of Massachusetts Bay, and the whole Province of New Hampshire . . . together with the Rivers of St. John's, Pentagoet, and Kennebeck with the whole fishery to the Westward of Newfoundland' would soon be in French hands. It was this conviction that fuelled Shirley's support of Lawrence and ensured a sympathetic reception for the latter's request for assistance when it reached him in the first week of December.

[. . .]

Shirley's rhetoric on the opportunity for 'ridding the Province of its dangerous Neighbours, with all the Mischiefs that threaten'd it from their remaining so near'[8] was not the sole argument in favour of Massachusetts endorsing the governor's proposal for raising 2,000 volunteers. There was also the matter of the immediate financial benefits to Boston merchants, since it was they who would provide supplies and services for the men. There would also be further economic advantages to the Commonwealth, flowing from the terms under which the men would serve. They were promised 'the King's Bounty Money, pay, uniform, Cloathing (the most that can be got here) and Arms, and have everything provided for them which is necessary for their comfortable Subsistence.' The question of security and the possibility of financial gain proved useful arguments for John Winslow, who was given the rank of lieutenant-colonel and put in charge of recruiting for the new regiment. [. . .] The commander-in-chief of the expedition remained Lieutenant-Colonel Monckton, aged 29, a regular army officer who would end his career as a lieutenant-general, governor of Portsmouth, England, and an *MP*.[9] [. . .]

During the months that Monckton had spent in Boston, overseeing the preparations for the expedition, Lawrence had been considering what would follow the capture of Beauséjour. The lieutenant-governor had been aware that those Acadians who had lived in the area, some only since Beaubassin had been set on fire in 1750, would present political difficulties. Many of the Acadians had established farms on land which had previously been under British supervision but which had not yet been surveyed. As a result, the Nova Scotian administration considered their title to the land dubious at best. As far as Lawrence was concerned, the attitude of these Acadians could be expected to be the same as that of those who had asked to be readmitted to British-controlled territory: argumentative, disputatious, and motivated by a strong belief that they had political rights that the British must respect. But, as will be seen, Lawrence in January 1755 was still unclear as to what would be the appropriate measures to take once the fort was captured. When he had written to the Board of Trade at the beginning of August 1754, he had tentatively stated that, should these Acadians refuse the unmodified oath of allegiance, when the opportunity to take it was given to them, he was of the opinion that it would be 'better if they were away.'[10] The lieutenant-governor had hedged this suggestion by remarking that he 'would be very far from attempting such a step without your Lordships approbation.' The Board of Trade did not compose a response to this letter until 29 October 1754.[11] Their dispatch arrived in Halifax at the beginning of January 1755.[12] It was not, in any way, a clear directive for decisive action. [. . .] The best advice they could offer was that the matter should be referred to Chief Justice Jonathan Belcher, who had taken the oaths of office at the Council meeting of 21 October 1754.[13] [. . .] In sum, in shaping his policy towards the Acadians, Lawrence was left to his own devices and to what guidance and recommendations members of the Council could offer.

Their lordships were aware, of course, of the parameters within which Lawrence would work. He was a successful regular army officer, whose career showed the extent to which he accepted the ideas of the politically and socially powerful of the time. Eighteenth-century society, French or British, Germanic or Hispanic, was hierarchical and brutal and paid considerable attention to hereditary rights.[14] Government measures taken to control dissidents differed from state to state but were, without exception, ruthless, without mercy. [. . .] In Britain, transportation of the indigent, vagrants, and children without visible means of support had begun in the reign of James I. In 1617, for example, a hundred children were dispatched from London to Virginia, their passages paid for by collections from various parishes, where they were considered a burden.[15] [. . .] For those transported as punishment, bonded service could be little better than slavery. The English Civil War provided the greatest impetus to the practice of removing difficult subjects from the care of the home government to the colonies. In 1648, when Cromwell's forces were unquestionably victorious, transportation for the defeated Stuart forces became commonplace.[16] From this time on, the English colonies in North America, as well as in the West Indies, received diverse groups of dissidents, Scottish covenanters, youngsters from Ireland, and Scottish military exiles. The return of the monarchy did not end the practice. [. . .] Thus, by the middle of the eighteenth century, British authorities, civil and military, colonial and imperial, were accustomed to transporting a motley collection of subjects, under varying regulations, from one jurisdictional area of the realm to another.

Further, Lawrence would have been aware not only of the general use of transportation but of the deportation of some 2,000 French and Acadian inhabitants of Île Royale to France in 1745 and of the forced French relocation of a minimum of 1,500 Acadians from the Beaubassin area to Île Saint-Jean after 1750. And so there was nothing original, in late 1754 and early 1755, in Lawrence considering deporting the Acadians in the Beauséjour region, and it is clear from his correspondence with Monckton that the lieutenant-governor was, indeed, thinking seriously about such a possibility. In a letter to Monckton written on 30 January 1755, Lawrence told him that, once the fort had surrendered, he would not have the oaths of allegiance proposed to 'the French Inhabitants' of the Chignecto area 'as their taking them would tye our hands and disqualify us to extirpate them, should it be found (as I fancy it will) ever-after necessary.'[17] Lawrence, at this point, was in the process of making up his mind over the best way to secure Nova Scotia. He was hopeful of populating the Beaubassin area with English-speaking Protestants, concluding his letter to Monckton with the suggestion that, if any of the Massachusetts troops had the 'least disposition' to settle in the lands that were already controlled by the British but had been deserted since the burning of Beaubassin, they should be told that they would receive 'all the encouragement' he had the power to offer. [. . .]

At the same time [Lawrence's] attitude towards the Acadians was reinforced by the appointment of the chief justice, Jonathan Belcher, as a Council member. It was Belcher who, on the day that Nova Scotia Council resolved to deport the Acadians, wrote the legal and political defence of the action.[18] Belcher had been born in 1710 to an established New England family, his mother's father having been lieutenant-governor of New Hampshire. His other grandfather had been a successful Boston merchant and member of the Massachusetts Council. His own father was governor of Massachusetts and New Hampshire from 1730 to 1741 and governor of New Jersey from 1747 to 1757.[19] [. . .] Until his appointment as the first chief justice of Nova Scotia, at the age of 44, Belcher had spent his working life outside North America but his childhood and early adulthood had been as a privileged member of the New England elite. [. . .]

The absence of any major discussion about the Acadians during this period by the Council is no indication of the actual relationship that existed at the time between the Acadians within Nova Scotia and the British administration. The rancour of the previous autumn continued. News about the lives of relatives on the Chignecto isthmus and along the Memramcook, the Petitcodiac, and the Shepody, where Le Loutre was active, served to sharpen Acadian ambivalence. Le Loutre was engaged not only in overseeing the building the dyke on the Aulac River in the Beauséjour area but also in encouraging the construction of smaller dykes on the Memramcook and the Shepody.[20] His aim was to stabilize the Acadian settlements, within the territory controlled by the French, by strengthening the development of traditional Acadian farming practices. At the same time, he worked to persuade the Acadians to recognize his authority to confirm their rights to the lands they farmed. The Acadians were hesitant, especially those who had their lands granted to them before 1710. Many had no wish to accept greater regulation of their affairs from any source, whether from the military at Beauséjour or from Le Loutre personally.[21] As well, the abbé demanded that they swear loyalty to Louis XV, their 'legitimate sovereign',[22] a demand that the French government had made ever since 1751 with respect to the Acadians who came under their control.[23] [. . .] All this activity seemed to presage French determination to remain an effective power in the region and perhaps the possibility of French reoccupation of Nova Scotia.

But the most important determinant of the attitude of many of the Acadians, in the spring of 1755, must have been the manner and policies of the French officials in the region. There were four administrators, the most senior being Augustin de Boschenry de Drucour, who had arrived to take charge at Louisbourg in 1754. That same year, Gabriel Rousseau de Villejouin had been appointed as major and commandant of Île Saint-Jean. Charles Deschamps de Boishébert et de Raffetot, who had played such an important role in the engagement at Grand Pré in 1747, was at mouth of the Saint John River as commandant of Fort La Tour, and Louis Du Pont Duchambon de Vergor was the commandant of Beauséjour. [. . .] Vergor was joined at Beauséjour by the appointment that same year, 1754, of Louis-Thomas Jacau de Fiedmont as the chief engineer for the fort, and Louis-Léonard Aumasson de Courville as notary for the Acadian settlements in the area. Jacau left an account, from a military perspective, of the fall of Beauséjour and Gaspereau which, as Webster points out, sought to place the blame everywhere except upon his own shortcomings as the man in charge of the defences of the fort for the two previous years.[24] The memoir of Aumasson de Courville is a much longer work and includes a wide variety of comments on Vergor and Le Loutre.[25] Together with the journal of Thomas Pichon (Tyrell), a British spy who had somehow attached himself as a commissary officer to Beauséjour, these works provide a vivid picture of the disorganization among the officers stationed there and the general state of disrepair of the fort in 1755.[26] Vergor himself was convinced until the day the British force arrived that there would be no major fighting in the region that year, so nothing had been done to prepare a defence against an attack.[27] There had been no concerted effort during the last weeks of winter and the first weeks of more clement weather to recruit Acadians to strengthen the fort or to assemble those who had been given militia responsibilities.

So, before the anchoring of the Boston fleet in Annapolis Bay, little had taken place that would have alerted the Acadians to the possibility of a major outbreak of warfare in their lands. Evidently, only the vaguest of rumours about the recruitment of volunteers in Massachusetts for an expedition against Beauséjour had reached the Acadian population. Certainly, the possibility of a major disruption of Acadian life throughout the Acadian villages of Nova Scotia would not have entered their minds. As Lawrence prepared to make Nova Scotia a completely secure outpost of the British empire in North America and to establish once and for all British control of the colony, the Acadian population, as a whole, still believed that British administrators of Nova Scotia continued to take Acadian reactions into account when making policy decisions. The existence of Halifax, of a Protestant population within the colony that was more than ten times what it had been a decade before, was not something that had made the Acadians consider any revision of their political stance. For the majority of the population, the need to alter their religious beliefs and linguistic heritage in order to remain on their lands would have unimaginable. Even if the French never reclaimed Nova Scotia, the strong French presence in the region meant visible support for Acadian retention of their customs and traditions. French control of Île Royale and Île Saint-Jean did not appear to be weakening at this time, especially after the return of Louisbourg to France in 1748. Since then, the build-up of French forces in the Chignecto area had served to strengthen the conviction, among the British as well as among the Acadians, that France was prepared to defend its presence in the area and probably had plans to expand the territory under its control.

The rapid conquest of Beauséjour [in June 1755], followed by the fall of Fort Gaspereau, and the lack of any immediate French response fundamentally altered the military situation in the region. As a consequence, the political options for the British administration at Halifax were broadened and those of the Acadians narrowed. [. . .]

The establishment of Halifax and the founding of Lunenburg had presaged a decision, on the part of London, to make Nova Scotia as much a British colony as the other British colonies in North America. From the moment he was appointed as lieutenant-governor, Lawrence was eager to make this decision a reality. We have a great deal of information on how Lawrence saw his own policy. He wrote, at length, to Governor Shirley of Massachusetts, to other governors of British colonies in North America, and to the authorities in London. By the summer of 1754, Lawrence had decided that those Acadians who refused to take an unqualified oath of loyalty to the British crown were a major stumbling block to fulfilling his plans.[28] At the same time, he saw that the French control of the Chignecto isthmus was both a constant encouragement to those Acadians who were dissatisfied with the British government and a potential military threat to British control of Nova Scotia. While the attack on Beauséjour was taking place, his view of the unreliability of Acadian neutrality was strengthened. As has been previously mentioned, Lawrence had taken steps to prevent any major aid being sent to Beauséjour by the Acadians under his jurisdiction. He also had made an attempt to disarm the Acadians of the Minas Basin and Captain Murray had issued orders to this effect from Fort Edward in the first week of June.[29] As well, a number of Acadian canoes were confiscated. The extent to which the Acadians complied has been a matter of debate among historians but the evidence shows that the majority of them did surrender at least some of their guns. Judge Isaac Deschamps, who was in Pisiquid at the time, stated that just under 3,000 guns had been brought in.[30] The strongest evidence for their compliance, however, is the petition of the Acadians for the return of their guns, which was presented to Captain Murray on 10 June and forwarded to Lawrence within the week. It is hardly likely that the Acadians would have taken time and effort to ask for their guns back had they not given up sufficient to make the request worthwhile.

[. . .]

On 24 June the Acadians arrived with another communication to the captain, this one much shorter and signed by 44 of the settlers 'in the name of them all'.[31] Obviously, the news of Beauséjour's capitulation on 16 June had reached the Minas Basin for in this communication 'the Inhabitants of Mines, Pisiquid and the river Canard' begged Lawrence to understand that 'if there shall be found any error or want of respect towards the government' in their recent memorial this was 'intirely contrary to their intention'.[32]

It is unlikely that this memorial would have reached Lawrence until just before the Council meeting of 3 July. Certainly, he could not have received it before 25 June, on which day he sent a dispatch to Monckton about the treatment to be accorded to the Acadian settlers in the Chignecto area. In this communication, Lawrence showed his continued concern for the security of the colony, his exasperation with the settlers in the Chignecto isthmus, and the policy he wished to pursue towards them as well as the uncertainty he had about implementing that policy. He was convinced that 'unless we remain in possession undoubtedly the French will return and re-establish and we can never expect a lasting peace with the Indians, without first totally extirpating the French who incite make war . . .' [. . .] There is no doubt that Lawrence had a great wish to solve the Acadian problem, once and for all, but he hesitated over the imposition of truly Draconian measures. As well, he obviously considered that an unqualified oath of allegiance was something which would have to be taken into account. [. . .] Thus, on 3 July 1755, when Lawrence met with 15 Acadian leaders from the Minas area who had been summoned to Halifax to explain their reasons for the petition of 10 June, the lieutenant-governor was a man still unsure of the military security of his colony, wanting unequivocal proof that the Acadians had accepted the reality of British government of Nova Scotia and of their role as British subjects. He was also aware that, however inconvenient it might be, the Acadians had some civil rights under British law.

Nevertheless, Lawrence had written to the Board of Trade, four days before this Council meeting, about what he intended to do with the Acadians settled in the isthmus. His dispatch first reported the surrender of Beauséjour and Gaspereau and then went on to state that 'the deserting French' were surrendering their arms, after which they were 'to be driven out of the country', although they might very well be put to repairing Fort Beauséjour, now renamed Fort Cumberland, before they were sent into exile.[33] While there is no evidence that, at this point, Lawrence contemplated the wholesale deportation of the Acadian population, the possibility of the dispersal of a significant number of Acadians was definitely in his mind.

The attitude of the Acadians at the Council meeting of 3 July was in keeping with their past behaviour over close to a century. It did nothing to make Lawrence reconsider his position. [. . .] In fact, as the minutes of the Council meetings throughout the month of July 1755 show, Lawrence and his advisers considered the Acadians not only politically unreliable but also socially impertinent, lacking in proper deference to their betters.

It is not surprising, then, that the atmosphere at the Council meetings in the first week of July was one of mutual incomprehension.[34] Colonel Lawrence chaired this and all other Council meetings during July. There were four other Council members present on the meetings of the 3rd and 4th of the month. [. . .] None of them had any personal acquaintanceship with the Acadians, knowing them only as a French-speaking, Catholic people who claimed to be different from the French but whose behaviour in the face of French intrusions on the borders of the colony was, at best, unreliable.

It was clear from the outset that the councillors found the Acadians' rhetoric deeply offensive. Before the Acadians were called into the meeting, Council members had come to the unanimous conclusion that the memorial was 'highly arrogant and insidious, an insult upon His Majesty's Authority and Government, and deserved the highest Resentment . . . '[35] Once the Acadians were present, it became quickly apparent that the two parties were at complete odds. The Acadians had composed their petition in the belief that Lawrence and the Council regarded them as people to be accorded consideration. The inhabitants had tried to explain, in the second paragraph of their communication, their difficulties. 'Permit us, if you please, Sir, to make known the annoying circumstances in which we are

placed, to the prejudice of the tranquillity we ought to enjoy', words that showed that, in their own eyes, they had every right to complain to those governing them.[36] They went on to ask the Council to take their past conduct into consideration as proof of their loyalty to the British. To this, the councillors answered that 'their past Conduct was considered, and that the Government were sorry to have occasion to say that their Conduct had been undutifull and very ungrateful for the Lenity shown to them.' From that point on, the minutes show that the councillors were united in demonstrating to the Acadians that the latter had shown a 'constant disposition to Assist His Majesty's Enemies, and to distress his subjects.'

[. . .] Towards the end of the meeting, the essence of the administration's position became clear: the Acadians were told that their loyalty and obedience could best be properly demonstrated by 'their immediately taking the Oath of Allegiance in the Common form before the Council.' Until this point, and including the request for the oath, the members of Council, while more abrasive than their predecessors, had acted much as former administrations had done. But when the Acadians responded, as they had done in the past, by saying that 'they had not come prepared to resolve the Council on that Head', they were then informed that for 'these Six Years past, the same thing had often been proposed' and that they must have 'fully considered and determined this point with regard to themselves before now.' The Acadians next asked to return and 'consult the Body of the People . . . as they were desirous of either refusing or accepting the Oath in a Body.' The councillors rejected this reply as 'extraordinary' and gave them an hour to consult among themselves. On their return, the Acadians were of the same mind but offered to take the oath 'as they had done before.' The councillors answered that 'His Majesty had disapproved of the manner of their taking the Oath before' and that any such compromise was now unacceptable. At this point the meeting was adjoined until the next day at ten o'clock.

The next morning, the Acadians repeated their decision that they could not take the oath without consulting their communities. At this point, Lawrence and the Council, composed of the same people as the day before, informed the Acadians that they had now provided enough evidence to make the Council consider them 'no longer as Subjects of His Britannick Majesty, but as Subjects of the King of France, and as such they must hereafter be Treated; and they were Ordered to Withdraw.'[37] The minutes record that the Council members then decided among themselves that Captain Murray should order the 'French Inhabitants forthwith to Choose and send to Halifax new Deputies with the General Resolution of the said Inhabitants in regard to taking the Oath, and that none of them should for the future be admitted to Take it after having once refused to do but that effectual Measures ought to be taken to remove all such Recusants out of the Province.' The 15 Acadians were now required to return to the meeting and were told of this decision. They then offered to take the oath but were informed that 'they would not be indulged with such Permission, And they were thereupon ordered into Confinement.'

It is striking that the Council decided, at this point, that refusal to take the oath of allegiance as offered would deprive the Acadians of their status as British subjects. In fact, it was a judgment that even Belcher and Lawrence would not repeat. It went against the tradition of international law, which had been accepted, particularly in the case of the Acadians after Utrecht, by both France and Great Britain, that peoples whose territories changed governments through treaties became unequivocally subjects of their new rulers.[38] In also went against all previous arguments by British administrators, including Cornwallis, on the status of Acadians. Finally, it contradicted English legal tradition since before the Tudors, as it had evolved with the linking of Wales and Ireland to England. By the time of Henry VIII, those

born on territory ruled at the moment of their birth by England were considered as natural-born subjects.[39] The majority of the Acadian population within peninsular Nova Scotia had by this time, 42 years after Utrecht, been born on British territory. Belcher's influence on the matter is difficult to assess. His experience in Ireland ought to have prevented him making a judgment that the Acadians' status as subjects depended on an oath of allegiance. By the end of month, when he wrote a defence of the decision to deport the Acadians en masse, he based his opinions upon the question of their loyalty as subjects, rather than upon their position as aliens. This is the argument that would be used in the future to defend the deportation.

The legal argument over the link between the oath of allegiance and the rights of the Acadians as British subjects had little import for the immediate circumstances of the Acadians in July 1754. At that time, their fate depended upon the designs of Lawrence and the Council, designs that become clear when the complete records of the Council meetings for 4, 14, and 15 July are read. The brief minutes of the meeting of 4 July alone leave some question in one's mind as to whether the decision to remove out of the province those who refused the oath referred to just certain individuals from the Minas area or to the Acadians as a whole. [. . .]

On 9 July, Admiral Edward Boscawen dropped anchor in Halifax harbour. On 14 July, Lawrence called another Council meeting; it was attended by the same people who had attended the meetings of 4 and 5 July.[40] Lawrence informed the Council that he had received instructions, which had been sent from the secretary of state to all governors on 15 April, requesting them to cooperate with Admiral Boscawen and provide him with all obtainable intelligence.[41] [. . .] At the meeting that took place on the 15 July, once more attended by those members who had been present at the meetings earlier in the month but with the addition of the two admirals, Lawrence laid out 'the proceedings of the Council in regard to the French Inhabitants, and desired their opinion and advice thereon.'[42] The admirals agreed that 'it was now Time to oblige the said Inhabitants to Take the Oath of Allegiance to His Majesty, or to quit the Country.' At this meeting, it was also decided that it was 'absolutely necessary for the Good of His Majesty's Service and the Security of this His Province, to retain in pay the Two Thousand New England Troops . . . ' [. . .]

The support of the admirals for Lawrence was precisely that: support. Obviously, they had not arrived in Nova Scotia with instructions to take over the administration of the colony, nor did they have either the requisite knowledge or the interest to do so. What they did provide was an agreement by senior British naval personnel that the policy being pursued by the administration of Nova Scotia seemed sensible, considering the overall military situation. Boscawen's presence at Halifax until October 1755, and the presence of the fleet in the region, obviously encouraged Lawrence.[43] But Lawrence remained the person in charge of the colony and ultimately the one responsible for its security. [. . .]

Lawrence wrote to the Board of Trade, presenting his view of the situation that confronted him. Neither in this dispatch nor in any other of his letters to London did Lawrence suggest that anyone else was responsible for the evolution of his policy towards the Acadians. Of course, he sought, and gained, the approval of the Council at each stage of its development; it was not a policy that the lieutenant-governor had fashioned against the general beliefs and attitudes of his advisers. However, essentially, it was his policy and the administrations of Cornwallis and Hopson had shown that it would have been possible to pursue another course. One of its most important antecedents was Shirley's proposal after the capture of Louisbourg in 1745, but no dispatch from London, whether from the Board of Trade or from any of the secretaries of state, suggested anything similar. Ever since 1713 the policy of the British government was one of determined refusal to admit that there was

any great necessity to resolve the issue, one way or another, of the oath of allegiance. Further, Britain had consistently argued against sending the Acadians out of the colony and these arguments were repeated again in a letter from the secretary of state, Robinson, to Lawrence on 13 August 1755.[44] In it Robinson wrote that 'it cannot, therefore, be too much recommended to you, to use the greatest Caution and Prudence in your Conduct, towards these neutrals, and to assure such of Them, as may be trusted, especially upon their taking the Oaths to His Majesty and His Government, That they may remain in quiet Possession of their Settlements under proper Regulation . . . ' This dispatch was in reply to one sent by Lawrence on 28 June 1755, in which he had broached the possibility of deporting Acadians, primarily from the Beauséjour region. Unfortunately, Robinson's dispatch arrived in Halifax only in late October 1755. As has already been mentioned, Lawrence's dispatch of August 1754, in which he pleaded for guidance on the issue, had received no other answer than that the problem he raised was, indeed, interesting and he should seek the advice of Belcher, the newly appointed chief justice of the colony.

Now, on 18 July, Lawrence reported his actions to his superiors.[45] It is a highly intelligent dispatch and guilty less of direct lying than of suppressing evidence and suggesting misleading implications. In relating what had happened at the Council meetings of 4 and 5 July, he omitted to mention that he had not, in fact, informed the Acadians clearly, before the final request to take an unqualified oath of allegiance, that their refusal would see them imprisoned and deported to France at the first opportunity. Moreover, he concluded the dispatch by saying that he was 'determined to bring the Inhabitants to compliance, or rid the province of such perfidious subjects.' There is no evidence whatsoever to suggest that Lawrence was then determined to exile not only the 15 men from the Minas Basin but also the Acadians who had settled in the Chignecto area, let alone all the Acadians settled elsewhere. Indeed, the information in his dispatch concerning the incarceration of the deputies on George's Island, until they could be sent to France, increases the impression that Lawrence was considering only a small group of the population for exile. It is possible, of course, that Lawrence was convinced that the Acadian population, especially those of the Annapolis region, would not prove obdurate.[46] The dispatch of 18 July, however, quite plainly ruled out any possibility of negotiation with those who did prove recalcitrant. Any softening of this position became less than likely when rumours of Braddock's defeat reached Halifax on 23 July.[47]

In the meantime, of course, from the moment the men from Minas had been detained at Halifax, the Acadian communities had been forced to consider their position on the oath. They responded to the demand for their presence at Halifax, 30 men from Annapolis Royal arriving there on 25 July and 70 from the Minas settlements on 28 July. The written response brought by the Annapolis group emphasized their past conduct, asserting that 'several of us have risked our lives to give information to the government concerning the enemy; and have also, when necessary, laboured with all our heart on the repairs of Fort Annapolis.'[48] The memorial stated that the deputies had been 'charged strictly to contract no new oath.'[49] [. . .] Their answer was discussed at the Council meeting of 25 July. [. . .] On this occasion, the Acadians were told clearly that 'if they once refused the Oath, they would never after be permitted to Take it, but would infallibly lose their Possessions.' They were then dismissed but required to attend another Council meeting on Monday, 28 July.

The same men were present at this meeting as had been in attendance three days earlier. Belcher presented to this meeting a memorial bringing together his ideas as to why the Acadians should be expelled. It was not sent to London until the spring of 1756.[50] It was a mean-minded document, full of historical inaccuracies and of specious arguments. In

it the Acadians were accused of outright and continuous support of the French since 1713, and it was implied that all British administrators since 1713 had acted contrary to 'the spirit and letter of His Majesty's Instructions'. Belcher went on to assert that, to allow the Acadians to take the oath once they had refused to do so, would defeat 'the Intention of the Expedition to Beau Sejour'. He went on to say that the Acadian presence 'may retard the Progress of Settlement . . . since the French at Lunenburgh and the Lunenburghers themselves . . . are more disposed to the French than to the English.' In any case, Belcher wrote, even if the Acadians did take the oath, 'it is well known, that they will not be influenced' by it 'after a [papal] Dispensation'.[51] He concluded by remarking that the presence of Massachusetts forces in the colony had provided an opportunity to remove the Acadians which, 'once the armament is withdrawn', would be lost. At that point, the Acadians would 'undoubtedly resume their Perfidy and Treacheries and with more arts and rancour than before.' Belcher therefore advised that 'all the French inhabitants may be removed from the Province' from 'the highest necessity which is lex temporis, to the interests of His Majesty in the Province.'

And so, when the Acadians were called before the Council on 28 July, their fate had already been decided. [. . .]

There had been no attempt made, in any of the Council meetings, to persuade the Acadians that taking the oath would guarantee them the peaceful possession of their lands. From the beginning, Lawrence had treated the Acadian population as a liability and something to control by fear. His policy had been one of accusation and demand. He had a fundamental disbelief in the possibility of the Acadian population being of any value to Nova Scotia and thus his communications with the various settlements were always threatening: 'this will happen if you do not conform to my orders.' Such a policy was bound to be less than successful, given that the Acadians had heard threats of exile and eviction from British administrators before. For more than 40 years, such threats had been no more than words. It was unlikely that the Acadians were disposed to take Lawrence seriously at this point, even with the presence of much greater military resources in the colony than they had ever known. As well, their forced exile would have seemed an almost unimaginable possibility—they could not conceive of a worse fate than transportation to France. Thus, the Acadian delegates unanimously refused the request to take the oath. They were sent into confinement and the minutes record that 'as it had been before determined to send all the French Inhabitants out of the Province if they refused to Take the Oaths, nothing now remained to be considered but what measures should be taken to send them away, and where they should be sent to.' The final paragraph of the minutes of this momentous meeting noted that, 'after mature Consideration, it was unanimously Agreed That to prevent as much as possible their Attempting to return and molest the Settlers that may be set down on their lands it would be most proper to send them to be distributed amongst the several Colonies on the Continent, and that a sufficient Number of Vessels should be hired with all possible Expedition for that purpose.'

An understanding of the sequence of events that led to the deportation leaves unanswered a great many questions. But it goes a long way to answering how such a catastrophe, the destruction of an established community of people, who had built a thriving society over more than a century and a half, occurred. It even goes some of the way to disentangling the complex of ideas and decisions that turned the possibility of the removal of Acadians from Nova Scotia, broached at the time of the Treaty of Utrecht, into the reality of exile. Insistence upon the context of eighteenth-century European life leads to a greater place being given to the contemporary realities of communication through time and across space. It provokes questions about how the belief and opinions of the elites affected the actions of those who lived on the periphery of the European empires in North America. Above all, the reconstruction of who actually did what and when brings to the fore the political and social conventions that were widespread at the time.

The Acadian deportation, as a government action, was of a pattern with other contemporary happenings, from the deportations after the 1745 rebellion in Scotland to actions on the European continent during the War of the Austrian Succession. It was, in many ways, quintessentially an act of a time when the state rested its authority upon the hereditary right of the monarch and when, as Dummett and Nicol have pointed out, there was 'a vertical relationship between monarch and individual, not a horizontal one between the members of a nation or the citizens of a body politics.'[52] But this conclusion, that the Acadian deportation was not essentially an extraordinary incident, does little more than scratch the surface of the questions posed. There are at least three ways in which the events of 1755 were significantly different from the other such occurrences. First, as we have seen, the possibility of removing the Acadians from the colony had been a matter of discussion by both French and English from the time of Treaty of Utrecht in 1713.[53] It had a long history as a proposition whereas the other deportations were the immediate consequence of particular actions, the solution to recent and immediate problems. Secondly, the actual pressure for the deportation came as much from a neighbouring territory as from within the jurisdiction itself. The Commonwealth of Massachusetts and its governor, Shirley, were as fully implicated in the event as were the officials in place in Nova Scotia. Further, as has already been mentioned but bears repeating, the final authority, London, had consistently argued against such action since 1713 and reiterated this argument once more in a letter sent from Whitehall on 13 August 1755. Thirdly, the enterprise itself was significantly different from the deportations that followed the Monmouth and Jacobite rebellions. Those were organized after battles had been fought against those sent into exile and were the result of judgments made in a law court about individuals. As well, the number deported was, in each case, only a fraction of the communities concerned. The Acadian deportation involved the removal of almost an entire society, which had been judged as a collectivity. People were dispatched to other communities with a letter of recommendation by the man in charge of the operation, suggesting that, since the deportation would divide Acadian strength, 'they May be of some Use as Most of them are Healthy Strong People; And as they Cannot easily collect themselves together again, it be out of their Power to Do any Mischief And they May become Profitable and it is possible, in time Faithful subjects.'[54]

Finally, of course, the greatest difference between the Acadian deportation and the other events is what happened afterwards: neither Jacobite nor Huguenot went into exile with the capacity to retain a coherent identity. The Acadians did. They had always been involved in shaping their own lives. In 1713, when 'Acadia or Nova Scotia' was transferred to Great Britain, the Acadians themselves, as much as the French or the English, decided that they would remain as subjects of the British empire rather than move to Île Royale, territory that the French still held.[55] In fact, the Acadians' stance represented two political beliefs that confronted the principles of hereditary power. The first was their conviction that they were indeed a people, distinct from the French of France and therefore with different political ambitions. The second belief was that, despite the actions of empires and the decisions of princes, the Acadians had every right to debate and present ideas about how and where they should live to those who claimed them as subjects. However skeptical others have been about the existence of Acadian identity, the Acadians themselves never seem to have doubted it. In considering their history, one has to give this 'obstinacy' its due, particularly when 'what happened next', the aftermath of the deportation, is examined. The Acadians had not been a collection of uneducated, illiterate, and ignorant peasants—the goods and chattels of others—before July 1755.

NOTES

1. *Histoire philosophique et politique de l'établissment des Européennes dans les deux Indes*, 1766 ed., 7 vols.

2. 'des jalousies nationales, de cette cupidité des gouvernements qui dévorent les terres et les hommes': ibid., 6:364.

3. 'font telles qu'un coeur humain & généreux ne les adopte jamais qu'à regret': William Burck, *Histoire des colonies européennes dans l'Amérique en six parties . . .* (Paris: Merlin 1767), 2 vols., 2:319. My translation.

4. For a collection of opinions on the issue, see N.E.S. Griffiths, *The Acadian deportation: Deliberate perfidy or cruel necessity?* (Toronto: Copp Clark 1969).

5. For the nineteenth-century debate, see Francis Parkman, Montcalm and Wolfe (2 vols. Boston: Little, Brown 1884) and *A half-century of conflict* (2 vols. Boston: Little 1897), and H.R. Casgrain, *Un pèlerinage au pays d'Evangéline* (Quebec:

Demers 1887). The debate was continued in the twentieth century by a great number of writers, most recently by Robert Sauvageau, *Acadie: La guerre de Cents Ans des Français d'Amérique aux Maritimes et en Lauisiane, 1678–1769* (Paris: Berger-Levrault 1987); Yves Cazaux, *L'Acadie: Histoire des Acadiens du XVIIe siècle à nos jours* (Paris: Albin Michel 1992); and Geoffrey Plank, *An unsettled conquest: The British campaign against the peoples of Acadia* (Philadelphia: University of Pennsylvania Press 2001). The bibliographies produced by the Centre d'Études Acadiennes, at the Université de Moncton, New Brunswick, are the first place to begin a survey of this literature. See, in particular, *Inventaire général*, vol. 2, *Bibliographies acadienne . . . à 1975* (n.d.), and various supplements. Worthwhile consulting, too, is CGriffiths, 'The Acadian deportation: A study in historiography and literature' (M.A. thesis,

University of New Brunswick 1957), which provides a critical survey of what was published before 1956.

6.   A full account of their actions is found in Micheline Dumont-Johnson, *Apôtres ou agitateurs: la France missionnaire en Acadie* (Trois-Rivières: Boréal Express 1970), 116–28.

7.   Robinson had been secretary to the embassy at Paris from 1723 to 1730 and plenipotentiary at the peace negotiations leading to the Treaty of Aix-la-Chapelle in 1748. He was appointed a member of the Board of Trade in 1748–49. See Alan Valentine, *The British establishment, 1760–1784: An eighteenth century biographical dictionary* (Norman: University of Oklahoma Press 1970), 2:743–4.

8.   For Governor Shirley's speech in February 1755, see *Doc. Hist. St. Maine*, 12:350–62.

9.   I.K. Steele, 'Robert Monckton,' DCB, 4:540–2.

10.   NAC, CO 217, 15, Lawrence to the Board of Trade, 1 Aug. 1754; Thomas Beamish Akins, ed., *Acadia and Nova Scotia: Documents relating to the Acadian French and the first British colonization of the province, 1714–1758* (Cottonport: Polyanthos 1979. Repr. of Halifax: Charles Annand 1869 ed.), 213.

11.   NAC, CO 218, 5, Board of Trade to Lawrence, 29 Oct. 1754; partially printed in Akins, *Acadia*, 235–7.

12.   NAC, CO 217, 15, Lawrence to the Board of Trade, 12 Jan. 1755.

13.   NAC, CO 220, NS (B), 8, f.126, Council minutes.

14.   A short corrective to present-day visions of the eighteenth century as a time of highly civilized and compassionate behaviour, epitomized by the glorious music of Bach and Mozart and the paintings of Fragonard, is found in M.S. Anderson, *War and society in Europe of the old regime, 1618–1789* (Montreal and Kingston: McGill-Queen's University Press 1998). See also R.R. Palmer, *Age of the democratic revolution: A political history of Europe and America 1760–1800* (2 vols. Princeton: Princeton University Press 1964).

15.   Abbott Emerson Smith, *Colonists in bondage: White servitude and convict labor in America, 1607–1776* (New York: W.W. Norton 1971), 148.

16.   Ibid., 92.

17.   NAC, Vernon-Wager Papers, printed in Griffiths, *The Acadian deportation*, 108. It is clear from the body of Lawrence's correspondence that he is using the word 'extirpate' to mean 'to clear away persons from a locality' and not in the sense of 'to kill'. See *Oxford English Dictionary*.

18.   Included in a letter of 14 April 1756 from Secretary Fox to the Lords of Trade, printed in *PAC Report*, 1905, app. B, 63–5. As lieutenant governor of Nova Scotia, Belcher displayed a harsh attitude towards the Acadians: see Townsend, 'Jonathan Belcher'.

19.   Susan Buggey, 'Jonathan Belcher', DCB, 4:50–4.

20.   See Abbé de L'Isle-Dieu to Pontbriand, 25 March 1755, in 'Lettres et mémoires de l'abbé de l'Isle-Dieu,' RAPQ, 1935–36.

21.   Pichon to Surlaville, 12 Nov. 1754, in Gaston Du Boscq de Beaumont, *Les derniers jours de l'Acadie (1748–1759), correspondances et mémoires: extrait du portefeuille de M. le Courtois de Surlaville, lieutenant-général des armées du roi, ancien major des troupes du l'Île Royale, mis en ordre et annotés* (Genève: Slatkine-Megariotis Reprints 1975), 130.

22.   'legitime souverain': R. Rumilly, *Histoire des Acadiens* (2 vols. Montreal: Fides 1955), 1:436.

23.   Brebner, 'Canadian policy towards the Acadians in 1751', 284. This includes the proclamation of La Jonquière on the subject, as does Griffiths, *The Acadian deportation*, 82–3.

24.   See excerpts and analysis in J.C. Webster, *The Forts of Chignecto: A Study of the eighteenth century conflict between France and Great Britain in Acadia* (Shediac 1930), 58–60.

25.   Aumasson de Courville, *Mémoires sur le Canada, depuis 1749 jusqu'à 1760*, LHSQ ed. (Quebec: Imprimerie de T. Cary 1838).

26.   For an account of Pichon's career, with references to those of his papers held in PANS, see J.C. Webster, *Thomas Pichon, "the Spy of Beauséjour,"* an Account of his career in Europe and America (Sackville: Tribune Press 1937). For a précis of the sort of information that Pichon sent the British, see T.A. Crowley, 'Thomas Pichon', DCB, 4:630–2.

27.   J.C. Webster, ed., *Journals of Beauséjour: Diary of John Thomas, journal of Louis de Courville* (Halifax: Public Archives of Nova Scotia 1937), 16, 17, and 100.

28.   Akins, *Acadia*, 212–14.

29.   PAC *Report*, 1905, app. B, 60; a description of the disarming is in *Coll. Doc. Inédits*, 1:138–9.

30.   See, in particular, the evidence of Judge Isaac Deschamps in NAC, Brown Papers, Mss. 19073,

item 52; and Grace M. Tratt: 'Isaac Deschamps,' *DCB*, 5:250–2.

31. 'Signé par quarante-quatre des susdits habitants, au nom de tous': Council minutes, 5 July 1755, ff.166–7, printed in full in French in PAC *Report*, 1905, app. A, pt. 3, and in English in Akins, *Acadia*, 249–50.

32. 'si dans la Requette qu'ils ont eu l'honneur de présenter à votre Excellence il se trouvoit quelque faute ou quelque manque de respect envers le gouvernement, que c'est contre leur intention . . . ': ibid.

33. NAC, CO 217, 15, Lawrence to the Lords of Trade, 28 June 1755.

34. John Brebner believes that the British, clearly irritated, attempted to make the Acadians declare themselves unequivocally: *New England's outpost: Acadia before the conquest of Canada* (Hamden: ARchon 1927), 215ff. L.H. Gipson maintains that the British judiciously presented their position to the Acadians: *The British empire before the American revolution* (New York: Alfred A. Knopf 1942), 6:255ff.; Emile Lauvrière is convinced that the meeting was a Machiavellian inquisition, designed to make the Acadians appear guilty: *La tragédie d'un peuple: histoire du peuple acadien de ses origines à nos jours* (2 vols. Paris: Editions BRossard 1922), 1:428ff.

35. NAC, CO 220, NS (B), 8, Council minutes, 3 July 1755; printed in Akins, *Acadia*, 250.

36. 'Permettez-nous, s'il vous plait, d'exposer ici les circonstances genantes dans lesquelles on nous retiens au prejudice de la tranquillité dont nous devons jouir': ibid.

37. NAC, CO 220, NS (B), 8, Council minutes, 4 July 1755; printed in Akins, Acadia, 256.

38. See chapter 6 for a discussion of the decision by French jurists that the British crown was justified in demanding an oath of allegiance.

39. Anne Dummett and Andrew Nicol, *Subjects, citizens, aliens and others: Nationality and immigration law* (London: Wiedenfield and Nicholson 1990), 45.

40. Ibid., 14 July 1755; printed in Akins, *Acadia*, 257.

41. NAC, CO 218, 5, Secretary of State Robinson's circular to all governors, 15 April 1755.

42. NAC, CO 220, NS (B), 8, Council minutes, 15 July 1755; printed in Akins, *Acadia*, 258–9.

43. W.A.B. Douglas, 'Nova Scotia and the Royal Navy, 1713–1766', Ph.D. thesis, Queen's University 1973, 242.

44. CO 5, 211, BL, Mss. 19073, f.42, Robinson to Charles Lawrence, 13 Aug. 1755; printed in full in Griffiths, *The Acadian deportation*, 111.

45. NAC, CO 217, 15, Lawrence to the Lords of Trade, 18 July 1755.

46. In much the same way that officials in France were shaken in 685 when Protestants chose exile rather than conversion.

47. Brought by one of the ships, the brig *Lily* out of New York. See Macdonald, 'The Hon Edward Cornwallis', 42.

48. 'nous pouvons bien assurer votre Excellence que plusieurs d'entre nous se sont risqué la vie pour donner connoissance au gouvernement de l'ennemis et aussi lorsqu'il a été nécessaire de travailler pour l'entretient du Fort d'Annapolis . . . nous nous y avons porter de tout notre coeur': NAC, CO 220, NS (B), 8 Council minutes, 25 July 1755; PAC *Report*, 2, app. A, pt. 3, app. C, 61.

49. 'nous leurs enjoignons de ne contracter aucun nouveaux serment': ibid., 61.

50. This memorial was not sent to the Lords of Trade until 24 Dec. 1755. It was included in a dispatch from Belcher, the main body of which was concerned with the need for an assembly for Nova Scotia: NAC: CO 217,16; printed in full in PAC *Report*, 1905, 2, app. A, Pt. 3, app. C, 63–5.

51. Belcher obviously believed that the Catholic hierarchy might proclaim that oaths sworn to a Protestant monarch were not binding. Such a position was extreme, but, when one recalls that Belcher had lived in United Kingdom during the Stuart rebellion of 1745, which had been openly financed by France, it becomes understandable.

52. Dummett and Nicol, *Subjects, citizens, aliens,* 22.

53. For the French view, and their wish to have the Acadians as settlers on Île Royale, see NAC, AC, IR, C11B, 1, f.123, Costebelle to the minister, 1715; for the English view, and their fear that the departure of the Acadians would strip Nova Scotia of its population, see NAC, NS/A, 5:1, Caulfield to the Lords of Trade, 1715.

54. NAC, CO 217, 15, Lawrence, 'Circular letter to the governors of certain colonies', 11 Aug. 1755; printed in PAC *Report*, 1905, 2, app. B, 15–16.

55. See Antoine Bernard, *Le drame acadien depuis 1604* (Montreal: Clercs de Saint Viateur 1936), 247–85.

Chapter Five

Representing Acadia and Canada

READINGS

Primary Documents

1   *The Death of General Wolfe, 1770*, Benjamin West

2   *The Death of Montcalm, 1783*, François-Louis-Joseph Watteau

3   *The Death of the Marquis de Montcalm, 1783*, Juste Chevillet

4   *Sketches for the Death of Montcalm, 1902*, Marc-Aurèle de Foy Suzor-Coté

5   *A View of the Launching Place Above the Town of Quebec, 1763*, Francis Swaine

Historical Interpretations

6   'An Empire on Paper: The Founding of Halifax and Conceptions of Imperial Space, 1744–55', Jeffers Lennox

7   '"Taken on the Spot": The Visual Appropriation of New France for the Global British Landscape', John E. Crowley

Introduction

Although historians have tended to favour written sources (and, increasingly, oral ones) when attempting to interpret the past, visual representations of historical events play the same role that these more conventional sources do. Art historians have for a long while supplied us with the stories surrounding the creation of artworks, and we can use some of their more basic techniques as we examine the way that those with artistic talent tackled the job of depicting 'what happened'. We can see the artist's choice of subject, medium, scale, tone, and colour as interpretive choices, just as we have long considered the actual execution of the works to be a kind of language. However, these visual sources must be considered carefully, as their meaning may not be easily accessible.

Consider, for instance, that neither General Wolfe nor General Montcalm, both of whom died at Quebec in 1759, fell in the way depicted by the four artists who painted the dramatic tableaux featured in this section. Wolfe did not die surrounded by the representatives of the different groups in the colonies. As for Montcalm, he did not even die on the Plains of Abraham, let alone under a palm tree. But these facts do not mean that these paintings are untrue. Such imaginings of historical events were supposed to depict not so much the death of Wolfe and Montcalm as the 'essence' of the experience—an essence influenced greatly by accounts already circulating and by the political or cultural position of each artist. In order to file their own particular kind of historical reports, representing British and French imperial grandeur, the paintings did not need to be factually accurate. As for the artists, they didn't need to be present (and weren't). In other words, the scene was already set—not by the 'reality' of the deaths portrayed, but by the context in which the works were produced. In this sense, these paintings can be compared to the *The Death of the Earl of Chatham* (John Singleton Copley, 1779) or *The Death of Nelson, 21 October 1805* (William Arthur Devis, 1807). The primary sources here do not serve as primary sources about the battle on the Plains of Abraham, but as primary sources that reflect the moments in which they were created, moments that came along decades later.

In the secondary works on visual representation, we learn how maps were useful, but the works created were intended to familiarize viewers with the territory on an entirely different scale, the scale on which their countrymen (or perhaps they themselves) would be encountering it as the colonial project proceeded. Jeffers Lennox's article is actually about maps, and how maps have considerable ability to help people grasp spatial relationships, as well as turn those relationships to the advantage of those who controlled the land on the map. John Crowley shows us how depictions of landscape can do more than entertain or highlight the artist's talents. In his reading, he demonstrates that the territory formerly known as New France becomes British as it is visually catalogued, just as other parts of the empire were. Just as the map is not the territory, the picture is not the event. But thinking critically about the way that visual representations operate can perhaps help us understand more clearly that our written and oral sources are prone to the same pressures.

QUESTIONS FOR CONSIDERATION

1. Who, or what, was the focus of West's work? Why do we make this assumption?
2. Even if they were not prepared for the celebration of Quebec's 300th anniversary in 1904, how do you think the sketches from 1902 would have been received on that occasion? In other words, how might art that acknowledges the end of something be interpreted during a celebration of its beginning?
3. Do you consider artworks reliable historical documents? What about photographs?
4. Regardless of who controlled the land, what was the purpose of producing images of a colony?
5. What purpose do maps serve, and do you think that purpose has changed since the eighteenth century?

SUGGESTIONS FOR FURTHER READING

Clayton, Daniel, *Islands of Truth: The Imperial Fashioning of Vancouver Island* (Vancouver: UBC Press, 2003)

Coates, Colin M., '"Like the Thames towards Putney": The Appropriation of Landscape in Lower Canada', *Canadian Historical Review* 74(3) (1994): 317–43

McNairn, Alan, *Behold the Hero: General Wolfe & the Arts in the Eighteenth Century* (Montreal and Kingston: McGill-Queen's University Press, 1997)

Quimper, Hélène, and Daniel Drouin, *The Taking of Québec* (Québec: Musée national des beaux-arts du Québec; Ottawa: The National Battlefields Commission, 2009)

PRIMARY DOCUMENTS

1 Benjamin West, *The Death of General Wolfe, 1770*

SOURCE: Oil on canvas, 152.6 x 214.5 cm. National Gallery of Canada, Ottawa
Transfer from the Canadian War Memorials, 1921 (Gift of the 2nd Duke of Westminster, England, 1918) Photo © NGC.

2   François-Louis-Joseph Watteau, *The Death of Montcalm, 1783*

SOURCE: Brush and brown and grey wash over black and red chalk, heightened with white, on laid paper, 43.2 × 59.6 cm. National Gallery of Canada, Ottawa. Gift of W.A. Mather, Montreal, 1953. Photo © NGC.

3   Juste Chevillet, *The Death of the Marquis de Montcalm, 1783*

SOURCE: Engraving and etching on laid paper, 47.1 x 59.9 cm trimmed within platemark; image: 42.8 x 59.6 cm. National Gallery of Canada, Ottawa. Photo © NGC.

4   Marc-Aurèle de Foy Suzor-Coté, *Sketches for the Death of Montcalm, 1902*

SOURCE: Oil on canvas 54.4 x 85 cm, Collection Musée national des beaux-arts du Québec, 1943.176, Patrick Altman.

5 Francis Swaine, *A View of the Launching Place Above the Town of Quebec, 1763*

SOURCE: Library and Archives Canada, Acc. No. 1997-3-2.

HISTORICAL INTERPRETATIONS

6 Jeffers Lennox, 'An Empire on Paper: The Founding of Halifax and Conceptions of Imperial Space, 1744–55', *Canadian Historical Review* 88(3) (2007): 373–412.

INTRODUCTION

In March 1754 the Board of Trade and Plantations wrote to Nova Scotia's Lieutenant-Governor Charles Lawrence to enquire about provincial security. In light of a looming international conflict that would set French and Native forces against the British, the Board of Trade argued that it was impossible 'at this distance and without a more perfect knowledge of the geography of the country' to devise an adequate defence plan.[1] Put simply, British administrators needed accurate maps. The settlement at Halifax, from which the British would launch their campaign against the French in Canada, has a telling cartographic history. The geographic knowledge created during the settlement's formative years shaped local and imperial ideas of British space and influenced the socio-political organization of power.

As the late John Brian Harley has argued, maps are more than precise representations of physical space; they are tools of empire that create knowledge and power through their representative functions. Harley pioneered the field of 'critical cartography' and encouraged historians to engage with the social, political, and economic power of maps.[2] Geographic and cartographic knowledge can be interpreted in two ways: first, maps and geographic surveys attempt to reflect accurately the position and characteristics of physical landforms, thereby bestowing on cartography the status of a science; second, because of this perceived scientific authority, cartography can be manipulated by the map-maker or map-reader and infused with symbolic meaning to illustrate a certain point of view, be it political, social, or otherwise. Working from the tenets of critical

cartography, this article will examine the influence of cartographic and geographic knowledge on the founding of Halifax in 1749.

The British Empire employed cartographic and geographic information to support the founding of Halifax, but spatial concepts were not static. The presentation of geographic knowledge varied according to British goals, each of which will be examined in this article: first, reconnaissance maps and surveys delimited boundaries and provided data; second, early settlement geographic knowledge established Britain's claim to the Halifax region by attempting to control the Native presence and emphasizing British strength; and third, 'popular' cartography rallied support for the empire by promoting attractive imperial imaginaries among Britons. Maps, geographic reports, and the people who created them helped to secure British expansion into Nova Scotia in part by anticipating empire instead of simply reflecting the physical and geopolitical realities on the ground.

There is no shortage of studies focused on early imperial geopolitics, but there is room in the Canadian historiography to illustrate the importance of geographic knowledge. Canadian historians have long been fascinated with land.[3] As Harold Innis famously stated, Canada 'emerged not in spite of geography but because of it.'[4] Yet Innis's assertion takes geography for granted. To understand the importance of geography we must first investigate how land has been imagined. Ideas about geography changed over time, influenced social organization and political development, and shaped cultural interaction. Mapping—by which I mean the creation and representation of geographic knowledge—shaped the British relationship to the land by locating natural boundaries, creating political, social, and economic borders, and surveying natural resources. Once this relationship was established it influenced how British settlers and administrators interacted with each other and with hostile or resistant groups. Mapping and the cartographic record it produced is therefore a neglected but key independent variable in British North American and early Canadian social and political history.[5] [. . .]

Britons in Halifax, like those at home, relied on imported knowledge to inform their ideas of the wider world. Scholars focusing on Europe and Asia have produced excellent works that examine how people in those regions viewed the larger imperial or colonial world, but few Canadian historians have analyzed spatial knowledge as it relates to empire or to nation-building.[6] In 1966 Donald Thomson wrote a commissioned three-volume institutional history of Canadian surveying entitled *Men and Meridians*. Thomson provided the chronology of cartographic development in Canada, illustrating the roles of prominent surveyors and map-makers across the country and setting the stage for future work. In 1988, Barbara Farrell and Aileen Desbarats co-edited *Explorations in the History of Canadian Mapping*. The contributors focused on four themes: research background; exploring the coasts; routes and patterns of settlement; and surveys and resources. In the collection's strongest essay Richard I. Ruggles calls upon future historians to attend to the neglected areas of the field. Specifically, Ruggles laments the lack of scholarship on Atlantic Canada's cartographic history.[7]

R. Cole Harris and Geoffrey J. Matthew's *Historical Atlas of Canada* illustrates the forces, both natural and artificial, that have shaped the Canadian landscape. Graeme Wynn and Debra McNabb recount the founding of Halifax on plate thirty-one, which includes a landscape painting, a 1755 map created by a French prisoner at Halifax, information on shipping rates, and immigration and emigration patterns. The *Historical Atlas* is not a history of maps, but history on maps. Each beautifully illustrated plate in the *Historical Atlas of Canada* presents Canada's history on the area in which it occurred, providing the reader with both a written explanation of events and a visual understanding of the event's geography. The *Atlas* is a valuable historical resource, but it does not investigate how ideas of land or space influenced Canadian history.[8]

[. . .]

On the east coast, John G. Reid's 'The Conquest of "Nova Scotia": Cartographic Imperialism and the Echoes of a Scottish Past' investigates the process by which the name Nova Scotia survived the first attempt to colonize the province in 1632 and was revived to legitimize later settlement endeavours. Reid argues that the union of Scotland and Britain in 1707 renewed Nova Scotia's toponymic importance as it was 'subsumed into a context of increasing Scottish involvement in British imperial affairs.' The re-emergence of 'Nova Scotia'—a term that survived on maps despite the colony's early failure—had little to do with the seventeenth-century Scottish settlement. Instead the name was invoked during the early eighteenth century to reflect imperial demands that required justifying present actions through past events.[9]

At the local level, Joan Dawson's *The Mapmaker's Eye* provides an important account of Nova Scotia's cartographic history. Dawson examines maps and some of the events that may have influenced their creation, offers insightful arguments concerning the use of maps as tools to attract settlers, and lays a solid foundation for a critical cartographic analysis of Nova Scotia.[10] While Dawson is correct to argue that these maps were used to advertise potential areas of settlement, more context is required to situate Nova Scotia in its imperial setting. The British authorities had a vested interest in map-making, as the fate of their North American possessions depended on the ability to acquire, govern, and promote new geographies.

The founding of Halifax serves as an ideal case study for examining the cartographic and geographic implications of imperial expansion.

The settlement was state-funded to the tune of £700,000 and there was no guarantee the venture would succeed. As will be demonstrated, spatial information was Janus-faced: maps and reports negotiated a fine line between value-free spatial information and imperially favourable geographic imaginations. Quite often this distinction was intentionally blurred. Cartographic and geographic knowledge encouraged expansion by anticipating, facilitating, and projecting the desired results; in practice, however, the task was not so simple.

RECONNAISSANCE SURVEYS AND SETTLEMENT

The settlement at Chebucto, later renamed Halifax, was long in the planning. Calls for establishing a new imperial fortress originated in the 1720s from officials at the weakly fortified Annapolis Royal; in the late 1740s, however, Governor William Shirley of Massachusetts began repeatedly memorializing the Board of Trade and Plantations. Over time these pleas became more urgent and expressed a need for both a physical and cartographic presence in Nova Scotia. Shirley argued in a 1745 letter to the Board of Trade that the French presence at Louisbourg must be counterbalanced, possibly with a large fortified and garrisoned place 'erected at Chibougto'.[11] Shirley's concerns were heightened during the War of Austrian Succession when the French Admiral Duc d'Anville attempted to attack Nova Scotia via Chebucto.[12] [. . .]

With time, calls for a stronger British presence in Nova Scotia were expressed increasingly in cartographic and geographic terms. Using maps to secure land title was important in Britain and in the colonies.[13] That colonial authorities employed map imagery, therefore, whether intentional or not, is not surprising. In early 1748, Shirley wrote to the Duke of Bedford, Newcastle's replacement, complaining about French encroachments at 'Crown Point', a disputed area along the British-French boundary that Shirley argued must be secured for the British. Shirley pleaded with Bedford, arguing that it was 'absolutely necessary for commissioners to run lines between his Majesty's colonies and Canada, that the boundary may be settled in such a manner if possible as to take away all pretence of dispute which will otherwise perpetually arise between the subjects of the two crowns and to put an end to the continual encroachments of the French.'[14] These boundary lines between the colonies would appear on maps, and would thereby provide the British Empire with an official cartographic foundation upon which to base its land claims. Shirley understood that maps could be used as tools of imperial authority, and he therefore supported the creation of a cartographic record that would favour British territorial expansion over that of the French.

In that same letter, Shirley voiced his concern about the possibility of French inhabitants in Nova Scotia becoming loyal British subjects. Britain had neglected the administration of Nova Scotia since it captured the region in 1710, allowing the Acadians to live in a virtually unchanged province. As the War of Austrian Succession came to a close in both Europe and North America, careful land management was required to assert authority over long-ignored regions. Shirley doubted that the French in the province would transfer their allegiance to the British crown without the influence of British settlers. To that end, Shirley commissioned Captain Charles Morris, a surveyor and army officer from Boston, to create a survey of the Bay of Fundy. Shirley 'directed Capt. Morris in his survey to see what room there was for interspersing British settlements to be seated in a commodious and defensible manner among those of the French within the aforementioned tract, which he has done, and marked out in the enclosed plan.'[15] Morris's manuscript map and accompanying survey provided both local and imperial officials with the geographic and cartographic information necessary to make decisions concerning imperial expansion (Figure 1). [. . .]

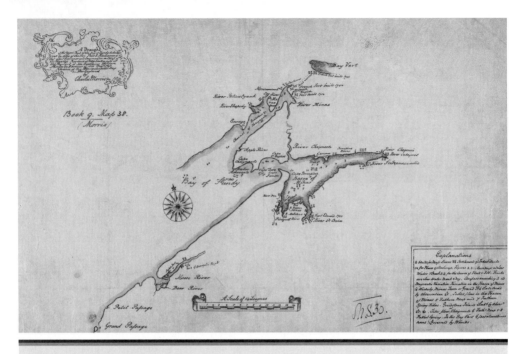

Figure 1. A copied extract from Charles Morris's 1748 survey of the Bay of Fundy. Included in this 'draught' are depth soundings and the location of French inhabitants. Library and Archives Canada, H3/205/[1745–1752](ca.1900), NMC 218.

The 1748 survey of the Bay of Fundy positioned Morris as the thin edge of an expansionist wedge. His work in the region established his imperial importance, and his cartographic contribution was rewarded with additional commissions.

After Morris completed his survey of the Bay of Fundy and supplied his draft of the region to William Shirley, the Massachusetts governor commissioned him to complete a survey of the entire province of Nova Scotia. Again, he was instructed to define the limits of the province, record areas of current French habitation, propose areas for English settlement, and describe the province's climate and geography. Defining the provincial limits was of great importance because the Treaty of Utrecht had left the issue unresolved, ceding to Britain the province according only to its 'ancient limits'. In 'A Brief Survey of Nova Scotia', Morris divided the province's geography into three

regions: lands bordering on the Canada (St Lawrence) River, lands bordering the northern part of the Bay of Fundy, and Nova Scotia's peninsula. Morris was well aware of Nova Scotia's imperial importance, and his surveys and reports suggested ways that Britain could strengthen its hold on North America. If settled with Protestants, he argued, Nova Scotia 'will then be not only a barrier to all other Brittish Colonies, but with their assistance may sooner or later, either ruin the French Provinces, or at least greatly distress them.'[16]

Morris provided a history of the province, beginning with Cabot's voyage of 1496 and ending with the Treaty of Utrecht, and compared the provincial boundaries as defined by the French and the English. The French boundaries were more fluid than were the English. France had stretched its claim from the mouth of the St Lawrence River in the north to the Penobscot River in the south when favourable relations with the Natives permitted. But the French could also claim that Acadia was limited to peninsular Nova Scotia—minimizing the amount of land ceded to Britain in 1713—since no record clearly indicated otherwise. Morris's 'Draught of the Northern English Colonies' notes that Nova Scotia must include the peninsula, present-day New Brunswick, and the Gaspé region of Quebec. The map also suggests that 'this country from Kennebeck river to Cape Rozier was always called by the French ACCADA' (Figure 2). As tools of British expansion, Morris's maps and reports were important for their geographic knowledge and their imperial presentation. These surveys made a significant contribution to the development of imperial policy because the extent of land under British control was of central importance to the metropolitan administrators.[17]

The pleas and plans for settlement that originated primarily from New England, Morris's reports and maps, and a plan for civil government drafted by William Shirley assisted George Montagu Dunk, the Earl of Halifax

and president of the Board of Trade, in creating 'A Plan for Settling Nova Scotia'. His direct involvement in the settlement's planning is characteristic of Dunk himself, who fought for 'his right, and the right of the board, to be regarded as the directing force in colonial affairs.'[18] Dunk's plan addressed most requirements for a successful settlement, but he emphasized the importance of surveys and cartography. Careful land management was important because the availability of land served as a primary attraction for potential settlers. Dunk had specific instructions for future governors and surveyors concerning how best to lay out towns and settle new citizens in Nova Scotia. Five settlements were proposed, with two townships to be marked out 'containing one hundred thousand acres or 12 miles each . . . at Chibucto, which is intended to be the metropolis.'[19] These townships were to be surveyed in such a way as to provide for expansion when required, so sufficient land was to be left surrounding the original settlement. As will be demonstrated, the plan was overly optimistic,

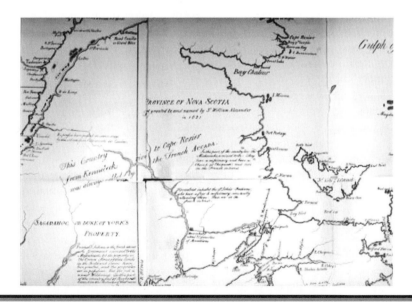

Figure 2. Extract from Charles Morris's 1749 'Draught of the Northern English Colonies'. Morris notes clearly that Nova Scotia's boundaries extend to the present-day Gaspé region. Dalhousie University, Call number E 198 P86 Sp. Coll. Courtesy, Special Collections, Killam Library.

and upon their arrival at Chebucto the settlers were able to establish only one of the proposed five towns.

Dunk also included instructions for specific placement of the townships and the general manner in which the towns should be laid out. Towns were to be surveyed to ensure that each lot shared a common boundary with its neighbour, 'taking care, however, that the said lands do not extend in length along the sea coast, but only a necessary part therefore do abut upon the sea.'[20] Dunk was explicit in his desire to establish an English grid style township, unlike the French-Canadian seigneurial system, in which each lot fronted onto the water to facilitate travel and communication.[21] He repeated this sentiment when he instructed the governor, with whom the final design for the town layout would ultimately rest, that 'a regular plan ought to be observed in the laying out the streets and buildings of each town', and that although some alterations to such regular plans might be required, that he 'should be directed to observe as much regularity as possible in this.'[22] A town laid out in a 'regular' fashion would stamp a British design onto the new geography.

Dunk was also aware that carefully placed surveys could bring the region's French inhabitants under the power of the British authorities, a concept that echoed Morris's surveys and maps. Surveyors were instructed to ensure that towns laid out for the proposed settlement, and any future settlements, include land currently inhabited by the French. As the number of towns grew, each carefully surveyed to encompass a section of Acadian settlement, French settlers' property rights would then be defined and controlled by the imperial authorities. Land surveys would also help British authorities keep track of French inhabitants whose lands could not be expropriated by careful town planning. Dunk instructed the governor promptly to make an account of French settlements, including their placement and the number of inhabitants at each. Furthermore, Dunk required

'that a survey be now likewise made of their lands now under actual improvement, specifying the numbers of acres cultivated by each particular person.'[23] Careful town planning, as far as Dunk was concerned, could control the French as long as detailed geographic surveys were employed as tools of imperial power to support the British military presence in the colony. Spatial knowledge, from Morris to Shirley to Dunk, served two important purposes during this early reconnaissance phase: first, the land was measured and mapped; second, geographic information was presented in terms favourable to imperial expansion.

SECURING TERRITORY AND CONTROLLING OPPOSITION

Upon his arrival at Chebucto, Cornwallis began corresponding with the Board of Trade. In his first letter, Cornwallis gave the commissioners an idea of the region's geography, informing them that 'the country is one of continued wood, no clear spot to be seen or heard of.'[24] Aside from the small area of land cleared by d'Anville's fleet during their aborted attack on Nova Scotia in 1746, the settlers recognized few changes in the region's natural geography.[25] A month later, Cornwallis again emphasized the labour required to clear the forests, but added that 12 acres had been cleared in July and that he was confident he could have all the settlers in homes by winter. Along with this letter Cornwallis intended to send a plan for the settlement drafted by military engineer John Brewse.[26] The plan merely anticipated construction, but Brewse's contribution was quite influential as the first of only a few maps sent to London.

Little is known of Brewse's career before he arrived in Halifax with Cornwallis. However, military engineers made a considerable contribution to European mapping and surveying during the early modern period. Since the sixteenth century, military engineers had surveyed potential battlegrounds, and in the 1740s they took a leading role in cartographic development,

often drafting town plans and fortifications.[27]
[. . .]

Brewse wasted no time in creating a 'Project for Fortifying the Town of Halifax in Nova Scotia, 1749' (Figure 3), which was sent to the Board of Trade in Cornwallis's letter of August 1749. This letter also included Captain Durell's map of the harbour, created in the 1730s; the combination of both charts gave the Board of Trade a visual representation of the region. [. . .] Brewse's map is less informative than other military plans, which usually included forests and other aspects of the natural environment to give military authorities enough information to make strategic decisions. The use of striations on Brewse's map was an attempt to provide an idea of relief, but the markings do little to portray accurately the incline upon which the city was to be built.[28] Stephen Hornsby has argued that 'the governor's residence, parade ground,

Anglican church, and citadel dominated the town's grid plan and symbolized British political, military, and religious authority in the colony.'[29] The planned palisade was substantial and included a proposed earthen ditch, a cross-section of which is provided on the map's lower right corner. Military engineers usually produced detailed maps, therefore Brewse's lack of detail is surprising. His contribution was little more than an architectural plan, which served limited strategic purposes. Specifically, the omission of any sign of Natives, from whom the settlers were trying to protect themselves, is particularly revealing.

The exclusion of Natives on Brewse's plan is not surprising. As J.B. Harley has argued, 'It is in the nature of all maps . . . to construct a world in the image of society rather than to hold a mirror to an "objective reality".'[30] When the settlers arrived at Halifax, they renamed the region,

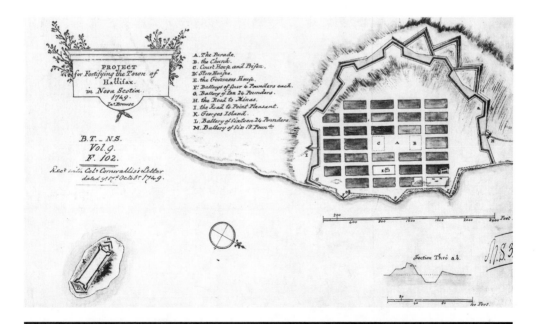

Figure 3. Brewse's plan for fortifying Halifax, 1749. There are no trees to be cut, and the well-organized town is surrounded by strong fortifications. The position of the church (marked B) and the government building (marked C) are reversed. This error was reproduced on Halifax maps long after both buildings were constructed on their respective ends of the Grand Parade. Library and Archives Canada, H3/240/Halifax/1749, NMC 18356.

replacing Native toponyms with British ones in an attempt to claim the land and superimpose British references that suited the purpose of the colony. Ignoring the Native presence and providing new names helped create order out of wilderness, which made the image of Halifax comprehensible and attractive to people in Britain.[31] Cleared of the surrounding dense forests and threatening Natives, Halifax appeared on maps as an ideally situated colony, heavily fortified against a seemingly non-existent enemy. However, as John G. Reid has argued, it is no longer possible to examine eighteenth-century northeastern North America in terms of 'colonialism'. Nova Scotia was the site of competition and negotiation between empires and Aboriginals, and there was no certainty that Europeans would be the victors.[32] Despite their reduced numbers, the local Mi'kmaq were formidable foes who controlled most of the region's geography until the arrival of the Loyalists in the mid-1780s.[33] An investigation into British

maps of the Halifax region must recognize this tension and not simply argue that Natives were ignored. Individual map-makers could choose to exclude Aboriginals from British maps, thereby denying Natives a place in the British image of Nova Scotia. Map-makers who did recognize Aboriginals could choose where and how they were represented. At the very least, British cartography imposed a European definition of the region's indigenous inhabitants.

Halifax maps of the mid-eighteenth century illustrate how cartographic representations had changed, especially in relation to the inclusion or exclusion of Natives. At the time of the Virginia settlement and Champlain's expeditions it was common to recognize and emphasize the presence of Aboriginals. John Smith, the first governor of Virginia and later a promoter of colonial settlement in New England, credited local Natives for their cartographic contributions and included depictions of Powhatan's tribe on his 1612 map of Virginia. Champlain had Native

Figure 4. Extract from Henry Popple's 1733 map of North America. The Native names Souriquois, Micmaques, and Etechemins feature prominently on this map and are positioned in close proximity to Annapolis Royal and the future Halifax site. Library and Archives Canada, H11/1000/1733, NMC 50738.

guides during his expeditions along the coast of Maine and New Hampshire, and Natives were periodically abducted from North America and taken to Europe, where they learned English and provided geographic information.[34] Natives in other areas of Canada left their own cartographic record, illustrating a developed knowledge of regional geography and the ability to represent in graphic form large areas of land unknown to Europeans.[35] Natives' maps and sketches did not conform to European standards, but their stylistic differences were purposeful. Map scale varied to correspond to the difficulty of passage, with a large area of easily navigable land appearing much smaller than a shorter, more treacherous passage. These maps included markers that indicated the approximate time needed for each section, which helped keep changes in scale manageable. Moreover, many of these Native maps came with verbal instructions to facilitate travel.[36]

Although the documentary evidence is limited, there is reason to suggest that eastern Algonkian Natives were able to express to British settlers their concepts of geographic space. In New England, seventeenth-century land deeds demonstrate Natives' use of cartography to sketch what lands they were willing to sell, even if the terms of sale were not always understood by both sides.[37] [. . .] There were multiple conceptions of space and myriad ways of rendering geographic information at the time of the Halifax settlement. Although the evidentiary record favours a Western interpretation, it would be irresponsible to ignore Native maps and mapping techniques during this period of geographic competition.

Despite the Natives' military prowess and geographic power, British cartography surrounding the founding of Halifax controlled and sometimes elided the Aboriginal presence in Nova Scotia. Comparing British cartographer Henry Popple's 1733 map with those that appeared at the time of the Halifax settlement illustrates cartography's ability figuratively to clear the land in preparation for settlement. Although Popple's rendering of

Nova Scotia's coastline leaves something to be desired, he indicates in large font the areas of three prominent Native groups: 'Micmaques', 'Souriquois', and 'Etechemins' (Figure 4). Less than twenty years later, when Thomas Jefferys was circulating his influential maps in Britain, this Aboriginal element was conspicuous in its absence. The Natives had not disappeared, but certain maps made it appear as if they had.[38] Jefferys's cartographic competition in London, Thomas Kitchin, did not ignore Natives but did exert power over their representation. *Ind. Vil.* appears in only three locations on peninsular Nova Scotia, although none on its Atlantic coast where Britain was to establish Halifax (Figure 5). Maps produced locally for official use, like Morris's 'Draught of the Northern English Colonies', were only marginally better than the popular cartography produced for public consumption in Britain. Morris's peninsular Nova Scotia is nearly empty, save for a small marker explained by the text 'Here is a church for the Cape Sable Indians' (Figure 6). Morris may have been more interested in justifying British claims to the region than in illustrating who was living within. Morris and the other geographers demonstrate a British cartographic ambivalence towards Natives. When included on maps, Aboriginals were often controlled and suppressed on paper in ways that were impossible in reality.

In practical terms, however, Mi'kmaq resistance to Halifax forced Britain to change its settlement plans. George Dunk wanted five settlements, but Cornwallis established only one, arguing that 'while there is any danger from the Indians the more compact we are the better.'[39] [. . .]

The Mi'kmaq resisted British settlement and influenced its development long after Halifax was founded. Yet maps of Halifax belied the presence and power of Aboriginals and did nothing to recognize Native conceptions of space; in so doing these maps demonstrate the discordance between the images and language of empire and the reality that settlers faced on the ground. [. . .]

Although the founding of Halifax was crucially important to the British Empire, there was no guarantee during the early period that the settlement would succeed. Spatial knowledge, especially when rendered as cartography, did not reflect Britain's tenuous position on Nova Scotia's Atlantic shore.

[. . .]

Cartography provided spatial information while also anticipating an imperial presence in the region that would be more difficult to secure than the maps suggested. By favouring a British image of the region over that of Natives or the French, geographic imaginings helped convince imperial authorities to support British efforts at Halifax.

GEOGRAPHIC KNOWLEDGE AND HALIFAX'S PROMOTION IN BRITAIN

[. . .]

'Geography is so necessary to illustrate history', wrote the French cartographer Jacques-Nicholas Bellin in the *Gentleman's Magazine* in 1746, 'that they ought to be inseparably connected.'[40] The monthly magazines published in Britain during the eighteenth century often emphasized this connection, and with a circulation of up to fifteen thousand copies for a single issue, these publications were effective vehicles for influencing public opinion.[41] In March 1749, the *London Magazine* printed Dunk's

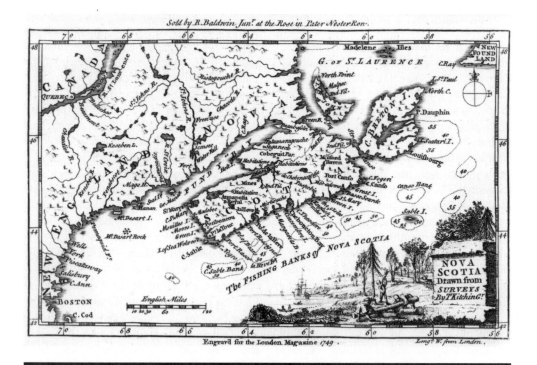

Figure 5. Thomas Kitchin's 1749 map of Nova Scotia. Note the three *Ind. Vil.* included on the peninsula. *Nova* is written on the mainland, and *Scotia* on the peninsula, supporting a larger British claim in the region. The St Croix River (Holy Cross River) divides Nova Scotia and New England. *Acadia* is not included on the map, effectively dispossessing the French of any claim to the region. New England and Boston feature heavily, while Newfoundland's presence is minimal. Published in the *London Magazine*, March 1749. Library and Archives Canada, H3/200/1749, NMC 93318.

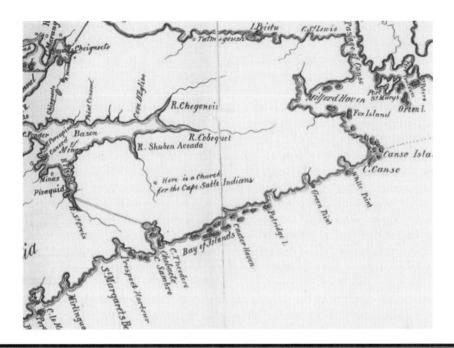

Figure 6. Extract from Charles Morris's 1749 'Draught of the Northern English Colonies' including an indication of a church for the 'Cape Sable Indians'. Dalhousie University, Call number E 198 P86 Sp. Coll. Courtesy Special Collections, Killam Library.

call for settlers to travel to Nova Scotia. A general description of the province and Kitchin's map accompanied this call (see Figure 5), providing potential settlers with a geographic depiction of the region. Other articles in these magazines supplied a historical context for the province's imperial significance, including details of the 1621 land grant issued to Sir William Alexander by King James I, which established the original land claim to Nova Scotia from which Britain could assert territorial authority.[42] More geographic descriptions followed. [. . .] Readers engaged with the geographic, cartographic, and historical depictions of Nova Scotia, and many editorial contributors were able to identify geographic imaginations with imperial aspirations.

Cartographic imperialism—the process by which maps delineate imperial possessions and lay claim to geographic areas—was central to accounts of Nova Scotia in the *London Magazine*. The Treaty of Utrecht in 1713 may have ceded to Britain the French possession of Acadia, but Britons realized that the French attempted to use maps to manipulate the size of the area that they were surrendering.[43] 'The French', one contributor to the *London Magazine* argued, 'since the property of this country has been vested in the English, affect to confine the name of Accadia to the peninsula only: but their own maps, made before the cession of this province, give it the limits we have now assigned. I will add, that the words of the treaty do not contact it within narrower limits than were before allowed to Accadia.'[44] [. . .] Informed Britons were aware of and concerned about cartography's ability to influence imperial development, especially when the result was detrimental to the British cause. That these discussions of cartographic imperialism took place in a public forum indicates an increased interest in cartographic and geographic knowledge among educated Britons during the years prior to the founding of Halifax.[45]

When the time came to announce plans to establish a new settlement, the British government placed advertisements in popular British newspapers and magazines. The advertisements and accompanying maps were so successful that the mayor of Liverpool wrote to the Board of Trade asking for money to support those 'who came from distant parts of the country' to travel to Nova Scotia. The mayor wrote a week later asking if any more ships would be leaving for Nova Scotia that season, to which the Board replied that it was too late in the year to arrange extra ships and suggested 'not to receive or enter more persons, than will be sufficient to fill the ship now receiving persons at that port.'[46] With the promise of free land, no taxes, and a year's worth of provisions, the Board of Trade was able to enlist 2,500 people to sail with Edward Cornwallis to Chebucto.

In the years following settlement, interested British citizens continued looking to printed maps, the popular press, and published travel accounts to learn more about Halifax. Although the information included in these media was not always detailed, the public discussion on geography and cartography that took place during this period, as in the pre-settlement era, suggests that many literate citizens were curious about developments at Halifax and relied on maps and geographic reports to inform their image of the settlement. Unfortunately for those who wanted to receive the most accurate maps and the most truthful reports on the colony, geographic information passed through several filters before being presented to the public. In the map-publishing trade, economic barriers and limited access to official information defined which maps could be published and how often each would appear. Periodicals such as the *Gentleman's Magazine* or the *London Magazine* were able to provide maps and colonial correspondence to a wide audience at an affordable price, but because

these publications relied on contributions from settlers or excerpts from other printed sources, many months could pass between updates.

The best example of a Halifax settler contributing to popular magazines is that of Moses Harris, whose unpublished map captured some of the dangers at Halifax while his printed efforts reflected the British settlement that imperialists wanted to see. In 1749, 19-year-old Harris and his wife arrived at Chebucto on the *Winchelsea* with the first group of settlers sent from England. Harris's interests included nature and geography; he had studied entomology since his youth, and at fourteen he began an apprenticeship with the London geographer Charles Price. Harris left for Halifax before he could complete his apprenticeship,[47] and shortly after his arrival he produced three maps of the infant settlement. Two of his surveys appeared in various forms in either the *Gentleman's Magazine*, as published maps, or both, but Harris's first survey was never printed or released to the public. Comparing his unpublished map to those made available to Britons illustrates the ways in which colonial promotion, the nature of the map trade, and the dual nature of cartographic representations influenced what kind of geographic knowledge was released to British citizens. Quite often geographic detail was sacrificed for both aesthetic appeal and imperial objectives; instead of a simple reflection of regional geography, these maps provided an idealized image aimed at striking an imperial chord in the metropole.

According to the extant records, Moses Harris was a sawyer. Joan Dawson has suggested that this entry was probably a misreading of 'surveyor', which would explain why Harris made a few maps and then quit the colony.[48] His work might have benefited from, but did not impinge upon, that of Morris and Brewse. The official surveyors and map-makers in Halifax were far more interested in facilitating expansion than submitting their maps for publication. The first map Harris created at Halifax was never published, for reasons that

Figure 7. Extract from Moses Harris's unpublished Halifax map, 1749. The trees are dense and the settlement seems isolated. Notice the bear in the top left corner. By permission of the British Library, Maps K.Top.119 f73.

seem obvious when the promotion of empire is weighed against a detailed geographic depiction. 'A Plan of Chebucto Harbour with the Town of Hallefax' (Figure 7) isolates the settlement on the edge of a densely wooded peninsula with only a single path cleared towards the Northwest Arm. Ships in the harbour represent the settlement's sole connection to Europe, but also emphasize its reliance on naval support for defence.[49] The town, as on his maps that would be published later, is well organized and surrounded by a palisade, but unlike other maps, this particular version includes the area's dangers. The cartouche features a bear wandering around a tree trunk, and the scale at the bottom of the map features an angry dragon, both of which symbolize the potential threat posed

by the region's wildlife.[50] Including dangerous animals—mythical or otherwise—was not common in maps aimed at colonial promotion, and in later versions of Harris's maps these predatory animals were replaced with much friendlier ones.[51]

Dangerous animals were not the only aspect of this map omitted from later versions. Trees were thinned, the topography was tamed, and all evidence of Natives was erased. Harris's first map is rare because it recorded the Native presence near Halifax (Figure 8). Across the harbour from the town, nestled among the trees at present-day Dartmouth, Harris drew a Native wigwam. Other maps might have included a Native presence, but it was often an abstracted rendering situated at

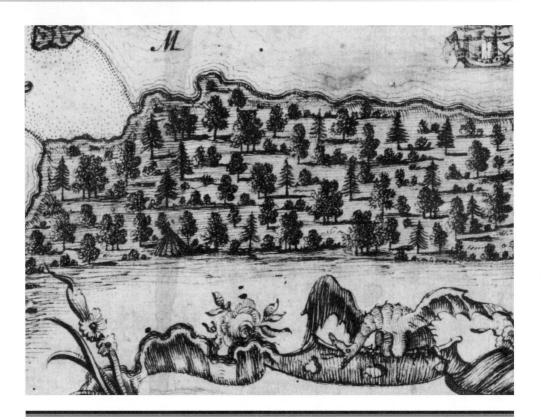

Figure 8. Extract from Harris's unpublished map. At the centre of this image is a Native wigwam that would be removed in future versions. A dragon in the bottom right corner decorates the cartouche. By permission of the British Library, Maps K.Top.119 f73.

a distance from the Halifax settlement. Harris, on the other hand, depicted the Mi'kmaq using a Native symbol and placed them within striking distance. Although Halifax settlers were well aware of the Native presence,[52] this image of Halifax was not to be the one that informed curious Britons. Harris's next two maps would provide a gentler image of the colony, one that emphasized the town's strength and imperial importance while at the same time pushing the dangers at Halifax off the page.

The 'Porcupine Map', (Figure 9) which appeared in the *Gentleman's Magazine* in 1750, is the most famous of Harris's collection and is often admired more for the inclusion of insects and animals than for the cartographic depiction of Halifax. The sketch itself provides little geographic information, instead offering its viewers a glimpse of wildlife and imperial symbols. The local animals and insects, especially the porcupine, which is the map's focal point, replace the daunting topography and Native presence in Harris's earlier map.[53] The map's scale is no longer guarded by a dragon but by a 'Musk Beetle'. Also included on the map is 'The Ensign of Nova Scotia', as well as the coat of arms of the colony's seven baronets,[54] an allusion to the imperial presence in the new colony. The names given to various locations on the 'Porcupine Map' reflected contemporary imperial figures. What was Rowses Island on Harris's first map became Cornwallis Island, Torrington Bay became Bedford Bay, and Hawk's River was renamed Sandwich

River for the First Lord of the Admiralty. This map was meant to render Halifax familiar to a British audience by employing common names and symbols, presenting a tame landscape, and offering a view of interesting wildlife. Geographic details were of secondary importance.

In 1749, the engraver and copperplate printer Edward Ryland published Moses Harris's 'A Plan of the Town of Halifax in Nova Scotia', which was a simple map indicating the layout of the town. The map resembled that of John Brewse, only Harris included some trees and wooden pickets surrounding the more formally constructed palisades. Thomas Jefferys, a London geographer who would become one of Britain's most influential map publishers,[55] was anxious to compile a new and impressive

map of Halifax and Nova Scotia. To that end, he combined Harris's 'Porcupine Map', the town map published by Ryland, and a chart of Nova Scotia based on the surveys of the French geographer Jean-Baptiste Bourguignon d'Anville. The result was 'A New Map of Nova Scotia' (Figure 10), an attractive map that did little to increase geographic knowledge in England but epitomized the process of British map-making.[56] Its geographic information came from a variety of sources, none of which were created from officially commissioned professional British surveys. The main section of the map is a version of the 'Porcupine Map', but instead of filling unknown areas with animals and insects, Jefferys included three insets. In the top left corner is a map of Nova Scotia oriented with Boston as a reference; in the top

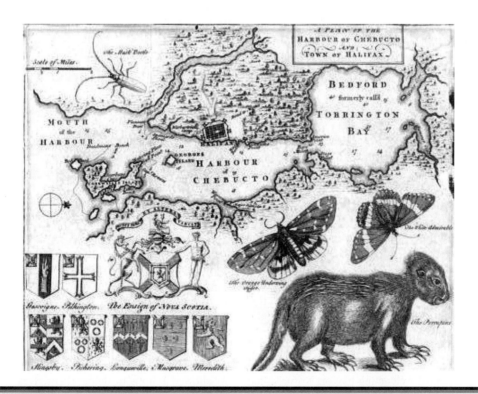

Figure 9. Harris's 'Porcupine Map', 1750. Wildlife and imperial symbols, not geography, dominate this chart. Dalhousie University, Morse Map #38. Courtesy Special Collections, Killam Library.

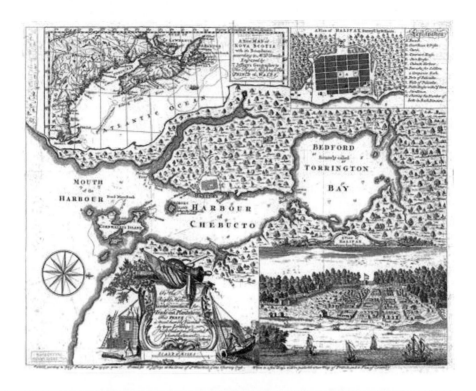

Figure 10. Thomas Jefferys's 'A New Map of Nova Scotia', 1750. Insets of dubious accuracy and a dedication to the Board of Trade take up most of the space on this map. Dalhousie University, Morse Map #40. Courtesy Special Collections, Killam Library.

right is a replica of Harris's 'A Plan of Halifax' with a legend to identify town buildings; and in the bottom right is a landscape portrait of the settlement, entitled 'A View of Halifax drawn from the topmasthead'. Examining the details of this map illustrates the difficulties and restrictions cartographers in Britain faced when compiling the latest geographic information.[57] The inset of Nova Scotia contains many of the same misrepresentations as other regional maps published in the mid-eighteenth century. Chebucto Harbour dwarfs St Margarets Bay, which is in reality the larger of the two, making Halifax appear to be situated on the most welcoming bay on Nova Scotia's eastern shore. Jefferys, unable to acquire original surveys for the Atlantic coast, used d'Anville's map. The inset of Harris's plan of

Halifax is an overly simplistic topographic representation. There is no attempt to indicate the slope upon which the city stood, the trees are sparse, and there is no indication of a Native presence.

The final inset, a landscape portrait of the town, illustrates the way in which landscape art was used to provide a 'British vision' of colonial settlements. British colonial landscape art during the mid- to late eighteenth century attempted to portray geography in a realistic fashion. But these paintings can also be interpreted as illustrating how the British wanted these regions to appear. Like maps, landscape art allowed Britons to define themselves as a 'civilised and civilising' people by presenting alien environments in an aesthetically familiar way,[58] minimizing the cognitive leap required to associate a strange wilderness with an imperial possession. The bird's-eye view of Halifax on Jefferys's map, although not picturesque like the typical landscape art of the era, provided a 'British vision' of Nova Scotia to which British readers could relate, emphasized by the British flag flying at the gates of the settlement.[59] The clearing upon which the settlers have built their homes is level, although both outside streets seem to be marked with striations that may be an attempt to indicate slope. Particularly important is the inclusion of tents on the outskirts of the settlement, nestled among felled trees and their stumps. Some settlers had yet to construct their homes at Halifax, so the inclusion of these tents hints at the harsh settler reality in an otherwise largely optimistic image of Halifax.

This Jefferys map, like many others, was dedicated to the Board of Trade and Plantations. But the Board was wary of maps published for the general public. The commissioners were receiving the latest manuscript surveys from Halifax and had no use for—and could recognize faults in—the published maps of Nova Scotia. The flow of official geographic knowledge from settlement to metropole, although not always fast, was direct, multifaceted, and largely unfiltered.[60] As a result, the Board attempted to distance itself from British geographers, allowing them to dedicate maps in its honour only to help with sales, even though the Board never 'superintended or approved' the manner in which these maps were executed.[61] A dedication to the Board of Trade gave maps an air of authority that would attract subscribers, even though the Board itself was not completely comfortable with the relationship. Geographers also inserted additional headings onto maps, hoping to increase sales by claiming them to be based on the 'most recent surveys', or calling them 'newly improved'. There was a cognitive disconnect between the language geographers used to explain their maps and the content on those maps, just as there was a tension between the map's image and the reality it represented.

British geographers catered to the public's curiosity, aesthetic tastes, and imperial outlook in an attempt to present a vision of Halifax that would convince Britons to support such an expensive endeavour.

CONCLUSION

[. . .]

The British experience in Nova Scotia was influenced heavily by the mapping of imperial space. Maps, mapping, and the creation of geographic knowledge provides a common theme with which to investigate the inter- and intra-cultural relationships that were constantly being developed and negotiated during the eighteenth century. At a cost to the government of £700,000, the Halifax settlement carried practical fiscal and political risks, yet the settlement's establishment has received little attention over the past generation. Critical cartography, with its focus on analyzing the forms and uses of spatial knowledge, enables historians to investigate how renderings of geography influenced the development of imperial policy. Maps and geographic knowledge acted as a vertical linkage between settlers, surveyors, local administrators, and their superiors in London, enabling imperial officials to visualize their North American possessions and plan military operations and future settlements. Cartographic information both influenced and adapted to imperial policy and realities on the ground, shaping the political and social world of early modern settlers.

[. . .]

British imperial culture was not static, and there was no single geographic image of Nova Scotia and Halifax that helped fuel the British desire to strengthen its North American holdings. Representations of space between 1744 and 1755 changed over three phases: reconnaissance information provided geographical data and delimited international boundaries; settlement maps and reports established and emphasized the British nature of the Halifax region by controlling oppositional forces; and finally, popular cartography and reports that circulated in Britain rallied imperial support for the settlement and influenced the British vision of Halifax. Establishing a settlement at Chebucto Harbour to address geopolitical threats in the region required more than money and military power; geographic knowledge provided an idea and an image of Halifax that encouraged a culture of imperial expansion.

The public in Britain did not have access to most maps and reports that crossed the Atlantic from Halifax to Whitehall. However, public geographers like Thomas Jefferys worked with the information they could secure to produce maps that engaged curious Britons and appealed to their aesthetic tastes. Charles Morris and John Brewse created maps and plans of Nova Scotia and Halifax to inform imperial officials, but like Jefferys

they presented an imperially favourable image of the settlement to encourage and anticipate future British expansion. Geographic information embodied a tension between what was and what could be, and the dual nature of maps facilitated a variety of interpretations of local geography and geopolitics. Boundaries, trees, and enemies were included or excluded from maps as the map-maker or map-reader saw fit. The founding of Halifax illustrates the ability of spatial information to blur the lines between image and reality; the cartography surrounding the Halifax settlement was powerful because it contained elements of both. When harnessed for the British cause, as it was from 1744 to 1755, geographic knowledge anticipated expansion by creating an empire on paper that inspired an empire on the ground.

NOTES

I am much indebted to Jerry Bannister and John G. Reid for their valuable comments and suggestions on this paper. John E. Crowley, Roger Marsters, and Bradley Miller read earlier drafts and provided useful suggestions, and the anonymous readers for the *Review* offered constructive insight and advice. A scholarship from the Social Sciences and Humanities Research Council provided financial assistance.

1.   Nova Scotia Archives and Records Management (NSARM), RG1, vol. 29, 25, Board of Trade and Plantations (BTP) to Lawrence, Whitehall, 4 Mar. 1754.

2.   Critical cartography examines maps as 'active, creative, and constitutive' texts or images that 'are implicated in creating the reality that they presume to reveal.' Raymond B. Craib, 'Cartography and Power in the Conquest of New Spain', *Latin American Research Review* 35, no. 1 (2000): 13. On critical cartography, see J.B. Harley, *The New Nature of Maps: Essays in the History of Cartography* (Baltimore: Johns Hopkins University Press, 2001). Harley's forays into cartographic theory, while influential, were not without their limits and critics. For an overview of Harley's intellectual legacy, see Matthew H. Edney, ed., 'The Origins and Development of J.B. Harley's Cartographic Theories', *Cartographica* monograph 54, vol. 40, no. 1–2 (Spring/Summer 2005).

3.   For three recent examples, see Rod Bantjes, *Improved Earth: Prairie Space as Modern Artefact, 1869–1944* (Toronto: University of Toronto Press, 2005); Julie Cruikshank, *Do Glaciers Listen? Local Knowledge, Colonial Encounters and Social Imagination* (Vancouver: UBC Press, 2005); and Gerald Friesen, 'Presidential Address of the Canadian Historical Association: Space and Region in Canadian History', *Journal of the Canadian Historical Association* n.s. 16 (2005): 1–22.

4.   Harold Adams Innis, *The Fur Trade in Canada: An Introduction to Canadian Economic History* (Toronto: University of Toronto Press, 1970), 393.

5. For more on the Atlantic example, see Jeffers Lennox, 'An Atlantic Borderland: Mapping, Geographic Knowledge, and Imagining Nova Scotia/L'Acadie/Mi'kma'ki, 1710–1784' (Ph.D. diss., Dalhousie University, in progress).

6. To name just three influential international works, see Benedict Anderson, *Imagined Communities: Reflections on the Origin and Spread of Nationalism* (New York: Verso, 1983); Mary Louise Pratt, *Imperial Eyes: Travel Writing and Transculturation* (New York: Routledge, 1992); and Edward W. Said, *Orientalism* (New York: Vintage Books, 1979). For a recent analysis of Occidentalism and Orientalism, see Jack Goody, *The Theft of History* (Cambridge: Cambridge University Press, 2006).

7. Donald W. Thomson, *Men and Meridians: The History of Surveying and Mapping in Canada* (Ottawa: Queen's Printer, 1996); and Barbara Farell and Aileen Desbarats, eds., *Explorations in the History of Canadian Mapping: A Collection of Essays* (Ottawa: Association of Canadian Map Libraries and Archives, 1988). For works that focus on Atlantic Canadian map history and publication, see William P. Cumming, *British Maps of Colonial America* (Chicago: University of Chicago Press, 1974); W.F. Ganong, *Crucial Maps in the Early Cartography and Place-Nomenclature of the Atlantic Coast of Canada* (Toronto: University of Toronto Press, 1964); and Donald P. Lemon, *Theatre of Empire: Three Hundred Years of Maps of the Maritimes* (Saint John: NBM Publications MNB, 1987).

8. Graeme Wynn and Debra McNabb, 'Pre-Loyalist Nova Scotia', in *Historical Atlas of Canada*, ed. R. Cole Harris and Geoffrey J. Matthews, *From the Beginning to 1800* (Toronto: University of Toronto Press, 1987), plate 31.

9. John G. Reid, 'The Conquest of "Nova Scotia": Cartographic Imperialism and the Echoes of a Scottish Past', *Nation and Province in the First British Empire: Scotland and the Americas, 1600–1800*, ed. Ned C. Landsman (Cranbury, NJ: Associated University Presses, 2001), 41.

10. Joan Dawson, *The Mapmaker's Eye: Nova Scotia through Early Maps* (Halifax: Nimbus and the Nova Scotia Museum, 1988).

11. Referred to in NSARM, RG1, vol. 11, 37, Mascarene to BTP, Annapolis, 17 Oct. 1748.

12. See James Pritchard, *Anatomy of a Naval Disaster: The 1746 French Expedition to North America* (Montreal and Kingston: McGill-Queen's University Press, 1995).

13. Roger Kain and Elizabeth Baigent, *The Cadastral Map in the Service of the State* (Chicago: University of Chicago Press, 1992), 335; Reid, 'The Conquest of "Nova Scotia".' An excellent investigation of cartography and British imperialism can be found in Matthew Edney's Mapping an Empire: The Geographical Construction of British India, 1765–1843 (Chicago: University of Chicago Press, 1997).

14. NSARM, RG1, vol. 12, 45, Shirley to Bedford, Boston, 18 Feb. 1748.

15. Ibid. In 1748, Lieutenant-Governor Mascarene received orders from Governor Shirley to provide support for Morris while he created his survey. The correspondence between Mascarene and Morris indicates the importance that Mascarene ascribed to this project. See NSARM, RG1, vol. 9, 235–6, Mascarene to Morris, Annapolis, n.d.; and NSARM, RG1, vol. 9, 242, Mascarene to Morris, Annapolis, 6 Aug. 1748.

16. Library and Archives Canada (LAC), MG18, F10, Charles Morris, 'A Brief Survey of Nova Scotia, 1748'.

17. In 1750, France and Britain established a committee to resolve the boundary dispute. Both sides were wary of cartographic evidence, and after five years no settlement had been reached. See Mary Pedley, 'Map Wars: The Role of Maps in the Nova Scotia/Acadia Boundary Disputes of 1750', *Imago Mundi* 50 (1998): 96–104. The commissioners did not refer specifically to Morris's survey, but the records suggest that it was in the Board of Trade's possession. In a 1749 letter discussing the need to settle the boundary issue, Governor Cornwallis explained to the Board of Trade, 'You will see by the map carried home by Governor Shirley the most accurate I have seen (done by Captain Morris).' NSARM, RG1, vol. 35, 9, Cornwallis to BTP, Halifax, 7 Dec. 1749.

18. Arthur Herbert Basye, *The Lords Commissioners of Trade and Plantations Commonly Known as the Board of Trade, 1748–1782* (New Haven: Yale University Press, 1925), 36. For a comparison of settlements founded by the King and those founded by Parliament, see Elizabeth Mancke, The Fault Lines of Empire: Political Differentiation in Massachusetts and Nova Scotia, 1760–1830 (New York: Routledge, 2005).

19. NSARM, MG1, vol. 160, 23, George Montagu Dunk, 'A Plan for Settling Nova Scotia, 1749.'

20. Ibid.

21. For a study on French land management, see R. Cole Harris, *The Seigneurial System in Early Canada* (Montreal and Kingston: McGill-Queen's University Press, 1966). The seigneurial system was employed in New France, but not in France's other American colonies. See James Pritchard, *In Search of Empire: The French in the Americas, 1670–1730* (Cambridge: Cambridge University Press, 2004), 80.

22. Dunk, 'Settling Nova Scotia'. As Stephen J. Hornsby as argued, eighteenth-century British towns were increasingly dominated by 'rigid geometry consisting of a gridiron of wide, straight streets; rectangular, standard-sized lots; and public squares.' See Stephen J. Hornsby, *British Atlantic, American Frontier: Spaces of Power in Early Modern British America* (Hanover: University Press of New England, 2005), 180–7.

23. Ibid. Dunk's instructions read, 'That care be taken in laying out the aforementioned townships, or any others that may hereafter be laid out, that some part of the lands belonging to the French inhabitants be taken into each township, so that the whole of their possessions may be comprehensive in so many townships as shall be laid out, by which means they will be subjected to Magistracy thereof, and to such rules and orders as may be made for the better governing of the same.'

24. NSARM, RG1, vol. 35, 2, Cornwallis to BTP, Halifax, 22 June 1749.

25. Cornwallis and the settlers may not have recognized the Native geographic influence, but L.F.S. Upton has argued that the local Mi'kmaq had cleared land and long used the sites on which Europeans settled. See *Micmacs and Colonists: Indian–White Relations in the Maritimes, 1713–1867* (Vancouver: UBC Press, 1979), 48. See also William Cronon, *Changes in the Land: Indians, Colonists, and the Ecology of New England* (New York: Hill and Wang, 1983).

26. NSARM, RG1, vol. 35, 2, Cornwallis to BTP, Halifax, 24 July 1749. It appears that Cornwallis intended to include this plan in his July letter, but his letter dated 20 August states 'from Mr Brewse's plan enclosed which I should have sent by my last.' NSARM, RG1, vol. 35, 5, Cornwallis to BTP, Halifax, 20 Aug. 1749.

27. David Buisseret, *The Mapmakers' Quest: Depicting New Worlds in Renaissance Europe* (Oxford: Oxford University Press, 2003), 114–16, 122–5, 150. See also R.A. Skelton, 'The Military Surveyor's Contribution to British Cartography in the 16th Century', *Imago Mundi* 24 (1970): 77–83.

28. Buisseret, *Mapmakers' Quest*, 116. Contour lines were not employed on maps 'until quite far into the nineteenth century', 118.

29. Hornsby, British Atlantic, American Frontier, 206.

30. Harley, *New Nature of Maps*, 187.

31. William Wicken, *Mi'kmaq Treaties on Trial: History, Land, and Donald Marshal Junior* (Toronto: University of Toronto Press, 2002), 174.

32. See Luca Codignola and John G. Reid, 'Forum: How Wide Is the Atlantic Ocean?' *Acadiensis* 32, no. 2 (Spring 2005): 74–87.

33. John G. Reid, 'Pax Britannica or Pax Indigena? Planter Nova Scotia (1760–1782) and Competing Strategies of Pacification', Canadian Historical Review 85, no. 4 (Dec. 2004): 669–92. For an opposing view, see Stephen E. Patterson, 'Indian–White Relations in Nova Scotia, 1749–61: A Study in Political Interaction', *Acadiensis* 23, no. 1 (Autumn 1993): 23–59.

34. Harley, *New Nature of Maps*, 173–4. See also Gwenda Morgan, 'Smith, John (bap. 1580, d.

1631)', in *Oxford Dictionary of National Biography* (ODNB), ed. H.C.G. Matthew and Brian Harrison (Oxford: Oxford University Press, 2004), http://www.oxforddnb.com.ezproxy.library.dal.ca/view/article/25835; and Alden T. Vaughan, *Transatlantic Encounters: American Indians in Britain, 1500–1776* (Cambridge: Cambridge University Press, 2006).

35. D. Wayne Moodie, 'Indian Map Making: Two Examples from the Fur Trade West', in *People Places Patterns Processes: Geographical Perspectives on the Canadian Past*, ed. Graeme Wynn (Toronto: Copp Clark Pitman, 1990), 57.

36. Ibid., 59–60.

37. Investigations into Native cartography are progressing despite the evidentiary challenges posed by the ephemeral nature of many Native maps, which were often scratched in the sand, sketched on tree bark, or explained using gestures. See Emerson W. Baker, '"A Scratch with a Bear's Paw": Anglo-Indian Land Deeds in Early Maine', *Ethnohistory* 36, no. 3 (Summer 1989): 235–56; G. Malcolm Lewis, ed., *Cartographic Encounters: Perspectives on Native American Mapmaking and Map Use* (Chicago: University of Chicago Press, 1998); J.B. Harley, 'Rereading the Maps of the Columbian Encounter', *Annals of the Association of American Geographers* 82, no. 3 (Sept. 1992): 522–36; and David Woodward and G. Malcolm Lewis, eds., *The History of Cartography*. Vol. 2, bk. 3, *Cartography in the Traditional African, American, Arctic, Australian, and Pacific Societies* (Chicago: University of Chicago Press, 1998).

38. Technically, the Etchemin and Souriquois had by 1730 been replaced by and/or evolved into the (Maliseet) and the Mi'kmaq, respectively. For an investigation into the changing Aboriginal presence in the region, see Bruce J. Bourque, 'Ethnicity on the Maritime Peninsula, 1600–1759', *Ethnohistory* 36, no. 3 (Summer 1989): 257–84.

39. NSARM, RG1, vol. 35, 11, Cornwallis to BTP, Halifax, 19 Mar. 1750.

40. Jacques-Nicholas Bellin, 'Remarks by M. Bellin in Relation to His Maps Drawn for P. Charlevoix's History of New France', *Gentleman's Magazine*, Feb. 1746, 72.

41. E.A. Reitan argues that *Gentleman's Magazine* in the 1740s published between five and six thousand copies per issue, but Anthony David Barker puts the number at ten to fifteen thousand for the same period. See E.A. Reitan, 'Expanding Horizons: Maps in the "Gentleman's Magazine", 1731–1754', *Imago Mundi* 37 (1985): 54; and Anthony David Barker, 'Cave, Edward (1691–1754)', ODNB.

42. See Reid, 'The Conquest of "Nova Scotia"', *passim*.

43. On cartographic deceptions, see Mark Monmonier, *How to Lie with Maps* (Chicago: University of Chicago Press, 1991).

44. *London Magazine*, Apr. 1749, 181–2.

45. On the rise of geography in the British education system, see Lesley B. Cormack, *Charting an Empire: Geography at the English Universities, 1580–1620* (Chicago: University of Chicago Press, 1997). On the use of geography in creating an English imperial identity, see Cormack, '"Good Fences Make Good Neighbours": Geography as Self-Definition in Early Modern England', ISIS 82, no. 84 (Dec. 1991): 639–61. For the early American example, see Martin Brückner, *The Geographic Revolution in Early America: Maps, Literacy, and National Identity* (Chapel Hill: University of North Carolina Press, 2006).

46. *Journal of the Commissioners for Trade and Plantations from January 1741–2 to December 1749, Preserved in the Public Record Office* (Nedeln: Kraus-Thomson, 1970), 415 and 419 covering the dates 23 and 29 May 1749, respectively.

47. Robert Mays, 'Harris, Moses (1730–c. 1788)', ODNB.

48. Dawson, *The Mapmaker's Eye*, 112.

49. Ibid.

50. On the use of the cartouche as a cultural symbol, see G.N.G. Clarke, 'Taking Possession: The Cartouche as Cultural Text in Eighteenth-Century American Maps', *Word and Image* 4, no. 2 (1988), 455–74.

51. Dawson, *The Mapmakers' Eye,* 112.

52. By the end of September 1749, Natives had killed at least four settlers. See T.B. Akins, *History of Halifax City* (1895; repr., Dartmouth: Brook House, 2002), 18.

53. Cleansing maps for colonial promotion was not a new phenomenon. See Louis de Vorsey, Jr, 'Maps in Colonial Promotion: James Edward Oglethorpe's Use of Maps in "Selling" the Georgia Scheme', *Imago Mundi* 38 (1986): 35–45. On the role of the *Gentlemen's Magazine* in supporting British imperial projects, see Reitan, 'Expanding Horizons'.

54. Dawson, *The Mapmakers' Eye*, 112.

55. See Laurence Worms, 'Jefferys, Thomas (*c.* 1719–1771)', ODNB.

56. An excellent overview and comparison of French and British cartography is provided in Mary Sponberg Pedley, *The Commerce of Cartography: Making and Marketing Maps in Eighteenth-Century France and England* (Chicago: University of Chicago Press, 2005).

57. The error of reversing the positions of St Paul's Anglican Church and the Government building persisted on British maps until 1755.

58. John E. Crowley, '"Taken on the Spot": The Visual Appropriation of New France for the Global British Landscape', *Canadian Historical Review* 86, no. 1 (Mar. 2005): 2, 6. See also Edney, *Mapping an Empire*, 57–76.

59. Mary Christine Sparling, 'The British Vision in Nova Scotia, 1749–1848: What Views the Artists Reflected and Reinforced' (master's thesis, Dalhousie University, 1978), 10–11.

60. Ian K. Steele has argued that the Atlantic Ocean was more of a highway than an obstacle. See Steele, *The English Atlantic, 1675–1740: An Exploration of Communication and Community* (New York: Oxford University Press, 1986). On France's significantly less successful communications infrastructure, see Kenneth J. Banks, *Chasing Empire across the Sea: Communications and the State in the French Atlantic, 1713–1763* (Montreal and Kingston: McGill-Queen's University Press, 2002).

61. J.B. Harley, 'The Bankruptcy of Thomas Jefferys: An Episode in the Economic History of Eighteenth Century Map-Making', *Imago Mundi* 20 (1966): 37. Quoting from the *Memorial of the English and French Commissaries, Nova Scotia. Vol. 1* (London, 1755).

7 John E. Crowley, '"Taken on the Spot": The Visual Appropriation of New France for the Global British Landscape', *Canadian Historical Review* 86(1) (2005): 1–28.

During the British invasion, occupation, and colonization of New France, artists appropriated the conquests visually with topographic renderings of the empire's new landscapes. Officers in the invasion forces made drawings of landmarks along the St. Lawrence, linking military events with striking physical features. During the occupation they portrayed the conquered province's capital as an exotic urban landscape. After the Treaty of Paris, military surveyors sought out the province's scenic attractions as they simultaneously mapped new British domains. Artistically inclined imperial agents represented the new British province as a place of natural beauty with a picturesque indigenous culture. They sent a visual message—to the king, ministers and aristocrats, parliamentary politicians, fellow officers and officials, their families, the viewing public at exhibitions—about a landscape whose scenic attractions and rustic tranquillity mitigated its appropriation by conquest.

The artists who created this imperial landscape claimed to have drawn their scenes first-hand—'taken on the spot'—in order to give them visual authenticity. These drawings conformed with a developing topographical imperative that required verisimilitude from representations of specific places of scenic interest.[1] Such topographic art cannot be taken for granted as artistically natural just because it was naturalistic. As Victoria Dickenson has shown, throughout the early modern period of colonization European artists lavishly represented the natural world of North America, but their empirical naturalism neglected landscapes and focused on studies of natural history. Until the arrival of topographic landscape artists with British forces in the 1750s, European representations of North American landscapes usually depended on artists' imaginations, with deliberately schematic and symbolic results.[2]

This paper analyzes post-conquest British representations of New France as part of the creation of a global British landscape, with Canada as a distinctive part. According to these representations, the sublime aspects of Canada's scenery confirmed the grandeur of the imperial project against New France, while the picturesque landscapes of towns, farms, and shorelines promised an easily governed population readily subject to British improvements. This aesthetic message is curiously harmonious with Allan Greer's summary of a revisionist historiography that considers 'French Canada' as a 'ceded colony' rather than a 'conquered nation', 'ruled by a different set of outsiders who happened to be British.'[3] In Canada's early landscape art as in its historiography, the conquest becomes a hazy background to localized multicultural scenes.

[. . .]

The British landscape of conquests in North America would differ markedly from preceding French representations of imperial New France. The topographical imperative for landscape art was much stronger for British than for French artists. The indigenous inhabitants—crucial both to the French Empire's fur trade and strategic survival—predominated as subjects for artists of New France. But French prints of Amerindians usually showed figures either as isolated studies or in schematic rather than identifiable settings. First-hand authority

was less important than artistic skill and creativity, and French representations of North American peoples often set them in imaginary landscapes.[4] Few images nominally of colonial New France purported to show how its landscape actually looked. The French colonists' favourite art form, votive images, often referred miraculous events to particular places in New France, but it was the event, not the place, that required faithful representation. The often reprinted view of Niagara Falls in Louis Hennepin's *Nouvelle découverte d'un très grand pays situé dans l'Amérique entre le Nouveau Mexique, et la Mer Glaciate* (1697) was an exception proving the rule. An anonymous engraver in Utrecht derived it from Hennepin's textual description (Figure 1), and there were no follow-up renderings by French artists on the spot.

French strengths in the visual representation of colonial landscapes were mainly cartographic and architectural. For the visual representation of colonial landscapes, French military engineers and architects applied their highly professional surveying and drafting skills to architectural plans, sections, and elevations and to town plans and models. With the exception of the models, these renderings of buildings deliberately abstracted them architecturally and isolated them from their settings. Printed representations of French colonial landscapes as they might actually be viewed were restricted to town views. These iconic views placed a premium on identifiably representing a town's most important buildings, and they often figured in architectural politics to secure royal favour. As landscapes, they typically presented a comprehensive, wide angle view of the respective town and invariably looked toward the commercial frontage of a port. They emphasized generic metropolitan connections, not creole colonial social life. Their authenticity was at a discount because metropolitan publishers often reissued them with a few imaginative updatings rather than go to the expense of engraving freshly taken views. In contrast to architectural drawing and

Figure 1. No first-hand renderings of Niagara Falls survive from the period of French rule in Quebec. Louis Hennepin, *Nouvelle découverte d'un très grand pays situé dans l'Amérique entre le Nouveau Mexique, et la Mer Glaciate* (Utrecht: Guillaume Broedelet, 1697), facing 44. Library and Archives Canada, C-004236.

cartographic surveying, topographical imperatives for landscape art were weak in New France.[5]

The topographical imperative did not preclude artistic licence. Topographic landscape artists intended their representations to be 'picturesque'. *Picturesque* meant literally 'like a picture', and the pictures most often in mind were those of the Roman Compagna painted by three seventeenth-century artists: Claude Lorrain, Salvator Rosa, and Gaspard Poussin. They had painted idealized landscapes as settings for Roman historical and mythological scenes, with panoramic perspectives, strong contrasts of light and dark, irregular terrain, and cultural nostalgia in architecture and

figures' dress. [. . .] As eighteenth-century British artists increasingly took an interest in their country's scenery, they adapted the idealizing style of the picturesque for their topographic representations. The popularity of the style encouraged the Reverend William Gilpin to make a series of tours, beginning in the 1760s, looking for picturesque scenery in the remoter parts of Britain, such as south Wales, Derbyshire, the Lake District, and Scotland. His enormously popular guidebooks located the exact spots where sensitive viewers could observe picturesque scenery.[6]

British topographic landscape art masked relations of power by privileging scenic representations over ones showing social, economic, or political relations.[7] Humphry Repton, Britain's foremost landscape architect in the late eighteenth and early nineteenth century, forthrightly asserted that aesthetically motivated 'appropriation' naturalized landowning and absolved it from charges of exploitation. Therefore the picturesque style also suited 'the creation of imperial space' that has interested so many cultural historians over the past quarter century.[8] Empires, like nations, are works of politically imaginative representation.[9] As an 'instrument of cultural power' in the politics of imperialism, landscape art 'naturalizes a cultural and social construction, representing an artificial world as if it were simply given and inevitable.'[10] Cultural historians now take for granted that the fine arts perform such political work: 'Members of the dominant groups invariably use art as a device to explain and justify their power, to express the mystique of rulers, and to illustrate their knowledge and command of the natural world.'[11] Imperial landscape art linked three crucial developments in eighteenth-century British culture and politics: 1) the creation of a British identity available to peoples throughout the British Isles and in settler colonies, 2) the imperial assertion of this identity through commercial expansion and strategic success, and 3) the commodified representation of these identities and successes to a viewing public.[12] Viewing imperial spaces in the picturesque style helped both colonists and metropolitans to maintain their identity and self-respect as civilized and civilizing Britons.[13] The picturesque style simultaneously created differences (topographically) and familiarity (aesthetically) among imperial spaces in ways that naturalized their appropriation as British rather than alien environments.[14]

Colonial landscapes claiming topographical accuracy became frequent at the same time that Britain extended its imperial interests through conquests and accessions on a global scale—in Canada, the trans-Appalachian West, India, and the Pacific. The Seven Years War, with its outcome for Great Britain of a global

territorial empire over non-British peoples, critically changed governmental relations between the metropole and its new peripheries. The regular army stationed troops in the Indian subcontinent and the interior of North America for the first time, increased their numbers in Ireland and the West Indian slave colonies, and sent massive forces to put down the rebellion in the thirteen colonies that became the United States.[15]

In accordance with this militarization of the empire, army and naval officers produced most of the topographical art representing Britain's new imperial landscapes. Yet their artistic creations sent home a curiously anti-triumphalist message. Their aesthetically appealing representations of previously alien places helped legitimize imperial projects that were subjects of lively controversy in British politics: the eradication of the Scottish clans, the assimilation of a French-Catholic population in Quebec, the maintenance of peace between First Nations and European settlers in the trans-Appalachian West, the acquisition of additional Caribbean colonies dependent on slave labour, the regulation of a nascent empire in Bengal, the intrusion of disease-ridden naval expeditions into unspoiled Polynesia, and the penal transportation of free-born Britons to Botany Bay. Mary Louise Pratt's interpretation of 'anti-conquest' themes in visual representations of Europeans' travel and natural history—'taking possession without subjugation or violence', as a bourgeois public sought to 'secure their innocence in the same moment as they assert European hegemony'—reduces the paradox of such anti-triumphalist landscapes of imperial conquests.[16] They mystified colonization with an apolitical appreciation of scenery.

[. . .]

In the wake of Britain's far-flung assertions of rule and territory, artists created works of topographic landscape art informing the metropolitan viewing public of its new imperial domains. [. . .] In Canada, British officers in the invasion forces during the Seven Years

War produced the first extensive landscape and genre art of European colonies in North America. [. . .]

Military art of the Seven Years War spanned the aesthetic spectrum, from the sublime through the picturesque and beautiful to the grotesque. Pictures could make the mayhem of battle 'awesome' and 'tremendous'—terms straight out of Edmund Burke's aesthetics of the sublime. A typical battle-scene print, *Britain's Glory, or the Reduction of Cape Breton* (1758), showed mortar bombs in mid-air, ships' cannon and shore batteries blasting each other, and assault troops taking cannon fire at point-blank range—all to exhilarating rather than gruesome effect. Thomas Davies, then a young artillery lieutenant, drew a fiercely illuminated nocturnal scene of the 'plundering and burning of the city of Grymross, Capital of the Neutral Settlements, on the River St. John's in the Bay of Fundy, Nova Scotia.' Representations of heroism raised the military genre to the highest realm of art: moralized history. Benjamin West's *Death of General Wolfe* became the most celebrated British painting of the eighteenth century because he aesthetically elevated a glorious contemporary scene to comparison with classical models. In popular art, the symbolic conventions of Victory represented the defeated as a beautiful, distressed woman. On a medal for distinguished service in the capture of Louisbourg, a British soldier and sailor stand on either side of a globe—oriented to eastern North America—as it crushed a female personification of France.[17] The triumphalism of military art was virtually a tautology.

Yet in the context of New France—over the course of the British conquest and occupation—British officers deployed a demilitarized, anti-conquest art for a benignly civilian, picturesque representation of a defeated enemy's landscape. The creation of Quebec's scenic landscape for the British viewing public began during the British invasion of 1759. Captain Hervey Smyth, an adjutant to General James Wolfe, made drawings 'on the spot' as the British expedition sailed up the St. Lawrence to Quebec. The resulting series of engravings, *Six Views of the Most Remarkable Places in the Gulf and River of St Laurence* (1760), dedicated to William Pitt, Britain's strategist in the Seven Years War, traced the campaign through a landscape at least as impressive for its scenic as its military interest. Every print juxtaposed British military force with arresting landscapes. The scene at the French settlement at Miramichi, 'destroyed by Brigadier Murray detached by General Wolfe for that purpose', forthrightly showed soldiers with bayonets ready for assault, but their pathetic object was set in a vast forested valley. The tumultuous waterfall at Montmorency and the steep hills framing the valley at Cape Rouge warranted inclusion for their sheer scenic interest, but Smyth's engravings also reported their crucial tactical importance in the siege of Quebec (Figure 2). The scene at Montmorency showed Wolfe's disappointing attack 'on the French Intrenchments near Beauport, with the Grenadiers of the Army, 31 July 1759', while that of Cape Rouge portrayed how 'from this place 1500 chosen troops at the break of Day fell down the River on the Ebb of Tide to the place of Landing 13 Sept. 1759.' Smyth also designed a separate print elaborately showing the geography of events on that fateful day. The print centred on the defile and cliffs at Anse-au-Foulon that Wolfe's troops climbed during the critical early stage of the attack. Despite a key to seventeen points of tactical importance, the print emphasized Quebec's most striking landscape features—its cliffs and broad river basin. Smyth placed the crucial battle scene to the side of the middle ground. At the climactic moment in Britain's conquest of New France, he implied, the landscape of the new imperial domain visually congratulated British military accomplishments there.[18]

This muted triumphalism carried over to the next series of British prints about Quebec, *Twelve Views of the Principal Buildings in Quebec* (1761), by Richard Short, purser aboard HMS *The Prince of Orange*. Short forthrightly showed how extensively the British bombardment had

Figure 2. The visual record of the invasion balanced military events with picturesque landscapes. William Elliott after Hervey Smyth, *View of the Fall of Montmorency and the Attack Made by General Wolfe on the French Intrenchments near Beaufort* (London: Thomas Jeffreys, 1760). Library and Archives Canada, C-041389.

wrecked the town. To underline their reportorial quality, several of the prints stated that they depended on drawings 'made on the spot' and noted where the artist stood to draw them. The series moved from square to square within the town, providing its first thorough topographical description. Only two pictures had a heavy military presence. One showed British troops being rowed toward Quebec from Point Levy. The other showed three ranks of troops drawn up before the Recollets' church—with a sunrise metaphorically bringing a new day to the town. The rest of the pictures showed British sailors, soldiers, and officers casually taking stock of the surrendered town in the company of townspeople. Numerous carts, carriages, and porters marked the unobstructed continuation of daily life, as French religious and judicial officials moved

freely about the town (Figure 3). Besides a few broken statues, the interior scenes of rubble in the Jesuits' and Recollets' churches barely hinted at iconoclasm: The devotional paintings and altarpieces and altar furnishings were miraculously intact.[19]

Short's tranquil presentation of Quebec corresponded with General James Murray's post-conquest assessment of the 'new subjects' for Lord Egremont, secretary of state. Murray painted a picture of cross-confessional succour in the aftermath of the conquest, as female Catholic religious tended to the wounded and ailing British soldiers, while later in the winter British officers and men drew up a subscription to relieve the starving inhabitants. As people from each nation gained trust in the others, Murray implied, a liberation had succeeded a conquest: 'Such uncommon generosity towards the conquered . . . convinced these poor deluded people how grossly they had been imposed upon . . . the daily instances of lenity, the impartial justice which had been administered, so far beyond what they had formerly experienced, have so altered their opinion with regard to us . . . that, far from having the least design to emigrate into any other of the French colonies, their greatest dread is lest they should meet with the fate of the Acadians and be torn from their native country.'[20] In emphasizing the beauty of newly acquired domains and the picturesqueness of their inhabitants, artists encouraged the metropolitan viewing public to consider the expanded empire as benign realms of amenable subjects. Such landscapes made it difficult to imagine Canadian insurgency.

[. . .]

Topographic landscape art helped Britons visualize their new Canadian landscape in the broad context of a North American empire. Thomas Davies published a series of engravings of waterfalls—on the Niagara, Passaic, Cohoes, and Genessee rivers—which he had drawn after the fall of Montreal when Lord Amherst sent him to survey the upper St. Lawrence and the rivers that flowed from New York into Lake Ontario.[21] Waterfalls had both strategic and scenic significance. They posed critical tactical problems along wartime communication routes, while their visual variety made them picturesquely attractive. More ambitiously, the *Scenographia Americana: Or, a Collection of Views of North America and the West Indies* (1768), presented a twenty-eight-print series of topographical landscapes in an arc across eastern North America from

Figure 3. Short's topography of Quebec's wrecked institutions implicitly asked what would replace them. Antoine Benoist after Richard Short, *A View of the Bishop's House with the Ruins as they appear in going up the Hill from the Lower to the Upper Town* (London: Richard Short, 1761). Library and Archives Canada, C-041514.

Montreal to Guadeloupe. Now the drawing master at the Royal Military Academy at Woolwich, Paul Sandby compiled the collection from 'Drawings taken on the spot, by several officers of the British Navy and Army'. The *Scenographia Americana* traced the geography of Britain's strategy during the Seven Years War. The series began in Canada with views of Montreal, Quebec, and Louisbourg, plus Hervey's five sights from the invading fleet in 1759. It then moved southward for views of Boston, New York, and Charleston—reminders that the war in North America had been about the security and growth of Britain's colonies there. Sandby also engraved six of Governor Thomas Pownall's drawings of dramatic landscape features in the middle colonies—the falls on the Passaic River in New Jersey, the highlands of Tappan Zee at the mouth of the Hudson, the Catskill Mountains further upriver, and the Great Cohoes Falls on the Mohawk River in northern New York. Pownall had drawn these impressive sights as part of a strategic survey of terrain for Britain's war with France in North America. From continental North America the *Scenographia* then shifted theatre to the Caribbean—just as the war had—and concluded with six views of Havana, one of Dominica, and three of Guadeloupe. Scenic attractiveness, as well as success by British arms, united these places in their connection to Britain's global landscape.[22]

British atlases complemented the *Scenographia* cartographically in placing Britain's new North American empire in a global context. The hundred maps in Thomas Jefferys and Robert Sayer's *General Topography of North America and the West Indies* (1768) covered both the Atlantic and Pacific coasts (including recent Russian explorations in the northern Pacific) and related them to the nearest African, Asian, and European coasts. Most of the maps described areas of British conquests during the Seven Years War—in Cuba, Florida, the Lesser Antilles, and Guyana. Twelve of them described the former New France—charts of the St. Lawrence, plans of Quebec and Montreal, and maps of Acadia and the fur trading country west of Hudson Bay and the Great Lakes.

The most important visual survey of Britain's new continental empire in North America was the *Atlantic Neptune* (1777–84), a monumental coastal charting initiated shortly after the Treaty of Paris. In 1763 the Admiralty directed Joseph Frederick Wallet DesBarres to chart the coastal waters of Nova Scotia and Cape Breton Island. In 1764 the Board of Trade appointed Samuel Holland as surveyor general of Quebec and of the Northern District (i.e., north of the Potomac River) and William De Brahm as surveyor general of the Southern District. In 1769 the board ordered them to cooperate with DesBarres in charting their respective coasts. For the first time the Atlantic coast of North America would have a continuous series of navigational charts based on direct hydrographic surveys: from the tidal reaches of the St. Lawrence in the west and the Strait of Belle Isle in the north, around Cape Breton Island and Nova Scotia, along the Atlantic seaboard of the British-settled colonies, and reaching south and westward to include the new British colonies of East and West Florida.[23] New France would be seamlessly integrated with the colonies of British settlement and accessions from Spanish America.

The strategic importance of this project was self-evident—it made the Royal Navy's patrolling of a lengthy imperial coastline safer and more thorough—but its aesthetic priorities are more surprising. As DesBarres compiled and revised the *Atlantic Neptune*, he added scenic aquatints (the first ones of North American landscapes) to the conventional charts and profiles dictated by his commission. The scenes often included waterfront activities as staffage, giving them a genre quality: careened ships being cleaned, lighters landing cargo on beaches, even—in a bit of reflexivity—boats making soundings for a chart. Most of the prints were of Nova Scotian scenes because that was where DesBarres mainly worked, and he respected the topographical imperative by only illustrating places he had

Figure 4. DesBarres' favourite subjects for landscapes were rocky promontories—features that navigators had little interest in seeing up close. 'A View of the Plaister Cliffs, on the West Shore of Georges Bay', *Atlantic Neptune* (London: Joseph Frederick Wallet DesBarres, ca. 1779). Library and Archives Canada, C-040998.

actually seen. Often coloured by hand, these views—over 130 of them—went well beyond the Admiralty's directions for a coastal survey. DesBarres's views gave a self-commissioned priority to British landscape aesthetics of the beautiful, the sublime, and the picturesque, as Edmund Burke and William Gilpin had defined them. Scenes drawn from near shore had picturesquely gnarled trees and varied rock formations. Some views even contradicted the cartographic project in order to represent impressive landscapes: the ships setting some of the scenes were so numerous that they obscured the coastal profile, and a few views were from land to sea—not a useful perspective for navigating a ship (Figure 4). Ships carried the *Atlantic Neptune* as a navigational aid, but DesBarres also aimed the work at armchair sailors interested in imagining themselves along Britain's new imperial coastline, especially so that they could follow events in the rebellious colonies.[24]

The outcome of the War of American Independence made Quebec Britain's largest, and potentially most important, colony in North America. Yet its imperial features received less visual emphasis than representations of its georgic potential, picturesque culture, and genteel leisure. Quebec's invitation of scenic tourism in a landscape simultaneously sublime and picturesque implied a happily governed colony, welcoming immigrants and encouraging imperial resources.

The watercolours and prints of James Peachey epitomized these trends, and in the mid-1780s they accounted for most of the representations of Quebec to British metropolitan viewers. In the early 1770s he had worked with Samuel Holland's survey of the Northern District; then he returned to England to produce maps for the *Atlantic Neptune*. He went back to Quebec in 1780, where he gained patronage as a draftsman for the governor of Quebec, General Frederick Haldimand. He flattered Haldimand's taste by painting a series of watercolours of the area around the

governor's country house on the bluff above Montmorency Falls. Haldimand counted himself a connoisseur of landscape: He built a Chinese-styled viewing seat upstream as well as a viewing lodge perched on stilts over the head of the falls.

Peachey also flattered his patron's benign rule with watercolours of the Quebec countryside. They showed a peaceful province whose cottages, outdoor ovens, horse-drawn sleighs, and habitants and Amerindians in colourful costumes marked it as distinctively Canadian (Figure 5). Peachey's views of Quebec and Montreal played down their fortifications. His *View of the City of Quebec* (ca. 1785) showed the citadel and outworks indistinctly in the background, while the foreground and middle ground showed a farm with large, well-fenced

Figure 5. Georgic symbols of Quebec's prosperous agricultural potential—notably bridges built at Haldimand's behest—complemented the province's picturesque landscape. James Peachey, *A View of the Bridge Built over the River Bertier by Order of General Haldimand in 1781* (1785). Library and Archives Canada, C-045559.

fields, heavily laden hay wagons, a well-maintained house and barn, and leisurely farm workers. *A View of the Citadel at Quebec* (1784), taken from the Heights of Abraham, showed outworks now fenced for pasture.[25]

[. . .]

In late 1784 Peachey returned to Britain with Haldimand and immediately began to publicize his landscapes of Quebec. Besides exhibiting paintings at the Royal Academy, he published aquatints of Montreal and Quebec and a series of coloured etchings of the area around General (now Sir Frederick) Haldimand's country house. These showed Montmorency Falls, from above and below, in summer and winter, as well as the river above the falls. Despite the awesome majesty of the falls, rapids, and cliff-lined river, the scenes' numerous gentlefolk out walking and fishing demonstrated that the Quebec landscape was readily approachable.

When Thomas Davies returned the third time to North America in 1786, now as a lieutenant colonel commanding artillery in Quebec, he elaborated on Peachey's themes. His watercolours returned to a favourite subject, waterfalls, but now he chose sites on rivers easily reachable from the city rather than ones important for military campaigns as in 1759–60 (Figure 6). Along these waters, habitants and gentlefolk fished, picnicked, and walked their dogs. His scenes of the countryside studied distinctively Canadian features of the landscape: hunters returning with a canoe on a wagon, weirs set along tidal marshes of the St. Lawrence, farmsteads strung along the road of the first *rang*, the church at Château-Richer, a traverse of a portage on the Ottawa River, and the annual encampment at Pointe-Lévis for First Nations peoples to receive their obligatory presents. His less frequent urban scenes

Figure 6. Davies helped to create a regional, genre landscape of Quebec. Thomas Davies, *Chaudière Falls near Quebec* (1792). Library and Archives Canada, C-013313.

showed a reconstructed Quebec with many of its old ways represented—female religious in habits, dog-drawn watercarts, one-horse carriages—with the British presence barely hinted at by an officer overseeing the scene, a single sentry, and three stands of guns for soldiers out of the picture.[26] Scenic, social, and political tranquillity implicitly complemented each other in reassuring ways for Britain's imperial presence in North America.

Elizabeth Posthuma Simcoe extended the British imperial landscape into areas of the Great Lakes uncolonized while part of New France. She arrived in Canada in 1791 as the wife of Lieutenant Colonel John Graves Simcoe, the first lieutenant-governor of the new Province of Upper Canada. During her nearly five years in the Canadas she sometimes wintered at Quebec, but she spent the rest of the time at her husband's bases in Upper Canada, first at Newark (later Niagara-on-the-Lake), then at York (formerly and eventually Toronto).[27] She recorded landscapes of the Canadas in several diaries and sketchbooks. She regularly revised her diaries and made finished watercolours from her drawings to send to her four older daughters, whom she had left in England, and to a friend, Mary Anne Burgess, a notable author (she updated *Pilgrim's Progress*) and illustrator of natural history. Though she never published her landscapes, she publicized them by private circulation. She had an artistic fellowship with British officers such as Peachey, Holland, and George Bulteel Fisher, with whom she compared and copied drawings (40, 55, 58, 74, 108). She drew maps for her husband's reports, and she gave King George III 32 watercolours on birchbark of scenes in the Canadas.[28]

Elizabeth Simcoe sought and found a picturesque Canada. In her diary 'picturesque' described dozens of scenes that caught her eye. Besides editorializing aesthetically with terms such as 'beautiful', 'prettiest sight imaginable', 'very fine sight' (76), 'very fine scene' (107), and 'sweet view' (184), she recommended the visual interest of Canadian scenes by comparing them with landscapes her correspondents already knew from European art and literature. An 'old-fashioned' Quebec inn 'resembled my idea of a Flemish house' (38); the 'pretty vale' at Sillery was just as Emily Montague described it (59); the 'Lake-like' St. Lawrence put her in mind of how 'Spenser, Ariosto etc., dwelt on the delight of sailing in a Boat on Lakes' (64); as she rode toward Niagara Falls she 'was struck by the similarity between these Hills & Banks & those of the Wye about Symond's Gate & the lime Rock near Whitchurch in Herefordshire' (76); a mill under construction 'has the appearance of a Sketch of a Ruin in Italy' (190). In providing positive comparisons between Canada and aesthetically prestigious European landscapes, Simcoe made a new part of the empire recognizable, familiar, and desirable for appropriation.

Simcoe constantly evaluated the landscape along her travels and frequently made scenic excursions. Within four days of arriving at her new home at Navy Hall near the mouth of the Niagara River, she went to see Niagara Falls. She was not disappointed: 'The fall itself is the grandest sight imaginable from the immense width of waters & the circular form of the great fall' (Figure 7). She immediately appreciated the artistic challenge of capturing the falls' distinctive features, 'the whole centre of the circular fall being of the brightest green & below it is frequently seen a Rainbow.' She venturesomely descended to Table Rock to get the full effect of 'the prodigious Spray which arises from the foam at the bottom of the fall [and] adds grandeur to the scene' (76–7). Happily for Simcoe, areas near where she lived in Upper Canada—the Niagara River, the eastern and western ends of Lake Ontario, and between the escarpment and the lake at York—provided her with ample opportunities to paint landscapes in both picturesque and sublime styles.[29]

In counterpoint to her husband's geopolitical strategies, Elizabeth Simcoe presented Upper Canada as a sub-boreal English landscape garden.[30] Her pictures showed a

Figure 7. Elizabeth Simcoe painted Niagara Falls many times. *Niagara Falls* (ca. 1795). Archives of Ontario, F 47–11–1-0–178, 10007030.

fascination with the scenic harmony between European settlement and heavily forested areas along wilderness shorelines: mills on the Gananoque and Napanee, tents on the heights above Queenston, houses in park-like water meadows along the upper St. Lawrence, and rustic Castle Frank with its pedimented facade supported by Greek columns of pine logs. The familiar picturesque style of her landscapes helped her metropolitan correspondents imagine Britain's imperial outposts in North America.

Such visual appropriation of Quebec for the global British landscape enjoyed continued success.[31] In 1795 George Bulteel Fisher, a frequent exhibitor at the Royal Academy, published *Six Views of North America from Original Drawings Made on the Spot* (1796)—of Cape Diamond, Grand River, and Montmorency and Chaudière Falls. Their example encouraged the deputy postmaster-general of the Canadas, George Heriot, to use his official

travels for a systematic survey of Canadian landscapes. Twenty-five aquatint landscapes and genre scenes illustrated his *Travels through the Canadas: Containing a Description of the Picturesque Scenery on Some of the Rivers and Lakes* (1807). Travel accounts of Britain's North American colonies increased, and with them, illustrations of Canada's scenery.[32] Joseph Bouchette, surveyor-general of Lower Canada, published the most important survey of Canadian scenery following Heriot's. His *Déscription topographique de la province du bas Canada* (1815) was published in London in English as well as French, with engravings of georgic mills and farms as well as picturesque villages and sublime waterfalls.

In Canada, as elsewhere in the empire, representations of picturesque, sublime, and georgic scenes in British colonies mitigated the forthrightness of their conquest and/or military rule. The supposed authenticity of topographic landscape art gave Britons at home confidence to identify with Britain's new possessions overseas, while the familiar picturesque style of these imperial landscapes diverted attention from the controversies surrounding them. Artists' representation of imperial landscapes harmonized the empire's implicit mayhem with its scenery. The sublime glory of British arms was reinforced by the picturesque landscape in which they had prevailed, and vice versa.

NOTES

1. Dean MacCannell, *The Tourist: A New Theory of the Leisure Class*, 2nd ed. (Berkeley and Los Angeles: University of California Press, 1999), 91–107.

2. Victoria Dickenson, *Drawn from Life: Science and Art in the Portrayal of the New World* (Toronto: University of Toronto Press, 1998), 105–39.

3. For revisionist historiography of New France and the conquest, see Allan Greer, 'Comparisons: New France', in *A Companion to Colonial America*, ed. Daniel Vickers (Maiden, MA: Blackwell Publishers, 2003); id., *The People of New France* (Toronto: University of Toronto Press, 1997), quoted 115; Marcel Trudel, 'La Conquête de 1760 a eu aussi ses avantages', in *Mythes et réalités dans l'histoire du Québec* (Montreal: Éditions Hurtubise HMH, 2001), 209–34.

4. Claude-Charles Bacqueville de la Potherie, *Histoire de l'Amérique septentrionale*, 4 vol. (Paris: Jean-Luc Nion and François Didot, 1722); Joseph François Lafitau, *Moeurs des sauvages ameriquains comparée aux moeurs des premiers temps* (Paris: Sauguin l'aîné and Charles-Estienne Hochereau, 1724).

5. Luc Noppen and Marc Grignon, *'L'art de l'architecte': Three Centuries of Architectural Drawing in Québec City* (Quebec: Musée du Québec and Université Laval, 1983), 27–53, 114–36; Rémi Chénier, *Québec: A French Colonial Town in America, 1660–1690* (Ottawa: National Historic Sites, Parks Service, Environment Canada, 1991), pl. 5–12, 20, 22, 27–8; Marc Grignon, 'Loing du soleil': *Architectural Practice in Quebec City during the French Regime* (New York: Peter Lang, 1997).

6. Malcolm Andrews, *The Search for the Picturesque: Landscape Aesthetics and Tourism in Britain, 1760–1800* (Stanford, CA: Stanford University Press, 1989).

7. John Barrell, *The Dark Side of the Landscape: The Rural Poor in English Painting 1730–1840* (Cambridge: Cambridge University Press, 1980); Ann Bermingham, *Landscape and Ideology: The English Rustic Tradition, 1740–1860* (Berkeley and Los Angeles: University of California Press, 1986); Hugh Prince, 'Art and Agrarian Change, 1710–1815', in *The Iconography of Landscape: Essays on the Symbolic Representation, Design and Use of Past Environments*, ed. Denis Cosgrove and Stephen Daniels (Cambridge: Cambridge University Press, 1988), 98–118.

8. Daniel Clayton, 'The Creation of Imperial Space in the Pacific Northwest', *Journal of Historical Geography* 26 (2000): 327–50.

9. Benedict Anderson, *Imagined Communities: Reflections on the Origin and Spread of Nationalism*, rev. ed. (London: Verso, 1991); Beth Fowkes Tobin, *Picturing Imperial Power: Colonial Subjects in Eighteenth-Century British Painting* (Durham, NC: Duke University Press, 1999).

10. W.J.T. Mitchell, 'Introduction', in *Landscape and Power*, ed. W.J.T. Mitchell (Chicago: University of Chicago Press, 1994), 1–2.

11. John M. MacKenzie, 'Art and the Empire', in *The Cambridge Illustrated History of the British Empire*, ed. P.J. Marshall (Cambridge: Cambridge University Press), 296.

12. Linda Colley, *Britons: Forging the Nation 1707–1837* (New Haven, CT: Yale University Press, 5992); Kathleen Wilson, *The Island Race: Englishness, Empire and Gender in the Eighteenth Century* (London: Routledge, 2003); John Brewer, *Pleasures of the Imagination: English Culture in the Eighteenth Century* (Chicago: University of Chicago Press, 1997), 201–51, 449–63, 615–61.

13. Colin M. Coates, 'Like "The Thames towards Putney": The Appropriation of Landscape in Lower Canada', *Canadian Historical Review* 74 (1994): 317–43 (Repton quoted 322).

14. Douglas Cole and Maria Tippett, 'Pleasing Diversity and Sublime Desolation: The

Eighteenth-Century British Perception of the Northwest Coast', *Pacific Northwest Quarterly* 65 (1974): 1–7; I.S. MacLaren, 'Samuel Hearne & the Landscapes of Discovery', *Canadian Literature* 103 (1984): 27–40.

15. P.J. Marshall, 'Empire and Authority in the Later Eighteenth Century', *Journal of Imperial and Commonwealth History* 15 (1987): 105–22.

16. Mary Louise Pratt, *Imperial Eyes: Travel Writing and Transculturation* (London: Routledge, 1992), 38–85 (quoted 7, 57).

17. R.H. Hubbard, ed., Thomas Davies in *Early Canada* (Ottawa: Oberon, 1972), 9; Bruce G. Wilson, *Colonial Identities: Canada from 1760 to 1815* (Ottawa: National Archives of Canada, 1988), 24–7 (victory medals); Dennis Montagna, 'Benjamin West's *The Death of General Wolfe*: A Nationalist Narrative', *American Art Journal* 13 (1981): 72–88; Bruce Robertson, 'Venit, Vidit, Depinxit: The Military Artist in America', in *Views and Visions: American Landscape before 1830*, ed. Edward J. Nygren (Washington, DC: Corcoran Gallery of Art, 1986), 86–103.

18. *A View of the Landing Place above the Town of Quebec*, Pierre-Charles Canot after Francis Swaine after Hervey Smith (London, ca. 1760).

19. *Twelve Views of the Principal Buildings in Quebec, from Drawings, Taken on the Spot, at the Command of Vice-Admiral Saunders,* Pierre Grignon et al. after Richard Short (London, 1761). On the bombardment and occupation, see Guy Frégault, *Histoire de la Nouvelle-France, vol. 9, La guerre de la conquête 1754–1760* (Montreal: Fides, 1975), 341–2, 359–63, 387; Marcel Trudel, 'Les surprises du régime militaire, 1759–1764', in *Mythes et réalités*, 193–207.

20. 'General Murray's Report on the State of the Government of Quebec in Canada, June 5, 1762', in Documents *Relating to the Constitutional History of Canada 1759–1791*, ed. Adam Shortt and Arthur G. Doughty (Ottawa: King's Printer, 5907), 60.21. R.H. Hubbard, ed., *Thomas Davies c. 1737–1812* (Ottawa: National Gallery of Canada, 1972), 28, 30, 54–6, 138–45, plates I–VI.

22. I.N. Phelps Stokes, *The Iconography of Manhattan Island 1498–1909*, 6 vol. (New York: Robert H. Godd, 1915), 1:281–95.

23. G.S. Ritchie, 'Introduction', in *The Sea Chart*, ed. Derek House and Michael Sanderson (New York: McGraw-Hill Books, 1973), 11–13.

24. Richard L. Raymond, *J.F.W. DesBarres: Views and Profiles* (Halifax: Dalhousie University Art Gallery, 1982); G.N.D. Evans, *Uncommon Obdurate: The Several Careers of J.F.W. DesBarres* (Toronto: University of Toronto Press, 1969), 9–26.

25. *James Peachey, in Archives Canada Microfiches*, 2 (Ottawa: Public Archives, 1975–1976); W. Martha E. Cooke and Bruce G. Wilson, 'James Peachey', DCB, 4:612–14; Stuart R.J. Sutherland and Madeleine Dionne-Tousignant, 'Sir Frederick Haldimand', DCB, 5:887–904.

26. Hubbard, *Thomas Davies in Early Canada*, 41–61; id., 'Art of Thomas Davies', 34–8; id., *Thomas Davies*, 118–30.

27. S.R. Mealing, 'John Graves Simcoe', DCB, 5:754–59; Edith G. Firth, 'Elizabeth Posthuma Gwillim Simcoe', DCB, 7:361–3; Mary Beacock Fryer, *Elizabeth Postuma Simcoe 1762–1850: A Biography* (Toronto and Oxford: Dundurn Press, 1989).

28. Tom Gerry, 'Extremes Meet: Elizabeth Simcoe's Birchbark Landscapes', *Queen's Quarterly* 106 (1999): 589–601. Mary Quayle Innis, ed., *Mrs Simcoe's Diary* (Toronto: Macmillan of Canada, 1965). Parenthetical references are to this edition.

29. Canada, 'The Visual Diary of Elizabeth Simcoe: A Journey through Upper and Lower Canada', http://collections.ic.gc.ca/elizabethsimcoe (accessed 27 January 2005).

30. Malcolm MacLeod, 'Fortress Ontario or Forlorn Hope? Simcoe and the Defence of Upper Canada', *Canadian Historical Review* 53 (1972): 177.

31. On Québécois art after the conquest, see John R. Porter, 'L'Abbé Jean-Antoine Aide Créquy (1749–1780) et l'essor de la peinture religieuse après la Conquête', *Journal of Canadian Art History/Annales d'histoire de l'art canadien* 7 (1983): 55–73. In the 1780s Québécois

painters developed an indigenous portrait tradition, but they produced few landscapes before Joseph Légaré's work in the 1820s; R.H. Hubbard, *Peintres du Québec: Collection Maurice et Andrée Corbeil* (Ottawa: Galerie nationale du Canada, 1973), 38–69; John R. Porter, Nicole Cloutier, and Jean Trudel, *The Works of Joseph Légaré 1795–1855: Catalogue raisonné* (Ottawa: National Gallery of Canada, 1978).

32. Patricia Jasen, 'Romanticism, Modernity, and the Evolution of Tourism on the Niagara Frontier, 1790–1850', *Canadian Historical Review* 72 (1991): 283–318.

This paper benefited from commentary on earlier versions presented at a conference called The World of Objects: Appropriation, Reappropriation, and Disappropriation organized by the Centre interuniversitaire d'études sur les lettres, les arts, et les traditions at the Musée de la civilisation, Quebec (March 2003), and at the Student-Faculty Seminar in the Department of History at Dalhousie University (March 2003). Jerry Bannister, Marian Binkley, Elizabeth Manche, Shirley Tilotson, and anonymous assessors for the *Review* provided helpful criticisms. A fellowship from the John Simon Guggenheim Memorial Foundation and research grants from the Dalhousie University Faculty of Graduate Studies and the Social Sciences and Humanities Research Council of Canada provided financial assistance.

Chapter Six

Loyalists

READINGS

Primary Documents

1   From 'The Diary of Sarah Frost, 1783', in *Kingston and the Loyalists of the 'Spring Fleet'
of 1783*

2   'The Petition of 55 Loyalists', 22 July 1783 and 'A Memorial of Samuel Hakes and 600
Others', 15 August 1783 in *Vindication of Governor Parr and his Council*

Historical Interpretations

3   From 'Patriarchy and Paternalism: The Case of the Eastern Ontario Loyalist Women', Janice
Potter

4   From 'An Ancestry of which Any People Might Be Proud: Official History, the Vernacular
Past, and the Shaping of the Loyalist Tradition at Mid-Century', in *Inventing the Loyalists: The
Ontario Loyalist Tradition and the Creation of Usable Pasts*, Norman Knowles

Introduction

The quality of loyalty that distinguished some North Americans from others during and after
the American Revolution is generally invoked to explain one of the biggest differences between
Canadians (especially Upper Canadians and Maritimers) and Americans, and the differences in
their values. The refusal of some colonists to seek safety, food, and comfort outside the British
Empire certainly affected the way that people came to live in these places. Was loyalty to the
British monarch during and after the Revolution the only factor that mattered? Might loyalists
have been just as loyal to, or eager to maintain, the positions they held as merchants or workers
regardless of who ruled them?

   In her diary entries, Sarah Frost, a woman of no great fortune, reflects on the choice she and
her fellow Loyalists have made, knowing that even though the road ahead looked daunting, to
remain in the new United States would have been worse. Prospects for re-making their lives after
being identified with the oppressive British regime meant that the only card they had left to play
was loyalty, and the language of loyalty was relocation. The documents petitioning for land and

compensation from the Crown show that those who left the US to dwell in British North America wanted the Crown to know that they expected to be accommodated and rewarded in proportion to their service.

The secondary sources here reveal that the experiences of Loyalists were hardly uniform. Janice Potter sketches the clear gender divisions within the group that settled in what would become Eastern Upper Canada (ultimately Ontario) in the early post-revolutionary period. However, the reasons that led the loyalists to emigrate into what became Upper Canada were more complex than it may seem at first. In his contribution, Norman Knowles explains that the 'loyalist myth', the idea that the loyalists who emigrated to what became Upper Canada had left everything behind mainly out of loyalty, was created almost a century after their arrival, mainly to reflect the conservative political identity that developed in Upper Canada in the 1860s and 1870s.

QUESTIONS FOR CONSIDERATION

1. Do you think Sarah Frost would have known any of the people who created the petition (Document 2), and why?
2. What was the purpose of the petition?
3. To what degree do you think the Loyalists were acting in their own interests?
4. Does Potter think that Loyalist women gained anything beyond political peace and quiet by coming to the area that is now Eastern Ontario?
5. What purposes did the loyalty myth serve?

SUGGESTIONS FOR FURTHER READING

Condon, Ann Gorman, *The Envy of the American States: The Loyalist Dream for New Brunswick* (Fredericton: New Ireland Press, 1984)

Errington, Jane, *The Lion, the Eagle, and Upper Canada: A Developing Colonial Ideology* (Montreal and Kingston: McGill-Queen's University Press, 1994)

Graymont, Barbara, *The Iroquois in the American Revolution* (Syracuse, NY: Syracuse University Press, 1972)

Knowles, Norman, *Inventing the Loyalists: The Ontario Loyalist Tradition and the Creation of Usable Pasts* (Toronto: University of Toronto Press, 1997)

MacKinnon, Neil, *This Unfriendly Soil: The Loyalists Experience in Nova Scotia, 1781–1791* (Montreal and Kingston: McGill-Queen's University Press, 1986)

Potter-MacKinnon, Janice, *While the Women Only Wept: Loyalist Refugee Women* (Montreal and Kingston: McGill-Queen's University Press, 1993)

Walker, James W. St. G., *The Black Loyalists: The Search for a Promised Land in Nova Scotia and Sierra Leone 1783–1870* (Toronto: University of Toronto Press, 1992)

Whitfield, Harvey Amani, 'The American Background of Loyalist Slaves', *Left History* 14(1) (Spring/Summer 2009): 58–87

PRIMARY DOCUMENTS

1   From 'The Diary of Sarah Frost, 1783', in Walter Bates, ed., *Kingston and the Loyalists of the 'Spring Fleet' of 1783* (Fredericton: Non-Entity Press, 1980), 30–2.

Friday, June 6.—We are still lying at anchor waiting for other vessels of our fleet. My father will come on board in the morning if my husband can go and fetch him. I do so long to hear from my dear mother and my brothers and sisters. We have had a very bad storm this evening. Our ship tossed very much, and some of the people are quite sick, but I am in hopes the storm will soon abate. It grows late as I conclude for the night, hoping to see 'Daddy' in the morning.

Saturday, June 7.—My husband went on shore and brought father on board to breakfast. Soon after breakfast he returned on shore, for he expected to go home in the same boat he came down in, but hearing there was a vessel coming from Stamford today, he concluded to stay and return in it, so he came on board again to dine.

Sunday, June 8.—We are still lying at anchor in the North River. We expected to sail tomorrow for Nova Scotia, but I believe we shall remain at Staten Island or Sandy Hook for some days, or until our fleet is all got together.

Monday, June 9.—Our women, with their children, all came on board today, and there is great confusion in the cabin. We bear with it pretty well through the day, but as it grows towards night, one child cries in one place and one in another, whilst we are getting them to bed. I think sometimes I shall be crazy. There are so many of them, if they were as still as common there would be a great noise amongst them. I stay on deck tonight till nigh eleven o'clock, and now I think I will go down and retire for the night if I can find a place to sleep.

Tuesday June 10.—I got up early, not being able to sleep the whole night for the noise of the children. The wind blows very high. My little girl has been very sick all day, but grows better towards evening.

Wednesday, June 11.—We weighed anchor in the North River about six o'clock this morning, and sailed as far as Staten Island, where we came to anchor. I went on shore with Mr. Goreham and his wife, and Mr. Raymond and his wife, and my two children. We picked some gooseberries. We staid but a short time. In the afternoon I went ashore again with Mr. Frost and several others.

Thursday, June 12.—Nothing seems to be worth mentioning today. We are so thronged on board, I cannot set myself about any work. It is comfortable for nobody.

Friday, June 13.—It is now about half after three in the morning. I have got up, not being able to sleep for the heat, and am sitting in the entry-way of the cabin to write. It storms so I cannot go on deck. My husband and children are still sleeping. Through the day I am obliged to lie in my berth, being quite ill.

Saturday, June 14.—I am something better this morning. My husband brings me my breakfast, which I relish. We are still lying at Staten Island. We expected to sail this morning.

Sunday, June 15.—Our people seem cross and quarrelsome today, but I will not differ with any one, if I can help it. At half-past twelve our ship is getting under way—I suppose for Nova Scotia. I hope for a good passage. About five o'clock we come to anchor within six miles of the lighthouse at Sandy Hook. How long we shall lie here I don't know, but I hope not long. About six o'clock this evening we had a terrible thunder storm, and hail stones fell as big as ounce balls. About sunset there came another shower, and it hailed faster than before. Mr. Frost went out and gathered up a mugful of hail stones. Such an instance I never saw before on the 15th day of June.

Monday, June 16.—*Off at last!* We weighed anchor about half after five in the morning, with the wind north-nor'west, and it blows very fresh. We passed the lighthouse about half after seven. We have twelve ships belonging to our fleet besides our commodore's. Two hours later a signal was fired for the ships all to lie to for the *Bridgewater*, which seems to lag behind, I believe on account of some misfortune which happened to her yesterday. At 9 a.m. we have a signal fired to crowd sail. Again we are ordered to lie to. I don't know what it is for, as the *Bridgewater* has come up. It is now two o'clock, and we have again got under way. The mate tells me they have been waiting for a ship to come from New York, and she has overhauled us. We have now got all our fleet together: we have thirteen ships, two brigs, one frigate. The frigate is our commodore's. The wind dies away. It is now three o'clock, and the men are fishing for mackerel. Mr. Mills has caught the first one. I never saw a live one before. It is the handsomest fish I ever beheld. . . .

Monday, June 23.—It grows brighter towards noon, and the fog disappears rapidly. This afternoon we can see several of our fleet, and one of our ships came close alongside of us. Mr. Emslie says we are an hundred and forty miles from land now. The wind becomes more favorable, the fog seems to leave us and the sun looks very pleasant. Mr. Whitney and his wife, Mr. Frost and myself have been diverting ourselves with a few games of crib.

Tuesday, June 24.—The sun appears very pleasant this morning. Ten ships are in sight. The fog comes on, and they all disappear. We have been nearly becalmed for three days. A light breeze enables us to sail this evening two miles and a half an hour.

Wednesday, June 25.—Still foggy; the wind is fair, but we are obliged to lie to for the rest of the fleet. The commodore fires once an hour. The frigate is near us, and judging by the bells, we are not far from some of the other ships, but we can't see ten rods for the fog. We have *measles* very bad on board our ship.

Thursday, June 26.—This morning the sun appears very pleasant. The fog is gone to our great satisfaction. Ten of our ships are in sight. We are now nigh the banks of Cape Sable. At nine o'clock we begin to see land, at which we all rejoice. We have been nine days out of sight of land. At half after six we have twelve ships in sight. Our captain told me just now we should be in the Bay of Fundy before morning. He says it is about one day's sail after we get into the bay to Saint John's River. Oh, how I long to see that place, though a strange land. I am tired of being on board ship, though we have as kind a captain as ever need to live.

Friday, June 27.—I got up this morning very early to look out. I can see land on both sides of us. About ten o'clock we passed Annapolis; after that the wind all died away. Our people have got their lines out to catch codfish, and about half after five John Waterbury caught the first one for our ship.

Saturday, June 28.—Got up in the morning and found ourselves nigh to land on each side. It was up the river St. John's. At half after nine our captain fired a gun for a pilot; an hour later a pilot came on board, and at a quarter after one our ship anchored off against Fort Howe in St. John's River. Our people went on shore and brought on board spruce and gooseberries, and grass and pea vines with the blossoms on them, all of which grow wild here. They say this is to be our city. Our land is five and twenty miles up the river. We are to have here only a building place of forty feet in the front and a hundred feet back. Mr. Frost has now gone on shore in his whale boat to see how the place looks, and he says he will soon come back and take me on shore. I long to set my feet once more on land. He soon came on board again and brought a fine salmon.

Sunday, June 29.—This morning it looks very pleasant on the shore. I am just going ashore with my children to see how I like it. *Later*—It is now afternoon and I have been ashore. It is, I think, the roughest land I ever saw. It beats Short Rocks, indeed, I think, that is nothing in comparison; but this is to be *the city*, they say! We are to settle here, but are to have our land sixty miles farther up the river. We are all ordered to land to-morrow, and not a shelter to go under.

2 'The Petition of 55 Loyalists', 22 July 1783 and 'A Memorial of Samuel Hakes and 600 Others', 15 August 1783 in *Vindication of Governor Parr and his Council* (Halifax: 1783).

THE PETITION OF 55 LOYALISTS (22 JULY 1783)

The affairs at Nova Scotia and New York went on amicably among the Loyalists till August 1783, when it was discovered that the Rev. John Sayre, with fifty-four other persons, had privately presented to Sir Guy Carleton the following letter:

NEW-YORK, JULY 22, 1783.

SIR,
Your Excellency's kind attention and offers of your support to us demand our warmest thanks, which we beg the favour of you to accept.

The unhappy termination of the war obliges us, who have *ever been steady in our duty, as loyal subjects*, to leave our homes; and being desirous of continuing to enjoy the benefits of the British constitution, we mean to seek an asylum in the province of Nova Scotia.

Considering our several characters, and our former situation in life, we trust you will perceive that our circumstances will probably be the contrast to which they have been heretofore; especially as, from our respective occupations, we shall be unable *personally* to obtain the means of a tolerably decent support, unless your Excellency shall be pleased to countenance us by your recommendation in the following proposals; which are, with the utmost deference, submitted to your Excellency's consideration.

1. That a tract or tracts of land, free from disputed titles, be laid out for us in Nova Scotia, in such part of that province as one or more gentlemen, whom we propose to send forward for that purpose, being first approved of by your Excellency, shall pitch upon for us.
2. That this tract be sufficient to put us on the same footing with field-officers in his Majesty's army, with respect to the number of acres.
3. That, if possible, these lands may be exonerated of quit-rents.
4. That they be surveyed and divided at the expence of Government, and the deeds delivered to us as soon as possible, remitting the fees of office.
5. That, while we make this application to your Excellency, we wish not to be understood as soliciting a compensation for the losses we have sustained during the war, because we are humbly of opinion, that the settling of such a number of Loyalists of the most respectable characters, who have *constantly* had great influence in his Majesty's American dominions, will be highly advantageous in diffusing and supporting a spirit of attachment to the British constitution, as well as to his Majesty's royal person and family.

We have only to add our earnest request of your Excellency's aid and support in carrying this matter into execution, as soon as it shall comport with your leisure; and to assure your Excellency, that we are, with great respect, your Excellency's most humble and obedient servants,

Signed by, Addison, Henry (and 54 others). . . .

A MEMORIAL OF SAMUEL HAKES AND 600 OTHERS (15 AUGUST 1783)

The Loyalists about this time (mid-August) discovered the art and designs of the Fifty-five: a meeting of them was held immediately; when they agreed upon . . . a Memorial to the Commander in Chief:

The Memorial of the Subscribers,
Humbly sheweth,
That your Memorialists, having been deprived of very valuable landed estates, and considerable personal properties, without the lines, and being also obliged to abandon their possessions in this city, on account of their loyalty to their Sovereign, and attachment to the British constitution, and seeing no prospect of their being reinstated, had determined to remove with their families, and settle in his Majesty's province of Nova-Scotia, on the terms which they understood were held out *equally* to all his Majesty's persecuted subjects.

That your Memorialists are much alarmed at an application which they are informed Fifty-five persons have joined in to your Excellency, soliciting a recommendation for tracts of land in that province, amounting together to *two hundred and seventy-five thousand acres*, and that they have dispatched forward Agents to survey the unlocated lands, and select the most fertile spots and desirable situations.

That, chagrined as your Memorialists are at the manner in which the late contest has been terminated, and disappointed as they find themselves in being left to the lenity of their enemies, on the dubious recommendation of their leaders, they yet hoped to find an asylum under British protection, little suspecting there could be found, among their fellow-sufferers, persons ungenerous enough to attempt engrossing to themselves so disproportionate a share of what Government has allotted for their common benefit, and so different from the original proposals.

That your Memorialists apprehend some misrepresentations have been used to procure such extraordinary recommendations, the applications for which have been most studiously concealed, until now that they boast its being too late to prevent the effect. Nor does it lessen your Memorialists surprize to observe, that the persons concerned (several of whom are said to be going to Britain) are most of them in easy circumstances, and, with some exceptions, more distinguished by the repeated favours of Government, than by either the greatness of their sufferings, or the importance of their services.

That your Memorialists cannot but regard the grants in question, if carried into effect, as amounting nearly to a total exclusion of themselves and families, who, if they become settlers, must either content themselves with barren or remote lands, or submit to be tenants to those, most of whom they consider as their superiors in nothing but deeper art and keener policy.— Thus circumstanced,

Your Memorialists humbly implore redress from your Excellency, and that enquiry may be made into their respective losses, services, situations, and sufferings; and if your Memorialists shall be found equally entitled to the favour and protection of Government with the former applicants, that they may be all put on an equal footing; but should those who first applied be found, on a fair and candid enquiry, more deserving than your Memorialists, then your Memorialists humbly request that the locating their extensive grants may at least be postponed, until your Memorialists have taken up such small portions as may be allotted to them.

And your Memorialists, as in duty bound, shall ever pray, &c.

New-York, Aug. 15, 1783.

Signed by Samuel Hake,
and above 600 others.

HISTORICAL INTERPRETATIONS

3 From Janice Potter, 'Patriarchy and Paternalism: The Case of the Eastern Ontario Loyalist Women', *Ontario History* 81(1) (1989): 3–24.

Although the American Revolution did not alter the legal or political rights of women, it changed their lives dramatically in other ways.[1] With the men away fighting, women were forced to shoulder the burden of running the farm, the estate, or the business, and as a result there was less rigidity in the sexual division of labour, women gained confidence in their abilities, and men had more respect for women and their contributions to society. Those experiences were reinforced by public recognition of women's contribution to the Revolution and by the ideology of the Revolution. For example, boycotts of British cloth meant that wearing homespun became a sign of patriotism and that spinning, one of the most time-consuming and clearly feminine domestic chores, was raised in status. Moreover, there was an anti-patriarchal aspect of the Revolution that fostered less authoritarian and more reciprocal relationships between men and women. Republican ideology, with its emphasis on voluntary consent, also allowed more scope for women. There was 'greater mutuality and reciprocity' in marriages and in some cases 'more egalitarian marital relationships'.[2] The belief in the need to raise a moral and upright citizenry also enhanced the status of motherhood and made it easier for women to obtain an education, since it was they who would be raising the children. The result was more confident, self-reliant women, some of whom decided not to marry, and a society that valued more highly the domestic sphere generally and women specifically.

But what was the situation of Loyalist women, whose actions did not receive the same recognition and for whom there was no equivalent to republican ideology? The existing material on Loyalist women includes books about individuals, papers about specific groups, such as Loyalist women who filed claims for compensation, and an interesting thesis discussing Loyalist women in general terms.[3] This paper, however, considers in a preliminary way the effect of the Revolution on one specific group of Loyalist women—those who lived on the frontiers of New York, New England, and Pennsylvania and eventually settled in the townships created along the St. Lawrence River and Lake Ontario between Longueuil and the Bay of Quinte in what is now eastern Ontario.

Despite the diversity of their ethnic origins, the eastern Ontario Loyalist women shared a common background characterized by paternalism and patriarchy, and their experiences during the Revolution were similar. Virtually all went through several stages in the course of becoming refugees: they were harassed or persecuted, they were forced to flee to British bases for protection, they lived under British military rule in what might be called refugee camps, and with aid from the British they were eventually resettled.

Information about these women can be found in the few personal letters and diaries that have survived, in the claims Loyalists made for compensation from the British government, and in the records of the Patriot committees that interrogated Loyalists and of the British authorities who had to supervise and provision them. And, from records such as military registers, provisioning lists, returns of Loyalists, and land grants, it is possible to compile a reasonably precise statistical profile of the eastern Ontario Loyalists.

The 1786 census reveals that the 1,800 families, or 4,661 individuals, living along the St. Lawrence River and the eastern end of Lake Ontario were an ethnically diverse group that included many recent immigrants. Of the eastern Ontario Loyalists whose birthplace is known, about 45 per cent were foreign and about 45 per cent American-born.[4] Many of the American-born belonged to ethnic groups that had retained their native language, group cohesiveness, and other aspects of their culture. The largest of the ethnic minorities were the Germans, who accounted for about 30 per cent of the total and of whom one-quarter were immigrants and the rest Americans of German ancestry. About 5 per cent were Dutch, mostly more traditional members of the Dutch Reformed Church who had kept their culture and language.[5] Another group of American-born Loyalists who had retained their distinctive culture were the Mohawk Indians, who had played an important military role in the Revolution.

The largest of the immigrant groups, constituting 24 per cent of the total, were the Scots. Many were Highlanders and Jacobites who had emigrated because of poverty and the enclosure of their lands. In the colonies they retained their Gaelic language, Catholic religion, and other aspects of their culture.[6]

Whether American- or foreign-born, the vast majority of eastern Ontario Loyalists had lived on the frontiers of colonial society and were farmers. Over 70 per cent came from the northern New York counties of Tryon, Charlotte, and Albany. About 2 per cent came from each of New Jersey, Connecticut, and Pennsylvania, and many of the Pennsylvanians were from the frontier settlements along the Susquehanna River.[7] They had all been part of the mass movement to the frontiers after the Seven Years War.

A common theme in the social relationships of many eastern Ontario Loyalists was paternalism. Paternalism has been variously defined as interference with people's liberty for their own good and as the determination by one person what is in the best interests of another. A paternalistic relationship need not be harsh, however, and can even be co-operative in that it is a close and affectionate relationship in which the dependent party feels the need for guidance and is willing to exchange some independence for security.[8] But in such a relationship there is a hierarchy or at least inequality—there are superiors and subordinates, leaders and followers—and the dominant party feels an obligation to protect the interests of the subordinate in return for loyalty and deference.

Eighteenth-century paternalism was exemplified in the relationship between some New York landlords and their tenants. In spite of the rush to the frontiers for land, not all colonial Americans managed to acquire land of their own. In the case of the eastern Ontario Loyalists, only 20 per cent had held their land in freehold, and some had shared land or squatted on disputed land, but the vast majority had been tenants on the northern New York manorial estates owned by families like the Johnsons; indeed, at least 20 per cent of the Loyalist claimants who settled in what is now eastern Ontario had been tenants of the Johnsons.

The Johnsons ran their 20,000-acre estate like quasi-feudal lords. They helped their tenants financially, burned the debtor bonds of over-extended tenants, and helped artisans like Richard Mandevell, a 'Breeches Maker' who later settled in eastern Ontario, establish themselves in the local village. They also built roads, schools, and mills; introduced sheep and new crops; and at Johnstown, the county seat, established a county fair and built the local jail, courthouse, and Anglican church.[9] In return for looking after the interests of their tenants, the Johnsons expected loyalty and deference—letters to them from tenants and others, for example, often began, 'May it Please your Lordship'. When the Revolution came, the Johnson's tenants formed an armed guard to protect their landlord, and when he fled to Canada, they followed.[10]

There were also other paternalistic relationships between eastern Ontario Loyalists and various authorities. Many of the colonists, of German Palatinate or French Huguenot ancestry were Protestants who had fled to England in search of religious freedom and who revered George III as a defender of Protestantism. The Highlanders were accustomed to an authoritarian society, and their family and clan structure was patriarchal. And the Mohawk, although they considered themselves an independent people, spoke of the king as a father and looked to the British government to protect them from the rapaciousness of the powerful New York landlords who spent much of the eighteenth century defrauding the Indians of their land. [. . .]

The social and family structure in which these Loyalists and other colonial Americans lived was also patriarchal if we take patriarchy to mean 'the manifestation and institutionalization of male dominance over women and children in the family and the extension of male dominance over women in society in general. . . . [It] implies that men hold power in all the important institutions of society and that women are deprived of access to such power.'[11] Colonial American society was patriarchal in several senses. Women could not participate in the political process, they could not get a higher education, and men controlled the most

basic commodity in the society—land. Not only was the title to the family's property in the man's name, but a widow who remarried lost ownership of her property to her new husband. A married woman's identity was subsumed in that of her husband's. 'A married couple', in the words of one historian, 'became like a legal fiction: like a corporation, the pair was a single person with a single will'—the husband's. Even within the household it was common for the man to make all of the major decisions about finances and even about raising the children, and in any marital separation the man retained custody of the children.[12]

Patriarchal relationships, like paternalistic ones, did not mean that there could not be affection between husband and wife. To cite one example, a 1776 letter from Alexander McDonald, a captain in the Royal Highland Emigrants stationed in Halifax, to his wife in the colonies began, 'My dear Susannah' and ended tenderly, 'I have no time to write more. . . . Kiss the children for me and believe the one forever to be yours.' Yet the patriarchal nature of the relationship was revealed in the instructions he gave her about all aspects of her life: 'Keep the Child always clean and well dress'd and you must appear in yr best Colours yourself.' Of a fellow soldier, he wrote, 'Keep the old gentleman always at a distance from you and never let him again appear in the House.'[13]

The subordination of women in the colonial American family was revealed in the diary of Dothe Stone, sister of the eastern Ontario Loyalist, Joel Stone. As Dothe's list of births illustrates, marriage and childbirth were central to women's lives. The average woman was married in her early twenties to a man from one to five years older; she could expect to be pregnant within 12 months, and her childbearing years became a cycle of pregnancy, birth, and lactation.[14]

The birth and care of children, combined with women's other tasks, meant that their life centred on the home. The family farm was the basic economic and social unit on the frontier, and although some women did have to help with clearing and farming the land, women's jobs were more often milking the cows, taking care of the chickens, planting and tending the garden, and harvesting the orchard. As well, they cared for the house, salted beef and pork, preserved fruit and stored vegetables, made cider and cheese, and dried apples. A major chore was making clothing: Dothe writes of spending days with her sisters at spinning wheels. Whereas her husband might get away from home by going fishing or hunting or by travelling to town for supplies or to do business, the woman, especially if she had small children (which was almost always), was tied to the home.[15]

Colonial women found security in what was familiar to them—their homes, their families, and their circle of community friends and relatives. Dothe wrote fondly of her favourite room, her 'once loved chamber', and her diary is full of excitement when describing social events, such as weddings, or gatherings at which a fiddler led the party in singing and dancing. Dothe also relied heavily on female companionship. Tasks like spinning were done in the company of other women; women helped each other in childbirth and child rearing, and most of them lived in the same house as, or close to, other female relatives. [. . .] Home, family, and female companionship were what mattered most to colonial women. [. . .]

Relationships within the colonial family were patriarchal, and even women themselves spoke of their own inferiority and dependence. Widows, like the strong-minded Patriot, Mary Fish, for example, described themselves as 'a poor weak and helpless creature, [who] could do nothing but lie at the foot of mercy and look for direction.' 'What', she asked rhetorically, 'Could a feble [sic] woman do.'[16] Statements like these do not necessarily mean that women inwardly accepted the notion of their helplessness and inferiority. What they do mean, however, is that the social norms were such that women felt the need to express their feminine dependence and weakness.

But the notions of female helplessness and dependence were brought into question by the Revolution, which posed new challenges for Patriot *and* Loyalist women and forced many to adopt new roles. To Loyalist women, attached to their homes and local surroundings, accustomed to the security of friends, relatives and neighbours, and used to relying on men to direct their lives and make important decisions for them, the Revolution was a shattering experience. Patriot women, it is true, were left to manage the family and farm or business in their husbands' absence; but at least most remained in their homes and communities. Many Loyalist women, however, lost everything they valued most. Their families were scattered and the men who had directed their lives, gone. Many were also wrenched from all that was familiar—their homes, their relatives, and their communities. What all Loyalist women shared was their experiences as refugees, which were far more challenging than those of most Patriot women.

The pattern was set in May 1776, when Sir John Johnson fled from his northern New York estate with 170 tenants to escape arrest by the Patriots and to seek refuge in Canada, leaving behind his wife, Lady Mary Watts Johnson, who was pregnant and already the mother of two children under two. Mary, or Polly, who was from a prosperous New York city merchant and banking family, had married Sir John in 1773 at the age of nineteen and moved north to live in Tryon County. When her husband fled, Polly could not accompany him because of her condition, the hastiness of his departure, and the extraordinary rigours of the trip. Disappointed at the escape of Sir John, the Patriots forced her to turn over the keys to 'every place'; her husband's private papers were seized, his 'books distributed about the country', and their home, Johnson Hall, plundered and 'made a Barrack.' Lady Johnson was held hostage in Albany, although she was in touch regularly with her husband through 'Indian and white men . . . sent through the Woods.' After some twenty months in captivity, Lady

Johnson escaped, travelling through enemy territory in the cold winter. Although she finally reached the British base in New York City, her youngest child died as a result of its traumatic experiences.[17]

Within months of Lady Johnson's escape the war that was to rage on the frontier for more than four years began, and the hostages in this vicious conflict were the women and the children. As the Patriots attempted to assert their control over the region by forcing suspected Loyalists to take oaths of allegiance or join the militia, many able-bodied Loyalist men were either arrested or followed Sir John Johnson's lead by escaping to British lines, reluctantly leaving their families behind. Once in Canada, most had to join the various Loyalist regiments that collaborated with the Indians to launch retaliatory raids on the American frontier. For the British, the raids had a military purpose; to harass the enemy and destroy food supplies for Patriot forces. For many Loyalist soldiers, the raids were an opportunity to seek revenge on their foes in the colonies, find new recruits, make contact with their families, and occasionally bring the families back to Canada. For the families, the raids complicated their already troubled lives by intensifying Patriot hatred of the Loyalists and compromising them even further, since the families often harboured or helped the raiding parties. As the raiding parties retreated to the safety of Canada, they left their families behind.[18]

With the men in their lives gone, Loyalist women were forced to assume new responsibilities, and some even actively engaged in the war effort. For example, three women were implicated in a plot to kidnap the mayor of Albany, and one, an Indian woman, confessed to having lured the mayor to the woods by reporting that she had found a dead body there.[19] Another woman was arrested and jailed along with twenty men for 'having assisted in the destruction of Currey Town.'[20] Women were arrested and some imprisoned for taking part in robberies, which were especially common at the manor of Rensselaerwyck in the late

1770s.[21] Loyalist women also provided intelligence and passed messages between the British in New York City and Canada.[22]

Two eastern Ontario Loyalist women who were unusually active in the war effort were associated with the Mohawk Indians. This is not surprising in light of the status of women in the matrilineal Mohawk society, where children belonged to the mother's rather than the father's clan and women chose and deposed the chiefs. The local economy of the predominantly agrarian Mohawk was controlled by the women, who were responsible for planting, harvesting, and distributing the crops. Mohawk matrons were also influential in war councils and in determining the fate of captives.[23]

One very influential Mohawk woman was Molly Brant, or Konwatsi'tsianienni. A member of a high-ranking Mohawk family, sister of the famous Mohawk chief, Joseph Brant, and a matron who had a great influence in the matrilineal Iroquois society, Molly Brant 'was a person of great prestige in her nation and throughout the Confederacy.' Her power and influence were heightened after 1759, when she became the wife in all but name of Sir William Johnson, superintendent of Indian affairs, with whom she had eight children. Equally at home in the Indian village, in the war council, as the charming and gracious hostess at Johnson Hall, or in running Johnson's huge estate during his frequent absences, Molly Brant was a remarkable woman.[24]

She helped many Loyalists escape to Canada, provided intelligence to the British, and played a decisive part in fostering the ties of loyalty, self-interest, and history that underpinned the Mohawk support for the British during the Revolution. After her home was plundered by the Patriots and she was forced to flee with her family to the safety of the Iroquois villages, Brant came to Canada in 1778 and moved from one British base to another, cementing the Mohawks' loyalty to the British. Daniel Claus, Indian agent and son-in-law of the late Sir William Johnson, said of Molly Brant, 'One word from her is more taken notice of by the five nations than a thousand from any white man without Exception.' The commanding officer at Carleton Island attributed the good behaviour of the Indians there to Brant's influence: 'The Chiefs were careful to keep their people sober and satisfy'd, but their uncommon good behaviour is in a great Measure to be ascribed to Miss Molly Brant's influence over them, which is far superior to that of all their Chiefs put together, and she has in the course of this Winter done every thing in Her power to maintain them strongly in the King's interest.' Brant's stature was recognized by the British government, which awarded her one of the largest pensions ever given to any Indian and built her a house at present-day Kingston, where she spent her last years.[25]

Another woman influential among the Mohawk was Sarah Kast McGinnis, an American-born Palatinate German, who as a child in northern New York lived with the Mohawks, was adopted by them, and learned their language. In the 1740s Sarah married an Irishman, Timothy McGinnis, who became involved with Sir William Johnson in the fur trade and as a captain in the Indian Department. After her husband was killed in the Seven Years War, the widow McGinnis carried on his trading business.[26]

When the Revolution broke out, both sides courted Sarah because of her close association with the Iroquois, the Patriots offering her twelve shillings York currency a day and a guard of fifteen men. But Sarah and her family sided with the British and worked to cement the Iroquois' loyalty, actions that caused them to be persecuted by the Patriots. In 1777, as news spread of Burgoyne's expedition from Canada through northern New York, the Patriots considered it necessary to neutralize Loyalists like Sarah and her family. In Sarah's case, this involved arresting her son-in-law and then confiscating all her property. Sarah, her daughters, and grandchildren watched helplessly as their belongings were sold at public auction; they were then arrested and 'so harshly used' that one granddaughter died. When the Patriots

mistakenly concluded that the British had the upper hand in the region, Sarah and her family were released. Before they could be recaptured, they 'escaped at night with only what they could carry on their backs' and left for Canada with British troops, although Sarah had to leave behind a son 'who was out of his senses and bound in chains . . . and who some time afterward was burnt alive.'[27]

After arriving in Canada, Sarah agreed to a British request to return to northern New York, winter with the Iroquois, and try to counter the harmful effects of Burgoyne's defeat. On her arrival at 'the most central village of the Six nations', the Indians 'flocked to her from the remotest villages and thanked her for coming . . . to direct and advise them in that critical time.' Soon after her arrival, the Patriots sent messages to the Iroquois, 'with a most exaggerated account of General Burgoyne's disaster' and 'belts', inviting them to join the Patriots along with 'threats' in case the Indians refused. In response to the Patriot overtures, the Indians 'consulted with' Sarah and sought her 'opinion and advice': 'Then after that with an Authority and privilege allowed to women of Consequence only among Indians, [she] seized upon and cancelled the [Patriot] Belts, telling them such bad news came from an evil Spirit and must endanger their peace and union as long as it was in their sight and therefore must be buried underground.'[28] When Sarah spent this long and difficult winter in the Indian villages, she was 64 years old.

Although Sarah Kast McGinnis's relationship with the Indians and her active participation in the Revolution were extraordinary, her other experiences were typical of those of other Loyalist women. As able-bodied Loyalist men on the frontiers either were arrested or fled, leaving their families behind, the sins of the fathers and husbands were visited on the wives and children. Patriot committees and mobs assumed, unless there was evidence to the contrary, that families were accomplices in the guilt of one member If one member of a family fled or was arrested, the rest were vulnerable either to official interrogation by committees or to unofficial harassment by mobs or Patriot neighbours.

The case of the Cartwright family was not unusual. The father, Richard, Sr., a prosperous innkeeper, landowner, and deputy postmaster of Albany, had shown his support for the Patriots in 1775 when he gave money to the Patriot expedition against Ticonderoga. But his daughter, Elizabeth, who was married to a British soldier and lived in Niagara, was in touch with his son, Richard, Jr., and when the local committee of correspondence discovered this in February 1777, it forced Richard, Jr., to give security for his future good behaviour. By October 1777 he could no longer give this guarantee, and with his young niece, Hannah, he left on a difficult journey through the northern New York wilderness to Canada. The parents, tainted by the Loyalism of their children, were mistreated, their property was confiscated, and within a year of their son's departure they were taken under guard to the border.[29]

The Cartwrights' experiences were shared by many Loyalist women who had to live with the consequences of their husbands' actions. With the men in their lives gone, the women not only had to assume responsibility for running the farm and taking care of their families, but also had to deal with Patriot harassment or persecution and in many cases they were forced to leave their homes to seek refuge behind the British lines. [. . .]

The severity of the treatment meted out to Loyalist women depended on their husbands' connections and reputation among the dominant faction in the community. The case of two Vermont Loyalist women illustrates this point. Sarah Bottum was the wife of Justus Sherwood, a Vermont landowner, speculator, and entrepreneur in the timber business. Originally from Connecticut, Justus had received his land in Vermont from the New Hampshire government, and he supported Ethan Allen and his brothers, the dominant faction in the disputed territory. When Justus fell afoul of the local Patriots for refusing to take an oath of allegiance and allegedly corresponding with the British, he

was threatened with execution and imprisoned, although he escaped and fled to Canada. The Patriots ransacked the Sherwoods' cabin and destroyed some of their belongings, but Sarah could look to her parents for help, and she was allowed to remain in Vermont until she decided to seek permission from the Patriots to join her husband in Canada.[30]

The treatment of another Vermont Loyalist, Mary Munro, was much harsher because her husband belonged to an unpopular faction in Vermont. John Munro, originally from Scotland, had been granted large tracts of land by New York, and this put him at odds with the dominant faction in Vermont, whose land grants came from New Hampshire. Munro became even more unpopular when he was appointed justice of the peace and given the unenviable task of imposing law and order on Ethan Allen and the Green Mountain boys, who harassed New Yorkers in Vermont. When the Revolution came and Munro supported the British, the Council of Safety drove him from his home and seized all his property, except 'a few personal articles left for the support of his wife.' Unlike Sarah Sherwood, who had the support of her family, Mary Munro was treated very harshly by her neighbours and shunned by her own family. She wrote to her husband of her plight:

> I am in a poor state of health and very much distresst. I must leave my house in a very short time and God knows where I shall get a place to put my head in, for my own relations are my greatest enemies. . . . They have distrest me beyond expression. I have scarcely a mouthful of bread for myself or children. . . . Is there no possibility of your sending for us? If there is no method fallen upon we shall all perish, for you can have no idea of our sufferings here . . . my heart is so full it is ready to break.

Luckily, Mary Munro and her eight children did make their way to Canada within a few months of this letter.[31]

Flight may have represented an end to persecution for many Loyalist women; yet, it was also difficult for them to leave their homes and cut their ties with their families, friends, and communities. Simon Schwartz, the son of tenants of the Johnson family, who described his father's flight to Canada with Sir John in 1776 and the harassment of other family members, stressed that his mother had left only when she had to; she 'would not come in [to Canada] before the House & builds [*sic*] were burnt.' Women like Mrs. Schwartz usually had no choice but to leave. If they left voluntarily, it was usually because their property had been confiscated or their homes destroyed and there were no relatives or neighbours to protect them.

Some Loyalist women simply fled, but many others sought permission to leave from Patriot committees. Either permission was granted and the women escorted to the frontiers, or they were exchanged for Patriot prisoners being held in Canada. Mary Cruger Meyers had been alone with seven children under thirteen since the summer of 1777, when her husband, John Walden Meyers, left to join Burgoyne. In October 1778 she and another Loyalist woman requested permission to go to New York.[32] After being dispossessed of their property, the wives of Loyalists in Tryon County petitioned the local Patriot committee to be either taken care of or allowed to join their husbands. Their latter request was eventually granted.[33] When women left, they could only take children under twelve with them; boys twelve and over were considered capable of bearing arms and had to be left behind.[34] Those going to British lines also had to pay all the costs of being escorted there and take fourteen days' provisions with them.[35]

By the late 1770s, however, many Loyalist women were forced to leave. Some were sent to Canada because they were destitute and 'subsisted at public Expense'. A more common reason for removing the women was that they had assisted the enemy. When their husbands, relatives, or friends returned to the frontiers from Canada to gather intelligence, to recruit, or to raid, the women provided food, shelter, and other forms of assistance, which only further incriminated them in the eyes of the Patriots. Rachel Ferguson and her daughters, for example, were brought before the local Patriot committee in 1779 'for harbouring and entertaining a Number of Tories who came down from Canada with an inte[n]tion of Murdering the Defenceless Inhabitants on the Western Frontiers.'[36] For their efforts the Ferguson women were jailed and later forced to leave.

By July 1780 it was official policy in New York to 'remove families of persons who [had] joined the Enemy.' The families were given twenty days to prepare for their departure, their goods and chattels were to be sold to pay the costs, and any who ignored the edict were to 'be liable to be proceeded against as Enemies of this and the United States.'[37] Some women asked for and received a reprieve; but this required that 'sundry well affected inhabitants' had to testify that the woman had 'behaved herself in a becoming manner.'[38] In other words, it was up to the woman to prove innocence by having well-known Patriots testify on her behalf. In the absence of such testimony, the woman was assumed to share the guilt of her husband.

Exile was the last stage in a process that profoundly altered the role and responsibilities of many Loyalist women. Like their Patriot counterparts, Loyalist women assumed the responsibility for running the household and farm in the absence of their husbands. But Loyalist women also had to endure harassment, persecution, and often poverty because of the actions of their husbands. Most difficult of all, perhaps, was the necessity of abandoning their homes, relatives, and communities. [. . .]

Women were also forced to take more responsibility for looking after themselves and families. A group of New York Loyalist women who had established themselves near Saratoga petitioned the Patriots in 1780 for permission to go to Canada; in 1781 they were still on the frontier and regarded as a serious enough threat that they were ordered to move to the interior. The 16-year-old daughter of John McDonell, a Scots Loyalist from Tryon county, 'was obliged to hire herself to an old Dutch woman to spin in order to prevent starving.' And there was the case of Elizabeth Bowman, who, after her house on the Susquehanna River had been sacked by the Patriots and her husband and eldest son carried off, was left to care for eight children. The Indians helped them through the winter, and in the spring she moved to the Mohawk River and joined other Loyalist women to grow corn and potatoes. When the British rescued them in the fall and took them to Canada, there were five women, thirty-one children, and one pair of shoes.[39]

Exile marked the end of one stage of Loyalist women's refugee experience and the beginning of another. The women had left the American colonies as disaffected citizens considered a threat to the security of the new nation. In British territory they were burdens, mouths to be fed and bodies to be clothed and housed. When they reached Canada, they were usually destitute and the British unprepared for their arrival. In 1777 an officer in Niagara described the refugees flocking to that base: 'They are almost naked and have been so long hiding in the woods, and almost famished that it is distressing to behold them. . . . I am informed that 50 are on their way, but so weak they can scarcely crawl. I wish your excellency's direction on how to dispose of them.'[40] From Crown Point, a base at the other end of the outer perimeter of British defences, came similar accounts of the arrival of Loyalists who 'had fled from persecution', especially in the winter when the lakes and rivers could be crossed by sleigh. Often British officials were uncertain what to do with the refugees, and families arriving in Niagara were often sent on to Montreal.[41]

When the women arrived at the bases, they were in need of food, clothing, and shelter. Most had been stripped of their property and many of their possessions before their flight. The journey itself across the wilderness of northern New York was gruelling. Reaching Canada involved either crossing one of the many lakes in an open boat or perhaps a sleigh in winter, or travelling along rugged trails since 'there [was] no road

by land to go with a carriage.' Sir John Johnson and his tenants who fled from northern New York in 1776 travelled for nineteen days, during which they almost starved, going nine days without provisions, except 'wild onions, Roots and the leaves of beech trees'. When they reached Canada, their shoes were worn through and their clothes ragged.[42]

Sarah Bottum Sherwood's greatest ordeal during the Revolution was her trip to Canada, which began with a wagon ride over trails to the shores of Lake Champlain. Next was a boat trip across the lake and a thirty-mile trek through the bush to the closest British outpost. When Sarah undertook the trek, it was November; she had with her a slave, a child of three, and a baby; and she was seven months pregnant. But she succeeded and was re-united with her husband.[43]

When Loyalists arrived at British bases, penniless and exhausted by the rigours of their journey, they were at the mercy of paternalistic and patriarchal British military regimes. Even Sarah McGinnis, the tough 64-year-old who had wintered with the Iroquois in 1777, was 'in dire need' in Montreal the following year. Her daughter was 'so scantily lodged' that her mother could not stay with her. She was also refused firewood by the officer in charge, who said that only the governor could make such a decision. Sarah and her family were left 'without any money or income except what they could earn by the needle.'[44] Thus, Loyalists had to look to the British government to provide shelter, clothing, and rations and at the end of the war to chart their future.

The British government took care of its charges but expected deference and service in return. The British regimes were military ones that dealt quickly and harshly with dissenters. In return for their keep, men had to fight in the Loyalist regiments and women had to do washing and other domestic chores for the army. Questioning of the regime was neither common nor tolerated. When a group of Loyalists in Quebec petitioned the governor for more aid, for example, they were informed that if the governor's plans for them were not acceptable, they could go to Nova Scotia.[45]

Patriarchy and paternalism were also apparent in the last phase of the Loyalists' experience—their resettlement in what is now eastern Ontario. Under the direction of British officials, the Loyalists were transported into the interior and provided with food, clothing, agricultural equipment, and seeds. They were settled on land surveyed by British officials, and British army officers were there to preserve order and ensure that the governor's instructions were obeyed. Although the new communities were on the frontier, from the beginning there was a structure and hierarchy. In a society where land ownership was central to status, the size of one's land grant varied according to one's military rank, the British government compensated Loyalists for their losses on the basis of the value of their former assets in the American colonies, and Loyalist officers received half pay after their regiments were disbanded.[46]

Thus, when Loyalist women reached British lines, they were re-integrated into a paternalistic and patriarchal power structure. Within this paternalistic order there was a hierarchy. There were those who needed to be cared for and those responsible for administering the care, those in leadership roles and those who were clearly subordinates. Deference to authority was built into the military regimes, and deference was accorded to those dispensing benevolent care and expected of those receiving it. Even more so than the civil regimes in the American colonies, the military regimes in Quebec and New York City had no place for women and even shunned them as extra mouths to be fed and families to be housed. Women could only fit into such paternalistic and patriarchal power structures as subordinates needing care and protection.

This subordination was reflected in the Loyalist women's petitions for rations, subsistence, or compensation for losses. The very act of petitioning those in authority for aid cast all Loyalists in the role of supplicant; 'the formulation of a petition', in the words of Linda Kerber,

'begins in the acknowledgement of subordination.'[47] Moreover, many Loyalist petitions were stylized litanies of loyalty, service, and sacrifice. But there was a difference in the substance of women's petitions: women based their claim to British assistance on their feminine frailty and on the service of their husbands. In fact, some did not even petition on their own behalf but had men request aid for them. When Catherine Peck, wife of one of Sir John's tenants who had fled to Canada in 1776, arrived in New York City 'in hope of getting a Passage to Canada' and found herself and her child 'destitute of any Sort of Support', it was an official from Indian Affairs who appealed to British officials to assist her.[48] Even Molly Brant, who had been so active in maintaining the loyalty of the Mohawk, had to seek male help when it came to approaching the British for support. She sought advice from her brother in 1779, and in 1780 two members of the Johnson clan and another associate discussed helping Molly and her daughters to get a pension from the British.[49] Of the 26 eastern Ontario Loyalist women who sought compensation from the British for their losses, four had men file their claims.[50]

Whether Loyalist women petitioned themselves or had others do it for them, what was stressed was their weakness, helplessness, and dependence. Citing a 'numerous, small and helpless family' as his main burden, one Loyalist appealed to the governor of Quebec for subsistence, while another asked for aid for his 'chargeable family'. The Loyalist Jean McConell summed up perfectly the notion of female incapacity when she described herself as 'feeble' and added that she also had 'a family of daughters'.[51] Feeble and helpless were the adjectives used most often by Loyalist women to describe themselves.[52]

These professions of feebleness were very much at odds with Loyalist women's recent experiences. The case of Phoebe Grant, or Grout, illustrates this point nicely. When her husband and son joined Burgoyne in 1777, the 'rebels' seized his property and 'effects' and turned her 'and three helpless Female children

Out of Doors destitute'. She then had to 'fly' to Quebec 'for protection'. Within days of her arrival in Quebec, her husband drowned and she was 'obliged to provide for herself and her three children without an allowance from government which ceased on the death of her husband.' After her husband's death she did 'everything in her power to support herself', even though she was 'in a country far from a single Friend and a stranger to the language.' When Phoebe finally had to throw 'herself and poor family at your Excellency's feet praying' for subsistence, she could not revel in her accomplishments and seek praise for even surviving such ordeals; all she could do was tell her story as a tale of suffering and depict herself, in her own words, as 'a Feeble Woman'.[53]

Why did Loyalist women describe themselves as feeble or helpless when their recent experiences suggested just the opposite? One reason was a practical reality. What the British needed from the Loyalists were able-bodied males to raid the frontiers, spy on the Patriots, bring in new recruits, supply British troops, or build fortifications. What they did not need or want was women and children, who, it was assumed, could perform none of these services and would be a burden to the British because they had to be fed, clothed, and housed. Thus, the only way for women to appeal to the British was to cite their husband's valued services, rather than their own undervalued ones, and to invoke the paternalism of the military regimes by stressing their vulnerability and need for protection.

Another reason, however, was that when they reached British lines, Loyalist women confronted a well-defined power structure in which there were clearly prescribed social roles. In the colonies during the Revolution, traditional relationships were disrupted and lines of authority far from clear. Women could and did do things they might have never dreamed of doing in peacetime, and their actions were of necessity considered socially acceptable, if only because the boundaries of socially acceptable behaviour are more flexible in wartime. However, at British

bases lines of authority were not only clear, but were better defined than they had been in the colonies. Though there had been elements of paternalism and patriarchy in the pre-Revolutionary experiences of many Ontario Loyalists, the British regimes were much more patriarchal and paternal. And women could fit into such a power structure only as frail subordinates.

But the fact that women used the language of enfeeblement does not mean that they themselves accepted their own weakness. They were supplicants who had to petition for assistance, and 'the rhetoric of humility is a necessary part of the petition as a genre, whether or not humility is felt in fact.'[54] Women had no choice but to stress their dependence and helplessness; whether they actually believed it is another matter.

Yet, whether or not women accepted their own weakness is beside the point. The language they used expressed accurately their position in the power structure. Whether or not they were weak and dependent, they were assumed to be so for all public purposes and were outwardly treated as such. On the other hand, the consistent use of certain words cannot be divorced from one's attitudes about oneself: if women were forced by circumstances to reiterate their helplessness again and again, how long was it before they came either to accept that helplessness was basic to their femininity or to allow their actions to be limited by their supposed weakness? The fact that the eastern Ontario Loyalist women were never allowed to speak of their achievements with pride meant that they never received in any measure the recognition accorded to Patriot women.

It is ironic that many eastern Ontario Loyalist women, though they overcame greater obstacles and met more devastating challenges during the Revolution than their Patriot counterparts, received less recognition. As well as having to take charge of their families and farms in the absence of their husbands, Loyalist women were dispossessed of their property, thrown out of their houses, and even jailed by the Patriots. They had to leave what was most dear to them—their homes, their relatives, and their friends—and travel through the wilderness to the British lines.

Yet these remarkable and heroic accomplishments were never recognized. When they reached British lines, they had to fit once again into a patriarchal power structure in which their inferiority and dependence were assumed. Needing British support, they had to stress their dependence and weakness to appeal to the paternalism of the British regime. Only their suffering and their husband's service counted with the British. Whereas republicanism at least potentially offered more scope to women, paternalism assumed inequality and deference. There were the weak and the strong, the leaders and the followers. Within such a framework, women could only be the weak followers.

Not only were the accomplishments of eastern Ontario Loyalist women not recognized by the British; they were also ignored by later generations. After the Revolution, myths

grew up about the Loyalists' undying devotion to the British Empire or their upper class backgrounds, and tales were told of the men's heroism. Virtually ignored, however, were the heroic feats of the Loyalist women. Whereas the contributions of Patriot women, such as their spinning of homespun cloth, became part of the American folklore, the memories of the travails and victories of the eastern Ontario Loyalist women died with them.

These women were also ignored by Canadian historians, who, by focusing on the Revolutionary war on the frontier as it was run by the British and fought by the Loyalist regiments, have overlooked the essential fact that the war was a civil war in which women and children were of necessity participants. The experiences of the eastern Ontario Loyalist women and their part in the civil war that raged on the frontiers are an important part of Canadian history. Recognition of their accomplishments is long overdue.

NOTES

1. Mary Beth Norton, *Liberty's Daughters: The Revolutionary Experience of American Women, 1750–1800* (Boston: Little, Brown, 1980); Linda Kerber, *Women of the Republic: Intellect and Ideology in Revolutionary America* (Chapel Hill, NC: University of North Carolina Press, 1980). For another view, see Joan Hoff Wilson, 'The Illusion of Change: Women and the American Revolution', In Alfred F. Young, ed., *The American Revolution: Explorations in the History of American Radicalism* (DeKalb: Northern Illinois University Press, 1976), pp. 383–446.

2. Jay Fliegelman, *Prodigals and Pilgrims: The American Revolution against Patriarchal Authority, 1750–1800* (Cambridge: Cambridge University Press, 1982); Norton, *Liberty's Daughters*, pp. 235, 229; Jacqueline S. Reinier, 'Rearing the Republican Child: Attitudes and Practices in Post-Revolutionary Philadelphia', *William and Mary Quarterly*, 3rd ser., 39 (1982), 150–63.

3. See, for example, Mary Beacock Fryer, 'Sarah Sherwood: Wife and Mother, an "Invisible Loyalist"', in *Eleven Exiles: Accounts of Loyalists of the American Revolution*, Phyllis R. Blakely and John N. Grant, eds. (Toronto: Dundurn, 1982), pp. 245–64; Mary Beth Norton, 'Eighteenth-Century American Women in Peace and War: The Case of the Loyalists', *William and Mary Quarterly*, 3rd ser., 33 (1976), 386–409; Katherine M.J. McKenna, '"Treading the Hard Road": Some Loyalist Women and the American Revolution' (M.A. thesis, Queen's University, 1979).

4. M.S. Waltman, 'From Soldier to Settler: Patterns of Loyalist Settlement in "Upper Canada", 1783–1785' (M.A. thesis, Queen's University, 1981), p. 58.

5. Waltman, 'From Soldier to Settler', p. 60; Walter Allen Knittle, *Early Eighteenth Century Palatine Emigration: A British Government Redemptioner Project to Manufacture Naval Stores* (Baltimore: Dorrance, 1937); Eula C.

Lapp, To *Their Heirs Forever* (Picton: Picton Publishing Co., 1970); Alice P. Kenney, *Stubborn for Liberty: The Dutch in New York* (Syracuse: Syracuse University Press, 1975); 'The Albany Dutch: Loyalists and Patriots', *New York History*, 42 (1961).

6. Waltman, 'From Soldier to Settler', p. 62; I.C.C. Graham, *Colonists from Scotland: Emigration to North America, 1707–1783* (Ithaca: Cornell University Press, 1956); Hazel C. Mathews, *The Mark of Honour* (Toronto: University of Toronto Press, 1965).

7. Waltman, 'From Soldier to Settler', pp. 39–42.

8. Gerald Dworkin, 'Paternalism', in Rolf Sartorious, ed., *Paternalism* (Minneapolis: University of Minnesota Press, 1983), pp. 19–34; Donald Van De Veer, *Paternalistic Intervention: The Moral Bound of Benevolence* (Princeton: Princeton University Press, 1986), pp. 16–23; John Kleinig, *Paternalism* (Totow, NJ: Rowman and Allaneld, 1984), pp. 4–5; Jack D. Douglas, 'Co-operative Paternalism versus Conflictual Paternalism', in Sartorius, *Paternalism*, pp. 171–200; David Roberts, *Paternalism in Early Victorian England* (New Brunswick, NJ: Rutgers University Press, 1979), pp. 4–6.

9. Abbott Collection, Ms. 420, Letter and Reference for Richard Mandevell, Sir William Johnson, June 11, 1771, quoted in Robert William Venables, 'Tryon County, 1775–1783: A Frontier in Revolution' (Ph.D. thesis, Vanderbilt University, 1967), pp. 72, 64; Edward Countryman, *A People in Revolution: The American Revolution and Political Society* (Baltimore: Johns Hopkins University Press, 1981), pp. 21, 33.

10. Countryman, *A People in Revolution*, p. 33.

11. Gerda Lerner, *The Creation of Patriarchy* (New York: Oxford University Press, 1986), p. 239.

12. Kerber, *Women of the Republic*, p. 120; Joan R. Gundersen and Gwen Victor Gampel, 'Married Women's Legal Status in Eighteenth-Century New York and Virginia', *William and Mary Quarterly*, 3rd ser., 39 (1982), 114–34.

13. NAC, Fraser Papers, MG 23, B 33, Alexander McDonald to his wife, in 'Letters Extracted from the Letter Book of Capt. Alexander McDonald of the Royal Highland Emigrants written from Halifax, Windsor and Cornwallis between 1775 and 1779.'

14. Archives of Ontario [hereafter AO], Joel Stone Papers, Dothe Stone Diary, 1777–1792 [hereafter Stone Diary]; Joy Day Buel and Richard Buel, Jr., *The Way of Duty: A Woman and her Family in Revolutionary America* (New York: Norton, 1984); Robert V. Wells, 'Quaker Marriage Patterns in a Colonial Perspective', in Nancy F. Cott and Elizabeth Peck, eds., *A Heritage of Her Own: Toward a New Social History of American Women* (New York: Simon and Shuster, 1979), pp. 81–106; Norton, *Liberty's Daughters*, pp. 71–72; Laurel Thatcher Ulrich, *Good Wives: Image and Reality in the Lives of Women in Northern New England, 1650–1750* (New York: Knopf, 1982).

15. See, for example, Stone Diary; Norton, *Liberty's Daughters*, pp. 3–14.

16. New Canaan Historical Society, Noyes Family Papers, pp. 39–47, Mary to Joseph and Rachel Fish, Aug. 6, 1769, May 30, 1772, privately owned, quoted in Buel, *The Way of Duty*, pp. 62–63, p. 67.

17. NAC, Claus Papers, C-1478, vol. 1, Sir John Johnson to Daniel Claus, Jan. 20, 1777.

18. Jack M. Sosin, *The Revolutionary Frontier, 1763–1783* (New York: Holt, Rinehart and Winston, 1967).

19. Victor Hugo Palsits, ed., *Minutes of the Commissioners for Detecting and Defeating Conspiracies in the State of New York: Albany County Sessions, 1778–1781*, 3 vols. (New York: J.B. Lyon, 1909), Aug. 13, 1781, vol. 2, 762–63.

20. Ibid., July 25, 1781, vol. 2, 751–52.

21. Ibid., Sept. 4, 1778, vol. 1, 224; May 20, 1778, vol. 1, 122; June 17, 1778, vol. 1, 146; Aug. 3, 1779, vol. 1, 398; Oct. 3, 1778, vol. 1, 252.

22. Ibid., Nov. 8, 1780, vol. 2, 563; Jan. 29, 1781, vol. 2, 624; June 9, 1781, vol. 2, 733.

23. Barbara Graymont, The Iroquois in the American Revolution (Syracuse: Syracuse University Press, 1972), pp. 17, 21–23.

24. Graymont, *The Iroquois in the American Revolution*, p. 47; *Dictionary of Canadian Biography*, vol. 4, 416–19; H. Pearson Gundy, 'Molly Brant, Loyalist', *Ontario Historical Society Papers and Records*, 45 (1953), 97–108.

25. NAC, HP, vol. 21, p. 774, Daniel Claus to Governor Haldimand, Aug. 30, 1779; NAC, HP, vol. 21, p. 787, Captain Frazer to Haldimand, Mar. 21, 1780.

26. NAC, HP, vol. 21, p. 774, Daniel Claus to Governor Haldimand, Nov. 5, 1778.

27. NAC, HP, vol. 27, p. 302, Petition of Sarah McGinn, Audit Office 14.

28. Ibid.

29. Janice Potter and George Rawlyk, 'Richard Cartwright, Jr.', *Dictionary of Canadian Biography*, vol. 5, 167–72.

30. *PAO Report*, Claim of Justus Sherwood; Ian Cleghorn Pemberton, 'Justus Sherwood, Vermont Loyalist, 1747–1798', (Ph.D. thesis, University of Western Ontario, 1973); Mary Beacock Fryer, *Buckskin Pimpernel: The Exploits of Justus Sherwood, Loyalist Spy* (Toronto: Dundurn, 1981), 'Sarah Sherwood: . . . ', *Eleven Exiles*, pp. 245–64; Queen's University Archives, H.M. Jackson, *Justus Sherwood: Soldier, Loyalist and Negotiator* (Kingston: n.p., 1958).

31. AO, John Munro Papers, Undated document; NAC, HP, series B, vol. 214, p. 35.

32. Palsits, *Minutes of the Commissioners*, Oct. 1, 1778, vol. 1, 248.

33. 'Petition of sundry women wives of tories for relief', n.d. Tryon County Committee of Safety Papers, in Kerber, *Women of the Republic*, p. 50.

34. Palsits, *Minutes of the Commissioners*, Aug. 1, 1778, vol. 1, 190.

35. Ibid., Introduction, vol. 1, 57.

36. Ibid., *Minutes of the Commissioners*, Sept. 21, 1778, vol. 1, 237–38; Sept. 8, 1779, vol. 1, 441.

37. Ibid., vol. 3, 795.

38. See, for example, the case of Elizabeth Hogel, in Palsits, *Minutes of the Commissioners*, vol. 2, 540.

39. Palsits, *Minutes of the Commissioners*, Oct. 29, 1780, vol. 3, 558; Apr. 30, 1781, vol. 3, 696; NAC, HP, vol. 73, p. 54, John McDonell to Mathews, Mar. 20, 1780; 'A Letter from Mrs. Elizabeth Bowman Spohn', in J.J. Talman, *Loyalist Narratives from Upper Canada* (Toronto: Champlain Society, 1946), 315–22.

40. NAC, Colonial Office 42 [hereafter CO 42], vol. 36, B 33, pp. 2–3, R.B. Lernoult to Haldimand, Apr. 28, 1777.

41. CO 42, Q13, vol 36, B 33, Sir Guy Carleton to Lord G. Germaine, May 27, 1777; NAC, Claus Papers, vol. 25, C 1485, Taylor and Diffin to Daniel Claus, Nov. 11, 1778, Claus Papers.

42. Claus Papers, C 1478, vol. 1, Johnson to Claus, Jan. 20, 1777.

43. Fryer, 'Sarah Sherwood: . . . ', *Eleven Exiles*, pp. 245–64.

44. NAC, HP, vol. 21, p. 774, Claus to Haldimand, Nov. 19, 1778.

45. NAC, HP, vol. B 211, pp. 133–4, Memorial: Michael Grass and Loyalists from New York, Sorel, Jan., 1784. NAC, HP, vol. B 63, pp. 109–10, Mathews to Stephen DeLancey. Mar. 2, 1784.

46. H.V. Temperley, 'Frontierism, Capital and the American Loyalists in Canada', *Journal of American Studies*, 13 (1979), 5–27.

47. Kerber, *Women of the Republic*, p. 85.

48. NAC, British Headquarters Papers, vol. 16, microfilm, reel M-348, [Name illegible] to Lt. Col Roger Morris, Apr. 22, 1779.

49. NAC, Claus Papers, C 1478, Mary Brant to Joseph Brant, Oct. 5, 1779; C 1485, Captain Frazer to Daniel Claus, June 26, 1780.

50. Lydia Van Alstine, Flora Livingston, widow Obenholt, Margaret Hare.

51. NAC, HP, vol. 21, p. 875, Petition to Haldimand, Jan. 3, 1783; HP, vol. 21, p. 874, Petition of George Christie, Dec. 16, 1778; HP, vol. 21, p. 874, Petition of Jean McDonell, Nov. 30, 1782.

52. Mary Beth Norton, 'Eighteenth-Century American Women in Peace and War: The Case of the Loyalists', *William and Mary Quarterly*, 3rd ser., 33 (1976), 386–409.

53. NAC, HP, A 776, Phoebe Grout, Petition.

54. Kerber, *Women of the Republic*, p. 85.

4   From Norman Knowles, 'An Ancestry of which Any People Might Be Proud:
     Official History, the Vernacular Past, and the Shaping of the Loyalist Tradition at
     Mid-Century', in *Inventing the Loyalists: The Ontario Loyalist Tradition and the
     Creation of Usable Pasts* (Toronto, University of Toronto Press, 1997), 26–47.

'No people', the Toronto *Globe* observed in October of 1856, 'has made a figure in the life of nations, without its heroes.' Fortunately, Upper Canada could claim heroic foundations. 'United Empire Loyalists', the *Globe* asserted, 'form an ancestry of which any people might be proud. They had every characteristic which can go to constitute an enduring substratum for a coming nation.' It was a matter of considerable concern to the *Globe*, however, that Upper Canadians displayed a decided 'ignorance' and 'indifference' towards the province's 'Loyalist Fathers'. 'No ignorance of history', the *Globe* warned, 'can be more reprehensible than that which we now censure. It amounts to an utter obliviousness of our peculiar story . . . Here, then, we are in the sixty-second year of our being in Upper Canada with the only men who would accurately inform, fast dying, if not already dead, and but grossly ignorant of our provincial parentage and birth . . . such carelessness is a cruel injustice to our fathers.' The *Globe* urged the superintendent of education, Egerton Ryerson, to take immediate action to preserve and record the province's Loyalist history. 'Something must be done', the *Globe* concluded, 'in justice alike to the past, and to coming generations.'[1] A small group of committed individuals, Ryerson among them, heeded the *Globe's* advice and set about collecting the reminiscences, memoirs, and papers of surviving Loyalists and creating a Loyalist history.

The *Globe's* interest in Upper Canada's history and its Loyalist origins attests to the emergence of a new historical consciousness in the 1850s. This development was largely a product of the nationalist sentiment and expansionist ambitions that accompanied the process of state formation and the province's economic growth. The past was invoked and recalled by provincial leaders interested in the creation of an official history that could be used to promote unity, build a national identity, and uphold social and political order. Promoters of Upper Canada's past sought a heroic and inspiring history that celebrated the province's past achievements and future potential. A concern with origins, the deaths of the last of the original Loyalists, the need to counter nationalist American histories, and the presence of Loyalist descendants in prominent positions of influence in the government ensured that much of this interest in the past became focused upon Upper Canada's Loyalist pioneers. The result was a concerted effort on the part of the state and Loyalist descendants to collect and preserve documents connected with the province's Loyalist origins and to construct a history worthy of the province's founders and its future aspirations. Creating an official history that preserved the memory of the Loyalists, celebrated their contributions, and pointed to a future of continued progress and achievement proved to be a difficult task. The papers and reminiscences of surviving Loyalists that were anxiously collected at the time were part of a vernacular past rooted in local conditions, personal recollection, and particular experience. As John Bodnar has demonstrated, the immediate concerns of the vernacular past frequently conflict with the abstract needs of official history.[2] This was certainly the experience in Upper Canada. The desire to create a heroic and forward-looking official history of progress and achievement confronted, in the reminiscences of surviving Loyalists, figures who were ambivalent and ambiguous rather than heroic, a nostalgic idealization of pioneer society, and a deep disenchantment with present conditions. Ignoring the reminiscences, the agents of official history recast the Loyalist pioneers of memory into a persecuted elite who heroically sacrificed their homes and comfort for the sake of principle. Ironically, the idealized past produced by Loyalist historians such as William Canniff and Egerton Ryerson was based to a considerable degree on the work of an American, Lorenzo Sabine.

By mid-century, Upper Canada was no longer an isolated colonial backwater but a self-governing and prosperous commercial society. A steadily rising population, the construction of railways, the beginnings of large-scale industry, and the growth of the professions, banking, and other financial institutions all provided evidence that the transition to a mature capitalist society was well under way.[3] A vigorous process of state formation followed the achievement of responsible government and resulted in a tremendous expansion in the size of the state and the scope of its activities.[4] At the same time, sectional conflict with Canada East and the expansionist sentiment that accompanied the province's economic growth and the disappearance of its agricultural frontier helped to define a distinctive Upper Canadian identity and sense of national destiny.[5]

The forces transforming Canada West gave birth to a growing historical consciousness among the province's political and social leaders. This development was not unique. A sense of continuity and identity with a national past, reverence for national heroes, and the commemoration of great national events were becoming commonplace in both Europe and the United States by the middle of the nineteenth century. The rise of mass democracy and the social changes wrought by the industrial revolution demanded new devices to ensure or express social cohesion and identity and to structure social relations. The result was a determined effort on the part of the state and other power groups to create what Benedict Anderson has termed 'imagined political communities'. According to Anderson, the creation of such 'imagined communities' required the active mobilization of periphery by cultural centre in order to create a shared history upon which a national identity could be erected. In this process, a particular view of the past is selected from all the different times and events possible in order to represent the nation. It is particularly important, Anderson asserts, to designate a founding moment of great significance from which a straightforward history of progress can be dated.[6]

Canadian legislators recognized the importance of the past in constructing community and a shared identity and actively supported the production of literary and historical works. A committee of the legislature was created to review applications shortly after the union of Upper and Lower Canada in 1841. In 1842 the Legislative Assembly made a grant to John Richardson to assist in the publication of his planned history of the War of 1812.[7] The committee responsible for the encouragement of 'literary enterprise in Canada' was dominated by members from Canada East, which ensured that most of the funds available were directed towards French-Canadian authors.[8] François-Xavier Garneau, G.B. Faribault, and Abbé J.B.A. Ferland all received parliamentary grants to assist in the collection, transcription, and publication of materials connected with French-Canadian history.

In 1855 John Mercier McMullen, an Irish immigrant and journalist, published the province's first narrative history, *The History of Canada from its Discovery to the Present Time*. For McMullen, the past was a guide to the future. 'To regard our national future with confidence', McMullen insisted, 'an acquaintance with the past is an absolute necessity.' If Upper Canadians understood the lessons of history, their future would be assured. McMullen's interest in the didactic uses of history was accompanied by an appreciation of the importance of the past in forging a national identity. In writing his history, McMullen hoped to overcome the ethnic, social, and political tensions that divided Upper Canadians and to create an 'identity of interests' by infusing 'a spirit of Canadian nationality into the people generally.'[9] Seeking to consolidate and celebrate the achievements of the past, McMullen used the rise of colonial self-government and the province's social and economic progress as the central themes of his narrative. McMullen's preoccupation with material progress and improvement reveals a great deal about the type of past Upper Canadians sought to create for themselves.[10]

The importance of the past in creating community and identity was appreciated by the founders of Upper Canada's system of public education. The province's public schools were designed to create social harmony and uphold the existing social structure and relations of authority by constructing a patriotic public with a common sense of identity.[11] To achieve these ends, the province's superintendent of education, Egerton Ryerson, sought to create a system that was 'not only British, but Canadian in form and content.'[12] The ability of the public schools to forge a common national identity was limited by the lack of domestically produced textbooks with local themes and illustrations. Concerned by the dominance of American textbooks, Ryerson authorized the adoption of the Irish National Readers. Although the readers better reflected the political, social, and religious values Ryerson felt should underlie Upper Canadian society, they did not satisfy the demand for Canadian texts.[13] Educators recognized the important role that history could play in fostering patriotism and inculcating moral lessons from the past. In 1849 the superintendent of common schools for the Ottawa district, Thomas Higginson, commented in his annual report on the urgent need for a Canadian history textbook. 'Such a work', Higginson asserted, 'would be a secure basis whereon our young people could and would rest their loyalty and patriotism; such a work would develope [sic] events and circumstances around which the associations of heart and memory might cluster, as around a common centre, making us what we should be, what we require to be, and what we have

never yet been—a united, a prosperous, and a contented people.'[14] Although Upper Canadian educators were astutely aware of the critical role that the study of history could play in creating the collective memory on which identity rests, it would be a number of years before a Canadian history text appeared for use in the public schools.

The appeal for Canadian history texts was finally answered by the publication of J. George Hodgins's *The Geography and History of British America and of the Other Colonies of the Empire in 1857*. Convinced that the British North American colonies were quickly emerging from their 'colonial infancy', Hodgins saw the study of history as an essential element in forging bonds of unity and forming a national identity. He insisted that British North Americans could no longer rely on the 'uncertain and inaccurate' information contained in European textbooks and the 'unfriendly interpretations' found in American publications, but they must acquire 'a fuller acquaintance' with their own 'history, condition and capabilities'.[15] Hodgins's history portrayed Upper Canada as a distinct British American society built upon the loyalty, patriotism, industry, and self-discipline of its Loyalist founders. Presented in this fashion, the Loyalist past became a useful means of conveying the values and virtues educators hoped to instill in the province's students. The increased importance attached to the study of Canadian history was evident the following year, when Egerton Ryerson acquired a collection of Canadian historical materials to be used to train teachers at the provincial normal school.[16]

The Loyalist past became the focus of the growing historical consciousness that emerged in the 1850s. It was widely believed throughout the nineteenth century that origins played a critical role in establishing the character of a people and setting the future course of a nation's or a people's development. 'The beginnings of a nation, or even of a colony', observed Nathanael Burwash at century's end, 'are always important. They are as the first track made across a hitherto untravelled prairie; they give direction to all that follows.'[17] An understanding of Upper Canada's destiny thus demanded an appreciation of its founders. 'If a man would know anything of the life of nations', the *Globe* asserted in October of 1856, 'he should first know a little about the origins of his own.' There thus emerged a growing interest in recovering the Loyalist past and extolling the virtues, principles, and accomplishments of the province's 'Pilgrim Fathers'.[18]

[. . .]

A sense of urgency surrounded the growing interest in the Loyalist past as the last of the Loyalists died. 'Our early settlers are fast passing away', the Cobourg *Star* warned, 'and with them many invaluable records and instances of the past', which 'must be secured very speedily or they will perish forever.'[19] This sense of irretrievable loss was reflected in the numerous obituaries that appeared throughout the press of the province during this period mourning the fall of 'another giant of the forest' or the removal of 'another landmark'. Loyalist descendants appear to have been especially influenced by the passing of the last of the Loyalist pioneers. Egerton Ryerson's lifelong interest in history did not become focused on the Loyalists until the death of his own father in 1854. Shortly after his father's death, Ryerson began to collect and compose Loyalist obituaries for publication in the *Journal of Education for Upper Canada*.[20]

Fearing that the opportunity to record and preserve Upper Canada's past was rapidly disappearing as the Loyalist generation died off, a number of concerned individuals urged the government to take immediate action to collect the recollections, memoirs, and family papers of surviving Loyalists. At the beginning of the 1859 sitting of the Legislative Assembly the Honourable William Hamilton Merritt presented a petition circulated by his son Jedediah calling on the government to support actively the collection of documents relating to Upper Canada's early history. [. . .] Feeling that Upper Canadian history was being neglected, William Hamilton Merritt used his political influence to displace the French-speaking majority on the library committee and managed to have his son Jedediah granted a sum of 200 pounds so that he could travel to England to collect documents.[21]

The Merritts' interest in the Loyalists was both personal and political. During the American Revolution, William Hamilton Merritt's father, Thomas, served under John Graves Simcoe in the Queen's Rangers. He moved to New Brunswick in 1783 but returned to the United States two years later. In 1796 the family settled in Upper Canada as late Loyalists.[22] A veteran of the War of 1812, William played a leading role in the erection of the second Brock monument on Queenston Heights and actively promoted the building of memorials on the sites of other battlefields.[23] Merritt's interest in the past was more than a little self-serving. A close friend observed that the Merritts did not hide their desire that 'posterity might know the energies pursued by them to establish an Independent Country and provide a good home as it had done to thousands of families now scattered throughout every portion of this Province.'[24]

Although such family egotism contributed to the Merritts' efforts to recover the Loyalist past, their historical interests also reflected their commercial and political concerns. Throughout his long career in business and politics, William Hamilton Merritt vigorously promoted efforts to improve Upper Canada's transportation system and enlarge its trade. Like many Upper Canadians, Merritt took pride in the growth of the province but feared that Upper Canada was outgrowing its boundaries. By the 1850s Merritt's interest in trade and transportation and his concerns for the future led him to take an active interest in the union of the British North American colonies and expansion into the northwest. Merritt's sudden interest in the province's past was closely linked to expansionist ambitions. He believed that history could play an important role in creating a shared sense of identity and destiny that would facilitate Upper Canada's political growth and national development within the British Empire. In the preface to Merritt's biography, Jedediah observed that his father was a man who 'loved Britain with a Briton's love, yet he loved Canada more' and 'longed for its prosperity.'[25] Such sentiments lay behind the Merritts' efforts to recover and preserve the Loyalist past.

William D. Eberts, Thomas D. Phillipps, and Duncan Warren presented another set of petitions to the Assembly in February and March, 'praying that an appropriation may be made out of the Provincial Treasury for collecting and re-printing original contemporary documents relating to the History of Upper Canada since its first settlement by the United Empire Loyalists.'[26] In April the Library Committee approved 'of the praiseworthy endeavours of those who have thus awakened public attention to the necessity of seeking to recover the lost fragments of our historical annals' and appropriated £100 for the collection of documents. George Coventry, a long-time associate of the Merritts, was engaged by the committee to collect and transcribe documents. Coventry and Jedediah Merritt received a further grant of 300 pounds in 1860 to continue their work.[27]

[. . .]

Inspired by the success of the Literary and Historical Society of Quebec and the formation of numerous historical and patriotic organizations in the United States, Jedediah Merritt and George Coventry circulated a 'Prospectus for the Formation of an Upper Canadian Historical Society' in 1861. [. . .] The movement to form a provincial historical society was endorsed by many of the province's leading political, business, and cultural leaders. The names of Egerton Ryerson, Chief Justice John Beverley Robinson, Sir Allan MacNab, Hon. W.H. Dixon, Rt Rev. John Strachan, J. George Hodgins, William Boulton, Hon. George Boulton, and Hon. Sydney Smith were listed among 'the gentlemen favourable to the formation of an historical society for Upper Canada' on a circular promoting the new association.[28]

The society's inaugural meeting was held on 14 November 1861 in Toronto. At the meeting it was resolved that members of the society should collect the reminiscences of the surviving pioneers of the province and furnish them to the society to be examined by a committee, which would publish the most 'worthy' manuscripts. It was hoped that the province would support the society in its endeavours to publish a documentary history of the province that would help to instill a 'sentiment of nationality' among the people of Canada West.[29]

The Historical Society of Upper Canada played a key role in the development of the Loyalist tradition. At the urging of the society, Egerton Ryerson issued a circular in 1861 addressed to the 'descendants of the British United Empire Loyalists' soliciting 'any Documents, Journals, Letters or other Papers which may relate to the Lives and Adventures of their forefathers and of their settlement in Canada, or any facts or information which may afford materials for a history of the venerated founders of our country.'[30] The work begun in 1861 for the Historical Society of Upper Canada culminated with the publication in 1880 of Ryerson's 'monument to the character and merits of the fathers and founders of my native country', *The Loyalists of America and Their Times from 1620–1816*.[31] It was also at that request of the society that the Belleville physician William Canniff undertook to interview surviving Loyalists and to write the paper— upon the settlement of the Bay of Quinte that was the genesis for his influential study, *The History of the Settlement of Upper Canada*.

A number of forces coalesced in the 1850s to generate an official interest in Upper Canada's past generally and the Loyalist past in particular. Economic growth and sectional tensions fostered expansionist ambitions and nationalist sentiment. The expansion of the state and the need to create a public produced an appreciation of the usefulness of the past in constructing a shared sense of identity, promoting patriotism, and instilling common values. The death of the last of the Loyalists and the desire to vindicate the province's founders in the light of nationalist American histories focused this growing historical consciousness on the Loyalists. All of these elements contributed to official efforts to construct a heroic history of origins that celebrated the achievements of the past and looked forward to a future of continued accomplishment. The attempt to construct an official history along these lines confronted a serious challenge in the reminiscences, memoirs, and documents collected at the time. Rooted in local particularities and personal experience and memory, the memoirs and reminiscences collected by Coventry, Merritt, Canniff, and Ryerson were part of a nostalgic vernacular past that lamented the loss of a simpler and purer world.

For those hoping to create a forward-looking history that presented the province's founders in heroic terms, the reminiscences were disappointing. Descendants did not dwell on the principles of their Loyalist parents or grandparents or the role they had played in the Revolution. The son of a Dutch Loyalist, James Dittrick, simply stated 'that his father was a 'strict Loyalist' and that the Revolution was 'a momentous struggle, a frightful warfare, where two parties were fighting to obtain ascendancy.'[32] Henry Ruttan asserted that his Huguenot grandfather was 'loyal to the backbone', but he did not elaborate on the reasons behind his grandfather's attachment to the Crown.[33] The Loyalists' mixed motives are evident in the reminiscences of Catharine White, the daughter of a Thurlow Loyalist. White recalled: 'hearing that sugar was made from Trees in Canada, and being thorough Loyalists, and not wishing to be mixed up with the Contest about to be carried on, we packed up our effects and came over to Canada.'[34] There were few stories of individual bravery and heroics, but bitter accounts of the losses endured by the Loyalists were plentiful. Such material did not lend itself easily to the portrayal of the Loyalists as heroic defenders of principle.

While the reminiscences provided little insight into the Loyalists' role in the Revolution, they did present the Loyalists as a group of hardworking men and women who toiled and suffered and triumphed over the obstacles of nature and in so doing laid the foundations of the province's progress and prosperity. [. . .] Wolves, wildcats, 'savage' Indians, swarms of mosquitoes, fever-infested swamps, and poisonous snakes were all mentioned as dangers encountered by the Loyalists. Particular attention was paid to the 'Hungry Year', days of 'dearth and famine' during which many were said to have been reduced to surviving on the leaves of trees, herbs, and ground nuts, or soup bones passed from family to family. [. . .]

The contributions made by Loyalist women during the Revolution and resettlement in Upper Canada received comment in many reminiscences. Roger Bates of Cobourg recalled that his grandmother was an 'active', 'intelligent', and 'wonderfully industrious' woman, who shared his grandfather's 'indomitable courage' and 'love of the British Constitution' and happily left the comforts of her former home to begin life anew in the wilderness.[35] While their husbands served in the Loyalist militia or sought refuge from Patriot harassment, many women found themselves solely responsible for the care and maintenance of their homes and property. 'The farms', James Dittrick asserted, 'were left to the care of the women, who seldom ate of the bread of Idleness.'[36] The many demands placed on Loyalist women during resettlement were described by Catherine White, who recollected that her mother 'used to help chop down trees' as well as attend to 'household duties'.[37] Life in the pioneer family was often characterized by mutual dependence, as husbands, wives, and children laboured together to fulfill the family's needs. John Clark asserted that 'everything was performed by a division of labour so that all performed their parts and imbibed a spirit of industry.' The importance of women's work to the economic success of the family was also noted by Clark, who observed that 'wherever the spinning wheel and loom were at work that family was industrious and prosperous.'[38]

Women were especially commended for their ingenuity and resourcefulness and their ability to persevere in difficult circumstances.

Descriptions of pioneer achievement and ingenuity served the interests of official history well and became an integral part of the Loyalist tradition. The utility of the reminiscences was severely limited, however, by a pervasive nostalgia that idealized pioneer society and denigrated the present. Pioneer society was repeatedly asserted to have been free of 'unsettled minds', 'political strife', and 'squabbling'.[39] Amelia Harris, the daughter of Long Point Loyalist Captain Samuel Ryerse, professed that during those 'halcyon days' the 'greatest good feeling existed amongst the settlers, although they were of all nations and Creeds, and no Creeds . . . Crime was unknown in those days, as were locks and bolts. Theft was never heard of, and a kindly, brotherly feeling existed among all.'[40] Notwithstanding the 'numerous privations' suffered by the Loyalist pioneers, John Clark referred to the period as 'the happiest hours of existence'.[41]

The idealization of the past was frequently followed by a profound sense of loss and declension. John Kilborn, the son of a Brockville Loyalist, insisted that 'At this early date, the State of Society, however humble, was in many respects I think superior to the present. All the parties then were more or less dependent on each other for favours and occasional assistance, and all felt more or less interested in each other's condition and prosperity . . . all were acquainted and were friends, entirely unlike our present position.'[42] The loss of community was also lamented by James Dittrick. 'We visited one another', Dittrick asserted, 'and all appeared like one family. There was then no distinction, as is the case nowadays—all were on an equality and ready to do any kind acts and services for one another.' 'I am decidedly of the opinion', Dittrick concluded, 'that true happiness, as far as human nature has the privilege of enjoying it, was far more abundant then than the present frivolities of the age.'[43]

To many of the Loyalist generation it appeared that the industry and perseverance that had built the province had been replaced by extravagance and false pretensions. Thomas Gummersal Anderson, the son of a lieutenant in the British army, recalled that 'in these primitive times every inhabitant in the country was striving might and main to earn an honest and comfortable living. None was idle. People were honest, attended to their own business and were kind, accommodating and friendly to each other. No banks to encourage extravagance and indolence with the proud spendthrift, or to excite envy in the breasts of his less presuming, though perhaps more worthy, neighbours.' Anderson had few doubts about the forces that had produced such degeneration. 'The young of the present day wallowing in wealth, yes, the hard-earned wealth of their forefathers', Anderson insisted, 'have became such lumps of stalking pride and arrogance, that to remind them of old times, when their fathers gained an honest livelihood by holding the plough and their mothers by household economy assisted in providing property for their offspring, is to bring upon your head every evil their weak minds can invent or command.'[44] Many contrasted the hardiness of pioneer wives, who 'gloried in their occupations', with the frivolous fashion concerns of the current generation of women.[45] Such sentiments conveyed a fear that the accomplishments of the Loyalists were in danger of being lost and forgotten in the prosperity and materialism of the present.

Although the vernacular past is based in personal experience, it needs to be stressed that recollections are malleable and undergo constant revision in the light of subsequent knowledge and present need. The reminiscences thus reveal as much, if not more, about the contemporary position and condition of the individuals concerned as they do about the reality of the past. The individuals contacted by Coventry, Ryerson, Merritt, and Canniff were well into their seventies, eighties, and nineties, usually of modest means, and typically lived in older rural areas of the province that were in a state of decline. The feelings of disenchantment with the present and idealization of the past expressed in the reminiscences are typical of the elderly and individuals and groups that feel marginalized by society. Psychologists attribute the nostalgia of the elderly to a naturally occurring mental process termed the 'life review.' Awareness of 'approaching dissolution and death' results in 'a progressive return to consciousness of past experience', which 'absorbs one in attempts to avoid the realities of the present.'[46]

'The nostalgic evocation of some past state of affairs', sociologist Fred Davis maintains, 'always occurs in the context of present fears, discontents, anxieties or uncertainties, even though they may not be in the forefront of awareness.'[47] The pervasive nostalgia of the reminiscences represented a search for continuity amid the discontinuity and disorientation that accompanied the transformation of Upper Canada into an increasingly complex commercial society. [. . .]

As society underwent increasing change, there was a sense that the contribution of the Loyalist pioneers would be lost and forgotten. Throughout the reminiscences collected by Coventry, Ryerson, Merritt, and Canniff, the current generation was repeatedly reminded of their indebtedness to the Loyalist pioneers and admonished to 'cherish the remembrance, and imitate the example of their forefathers.'[48] Roger Bates, the grandson of a late Loyalist, called upon Upper Canadians to 'forever remain faithful and loyal and 'pursue the old beaten track of their forefather[s].'[49] Henry Ruttan urged the 'rising generation' to 'remember the apparent hardships their ancestors had to undergo to obtain their present goodly heritage.'[50] In collecting Loyalist materials and chronicling their history, Loyalist descendants hoped to fulfill their filial obligations to preserve the memory of their forefathers' accomplishments. Some became obsessed with the task. Egerton Ryerson dedicated much of the last 20 years of his life to completing his history of the Loyalists. 'I am so absorbed in my

historical work', Ryerson wrote to his daughter, 'that I have little inclination to talk or write to anybody.'[51] The fear that he might not complete 'the chief legacy I can leave after me' weighed heavily upon Ryerson and was one of the principal reasons he finally decided to retire in 1875.[52] [. . .] When Ryerson finally completed *The Loyalists of America and Their Times* in 1880, he thanked God 'for sparing and enabling me to complete a work which has weighed upon my mind and occupied so much of my time and labour for more than a quarter of a century, and which I hope may do some honour to the fathers and founders of our country.'[53]

While the descendants of Loyalists felt compelled to persevere in their efforts to record and preserve the Loyalist past, official support for this work quickly evaporated. In May of 1862 George Coventry presented a report of his progress and a large collection of papers to the Legislative Assembly's Library Committee. On the basis of Coventry's report, the committee renewed his grant for another year. In September of 1863, however, the committee had second thoughts. 'After an examination of the material already collected' the committee reported that it did 'not think it advisable to recommend that his engagement should again be renewed.' Dissatisfied with the results of Jedediah Merritt's labours, the committee requested that he return the grant he had received in 1859 to collect documents in England.[54] The fortunes of the Historical Society of Upper Canada also suffered. Despite repeated attempts, the society was unable to secure government financing for the collection and publication of documents. Unable to live up to the expectations of its founders, the society quickly dissipated.[55] The government's decision to withdraw its support appears to have been based largely on the content of the materials already collected. Ambivalent in their description of the Loyalists' motives and ideas, nostalgic in tone, and pessimistic about the province's present and future prospects; the reminiscences and memoirs simply did not

lend themselves to the creation of a heroic, unifying, and future-oriented official history that
legitimized the ambitions and aspirations of the
province's political and economic elites.

Although the state could simply withdraw
its financial support when it became evident
that the materials being collected did not support its official agenda, Loyalist descendants
could not ignore the voices of their forebears so
easily. A sense of filial duty obliged them to preserve the memory of their ancestors by writing
their history. Loyalist historians such as Egerton
Ryerson and William Canniff, however, shared
the aims and objectives of official history. The
imperative to create a history that was heroic,
celebratory, and forward looking dictated that
the vernacular past of the reminiscences would
be largely ignored and forgotten in a deliberate
act of historical amnesia. Despite the considerable time and effort each had devoted to the
collection of documents and reminiscences,
in their respective works Ryerson and Canniff
made little use of the reminiscences and memoirs they had collected from surviving Loyalists.
Canniff cited the popular folklore surrounding
incidents such as the Hungry Year, and Ryerson
published excepts from several memoirs, but
neither integrated the material into his central
argument. In place of the vernacular past of the
reminiscences Canniff and Ryerson constructed
an invented past that satisfied the needs of official history.

William Canniff's *The History of the
Settlement of Upper Canada*, first published in
1869, and Egerton Ryerson's *The Loyalists of
America and Their Times*, completed in 1880,
represented the culmination of the research
they had begun on behalf of the Historical
Society of Upper Canada. Although their works
differed in style and organization, Canniff and
Ryerson each wrote a history of the Loyalists
designed to 'vindicate their character as a body,
to exhibit their principles and patriotism, and
to illustrate their treatment and sufferings.'[56]
In both histories the Loyalists are portrayed
as a noble elite persecuted for their principles.
Adhering faithfully to their convictions, the

Loyalists took up arms for the king, passed
through the horrors of civil war, sacrificed their
homes and possessions, endured the hardships
and privations of the Upper Canadian wilderness, and laid the 'foundations for the nation's
future progress and prosperity.'

The forms and structures of historical
writing have recently attracted a great deal of
attention from literary critics. Theorists such
as Hayden White and Dominick LaCapra have
demonstrated the important role of language
and form in the creation and description of
historical reality.[57] When analyzing the Loyalist
histories written by Canniff and Ryerson, it
is thus essential that we distinguish between
'story', the sequence of events to which historians refer in constructing their narratives, and
'discourse', the rhetorical overwriting that colours and shapes the direction of the narrative.
Throughout most of the nineteenth century,
history was viewed as a branch of literature
rather than a science. As a branch of literature,
history was expected to conform to the literary form and style of the period. The idealized
portraits of the Loyalists drawn by Canniff and
Ryerson were greatly influenced by the literary
conventions of their day. The most important
of these influences came from the romantic
movement, with its emphasis on the struggle between the forces of light and darkness,
the role of great men, and its vivid pictorial
descriptions. [. . .] Canniff and Ryerson drew
upon the conventions of romance in order to
fit the Loyalist past into a 'master narrative'
that generated meanings on both a literal and
an allegorical level. The 'story' of the Loyalists
was overlaid with a discourse that appealed to
the emotions and attempted to create the same
sense of ancestry and unimpeachable morality
and character. [. . .]

Both Canniff and Ryerson cast the
American Revolution as a struggle between
noble and principled Loyalists motivated
by 'all the ardor of a lofty patriotism' and a
rebel minority 'actuated mainly by mercenary
motives, unbounded selfishness and bigotry.'[58]
Ryerson traced the struggle back to the original

settlement of New England by the Puritans and Pilgrims. 'The government of the Puritans', Ryerson maintained, 'was deceptive and disloyal to the Throne and the Mother Country from the first, and sedulously sowed and cultivated the seeds of disaffection and hostility to the Royal government, until they grew and ripened into the harvest of the American revolution.' 'The government of the Pilgrims', on the other hand, 'was frank and loyal to the Sovereign and people of England.'[59] A graphic description of the persecution endured by the Loyalists followed both authors' assessment of the causes of the Revolution. Ryerson condemned the Loyalists' 'cruel treatment from the professed friends of liberty', and Canniff denounced the rebels' 'bloodthirsty and vindicative' treatment of 'innocent old men, women, and children'.[60] The depiction of the Loyalists as 'men of property and character' drawn from the ranks of the 'most wealthy and intelligent' inhabitants of the colonies further emphasized the degree to which the they suffered for their convictions.[61] Both Canniff and Ryerson contrasted the Loyalists' comfortable lives in the American colonies with the 'hardships, exposures, privations and sufferings' encountered in the Upper Canadian wilderness. The 'spirit and determination' displayed by the Loyalist pioneers, however, transformed the primeval forest into 'a fruitful field' and laid the foundation of the province's 'growth and prosperity' and 'future greatness.'[62] Both Canniff and Ryerson included a large section on the War of 1812 in their histories. For both historians, the War of 1812 vindicated the defeat of 1783. 'The true spirit of the Loyalists of America', Ryerson concluded, 'was never exhibited with greater force and brilliancy than during the war of 1812–15.'[63] In constructing their discourse in this fashion, Canniff and Ryerson fit the Loyalists into a master narrative of progress and redemption in which the Loyalists' convictions, heroic fortitude, and sufferings and privations were ultimately rewarded as they overcame adversity and succeeded in creating a prosperous society built upon noble principles of honour, loyalty, and patriotism.

Although the vital contribution of women to the Loyalists' settlement and success in Upper Canada was frequently commented on in the reminiscences of Loyalist descendants, women did not figure prominently in the histories written by Canniff and Ryerson. Both authors produced a gendered past that emphasized the strength, courage, endurance, and dedication of the province's heroic 'founding fathers'. When women were mentioned at all, they were typically portrayed as fragile victims of Patriot harassment or as helpless refugees in need of protection and assistance. Men, in contrast, were depicted as brave defenders of the Empire and industrious pioneers. The masculine images that filled the histories written by Canniff and Ryerson reflected the assumptions of female frailty and domesticity that characterized the period. As Janice Potter has pointed out, the manly patriotism attributed to the Loyalists had 'obvious and unequivocal gender implications' in a society that excluded women from politics and confined them to the domestic sphere—a fact recognized by advocates of women's rights, who set out at the end of the nineteenth century to reclaim a place for women in Loyalist history.[64]

One of the most striking features of both Canniff's *The History of the Settlement of Upper Canada* and Ryerson's *The Loyalists of America and Their Times* is the degree to which their characterizations of the Loyalists are based on American paradigms and sources. Each author refers to the Loyalists as 'Canada's Pilgrim Fathers'. Much of the material used by Canniff and Ryerson was drawn from the works of an American historian, Lorenzo Sabine. [. . .] Sabine was a Whig in a frontier town at the time Jacksonian democracy was at its height. As men of education and property, Whigs believed themselves to be worthy of emulation and electoral deference from the majority. Sabine saw a parallel between the position of the Loyalist elite and that of the Whigs.[65] Sabine's interest in the Loyalists resulted in a review of

Simcoe's military journal in October of 1844 for the *North American Review* and ultimately in the publication of *The American Loyalists, or Biographical Sketches of the Adherents to the British Crown in the War of the Revolution* in 1847. A two-volume, enlarged edition, retitled *Biographical Sketches of the Loyalists of the American Revolution*, appeared in 1864.

[. . .]

Sabine's attempt to provide a balanced treatment of the Revolution and the Loyalists was widely condemned in the United States.[66] While he argued that the Loyalists deserved better treatment than they had received at the hands of most American historians, Sabine was by no means pro-Loyalist and was equally determined to expose Loyalist mythology. 'The Loyalists, and those of their descendants who repeat their fathers' accusations' that the Patriots 'were mere needy office-seekers', Sabine asserted, 'are to be turned upon in quiet nature, and to be put upon their own defence.'[67] 'Place and patronage', 'timidity of character', 'the dread of bloodshed', and 'a sense of the overpowering strength and resources of England, and of the utter impossibility of successfully resisting her', he concluded, 'appear to have been general among those who made shipwreck of their patriotism.' Those Loyalists who 'clung to the cause of the King' because of 'a calculation of personal advantage, or from the love and expectation of place and power', Sabine insisted, 'deserve to be held up to public scorn', as did those who entered the British service and 'fought against their brethren'.[68]

In his analysis of the causes of the American Revolution and the motives of both Patriots and Loyalists, Sabine displayed a sophistication and balance unique in his generation. His revisionism did not have a significant impact on American historiography. [. . .] The story was different in Canada, where Sabine's *The American Loyalists* had a considerable impact on the development of the Loyalist tradition. [. . .] A selective reading of Sabine provided exactly the kind of material lacking in the Loyalist reminiscences and memoirs and

from which a heroic and redemptive narrative could be constructed.

The publication of William Canniff's *The History of the Settlement of Upper Canada* and Egerton Ryerson's *The Loyalists of America and Their Times* marked the culmination of the efforts begun at mid-century to create a history for the province. With the appearance of both works, all of the constituent elements of the Loyalist tradition were in place: the Loyalists' dedication to the British Empire, the persecution they suffered for their principles, the hardships and privations they endured in the Upper Canadian wilderness, their vigilant anti-Americanism, and finally, their elite social status. The forces underlying this process of transformation were complex. The province's economic growth, expansionist ambitions, and sectional tensions combined to produce a growing national sentiment and a desire for a celebratory history of origins that would sanction future aspirations. At the same time, the growth of the state and the need to construct a public out of the province's diverse population contributed to official interest in the production of a unifying and future-oriented past. The anxiety produced by the passing of the last of the Loyalist pioneers, the vilifying treatment of Upper Canada's founders presented in nationalist American histories, and the filiopietism of Loyalist descendants ensured that much of this emergent historical consciousness was focused on the province's Loyalist origins. Although the legislature financially backed the first efforts to collect and preserve historical materials connected with the province's Loyalist founders, state support for Loyalist history was withdrawn when it became evident that the nostalgic and idiosyncratic vernacular past contained in the reminiscences and memoirs of surviving Loyalists did not meet the needs of official history. A sense of filial obligation compelled Loyalist descendants such as Canniff and Ryerson to persevere in their work. Heavily influenced by the conventions of romance and the works of the American historian Lorenzo Sabine, Canniff and Ryerson produced an idealized version of the Loyalist past that greatly influenced the way in which the Loyalists were portrayed by publicists and promoters in later years.

NOTES

1. Toronto *Globe*, 30 Oct. 1856

2. John Bodnar, *Remaking America: Public Memory, Commemoration and Patriotism in the Twentieth Century* (Princeton: Princeton University Press, 1992)

3. The most valuable general study of the political, economic, and social maturing of Upper Canada remains J.M.S. Careless, *The Union of the Canadas: The Growth of Canadian Institutions, 1841–1857* (Toronto 1967), 149–58. On the disappearance of the agricultural frontier see David Gagan, *Hopeful Travellers: Families, Land, and Social Change in Mid-Victorian Peel County, Canada West* (Toronto 1981). On the transportation revolution see Peter Baskerville, 'Transportation, Social Change and State Formation: Upper Canada, 1841–1864', in *Colonial Leviathan: State Formation in Mid-Nineteenth-Century Canada*, ed. Allan Greer and Ian Radforth (Toronto 1992). On the growth of the professions and banking see R.D. Gidney and W.P.J. Millar, *Professional Gentlemen: The Professions in Nineteenth-Century Ontario* (Toronto 1994) and Peter Baskerville, *The Bank of Upper Canada* (Ottawa 1987).

4. On the process of state formation see Greer and Radforth, eds, *Colonial Leviathan* and J.E. Hodgetts, *Pioneer Public Service: An Administrative History of the United Canadas* (Toronto 1955).

5. On the growth of national sentiment and Upper Canadian expansionism see Doug Owram, *Promise of Eden: The Canadian Expansionist Movement and the Idea of the West, 1856–1900* (Toronto 1980), chap. 2; Allan Smith, 'Old Ontario and the Emergence of a National Frame of Mind', in *Aspects of Nineteenth-Century Ontario*, ed. F.H. Armstrong, H.A. Stevenson, and J.D. Wilson (Toronto 1974) 194–217; M. Brook Taylor, *Promoters, Patriots and Partisans: Historiography in Nineteenth-Century English Canada* (Toronto 1989), chap. 5.

6. Benedict Anderson, *Imagined Communities: Reflections on the Origins and Spread of Nationalism* (London and New York 1983)

7. *Journals of the Legislative Assembly of the Province of Canada*, (8 October 1842), 11

8. *Journals of the Legislative Assembly of the Province of Canada* (18 August 1851), 292–4

9. J.M. McMullen, *The History of Canada from its Discovery to the Present Time* (Brockville 1855), preface

10. See Taylor, *Promoters, Patriots and Partisans*, 165–7.

11. On the use of the public school system to create a public see Bruce Curtis, *Building the Educational State: Canada West, 1836–1871* (London, Ontario 1988). Alison Prentice uses a more traditional social control model in *The School Promoters: Education and Social Class in Mid-Nineteenth Century Upper Canada* (Toronto 1977).

12. UCA, Egerton Ryerson Papers, Address, 1841. Ryerson's conviction that it was the function of public education to promote local and imperial patriotism, social harmony, and loyalty to properly constituted authority are most clearly expressed in his *Report on a System of Public Elementary Education for Upper Canada*, published in 1847.

13. On the debate over textbooks see Susan E. Houston and Alison Prentice, *Schooling and Scholars in Nineteenth-Century Ontario* (Toronto 1988), chap. 8.

14. Cited in Smith, 'Old Ontario and the Emergence of a National Frame of Mind', 195.

15. J. George Hodgins, *The Geography and History of British America and of the Other Colonies of the Empire* (Toronto 1857), iii–iv

16. *Journals of the Legislative Assembly of the Province of Canada*, XVIII (31 Jan. 1869), Appendix I, 1–7

17. Nathanael Burwash, 'U.E. Loyalists, Founders of Our Institutions', UELO, *Transactions* (1901–2), 35

18. *Globe*, 30 Oct. 1856

19. *Cobourg Star*, 20 Nov. 1861

20. Loyalist obituaries published in the *Journal of Education for Upper Canada* by Ryerson included those of Nicholas Brouse, 12 (April 1859), 58; D. Burritt. 12 (May 1859), 75; Hon. George Crookshank, 12 (Aug. 1859), 121; George Brouse, 13 (31 March 1860), 44; John Willson, 13 (June 1860), 94; William Woodruff, 13 (July 1860), 108.

21. J.P. Merritt, *Biography of the Hon. W.H. Merritt, M.P.* (St Catharines 1875), 424

22. J.J. Talman, 'William Hamilton Merritt', DCB, vol. 9, 544–8

23. Merritt, *Biography of the Hon. W.H. Merritt*, 215, 406–7

24. George Coventry quoted in Gerald Killan, *Preserving Ontario's Heritage: A History of the Ontario Historical Society* (Ottawa 1976), 7.

25. Merritt, *Biography of the Hon. W.H. Merritt*, preface

26. *Journals of the Legislative Assembly of the Province of Canada, 1859, XVII* (10 Feb. 1859) 38, (2 March 1859) 137, (7 March 1859) 156

27. *Journals of the Legislative Assembly of the Province of Canada, XVII* (April 1859) 525–6, 928; XX (1862) 246

28. AO, Historical Society of Upper Canada, Merritt Papers, MU 4374, Series E, Envelope 1

29. *Globe*, 15 Nov. 1861

30. UCA, Egerton Ryerson Papers, 'History of the British United Empire Loyalists of America', Box 13, File 365

31. Egerton Ryerson, *The Loyalists of America and Their Times from 1620–1816*, vol. I (Toronto 1880), v

32. 'Reminiscences of Captain James Dittrick', in J.J. Talman, *Loyalist Narratives* from Upper Canada (Toronto 1946) 63. The original transcripts of many of the reminiscences can be found in the George Coventry Papers at the National Archives of Canada.

33. 'Reminiscences of the Hon. Henry Ruttan of Cobourg', *Loyalist Narratives*, 298

34. 'Reminiscence of Mrs White of White Mills near Cobourg, Upper Canada. Formerly Miss Catherine Chrysler (Cysdale) of Sydney, near Bell(e)ville. Aged 79', *Loyalist Narratives*, 353

35. 'Testimonial of Roger Bates', *Loyalist Narratives*, 31

36. 'Reminiscences of Captain James Dittrick', *Loyalist Narratives*, 63

37. 'Reminiscence of Mrs White', *Loyalist Narratives*, 354

38. 'Memoirs of Colonel John Clark of Port Dalhousie, C.W.', *Ontario Historical Society Papers and Records VII* (1906), 162, 164

39. 'Reminiscence of Mrs White', *Loyalist Narratives*, 355

40. 'Historical Memoranda of Mrs. Amelia Harris, of Eldon House, London, Ontario, only daughter of the Late Colonel Samuel Ryerse, and sister of the late Rev. Geo. J. Ryerse', in Ryerson, *Loyalists*, vol. II, 236, 245

41. 'Memoirs of Colonel John Clark', *Ontario Historical Society Papers and Records*, 163

42. NAC, George Coventry Papers, 'Reminiscence of John Kilborn, Esq. born at Brockville, U.C., 1794, whose Grandfather was with General Amherst, and left in charge of Fort Oswego, 1759', 219

43. 'Reminiscences of Captain James Dittrick', *Loyalist Narratives*, 68

44. 'Reminiscences of Capt. Thomas Gummersall Anderson', *Loyalist Narratives*, 2–3, 14, 8

45. 'Reminiscences of the Hon. Henry Ruttan' and 'Testimonial of Roger Bates', *Loyalist Narratives*, 302, 38

45. Robert N. Butler, 'The Life Review: An Interpretation of Reminiscence in the Aged', *Psychiatry: Journal for the Study of Interpersonal Processes*, 26 (1963), 66–73

47. Fred Davis, *Yearning for Yesterday: A Sociology of Nostalgia* (New York 1979), 34. Also see Christopher Shaw and Malcolm Chase, eds., *The Imagined Past: History and Nostalgia* (Manchester and New York 1989).

48. 'Susan Burnham Greeley's "Sketches of the Past"', *Loyalist Narratives*, 107

49. 'Testimonial of Mr Roger Bates', *Loyalist Narratives*, 40

50. 'Reminiscence of the Hon. Henry Ruttan', *Loyalist Narratives*, 302

51. 'Egerton Ryerson to Sophia Harris, 11 August 1872; 1 Jan. 1871', in *My Dearest Sophie: Letters from Egerton Ryerson To His Daughter*, ed. C.B. Sissons (Toronto 1955) 227, 201

52. 'Egerton Ryerson to Sophia Harris, 9 October 1875', in *My Dearest Sophie*, 283

53. UCA, Ryerson Papers, Box 2, 'Egerton Ryerson to Sophia Harris, 14 April 1880'

54. *Journals of the Legislative Assembly of the Province of Canada, XXII* (15 Sept. 1863) 126, (24 Sept. 1863), 177

55. Gerald Killan, *Preserving Ontario's Heritage: A History of the Ontario Historical Society* (Ottawa 1976), 8

56. Ryerson, *Loyalists*, Vol. I, 191

57. See: Hayden White, *The Content and the Form: Narrative Discourse and the Historical Representation* (Baltimore 1987); Dominick LaCapra, *Rethinking Intellectual History: Texts, Contexts, Language* (Ithaca 1983).

58. Canniff, *History of the Settlement of Upper Canada with Special Reference to the Bay of Quinté* (Toronto: Dudley and Burns, 1869), 50, 45

59. Ryerson, *Loyalists*, Vol. I, 12

60. Ibid., 265; Canniff, *Settlement of Upper Canada*, 54–5

61. Ryerson, *Loyalists*, Vol. I, 408, 507. Also see Canniff, *Settlement of Upper Canada*, 51.

62. Ryerson, *Loyalists*, Vol. II, 189; Canniff, *Settlement of Upper Canada*, 580–1

63. Ryerson, *Loyalists*, Vol. III, 316 Also see Canniff, *Settlement of Upper Canada*, 633–4.

64. Janice Potter-Mackinnon, *While the Women Only Wept: Loyalist Refugee Women in Eastern Ontario* (Montreal and Kingston 1993), 158

65. Gregory Palmer, 'Introduction', *Biographical Sketches of the Loyalists of the American Revolution* (1864; rpt Westport and London 1984), xxvii

66. Hale, 'Memoir of the Hon. Lorenzo Sabine, A.M.', *Proceedings of the Massachusetts Historical Society*, xvii (1879–80), 377

67. Lorenzo Sabine, *Biographical Sketches of the Loyalists of the American Revolution* (1864; rpt Westport and London: Meckler, 1976), 40

68. Lorenzo Sabine, 'A Review of *The History of the Operations of a Partisan Corps Called the Queens Rangers*', *North American Review* (Oct. 1844): 262–3, 278

Chapter Seven

The Fur Trade in the Northwest

READINGS

Primary Documents

1   From *The English River Book: A North West Company Journal and Account Book of 1786*, Harry W. Duckworth

2   From *A Sketch of the British Fur Trade* (1815), Lord Selkirk

Historical Interpretations

3   From *'Many Tender Ties': Women in Fur Trade Society in Western Canada, 1670–1870*, Sylvia Van Kirk

4   From *Making the Voyageur World: Travelers and Traders in the North American Fur Trade*, Carolyn Podruchny

Introduction

It is really difficult to 'get' the fur trade. We can follow the great economic historian Harold Innis in considering it as one of the activities that pushed European domination of North America northward and westward. We can think about it as the business that created the Métis when traders took up with Aboriginal women for various reasons, not all of them business-related. We can think of the trade as a form of government, a territorially based alternative to the looser control that individual First Nations exercised over their own people. With the trade came new yearly rhythms; competition for furs and the goods they bought; the creation of a new kind of employment for Europeans and North American colonists alike; a threat to New France as young men often preferred the trade to farming; and an increased knowledge of regions that without the trade might have been virtually ignored by the indigenous population and by newcomers.

It is clear that the fur trade moved the territory that would become Canada closer to the industrial age, as the companies involved sought to make their ventures predictable and steadily profitable through efficient deployment of their capital. In other words, they sought to make what might seem like a rather sloppy, outdoor pursuit of animal skins into something that we might now call a 'day at the office'. Thankfully, this process had several points of interest. As we see in the primary material, a fur trade post was not exactly the local convenience store. It had to respond to the needs of those bringing the furs to the posts, needs that sometimes included winter accommodation.

As competition became most intense between the Hudson's Bay Company and its rivals, colonial enterprises (such as those at Red River) were directly affected. Account books and chronicles can tell us a great deal, but historians have done much more recently to flesh out our understanding of the social relationships created and sustained via the trade. Sylvia Van Kirk's classic study of the role of women in the trade, from the formation of the Hudson's Bay Company through to the point where the tradition begins to decline, shows how crucial fur trade marriages and alliances were to the shape and progress of the trade. We learn also, thanks to Carolyn Podruchny, how complex the culture of the trade was, even when the traders and voyageurs were performing tasks that should have left them little time or energy for anything else but sleep. The trade created its own rules, its own atmosphere, and most certainly changed the course of North American history.

QUESTIONS FOR CONSIDERATION

1. What does the inventory of trade goods from a North West Company journal tell us about the western fur trade?
2. What is Lord Selkirk's opinion of the way that the NWC ran their business? Did he admire them or reject their way of doing things?
3. Thinking about both the primary and secondary sources, what sort of personality type do you think might be suitable for a career with the Hudson's Bay Company or one of its rivals?
4. Thinking about Van Kirk's article, what do you think were the main advantages of fur trade marriages? Disadvantages?
5. Did Podruchny's account of voyageur life change your assumptions about what such a career might be like?

SUGGESTIONS FOR FURTHER READING

Binnema, Theodore, Gerhard J. Ens, and R.C. Macleod, eds., *From Rupert's Land to Canada: Essays in Honour of John E. Foster* (Edmonton: University of Alberta Press, 2001)

Bumsted, J.M., *Lord Selkirk: A Life* (East Lansing, MI: Michigan State University Press, 2009)

Francis, D., and Toby Morantz, *Furs: A History of the Fur Trade in Eastern James Bay, 1600–1870* (Montreal and Kingston: McGill-Queen's University Press, 1983)

Freeman, Donald, and Arthur J. Ray, *'Give Us Good Measure': An Economic Analysis of Relations between Indians and the Hudson's Bay Company before 1763* (Toronto: University of Toronto Press, 1978)

Podruchny, Carolyn, *Making the Voyageur World: Travelers and Traders in the North American Fur Trade* (Toronto: University of Toronto Press, 2006)

Skinner, Claiborne A., *The Upper Country: French Enterprise in the Colonial Great Lakes* (Baltimore: Johns Hopkins University Press, 2008)

Van Kirk, Sylvia, *'Many Tender Ties': Women in Fur Trade and Sierra Leone 1783–1870* (Toronto: University of Toronto Press, 1992)

PRIMARY DOCUMENTS

1   From *The English River Book: A North West Company Journal and Account Book of 1786*, Harry W. Duckworth, ed. (Montreal and Kingston: McGill-Queen's University Press, 1990), 30, 101, 116–8.

page 60d

Inventory of Goods left at L'Isle a la Crosse in the Hands of Mr Le Sieur—4 June 1786

5½ yds English Strouds
2½ yds Aurora[1] do
14 yds Red Strouds
8½ yds blue do
———
30½
3 Chiefs Coats
1 Cased Capot[2]
4 Capots 3 Ells[3]
3 do 2½
9 do 2
2 do 1½
1 do 1
4 Mens white Shirts
1 Boys do
2 Cased Hatts

14 pr small Sleeves
2 pr Moyen do
9 Skaines Worsted
16 Rom as Hhdss[4]
4 ps Gartering
15 li large Brass Wire
4 li small do
1 doz: Japan'd Boxes wt Glasses[5]
3 Spring Tobaco do[6]
3 Bunches Beads
8½ Groce Thimbles
[blank] Hawks Bells[7]
7 doz: Gunworms
38 fire Steels
36 Gun flints

Continued

page 61

Inventory of Goods left at L'Isle a la Crosse con^d—

1 large Nattataned [?] Coleur[8]
1 small do do
1 pr Nons aprituss
7 doz: Box wood Combs
11 Horn Combs
1 doz Ivory Combs
10 doz large Knives
12 doz + 4 small do
2 Cartouche do
10 Buck handled knives
19 doz: Rings
3 pr Scizzars
1 doz: Stone Crosses[9]
8 li Vermillion
1/2 li Cotton Wick
1 Groce Awls

12 yds Lace
14 files (7 of which Damaged)
1 Round —
5 pr Arm Bands
6 fine plain Dagues[10]
28 maces B Corn Beads[11]
2 Tin Basons
5 Plain Dags[12]
4 Battle Axes
1 Blkt 2½ Points
2 do 2 —
1 do 1 —
5 packs Cards —
1 Stock Lock —
1 Poudre Horn —

Continued

The Account Book

Dr Francois Raimond	Devant	
1785		
July 29	To Balance from last years Book	288
Augt 6	To Sund^ies at L. La Pluis P. Blotter	369
1786		
June	To Amt of your acct P A. Book	462
	To amunition & 1½ fath^m Tob° Isle a la Cross	50
	To Passage of your Woman	100
		1269
	To Balance due by you	341
Contra		
1786		
June 1	By so much to your Cr P Araba Bk	28
	By one years Wages	900
	By Balance due by you	341
		Lvs 1269

pages 47d–48

Pages 20d–21

Dr Francois Le Blan [Leblanc]	Devant		
1785			
July 29	To Balance from last years Book		182
Augt 6	To Sund^ies at Lac la Pluis p Blotter		347
	To 1 Tobacco Box at do		6
	To Sundries on the road p Blotter		62
1786			
May 30	To 2 Meas. Powder & Balls for Isle Crosse		24
	To 1 fath^m Tob°		20
	To amt of your acct at Lac La Ronge		78
June 1	To Balance due you		81
			Lvs 800
*July**	*To Francois Monette*	*80*	
	To Balce	*1*	
		91	
Contra			
1786			
June 1	By one years Wages		800
			Lvs 800
	By Balance due you		81
	By Balce		*1*

* Italicized entries were added later than the main entries, but in the same hand.

NOTES

1. Aurora, 'a rich orange colour, as of the sky at sunrise' (*OED*, noted 1791).

2. 'Cas'd' or 'cased', also used in connection with hats, may mean 'lined'; cf. 'cased cats', wildcat skins taken off the animal in such a way that the fur was inside. [Ed.: A 'capot' is 'a long coat with a hood, esp. (in Canada) tied with a colourful sash' (*Oxford Canadian Dictionary*).]

3. These would have been cloth. The ell (French *aune*) measured 45 inches in England (*OED*) and 1.188 metres or 46½ inches in France and French Canada, and *capots* varying from 4½ *aunes* to 1½ *aunes* appear in inventories. Although the width of these garments is not specified, the largest *capots* would have been very large indeed and, like the Scotsman's plaid, useful when sleeping in the open air.

4. An uncertain reading, which could mean 'rum as hogsheads', although the amount of spirits implied is very large, and actual hogsheads (of 52½ imperial gallons) would never have been portaged. In another inventory 120 gallons of *double force* rum was contained in 14 barrels (Hudson's Bay Company Archives, F.4/1,3), for an average content of 8.57 gallons and

weight of almost 86 pounds plus the keg—a typical 'piece' of ninety pounds.

5. Japanned boxes containing looking glasses (mirrors) or perhaps drinking tumblers.

6. Tobacco boxes presumably with spring-closed lids.

7. The smallest size of bells in the trade, and the commonest traded. The Hudson's Bay Company's Athabasca outfit for 1820–1 listed 2,000 hawks bells, and also 60 dogs bells and 58 horses bells.

8. This item defeats me. 'Nattataned' could just as easily be read 'Nallataned' or 'Nattalaned'; 'Coleur' is probably collar.

9. This may have been the North West Company's contribution to religion in the wilderness.

10. Probably *dag*, 'a kind of heavy pistol or hand-gun formerly in use' (*OED*), though it could also be for *dagger*.

11. These beads were the same as 'Beads barley corn', so called because of their size, which are listed in the Hudson's Bay Company's Moose Fort standard of trade for 1784, and in other inventories.

12. See note 10.

---

2 From Lord Selkirk, *A Sketch of the British Fur Trade* (1815), in J.M. Bumsted, ed., *The Collected Writings of Lord Selkirk 1810–1820*, vol. 2, *Writings and Papers of Thomas Douglas, Fifth Earl of Selkirk* (Winnipeg: Manitoba Record Society, 1987), 48–55.

I. Remarks on the respective systems adopted in Canada prior and subsequent to the Cession of that Colony to Great Britain.—General View of the Canadian Fur Trade.— Origin and Constitution of the North-West Company of Montreal.

The commercial benefits which were expected to accrue from the Fur Trade in Canada, formed the principal object in the original settlement of that colony.[1] For a long period that branch of trade furnished the chief employment of the colonists; but of late years the progress of population, and the increase of wealth, have given rise to other and more valuable branches of traffic.[2] The Fur Trade, however, still constitutes an important branch of Canadian commerce. An inquiry into the principles on which this trade has been conducted may be interesting, in many respects, not only to those who are connected with the colony, but to all who have turned their attention to the commercial resources, and colonial prosperity, of the British Empire: and the inquiry may be the more important, because the mode in which the Fur Trade is conducted does not appear to be generally understood, or justly appreciated, even in Canada.

While that province was in the possession of France, the Fur Trade was carried on under a system of exclusive privileges.[3] In each district of country, or nation of Indians, a licence was granted by the governor of the province, assigning to some favoured individuals the privilege of trading within the prescribed limits. The persons who obtained these privileges were generally officers of the army, or others of respectable family connection. Whatever were the motives in which this system originated, there can be no doubt that it contributed, in a very great degree, to the main object of the French government in their transactions with the Indian nations of America: *viz.* to establish and extend their political influence.[4] Whoever possessed the exclusive trade of a district was the only person to whom the Indians could apply for such articles as an intercourse with Europeans had introduced among them; and, independent of the ordinary transactions of barter, the natives had frequently occasion to solicit favours which they could only expect from the indulgence of the privileged traders. These were generally men of liberal education, who knew how to promote the views of government; and they had the greater anxiety on this head, as it was well known that if any of them abused their privileges, or otherwise failed in promoting the general objects expected from them, their exclusive rights would be withdrawn. The conduct of the traders was at the same time closely watched by the Missionaries, whose anxious attention was directed to prevent the abuses which had been found to arise from the sale of spirituous liquors among the savages; an object in which they appear to have been in general zealously seconded by the Provincial Government.[5]

This system appears to have been wisely adapted to increase the comforts, and improve the character, of the natives; as a proof of which, we need only compare the present state of the Indians in Canada, with that in which they stood immediately after the conquest of that province by Great Britain, at which period populous villages existed in many districts, where at present we meet only two or three wandering families, and these addicted to the most brutal excesses, and a prey to want and misery.

A few years after the conquest of Canada, the former system of traffic with the Indians was laid aside, as inconsistent with the received principles of freedom of trade; and, with the exception of one district, no more exclusive privileges were granted. After the trade was thrown open to the public, the first adventurers who arrived in the Indian country made very large profits, and this circumstance soon gave rise to a keen commercial competition, the result of which, however, was very different from that which would have taken place in a civilized country, where the effect of rivalship tends only to compel the trader to supply his customers with better goods, and on more reasonable terms.[6] Among the Indians it was found that a profuse supply of spirituous liquors was a shorter and more certain mode of obtaining a preference, than any difference in the quality or price of the goods offered for sale.[7] The ungovernable propensity of the Indians to intoxication is well known, and it is easy to imagine the disorders which would arise, when this propensity was fostered by unbounded temptation. But, to comprehend the full extent of the mischief, it must be recollected, that these rival traders were scattered over a country of immense extent, and at such a distance from all civil authority, as to lead them to believe that the commission of almost any crime would pass with impunity. In such a situation every art which malice could devise was exerted without restraint, and the intercourse of the traders with each other partook more of the style of the savages by whom they were surrounded, than of the country from which they had sprung. The only difference was that their ferocity was mixed with a greater portion of cunning. Direct personal violence was perhaps seldom resorted to, because it was more easy to succeed when the object was disguised, and effected through the agency of the Indians. Those of the natives who had formed a connection with one trader might be led by him to believe the most atrocious calumnies of another, and to credit the most absurd tales of his hostile and wicked designs; and, under the influence of continued intoxication, there was no pitch of fury to which an Indian might not be roused, nor any act of ferocity which he might not be impelled to commit. Mr. Henry, one of the first British subjects who engaged in the Canadian Fur Trade, in the very interesting account which he has published of his Travels and Adventures, observes, that on his arrival at the Grand Portage on Lake Superior, in the year 1775, 'he found the traders in a state of extreme reciprocal hostility, each pursuing his own interests in such a manner as might most injure his neighbour. The consequences,' he adds, 'were very hurtful to the morals of the Indians.' (*Page 239*).[8] The same facts are stated more at large by Sir Alexander M'Kenzie, who, in his Account of the Fur Trade, (prefixed to his Voyage through North America,) states, that 'this trade was carried on in a very distant country, out of the reach of legal restraint, and where there was a free scope given to any ways or means in attaining advantage. The consequence was, not only the loss of commercial benefit to the persons engaged in it, but of the good opinion of the natives, and the respect of their men, who were inclined to follow their example; so that with drinking, carousing, and quarrelling with the Indians along their route, and among themselves, they seldom reached their winter quarters; and if they did, it was generally by dragging their property upon sledges, as the navigation was closed up by the frost. When, at length, they were arrived, the object of each was to injure his rival traders in the opinion of the natives as much as was in their power, by misrepresentation and presents, for which the agents employed were peculiarly calculated. They considered the command of their employer as binding on them, and however wrong or irregular the transaction, the responsibility rested with the principal who directed them:—this is Indian law.' (*Page x.*)[9] The agents here alluded to, were the Coureurs des Bois, whom the Author had previously described, (*page ii.*) as French Canadians, who, by accompanying the natives on their hunting and trading excursions, had become so attached to the Indian mode of life, that they had lost all relish for their former habits, and native homes. Of these people the Author remarks, that they often brought home rich cargoes of furs, but that during the short time requisite to settle their accounts with the merchants, and procure fresh credit, they generally contrived to squander away all their gains. He adds, that 'this indifference about amassing property, and the pleasure of living free from all restraint, soon brought on a licentiousness of manners, which could not long escape the vigilant observation of the missionaries, who had much reason to complain of their being a disgrace to the christian religion, by not only swerving from its duties themselves, but by thus bringing it into disrepute with those of the natives who had become converts to it.' Sir Alexander M'Kenzie goes on to state, that from this conduct of the traders and their servants, the winter was passed among them in a continual scene of disagreement and quarrels; that the natives could entertain no respect for persons who conducted themselves with so much irregularity and deceit; that from the consequences of this licentious conduct, the traders were in continual alarm, and frequently laid under contribution by the Indians,—in short, that matters were daily becoming worse and worse, so that the merchants who furnished the traders with goods, and participated in their adventures, became disgusted with their ill success, and were with difficulty persuaded to continue their advances. The same Author specifies a few individuals, who, from greater precaution and good sense, were more successful than others, but observes, that these partial advantages 'could not prevent the people of Canada from seeing the improper conduct of some of their associates, which rendered it dangerous to remain any longer among the natives. Most of them who passed the winter at the Saskatchawan, got to the Eagle Hills, where, in the spring of the year 1780, a few days previous to their intended departure, a large band of Indians, being engaged in drinking about their houses, one of the traders, to ease himself of the troublesome importunities of a native, gave him a dose of laudanum in a glass of grog, which effectually prevented him from giving further trouble to any one, by setting him asleep for ever. This accident produced a fray, in which one of the traders and several of the men were killed, while the rest had no other means to save themselves but by a precipitate flight, abandoning a considerable quantity of goods, and near half the furs which they had collected during the winter and spring. About the same time, two of the establishments on the Assiniboin River were attacked with less justice, when several white men and a greater number of Indians were killed. In short, it appeared that the natives had formed a resolution to extirpate the traders; and, without entering into any further reasonings on the subject, it appears to be incontrovertible, that the irregularity pursued in carrying on the trade has brought it into its present forlorn situation.' (*Page xiii, xiv.*) 'The traders,' he adds, 'were saved from the indignation of the natives, only by the ravages of the small pox, which at this period spread among the Indians like a pestilence, and almost depopulated the country. By this calamity, the traders were rescued from personal danger, but the source of their profits was cut off, and very few peltries were to be obtained. Even such of the natives as escaped the contagion, were so alarmed at the surrounding destruction, that they were dispirited from hunting, except for their own subsistence.' In this deplorable state of things, it is not wonderful that the traders should have been (as the Author states) very much reduced in number, and that the merchants in Canada, who supported them, having foreseen that the continuance of such proceedings would be altogether fatal to their interests, should have been inclined to form a junction for carrying on the trade in partnership. Accordingly, during the winter 1783–4, these merchants formed an Association under the name of The North-West Company, in which the leading persons were Messrs. B. and J. Frobisher, and Mr. Simon M'Tavish, by whose influence chiefly the coalition had been brought about. The main principle of the arrangement was that the separate capitals of the several traders were to be thrown into a common stock, in consideration of which, each individual held a proportionable share of the combined adventure. In the arrangement of this co-partnership, difficulties were found, from the claims of some individuals (chiefly Messrs. Pangman and Gregory), who were not satisfied with the shares assigned to them, and who, refusing to concur in the coalition, continued to carry on a separate trade. This retarded for some time the formation of a general union, and, after that was effected, it was again dissolved by differences of a similar nature. This led, in the year 1798, to a great secession from the North-West Company, and to the formation of a New Company (known in Canada by the name of The X.Y. Company), which traded for some years in competition with the former establishment. A coalition, however, was at length effected between these rival bodies in the year 1805, at which time the North-West Company took its present shape.—The means by which this Association acquired a preponderance which has enabled the Company to secure to themselves so extensive and lucrative a trade, will be found well deserving of public attention.[10]

After the junction of the Old and New North-West Companies, the whole concern came to be divided into a hundred shares, of which a considerable proportion is held by the mercantile houses in London or Montreal, which had contributed the capital for the companies; and other shares are held by individuals who are termed *wintering partners*, and who take upon themselves the charge of managing the affairs of the Company in the interior. Of seventy-five shares assigned to the Old Company, thirty are held by one house at Montreal, the successors of those who planned the original coalition in 1783. Of twenty-five assigned to the New Company, eighteen or nineteen are appropriated to the different houses in Montreal or London, which had contributed a capital for the undertaking. All the remaining shares are distributed among the wintering partners, some of whom possess one share, and some two. The partners hold a general meeting every summer, at the rendezvous at Fort William, at the Grand Portage on Lake Superior, where all matters are decided by a majority of votes, every share giving one vote, and the absentees voting by proxy. At this meeting, the operations to be carried on during the succeeding year are arranged, and the station to be assigned to each individual is determined; the accounts of the former year are settled; and every partner brings a statement of the transactions of the department which has been under his charge.

When a wintering partner has served for a certain number of years, he is at liberty to retire from the concern; and, without doing any further duty, to receive not only his share of the capital of the Company, but also, for seven years, to draw one-half of the profits of the share which he had held. Upon his retiring, the vacancy is filled up by the election of a new partner. The candidates for this situation must have served the Company for a certain number of years as clerks, of whom a great number are employed under the direction of the wintering partners, and are entrusted with the command and immediate management of one or more trading posts situated in the interior. The election of a new partner is decided, like the other affairs of the Company, by the majority of votes at the general annual meeting of the partners: and, as the conduct of the new partner may affect in a material degree the personal interest of every one who has a right to vote in the election, it is not likely that the choice should fall upon a person destitute of those qualifications which are considered requisite for promoting the common interest. No candidate can have much chance of success, unless he be well acquainted with the nature of the trade, the character and manners of the Indians, and the mode of acquiring influence with them. He must also be of an active disposition, and likely to pursue with perseverance and vigour any object that can tend to promote the interest of the Company. The hope of obtaining the envied station of a partner, being kept alive among all the senior clerks, excites among them an activity and zeal for the general interests of the concern, hardly inferior to that of the partners themselves. They act under the immediate inspection of those who have a direct interest in the result of their management, and are sensible that all their ability must be exerted to secure the favour of their superiors. Every wintering partner watches closely the conduct of the clerks who are under his immediate command; he is excited to this vigilance, not merely by the common interest in which he participates as a partner, but also by feelings of personal responsibility. He comes to the general meeting to give an account of the transactions of his department; and the praise or the censure of his associates is dealt out to him, in proportion to the profit or loss which has occurred in the trade under his direction, and to the success, or failure, of the plans entrusted to his management.

Nothing certainly could be devised more admirably calculated than this system, to infuse activity into every department of so extensive a concern, and to direct that activity, in the most effectual manner, and with complete unity of purpose, towards the common interest. But however much this community of interest among all the partners, and the responsibility thus imposed upon each individual, tend to keep alive an active attention to the Company's affairs, it must be admitted that they are by no means calculated to produce much respect for the rights of others:—On the contrary, the very nature of the Association, and the extensive range which their operations embrace, cannot fail to produce an *esprit de corps* not very consistent with the feelings of propriety and justice.—This observation will be found particularly applicable to the wintering partners. In the common intercourse of civilized society the necessity of maintaining a fair character in the estimation of the public forms a continued check to that inordinate stimulus of self-interest which too often causes individuals to deviate from the principles of honour and honesty. But a wintering partner of the North-West Company is secluded from all society, except that of persons who have the same interests with himself; and if, in the pursuit of these, he should be induced to violate the rules of justice, he must feel that he is not likely to be judged with extreme rigour by the only persons for whose approbation he is solicitous. The civilized world is at so great a distance, that he cannot be very deeply affected by the chance of his conduct meeting with public reprobation; and he naturally flatters himself that his proceedings will never be investigated, or that if they should, there are so many persons to share in the responsibility, that it cannot fall very heavily on himself. In these remote situations, the restraints of law cannot operate as in the midst of a regular society.—When a plaintiff has to travel thousands of miles to find the court from which he is to seek redress, and when witnesses are to be brought from such a distance, at a vast expense, and to the total interruption of their ordinary pursuits, it must be a case of extraordinary importance, which would induce even a wealthy man to encounter the difficulty of obtaining it.[11] Every wintering partner, therefore, must naturally be aware of the extent of his power over individuals who are not rich enough to contend with the whole Association of which he is a member; and if under these circumstances, acts of injustice and oppression be committed against weaker neighbours, however greatly they are to be regretted, they cannot form a subject of much surprise.

Thus, from the very nature and organization of the Company, a conclusion may reasonably be drawn as to the line of conduct which they are most likely to pursue. That indeed may be varied in a certain degree by the personal character of the individuals at the head of the concern; but even supposing that these were men of the most honourable principles, and incapable of countenancing a systematic violation of justice, it would be with the greatest difficulty that they could restrain this tendency in others.

NOTES

[Editor's note: The reference numbers in the text are Selkirk's page references to the original books.]

1. Modern scholars might dispute Selkirk's assertion here; see, for example, Marcel Trudel, *The Beginnings of New France 1524–1663* (Toronto, 1973).

2. In general, see Fernand Ouellet, *Social and Economic History of Quebec, 1760–1850* (Toronto, 1980).

3. For a general description of the workings of the French fur trade, see Harold A. Innis, *The Fur Trade in Canada* (rev. ed., Toronto, 1956). But consult also William J. Eccles, 'A Belated Review of Harold Adams Innis's *The Fur Trade in Canada*', *Canadian Historical Review* 60 (1979): 419–44.

4. Most modern scholars would agree that Selkirk here overemphasizes the extent to which the French were able to exercise their monopoly through licensing.

5. Again, Selkirk overemphasizes the success of the government in controlling matters, especially in the so-called Brandy Trade. See, for

example, J.E. Lunn, 'The Illegal Fur Trade Out of New France, 1713–1760', *Canadian Historical Association Annual Report* (1939): 61–76.

6. For modern scholarly accounts of the changes in the fur trade after 1763, consult E.E. Rich, *The Fur Trade and the Northwest to 1857* (Toronto, 1967), 130–85; Arthur J. Ray, *Indians in the Fur Trade: their role as hunters, trappers and middlemen in the lands southwest of Hudson Bay 1660–1870* (Toronto, 1974), 94 ff.

7. For recent analyses, see Ray, *Indians in the Fur Trade*, and Arthur J. Ray and Donald Freeman, *'Give Us Good Measure': An Economic Analysis of Relations between the Indians and the Hudson's Bay Company before 1763* (Toronto, 1978), 192–7.

8. Alexander Henry, *Travels and Adventures in Canada and the Indian Territories between the years 1760 and 1776* (New York, 1809).

9. Alexander Mackenzie, *Voyages from Montreal, on the River St. Laurence, through the Continent of North America, to the Frozen and Pacific Oceans; in the Years 1789 and 1793; With a Preliminary*

Account of the Rise, Progress, and Present State of the Fur Trade of that Country . . . (London, 1801).

10. For the North West Company, see Marjorie Wilkins Campbell, *The North West Company* (Vancouver, 1983); Gordon Charles Davidson, *The North West Company* (New York, 1967); W. Stewart Wallace, ed., *Documents Relating to the North West Company* (Toronto, 1934); L.R. Masson, ed., *Les bourgeois de la Compagnie du Nord-Ouest . . .* (Quebec, 1889–1890).

11. The British government attempted to deal with these questions in 1803 with the passage of the so-called Canada Jurisdictions Act, which made the courts of Upper and Lower Canada responsible for the obtaining of justice in the western territories. This legislation, of course, became one of the major bones of contention between the Hudson's Bay Company (which denied that the act applied to territory in their charter) and the North West Company backed by the Canadian government (which insisted the act did apply). In general, see A.S. Morton, 'The Canada Jurisdiction Act and the North-West', *Transactions Royal Society of Canada* 3rd ser., 32 (1938): 121–38.

HISTORICAL INTERPRETATIONS

3 From Sylvia Van Kirk, *'Many Tender Ties': Women in Fur Trade Society in Western Canada, 1670–1870* (Winnipeg: Watson and Dwyer, 1980), 53–73.

The economic role played by Indian women in fur-trade society reflected the extent to which the European traders were compelled to adapt to the native way of life. The all-encompassing work role of Indian women was transferred, in modified form, to the trading post, where their skills not only facilitated the traders' survival in the wilderness but actual fur-trade operations. At the North West Company posts and at Hudson's Bay Company posts especially, native women came to be relied upon as an integral if unofficial part of the labour force. Their economic assistance was a powerful incentive for the traders to take Indian wives; even within their own tribes, the women exercised a role in the functioning of the trade which has been little appreciated by historians of this period.

The Nor'Westers had a first-hand knowledge of the usefulness of Indian wives which they gained from the French, and this was an important reason for the Company allowing its men to intermarry with the natives. Besides familiarizing the Frenchman with the customs and language of her tribe, the Indian woman had performed a wide range of domestic tasks. When the Jesuit Father Carheil castigated the French traders at Michilimackinac for keeping Indian women, the traders argued that their primary motive was economic necessity. Their wives ground the corn to make the staple food known as sagamité, made moccasins and leather garments, and performed other essential services such as washing and chopping firewood for the cabins. Carheil's remonstrance that the carrying out of these duties provided but 'a proximate occasion for sin' was a gross underestimate of the genuine importance of the women's tasks.[1] Given that the Nor'Westers with their large force of skilled engagés still relied upon the services of Indian women, it can be appreciated that the Hudson's Bay Company with its limited and inexperienced personnel had an even greater need for their assistance. Throughout the eighteenth century, officers on the Bay argued with the London Committee that it was essential to keep Indian women in the posts, as they performed important tasks which the British had not yet mastered. The Council at York Factory even protested to the Committee in 1802 that the women should be regarded as 'Virtually your Honors Servants.'[2]

Perhaps the most important domestic task performed by the women at the fur-trade posts was to provide the men with a steady supply of 'Indian shoes' or moccasins. The men of both companies generally did not dress in Indian style (the buckskinned mountain man was not part of the Canadian scene), but they universally adopted the moccasin as the most practical footwear for the wilderness. The first step in making moccasins or other leather apparel such as leggings and mittens was the laborious process of tanning the moose or deer skins:

> The skin they scrape and . . . take the braines of the animal and rub it upon the skin to make it pliable and soft; afterwards they smoke it well and then soak it in warm water for the night in order to render it easy to work with a piece of iron made for that purpose.[3]

Even Joseph Isbister, a stern disciplinarian, stressed the necessity of admitting women into the Bayside forts to provide a constant supply of shoes for the men. Large quantities were needed, for moccasins wore out quickly; at York Factory in 1800, the women made 650 pairs for the men's use in the summer season.[4] On his 1789 expedition, Alexander Mackenzie depended upon the wives of his two French-Canadian voyageurs to keep his party in footwear. The women scarcely ever left the canoes, being 'continually employ'd making shoes of moose skin as a pair does not last us above one Day.'[5]

Closely related to the manufacture of moccasins was the Indian woman's role in making the snowshoes which made winter travel possible. Although the men usually made the frames, the women prepared the sinews and netted the intricate webbing which provided the support. When Samuel Hearne and his small party went inland in 1774 to establish Cumberland House, the first Hudson's Bay Company post inland, they looked to Indian women for assistance. On October 21, Hearne recorded that all the Indians had gone away 'Except 2 or 3 Women who Stays to Make, Mend, Knitt Snowshoes &c for us dureing the Winter.'[6] A man could not even venture outside the post to collect firewood or hunt small game in winter without snowshoes. To be without women to make them was to invite disaster, as Alexander Mackenzie's well-known lament to his cousin Roderic at Fort Chipewyan in 1786 indicates:

> I have not a single one in my fort that can make Rackets [racquettes]. I do not know what to do without these articles see what it is to have no wives. Try and get Rackets—there is no stirring without them.[7]

Without women to provide them with moccasins and snowshoes, Hudson's Bay Company officers stressed, the Company would be seriously restricted in its efforts to compete with its rivals.[8]

In the provision and preservation of food, always a serious concern to the fur traders, Indian women also made an important contribution. For the North West Company, the expense of importing foodstuffs was prohibitive. The problem of supplying its canoe brigades was ideally solved by the use of the Indian food, pemmican—a nutritious, compact mixture of pounded buffalo meat and fat which kept well and took up relatively little space. Pemmican became the staple food of the fur trade, and Indian women performed most of the steps required in its preparation. At posts on the plains, buffalo hunting and pemmican making formed an essential part of the yearly routine, each post being required to furnish an annual quota for the support of the brigades. In accordance with Indian custom, once the hunters had killed the buffalo, the women's work began. They skinned the animals, cut the meat off the carcasses and collected the marrow and fat for rendering. After the meat was sliced into thin strips, it was dried on racks in the sun or over a slow fire. 'The women employed all day Slicing and drying the meat' was a typical diary entry in the early summer months.[9] When the meat was dry, the women pounded it into a thick flaky mass. About 50 pounds of this meat would then be mixed with 40 pounds of melted fat and packed in a *taureau* to make up the standard 90-pound lot of pemmican. Previously, during the winter, the women had been kept busy making the *taureaux* which were flattish sacks of buffalo hide with the hair on the outside. 'Women all busy stretching buffalo hides to make pemmican bags'; 'All the women at work sewing Bags' were common remarks in many fort journals.[10]

Although pemmican was the staple food of the transport brigades, it was too precious a commodity to form the chief diet at the posts themselves. Fresh meat could be kept in the ice-houses at most of the posts on the plains, but to the north, where game was scarce, the people subsisted mainly on fish and fowl. The women at the posts of both companies on Lake Athabasca were adept fisherwomen, since tending the nets was part of a woman's role in more northerly tribes. After a successful fall fishery, the women were busily occupied splitting and drying hundreds of whitefish for the winter.[11] Across the Rockies, the women preserved vast quantities of salmon, the basic food for the districts of the Columbia and New Caledonia.[12] At the posts around Hudson Bay, geese, either dried or salted by the Indian women, formed an important part of the 'country provisions'.[13]

Apart from curing the produce of the hunt, Indian women were also responsible for collecting auxiliary food supplies which, besides adding variety to the diet, could sometimes mean the difference between life and death. In the area to the west and southwest of Lake Superior, wild rice was a staple food of the Ojibwa. The women harvested the rice from the marshy shores of the lakes and rivers by shaking the ripe heads into the bottom of their small canoes. The rice was then parched and stored in fawn skins. The traders in the area were frequently grateful for such food,[14] and for maple sugar which constituted an important addition to the diet in the Shield area. The spring trip to the sugar bush provided a welcome release from the monotony of the winter routine, and the voyageurs with their families and Indian relatives all enjoyed the annual event. In April 1805, as a typical instance, all the women from the Nor'Westers' post on Rainy Lake were out making sugar. 'Mr. Grant's Girl' seems to have been especially expert at the job and on one occasion traded about thirty pounds of sugar for rum.[15] A kind of sugar could also be made from the Manitoba maple which grew as far west as Fort Carlton. Chief Factor John Stuart noted in April 1825 that the only subject of interest was that all the women were busy making sugar, 'some of it very fine.'[16]

The entire Indian Country teemed with many varieties of berries which the women looked forward to collecting annually. When the Nor'Westers were tracking up the higher reaches of the Saskatchewan, the younger Henry observed: 'the women generally keep on by land, during the use of the line, to gather fruit, which alleviates the labor and revives the spirits of the men.'[17] Later at Rocky Mountain House, he reported that the women would all go off on horseback and return with great quantities of poires, raspberries and strawberries. Dried berries, especially saskatoons, were added to the high-grade pemmican made for the officers. But berries were more than a luxury item. David Thompson declared that berries had kept him alive after he became incapacitated by breaking his leg in 1788:

> I became emaciated till the berries became ripe and the kind hearted Indian women brought me plenty . . . for my support. This was pure charity for I had nothing to give them and I was much relieved.[18]

In New Caledonia and the Columbia, berries and 'wappitoo root' gathered by the women were necessary to alleviate hunger in the spring when supplies of salmon invariably ran low.[19]

Although the wilds of Western Canada gave the appearance of providing abundant sustenance, all regions suffered from seasonal fluctuations and poorer areas faced frequent starvation. In times of scarcity, an Indian woman's skill and resourcefulness came into their own. At Lake Athabasca, it was common for the women to be sent away to the fishery to support themselves and their children when provisions ran low.[20] After his fisherman deserted to the Nor'Westers at Île à la Crosse in 1810, Peter Fidler's Cree wife Mary virtually saved the English from starvation since she was the only one who knew how to mend and set the nets.[21]

The fact that it was also the woman's role in Indian society to snare small game served the traders well. On one occasion, the Indian wife of the bourgeois John Dugald Cameron reputedly kept the people at her husband's post alive with the catch from her snares.[22] The young Nor'Wester George Nelson was certainly grateful for his Ojibwa wife when he found himself in dire straits at a small outpost north of Lake Superior in 1815.[23] After provisions became almost exhausted in February, Nelson's wife set out, well equipped with snares of wire and twine, to catch small game. At first, she had little success because wild animals were devouring her catch before she could return to the snares. After about a week, however, she came in with sixteen partridges and went off with one of the men next day to bring home the thirty hares which she had cached. Nelson's wife had been accompanied by the wife of one of his Hudson's Bay Company competitors, but although the Nor'Wester knew he might be censured for allowing this, he felt his wife's welfare must come before commercial rivalry:

I am happy of it because it is company, she will have less trouble to chop wood & if misfortunately she cuts herself or gets otherwise sick, the others will help her.

The 'she-hunters' returned with all their equipment after about three weeks, having added much to the kettles of both companies. 'My woman brings home 8 hares & 14 Partridges' wrote Nelson with satisfaction on March 3, 'making in all 58 hares and 34 Partridges. Good.' Occasionally even the well-established post of York Factory could run out of fresh provisions, so essential for the prevention of scurvy. In December 1818, Chief Factor James Swain was forced to send his wife and one of his daughters out to try to catch fish or rabbits. They returned a fortnight later in bitterly cold weather with grim news: there were no fish and they had had to walk many miles to secure a few rabbits.[24]

Although Indian women played an important part in preserving and procuring country provisions, they did not take over the official role of cook at the fur-trade posts as might be expected. Usually an Orkneyman or a French Canadian was specifically designated to serve as cook for the officers' mess. At some posts the servants took their meals in a military-type mess, but as families increased it became common for the women to prepare their families' daily rations in the servants' quarters.[25]

Apart from domestic duties relating to the traditional female roles of making clothes and preparing food, the Indian woman was also involved in specific fur-trade operations. Of particular importance to the inexperienced Hudson's Bay Company men was the women's knowledge of dressing furs. As the York Council emphasized to its London superiors, the Indian women 'clean and put into a state of preservation all Beaver and Otter skins brought by the Indians undried and in bad Condition.'[26] Since the North West Company had adopted the birch-bark canoe as the basis of its transport system, Indian women continued in their traditional role of helping in its manufacture. It was the women's job to collect wattappe (wattap), roots from the spruce tree, which they split fine for sewing the seams of the canoe. The numerous references in the journals testify to the vast quantities needed: 'Women raising wattap—33 women, 8 bundles each'—'Mr. Grant's Girl brought us 75 Bundles Wattap to day.' On Lake Athabasca, the women at the Hudson's Bay Company post were expected to provide an annual quota of 50 bundles of watt-appe each.[27] Having collected the wattappe, the women helped to sew the seams of the canoes and then caulk them with spruce gum which they also collected. At Rocky Mountain House in 1810, Alexander Henry observed the voyageurs' wives busy gathering gum for the Columbia canoes; a brigade which departed without adequate supplies of bark, wattappe and gum for repairs could find itself in dire straits.[28] At York Factory, the women helped to pay for their keep during the winter by making canoe sails.[29]

Besides assisting in the making of canoes, Indian women, because of their traditional training, could readily lend a hand to help man them. Two women assisted in paddling the canoes on Mackenzie's voyage in 1789,[30] but with a large force of voyageurs, it was seldom necessary for the North West Company to call upon this reserve. This was not the case with the Hudson's Bay Company in the early stages of its moving inland. With few experienced canoemen, the Hudson's Bay Company turned to women, who often rendered valuable assist-ance. John Thomas, on his return to Moose Factory in 1779, told of meeting another offi-cer in charge of three small canoes loaded with provisions for a new inland post; each canoe was manned by an Englishman and an Indian woman, the woman acting as steersman.[31] In the 1790s Chief Factor Joseph Colen declared that one of the reasons for the declining num-ber of canoes coming down to York Factory was that the women were no longer allowed to accompany their husbands and help paddle the canoes.[32] . . .

Altogether, the multifaceted work role of Indian women in the fur trade merits their description as 'Your Honors Servants'. But they were servants who never received wages in any real sense and undoubtedly both com-panies profited by this source of cheap labour. Significantly, in fur-trade society, it was the Indian woman's traditional skills which made her a valuable economic partner, a fact which serves to underscore the initial dependence of the traders upon the Indians. . . .

NOTES

1. Jesuits. Letters from Missions. Black gown and redskins; adventures and travels of the early Jesuit missionaries in North America, 1610–1791, edited by Edna Kenton (New York, 1956), 401–2.

2. HBCA, B.239/b/79, fos. 40d–41; see also J.B. Tyrrell, ed., *Journals of Samuel Hearne and Philip Turnor, 1774–1792* (Toronto: Champlain Society, XXI), 327, n.6; HBCA, A. 11/116, fo. 77d.

3. PAC, Masson Collection, No. 3, 'An Account of the Chipwean Indians', 22.

4. HBCA, B.239/a/105, fo. 11; B.42/a/36, fo. 23; B.42/a/5, fo. 7.

5. W. Kaye Lamb, ed., *The Journals and Letters of Sir Alexander Mackenzie* (Cambridge, England, 1970), 220.

6. Tyrrell, *Journals of Hearne and Turnor*, 125.

7. Lamb, *Journals of Mackenzie*, 424.

8. HBCA, B.239/b/79, fo. 41.

9. PAC, Masson Collection, No. 6, John Porter's Journal, 29; HBCA, B.121/a/4, fo. 48d.

10. Elliott Coues, ed., *New Light on the Early History of the Greater Northwest: The Manuscript Journals of Alexander Henry and of David Thompson, 1799–1814* (Minneapolis, 1965), 582–3; Charles M. Gates, ed., *Five Fur Traders of the Northwest* (St Paul, Minn., 1965), 161; L.R.F. Masson, *Les Bourgeois de la Compagnie du Nord-Ouest* (New York, 1960), I: 288.

11. HBCA, B.39/a/16, fo. 21.

12. Gabriel Franchère, *Narrative of a Voyage to the Northwest Coast of America, 1811–1814*, edited by R.G. Thwaites (Cleveland, 1904), 5.

13. HBCA, B.239/a/131–3 passim.

14. Michel Curot, 'A Wisconsin Fur-Trader's Journal, 1803–04', *Wisconsin Historical Collections* 20: 442–3.

15. Gates, *Five Fur Traders*, 237; Curot, 'Journal, 1803–04', 441.

16. HBCA, B.27/a/14, fo. 98.

17. Coues, *New Light on Greater Northwest*, 485.

18. Richard Glover, ed., *David Thompson's Narrative, 1784–1812* (Toronto: Champlain Society, 1962), 55.

19. Coues, *New Light on Greater Northwest*, 859; Ross Cox, *The Columbia River*, edited by Edgar and Jane Stewart (Norman, Okla., 1957), 266.

20. HBCA, B.39/a/16, fos. 4d–13 passim.

21. HBCA, B.89/a/2, los. 7, 10d.

22. Margaret A. MacLeod, ed., *The Letters of Letitia Hargrave* (Toronto: Champlain Society, XXVIII), lii.

23. The following account is taken from the George Nelson Papers, Journal, 29 Jan.–23 June 1815.

24. HBCA, B.239/a/126, fo. 14.

25. MacLeod, *Letitia's Letters*, 85.

26. HBCA, B.239/b/79, fo. 40d; see also Tyrrell, *Journals of Hearne and Turnor*, 237, n.6.

27. Coues, *New Light on Greater Northwest*, 615; Gates, *Five Fur Traders*, 217; E.E. Rich, ed., Simpson's *Athabasca Journal and Report, 1820–21* (London: HBRS, I), 342.

28. Coues, *New Light on Greater Northwest*, 622; Gates, *Five Fur Traders*, 250–2; Curot, 'Journal, 1803–04', 460.

29. HBCA, B.239/a/130, fos. 22d–28 passim.

30. Lamb, *Journals of Mackenzie*, 165.

31. HBCA, A. 11/44, fo. 95.

32. HBCA, B.239/a/99, fo. 18d: Colen further adds that 'this occasions much murmuring among the Men and forces many to leave the Service sooner than they wished to'. Unfortunately, no further information has been found to explain either the cause or ultimate outcome of this action.

4   From Carolyn Podruchny, *Making the Voyageur World: Travelers and Traders in the North American Fur Trade* (Toronto: University of Toronto Press, 2006), 165–200, 337–44.

RENDEZVOUS: PARTIES, TRICKS, AND FRIENDSHIPS

Fort William is the great emporium for the interior. An extensive assortment of merchandise is annually brought hither from Montreal, by large canoes, or the Company's vessels on the lakes, which, in return, bring down the produce of the wintering posts to Canada, from whence it is shipped for England . . . Fort William may therefore be looked upon as the metropolitan post of the interior, and its fashionable season generally continues from the latter end of May to the latter end of August. During this period, good living and festivity predominate; and the luxuries of the dinner-table compensate in some degree for the long fasts and short commons experienced by those who are stationed in the remote posts.

The voyageurs *too enjoy their carnival, and between rum and baubles the hard-earned wages of years are often dissipated in a few weeks.*[1]

The Montreal fur trade was a far-flung enterprise spanning thousands of miles. Central administrative posts were established in the interior of the pays d'en haut to facilitate the organization of trading and the transfer of goods. Ross Cox's description of Fort William quoted here, from his *Adventures on the Columbia River* (1831), conveys an image of a bustling and diverse centre of commerce and cavorting. At these administrative nodes fur traders and labourers congregated in midsummer to exchange furs for European trade goods. These gatherings, called rendezvous, became a time of celebration and feasting. Arriving voyageurs were relieved to have survived their gruelling journey, pleased to meet up with friends, and excited about fresh supplies of food and drink. In the 1770s trader Peter Pond described the rendezvous at Mackinac (at the junction of Lakes Michigan and Huron), where many 'ware amuseing themselves in Good Cumpany at Billards Drinking fresh Punch Wine & Eney thing thay Please to Call for while the Mo[re] valgear Ware fiteing Each other feasting was Much atended to Dansing at Nite.'[2] After 1803 the most famous rendezvous was at Fort William, at the western end of Lake Superior, which became a 'great emporium', as Ross Cox aptly described it. Here pork eaters and northmen unloaded and loaded their ladings, the bourgeois held their annual meetings to plan business operations for the coming year, independent merchants set up shops to sell wares, and retired voyageurs who had settled in the area came to the fort to hear about the past year's adventures.[3] In the midst of all this activity, voyageurs' celebrations dominated the scene. When clerk George Nelson arrived at Grand Portage for the first time in 1802, he observed high levels of 'Gambling, feasting, dancing, drinking & fighting'.[4]

Although voyageurs were hired for extremely difficult work, a large part of their lives was occupied with celebrations, festivity, and play. [. . .] Perhaps play came to comprise a significant part of voyageurs' lives because they worked in a liminal space, on the boundaries between French Canada and Aboriginal societies, constantly moving through the pays d'en haut. Scholars have argued that liminality encourages playfulness and trickery; in particular cultural anthropologist Victor Turner asserted that 'liminality is particularly conducive to play. Play is not to be restricted to games and jokes; it extends to the introduction of new forms of symbolic action . . . parts of liminality may be given over to experimental behaviour.'[5] Voyageurs regularly moved across the thresholds of new worlds, and the thrill and adventure of travelling into the unknown were expressed in their parties, tricks, and friendships.

Following Turner's lead, this article takes a broad view of the concept of play, not simply

as an opposite to work, but rather as a comprehensive term for festivities, pastimes, relief from work, and trickery. Parties, singing, dancing, gaming, and joking made up the play of voyageurs when they were working as well as resting. Play offered them amusement and diversion, but it also became a means through which they could shape their world.

CARNIVAL ON CANOE JOURNEYS

Group celebrations were an especially revealing aspect of the play of voyageurs, and historians have developed lines of analysis to interpret the celebrations of lower orders of people, such as peasants and workers. In play Mikhail Bakhtin found a window to late medieval and early renaissance European folk culture. Bakhtin saw 'carnival' as providing

> [a] boundless world of humorous forms and manifestations opposed to the official and serious tone of medieval ecclesiastical and feudal culture. In spite of their variety, folk festivities of the carnival type, the comic rites and cults, the downs and fools, giants, dwarfs, and jugglers, the vast and manifold literature of parody—all these forms have one style in common: they belong to one culture of folk carnival humor. . . . All these forms of protocol and ritual based on laughter and consecrated by tradition existed in all the countries of medieval Europe; they were sharply distinct from the serious official, ecclesiastical, feudal, and political cult forms and ceremonials. They offered a completely different, nonofficial, extraecclesiastical and extrapolitical aspect of the world, of man, and of human relations; they built a second world and a second life outside officialdom, a world in which all medieval people participated more or less.[6]

In the fur trade the same applied to voyageurs, who constructed a world that differed dramatically from that of their masters.

Voyageurs' distinctive identities and practices were not confined to specific celebrations, such as rendezvous, but permeated all their forms of play. [. . .]

As in other early modern folk settings, carnivals, and especially rendezvous, helped to shape the voyageurs' world. Literally translated as 'meeting', rendezvous represented a time when fur traders came together to celebrate, encouraging camaraderie, competition, and social distinctions among everyone in the trade. Earlier we noted the omnipresent divisions between voyageurs and their masters. During rendezvous, however, divisions among voyageurs themselves became more pronounced. Throughout the rest of the year, celebrations served the same functions: they unified men in camaraderie but also fostered social fissures.

In fur trade departures festivity pervaded the chaos of last-minute hirings, packing, and planning. This flurry of activity was most intense at the large annual leave-taking from the St. Lawrence valley at the beginning of a season.[7] People gathered around the crews at Montreal and Lachine, the departure point just west of the rapids near Montreal, to send off the brigades.

Clerk George Nelson reminisced that the young men bade farewell to their relatives and friends 'with tears in their eyes & singing as if going to a banquet!'[8] Large parties were held at Lachine the night before the brigades intended to set out, and most people became intoxicated. In his biography of the voyageur Jean-Baptiste Charbonneau, Georges Dugas described the parties that were held before crews set out: 'During fifteen days, it was, for these old wolves of the North, a series of celebrations and amusements; they invited all their friends, and reveled; one had to say that they kept spending down to the last cent, and left their gusset [pocket] completely empty. The drink was flowing in torrents; in the evening they had a dance. . . . On the day of departure, a crowd of people went to Lachine to witness the spectacle.'[9] [. . .]

The pageantry of departures and arrivals was heightened with 'Indian war whoops' and firing muskets.[10] The yelling and musket fire were a form of salute to the brigades, a gesture of respect, and a wish of goodwill. 'Indian war whoops' may have symbolized entry into a 'savage world', unknown, exotic, and dangerous to voyageurs, and perhaps marked the beginning of the men's transition from French Canadian habitants to voyageurs who lived among Aboriginal peoples. The war whoops probably reflected both a fear of Aboriginal peoples as well as admiration for them. Dugas described the desires of new voyageurs to imitate Aboriginal people: 'The savage life appealed to them; it seemed to them that down there, that could be rid of all brakes, dressed like the Indian, sleeping with him the tent, and hunting like him for livelihood.'[11] The most common of voyageur labour, canoeing, was a practice learned from Aboriginal peoples. The war whoops symbolized the extensive cultural borrowing of Canadians from Aboriginal peoples, but they also symbolized French colonists' view of Aboriginal peoples as an undifferentiated and exotic 'other'.[12] Philip Deloria has found similar cultural ambiguity in American appropriation of Aboriginal actions. He argues that '[t]he indeterminacy of American identities stems, in part, from the nation's inability to deal with Indian people. Americans wanted to feel a natural affinity with the continent, and it was Indians who could teach them such aboriginal closeness. Yet, in order to control the landscape they had to destroy the original inhabitants.'[13] Voyageurs did not want to control the landscape to the same degree as American colonists, but they knew they were at the mercy of those who did. Thus voyageurs had to appease Aboriginal peoples, despite their fear. Imitating Aboriginal customs was a way in which voyageurs could familiarize themselves with these strange new people. Yet voyageurs' behaviour was similar to that of American colonists in other ways. Deloria asserts that in the context of carnivalesque holidays, such as in Tammany societies, when the 'real' world was suspended in favour of a topsy-turvy world of unstable power, the figure of the Indian became central. The Indian became a means through which to articulate a revolutionary identity separate from Europe and attached to the North American continent.[14] Likewise, 'Indianness' or 'Aboriginality' was evoked in the formation of the voyageurs' distinct identity.

The pattern of celebrations at departures carried over into the interior. Alexander Henry the Younger described his men's party in the summer of 1800 after the first day on the route from Grand Portage to Lake Winnipeg: 'All were merry over their favourite regale, which is always given on their departure, and generally enjoyed at this spot, where we have a delightful meadow to pitch our tents, and plenty of elbow-room for the men's antics.'[15] This treat was especially appreciated after the arduous portage at that site.

Arrivals were marked with the same festivity and pageantry as departures. A sense of relief rather than excitement dominated the occasions, as men celebrated the completion of a safe and successful journey. Arriving back in Montreal was an especially momentous occasion, as it marked passage out of the fur trade world. When Ross Cox's crew arrived at the Lake of Two Mountains, near Montreal, in September 1817, he presented his voyageurs with a keg of rum as a 'valedictory allowance' and shook hands with each man.[16] At Fort William and Grand Portage men were treated with regales of bread, pork, butter, liquor, and tobacco, and usually held parties.[17] At smaller posts men were treated with drams when disembarked.[18] The fur trade arrivals were reminiscent of sailors reaching ports after long bouts at sea or lumbermen completing a river drive. Drunken merriment and unruly rioting were expressions of joy in finishing a round of gruelling labour. [. . .]

Incoming crews were usually met by the inhabitants of a post, including families that the men had left behind for the summer. Especially large crowds gathered at Grand Portage and Fort William.[19] Alexander

Ross described the pageantry and pomp that could accompany the arrival of a crew: 'On this joyful occasion, every person advances to the waterside, and great guns are fired to announce the bourgeois' arrival. A general shaking of hands takes place, as it often happens that people have not met for years: even the bourgeois goes through this mode of salutation with the meanest.'[20] At smaller posts flags were raised and crews were saluted with musket shots.[21] Men were often sent out to meet expected canoes to help guide the crews into the posts.[22] Boisterous arrivals seemed to be a long-standing custom.[23] [. . .]

Parties at the start and the end of journeys were not unique to voyageurs or French Canada in the eighteenth century, but these celebrations became distinctive social markers of the voyageur's journey, underscoring the journey's importance to the trade, its danger, as well as its defining status for voyageurs. The pageantry and festivities helped to separate the voyageur social order from French Canada and marked the transition between the distinct social spaces and the emergence of a new voyageur world. The designated (though limited) space for revelry allowed voyageurs an opportunity to express their fear, anxiety, sadness, and excitement at travelling between these different worlds. By 'letting go' or 'going wild' at the parties, men were then better able to focus on the task of efficient travelling, so necessary to the effective functioning of the trade.

The rendezvous, on the other hand, was unique to the fur trade. It assumed great significance because it brought together most parts of the disparate trading operations and underscored the extreme division of times of plenty from times of want in the trade. Some rendezvous may have been modelled on Aboriginal trading fairs, such as those at Montreal in the second half of the seventeenth century.[24] In the continental interior many Aboriginal peoples met with one another in large groups on an annual basis.[25] Among the most significant of these gatherings on the plains were the annual summer trading fairs at the Mandan-Hidatsa villages, but smaller fairs also occurred among the Crees, the Ojibwes, the Assiniboines, the Shoshones, and the Blackfeet.[26] David Meyer and Paul Thistle contend that fur traders built their posts along the Saskatchewan River in the vicinity of annual religious gatherings of Cree people.[27] Ironically the fur trade rendezvous could become a source of consternation for Aboriginal peoples. Victor Lytwyn has shown that Ojibwe hunters and trappers were intimidated by traders at Grand Portage, especially during the rendezvous, when revelry got out of hand.[28]

ANNUAL CYCLE OF CARNIVAL AT TRADING POSTS

Voyageurs had much more leisure time during the winter months spent at interior posts than they did during the canoe journeys of the summers. Yet here they also had more time to feel homesick and anxious in the midst of a foreign world. Much of their play was reminiscent of French Canada, such as celebrating annual holidays, drinking, and holding balls; these festivities helped voyageurs create a sense of home away from home. Voyageurs also had the time to create new connections, form new families, and solidify a distinctive society in the Northwest. Their celebrations helped them create new memories and new traditions rooted in their new locations.

An annual schedule of holiday celebrations accompanied the yearly round of labour, which was especially important to the men living at isolated posts, away from their families and friends. Men often journeyed from outlying posts to congregate at larger central forts to celebrate the holidays and gladly risked the dangers and discomfort of winter travel, even a week of walking with snowshoes, to avoid spending a holiday alone.[29] Holidays helped mark the passage of time and provided structure during the long, dreary, and often lonely months at the interior posts. Coming together

to celebrate at specific times helped to generate camaraderie and fellow feeling with one another, their masters, and Aboriginal peoples.

Christmas and New Year were the most popular holidays for the fur traders and were rarely forgotten or ignored. Other holidays that were sometimes celebrated included All Saint's Day on November 1, St. Andrew's Day on November 30, and Easter in early April.[30] Similar celebrations occurred at HBC posts.[31] The occasional mention of celebrations occurred on Palm Sunday, the king's birthday (June 4, George III), and Epiphany, or 'little Christmas' (January 6).[32] Men seemed willing to commemorate any day, regardless of its origins or significance to them, because it served as an excuse for a celebration and drams from the bourgeois. Commemorating St. Andrew, the patron saint of Scotland, and observing the birthday of George III, king of Great Britain, were probably holidays introduced by the Scottish and English bourgeois and clerks, while Christmas, New Year's, All Saint's Day, and Easter would have been common celebrations in French Canada.[33] George Landmann noted that in late eighteenth-century Montreal, New Year's Day was 'a day of extraordinary festivity, which was extended to the two or three following days. Amongst the Canadians it was . . . the fashion for everybody to visit everybody during one of the three first, days of the year, when a glass of noyeau or other liquor was, with a piece of biscuit or cake, presented to the visitor, which, after a hard day's work in calling at some twenty or thirty houses, frequently terminated in sending a number of very respectable people home in a staggering condition toward the close of the day.'[34] Feasting, drinking, and levees, or paying courtesy calls on masters (particularly on New Year's Day) were characteristic of celebrations in fur trade society.

The holiday celebrations seemed to follow a formula. Specific rituals and ceremonies, giving the day a sense of orderly formality and tradition, were followed by chaotic parties, where wild abandon and heavy drinking predominated. Alexander Henry the Younger complained on New Year's Day in 1803 that he was plagued with ceremonies and men and women drinking and fighting 'pell mell'.[35]

During most holiday celebrations at fur trade posts, men generally did not have to work.[36] During the Christmas and New Year's holidays, voyageurs and bourgeois frequently arranged to visit other posts or invited visitors to their post for the day or for the entire holiday season.[37] Many men tried to organize their work schedules so they would not miss any of the festivities. [. . .]

The day's festivities on Christmas and New Year's usually began early in the morning. Voyageurs ceremoniously called on their bourgeois or clerk to formally wish him well and pay their respects.[38] The early morning firing of muskets or cannons usually woke the masters.[39] In 1793 Alexander Mackenzie wrote: 'On the first day of January, my people, in conformity to the usual custom, awoke me at the break of day with the discharge of firearms, with which they congratulated the appearance of the new year. In return, they were treated with plenty of spirits, and when there is any flour, cakes are always added to the regales, which was the case, on the present occasion.'[40] Like the firing of muskets when a brigade arrived at a post, this salute was a symbolic welcome and a formal honouring of the holiday.

After the firing of muskets, all the residents of the fort gathered together in a general meeting where the bourgeois or clerk would provide regales to the voyageurs. Depending on the wealth of the post, regales as little as a single dram or as much as great quantities of alcohol, especially if there was a shortage of food.[41] At the beginning of 1802, Daniel Harmon gave his men a dram in the morning and then enough rum to drink throughout the course of the day, to help distract them from the scarcity of meat.[42] In an effort to secure more alcohol for the day's festivities, men would go to great lengths to salute their bourgeois or any passing visitor or dignitary, in hopes of gaining a treat.[43] Regales on New Year's seemed to be slightly more generous than those at Christmas, as men were frequently given tobacco in addition to drams.[44] At wealthier posts the men's regales included food, usually specialty items that were hard to procure, such as flour and sugar, though the regale could include meat and grease.[45]

Regardless of wealth most posts mustered some kind of feast on Christmas and New Year's as part of the day's ceremonies. Voyageurs took great pleasure in their food and in feasting, especially since survival could be so precarious in the pays d'en haut, and their victuals were often mundane and limited. In 1812 Gabriel Franchère commented: 'The 25th of December, Christmas Day, was spent most pleasantly. We treated our men to the best that the post could offer, which delighted them as they had lived for nearly two months on fish dried by fire, which is very poor food.'[46] Bourgeois were not always so generous. Alexander Henry the Younger wrote on 1 January 1814, that the bourgeois could scarcely collect liquor enough out of the kegs to give the men one dram each, so they provided them with rice, salt beef, and swans as wel. The bourgeois, however, provided themselves with a great feast of rice soup, boiled swans, roast wild fowl, roast pork, potatoes, rice pudding, wild fruit pie, cranberry tarts, cheese and biscuits with porter, spirits, and two bottles of Madeira.[47] However, it seemed to be more usual for the bourgeois and the voyageurs to celebrate the day together.[48] This temporary lowering of class barriers probably stemmed from the loneliness of the bourgeois and the clerks who were isolated from other masters. [. . .] By providing voyageurs with a decent feast, masters could ensure goodwill from their men. Working together to create a celebratory feast fostered a feeling of fellowship among the men.

After the formal ceremonies of honouring the day, exchanging gifts, and feasting, the real party began: Men celebrated by drinking liberally.[49] Serious drinking could last for several days after the holiday.[50] Both Edith Burley and Anne Morton found that at HBC posts,

Christmas and New Year's could be celebrated with almost a week of 'incessant carousing'.[51] Drinking heavily usually led to fighting among the men.[52] Duncan McGillivray commented that 'the Holidays [had been] spent as usual in dissipation & enjoyment, intermixed with quarreling and fighting—the certain consequences of intoxication among the men.'[53] Dancing, fiddle playing, and singing were also significant ingredients of the parties.[54] During this part of the day's festivities, disorder and subversion dominated. In the word of Mikhail Bakhtin, '[w]hile carnival lasts, there is no other life outside it. During carnival time life is subject only to its laws, that is, the laws of its own freedom.'[55] Yet the chaotic mayhem was constrained and limited by its designated site and meaning. It was a socially sanctioned time where voyageurs as well as their masters were allowed to carouse to the extreme.

This style of celebrating holidays—starting with formal ceremonies then moving on to wild abandon—lasted well into the mid-nineteenth century at the interior fur trade posts. [. . .]

Many groups of all-male sojourners seemed to enjoy music and dances in their leisured moments. Nearly all shanty camps in northern Ontario had a fiddler, and singing and dancing were popular Saturday-night pastimes.[56] [. . .]

Holding a formal ball was an importation from French Canada, but the dancing and music were culturally distinctive. The 'old fiddle and Indian drum' symbolized the mixing of European and Aboriginal forms.[57] Dancing was not restricted to holidays but continued throughout the seasons at fur trade posts. Having dances or 'balls' was a fairly common occurrence both at the Great Lakes posts and in the interior.[58] Either fiddlers or singers provided the music. Fast and spirited dancing predominated. The descriptions of the 'lively reels' of country dances reflected a rough and tumble joie de vivre that was characteristic of many voyageurs' activities. Balls at Grand Portage during the rendezvous, however, were genteel affairs for the benefit of the bourgeois, with

music from the bagpipe, violin, and fife.[59] Yet even at these balls, 'country music' combined musical from Canada, Scotland, England, and Aboriginal peoples. Dances were often held to celebrate specific events, such as the coalition of the XYC and the NWC in 1804, but the most common occasions were weddings and to honour visitors to the post.[60] Men from different companies frequently attended each others' dances.[61] Sometimes dances were held for no particular reasons other than to have fun and enliven the monotony of post life, especially during the long winters.[62]

ALCOHOL

In eighteenth-century European and colonial settings, most people drank a significant amount of alcohol.[63] Historian Craig Heron explains that 'alcohol was regularly consumed in the home as a beverage and a tonic, and to a degree now unimaginable it also saturated almost all arenas of work and leisure. European settlers, especially men, drank often, though only occasionally to get drunk.'[64] The voyageurs' use of alcohol or attitudes toward it probably did not differ from those of habitants or other groups of labouring men. A key difference, however, was that alcohol was restricted and controlled by the bourgeois, and voyageurs did not have habitual access to it as they would have had in French Canada. The bourgeois and the clerks controlled the rations of alcohol to save money and to exert control over their men. Although the bourgeois and the clerks probably drank as much as their men, they often disparaged voyageurs as useless drunks. They frequently reprimanded their men for drunkenness.[65] Bourgeois and clerks sometimes refused to sell alcohol to their men in an effort to curb their drinking practices, especially when the bourgeois wanted voyageurs to pay their debts.[66] Seeing themselves as distinct from their men in regard to drinking helped the bourgeois to distance themselves socially from their voyageurs, which helped them maintain authority. These attitudes are ironic when compared to the behaviour of the bourgeois at the Montreal Beaver Club and annual rendezvous, where the dinners were notorious for excessive drinking and revelry.[67] After the merger of the HBC and the NWC in 1821, the new governor, George Simpson, imposed stringent temperance regulations on posts but met with little success.[68]

Drinking also occupied a central place in seafaring culture. Unlike the Northwest, where cargoes had to be physically hauled over unending portages, deadly excesses of drinking were common. Drink offered respite from an often punishing life on ship. Marcus Rediker speculates that '[t]oo much plain dealing, with the elements and with the conditions of life at sea, led to a lot of plain old drinking.'[69] Unfortunately for the voyageurs, they could not carry enough liquor to offer respite from their journeys. Yet, as for sailors, drinking served critical social functions for voyageurs, allowing the men to bond with one another and form enduring friendships.

The masters' control over supplies and the frequent shortage of alcohol on canoe voyages and in the interior probably encouraged voyageurs to develop a 'feast-famine' attitude toward drinking. If they knew that the supply of alcohol was precarious, they would drink with abandon while it was available. Although these occasions were described in considerable detail in the journals of the bourgeois and the clerks, limited supplies of alcohol made them exceptional rather than routine.

In some extreme cases voyageurs were drunk when they worked.[70] Periodically a master mentioned that the drunkenness of the voyageurs had impeded their work. One bourgeois could not send off his goods as early as he wished because his men 'were amusing themselves and not fit to travel.'[71] Voyageurs sometimes began to drink their regales while paddling, and journeys had to be interrupted because the voyageurs were not fit to continue.[72] A few posts were known for general drunkenness, but more commonly heavy and raucous drinking had a designated time and form at all posts, such as during holiday celebrations.[73] On canoe journeys and at interior posts men usually confined their heavy drinking to the occasional evening.[74] The bourgeois and the clerks sometimes used alcohol as a means of maintaining good faith among their men on a particularly difficult journey. In the summer of 1793 while on an arduous mission to find an overland passage to the Pacific Ocean, Alexander Mackenzie described the end of one hard day of work: 'At the close of the day we assembled round a blazing fire; and the whole party, being enlivened with the usual beverage which I supplied on these occasions, forgot their fatigues and apprehensions.'[75]

Heavy drinking was reserved for special occasions, such as when supplies arrived and during parties and 'balls', and especially the rendezvous, where voyageurs received generous *regales*.[76] Some instances of 'wild excess' are to be found further in the interior. One small creek near the Red River earned the name 'Drunken River' when a carousing group of voyageurs had a particularly memorable party.[77] At least one voyageur was nicknamed 'the Drunkard', and this mark of notoriety made it into official correspondence.[78]

Often excessive drinking led to violence. A voyager named Voyer, between forty and fifty years of age and described as 'a great drunkard', went to Grand Portage to visit friends. When he became drunk, some of the clerks and bourgeois smeared his face with 'caustie' (encaustic?) and drew lewd figures on it. Voyer became enraged when he sobered and swore revenge on those who had marked him. The following summer, when the same bourgeois denied him alcohol and chided him for his drunkenness, he killed several of their horses and threatened them with a knife.[79] These exceptional cases of 'drunkards' can be found in most early modern societies; they represent the edges of social acceptability rather than the norm.

Despite the outbreaks of violence, drunkenness was contained rather than excessive.

Drinking did not seriously threaten the social order of the fur trade; rather it provided an outlet for debauchery and disorder. Michael found the same pattern at York Factory—although excessive drinking caused some social tensions, alcoholism was not widespread and fatalities resulting from drinking were limited.[80] The 'boundaries of containment' were set by the availability of alcohol and the commonly accepted social sites for heavy drinking. Voyageurs became apprehensive when violence became excessive, when the functioning of the fur trade was disrupted for a great length of time, and when food was in short supply. In one extreme case a bourgeois named Duncan Campbell, charged with drunkenness by the NWC in 1809, had allowed his trading post to become a corrupt, filthy, and starving 'heart of darkness'. He lost all his trade goods, ran out of food, drank himself into oblivion, and neglected his paternal duties to his servants. He was court-martialed, and his voyageurs testified that they were disgusted by his behaviour.[81]

GAMES AND CONTESTS

The voyageurs' ethic of nonaccumulation derived in part from the fact that they could not carry many material goods while working in the fur trade. But for many money became less important the longer they worked in the trade and were away from their families in French Canada. Wealth became measured in different ways. Pierre Bourdieu's economic metaphor of 'capital' provides a way to understand voyageurs' notions of wealth and how this connected to their play.[82] Bourdieu expands the notion of capital beyond its economic conception to the realm of the cultural, social, and symbolic. Different types of capital can be acquired, exchanged, and converted into other forms. Cultural capital refers to the value that can be found in family background, social class, education, and other factors that may lead to success. For voyageurs cultural capital would have included knowledge of

skills such as making canoes and snowshoes. Cultural capital can be inherited, purchased, or earned. Bourdieu defines social capital as connections among people. Voyageurs could enhance their social capital through their relationships with Aboriginal people, with the bourgeois and clerks, and with each other. Symbolic capital represents prestige and honour, which voyageurs could earn by demonstrating their manliness. The masculine values of strength, courage, and risk taking became expressions of symbolic or masculine capital. Play, especially games and contests that demonstrated these qualities, became a means of accumulating masculine capital.

Because voyageurs had few possessions and could not carry many personal belongings with them into the interior, games could not involve elaborate equipment.[83] Playing cards and gambling were common pastimes.[84] Michael Payne also found small board games such cribbage and dominoes at York Factory.[85] Voyageurs played games from French Canada, such as those with a ball.[86] Other games or amusements, such as 'pagessan' or 'le jeu au plat' and body tattooing, were learned from Aboriginal peoples.[87] John Richardson, a surgeon in the Royal Navy and a travelling companion of John Franklin, described games played by Crees at Cumberland House. The game *puckesann* involved betting on the number of stones tossed out of a small wooden dish. In the 'game of the mitten', one marked and three unmarked balls were placed under four mittens, and contenders had to guess under which mitten the marked ball lay. These games, along with lacrosse, required little equipment, which could be easily made from materials in the surrounding environment.[88]

Voyageurs gained symbolic currency both by enhancing their reputations for toughness and skill and by their own belief in their strength and ability. In reminiscing about his life, the elderly voyageur on Lake Winnipeg bragged to Alexander Ross: 'I beat all Indians at the race, and no white man ever passed me in the chase.'[89] The value of beating Aboriginal peoples implies that Aboriginal men were faster and stronger and thus more manly than European Canadians. The desire to excel at skills necessary for survival in the Northwest, skills that were usually learned from Aboriginal peoples, was a clear example of shifting cultural values among voyageurs. Being more 'Indian' than the 'Indians' was a measure of manliness and success in adapting to new social and physical spaces.

Currency could also be earned in physical contests among voyageurs. In canoe races, a popular form of competition, crews would race against one another within a brigade or race against other brigades.[90] These contests built a sense of fellowship, trust, and co-operation among the crews. Masters encouraged their men to race, and they often set out to break one another's records for the fastest time between major posts. Recall George Landmann's record for the journey from St. Joseph's Island, near Detroit, to Montreal, which his crew completed in seven and one-quarter days.[91] After the 1821 merger, Montreal canoes and York boats frequently raced at York Factory.[92]

Brawling was a common social activity and had a variety of meanings among the voyageurs. Fighting frequently accompanied parties and heavy drinking and in these contexts hostilities and maliciousness sometimes led to mayhem or riots.[93] However, brawling was often an organized event or competition in which men sought to demonstrate their prowess, boost their reputations, and amuse their mates.[94] They often 'fought for a set', and a 'drawn battle' could be decided with 'fair boxing at head quarting'.[95] Brawling could demonstrate strength and toughness, and it underscored the dimension of physicality in voyageur culture, which was encouraged by the nature of the job. One Métis voyageur, Paulet Paul, achieved fame as a fighter after the 1821 merger.[96]

Fur trade journals are filled with stories about the difficulty of fur trade work and the almost mythical strength, endurance, and joviality of the voyageurs. The literate in the fur trade frequently referred to voyageurs as 'beasts of burden', which both reduced them to animals and elevated them to 'hyper-masculine' superheroes. Clerk George Nelson wrote: '[Voyageurs] seem to do more than ever was meant for human nature; . . . [they] rise at dusk in the morning and until near sunset, are either pulling on their paddles, or running with 180, or 200 lbs wt. on their backs, as if it were for life or death; never stop to take their meals peacably, but with a piece of pemmican in their hands eat under their load.'[97] He went on to marvel that voyageurs seemed tougher, stronger, and swifter than dogs or horses. Voyageurs tried to outperform one another to demonstrate their masculine capital. Contests were not limited to physical prowess but extended to almost any area. Competing to see who could eat or drink the most functioned like gaming; voyageurs could gamble small amounts of their symbolic capital for entertainment's sake. In the spring of 1808 while journeying between interior posts, two of George Nelson's voyageurs, Leblanc and Larocque, decided to see who could eat the most during one of their meals. Both unfortunate men began to feel ill and shake, when lynx excrement was discovered at the bottom of the pot, which elicited 'many coarse & filthy jokes'.[98]

[. . .]

Although play became an area for the expression of new social practices that made voyageurs distinct from habitants and other early modern peasants, it did not threaten the paternalistic order of the fur trade or the masters' subordination of the voyageurs. Most of the play of voyageurs was highly structured and occurred within designated and contained contexts. It provided a safe space for voyageurs to express their anxiety and fear at the exotic pays d'en haut, their anger at unfair masters and unreliable colleagues, and their excitement at setting off on new adventures. Forms of play generally sanctioned by the bourgeois allowed voyageurs to frolic without threatening the pace or effectiveness of their work and encouraged values that were consistent with effective working skills, such as strength, bravery, risk taking, and perseverance.

Play and sociability were central to voyageurs' working lives. All forms of play, including carnivals, games, contests, tricks, and friendship, helped to create and support a distinctive voyageur world by both encouraging social bonding and facilitating the growth of social fissures and divisions. Three dominant themes emerged in the play of voyageurs.

Contests provided men with 'symbolic capital' in their efforts to bolster their reputations as strong men. The liminal space particularly encouraged jokes and trickery. Finally, voyageurs tried to form a unified and somewhat collective culture in the face of centrifugal forces caused by their transience and mobility of the job. These ideals and themes distinguished voyageurs from habitants in French Canada, fur trade bourgeois and clerks, and Aboriginal societies.

NOTES

1. Ross Cox, *Adventures on the Columbia River, including the Narrative of Residence of Six Years on the Western Side of the Rocky Mountains, among Various Tribes of Indians Hitherto Unknown: Together with a Journey across the American Continent*. 2 vols. London: Henry Colburn & Richard Bentley, 1831; 2:287.

2. Peter Pond, 'The Narrative of Peter Pond', 47. In Gates, *Five Fur Traders* of the Northwest, St. Paul: Minnesota Historical Society, 1965, 9–59.

3. For the central position of Grand Portage and Fort William in the Montreal fur trade, see Carolyn Gilman, *The Grand Portage Story*. St. Paul: Minnesota Historical Society, 1992; and Jean Morrison, *Superior Rendezvous-Place: Fort William in the Canadian Fur Trade*. Toronto: Belfords, Clarke, 1880.

4. Toronto Metropolitan Reference Library Baldwin Room (TBR), S13, George Nelson's journal 'No.1', 15–16. See also Nelson, *My First Years*, 42.

5. Victor Turner, 'Variations of a Theme of Liminality', 57. In Turner, *Blazing the Trail: Way Makers in the Exploration of Symbols*. Tucson: University of Arizona Press, 1992, 48–65.

6. Mikhail Bakhtin, *Rabelais and His World*. Translated by Hélène Iswolsky. Bloomington: Indiana University Press, 1984, 4, 5–6.

7. George Nelson, *My First Years in the Fur Trade: The Journals of 1802–1804*. Edited by Laura Peers and Theresa Schenck. St. Paul: Minnesota Historical Society Press, 2002, 32–33.

8. Nelson, *My First Years*, 32–33; see also Library and Archives of Canada (LAC), MG19 A17, June 15, 1791, 15.

9. Georges Dugas, *Un Voyageur des pays d'En Haut*. (1890) St. Boniface, MB: Editions des Plaines, 1981, 25, 30 (my translation). Original French: 'Pendant quinze jours, c'était, pour ces vieux loups du Nord, une suite de fête et de divertissements; ils invitaient tous leurs amis, et faisaient bombance; on aurait dit gu'ils tenaient à dépenser jusqu'à leur dernier sou, et à partir le gousset complètement vide. La boisson coulait à flots; le soir il y avait bal. . . . Le jour du depart, une foule de personnes se rendaient à Lachine pour être témoins du spectacle.'

10. For one example of muskets being fired at departure, see Captain John Franklin, *Narrative of a Journey to the Shores of the Polar Sea in the Years 1819, 20, 21 and 22*. London: J.M. Dent, 1819, February 8, 1820, 109. Muskets were fired on both arrival and departure on February 16, 1820, 112–3.

11. Dugas, *Un Voyageur*, 27 (my translation). Original French: 'La vie sauvaage leur souriait; il leur semblait que là-bas, débarrassés de tout frein, vêtus comme l'Indien, couchant avec lui sous la tente, et chassant comme lui pour vivre.'

12. For the influence of Aboriginal cultures on French Canada, see Delâge, 'L'influence des Amérindiens sur les Canadiens et les Français au temps de la Nouvelle France.' *Lekton* 2, no. 2 (Autumn 1992): 103–91.

13. Philip J. Deloria, *Playing Indian*. New Haven: Yale University Press, 1998, 5.

14. Deloria, *Playing Indian*, 11–20.

15. Alexander Henry (the Younger), *New Light on the Early History of the Greater Northwest: The Manuscript Journals of Alexander Henry*. Edited by Elliott Coues. 2 vols. Minneapolis: Ross & Haines; New York: F. Harper, 1897, July 20, 1800, 1:8. Similarly, at York Factory, the main administration post of the HBC, the departure of ships for England was always marked by a celebration. Michael Payne, *The Most Respectable Place in the Territory: Everyday Life in Hudson's Bay Company Service, York Factory, 1788 to 1870*. Ottawa: Ministry of the Envrionment, Canadian Parks Service, 1989, 87.

16. Cox, *Adventures on the Columbia River*, September 19, 1817, 304–5.

17. Alexander Mackenzie, 'A General History of the Fur Trade from Canada to the North-West', 52. In Mackenzie, *Voyages from Montreal on the River St. Laurence through the Continent of North America to the Frozen and Pacific Oceans in the Years 1789 and 1793 with a Preliminary Account of the Rise, Progress, and Present State of the Fur Trade of That Country*. London: R. Noble, Old Bailey, 1801; and Nelson, *My First Years*, 40–42.

18. Ontario Archives (OA), MU 2199, Edward Umfreville, July 24, 1784, 26; and Rare Books and Special Collections Division of the McGill University Libraries (MRB), MC, c.28, October 2 and 3, 1807, 8. See also Lloyd Keith, ed., *North of Athabasca: Slave Lake and Mackenzie River Documents of the North West Company, 1800–1821*. Montreal: McGill-Queen's Press, 2001, 311–12.

19. TBR, S13, George Nelson's diary of events on a journey from Cumberland House to Fort William, June 19, 1822; and John McDonell, 'The Diary of John McDonnell', in Gates, *Five Fur Traders of the Northwest*, 92.

20. Alexander Ross, *Fur Hunters of the Far West: A Narrative of Adventures in the Oregon and Rocky Mountains*. 2 vols. London: Smith, Elder, 1855, 1: 303–4.

21. OA, MU 842, September 27, 1818, 3.

22. Nelson, *My First Years*, August 22, 1803, 103; and LAC, MG19 A9, Simon Fraser Collection, vol. 3, Fraser to Mr. McDougall, Sturgeon Lake, August 6, 1806, 15.

23. John Henry Lefroy, *In Search of the Magnetic North: A Soldier-Surveyor's Letters from the North-West, 1843–1844*. Edited by George F.G. Stanley. Toronto: Macmillan, 1955, Lefroy to his mother, Toronto, November 20, 1844, 136; and Robert M. Ballantyne, *Hudson Bay; or, Every-Day Life in the Wilds of North America during Six Years' Residence in the Territories of the Honourable Hudson's Bay Company*. London:William Blackwood & Sons, 1848. Reprint, Edmonton: Hurtig, 1972, 212.

24. Nicholas Perrot, *The Indian Tribes of the Upper Mississippi Valley and the Region of the Great Lakes*. Edited and translated by Emma Helen Blair. 2 vols. Cleveland: Arthur H. Clark, 1911, 1:174–75, 210–20; Louise Dechêne, *Habitants and Merchants in Seventeenth-Century Montreal*. Montreal: McGill-Queen's University Press, 1992 (first published as *Habitants et marchands de Montréal au XVIIe siècle* (Paris: Editions Plon, 1974); and Allan Greer, *The People of New France*. Toronto: University of Toronto Press, 1997, chapter on 'French and Others'.

25. See Helen Hornbeck Tanner, ed., *The Settling of North America: The Atlas of the Great Migrations into North America from the Ice Age to the Present*. New York: Macmillan, 1995, 28–29.

26. John S. Milloy, *The Plains Cree: Trade, Dimplomacy and War, 1790 to 1870*. Winnipeg: University of Manitoba Press, 1988, II, 17, 51–52, 54; and Laura Peers, The Ojibwa of Western Canada, 1780 to 1879. Winnipeg: University of Manitoba Press, 1994, 30.

27. David Meyer and Paul C. Thistle, 'Saskatchewan River Rendezvous Centers and Trading Posts: Continuity in a Cree Social Geography.' *Ethnohistory* 42, no. 3 (Summer 1995): 403–4.

28. Victor P. Lytwyn, 'The Anishinabeg and the Fur Trade', 32. In *Lake Superior to Rainy Lake: Three Centuries of Fur Trade History*, edited by Jean Morrison, 27–45. Thunder Bay: Thunder Bay Historical Museum Society, 2003.

29. Lefroy, *In Search of the Magnetic North*, Lefroy to Isabella, Lake Athabasca, Christmas Day, 1843, 84.

30. For examples of All Saint's Day, see LAC, MG19 C1, vol. 12, November 1, 1804, 25; MRB, MC, c.28, November 1, 1807; and Keith, *North of Athabasca*, 316. For examples of St. Andrew's Day, see OA, reel MS65, Donald McKay, Journal from January to December 1799, November 30, 1799, 43 (my pagination); and MRB, MC, c.24, Sunday, November 30, 1800, 6. For examples of celebrating Easter, see LAC, MG19 C1, vol. 1, April 8, 1798, 53; LAC, MG19 C1, vol. 14, April 12, 1800, 23; and, OA, MU 842, April 11, 1819, 43.

31. Anne Morton, 'Chief Trader Joseph McGillivray.' Paper presented at the Rupert's Land Colloquium 1998, Winnipeg and Norway House, June 1998; and Payne, *Most Respectable Place*, 65, 87–92.

32. For an example of celebrating Palm Sunday, see OA, MU 842, April 4, 1819, 42. For examples of celebrating the King's birthday, see TBR, S13, George Nelson's journal, April 1, 1810–May 1, 1811, June 4, 1810, 11 (my pagination); and George Landmann, *Adventures and Recollections of Colonel Landmann, Late of the Corps of Royal Engineers*. 2 vols. London: Colburn, 1852, 2:167–68. For an example of celebrating Epiphany, see Henry (the Younger), *New Light*, January 6, 1801, 1:165.

33. For comments on New Year's celebrations as a French Canadian custom, see Daniel W. Harmon, *Sixteen Years in Indian Country: The Journal of Daniel Williams Harmon, 1800–1816*. Edited by W. Kaye Lamb. Toronto: Macmillan, 1957, January 2, 1801, 41; see also Grenon, *Us et coutumes du Québec*. Montreal: La Presse, 1974, 153–68; Sophie-Laurence Lamontagne, *L'hiver dans la culture québécoise (xviie–xixe siècles)*. Quebec: Institut québécois de recherche sur la culture, 1983, 101–3; and Jean Provencher, *Les Quatre Saisons dans la vallée du Saint-Laurent*. Montreal: Boréal, 1988, 499–57, 463–70.

34. Landmann, *Adventures and Recollection*, 1:239–40.

35. Henry (the Younger), *New Light*, January 1, 1803, 1:207.

36. OA, reel MS65, Donald McKay, Journal from January 1805 to June 1806, December 25, 1805, 47 (my pagination); TBR, S13, George Nelson's journal, November 3, 1807–August 31, 1808, December 25, 1807, 14; November 1, 1807, 7; and Henry (the Younger), *New Light*, November 1, 1810, 2:660.

37. OA, reel MS65, Donald McKay, journal from January to December 1799, December 24, 1799, 46 (my pagination); TBR, S13, George Nelson's journal, November 3, 1807–August 31, 1808, December 25, 1807, 14; George Nelson's journal, April 1, 1810–May 1, 1811, December 23, 1810, 39 (my pagination).

38. LAC, MG19 C1, vol. 14, January 1, 1800, 9; Hugh Faries, 'The Diary of Hugh Faries.' In Gates, *Five Fur Traders of the Northwest*, January 1, 1805, 244; LAC, MG19 C1, vol. 8, January 1, 1805, 37; and Keith, *North of Athabasca*, 197.

39. MRB, MC, C.13, January 1, 1800, 11 (my pagination); Henry (the Younger), *New Light*, January 1, 1801 and 1802, 1:162, 192; TBR, S13, George Nelson's journal, November 30, 1815–January 13, 1816, Monday, December 25, 1815, 91; George Nelson's journal and reminiscences, 84; and Gabriel Franchère, *Journal of a Voyage on the North West Coast of North America during the Years 1811, 1812, 1813 and 1814*. Toronto: Champlain Society, 1969, 107–8.

40. Mackenzie, *Voyages from Montreal*, January 1, 1793, 252. On other comments of the long-standing custom, see MRB, MC, C.28, January 1, 1808, 20; Keith, *North of Athabasca*, 326; and Franklin, Narrative of a Journey, January 1, 1802, 53.

41. For drams, see LAC, MG19 C1, vol. 1, November 1 and December 25, 1797, 17, 27; MRB, MC, C.24, December 25, 1800, 13; LAC, MG19 C1, vol. 6, December 25, 1800, 72; vol. 8, December 25, 1804, 34; and MRB, MC, C.28, December 25, 1807, 20; see also Keith, *North of Athabasca*, 122, 196, 325. For large quantities of alcohol, see LAC, MG19 C1, vol. 7, December 25, 1798, 23; MRB, MC, C.13, December 25, 1799, 10 (my pagination); Harmon, *Sixteen Years*, December 25, 1801, 52; and LAC, MG19 C1, vol. 12, November 1 and December 25, 1804, 25, 34.

42. Harmon, *Sixteen Years*, January 1, 1802, 53.

43. TBR, S13, George Nelson's journal, November 30, 1815–January 13, 1816, December 25, 1815, 91.

44. MRB, MC, C.7, January 1, 1794 and 1795, 6, 23; OA, MG19, C1, vol. 1, January 1, 1798,

29; LAC, MG19, C1, vol. 7, January 1, 1799, 24; and vol. 12, January 1, 1805, 35.

45. Mackenzie, *Voyages from Montreal*, January 1, 1793, 252; Henry (the Younger), *New Light*, December 25, 1800, 1:161; LAC, MG19 C1, vol. 9, January 1, 1806, 21; Cox, *Adventures on the Columbia River*, 305–6; and MRB, MC, c.8, January 1, 1806, 10.

46. Franchère, *Journal of a Voyage*, 107. See also LAC, MG19 A14, January 1, 1806, 6.

47. Henry (the Younger), *New Light*, 2:781.

48. OA, reel MS65, Donald McKay, journal from August 1800 to April 1801, December 25, 1800, 17; and TBR, S13, George Nelson's journal, September 1, 1801–March 31, 1810, January 1, 1809, 14 (my pagination).

49. OA, MG19, C1, vol. 1, January 1, 1798, 29; Harmon, *Sixteen Years*, January 2, 1801, 40; and Montreal, McCord Museum, M-22074, James Keith, Fort Chipewyan to McVicar, January 31, 1825, 2.

50. Faries, 'Diary', December 25–27, 1804, 223.

51. Morton, 'Chief Trader Joseph McGillivray'; and Edith I. Burley, *Servants of the Honourable Company: Work, Discipline, and Conflict in the Hudson's Bay Company, 1770–1879*. Toronto: Oxford University Press, 1997, 133.

52. Henry (the Younger), *New Light*, January 1, 1802 and 1803, 1:192, 207; Harmon, *Sixteen Years*, January 1, 1811, 136; and Faries, 'Diary', January 1, 1805, 224.

53. Duncan McGillivray, *The Journal of Duncan McGillivray of the North West Company at Fort George on the Saskatchewan, 1794–5*. Edited by Arthur S. Morton. Toronto: MAcmillan, 1929, Fort George, January 26, 1795, 51.

54. Harmon, *Sixteen Years*, January 2, 1801, December 25, 1805, 40, 99; TBR, S13, George Nelson's journal, April 1, 1810–May 1, 1811, December 1810 to January 1811, 39 (my pagination); and George Nelson's journal, September 1, 1808–March 31, 1810, January 1, 1809, 14 (my pagination).

55. Bahktin, *Rabelais and His World*, 7.

56. Ian Radforth, 'The Shantymen.' In *Labouring Lives: Work and Worker in Nineteenth-Century Ontario*, edited by Paul Craven, 204–76. Toronto: Uniersity of Toronto Press, 1995, 231–32.

57. See also Sylvia Van Kirk, *'Many Tender Ties': Women in Fur-Trading Society, 1670–1870*. Winnipeg: Watson & Dwyer, 1980, 126–29.

58. For examples of balls at Great Lakes posts, see Pond, 'Narrative', Mackinaw, 47; and OA, MU 1146, Frederick Goedike, Batchiwenon, to Geroge Gordon, Michipicoten, February 11, 1812, 1–3. For examples of balls at interior posts, see TBR, S13, George Nelson's journal, November 3, 1807–August 31, 1808, Fort Alexandria, June 18, 1808, 42; and Alexander Ross, *Adventures of the First Settlerson the Oregon or Columbia River: Being a Narrative of the Expedition Fitted Out by John Jacob Astor, to Establish the 'Pacific Fur Company' with an Accoun of Some Indian Tribes on the Coast of the Pacific*. Ann Arbor: University Microfilms, 1966 (first published in 1849 by Smith, ELder, London), Spokane House, summer 1812, 212.

59. Harmon, *Sixteen Years*, Grand Portage, July 4, 1800, 22.

60. TBR, S13, George Nelson's coded journal, June 28, 1821, 29; Henry (the Younger), *New Light*, September 6, 1810, 2:626; and Faries, 'Diary', December 16, 1804, February 24, March 31, April 28, May 12 and 17, 1805, 222, 230, 234–5, 238, 240–1.

61. For an example of NWC and HBC men dancing together at Fort George, see McGillivray, *Journal*, March 22, 1795, 66. For an example of NWC, XYC, and HBC men dancing together, see Faries, 'Diary', January 11, 1805, 244–25. For an example of NWC, XYC, and HBC men dancing together at Rivière Souris, Fort Assiniboine, see Harmon, *Sixteen Years*, May 27, 1805, 89–90.

62. Henry (the Younger), *New Light*, January 27, 1810, 2:584.

63. Thomas Brennan, *Public Drinking and Popular Culture in Eighteenth-Century Paris*. Princton: Princton University Press, 1988. For a discussion of how drinking can be understood as part of the social order, see Mary Douglas, ed., *Constructive Drinking: Perspectives on Drink from Anthropology*. Cambridge: Cambridge University Press, 1987.

64. Craig Heron, *Booze: A Distilled History*. Toronto: Between the Lines, 2003, 17.

65. For one of many examples of bourgeois drunkenness and brawling, see TBR, S13, George Nelson's journal and reminiscences, 57.

66. MRB, MC, C.24, January 2, 1801, 15; and OA, MU 842, March 3, 1819, 34–35.

67. See Carolyn Podruchny, 'Festivities, Fortitude and Franternalism: Fur Trade Masculinity and the Beaver Club, 1785–1827', in *New Faces in the Fur Trade: Selected Papers of the Seventh North American Fur Trade Conference*, Edited by William C. Wicken, Jo-Anne Fiske, Susan Sleeper-Smith, 31–52. East Lansing: Michigan State University Press, 1998.

68. Burley, *Servants of the Honourable Company*, 134–35; and Jan Noel, *Canada Dry: Temperance Crusades before Confederation*. Toronto: University of Toronto Press, 1995, 189–93.

69. Marcus Rediker, *Between the Devil and the Deep Blue Sea: Merchant Seamen, Pirates,and the Anglo-American Maritime World, 1700–1750*. Cambridge: Cambridge University Press, 1987, 192.

70. For two examples see Cox, *Adventures on the Columbia River*, June 29, 1812, and July 30, 1817, 74, 280. However, Alexander Mackenzie characterized it as a regular occurrence, in his 'General History', 17–18.

71. LAC, MG19 B1, A. McKenzie to John Layer [Sayer?], Grand Portage, August 9, 1799, 87. For another example of drunk voyageurs preventing a departure, see LAC, MG C1, vol. 12, September 20, 1804.

72. Nelson, *My First Years,* 100–101, August 5, 1803.

73. Regarding posts known for heavy drinking, see MRB, MC, C.7, October 27, 1793, 2.

74. MRB, MC, C.7, December 14, 1794, 22; LAC, MG19, C1, vol. 14, November 11–12, 1799, 3a; MRB, MC, C.26, October 10, 1800, 9; and Keith, *North of Athabasca*, 133.

75. Mackenzie, *Voyages from Montreal*, June 15, 1793, 329.

76. For an example of drinking when supplies arrived, see Henry (the Younger), *New Light*, March 7, 1814, 2:851. For examples of drunkenness during parties, see McGillivray, Journal, March 22, 1795, 66; Faries, 'Diary', January 11–12, 1805, 224–5; and Harmon, *Sixteen Years*, May 27, 1805, 89–90. For examples of heavy drinking at a rendezvous, see Nelson, *My First Years*, 42–3; and Mackenzie, 'General History', 1789, 52.

77. Ross, *Fur Hunters*, 2:249–50.

78. LAC, MG19 B1, Alexander Mackenzie to the proprietors of the NWC, Grand Portage, June 16, 1799, 71.

79. TBR, S13, George Nelson's journal and reminiscences, 57.

80. Payne, *Most Respectable Place*, 83.

81. TBR, S13, George Nelson's journal 'No. 5', June 1807–October 1809, 20–1 (my sequential pagination)/204–5 (Nelson's pagination).

82. Pierre Bourdieu, 'The Forms of Capital.' *In Handbook of Theory and Reserach for the Sociology of Education*, edited by John G. Richardson, 242. See also Pierre Bourdieu, *The Logic of Practice*. Translated by Richard Nice. Stanford: Stanford University Press, 1980, 112–21; and Pierre Bourdieu and Loïc J.D. Wacquant, *Invitation to Reflexive Sociology*. Chicago: University of Chicago Press, 1992, 119.

83. In his discussion of the cargoes carried in canots du maître, Bruce M. White notes only the basic necessities of food, clothing, and alcohol as equipment for voyageurs, in his 'Montreal Canoes and their Cargoes', 185–7. In *Le Castor Fait Tout: Selected Papers of the Fifth North American Fur Trade Conference, 1985*. Edited by Bruce Trigger et. al., 164–92. Montreal: St. Louis Historical Society, 1987.

84. For an example of playing cards, see Harmon, *Sixteen Years*, November 16, 1800, 37. For an example of playing a game called 'La Mouche' with cards and chips, see TBR, S13, George Nelson's journal and reminiscences, 63. On gambling as a widespread practice, see Cox, *Adventures on the Columbia River*, 306.

85. Payne, *Most Respectable Place*, 69.

86. OA, reel MS65, Donald McKay, Journal from August 1800 to April 1801, Sunday, December 28, 1800, 17.

87. For an example of voyageurs playing Aboriginal games, see Johann Georg Kohl, *Ktichi-Gami: Life among the Lake Superior Ojibway*. Translated by Lascelles Wraxall. St. Paul: Minnesota Historical Society Press, 1985 (first published in Germany in 1859), 82. On voyageurs tattooing themselves, see MRB, MC, C.24, January 22–23, 1801, 19. On Cree tattooing, see Dr. Richardson's account in Franklin, *Narrative of a Journey*, 67.

88. Franklin, *Narrative of a Journey*, 63, 68.

89. Ross, *Fur Hunters*, 2:236–37.

90. Henry (the Younger), *New Light*, August 11, 1800, 1:30–31; McGillivray, *Journal*, August

18, 1794, 11–12; and TBR, S13, George Nelson's diary of events, July 9, 1822, July 21–August 22, 1822, August 19, 1822.

91. Landmann, *Adventures and Recollections*, 1:167–9.

92. Payne, *Most Respectable Place*, 68–9.

93. Henry (the Younger), *New Light*, May 6, 1804, 1:243; and MRB, MC, C.24, April 10, 1801, 31.

94. LAC, MG, C1, vo. 14, April 11, 1800, 23. For another example of brawling referred to as a sport or competition, see TBR, S13, George Nelson's journal, April 1, 1810–May 1, 1811, May 13, 1810, 7 (my pagination), which mentions two voyageurs fighting 'rough and tumble' and a 'pitch battle'.

95. OA, MU 1146, Athabasca River, May 3, 1819, 69.

96. Payne, *Most Respectable Place*, 69; and John E. Foster, 'Paulet Paul: Métis or "House Indian" Folk Hero?' *Manitoba History*, no. 9 (Spring 1985): 2–7.

97. TBR, S13, George Nelson's diary of events, June 21, 1822. For other examples see diary entries for July 4 and 9, and August 6, 1822; Mackenzie, *Voyages from Montreal*, 251–52; Ross, *Fur Hunters*, 1:303 and 2:179, 186; Heriot, *Travels through the Canadas*, 246–47; and Extracts from a Letter of Andrew Graham, master at York Fort, to the Governor and Committee of the HBC, dated York Fort, August 26, 1772, in W. Stewart Wallace, ed. *Documents Relating to the Northwest Company*. Toronto: Champlain Society, 1934, 43.

98. TBR, S13, George Nelson's journal, 'No. 5', 28–29 (my sequential pagination)/212–13 (Nelson's pagination).

Chapter Eight

Immigration in the Early Nineteenth Century

READINGS

Primary Documents

1   From 'Testimony of Alexander Buchanan', *Third Report of the Select Committee on Emigration from the United Kingdom*

2   From *Statistical Sketches of Upper Canada, for the Use of Emigrants: by a Backwoodsman*, William Dunlop

Historical Interpretations

3   From 'Transatlantic Webs of Kin and Community', in *Emigrant Worlds and Transatlantic Communities: Migration to Upper Canada in the First Half of the Nineteenth Century*, Elizabeth Jane Errington

4   From 'Irish Immigration and Settlement in a Catholic City: Quebec, 1842–61', Robert J. Grace

Introduction

One method of successful colonization is to increase the population of residents within the colonial space—but not just anyone will do. Residents who are likely to be so absorbed in earning their own livelihoods that they will offer little opposition to the colonial administration are good candidates, as are residents likely to view the move to the colony as a step forward. In the early part of the nineteenth century, British North America had the capacity to accept such migrants, and the elites in the colonies were eager to settle newcomers on their lands. One of the ways this project moved forward was to offer subsidized ship transport and settlement assistance to willing Irish and Scottish people. During the eighteenth century, thousands from these groups had come to the territory that became the United States, so it was not as though the promoters of migration to British North America were treading entirely new ground. However, these later migrations were state-sponsored, and began to affect the demographic profiles of the receiving colonies almost immediately.

The primary sources here address all phases of the project to settle new people in the Canadas. First, an inquiry into the conditions on the ships bringing the migrants across the Atlantic conveys the sense that these passengers were considered only a notch or two above cargo. The second primary source is directed to the prospective migrants themselves, and advises them to bring certain goods along, while leaving others behind—a clear ranking of the strengths of industrial Britain and the North American frontier, as well as a commentary on the voyage.

Of course, the trip and the early prospects facing migrants were not the only considerations. Jane Errington's reading focuses on Upper Canada, and how connected migrants were to the kin and communities they had left behind. Correspondence maintained this connection, informing potential migrants of what they might expect and helping those who had already relocated to feel like they were still part of a family, even though the possibility of daily contact had vanished. Robert Grace's reading on the Irish and their settlement in Quebec City assesses the impact of their Catholic faith and origins in the British Isles on their ability to adjust to a new reality. The Irish in Quebec City did not fit the patterns that other historians have noted when writing about the broader topic of Irish migration to North America.

QUESTIONS FOR CONSIDERATION

1. What does Buchanan tell us about the experiences of these immigrants? Are officials holding to the spirit or the letter of regulations regarding passage?
2. Why might passengers be suspicious of assisted immigration schemes?
3. If you were a potential immigrant to the Canadas, how might you find Dunlop's information helpful?
4. Do you think that some of the letter writers that Errington discusses were really the best candidates for immigration after all? Why or why not?
5. Why do you think Quebec City became such a haven for Irish Catholics after the Great Famine in Ireland?

SUGGESTIONS FOR FURTHER READING

Cameron, Wendy, and Mary McDougall Maude, *Assisting Emigration to Upper Canada: The Petworth Project, 1832–1837* (Montreal and Kingston: McGill-Queen's University Press, 2000)

Elliott, Bruce S., *Irish Migrants in the Canadas: A New Approach* (Montreal and Kingston: McGill-Queen's University Press, 2004)

Errington, Elizabeth Jane, *Emigrant Worlds and Transatlantic Communities: Migration to Upper Canada in the First Half of the Nineteenth Century* (Montreal and Kingston: McGill-Queen's University Press, 2007)

Hepburn, Sharon A. Roger, *Crossing the Border: A Free Black Community in Canada* (Urbana: University of Illinois Press, 2007)

Houston, Cecil, and W.J. Smyth, *Irish Emigration and Canadian Settlement: Patterns, Links, and Letters* (Toronto: University of Toronto Press, 1990)

McGowan, Mark, *Creating Canadian Historical Memory: The Case of the Famine Migration of 1847* (Ottawa: The Canadian Historical Association, 2006)

Wilson, Catharine Anne, *A New Lease on Life: Landlords, Tenants and Immigrants in Ireland and Canada* (Montreal and Kingston: McGill-Queen's University Press, 1994)

PRIMARY DOCUMENTS

1 From 'Testimony of Alexander Buchanan', *Third Report of the Select Committee on Emigration from the United Kingdom* (London, 1827), 106–13.

Sabbati, 3° die Martii, 1827.
Alexander Carlisle Buchanan, Esq. called in; and Examined.

815. YOU are generally acquainted with the circumstances of the trade in the carrying of passengers between this country and the United States, as well as between this country and Canada?—From Ireland I am perfectly.

816. Have you made any comparison between the expense that will be occasioned by the restraints proposed in this Act, which has been laid before the Committee as a substitution for a former Act, and the expense occasioned by the Act of the year 1825?—I have.

817. What would be the difference of expense between the two Acts?—About 12 s. 6 d. for each passenger.

818. What do you consider would be the expense at present?—It is now perhaps 40 s. for an adult, or 3 l.

819. From what port to what port?—From Londonderry and Belfast, which are the great ports of emigration to our colonies; to the United States it is about 5 l. or 6 l.

820. What would be the expense of the poorest class of passengers from Belfast to Quebec?—About 50 s., finding their own provisions.

821. By this Act, a certain quantity of provisions is necessary?—They are; but the representations were so numerous from the poor people, that the provisions prescribed by the Act were so expensive, that the officers of His Majesty's Customs saw that it would in effect almost prohibit emigration if it were enforced, and they took upon themselves, I believe, to wave that part of the Act.

822. Do you consider that in point of fact, with respect to emigrants going from Ireland generally, the provisions of that Act have virtually been waved?—Not generally; the restriction as to numbers, and a proper supply of water, surgeon, &c. was particularly attended to by the officers of Customs, and although they waved that clause respecting a certain description of provisions, they generally made inquiry into the supply the passengers had.

823. Have you an opportunity of knowing that to be the case with respect to the south of Ireland as well as the north?—I have not.

824. Is it your impression that it has been so in the south?—I should think it has been. I dare say I have accompanied 6,000 emigrants to America myself, within the last ten years.

825. In those cases, the provisions of that Act were not enforced?—Not to any great extent; it has been the custom, for the last six or seven years, for the passengers to find their own provisions; formerly the ships found them.

826. Then in point of fact, the passengers themselves took that quantity of provisions which they thought necessary?—They did.

827. Do you imagine that the amount of provisions proposed to be required by this new Act, is greater than what is taken by the poorest of the emigrants who provide for themselves?—I do not think it is near so much.

828. The question applies to the quality as well as the quantity?—I understand it so.

829. Do the emigrants take pork or meat, for instance?—Very seldom; they take a little bacon.

830. Have the provisions which the Act prescribed with respect to tonnage, been actually observed?—They have.

831. The Custom-house officers have uniformly taken care, although they have relaxed with respect to provisions, to have the proportions of passengers to tonnage preserved?—They examine the list of passengers going out, to see that it corresponds with the licence; the licence is granted in proportion to the registered tonnage.

832. Is it the custom after the Customhouse-officer has examined the list, that passengers are taken off the coast?—I do not think it is; I have heard of trifling instances of the kind; the price paid for passage to our own colonies is so trifling, that a captain of a ship would hardly take the trouble.

833. Did you ever know it to happen in any vessel which you yourself were on board?—Never; I have repeatedly seen some relanded that have hid away on board; on the captain examining on leaving port, if he found he had any above his number, he would hove to, and put them on shore.

834. What practical inconvenience do you anticipate from allowing passengers to take with them such provisions as they may think fit, without any legislative enactment on the subject?—I think that the description of emigrants from Ireland particularly are very ignorant, and they have latterly got such an idea of the quick dispatch to America, that they would take a very short supply; they hear of packets coming over from New York to Liverpool in twenty or twenty-five days, and many of them come into Derry, calculating upon a twenty days passage, and without a quantity of oatmeal and other necessaries in proportion, and they are obliged to provide themselves with a larger quantity before they go on board.

835. Have you ever known any inconvenience actually to arise in consequence of a deficiency of provisions?—I have not known any myself, but formerly I have understood there were very great privations suffered, and a great many lives lost, before the Passengers Act passed.

836. Is that an opinion which you have heard from so many quarters as to leave no doubt in your mind of it being the fact?—I am perfectly satisfied of it.

837. Have you not stated that these legislative regulations have, in point of fact, not been adhered to?—They have not, as regards provisions.

838. But although they were not adhered to, they were not so entirely evaded as not to leave them in considerable operation?—Decidedly not.

839. Supposing a passenger, under the expectation of a quick passage, had brought only half the food which this new Act contemplates, what would have taken place in that instance; is any inquiry made by the captain of the passenger, as to the quantity of provision he has?—Always.

840. If the quantity of provisions he had brought was manifestly under what was necessary for an average voyage, would not the captain insist on his taking more?—Decidedly, he would not receive him without.

841. With respect to the tonnage, will you state to the Committee the reason why you are of opinion that there is a necessity for requiring the height of five feet six inches between the decks, and for prohibiting all stores from being placed between the decks?—I consider it indispensable in a ship carrying at the rate of one passenger to every two tons, to reserve the entire space between decks for their accommodation, and the deck of the ship not being at least five feet and a half, it would not be proper to have it double birthed; and

a ship carrying at the rate of one passenger to every two tons, will require to be double birthed, and to have six persons in each birth.

842. Are the double-decked merchant vessels usually of that height between the decks?—Generally more; there are very few that are not.

843. Then have you any reason to anticipate that ships would be built for the express purpose of carrying out emigrants, which would be of a less height between decks than the ordinary merchant vessels, or that the vessels that would be used for that purpose would probably be old merchant vessels?—Not at all; there are very few ships that trade to America that are not five feet and a half high between decks, and over.

844. Then do you conceive that there is any necessity for any regulation enforcing that which actually exists without any regulation?—The reason of that clause is, that ships carrying one to every five tons would be saved the necessity of any delay in making an application for a licence; they could take their one to five tons, and proceed on their voyage in the ordinary way; whereas if they take in a greater number than that, some restriction should be imposed.

845. Do you imagine that there will be any practical inconvenience in these regulations being enforced, either at the Custom-house at the port from which they go in England, or at the Custom-house at the port at which they land in the colony?—None whatever.

846. Do you consider that any expense would be incurred in consequence of those regulations, which would of necessity add to the expense of the passage?—None whatever.

847. Then you are of opinion, that if those regulations were considered to be necessary, there would be no objection against them upon the ground of any real inconvenience being sustained by the trade in consequence of them?—None whatever; I am satisfied they would be approved of, both by the emigrants and the shipowners.

848. Do you entertain the opinion, that the parties going out would rather be protected by legislation to the extent proposed, than to have no legislation upon the subject?—I am perfectly satisfied they would.

849. Are the Committee to understand that they object very much to those extreme regulations, which make the expense of the passage beyond their means?—They have a great objection to being obliged to have a particular description of provisions, but that has been latterly dispensed with.

850. Then, in point of fact, has emigration from Ireland been prevented, in consequence of that part of the Act which relates to provisions?—I do not think it has.

851. As you have stated that the restrictions of this Act with respect to provisions have been virtually superseded in practice, it is presumed that emigration from Ireland cannot have been prevented by the operation of this Act?—To a very small extent; perhaps to the amount of 100 a year or 200 a year more at the outside might have gone; the difference can only be about 10 or 12 shillings in the expense. I have heard a great many statements made about the Passengers Act; as to the Act increasing the expense of passage to the United States, and amounting to a prohibition of emigration, I am satisfied that if the Act were repealed the price would not be diminished one farthing, as the American law imposes a greater limitation as to number than the British and other local regulations.

852. Supposing this Act were not to be passed, requiring the emigrant to take with him a certain specified quantity of food for 75 days, do you imagine that the emigrant could in prudence take a less quantity?—I do not think he could, for I have known instances of very fast sailing ships from Liverpool being 75, 80 or 90 days going out to New York, and frequent instances occur of ships being 60, 70 and 80 days going to Quebec.

853. You say, that you think the emigrants would not take a less quantity of provisions than that which is prescribed by the Act?—I do not think they would; they generally consult the captain; they tell the captain of the ship what quantity they have got, and if he thinks they have not got enough, they put on board more.

854. That Act provides for a certain quantity of bread, meal and flour; is that the species of provision upon which the lower Classes in Ireland live, either entirely or in a great measure?—It is generally their chief support.

855. You are not much acquainted with the south of Ireland?—Not particularly; I consider that oatmeal and potatoes form the principal food of the Irish peasantry generally; I include potatoes when in proper season, say in the spring of the year, very necessary, but in case of bad weather or other casualty, oatmeal, flour or biscuit can only be depended on.

856. You are not aware that in the south of Ireland the peasantry never taste bread from one year's end to another?—I am not aware that they never taste bread, they chiefly live on potatoes; but this Act merely says, that there shall be that quantity of that or any other wholesome food equivalent thereto; I only submit that there should be a certain quantity of something on board, enough to keep them in life for 75 days.

857. If there were no restriction whatever by law as to the food to be taken by the passengers, do not you think that the captain of every ship carrying out passengers would for his own sake take care that no person should be taken on board who had not a proper quantity of provisions?—I think he would, or ought to do.

858. Have not you stated that that is the habit?—They generally inquire what quantity of provisions the passengers have brought; the ship is under a very heavy responsibility; I have known instances where the ship has taken on board a quantity of meal to guard against the possibility of the passengers falling short; I have done so myself, I have taken in a few tons of oatmeal, at the expense of the ship, to prevent any accident.

859. In case of a passenger falling short of provisions, would not the captain have to supply that deficiency?—Perhaps the captain might not have any to spare.

860. Does the captain generally go to sea so short of provisions?—A ship going to sea in the North American trade, if she victuals at home, may take in three or four months provisions, but what would a redundancy of a barrel of biscuit or a barrel of meal be among 300 emigrants.

861. What is the general burthen of those ships that carry 300 persons?—From 300 to 400 tons.

862. How many emigrants, according to the regulations of this Act, would be shipped on board a vessel of 350 tons?—I have put on paper a few observations with respect to the points of difference between the proposed Act and the former Act, which I will read to the Committee. In the first place, the proposed Act permits the ship to carry her full number, say one to two tons register, children in proportion, exclusive of the crew; the former Act included the crew. Secondly, it dispenses with carrying a doctor; the former Act imposed that necessity. Thirdly, it permits the ship carrying cargo, reserving a sufficiency of space, with the whole of the between-decks, for passengers, provisions, water, &c.; the former Act prohibited carrying cargo, or it was so construed by the Irish Board of Customs. Fourthly, it relieves the shipowner and captain from obnoxious and frivolous clauses and expenses that never perhaps would be resorted to, but operated in the calculation of a conscientious shipowner, not to permit his ship to embark in such trade. Fifthly, it permits the passenger or emigrant to lay in his own provisions, or to make any contract they think fit with the captain for that purpose, the captain being responsible that a sufficiency of

wholesome food for 75 days of some kind is on board for each adult passenger; the former Act obliged the ship to have on board a particular description of provisions, not suited to the habits of emigrants, and of increased expense. And the proposed amended Act gives every protection to the emigrant, at the same time removing many absurd difficulties to the ship, and permits as many passengers to be put on board as could possibly be justified with any due regard to their health and lives. I shall state in my humble opinion how it operates in a pecuniary way: first, a ship 400 tons by the former Act could only carry, deducting crew, about 180 adults; now 200; difference 20, at 40 s. per head, deducting expense of water, &c. 40 l.: secondly, free from expense of doctor, at least 50 l.: thirdly, giving liberty to carry cargo, is at least worth equal to 25 l.: fourthly, I consider that dispensing with the obligation that many ships are under, to put salt provisions on board to conform to old Act, although not used equal with other matters, to 25 l.; making a total of 140 l., which on two hundred emigrants would be equal to 12 s. or 14 s. per adult; and supposing that a ship was taking in emigrants, and that plenty were offering, it would enable the ship to carry them for so much less than under the former Act, and form as much actual gain on the passage as charging so much higher, so that in fact the emigrant gets his passage for so much less, and without any loss to the ship. A ship of four hundred tons has about seventy-five feet in length of space, and twenty-six feet wide between decks; so, to have her doubled birthed, would give you about twenty-six births aside, or fifty-two in all; and allowing six persons to each birth, would accommodate three hundred and twelve persons, which a ship of four hundred tons is permitted to carry; say two hundred adults, with average proportion of children, would at least make (if not more) the number stated, and with twenty of crew, would give on board altogether 332 persons in a space about 95 feet long, 25 to 26 feet wide, and 5½ or 6 feet high.

863. If there were no responsibility imposed upon the captains of vessels, either with respect to provisions or with respect to tonnage, are you apprehensive that captains might be found who would be willing to incur risks from which great evils might occur to the passengers?—I am afraid many instances might occur, and unless some legislative regulation existed, I fear captains and shipbrokers would be found that would cram them into any extent, and great hardship would be likely to follow.

864. Do you know of any serious consequences that did arise previous to the passing of the Passengers Act?—I know instances where passengers were carried a thousand miles from the place they contracted for.

2   From William Dunlop, *Statistical Sketches of Upper Canada, for the Use of Emigrants: by a Backwoodsman* (London: John Murray, 1832), 14–20.

PREPARATIONS FOR EMIGRATION

When a man has determined to quit home, and settle himself in a foreign land, and he should not do so on slight grounds, much trouble and vexation may be saved by his taking a little good advice, and that we are about to give in this chapter, in so far as emigration to Canada is concerned.

It cannot be too strongly impressed upon emigrants the inexpediency of carrying to the woods of Upper Canada heavy lumbering articles of wooden furniture. All these can be procured here for far less than the cost of transport from Quebec and Montreal. The only exception to this rule is, when a person has valuable furniture for which he cannot get any thing like a reasonable price at home; and in that case, it may be cheaper to carry it to Canada than to sacrifice it in England. [. . .] Clothes, more particularly coarse clothing, such as slops and shooting jackets, bedding, shirts, (made, for making is expensive here,) cooking utensils, a clock or time-piece, books packed in barrels, hosiery, and, above all, boots and shoes, (for what they call leather in this continent is much more closely allied to hide than leather, and one pair of English shoes will easily outlast three such as we have here,) are among the articles that will be found most useful. As a general rule also, every thing that is made of metal, (for ironmongery is very dear,) as well as gardening and the iron parts of farming tools, and a few of the most common carpenters' tools, can never come amiss; for, though a man may not be artist enough to make money as a carpenter for other people, he may save a great deal himself by having the means within his reach of driving a nail or putting in a pane of glass. A few medicines ought to be taken for the voyage, and those chiefly of the purgative kind, as ships are very frequently but indifferently furnished with a medicine chest. Among these I would recommend Anderson's, or any other of the aloetic and colocynth pills, Epsom salts, magnesia and emetics, made up in doses. If you take Seidlitz powders, or soda powders, or any of that tribe of acids and alkalies, let them be made up in phials, well stopped, not, as usual, in papers, for in that case they will get melted, or (as the learned express it) deliquate, before the passage is half over. With these phials will of course be required measures, to take out the proper proportions of each powder. Fishing and shooting tackle ought, also to be taken; but of these I shall come to speak more at large when I treat, as I mean to do in a separate chapter, of the field-sports of Upper Canada.

In the choice of a ship, steerage passengers should look out for one high, roomy, and airy between decks; and there can be no great difficulty in finding one of that description, as a very great number of the timber ships are so constructed. A fast sailer also should be preferred; for the difference of a fortnight or three weeks in arriving at your destination may make the difference of nearly a year's subsistence to the emigrant. If he arrive in time to put in a small crop of potatoes, turnips, oats, Indian corn, and a little garden stuff, it will go a great way towards the maintenance of a family for the first year, as it will enable them to feed pigs and keep a cow, which they could not otherwise accomplish. For a similar reason, it will be to the obvious advantage of all settlers to come out in the earliest ships that sail.

To all passengers, but more especially to those of the cabin, a civil, good-tempered captain ought to be a very great inducement to sail in his ship,—as much of the comfort or discomfort of a voyage depends upon him. There are many of the regular traders between Montreal and Greenock and Liverpool who answer this description, as well as on the London and Liverpool lines to New York. And to any person who goes by the latter route, I would strongly recommend my worthy, though diminutive friend, Captain Holridge of the Silas Richards. Above all, passengers of every description should ascertain, that the captain with whom they sail is a sober man; for the most fatal accidents may occur, and have occurred, from drunkenness on the part of the officers of the ship. I prefer coming to Canada *via* Montreal, as it saves money, time, and transhipment of baggage.

It is a question often asked, how should money be taken to Canada? I reply, in any way except in goods. Not that I have not often known that mode of bringing it prove highly profitable; but it is a risk; few who come out being good judges of the price of goods at home, and none of them knowing what kind of goods will suit the Canada markets. British silver or gold make a very good investment; as the former is bought up by merchants and tradesmen, and used to purchase bills on the Treasury through the Commissariat, and the latter is remitted by the same classes to meet their engagements in England. A Sovereign generally fetches 23s. or 24s. currency, that is 5s. to the dollar;—1s. sterling passes for 1s. 2d. currency;—so that either description of bullion gives a good remittance. One great objection, however, to bringing out money, is the liability there is of losing or being robbed of it: so that, upon the whole, the better way perhaps may be, to lodge it with T. Wilson and Co. of Austin Friars, Agents for the Bank of Upper Canada, or at the Canada Company's Office in St. Helen's Place, taking an acknowledgment; and then you can draw upon the fund from Canada, receiving the premium of the day on the exchange.

People who find themselves on the outward voyage, should lay in a very considerable quantity of potatoes and oatmeal, not only because these articles are cheap, but because they have a tendency to correct the scorbutic qualities of salt meat. A few onions and leeks likewise will be found a great comfort on a long voyage, as also a good supply of vinegar and pickles.

Emigrants would find their account in bringing out small quantities of seeds, particularly those of the rarer grasses, as lucern, trefoil, &c.; for if they did not need such articles themselves, they would find plenty who would buy them at a high price. To these may be added some small parcels of potato oats, and of the large black oat of the south of Ireland for seed, as that grain, if not renewed, degenerates into something little better than chaff in the course of time.

All kinds of good stock are wanted here, and those who can afford it will always find their account in bringing such. Pigs are valuable, in many parts of this country, according to the size to which they can be fatted. Thus, supposing a hog which weighs 2 cwt. fetched twopence halfpenny per lb., one weighing 3 cwt. would fetch threepence, and so on, adding a halfpenny per lb. for each cwt. of the weight. A good bull would also be of great value; and it is my firm belief, that we have not a first-rate draught stallion in the province. I have no doubt, moreover, that a Clydesdale cart-horse, a Suffolk punch, or even a moderate-sized Flanders stallion, would be a good speculation. The best description of working cattle we have is the Lower Canadian horse, which has many of the properties and much the appearance of the Scotch galloway: he is strong, active, and indefatigable in harness, but makes a bad saddle horse, as he is often not sure-footed. A breed between this and the American horse makes a good, useful farm-horse; and it is possible that a cross between the Canadian mare and the Flanders horse would make something like the Clydesdale,—tradition asserting, that the ancestors of the Carnwath breed sprang from a cross of some Flanders mares brought to Scotland by the Duke of Hamilton with the galloway stallions of the country.

As to dogs for household use, the English sheepdog or Scotch colley, or the lurcher, would be highly valuable, particularly if trained to bring home the cattle, which often stray in the woods and get injured by not being regularly milked. With careless settlers, indeed, one half the day is often spent in hunting up and driving home the oxen.

It has often struck me, that much time and trouble might be saved in collecting and bringing home the cattle, by taking out a few hundred weight of rock salt from Liverpool. In Cheshire they used to prepare lumps, for the purpose of putting in sheepwalks, by cutting them in the form of a ball, so that the rain ran off them without melting them. These might be put in certain places of the woods, and the cattle would not stray far from them; and they might be removed from time to time, as the pasture became scarce. Wherever there is a salt spring, or a salt 'lick,' as salt earth is called in this country, the deer and cattle flock to it from all quarters. A friend of mine had one on his farm, and no fence could keep off these intruders; till at last he was obliged to come to a compromise with the four-footed congress, and fairly fenced in a road to the spring, and by this species of Whig conciliation, by a sacrifice of part of his rights, saved the rest of his property.

When you arrive in the St. Lawrence, having been on shortish allowance of water, you will be for swallowing the river water by the bucket full. Now, if you have any bowels of compassion for your intestinal canal, you will abstain from so doing;—for to people not accustomed to it, the lime that forms a considerable constituent part of the water of this country, acts pretty much in the same manner as would a solution of Glauber's salts, and often generates dysentery and diarrhoea; and though I have an unbounded veneration for the principles of the Temperance societies, I would, with all deference, recommend, that the pure fluid be drank in very small quantities at first, and even these tempered with the most impalpable infusion possible of Jamaica or Cognac.

HISTORICAL INTERPRETATIONS

3   From Elizabeth Jane Errington, 'Transatlantic Webs of Kin and Community', in *Emigrant Worlds and Transatlantic Communities: Migration to Upper Canada in the First Half of the Nineteenth Century* (Montreal: McGill-Queen's University Press, 2007), 136–58.

When young Harriet Pengelly finally arrived in Upper Canada, she was exhausted, bewildered, and miserable. The difficult voyage from Plymouth to New York had been followed by a slow and disagreeable journey by way of Albany and Oswego to Toronto and then west to Flamborough. 'Alas! What am I come to! My heart is breaking with grief', she wrote at the end of May 1835.[1] She was almost overwhelmed by 'the dirt and misery'[2] of their new lodgings; and while Robert travelled about looking for land, she was desperately lonely. 'I feel very low in spirits, would I were home', she cryptically reported after a week in the colony.[3] The arrival of the first letters from home was bittersweet: 'I am still very low.

Wept when I read Sophy's and Uncle Irving's kind letters, such prayers for my happiness, dear friends may God bless you all.'[4] To help her assuage her sense of alienation and, when Robert was away, her feeling of being 'all alone in this second Siberia',[5] Harriet reached across the Atlantic. She frequently wrote to sister Sophy and to other friends and relations in Guernsey. When not writing, she was thinking of her 'absent friends';[6] and when letters arrived from home, she 'felt happier than [she] had done for some time.'[7]

Harriet's correspondence with home provided an emotional lifeline. It is clear from her journal that, from the beginning, she had been hesitant about emigrating to the colonies.

Married in September 1834, in the space of six months she had had to adjust to life as a newly-wed and to leaving her 'happy home' and 'dear Guernsey friends', along with all she loved 'so dearly', for a foreign land.[8] Letters home were a way of maintaining contact with the familiar world of her youth. They also reaffirmed the emotional, if not physical, proximity of friends and family. On the very day the couple boarded the packet at Plymouth and also on the day they landed in New York, Harriet sent letters home.[9] Especially in the early months of her journal, Harriet's notations that she had written home often appeared in entries that recounted some disappointment, whether it was the abrupt decision of her maid Emily not to accompany the couple to America or the failure of the luggage to arrive; or, once they were in the colony, the realization that their original choice of land 'was mistaken'.[10]

Even after the Pengellys had bought a farm and built a home on Rice Lake and had begun to settle into the rhythms of their new lives, Harriet maintained an active correspondence across the Atlantic. She was 'truly miserable' when anticipated letters from home did not arrive.[11] One 'disagreeable' day in August 1835, for example, she recorded, 'No letters from home, could eat no dinner—very, very unhappy.'[12] Even after the couple had decided to return to Guernsey for a visit after two years and Harriet's sense of exile began to abate, letters from home remained a vital part of her daily life, something to be cherished and read 'over and over'.[13] As she read of the comings and goings of kith and kin in Guernsey and England, she was able to maintain a sense of belonging to a community that was far removed from her daily round of housekeeping and visiting neighbours, and at times 'the awful silence of the woods of Canada'.[14] [. . .]

Until her death a little more than a year after she arrived in the colony, Harriet remained emotionally rooted in a world that lay more than three thousand miles away. Although she had 'the smiles and love of a very dear husband', on New Year's Day 1836

she longed for her mother's smile and 'a kind mother to wish me many happy returns of the day.'[15] Letters provided Harriet with the means of participating, at least vicariously, in the community of family and friends 'at home' even while she was forging new friendships and becoming part of a new community at Rice Lake. For Harriet, letters were also tangible evidence that she had not been forgotten and had not lost her place in the family circle. As was the case for many around her, letters from home were a touchstone, an affirmation of who one was and, for a time at least, where one continued to belong.

Certainly, not all or even most emigrant settlers maintained such an active transatlantic correspondence. Like her husband Robert, a former British officer and a gentleman of some means, Harriet was a member of the 'letter writing classes'.[16] The couple could afford to travel in a cabin on a packetship, and Robert had the capital to buy land and hire neighbours to help build his house and clear his fields. And when they arrived in the colony with their letters of introduction to the lieutenant-governor, they became part of a society that was directly tied to London and the Colonial Office. Harriet was determined 'to do without' a servant after she had sacked, for insolence, the one they had brought from Guernsey; she hoped, she said, that work would keep her 'alive in this dull disagreeable country.' But the young wife obviously had considerable time on her hands.[17] She had no children to attend to and was often alone when Robert worked in the fields.

Most new arrivals had not the time, the means, or perhaps the inclination to write home so often or at such length. As George Pashley recorded in his diary, his first letters home—one to his father, a second to a friend, and the third to his 'dear partner's' father—were not sent until three months after he landed in British America: 'I could not get Money to Pay the Postage till then.'[18] Of course, some emigrants may have chosen not to write. They wanted to sever ties with home—whether because they were fleeing from particular responsibilities (as in the case of absconding husbands) or from the court, or because they were determined to grasp the new opportunities of America and, in the process, reinvent themselves. However, it is clear that for many, re-establishing contact with home was an integral part of the process of making a new life away from home. As the new arrivals joined kin, former neighbours, and even just acquaintances who were already settled in Upper Canada and were integrated into or helped to create new families and communities and gradually become residents, the desire to maintain contact with those at home persisted. Frequently, the responsibilities attendant on kinship—coping with the needs of an elderly parent, providing aid to a young sibling or cousin, or settling disputes over parents estates—continued to tie emigrant settlers to those they had left behind. Letters were also a means of integrating the Old World and the New, of tying the familiar domestic landscapes, people, and relationships of home into the new and increasingly familiar world of a face-to-face colonial community. On both sides of the Atlantic, receiving or sending even one brief letter reaffirmed who one was and where one fitted into the world.

The transatlantic community sustained by correspondence was for many intensely personal, and despite distance in time and space, remained surprisingly immediate. Letters became an integral part of the ongoing cycle of British emigration and were one of the central pillars of the emigrants' world. Throughout Great Britain and Ireland, they frequently became the centrepiece of discussions in family parlours, churches, and taverns about the viability of 'going to America'. Letters from Upper Canada that included personal accounts of the journey and life in the New World helped to make the imagined world of emigration more real and tangible; at the same time, letters that arrived in the backwoods of the colony nourished the imagination of emigrant settlers with images of familiar landscapes and faces. The arrival of family members or friends of former neighbours, sometimes years later, reinforced these rather ethereal transatlantic communities. The receipt of letters, parcels, and even newspapers—even the appearance of a complete stranger with an introduction from a former acquaintance—was enough to sustain this world, both in its tangible form and in its participants' imagination.

[. . .]

Each year, hundreds if not thousands of emigrants of all social classes and occupations wrote home to announce their arrival and to report on the state of their health and that of their companions.[19] Sometimes these first letters were sent almost as soon as the family or the individual landed at Montreal or Quebec (or, in the case of Harriet Pengelly and Anne Langton, New York). A number included a journal or an account of the voyage and a promise to write again when settled.[20] Many emigrants waited and wrote their first letters weeks or even months after they had landed, and they included some 'account of Canada' or a commentary about 'the state of the country' (as they had apparently promised their readers before they left home), in addition to information about their own circumstances. As William Knox's first letter home to his uncle explained, 'I would have written you before this time to have acquainted you of our safe arrival in this country. But knowing that Mr George Gounlock had written to Greenhill shortly after we arrived here I told him to let you know that we were all well and I would write you as soon as we got a settlement.'[21]

Not surprisingly, emigrants' first letters home varied widely in tone and content. Some had to report the death of a companion or child on the voyage or how ague, scarlet fever, cholera, or other diseases had devastated family and friends.[22] Others noted that the country was 'discouraging at first' or that because of injury or ill health, they had initially had problems finding work.[23] But most letters, particularly those written after emigrants had found work or taken up land, expressed satisfaction with the country and the writer's situation; and implicitly, and often explicitly, they included assurances that they 'did not repent [their] journey.'[24] George Hill's mother and father must have received some comfort when their son concluded his letter, 'We left you almost broken-hearted, but you may be satisfied that we have bettered our condition by coming here.'[25] Perhaps most importantly, the arrival of George's letter was concrete proof that he was still alive.

For most newly arrived emigrants, the purpose of their first letter was to make contact and to renew what they obviously hoped would be an ongoing relationship with those at home. Many expected that not only would the initial recipient read their letter but that its contents and often the letter itself would be passed among 'Dear Friends And Relations'.[26] Mary and Arthur Stokes explicitly asked that their brothers and sisters write and they added, 'Please pass this letter to others.'[28] William Upton's letter to his mother asked that she give his love to all his brothers and sisters, and said, 'Tell them that can write to write to me soon.'[28] [. . .] Others sent salutations to specific neighbours, former employers, or members of the extended family.

[. . .]

Sending news, information, and messages to family and friends was clearly only one purpose of an emigrant's first letter home. Just as important was to urge the readers to reply as soon as possible. Almost without exception, the letters included such statements as, 'I long to hear from them all'[29] or pleaded, 'Please to let us hear from you as soon as convenient after receiving this; and acquaint us with all particulars, and how you all are.'[30] John Luff, an apprentice and one of the Petworth emigrants, wrote to his aunt saying, 'Whether we shall have the pleasure of seeing each other in this world again, lord only knows; if we should not, I wish you would join me in writing, it seems to be the only satisfaction we can truly have here.'[31]

It was clearly important to those who had newly arrived in Upper Canada to know that they had not been forgotten and, indeed, that they remained part of their communities at home. For the first few weeks or months, many must have felt betwixt and between. They were no longer residents of a particular village or neighbourhood in Great Britain or Ireland; at the same time, they had few connections or commitments to new communities in America. First letters were a way of asserting their continuing relationship with communities at home; and the responses to these letters reassured them that they still had a place in the world, an identity that was firmly rooted in place and time—one which they had taken with them to America and on which they could forge new relationships. Many new arrivals therefore waited anxiously for some acknowledgment from those they had left behind.[32]

Not all (and perhaps not even most) emigrants wrote to reassure the family of their safe arrival. As many of the 'information wanted' notices suggest, some men had emigrated to escape family or financial responsibilities. Even those with the best of intentions may have found that once they were in America, it was easy to disappear, leaving wives and children at home unknowingly deserted.[33] Many more new arrivals probably did not have the ability or the means to write. Most were nonetheless determined to let those at home know that they had arrived safely and, later, to tell them how they were settling in.

Those who arrived in Upper Canada as part of a group, like John Gemmill or members of the Petworth expeditions ten years later, or those who joined family or former neighbours already established in the colony, could always find someone to write on their behalf or, at the very least, could send greetings that would be expected to reach those at home. In the 1820s John Gemmill frequently sent messages from former shipmates and current neighbours in Lanark County, through his son Andrew, to friends and relatives in the old neighbourhood.

In the summer of 1823, for example, he asked Andrew to 'acquaint all Enquiring friends that Dr. Gemell John McFarline Walter Stirling James Cohune's family are all well.'[34] Three years later, in a postscript to a letter, he wrote, 'James Colquhoun wishes us to mention to you if you could hear anything of his brother Robert to let him know that he is well & is surprised that he has not heard from him for more than two years.'[35] Andrew tracked down James Colquhoun's brother and reported back to his father. Unfortunately, the situation in Upper Canada had changed. 'In your letter you desired me to let James Colquhoun know that you [had heard] from his brother', John wrote Andrew the following August, 1827. But now John had to ask Andrew to break the news to the brother that James was 'no more': 'He was killed in April last while at work upon his own land.'[36] More often, Andrew was given a happier commission. A year after John reported James's death, he asked his son, 'Give James Wrights Compliments to Mr David Strachan and Wife' and 'if David Strachan be writing to his sister he may let James Wrights Relations know that he is in good health.'[37]

Various members of the Petworth parties also regularly wrote home on behalf of their companions and neighbours. [. . .] James Rapson, another member of the first Petworth group, not only wrote letters on behalf of other emigrants[38] but also regularly sent his family news about his companions (some of whom were now near neighbours, and others he had heard about second or third hand), knowing that this information would be passed on.[39] For both John Gemmill and James Rapson and their friends, the world of emigration was a small world and continued to be characterized by face-to-face communication even when such conversations spanned the Atlantic. The intimacy of this world was also apparent to other Petworth emigrants who arrived in subsequent years and sought out James Rapson for advice and assistance.

In many ways, emigrant correspondence recreated and was an extension of the familiar relationships of village life. What is striking is that even with only intermittent correspondence, or with news received second or third hand and months if not years out of date, the assumption of a shared community persisted. So, too, did the apparent immediacy of the relationships. This was undoubtedly one of the factors that encouraged some family members or friends who emigrated years later to assume that a face-to-face relationship could be resumed and that they could call on those in the New World for emotional and physical support when they arrived in the colony.

Not all, of course, participated in or maintained their connections with this dynamic transatlantic community. Many new arrivals to British North America were restless and moved frequently to look for work or for better opportunities. Friends and family in Great Britain and Ireland too might move in response to local circumstances. Many on both sides of the Atlantic refused to give up hope that some lost family member or friend could be found, however. In addition to the hundreds of 'information wanted' notices placed by emigrants and settlers looking for a particular individual or family, colonial newspapers sometimes printed cards of family members or friends 'at home' who were hoping to get in touch with 'lost' relatives abroad. In 1835, for example, English friends offered a reward to anyone who had information about Ann Hall. 'A native of London', Ann had come to Canada three years earlier with a Chelsea pensioner and his wife, who had subsequently died. No one had heard from Ann since she had written in July 1832.[40] [. . .]

Often the problem for those in the British Isles was finding the beneficiary of an estate. In some instances, executors used a local agent to conduct the search. In 1829, for example, 'A.B.' began to look for George Long, 'a Tailor by trade' who had left England ten years earlier with his wife and four children. It was thought that he now lived 'somewhere near Philadelphia' and was a farmer. His wife's family, who lived near Knightsbridge,

London, were trying to contact him, for he would 'hear something to his advantage'.[41] In 1829 Catherine Evans of Colham, Shrewsbury, Shropshire, contacted the *Herald* office in Kingston for help finding her brother Spencer Evans, who had been discharged from the Queen's Rangers some 25 years earlier and was, she thought, now living in Upper Canada.[42] At other times, the family or its agent in Great Britain or Ireland made a direct appeal.[43] Infrequently, an anxious parent or sibling would write directly to the postmaster of the relative's last known address in America to try to track the person down.

Many emigrants and their families were determined not to lose touch. A sense of familial obligation, ongoing business affairs, or just the need to maintain the image of familiar faces and places promoted an extensive correspondence which, in a few instances, continued into the second generation. Maintaining such a correspondence had significant difficulties. Paper was often scarce, and postage, which was paid in part by the recipient, was relatively expensive and beyond the means of many.[44] Moreover mail 'service' was haphazard at best. Although the larger centres in Upper Canada had postal service that linked Halifax, Quebec, and Montreal to the interior, for much of the period the most economic and quickest route for mail was through New York.[45] [. . .] Even so, to the frustration of correspondents on both sides of the Atlantic, letters were often misdirected or lost in transit.

Almost a year after arriving in Lanark, John Gemmill grew increasingly concerned that he had heard nothing from his wife Ann. He had already written twice and 'had got no answer'. Ironically, even this third letter, which included detailed instructions about the family's reunion, took almost nine months to reach Glasgow and arrived long after Ann had already left home.[46] The frustration with mail to Scotland persisted. In one of his first letters to son Andrew, John noted, 'We are sorry to here that you have only received one letter in the course of two years. We have not been neglectfull of writting to you neither is the Country as poor but it can produce plenty of Paper but it is the post offices that must be neglectfull of not forwarding them.'[47] [. . .]

In Upper Canada, some letters from home arrived at their destination only to languish because the intended recipient did not know they were there or, as often seemed to happen, because the emigrant had left the area altogether. Local newspapers regularly published lists of letters waiting to be picked up. Isaac Wilson, the pre-War of 1812 emigrant living just outside York, discovered to his dismay in 1821 that 'they now have a regulation at the post office . . . to send all letters remaining unclaimed after three months down to the General Post Office at Quebec.' He had not been to York for some time, and the new clerk did not know him; as a result, he explained to his brother Jonathan his letter 'was sent with a raft'.[48] Harriet Pengelly, on the other hand, ever anxious to receive news from home, made a point of checking the post regularly and was always sorely disappointed when there was 'none from home'.[49] Mary Gapper, after deciding to marry Edward O'Brien and remain in the colony, remarked that mail sent by way of York in 1836 was delivered by 'an Indian . . . who now calls regularly at very irregular times.'[50]

To avoid expensive postage and problems with the mail service, letter writers on both sides of the Atlantic frequently relied on friends, acquaintances, or agents who were travelling overseas to carry their mail. It appears that a few Lanark residents returned home to visit, to fetch their family, or to go to college. Each time they left, they carried letters from John Gemmill to his son.[51] [. . .]

Personally delivered letters were a double benefit to the recipient. When the son of the Reverend William Bell from Lanark went 'home' to college and delivered John Gemmill's letter, Andrew also received a first-hand account of his father and the family and could get detailed answers to the myriad questions that could not be answered by post.[52] Isaac Wilson was 'pleased to inform' his brother Jonathan in the summer of 1821 'that John Barnes and his wife [had] arrived at York' and he had received Jonathan's note. 'I am much obliged to you for your kindness', he wrote, 'as they will afford me much information and entertainment.' As Barnes had arrived with a letter from Jonathan asking Isaac to assist the bearer in any way he could, Isaac ruefully concluded that they would also afford him 'some vexation, no doubt.'[53] [. . .]

Entrusting acquaintances, friends, or family members with letters did not guarantee their speedy or safe arrival. Before Allanason delivered the letter, he had already spent some time travelling around America. Even so, for much of the period, 'private conveyance' was less expensive and could be more reliable than the 'regular' post.[54] However, sometimes the traveller or acquaintance forgot to put the letter in the post on the other side of the Atlantic or found it too much trouble to deliver it. George Pashley was disconcerted to find that his letters had not been delivered as promised. 'This week I was informed that our Letters we had sent to Eng were within 2 miles of our own house because the man we expected to take them had fallen sick so they did not set off till the end of Jan.'[55] Nonetheless, the imminent departure of a friend, or a visitor returning home, or the sailing of a particular ship presented an opportunity to write and make contact. [. . .]

Whether letters were mailed or sent with a traveller on the day they were written, they usually took months to reach their destinations. Correspondence between family and friends often crossed each other. News and information might be repeated in a subsequent letter when the writer realized, or feared, that the first had not arrived. This may help explain, in part at least, why some correspondents waited weeks if not months to reply to a letter; or if one arrived particularly late, saw no need to reply at all.[56] And there was, of course, the perpetual problem that

writing took time and considerable thought and effort, all of which were at a premium in most new settlers' lives. What is so startling, therefore, is the sense of immediacy and often the conversational tone of many letters.

[. . .]

Of prime and increasing importance, however, was news about the health and welfare of various family members, and the primary focus of most of the transatlantic conversations revolved around family affairs. Each letter from Upper Canada began with an almost formulaic greeting. In June 1823, for example, John [Gemmill] began, 'Dear son, We received your letter darted the 26TH of March on the 26 of May and the other Dated the 29 of March which Gave us Great Pleasure to hear of your Well fare and they find us all in good health at Preasant thank God for it.'[57] Such almost ritualized openings were not empty rote; they were a crucial affirmation of the intimacy that existed between the writer and the recipient and a clear declaration of what was of greatest concern to both. Each of John and Ann Gemmill's letters included references to their and their children's health; they also specifically alluded to the power of the Almighty. In November 1825, Ann and John told Andrew, 'This at present leaves us in the full enjoyment of that valuable Blessing for which we have great reason to praise God.'[58] The letters also always asked after family members still in Scotland, and they admonished Andrew when he did not include information concerning his sisters' welfare. 'We were very much Surprised', the couple wrote in May 1823, 'that you never Mention nothing about your two Sisters Margeret and Jane.'[59] A month later, they asked Andrew to 'be so good as to lett them know of our Welfare.'[60] The Gemmills' letters presumed that the ongoing relationship between Lanark, Upper Canada, and Glasgow rested on far more than passive interaction. John expected Andrew to pass on information and to assume some responsibility for the welfare of his sisters.

At the same time, John and Ann were ensuring that Andrew remained part of the family circle in Upper Canada. Their letters reported major family events. Andrew vicariously followed his sisters as they went 'out to service' and watched as the little ones, including David, who had been an infant when he left home, go to school. In 1826 Andrew heard of the marriages of sisters Ann and Mary, and in turn he related his own marriage in 1827. To John, this was an opportunity to extend the family network, and thereafter his letters included greetings to 'all your [Andrew's] relations in Scotland'. Two years later, while rejoicing with Andrew over the birth of his first child, John wrote, 'We think that you forgot to mention her name and hope you will have a better memory when you write next.'[61]

Especially in the early years, when all the children were living in the parental household, Andrew was drawn farther into life in Lanark when John's letters included notes of specific greetings from other members of the family. Sometimes, it was a brief 'Jennet sends her best respects to you'[62] or, somewhat later, 'Your Brothers & Sisters all join in love to you & your Family, David [the youngest son] has some recollection of you . . . but says he would know you better if you would send him the suit of cloaths.'[63] Through her father's letters, Jennet, who was two years younger than Andrew, teased him about being a bachelor: 'She thinks that if you do not bring a wife with you that you will remain an Old Batchelor that you would not get a Negor or Indian Squaw in the Country they will think so little of you.'[64] In one of the few letters from Andrew that have survived, he replied, 'Tell Janet to belief herself besides those black Ghosts of Indians.'[65]

The occasion of Jennet's engagement to be married about six months later best illustrates the texture of this imagined familiar fireside. At the end of April 1824, a postscript cryptically noted, 'Janet will be married before you come here so you put on spurs.'[66] There may have been some hope that Andrew would arrive in time to be the best man. But John reported in November, 'Since you did not come forward to be the best man, they made as merry as they could without you.' And later in the same letter he passed on a message from Jennet: 'As soon as you send intimation of your comming they [Jennet and her new husband] will Joyfully saddle the Tea Kettle and have everything ready to make you comfortable but they dare not put it on yet lest the bottom boil out of it before you come.'[67] A year later, as John continued to hope that Andrew and his sisters would arrive, he bemoaned, 'If you don't come soon, the Bottom will be out of the kettle.'[68] One of Andrew's brothers, John, reintroduced the teapot to the transatlantic conversation many years later: 'But my Mother says that if you don't come soon she is afraid that you have to take your tea out of the pot for the botem is out of the old tea ketel and she has got A new one and she is afraid that it will go the same way before you reach this place.'[69]

The references to the familiar and domestic tea kettle—which in many Scottish homes was the symbol of welcome—helped create the illusion of a continuing and face-to-face relationship within a family divided by the Atlantic. By 1832, it must have been clear to all that Andrew and his new young family were unlikely to emigrate. Three years earlier, John had told Andrew that he 'had almost despair[ed] of the realization of your wishes of our meeting again with the rest of my family around my fireside.' He turned to his faith to help sustain him. The Gemmills shared an unshakable belief that 'Kind Providence . . . provided all things liberally.'[70] All their trials and tribulations, including family separations, were 'from the Supreme Disposer of Events', John observed, and were 'generally for our good.'[71] Thus, he took solace that 'though that [the family's reunion] may not take place upon earth, let us with the Divine assistance conduct ourselves in such a manner that we look forward to our meeting together in another and better world.'[72]

In the meantime, the Gemmills created their own world—one with a tea kettle on the hob—in which, through their imagination, they shared their concerns, their triumphs, and their sorrows. And the whole family took part in the conversation that lasted for more than ten years. After the birth of the first of Jennet's children, John told Andrew that she was 'living in great hopes of her son being heir to your inheritance . . . You made this promise & she will make you keep it.'[73] At the age of eight, young David was proud of the gold piece that Andrew had sent from home.[74] And when Andrew's brother, young John, wrote his first letter (and apologized for his spelling), it was sent to Andrew with the hope, wrote John, 'that you are intending to pay us a visit sure that would be a hapy meting.'[75] This was a world that offered all its participants emotional support—and a continuing sense of security. And for John Gemmill and his family, it provided a means of remaining part of the larger community of the extended family and friends at home in Scotland while they helped to create a new community abroad.

Frances Stewart, Mary Gapper O'Brien, and such women as Catharine Parr Traill and Susanna Moodie too maintained a regular transatlantic correspondence with family and friends in Britain. For Mary, like a young Harriet Pengelly, the arrival of letters and packages from home were a delightful treat, particularly after she had decided to marry Edward O'Brien and remain in the colony.[76] As she explained to her sister Lucy in England in 1832, 'The real event of importance which glads the day is the arrival of letters.'[77] [. . .] Even letters with bad news were welcomed. Mary 'fretted' when letters did not arrive, and when they did they were cherished and often reread time and again.[78] In the summer of 1836, just after the birth of her third child, she wrote in her journal, 'A letter from Lucy arrived a few hours after my baby & I am not very sure which was the more welcome.'[79]

For women and men, both the newly arrived in the colony and those who had become well settled, letters were part of a sustained transatlantic conversation. As the

Peterborough area resident Isabelle Brownlie wrote to her brother at home in a lengthy letter, 'But I will tire you with my talk for I think I am talking to you but I dought I will never have the pleasure to do but if we never meet in this world I hope we will meet in the happier one.'[80] Until that day, the very act of writing allowed one to enter the familiar world of family and friends. Although one might be replying to news that was months old or renewing contact after a lengthy silence, the transatlantic correspondence nearly always had a sense of immediacy. For Isabelle, as for Mary O'Brien and thousands of others, this imaginary world was as real and present as the physical world in which they now lived.

For many, the continuing connection to home was reinforced by unfinished business or family obligations. John Gemmill seems to have expected Andrew, as the eldest son, to assume some responsibilities for the two sisters who were still in Scotland.[81] John also gave Andrew authority to deal with various financial matters on his behalf. In October 1824, for example, he gave his son power of attorney to settle Ann's father's estate on the family's behalf. [. . .] Three years later, Andrew was again given authority, this time to settle a debt claimed by a former neighbour.[82] Throughout the years, John offered Andrew advice on how he might proceed, but it is clear that he had confidence in his son. Five years after the affair of the will had begun, he told Andrew, 'You have at least got the better of your Uncle', and expressed his satisfaction that the estate was finally settled.[83]

Isaac Wilson, a settler in Upper Canada, too relied on his younger brother Jonathan to represent his interests at home. Isaac and Jonathan maintained a regular correspondence from the time of Isaac's arrival in the colony in 1811 until his death in 1838.[84] Like many other emigrant settlers, Isaac does not seem to have written letters per se, although Jonathan apparently did. Instead, Isaac sent home an annual or semi-annual journal that was filled with details about the landscape and local politics and described his health, his work establishing his farm, and gave news of his neighbours; and, after his sister and family arrived in 1819, their news too. In 1811 Isaac was not sure that he intended to remain in the colony. The coming of war in 1812 'confounded' his plans to travel and see something of America; it also permanently interrupted Jonathan's plan to join him in Upper Canada.[85] Isaac made a brief visit home in 1814 to settle some affairs after his father's death in 1812 and undoubtedly to see his mother. He was restless, however, and he returned to his farm outside York a year later, explaining to his brother, 'I have fixed myself here for some time to come if not for life.'[86] Even so, for the next 20 years, Isaac still considered himself very much part of the old household and community. He kept up to date with 'the state of affairs at home'[87] from Jonathan's letters, from newspapers Jonathan sent him, and from the first-hand reports of newly arrived emigrants or travellers who occasionally appeared with letters or packages. He also periodically offered advice to his brother about how to manage various family affairs.[88]

[. . .]

The tangible bonds of family obligations and entitlements bound many emigrants to Britain long after they had begun to settle into their new homes. Only a relative few, however, would have had an inheritance to collect or were entitled to the proceeds from an ongoing business interest. Yet sons and daughters, sisters and brothers, parents and children often continued to feel a sense of responsibility for kin—especially for their parents—on the other side of the Atlantic. Shortly after Isaac Wilson returned from his visit home, he wrote to his brother saying, 'I hope my mother and you are living agreeably together in the way I left you. You must indulge her as much as you can to preserve peace among you.'[89] Mother and son obviously did not live together for long. In 1824 Mrs Wilson's house was broken into. After expressing his sorrow at the damage, Isaac wrote, 'It is gratifying to me to hear

that things are taken care of', and he thanked his brother for his efforts.[90] Three years later, Isaac commented, 'I am sorry to hear my Mother has not her health so well as usual. I think it would be better for her to try to live along with Ann or somebody than to live any longer by herself, so that she could be taken care of in case of sickness.'[91] Divided by the Atlantic, there was little that Isaac could do directly for his mother, however, except provide advice and encouragement to her and his brother.

When all the children had left home, the situation could become even more complicated and worrying. For some, the problem was resolved when their parents decided to join them in America. A number of letters from Upper Canada urged parents to come, offering to send them 'some assistance' for the passage.[92] Others asked friends or relations still in Britain to ensure that Mother or Father was settled and healthy. Two Petworth emigrants, for example, George and Mary Boxall, asked friends to 'pray leave' their 'poor mother at Henly, a sovereign' before they left.[93]

Emotional and financial support flowed both ways. John Scott's first letter to his uncle Andrew Redford was prompted by the loan of fifty pounds received from Andrew and 'other kind friends'.[94] Mary O'Brien periodically received monetary gifts from Aunt Sophie, for which she was always most grateful.[95] And for the first few years in the Belleville area, Fanny and William Hutton relied on funds they received from his parents to offset their growing debts. Although Fanny was a hesitant and apparently infrequent correspondent, she explained in a lengthy letter to 'Dear Mrs Hutton' (as the letter began) the specific circumstances that had given rise to one particular request for assistance in this 'time of trouble'.[96] The details of the problems concluded with a plea for help: 'The present exigency of our circumstances had prompted me to through ourselves on your kindness.' If the immediate family could not lend them the 'sum asked by William', she said, or 'if you take a different view of our affairs from us', then she and William 'would be glad' of 'any suggestions which may at any time strike any of you as useful or necessary to us.'[97]

Although most new arrivals could not expect financial assistance, a number did look forward to receiving parcels from family and friends at home. Isaac Wilson was 'much obliged' to his brother for sending local newspapers, and he offered, 'If you would like to have a newspaper from York, I could send you one.'[98] Isaac also often received parcels from his brother that had been brought by recently arrived emigrants. 'I believe I received everything safe', he wrote to Jonathan in 1822. 'Both newspapers, one pair of good stockings, and the spectacles I find very useful.'[99] Fanny Hutton, John and Anne Langton, and Mary O'Brien were delighted when packages arrived containing cloth, books, and clothing that were often difficult to find in Upper Canada. Often as important were small tokens or presents from family and friends at home. David Gemmill's new watch, Anne Langton's pictures drawn by her brother, and other mementos became treasured possessions. They were physical representations that the recipient was not forgotten;[100] they reinforced the emotional ties to home, and they helped keep alive the images of family and friends and the landscape of their youth.

Six years after he left home, John Scott wrote to his cousin, 'My heart still warms when I think on many localities in my native land I used to frequent and the friends and acquaintances I have left behind—tho' I have forgotten the names of many persons and many places, with the Poet I can still exclaim—"yet he behold her with the eyes of spirit—He sees the form which he no more shall meet—She like a passionate thought is come and gone—while at his feet the bright well bubbles on."'[101] John Scott was certainly not the only emigrant who wrote home with vivid images in his mind. As one of his brothers wrote, 'You can scarcely form any idea of a person's feeling and Emotion who has been absent from his native country so long as I have been.' He explained, 'Time and distance gives a sort of enchantment, a melancholy pleasure which words are quite unable to express.'[102] For the two brothers, even after years away, the landscape of Scotland continued to capture their imagination and give them a connection to home. In his letters, Archibald Scott remembered walking to school with friends past local landmarks and wondered what had happened to his old schoolmaster. This was the place, he wrote, where he was born and spent his childhood: 'It seems as I was then completely happy.'[103]

Such racking homesickness was not shared by all in the family. John explained to his cousin in 1844 that most of his brothers and sisters, who were all younger than he, did not 'care much about seeing Scotland again.' Of course, his parents could 'never forget old friends, old faces and bygone times in Scotland', but after ten years in the colony he and his siblings were 'all naturalized now'. John continued, 'I am now become part Dutchman, part Canadian and part everything else for I live among all kinds of people and feel at home with them all.'[104] A year later, he commented that he understood when many of his acquaintances who had gone home for a visit had thankfully returned 'home' to Upper Canada. 'They could nor remain in the Old Country' he explained, because they were 'so accustomed to American habits.' John felt the same and declared, 'We are now, of course, all Canadians.'[105]

[. . .]

Even after years away, for the Scott children and cousins living in Upper Canada, letters and newspapers from home were tangible evidence that they had not been forgotten. As William Knox wrote to his cousin in 1843, 'I was beginning to think you had forgotten me altogether as it was such a very long time since I had received a Letter from Hermiston [the home farm]. I can assure you nothing for this long time gave me more pleasure than your Letter which I received last Month.'[106] Letters and newspapers evoked images of home.

Emigrant settlers knew that this was often an imaginary world. But they maintained the sense of a shared landscape and a shared past with those they had left behind. Although relationships were often idealized and landscapes unchanging, this increasingly imaginary world was very real in many emigrant settlers' minds. As they wrote home, they could see the faces and places of those they wrote to; they could smell the teapot brewing on the hearth and could hear the sounds of cattle or sheep, or the marketplace. This provided much of the foundation for the conversational nature of emigrant letters and the immediacy of their tone. Many, like John Scott, 'fondly yet wish again to see my old Fetherlaw and my friends there.'[107] In the meantime, letters would have to suffice.

[. . .]

For those who remained behind, maintaining the transatlantic community may well have been more difficult, particularly if emigrant settlers did nor have the means or desire to return for a visit. But maintain it many did, and in the process they vicariously became part of the emigrants' world. For those waiting for letters from home and then responding often months and sometimes years later, the post was a vital part of their new lives. Maintaining contact over a great distance was not easy. The vagaries of the mail complicated the problems created by mobile populations and accidents, illness, or even death that abruptly ended such connections. Many emigrants, either by choice or by chance, lost touch with family at home. Many others were determined not to. Even those who did not write sent and received 'reports' to and from family and friends at home. The arrival of visitors from the other side of the Atlantic certainly strengthened these long-distance relationships; for most, however, their continuing ties to home depended on the vital links of letters.

Transatlantic correspondence was an integral part of the emigrants' world. In the early years, it provided a sense of place and reassurance as they negotiated their way through a strange land. Many wrote home, either regularly or after years of silence, to renew bonds of affection. Sending and receiving letters also affirmed their identity as fathers, mothers, sisters, brothers, and cousins—in short, as part of a familial network that was rooted not in time and place but in relationships of affection and obligation. In many ways, this part of the emigrants world rested on imagined landscapes, faces, and relationships. For the Gemmills, the Scotts, the Wilson brothers, and the thousands of others both at home and away, this transatlantic web of kin and community was central to their lives.

NOTES

1. Pengelly Family Papers, Harriet Pengelly Diary, 27 May 1835, Trent University Archives (TUA), 70–001/1/4.
2. Ibid., 26 May 1835.
3. Ibid., 29 May 1835.
4. Ibid., 5 June 1835.
5. Ibid., 8 June 1835.
6. Ibid., 10 June 1835.
7. Ibid., 14 July 1835. See also 26 August 1835, when Harriet wrote: 'Received a nice long letter from Sophy . . . very, very happy.'
8. Ibid., 14 March, 12 April 1835.
9. Ibid., 6 April, 8 May 1835.
10. Ibid., 26 March, 28 May 1835; also 3 March 1836, when she noted 'a very disagreeable day' and that she had written three letters.
11. Harriet Pengelly Diary, 20 August 1835; also 14 August; 5, 10, 12 and 22 September, 1 October 1835.
12. Ibid., 21 August 1835. See also 27 February, 5 March 1836.
13. Ibid., 4 October 1835. See also reference to returning home, 21 July 1835.
14. Ibid., 3 January 1836. See also 16 December and 29 November 1835.
15. Ibid., 1 January 1836.

16. Charlotte Erickson, *Invisible Immigrants* (Ithaca & London: Cornell University Press, 1972) was one of the first historians to gather and analyze nineteenth-century immigrant letters. Not surprisingly, she discovered that most surviving letters were from immigrants of the literate, 'middling' ranks of British society. David Fitzpatrick's ground-breaking study, *Oceans of Consolation: Personal Accounts of Irish Migration to Australia* (Ithaca & London: Cornell University Press, 1994), gathers and rests on letters from those who travelled steerage.

17. Harriet Pengelly Diary, 3 August 1835.

18. Journals of George Pashley, 2 or 3 December, Archives of Ontario (AO) MU843.

19. Jane Harrison, *Until Next Year: Letter Writing and the Mails in the Canadas, 1640–1830* (Ottawa: Canadian Postal Museum and the Canadian Museum of Civilization, 1997), 2, notes that in a somewhat earlier period, literacy, at least in Lower Canada, was relatively high. The collection of letters in Wendy Cameron, Mary McDougall Maude, and Shiela Haines, eds., *English Immigrant Voices* (Montreal and Kingston: McGill-Queen's University Press, 2000), attests to this in the Upper Canadian situation; Cameron notes that among the Petworth emigrants, about one-third were literate (ibid., xxvii–ix).

20. In addition to those in *Voices*, see letter of John Connel, 12 July 1845, National Library of Scotland (NLS), ACC7021. See also journal of George Forbes from Canada to Aberdeenshire, included in letter of 18 July 1845; Forbes's first letter was sent to 'Dear Parents' on 23 May 1845 (Forbes Letters, Scottish Record Office [SRO], RH4/80).

21. William Knox to Andrew Redford, 28 October 1838, Redford Papers, SRO, GD1/815/15.

22. See, for example, the letter of Rebecca Longhurst to Mrs Weller (mother), 4 October 1832, no. 31, *Voices*, 61.

23. See letter of Simeon Titmouse to — Jackson, 11 September 1832, no. 23, *Voices*, 47.

24. William Hewitt to father and mother, William and Elizabeth Hewitt, 6 July 1836, no. 108, *Voices*, 206. See also Henry Smart to James Napper, 5 November 1832, no. 44, *Voices*, 77.

25. 5 August 1832, no. 16, *Voices*, 33.

26. This is the salutation for the letter of Richard Neal, 20 July 1832, no. 5, *Voices*, 16.

27. Letter to John Colquhoun, 10 December 1823, 'Emigrant Letters', SRO, GD1/814/5. See also John Barnes to his father, 1 January 1837, no. 126, *Voices*, 246–50, which included specific directions on how and to whom it was to be distributed; also letter of Jesse Penfeld to Mr and Mrs Hill, 1 January 1833, no. 50, *Voices*, 94.

28. Upton to mother, 19 September 1832, no. 27, *Voices*, 52–3.

29. William Phillips to Mrs Newall, 5 August 1832, no. 13, *Voices*, 30.

30. Simeon Titmouse to — Jackson, 11 September 1832, no. 23, *Voices*, 48.

31. John Luff to Aunt Foster, 29 July 1832, no. 11, *Voices*, 25–6.

32. References to this appear in almost all letters or journals. See, for example, letter of Richard Neal to William and Abigail Neal, 18 November 1832, no. 46, *Voices*, 79, which stated, 'I have sent you a letter in July; but I have not had any answer yet: but Hope you will send me one soon.' See also Edward and Hannah Bristow letter to brother, 20 July 1833, no. 82, *Voices*, 138.

33. See chapters 1 and 4 above and Elizabeth Jane Erringron, *Wives and Mothers, School Mistresses and Scullery Maids* (Kingston & Montreal: McGill-Queen's University Press, 1995), chap. 3, for discussion of desertion within the colony.

34. Gemmill Family Papers, John Gemmill to Andrew Gemmill, 25 June 1823, SRO, TD293.

35. Ibid., 6 December 1826. See also a later letter, 2 May 1828, asking Andrew to find the brother of William Miller, who wanted him to write because he was 'anxious'.

36. John Gemmill to Andrew Gemmill, 6 August 1827.

37. Ibid., 17 September 1828.

38. See Thomas Adsett to his father, 25 June 1833, no. 71, *Voices*, 123, which ended: 'Wrote by James Rapson: his wife and family are all well.' Also Elizabeth Wackford to Mrs Sarah Green, 25 June 1833, no. 71, Voices, 124–5. See discussion in *Voices*, xix. The problems of literacy went both ways. For example, Charles Johnston wrote to his former employer, Thomas Tryon, Esq., announcing his arrival and asking him to pass on news to family members; he also asked Tryon to

let him know how his wife's parents were, since they could not write; and he sent on a message to his brother that if he intended to emigrate, he should write and Johnston would 'remain here till he comes' (Tryon of Bulwick Collection, Northamptonshire Record Office [NRO], TB869).

39. For example, his August 1836 letter concluded, 'John Heather from Petworth wishes you to call at Botting's, to know how his sister is at Redhill: he is well' (James Rapson letter, 30 August 1836, no. 115, *Voices*, 214). See also Rapson letters nos. 2, 12, 38, 76, in *Voices*, and letters of his in-laws, the Tribes, Henry and Charlotte Tribe (12 February 1833, no. 54, *Voices*, 102). The annotations in the published letters of the Sussex emigrants suggest that sometimes letters were communal undertakings, with two or three people writing individual notes to different recipients, well aware that all would read their news (*Letters from Sussex Emigrants* [Chichester, 1837], 37–41).

40. *Chronicle and Gazette*, 11 July 1835. A reward was also offered for information about James Honey, a tailor—either his current place of residence or a certificate attesting to his death (ibid., 19 August 1835).

41. *Farmer's Journal*, 13 May 1829. See also *Kingston Gazette*, 25 August 1818, looking for Alexander Langton, who had last been heard of in 1799 or 1800; *Kingston Chronicle*, 3 August 1819, looking for John Spence; *Kingston Chronicle*, 13 April 1821, looking for Donald Campbell, originally of Argyleshire, by agent in York.

42. *Kingston Chronicle*, 13 June 1829. See also *Cobourg Star*, 30 August 1843, Thomas Eyre of Cobourg and Richard Dingley, Esq., of Launceston, England, were looking for Edmund Turner Colwell, from Devon, who would learn something to his advantage.

43. See, for example, *Kingston Chronicle*, 4 July 1823, looking for William Holliday, native of Yorkshire; *Christian Guardian*, 19 April 1837, looking for 'Edward, the son of Anthony and Sarah Brown' of London, who was entitled to £2,000 from the estate of his maternal uncle: the solicitors were looking for him. Also *Cobourg Star*, 2 October 1844, Messrs Trehern & White, solicitors, in London were looking for John Blomfield, who had left home nine years before.

44. See discussion in *Voices*, xxxiii–xxxv.

45. See Harrison, *Until Next Year*, 125–7. David Gerber notes in *Authors of Their Lives* (New York: New York University Press, 2006) that sending letters overseas could be expensive and required planning and some knowledge of the postal system. For an intriguing discussion of 'Using the Postal Service', see ibid., chap. 4.

46. John Gemmill to 'Dear Wife and Family', 2 March 1822, with annotations that it was received on 23 November 1822, SRO, TD293.

47. Ibid., John to Andrew, 19 September 1823.

48. Isaac Wilson, Dear brother, 24 June 1821, Isaac Wilson Diaries.

49. Harriet Pengelly Diary, 5 September 1835, Pengelly Family Papers. In this particular sequence, Harriet became increasingly anxious, because she continued to check the mails (10 September, 12 September, 22 September, 1 October), but the long-awaited letters did not arrive until 3 October 1835. She noted similar delays and frustrations in later months.

50. Mary O'Brien Journals, 1 January 1836, AO.

51. See, for example, letters to Andrew of 1 June and 17 September 1823, SRO, TD293/1.

52. John Gemmill to Andrew, 21 June 1823.

53. Dear Brother, 24 June 1821, Isaac Wilson Diaries.

54. Wilson noted in a letter to his brother, 13 December 1834, Isaac Wilson Diaries, that he intended to send deeds home by private conveyance for exactly this reason.

55. Journals of George Pashley, February 1834, 16.

56. See Wilson letter to his brother, 26 April 1832, Isaac Wilson Diaries.

57. John Gemmill to Andrew, 21 June 1823.

58. Ibid., 21 November 1825.

59. Ibid., 21 May 1823.

60. Ibid., 21 June 1823.

61. Ibid., 8 June 1829.

62. Ibid., 17 September 1823.

63. Ibid., 6 December 1826.

64. In a remarkable passage, John passed on remarks from Jennett: 'She has not got the imitation of that Black Man you sent her yet', ibid.

65. Andrew to Mother and Father, 2 October 1824, ibid.

66. Ibid., John to Andrew, 30 April 1824.

67. Ibid., 8 November 1824.

68. Ibid., 21 November 1825. This image of the kettle was also invoked by John and Caroline Dearling to Brothers and Sisters (15 July 1838, no. 134, *Voices*, 276–7).

69. Ibid., John Gemmill to Andrew Gemmill, 25 September 1832.

70. Ibid., 8 November 1824.

71. Ibid., 24 November 1829. Five years earlier, John had replied to what appears to have been a thoughtful letter from Andrew: 'I take you kind advice . . . and I hope you will daily and hourly take to yourself the uncertainty of time and the precarious nature of all its enjoyments ought never to be forgot and our preparation for our eternal state ought to be our daily or hourly our constant study and employ as the basis of our Eternal felicity' (4 October 1824).

72. Ibid., 24 November 1829.

73. Ibid., 6 December 1826.

74. Ibid., 6 August 1827.

75. Ibid., 25 September 1832.

76. See Errington, *Wives and Mothers*, chap. 1, for an account of Mary making her decision.

77. Mary O'Brien Journals, AO, 13 February 1832.

78. Ibid., 15 April 1830, 14 February 1832, 13 July 1836.

79. Ibid., 25 July 1836.

80. The Miller Letters, TUA, B–70–1001, 24 March 1845.

81. See, among others, John Gemmill to Andrew, letters of 11 May and 21 June 1823, John Gemmill Family Papers, SRO.

82. Ibid., 6 August 1827.

83. Ibid., 8 June 1829.

84. Isaac Wilson Diaries. Isaac and his father had arrived in the colony in mid-1811. His father apparently returned home and John stayed. See 21 June and 19 November 1811.

85. Ibid., mentioned in letter of 24 May 1815.

86. Ibid., 30 August 1815. The letters/journal included considerable detail about the War of 1812, Wilson's sympathy with the Reformers in the 1830s, and a host of other political, social, and economic events in the colony.

87. See Isaac Wilson Diaries, 24 June 1817, 7 September 1819, and 15 November 1830.

88. See ibid., 24 June 1817 and 13 July 1822.

89. Isaac Wilson Diaries, 20 August 1815.

90. Ibid., 27 April 1824.

91. Ibid., 31 March 1827.

92. See, for example, letter of William Upton to his mother, 16 September 1832, no. 27, *Voices*, 53. See also Ann Thomas to Father, 15 October 1832, no. 37, *Voices*, 68–9; Thomas Adsett to Rev. Robert Bidsall, 21 December 1832, no. 49, *Voices*, 87–8. Charles Moore, on the other hand, in a letter to his father (c June 1833, no. 69, 110–11), told his father not to come: 'It is not fit for old people.'

93. George and Mary Boxall and William Tilly to family, 16 September 1832, no. 25, *Voices*, 50. See also George and Anna Hills to Father, Mother, Brother, and Sister, 8 March 1833, no. 63, *Voices*, 108–9, who 'hoped' that family members would 'ever be kind' to mother and father now living with them. John and Caroline Dearling to brother and sister, 15 July 1838, no. 134, ibid., 276–7.

94. Redford Papers, John Scott to Andrew Redford, 29 September 1835.

95. Mary O'Brien Journal, 20 June 1830 and 24 September 1835.

96. *Hutton of Hastings*, ed. Boyce, 2 July 1837, 57.

97. Ibid., 61.

98. Isaac Wilson Diaries, 28 October 1828. Newspapers were sent on 26 July 1830. In the early 1820s there were apparently problems having newspapers forwarded from Montreal (9 September 1820).

99. Ibid., 13 July 1822. See also 24 June 1821 and package that arrived with emigrant William Brown, 26 July 1830.

100. See, for example, Redford Papers, letter of Isabel Scott to her aunt Mrs Redford, 16 April 1840.

101. Ibid., John Scott to George Redford, 18 September 1840.

102. Ibid., undated letter, Archibald to his cousin.

103. Ibid.

104. Ibid., John Scott to cousin, October 1844.

105. Ibid., John Scott to Uncle Andrew Redford, 12 November 1845.

106. Ibid., William Knox to cousin, John Redford, 24 April 1843.

107. Ibid., John Scott to uncle Andrew Redford, 12 November 1845

4   From Robert J. Grace, 'Irish Immigration and Settlement in a Catholic City: Quebec, 1842–61', *Canadian Historical Review* 84(2) (2003): 217–251.

As British North America's leading port of entry in the first half of the nineteenth century, Quebec City witnessed an important influx of immigrants from Europe. Most of these people had embarked somewhere in the British Isles, and the Irish formed the largest group for much of the half-century. While the destination of most Irish immigrants lay to the west (Upper Canada) or south (United States) of the city, Quebec attracted its share of this Irish migration to the extent that, by 1861, over one-quarter of the total urban population was composed of Irish natives and their children.

Quebec was joined by other areas of major Irish settlement in British North America in the period: the Maritimes, rural Lower Canada, Montreal, Toronto, Hamilton, Kingston, and rural Upper Canada. Ontario has been the focus of several important studies of the Irish,[1] while Cecil Houston and William Smyth have examined Irish emigration to Canada and produced a geography of Irish settlement in the country.[2] The relative lack of research on the Irish in Quebec led me to complete a survey of the historiography for the province which was intended to stimulate further research in the field.[3] Montreal's Irish community has also been the object of recent study,[4] and work has likewise been done on the Irish in Halifax, Newfoundland, and New Brunswick.[5]

The main focus of most of these studies has been the pre-Famine period. Houston and Smyth note important regional differences in Irish emigration and settlement in central Canada, though they point out that most Irish in Canada were Protestants, that they settled mainly in rural areas, and that the pre-Famine era may be seen 'as definitive in the formation of Canadian Irish communities.'[6] In this article, I will investigate a neglected area of Irish settlement—in Quebec City—and analyze the Irish

community there before and after the Famine of 1845–9. As we shall see, the Catholic element within Quebec's Irish community was predominant throughout, but the character of the city's Irish population changed with the arrival of immigrants during the Famine and post-Famine years.[7] Thus, the common generalizations in the historiography on the Irish in Canada—a mostly pre-Famine rural settlement of Protestants—do not apply in Quebec City.

[. . .]

The principal sources for this study are the correspondence and annual reports and returns of the emigration agents posted at Quebec (A.C. Buchanan senior and his nephew of the same name, who took over the office in 1835), in addition to the manuscript censuses of Quebec City for 1842, 1852, and 1861. The Buchanans' annual reports were published in the *British Parliamentary Papers* from 1831 onwards, and all except those for 1844 and 1845 have been located in the various volumes of the 'Emigration' and 'Colonies–Canada' series.[8]

[. . .]

One problem that confronted the Buchanans every season was the tendency of many immigrants to go directly to the United States once they disembarked at Quebec. Given Buchanan's role, his estimates as to the numbers settling in the province each year are informed guesses and have a tendency to overstate the total actually remaining in the country. For example, Buchanan noted in 1831 that two-thirds of the immigrants who had arrived at Quebec from 1815 to 1828 went on to the United States. Buchanan himself arrived only in 1828, but, as Adams noted, the two-thirds proportion 'is perhaps as good a guess as any.'[9] This through migration continued to plague Buchanan and his nephew.[10] Indeed, between 1830 and 1841, over 250,000 Irish immigrants entered British North America, yet the number of Irish-born in the colony in the early 1840s was less than half that number (122,000).[11]

While the Buchanans' estimates on the number of immigrants who settled in Lower and Upper Canada were likely somewhat inflated, other data in their reports are particularly useful for the present study. Natives of County Tyrone, the Buchanans knew Irish emigration from the north of Ireland firsthand, especially the movement out of the ports of Belfast and Derry.[12] In giving evidence before Wilmot Horton's committee on emigration in 1827, the elder Buchanan stated: 'I dare say I have accompanied 6000 emigrants to America myself, within the last ten years.'[13] Thus, the Buchanans' familiarity with Irish emigration render their reports informative, at least with respect to the behaviour of the emigrants (the provisions they brought with them, the means by which they emigrated, their social status), if not their ultimate place of settlement. These reports further indicate the relative numbers of English, Irish, and Scottish natives in the movement to Quebec from year to year. Moreover, the annual distribution of Irish ports of embarkation is furnished, indicating the main source regions for Irish immigrants coming to Quebec before, during, and after the Great Famine. Throughout these reports,

the emigration agents comment on the general character of each year's immigration, and, after 1843, Buchanan junior began to compile the 'Trades or Callings' of the immigrants as they disembarked, allowing an assessment of the social status of the Irish entering the country.

While the emigration agents' reports indicate the rhythm, volume, source regions, and eventually the social status of the Irish coming to Canada by way of Quebec, the manuscript censuses provide detailed information on those who settled in Quebec City. The censuses, too, have their strengths and weaknesses. While the 1852 and 1861 censuses furnish several items of information for every individual in each household (name, age, sex, marital status, occupation, birthplace, religion), that of 1842 identifies only the name and occupation of the household head. The other individuals in the household remain masked behind subtotals (number of natives of Ireland, number of members of the Church of England, of the Church of Rome, etc.). The 1842 census contains a column entitled 'Number of years each person has been in the Province, when not natives thereof.' Census officials dutifully collected this information in five of the six Quebec City wards; the enumerator of Saint Peter's ward left the column blank, for some unknown reason.

Table 1 Total Urban Population by Birthplace, Quebec City, 1842–71

Year	England	Scotland	Ireland	Canada: French Origin	Canada: Not French Origin	Other	Total
1842	1,301	735	5,023	19,251	5,142	350	31,802
1852	1,280	648	6,344	24,506	6,985	2,169	42,052
1861	1,488	792	7,373	28,689	11,346	732	51,109
1871	1,127	487	4,941	40,890	11,786	468	59,699

Source: 1842 Census Recapitulation by Ward; *Census of the Canadas, 1851–52* (Quebec 1853); *Census of the Canadas, 1860–61* (Quebec 1863); *Census of Canada, 1870–71* (Ottawa 1873).

To better understand the evolution of Quebec City's Irish population, I used the 1842, 1852, and 1861 censuses to construct three comprehensive data sets. For the 1842 census, by carefully examining the surnames of household heads, the number of Irish-born in each household, and the number of years immigrants had been in the province, I established a data bank of the identifiable Irish population of the city, made up of 1267 households containing a total of 3,811 Irish natives. This number works out to a proportion of the total Irish-born population as indicated by the recapitulation of the city by wards (5,023) of 76 per cent. For the 1852 and 1861 censuses, however, I selected all enumerated Irish-born individuals and co-residents from all city wards (six in 1852, eight in 1861).

[. . .]

Using the data on birthplace in these censuses, we can arrive at an approximate distribution of the various ethnic groups of the city (see Table 1). No estimate is needed for the largest group, the French Canadians, because a column is reserved for natives of Canada of French origin. For the others—the English, Scots, and Irish—we have the relative proportions of natives of each country and 'Natives of Canada Not of French Origin', in other words, the sum of the Canadian-born offspring of the above three groups of foreign-born. To complete the table and for comparative purposes, the data for 1871 have been added.

The quality of these four census reports varies greatly. The 1842 and 1871 censuses were well conducted and do not appear to contain serious errors. The 1852 and 1861 census reports, however, each have their share of anomalies.[14] Most significant, the numbers of English, Scottish, and Irish natives are inflated in 1861. In fact, the number of Irish natives found in the manuscript schedules (6,531) comes nowhere near the figure reported in the published report (7,373). [. . .] According to historian John Hare and colleagues, the anomalies are due to the enumerators' inclusion of British soldiers or others in Saint Louis ward.[15]

In addition to the errors in the compilation procedures for 1852 and 1861, what is striking in Table 1 is the number of Irish-born in the city before (1842) and after (1871) the Great Irish Famine of 1845–9. Indeed, the figures are nearly identical, 5,023 in 1842 and 4,941 in 1871. However, as we shall see shortly, the cultural or religious composition of the Irish-born population of the city had changed markedly by 1871.

[. . .]

In their study of Irish emigration to Canada, Houston and Smyth have examined the flow of emigrants from Irish ports to Canadian destinations. They note, for example, important trading links between Belfast and Dublin and the port of Quebec and between Derry and Saint John.[16] I will add to these findings through a systematic analysis of the distribution of Irish ports of embarkation in the movement to Quebec in the first half of the nineteenth century. Since Buchanan's reports for 1844 and 1845 have not been located, the data on the relative distribution of Irish ports in the migration to Quebec are presented for two periods: 1831–43 and 1846–54. To provide perspective, Table 2 presents the Irish proportion of total immigration to Quebec for eight four-year periods between 1829 and 1860.[17]

Over the entire period the Irish proportion of total immigration at the port of Quebec stood close to 60 per cent, though the 1840s show the highest Irish component—between 70 and 74 per cent of the total. Of course, these four-year periods hide some exceptional years, such as 1840, when 88 per cent of all immigrants (22,234) were Irish natives. Other years of important Irish immigration were 1831 (34,000 of a total of 50,000), 1841 (21,000 out of 28,000), 1842 (31,000 out of 44,000), and 1846 (26,000 out of 32,000). The exceptional year of 1847 witnessed the all-time high of the period in terms of both total immigration (100,000) and the number of Irish natives (70,000). The Irish continued to arrive in numbers and constituted the majority until 1854, when the Irish proportion fell to 39 per cent. Thereafter, English, Scots, Germans, and Norwegians made up the bulk of immigrants arriving at Quebec.

Considering Irish migration to Quebec in this period as a whole, the pre-Famine period (up to and including 1844) accounted for 48 per cent of the total. The Famine and post-Famine period (1845–60) saw the arrival of 52 per cent.[18] Furthermore, as we have seen, less than half of the pre-Famine arrivals were still in Canada at the first censuses in the early 1840s. Of course, some Irish of the Famine and post-Famine years also passed through on their way south.[19] Those who remained can be found in the 1852 and 1861 censuses. [. . .]

The Buchanans, while meticulous in their compilations of the ports of embarkation of immigrants arriving at Quebec, were usually silent on the religion of the people. One exception to this rule may be found in the evidence given before Horton's committee on emigration by the elder Buchanan. In 1826 he stated that, for the past ten years, 'three-fourths were Protestants and Dissenters and about one-fourth Catholics. Latterly, there are more Catholics than there were.'[20] Presumably, Buchanan is here describing the movement out of the north of Ireland with which he was most familiar. [. . .]

David Fitzpatrick's survey of Irish emigration in the nineteenth century has shown that, from the 1840s onwards, the vast majority of Irish emigrants were Roman Catholics.[21] Adams noted this long ago, and Ó Gráda's more recent study of Irish immigration through New York and Boston has confirmed the increasingly Catholic and proletarian nature of the movement from the mid-1830s.[22] The shift in

Table 2 Total and Irish Immigration to Quebec by Four-Year Periods, 1829–60

Years	Total	Irish	% Irish
1829–32	145,945	90,251	61.8
1833–36	92,942	50,917	54.8
1837–40	54,840	40,706	74.2
1841–44	114,329	79,774	69.8
1845–48	182,951	136,173	74.4
1849–52	148,925	96,692	64.9
1853–56	132,242	46,620	35.3
1857–60	63,835	3,962	6.2
Total	**936,009**	**545,095**	**58.2**

Source: Buchanans' annual reports, *British Parliamentary Papers* (BPP).

Pre famine it was a mix

777

Table 3 Percentage of Catholics and Protestants in Irish Households by Period of Immigration of Household Head, Quebec City, 1842 (N=1067)

Period of Immigration	Number of Households	Catholics (%)	Protestants (%)	Irish-Born (%)
1800–19	74	49	51	43
1820–23	118	60	40	49
1824–27	140	72	28	54
1828–31	178	68	32	57
1832–35	244	60	40	63
1836–39	138	70	30	71
1840–41	175	71	29	89

Source: Based on a total of 1067 Irish households enumerated in the 1842 manuscript census of Quebec City, which indicated the year of arrival of the household head.

source regions from the north to the southwest observed in the movement to Quebec points to an increase in the proportion of Catholics leaving during the Famine and post-Famine periods. However, even before the Famine, among those Irish who chose to settle in Quebec City, Catholics formed the larger group. According to our data from the 1842 census, Protestants constituted 35 per cent of the total Irish population in the city.[23]

As stated previously, the 1842 census contains a column on the number of years immigrants had been in the province. In the case of the Irish in Quebec City, this information is provided for 1,067 Irish households, the enumerator of Saint Peter's ward having left the column blank. Since data on religion and birthplace were presented as subtotals, there is no efficient way to separate out the locally born children of the immigrants in Table 3, which summarizes the data on the period at which Irish household heads migrated. Therefore, to

keep matters in perspective, the proportion of Irish-born people in each cluster of households is provided in the last column on the right. To avoid disproportionately large and small clusters, the data are presented in four-year periods, except for the very early years (1800–19) and the last period of heavy Irish immigration (1840–1).

Thus, although imperfect because of the presence in each household of locally born individuals, these data show a Catholic majority for every period except that of 1800–19 when the Protestant presence is just over one-half. Despite the overall Catholic majority, an ever increasing Catholic presence is not observed. Rather, in addition to the first two decades, significant Irish Protestant settlement in the city occurred in the early 1820s and early 1830s, while relatively more Catholics settled in the mid-to-late 1820s, late 1830s, and early 1840s.

Further evidence of the increasingly Catholic composition of the migration stream from the 1840s may be obtained from the 1852 and 1861 manuscript censuses and studies of Irish communities elsewhere in Canada in the period. It is possible, for example, to ascertain the relative size of the Protestant and Catholic elements among Irish immigrants to Quebec in the Famine and post-Famine years by using the censuses of 1852 and 1861. The relative size of each group in the migration stream beginning in 1845 may be obtained by restricting analysis to the Irish-born ages zero to six in the 1852 census. The results show an Irish-born population in that age cohort composed, respectively, of 85.5 per cent Catholics and 14.5 per cent Protestants.[24] In 1861, choosing Irish-born individuals ages zero to fifteen (to reach back, as it were, to the beginning of the Famine in Ireland), the proportion of each group is as follows: 84.3 per cent Catholic, 15.7 per cent Protestant.[25] It could be argued that Quebec City, being a predominantly Catholic society, was attracting a disproportionately large Catholic segment of the flow of Irish immigrants to Canada in the period. However, in his study of the population of Hamilton, Ontario, Michael Katz observed a similar phenomenon from 1852 to 1861: 'their [Irish Catholics'] assessed population increase, 76 percent, nearly doubled that of the city as a whole', while that of Irish Protestants stagnated 'with a small 7 percent increase.'[26] A similar situation prevailed elsewhere as well. Bettina Bradbury's study of Montreal's working families shows a net predominance of Irish Catholics over Irish Protestants beginning in the early 1840s.[27]

[. . .]

The foregoing analysis of the religious affiliations of the Irish population of Quebec City from 1842 to 1861 shows the increasingly Catholic composition of that population over the period. Not only were fewer Irish Protestant families settling in the city in those years but some were leaving the city. [. . .]

The historiography on the question of the social status of the Irish immigrants who came to Canada presents two conflicting images. On the one hand, some historians who have

written on the Irish in Canada interpret the movement out of Ireland as one of small tenant farmers.[28] On the other hand, several studies have shown this migration to have been composed of a majority of unskilled labourers and female domestic servants.[29] [. . .]

As we shall see shortly, there is ample evidence of an initial immigration of Irish farmers to Quebec in the twenty years after Waterloo. However, in the mid-1830s, several contemporaries noted a change in status among the Irish disembarking at Quebec, as agricultural and common labourers replaced farmers and came to constitute a dear majority during the Famine and post-Famine periods.

While there is little doubt about the destitution of these Irish labourers in nineteenth-century Ireland, many thousands were able to emigrate because of an important and widespread Irish institution in the period—the remittance system. This practice, whereby the initial 'pioneer' emigrant in a family wasted little time in sending back from North America money or a pre-paid passage to permit the emigration of others, was very common. As Fitzpatrick has noted: 'The assistance offered by state, landlords and philanthropists was dwarfed by that sent home by emigrants to their families . . . It seems certain that the great majority of Irish emigrants owed their basic passage money to their predecessors.'[30] Furthermore, MacDonagh has pointed out that more than a half of all Irish emigrants of the nineteenth century, regardless of destination, were unable to raise their passage from their own resources. Their emigration was financed by remittances or prepaid passages from friends and relatives gone out before them.[31]

Both before and after he came to Quebec, the elder Buchanan observed the role of remittances in financing Irish emigration to Canada. Giving evidence before Horton's committee, he stated in 1826 that 'we can always tell in the season before, in the north of Ireland, whether we are likely to have a large emigration; it depends upon the success that the emigrants met with in the preceding year;

they write home letters, and if the season has been favourable . . . they send home flattering letters, and they send home money to assist in bringing out their friends.'[32] In his annual report for 1832, the emigration agent noted 'a very great disposition among the working Emigrants of last and preceding seasons to find opportunities to get transmitted their little earnings to the United Kingdom to aid their friends coming out to join them.'[33] A few years later, the younger Buchanan observed a similar disposition among the arrivals of the 1838 season. 'It may be remarked that most of these emigrants came out from home to join friends who have preceded them, and who, having advantageously established themselves in these provinces, had remitted money to Europe to enable their relatives to join them here.'[34]

[. . .]

Some Irish merchants and their agents based in Quebec were in the habit of facilitating the transfer of these remittances or prepaid passages from Canada to Ireland. In a letter to the Select Committee on Emigration dated 31 May 1827, the Dublin merchant John Astle explained how this system worked. 'During the past three years, I have authorized my agent in Quebec to receive cash from persons who wish to provide passage, and, if required, food, for their nominees from this country to Canada . . . The persons who pay the money are generally relatives, and quite capable of receiving and providing for their friends.'[35] The merchants Ryan Brothers and Co. of Quebec were also involved in the remittance business. In an advertisement entitled 'Emigration for 1843', which appeared in the local papers, the Ryan Brothers, 'Agents for P.W. Byrne, Liverpool . . . will give orders for passages to Canada from the ports of Liverpool, Dublin, Cork, Belfast, and Londonderry, in good and seaworthy Vessels, to sail next Spring . . . Money orders will also be given on the above places, for small sums, if required, for the accommodation of persons taking passage by Mr Byrne's ships.'[36]

[. . .]

In later reports, Buchanan continued to describe the means by which Irish emigrants were able to reach Quebec. Noting in 1844 that 'a very considerable portion of the year's emigration' consisted 'in persons and families whose means are very limited', the emigration agent went on to comment on the cumulative effect of the chain migration of the poor. 'This description of emigrants may be expected to be constantly on the increase; as the family pioneers who annually arrive here, permit only a short time to pass over without sending to assist some of their relatives to join them.'[37] Anthony B. Hawke, emigration agent for Upper Canada based in Kingston, also noted this trait among Irish emigrants to the country. Commenting on the 1846 season, he noted 'a large number of the Irish emigrants in a state of destitution as to clothes and bedding far exceeding anything I ever before witnessed'. Hawke wrote further that 'a very considerable amount is remitted annually from this colony in small sums, by those who have emigrated in previous years, to assist their relations to come to Quebec.'[38]

[. . .]

As previously mentioned, the social status of the Irish emigrant who disembarked at Quebec changed as the half-century progressed. Adams and, more recently, Ó Gráda both observed a modification in the class of Irish emigrants from the mid-1830s: initially a movement of small farmers and artisans from the north of Ireland, after the mid-1830s the labourer became omnipresent. The observations of the two Buchanans and Hawke, in addition to studies of nineteenth-century Irish society, appear to bear out this trend.

Indeed, the higher status of the immigrants disembarking at Quebec in the first three decades of the nineteenth century comes through clearly in the statements made by Buchanan. In his testimony before Horton's committee on colonization in 1827, Buchanan observed that 'we cannot call the emigrants that pass through Quebec a pauper emigration.'[39] In his annual report on emigration to Quebec in 1831, when a record 34,000 Irish settlers arrived, Buchanan went into some detail in describing the Irish he saw: 'Very many respectable and wealthy farmers came out this year from almost every portion of Ireland, but more particularly from the counties of Armagh, Fermanagh, Cavan, Leitrim, Mayo, Sligo, Tyrone, Dublin, Limerick and Wexford.' The capital brought to the colony by these emigrants he notes as 'exceedingly great'. In his weekly returns the following year, Buchanan again noted this wealthier type of emigrant: 'The majority of emigrants continues of a class superior to former years.'[40] However, in his report for 1840, Hawke remarked that the status of the immigrants arriving in Canada changed in 1834. 'Previous to the year 1834 a considerable proportion of the emigrants to the Canadas were persons of capital . . . but since 1834 the character of our emigrants has undergone a rapid change. We have had few settlers of capital, and, generally speaking, the voluntary emigrants have been persons in very narrow circumstances.'[41]

This change to a more humble status among the Irish to Canada in the mid-1830s is evident in Buchanan's reports. Thus, for the week ending on 21 June 1834, he notes that a 'considerable number of the working classes arrived this week, principally from Ireland.' In his annual report on emigration for 1840, a year in which the Irish component of total arrivals stood at nearly 90 per cent, Buchanan again comments on the status of the emigrants: 'The majority of the emigrants this year were common labourers, very poor, in the possession of mere physical strength, without much capacity for using it even in their humble vocation . . . Fully one-half were of this class, unacquainted with the ordinary duties of a farm servant, and unfit for any work beyond the use of spade and pick-axe. They came chiefly from the west and south of Ireland . . . from Sligo, Westport, Killala and Limerick and landed generally in good health, but in a state of great destitution.'[42] A similar situation prevailed in the Irish migration to New Brunswick. In his study of Saint John, T.W. Acheson notes that the 'composition of the immigration began

to change in the early 1840s and was characterized by a high proportion of agricultural labourers—a euphemism for those possessing neither urban skills nor knowledge of the more important agricultural technologies.' The emigration agent at Saint John, Israel Perley, claimed that 82 per cent of the immigrants of 1845 were agricultural labourers.[43]

This progressive predominance of Irish labourers in the movement to North America is not surprising, given their numbers in mid-nineteenth-century Ireland. Of the 8.2 million inhabitants of the island on the eve of the Famine in 1845, an estimated 3.3 million were labourers; 1.4 million, cottiers; and 500,000, small tenant farmers.[44] As we have seen, Irish agricultural labourers, the largest group in Ireland in this period, disappeared as a class because of their emigration to North America among other things. And Quebec was on the receiving end of this important migration.

[. . .]

In September 1851 the *Morning Chronicle* in Quebec City made note of this continuing exodus. 'The rush across the Atlantic shows no sign of subsidence . . . Farm labourers are now so scarce in the South of Ireland that agriculturists have to pay them 7s a week with diet, for cutting hay alone; while, in some instances, they demand 9s for saving the corn crops.'[45] As this contemporary's observation demonstrates, it was the Irish labourer whose absence was felt in post-Famine Ireland. Lacking the skills of the artisan and the resources to begin farming, these labourers were dependent on immediate employment for their family's survival. That is why many are to be found on the public works and in the cities in nineteenth-century Canada. However, important regional differences in Irish settlement patterns are evident: the Irish in Quebec were more Catholic and urbanized, while those in Ontario were largely Protestant and settled mainly in rural areas.

[. . .]

The Quebec Irish were both more Catholic and more urbanized than their Ontario counterparts, and the place of the Irish in each province's total population differed. In Ontario in 1871, for example, the number of people of Irish origin was 559,442, while the number of people of English and Scottish origin was 768,318. In the province of Quebec in the same year, people of Irish origin, 123,478, outnumbered those of English and Scottish origin combined (119,280). Overall, in 1871 people of Irish origin accounted for 34.5 per cent of the total population of Ontario (1,620,851) and 10.4 per cent of the total population of Quebec (1,191,516), but a greater proportion of people of Irish origin in Quebec were Irish natives (29 per cent) than was the case in Ontario (27.5 per cent).[46] Whether of Irish birth or origin in the province of Quebec, these people could be found from the Gaspé peninsula in the east to the Ottawa Valley in the west, with concentrations in Montreal, Quebec City, and the Eastern Townships.[47]

Further differences in Irish settlement patterns between the two central Canadian provinces are apparent when we compare degrees of urbanization. In Ontario in 1871, for example, 18 per cent of Irish natives lived in cities of over 5,000 inhabitants, a proportion similar to that of the general population. In the province of Quebec in 1871, over 44 per cent of Irish immigrants were in the cities, a level of urbanization nearly three times that of the general population (16 per cent). While Montreal, Canada's largest city, was home to most of these Irish city dwellers, Quebec City also harboured an important Irish population. As Table 4 shows, although they were present throughout the city, the Irish were most concentrated in the Lower Town, near the waterfront.

Some clear patterns emerge in an analysis of the spatial distribution of the city's different ethnic groups in the mid-nineteenth century. The Upper Town (Palace and Saint Louis wards) was the home of the city's élite and was the most cosmopolitan area of town. And while Saint Roch (with Jacques-Cartier ward) was the stronghold of the French Canadian population, nearly two-thirds of the Irish lived to the west, along the waterfront in Champlain and Saint Peter wards (Lower Town). The 'suburbs' in the above table include Saint John and Montcalm wards; in the former, the French constituted three-quarters of the population, while in the latter the Irish and French shared the territory with, respectively, 46 and 37 per cent of the ward's total population.[48]

Table 4 Estimated Ethnic Origins of Total Population by City Area, Quebec City, 1861

City Area	Anglo-Scots (%)	Irish (%)	French Canadian (%)	Other (%)	Total Number
Upper Town	26.7	33.7	32.8	6.8	6,904
Lower Town	6.4	62.6	28.5	2.5	8,403
Saint Roch	5.1	9.9	82.5	2.5	18,770
Suburbs	11.2	29.7	55.6	3.5	15,386
Total	**10.3**	**28.3**	**58.0**	**3.4**	**49,463**

Source: Derived from *Census of the Canadas 1860–61*, vol. 1 (Quebec 1863)

Table 5 Total Irish Population by City Area and Religion, Quebec City, 1861

City Area	Irish Protestants (%)	Irish Catholics (%)	Total Number
Upper Town	27.3	72.7	1,625
Lower Town	9.5	90.5	4,814
Saint Roch	32.4	67.6	1,751
Suburbs	28.3	71.7	3,952
Total	**21.3**	**78.7**	**12,142**

Source: 1861 manuscript census. Religion not available in one case. Total Irish population is 12,143.

The spatial distribution throughout the city of the two Irish cultural groups, Protestants and Catholics, reveals these settlement patterns in greater detail (see Table 5). Thus, overall, Irish Catholics outnumbered their Protestant counterparts by nearly four to one, but the latter were relatively more present in Saint Roch (where they were significantly involved in shipbuilding), in the suburbs (especially Montcalm ward), and in the Upper Town, where many senior civil servants, clergy, professionals, and merchants had their residences. A sizeable proportion of Irish residents of the Upper Town were Irish Catholic women employed as domestics.[49] The Irish Catholics were most heavily concentrated in the Lower Town (Champlain and Saint Peter wards), where they represented nine out of ten Irish people. Here, a majority of Irish men worked at ship labouring, loading and unloading vessels in the transatlantic trade in timber. Yet, despite this 'Little Ireland' of the waterfront, among the Irish, Catholics constituted the majority in all areas of the city and, as we shall see, were involved in nearly all sectors of the local economy.

[. . .]

The population of Quebec City, contrary to that of most other Canadian cities in the nineteenth century, was mostly Catholic.

Indeed, in 1871, nearly nine out of ten individuals professed that religion.[50] By contrast, in most other Canadian cities in this period, Irish Catholics faced the sustained and often well-organized opposition and competition of a large Protestant working class. [. . .] In Quebec City, in contrast, the very Catholic composition of the population appears to have favoured the Irish Catholics who settled in the city in that they were able to diversify their occupational choices. According to a study of the city's police force, a two-thirds majority of the policemen were Irish Catholics.[51] In fact, the chief police magistrate or superintendent and inspector of police in the 1850s and 1860s, John Maguire, was himself an Irish-born Catholic. In other areas too, such as tide waiting, customs, and timber culling, the number of Irish Catholic males in these jobs increased over the 1850s in Quebec City.[52] Moreover, most Irish cullers were Catholic, as was their Irish-born supervisor, William Quinn.[53] Furthermore, the city elected two Irish Catholic mayors in the nineteenth century (Charles Alleyn, 1854–5, and Owen Murphy, 1874–8).[54] Irish men working at loading and unloading ships involved in the transatlantic trade in timber founded a benevolent society in 1862 which soon became an important trade union—the most powerful of its kind in the nineteenth century, according to some historians.[55] It would appear that being Catholic in a predominantly Catholic society helped rather than hindered Irish integration into the city's economy. Research on the Irish and others in Montreal in the second half of the nineteenth century also shows some upward social mobility for Irish Catholics.[56]

In conclusion this brief look at Irish immigration and settlement in Quebec City confirms [. . . that] among those who chose to settle in the city, a clear Catholic majority was evident before and after the Famine—pointing to the presence of Ulster Catholics in the earlier period. In fact, both the superintendent of police, Maguire, and the supervisor of cullers, Quinn, were Catholics from the Ulster counties of Fermanagh and Derry, respectively.

[. . .] Initially a movement of farmers, farmers' sons, artisans, and labourers in which Protestants appear to have constituted a majority (especially in the first three decades of the century), the migration to Quebec became progressively more Catholic and proletarian. Buchanan's compilations of the trades of male immigrants arriving at Quebec in the 1846–54 period show a clear predominance of common and agricultural labourers. As several studies of Irish emigration have shown, at least 80 per cent of these people were Catholics. Thus, although statistics based on Irish origin data

from the 1871 census show a Protestant majority, Catholics were the larger group among the Irish-born in Canada in that year. Such was the case, for example, in Montreal, Hamilton, and Quebec City. Indeed, Quebec harboured an Irish-born population of around 5,000 both before (1842) and well after the Famine (1871), indicating an important settlement of Irish people in the Famine and post-Famine years. This Irish population became progressively more Catholic because of both the very Catholic immigration of the period and Protestant out-migration.

A comparison of settlement patterns with Ontario shows a much more urbanized Irish population in the province of Quebec. Moreover, the Irish were by far the largest non-French group in the province. In the city of Quebec, they settled in all areas but were concentrated in the western part along the waterfront, where nearly two-thirds of the total Irish population lived and worked. [. . .]

Unlike the situation in most other Canadian cities in the period with majority Protestant populations, in very Catholic Quebec Irish Catholics participated more fully in the local power structure. This was seen in policing, timber culling, and customs work, and in the fact that the city could boast two Irish Catholic mayors in the second half of the nineteenth century.

NOTES

1. See, for example, Donald H. Akenson, *The Irish in Ontario: A Study in Rural History* (Kingston: McGill-Queen's University Press 1984); Bruce S. Elliott, *Irish Migrants in the Canadas: A New Approach* (Kingston and Montreal: McGill-Queen's University Press 1988); Glenn J. Lockwood, *Montague: A Social History of an Irish Ontario Township, 1783–1980* (Smith Falls, Ont.: Corporation of the Township of Montague 1980).

2. Cecil J. Houston and William J. Smyth, *Irish Emigration and Canadian Settlement: Patterns, Links and Letters* (Toronto: University of Toronto Press 1990)

3. Robert J. Grace, *The Irish in Quebec: An Introduction to the Historiography* (Quebec: Institut québécois de recherche sur la culture 1993)

4. Patricia A. Thornton and Sherry Olson, 'The Tidal Wave of Irish Immigration to Montreal and Its Demographic Consequences', *Shared Spaces/Partage de l'espace*, 13 (Nov. 1993): 1–30

5. Terence M. Punch, *Irish Halifax: The Immigrant Generation, 1815–1859* (Halifax: International Education Centre, Saint Mary's University 1981); John J. Mannion, *Irish Settlements in Eastern Canada: A Study of Cultural Transfer*

and Adaptation (Toronto: University of Toronto Press 1974); Peter M. Toner, 'The Origins of the New Brunswick Irish, 1851', *Journal of Canadian Studies* 23, 1–2 (1988): 104–19

6.   Houston and Smyth, *Irish Emigration and Canadian Settlement*, 3–9; 23

7.   See Robert John Grace, 'The Irish in Mid-Nineteenth-Century Canada and the Case of Quebec: Immigration and Settlement in a Catholic City', 2 vols. (PhD dissertation, Université Laval 1999).

8.   *British Parliamentary Papers* (*BPP*) (Shannon: Irish University Press 1968–)

9.   W.F. Adams, *Ireland and Irish Emigration to the New World from 1815 to the Famine* (1932; New York: Russell & Russell 1967), 93

10. Oliver MacDonagh, *A Pattern of Government Growth, 1800–1860: The Passenger Acts and Their Enforcement* (London: MacGibbon and Kee 1961), 132

11. Adams, *Ireland and Irish Emigration*, 199

12. See Wesley B. Turner, 'Alexander Carlisle Buchanan', *Dictionary of Canadian Biography* 9 (Toronto and Quebec: University of Toronto Press and Les Presses de l'Université Laval 1977), 106–7.

13. 'Third Report from the Select Committee on Emigration from the United Kingdom': Evidence of A.C. Buchanan in *BPP–Emigration*, 2. These committees were appointed by the House of Commons in 1826 and 1827 to examine the broad subject of a national system of emigration. They were commonly known as Horton's committees, after the name of the chairman, Wilmot Horton. For the context surrounding their formation, see H.J.M. Johnston, *British Emigration Policy, 1815–1830. 'Shovelling Out Paupers'* (Oxford: Clarendon Press 1972), 91–128.

14. In the 1852 census report, for example, the birthplace for no fewer than 1819 people in the city is listed as 'Not Given'. In the 1861 census, a mere three people fall under this column, while in 1871 a birthplace is provided for the entire population. Thus, while for 1842, 1861, and 1871 the 'Other' column in Table 1 represents around 1 per cent, in 1852, owing to the latter problem, this proportion climbs to over 5 per cent. At the same time, the number of Irish-born in the 1852 census report (6,344) comes relatively close to the number of Irish natives found in the manuscript schedules (6,035). The 1861 census report reveals problems of another nature.

15. 'Il est probable que les recenseurs ont compté soit les militaires britanniques soit des immigrants de passage . . . En comparant le recensement de 1860–1861 à ceux qui précèdent et à celui de 1870–1871, il paraît évident que la population du quartier Saint-Louis est surévaluée en 1860–1861.' John Hare et al., *Histoire de la Ville de Québec, 1608–1871* (Montreal: Boréal Express et Musée canadien des civilisations 1987), 272 n. 27. The apparent great increase in the French population from 1861 (28,689) to 1871 (40,890) is due to the fact that the 1861 figure does not include the outlying areas of Saint Roch, 'la banlieue' (suburbs), which harboured at least 8,800 people in 1861, most of whom were French. Adding the latter figure to the French total in 1861 gives the more reasonable figure of 37,489. The increase of the French element from 1861 to 1871 is, therefore, on the order of 8 per cent. However, since the 1861 census report does not provide the various birthplaces of the population of the 'banlieue', we shall have recourse to the population of the city proper.

16. Houston and Smyth, *Irish Emigration and Canadian Settlement*, chap. 2: 'Emigrant Origins', 14–42

17. To account for the growing importance of Liverpool as a port of embarkation in the Irish migration to Quebec, the totals for 1844 and 1845 in Table 2 include the numbers who embarked at Irish ports in addition to 75 per cent of the total from England. Thus, the total for 1844 (15,068) is made up of Irish ports (9,498) and three-quarters of the total from England (5,570 of 7,426). For 1845, the proportions are as follows: 13,668 from Irish ports plus 6,337—that is, 75 per cent of the total from England (8,449).

18. The grand total of Irish for the entire period was 545,095, as indicated in Table 2. A total of 261,648 (or 48 per cent) disembarked at Quebec during the 1829–44 period. The years 1845–60 saw the arrival of 283,447 (or 52 per cent).

19. Such appears to have been the case in 1850 especially. Buchanan noted that 'the number who

have left the province is unusually large.' A.C. Buchanan, 'Annual Report on Emigration for 1850', in *BPP: Colonies–Canada*, 19. However, the reverse held true in some years when Irish labourers came up to Canada from the United States for work. In 1853, for example, an estimated 5,000 railroad labourers left the United States because of the depressed money market there and came north in search of work. See Hawke's report in the 'Annual Report on Emigration for 1853' in *BPP: Colonies–Canada*, 20. In correspondence with Buchanan the following year, Hawke again noted 'this disposition to leave the States and settle in Canada' and that 'the recent movements of the "native American", or as it is more generally called the "know-nothing" party, against foreigners, and more especially against the Irish Roman-Catholics, have been the chief cause.' 'Annual Report on Emigration for 1854', in *BPP: Colonies–Canada*, 21. On this question of through migration to the United States in the late 1840s and early 1850s, Gilbert Tucker remarked that there 'are no statistics to help us here. But there is good reason to think that in this period the population movements from Canada to the United States, and vice versa, came very close to balancing each other.' Gilbert Tucker, 'The Famine Immigration to Canada, 1847', *American Historical Review 36* (Oct. 1930): 548

20. 'First Report from the Select Committee on Emigration from the United Kingdom' in *BPP: Emigration*, 1 (1826): Evidence of A.C. Buchanan

21. David Fitzpatrick, *Irish Emigration, 1801–1921, Studies in Irish Economic and Social History 1* (Dublin: Dundalgan Press 1984), 13

22. 'Overall the data are in broad agreement with Adams's claim of a lowering of the socio-economic status of the emigrants after 1835 or so.' Cormac Ó Gráda, 'Across the Briny Ocean: Some Thoughts on Irish Emigration to America, 1800–1850', in Ira A. Glazier and Luigi De Rosa, eds., *Migration across Time and Nations: Population Mobility in Historical Contexts* (New York and London: Holmes & Meier 1982), 86

23. Grace, 'The Irish in Mid-Nineteenth-Century Canada', 1: table 3.14, 209

24. The total number of enumerated Irish-born individuals ages zero to six in Quebec City in

1852 was 228 (195 Catholics, 33 Protestants). Ibid., table 2.2, 152

25. The total number of enumerated Irish-born individuals ages zero to fifteen in Quebec City in 1861 was 489 (412 Catholics, 77 Protestants). Ibid., table 2.3, 153

26. Michael B. Katz, *The People of Hamilton, Canada West: Family and Class in a Mid-Nineteenth-Century City,* Harvard Studies in Urban History (Cambridge, Mass.: Harvard University Press 1975), 63

27. 'While Montreal had a sizeable component of Protestant Irish, the vast majority were Catholic.' Bettina Bradbury, *Working Families: Age, Gender, and Daily Survival in Industrializing Montreal* (Toronto: Oxford University Press 1993), 40, n. 57. See also figure 1.1, 42.

28. Houston and Smyth, *Irish Emigration and Canadian Settlement*; Donald H. Akenson, *Being Had: Historians, the Evidence and the Irish in North America* (Port Credit: P.D. Meany 1985); Wilson, *The Irish in Canada*

29. Kenneth Duncan, 'Irish Famine Immigration and the Social Structure of Canada West', *Canadian Review of Sociology and Anthropology* 12 (1965): 19–40; H. Clare Pentland, Labour and Capital in Canada, 1650–1860 (Toronto: James Lorimer 1981); Katz, *The People of Hamilton*; Peter Michael Toner, 'Occupation and Ethnicity: *The Irish in New Brunswick*', *Canadian Ethnic Studies* 20, 3(1988): 155–65; H.C. Pentland, 'The Lachine Strike of 1843', *Canadian Historical Review* 29, 3(1948): 255–77

30. Fitzpatrick, *Irish Emigration*, 1801–1921, 20–1

31. MacDonagh, *A Pattern of Government Growth*, 27–9. For a detailed and informative discussion of how the system of remittances worked, see chapter 2. 'The Problem'.

32. 'Second Report of the Select Committee on Emigration from the United Kingdom', in *BPP: Emigration*, 2 (1826–27): Evidence of A.C. Buchanan

33. A.C. Buchanan, 'Annual Report on Emigration for 1832', in *BPP: Emigration*, 19

34. A.C. Buchanan, 'Annual Report on Emigration for 1838', in *BPP: Emigration*, 20

35. Appendix No. 6 to 'Third Report of the Select Committee on Emigration', in *BPP: Emigration*, 2. Astle also stated in the letter

that since 'nearly all the parties, whose passage is so paid, are paupers and orphans, I have in future declined their conveyance . . . These unfortunate destitutes, however unfit for mercantile speculation, are exactly the parties, whose removal in a national view is most desirable; I would therefore strongly recommend that the colonial authorities be authorized to receive cash, or security, for passage from Ireland to Canada.'

36. Quebec Gazette, 18 Nov. 1842. The Ryan Brothers also handled landing money for the inmates of some of the Irish Poor Law Unions that sent out immigrants during and after the Famine. See Buchanan's weekly returns for 1852: '171 persons from the Rathdrum union were paid their landing money, amounting to 114 £ through Messrs. Ryan Brothers and Co. of this city.' A.C. Buchanan, 'Annual Report on Emigration for 1852', in BPP: Colonies–Canada, 20

37. Excerpt from Buchanan's annual report dated 'Quebec, 20th December, 1844', in Fifth General Report of the Colonial Land and Emigration Commission (1845) in BPP: Emigration, 10

38. Hawke's report in A.C. Buchanan, 'Annual Report on Emigration for 1846', in BPP: Colonies–Canada, 17

39. 'Second Report of the Select Committee on Emigration from the United Kingdom', in BPP: Emigration, 1 (1827): Evidence of A.C. Buchanan

40. A.C. Buchanan, 'Annual Report on Emigration for 1831', in BPP: Emigration, 19; A.C. Buchanan, 'Weekly Returns on Emigration for 1832', ibid.

41. A.B. Hawke, 'Report on Emigration to Upper Canada', in BPP: Colonies–Canada, 15

42. A.C. Buchanan, 'Weekly Returns for 1834' in BPP: Emigration, 19; 'Annual Report on Emigration for 1840', in BPP: Colonies–Canada, 15

43. T.W. Acheson, Saint John: The Making of a Colonial Urban Community (Toronto: University of Toronto Press 1985), 96

44. Cormac Ó Gráda, The Great Irish Famine, New Studies in Economic and Social History (Cambridge: Cambridge University Press 1995), table 1.2, 18

45. Morning Chronicle, 15 Sept. 1851

46. Census of Canada, 1870–71, vol. 1

47. For a survey of these settlements, see chapter 3, 'The Dynamics of Irish Settlement', in Grace, The Irish in Quebec.

48. These proportions are discussed in greater detail in chapter 3, 'Settlement Patterns', in Grace, 'The Irish in Mid-Nineteenth-Century Canada', 1: 171–265.

49. Of the 1034 Irish immigrants in Saint Louis and Palace wards in 1861, 679 were women. Of this number, 548 (or 80.7 per cent) were Catholics.

50. Hare et al., Histoire de la Ville de Québec, tableau 13, 327

51. Michael McCulloch, 'Most Assuredly Perpetual Motion: Police and Policing in Quebec City, 1838–1858.' Urban History Review/Revue d'histoire urbaine 19, 2 (1990): 100–12. This statistic is for the year 1854.

52. Grace, 'The Irish in Mid-Nineteenth-Century Canada.' 2: tables 6.1 to 6.6, 432–42

53. See, for example, William Quinn, Report of the Supervisor of Cullers, on the Lumber Trade (Quebec: 'Morning Chronicle' 1861).

54. See Les Maires de la Vieille Capitale (Quebec: La Société Historique de Québec 1980).

55. Jacques Rouillard and Judith Burt, 'Le monde ouvrier', in Noel Bélanger et al., Les travailleurs québécois, 1851–1896 (Montreal: Presses de l'Université du Québec 1973), 67–70

56. Jason Gilliland and Sherry Olson, 'Claims on Housing Space in Nineteenth-Century Montreal', Urban History Review/Revue d'histoire urbaine 26, 2 (1998): 3–16

I wish to thank Jacques Bernier of the History Department, Université Laval, for his helpful comments on an earlier draft of the essay and Philippe Desaulniers of the Centre interuniversitaire d'études québécoises (CIÉQ) for his preparation of the map of Ireland.

Chapter Nine

Rebellions in Lower Canada

READINGS

Primary Documents

1   From Ninety-Two Resolutions, in *Journals of the House of Assembly of Lower Canada*, 4th session of the 14th Provincial Parliament (January 7–March 8, 1834)

2   From Lord Durham to Lord Glenelg, 9 August 1838, in *The Report and Despatches of the Earl of Durham Her Majesty's High Commissioner and Governor-General of British North America*

Historical Interpretations

3   From 'The Failure of the Insurrectionary Movement, 1837–1839', in *Economic and Social History of Quebec, 1760–1850: Structures and Conjunctures*, Fernand Ouellet

4   From *The Patriots and the People: The Rebellion of 1837 in Rural Lower Canada*, Allan Greer

Introduction

Like the seigneurial regime we addressed in Chapter 3, the Rebellions of 1837 and 1838 in Upper and Lower Canada are a touchstone in the history of the colonial period. They mark the culmination of two processes: the growth of a reform movement in Lower Canada that resented its limited influence in the colony's political life, and the growth of an alternative to unquestioned Loyalism in Upper Canada. In the case of Lower Canada, the colonial administration (especially Governors Craig and Dalhousie) had made it difficult for French speakers to exercise real power in the colony, even though they formed the majority of the population. Although the Lower Canadian reformers framed all their demands within the British constitutional framework, until 1828 they achieved nothing. Their failure encouraged them to adopt more radical demands (inspired by republicanism) which were embodied in the Ninety-Two Resolutions in 1834. This radicalization oriented the reformers (who were called *patriotes* in the 1830s) toward rebellion.

In Upper Canada, the desire among the governing group and their wealthy allies to fulfill the vision of the colony as a kind of Britain in miniature led to a society that was more stratified than many citizens (reformers and radicals alike) would have preferred, and contrasted sharply with the egalitarian aura that Americans cast about themselves. As a result of the rebellions, the British government appointed a new governor in the colony, Lord Durham. In order to prevent a new rising, Durham proposed to assimilate French Canadians and to unite Upper and Lower Canada. In his *Report on the Affairs of British North America* (1839), he also advocated for more colonial autonomy through a certain kind of local ministerial responsibility. Flowing in part from Durham's reading of the colonial situation, the unification of the colonies brought on its own problems, resolved to the satisfaction of few by Confederation in the mid-1860s. Durham's letter to Glenelg reflects a simplistic view of a situation that colonial administrators had not stuck around in either colony long enough to grasp.

The secondary sources focus rightly on Lower Canada. The Upper Canadian activities of 1837, though indicative of the colony's own distinctive problems and tensions, were encouraged by the beginning of the more urgent and distinctly complex hostilities further east. Fernand Ouellet attributes the long-brewing unrest that boiled over in 1837 to both a deep economic crisis and the rise of French Canadian nationalism. In his estimation, rebellion was not a delayed reaction to the Conquest but the result of an economic crisis affecting Lower Canadians' ability to take advantage of being part of a more commercially dynamic British Empire. In Allan Greer's estimation, the *patriotes*' discourse was more influenced by republicanism than nationalism. However, despite the adoption of a republican rhetoric based on freedom and equality, the *patriotes* did not acknowledge women's equality. In his reading on attitudes toward women's participation in political protests and processes, Greer shows how the debate could persist even in the midst of (and perhaps because of) the rebellion against British authority, authority which had recently been invested in the young Queen Victoria.

QUESTIONS FOR CONSIDERATION

1. Which of the 92 Resolutions do you find most radical or confrontational?
2. Based on his letter to Glenelg, do you think that Durham understood the grievances of Lower Canadians? Why or why not?
3. Why were the spectacular instances of harassment and discipline that Greer mentions (such as the case of Rosalie Cherrier) effective?
4. Looking at Ouellet's account, do you agree that the political actions of a person or group are dependent upon their economic status or fortunes?

SUGGESTIONS FOR FURTHER READING

Buckner, Phillip A., *Transition to Responsible Government: British Policy in British North America 1815–1850* (Westport: Greenwood Press, 1985)

Coates, Colin, 'The Rebellions of 1837–38, and Other Bourgeois Revolutions in Quebec Historiography', *International Journal of Canadian Studies* 20 (1999): 29–34

Creighton, Donald G., *The Empire of the St. Lawrence* (Toronto: MacMillan of Canada, 1956)

Ducharme, Michel, 'Closing the Last Chapter of the Atlantic Revolution: The 1837–1838 Rebellions in Upper and Lower Canada', *Proceedings of the American Antiquarian Society*, 116(2) (2006): 411–428

Greenwood, F. Murray, and Barry Wright, eds., *Canadian State Trials*, vol. 2: *Rebellion and Invasion in the Canadas, 1837–1839* (Toronto: University of Toronto Press, 2002)

Greer, Allan, *The Patriots and the People* (Toronto: University of Toronto Press, 1993)

Ouellet, Fernand, *Economic and Social History of Quebec, 1760–1850: Structures and Conjunctures* (Toronto: MacMillan of Canada, 1980)

Read, Colin, *The Rebellion of 1837 in Upper Canada* (Ottawa: Canadian Historical Association, 1988)

Wilton, Carol, *Popular Politics and Political Culture in Upper Canada 1800–1850* (Montreal and Kingston: McGill-Queen's University Press, 2000)

PRIMARY DOCUMENTS

1 From Ninety-Two Resolutions, in *Journals of the House of Assembly of Lower Canada*, 4th session of the 14th Provincial Parliament (January 7 -March 18, 1834).

1. Resolved, That His Majesty's loyal subjects, the people of this province of Lower Canada, have shown the strongest attachment to the British Empire, of which they are a portion; that they have repeatedly defended it with courage in time of war; that at the period which preceded the Independence of the late British Colonies on this continent, they resisted the appeal made to them by those colonies to join their confederation.

9. Resolved, That the most serious defect in the Constitutional Act, its radical fault, the most active principle of evil and discontent in the province; the most powerful and most frequent cause of abuses of power; of the infraction of the laws; of the waste of the public revenue and property, accompanied by impunity to the governing party, and the oppression and consequent resentment of the governed, is that injudicious enactment, . . . which invests the Crown with that exorbitant power (incompatible with any government duly balanced, and founded on law and justice, and not on force and coercion) of selecting and composing without any rule or limitation, or any predetermined qualification, an entire branch of the legislature, supposed from the nature of its attributes to be independent, but inevitably the servile tool of the authority which creates, composes and decomposes it, and can on any day modify it to suit the interests or the passions of the moment.

17. Resolved, That . . . the principal Agent of His Majesty's Government in this Province . . . has destroyed the hope which His Majesty's faithful subjects had conceived of seeing the Legislative Council reformed and ameliorated, and has confirmed them in the opinion that the only possible mode of giving to that body the weight and respectability which it ought to possess, is to introduce into it the principle of election.

41. Resolved, . . . that the neighbouring States have a form of government very fit to prevent abuses of power, and very effective in repressing them; that the reverse of this order of things has always prevailed in Canada under the present form of government; that there exists in the neighbouring States a stronger and more general attachment to the national institutions than in any other country, and that there exists also in those States a guarantee for the progressive advance of their political institutions towards perfection, in the revision of the same at short and determinate intervals, by conventions of the people, in order that they may without any shock or violence be adapted to the actual state of things.

44. Resolved, That the unanimous consent with which all the American States have adopted and extended the elective system, shows that it is adapted to the wishes, manners and social state of the inhabitants of this continent; . . . and that we do not hesitate to ask from a Prince of the House of Brunswick, and a reformed Parliament, all the freedom and political powers which the Princes of the House of Stuart and their Parliaments granted to the most favoured of the plantations formed at a period when such grants must have been less favourably regarded than they would now be.

49. Resolved, That this House and the people whom it represents do not wish or intend to convey any threat; but that, relying as they do upon the principles of law and justice, they are and ought to be politically strong enough not to be exposed to receive insult from any man whomsoever, or bound to suffer it in silence; that the style of the said extracts from the despatches of the Colonial Secretary, as communicated to this House, is insulting and inconsiderate to such a degree that no legally constituted body, although its functions were infinitely subordinate to those of legislation, could or ought to tolerate them; . . .

52. Resolved, . . . That the majority of the inhabitants of this country are in nowise disposed to repudiate any one of the advantages they derive from their origin and from their descent from the French nation, which, with regard to the progress of which it has been the cause in civilization, in the sciences, in letters, and the arts, has never been behind the British nation, and is now the worthy rival of the latter in the advancement of the cause of liberty and of the science of Government; from which this country derives the greater portion of its civil and ecclesiastical law, and of its scholastic and charitable institutions, and of the religion, language, habits, manners and customs of the great majority of its inhabitants.

64. Resolved, That the claims which have for many years been set up by the Executive Government to that control over and power of appropriating a great portion of the revenues levied in this province, which belong of right to this House, are contrary to the rights and to the constitution of the country; and that with regard to the said claims, this House persists in the declarations it has heretofore made.

73. Resolved, That it was anciently the practice of the House of Commons to withhold supplies until grievances were redressed; and that in following this course in the present conjuncture, we are warranted in our proceeding, as well by the most approved precedents, as by the spirit of the constitution itself.

75. Resolved, That the number of the inhabitants of the country being about 600,000, those of French origin are about 525,000, and those of British or other origin 75,000; and that the establishment of the civil government of Lower Canada for the year 1832, according to the yearly returns made by the Provincial Administration, for the information of the British Parliament, contained the names of 157 officers and others receiving salaries, who are apparently of British or foreign origin, and the names of 47 who are apparently natives of the country, of French origin: that this statement does not exhibit the whole disproportion which exists in the distribution of the public money and power, the latter class being for the most part appointed to the inferior and less lucrative offices, and most frequently only obtaining even these by becoming the dependents of those who hold the higher and more lucrative offices; . . .

79. Resolved, That this House, as representing the people of this province, possesses of right, and has exercised within this province when occasion has required it, all the powers, privileges and immunities claimed and possessed by the Commons House of Parliament in the kingdom of Great Britain and Ireland. . . .

84. Resolved, That besides the grievances and abuses before mentioned, there exist in this province a great number of others (a part of which existed before the commencement of the present administration, which has maintained them, and is the author of a portion of them), with regard to which this House reserves to itself the right of complaining and demanding reparation, and the number of which is too great to allow of their being enumerated here: that this House points out, as among that number,

     lstly. The vicious composition and the irresponsibility of the Executive Council, . . . and the secrecy with which not only the functions, but even the names of the members of that body have been kept from the knowledge of this House, . . .

     2dly. The exorbitant fees illegally exacted in certain of the public offices, and in others connected with the judicial department, under regulations made by the Executive Council, by the judges, and by other functionaries usurping the powers of the legislature. . . .

     4thly. The cumulation of public places and offices in the same persons, and the efforts made by a number of families connected with the administration, to perpetuate this state of things for their own advantage, . . .

     5thly. The intermeddling of members of the Legislative Councils in the election of the representatives of the people, for the purpose of influencing and controlling them by force, and the selection frequently made of returning officers for the purpose of securing the same partial and corrupt ends; the interference of the present Governor-in-chief himself in the said elections; his approval of the intermeddling of the said legislative councillors in the said elections; . . .

     6thly. The interference of the armed military force at such elections, through which three peaceable citizens, whose exertions were necessary to the support of their families, and who were strangers to the agitation of the election, were shot dead in the streets, . . .

     7thly. The various faulty and partial systems which have been followed ever since the passing of the Constitutional Act, with regard to the management of the waste lands in this province, and have rendered it impossible for the great majority of the people of the country to settle on the said lands; the fraudulent and illegal manner in which, contrary to His Majesty's instructions, Governors, Legislative and Executive Councillors, Judges and subordinate officers have appropriated to themselves large tracts of the said lands; . . .

85. Resolved, . . . that this House expects from the honour, patriotism and justice of the reformed Parliament of the United Kingdom, that the Commons of the said Parliament will bring impeachments, and will support such impeachments before the House of Lords against the said Matthew Lord Aylmer, for his illegal, unjust and unconstitutional administration of the government of this province; and against such of the wicked and perverse advisers who have misled him, as this House may hereafter accuse, . . .

86. Resolved, That this House hopes and believes, that the independent members of both Houses of the Parliament of the United Kingdom will be disposed, both from inclination and from a sense of duty, to support the accusations brought by this House, to watch over the preservation of its rights and privileges which have been so frequently and violently attacked, more especially by the present administration; and so to act, that the people of this province may not be forced by oppression to regret their dependence on the British Empire, and to seek elsewhere a remedy for their afflictions. . .

2 From a despatch from Lord Durham to Lord Glenelg, 9 August 1838, in *The Report and Despatches of the Earl of Durham Her Majesty's High Commissioner and Governor-General of British North America* (London: Ridgways, 1839), 305–9.

Castle of St. Lewis, Quebec, 9 August 1838.

My Lord,

The information which my residence here has enabled me to obtain as to the condition of the two Canadas is of such a nature as to make me doubt whether, if I had been fully aware of the real state of affairs in this part of the world, any considerations would have induced me to undertake so very difficult a task as is involved in my mission. I do not, however, wish it to be understood that I consider success impossible. On the contrary, I indulge a hope that if the difficulties and dangers that are now so apparent to me are appreciated by Her Majesty's Government, so as to lead to their adoption of measures sufficiently comprehensive and decided to meet the emergency, the objects of my mission may be accomplished. My sole purpose, therefore, in adverting to circumstances which threaten a different result is to impress upon your Lordship my own conviction, which has been formed by personal experience, that even the best informed persons in England can hardly conceive the disorder or disorganization which, to the careful inquirer on the spot, is manifest in all things pertaining to Government in these colonies. Such words scarcely express the whole truth: not Government merely, but society itself seems to be almost dissolved; the vessel of the State is not in great danger only, as I had been previously led to suppose, but looks like a complete wreck. It is needless to point out the wide difference between this representation and the opinions on the subject which were, and probably still are, held by Her Majesty's Ministers; but since one who had the benefit of whatever information they possessed is nevertheless compelled to acknowledge that the truth, as it now appears to him, differs so much from his previous conceptions of it, what can he infer but that distance has precluded them from acquiring an accurate knowledge of the whole subject? This is my belief, and it becomes, therefore, an imperative duty on my part to convey to your Lordship the exact impressions which I have derived from personal inquiry and observation. I will not shrink from the performance of that duty.

On the present occasion, however, I propose to confine myself to a particular class of circumstances; that is, to those which relate to the Lower Province, and are of the most unfavourable character; my object in making such a selection being to state without reserve, in a separate despatch, certain facts and opinions, to which, as coming from me, it is most inexpedient that any publicity should be given for the present; this despatch will therefore be marked 'Secret.'

The first point to which I would draw your attention, being one with which all others are more or less connected, is the existence of a most bitter animosity between the Canadians and the British, not as two parties holding different opinions and seeking different objects in respect to Government, but as different races engaged in a national contest.

This hatred of races is not publicly avowed on either side; on the contrary, both sides profess to be moved by any other feelings than such as belong to difference of origin; but the fact is, I think, proved by an accumulation of circumstantial evidence more conclusive than any direct testimony would be, and far more than sufficient to rebut all mere assertions to the contrary.

If the difference between the two classes were one of party or principles only, we should find on each side a mixture of persons of both races, whereas the truth is that, with exceptions which tend to prove the rule, all the British are on one side, and all the Canadians are on the other. What may be the immediate subject of dispute seems to be of no consequence; so surely as there is a dispute on any subject, the great bulk of the Canadians and the great bulk of the British appear ranged against each other. In the next place, the mutual dislike of the two classes extends beyond politics into social life, where, with some trifling exceptions again, all intercourse is confined to persons of the same origin. Grownup persons of a different origin seldom or never meet in private society; and even the children, when they quarrel, divide themselves into French and English like their parents. In the schools and the streets of Montreal, the real capital of the province, this is commonly the case. The station in life, moreover, of an individual of either race seems to have no influence on his real disposition towards the other race: high and low, rich and poor, on both sides—the merchant and the porter, the seigneur and the habitant—though they use different language to express themselves, yet exhibit the very same feeling of national jealousy and hatred. Such a sentiment is naturally evinced rather by trifles than by acts of intrinsic importance. There has been no solemn or formal declaration of national hostility, but not a day nor scarcely an hour passes without some petty insult, some provoking language, or even some serious mutual affront, occurring between persons of British and French descent. Lastly, it appears, upon a careful review of the political struggle between those who have termed themselves the loyal party and the popular party, that the subject of dissension has been, not the connection with England, nor the form of the constitution, nor any of the practical abuses which have affected all classes of the people, but simply such institutions, laws, and customs as are of French origin, which the British have sought to overthrow and the Canadians have struggled to preserve, each class assuming false designations and fighting under false colours—the British professing exclusive loyalty to the Crown of England, and the Canadians pretending to the character of reformers. Nay, I am inclined to think that the true principles and ultimate objects of both parties, taken apart from the question of race, are exactly the reverse of what each of them professes, or, in other words, that the British (always excluding the body of officials) are really desirous of a more responsible Government, while the Canadians would prefer the present form of Government, or even one of a less democratic character. I shall have more to say on this head presently, having mentioned the subject here only for the purpose of citing another fact which tends to prove the existence of a deep-rooted national sentiment on both sides. Such a contradiction between the real and avowed principles of each party, could not have occurred if all the people had been of one race, or if every other consideration had not given way to the sentiment of nationality.

This general antipathy of the Canadians towards the British, and of the British towards the Canadians, appears to have been, as it were, provided for at the conquest of the province, and by subsequent measures of the British Government. If Lower Canada had been isolated from other colonies, and so well peopled as to leave little room for emigration from Britain, it might have been right at the conquest to engage for the preservation of French institutions, for the existence of a 'Nation Canadienne;' but, considering how certain it was that, sooner or later, the British race would predominate in the country, that engagement seems to have been most unwise. It ensured such a strife as has actually taken place; for, notwithstanding the division of Canada into two provinces, for the purpose of isolating the French, the British already predominate in French Canada, not numerically of course, but by means of their superior energy and wealth, and of their natural relationship to the powers of Government. It was long before the Canadians perceived that their nationality was in the course of being overridden by a British nationality. When the Constitutional Act bestowed on them a representative system, they were so little conversant with its nature, and so blind to the probable results of British emigration, that they described the constitution as a 'machine Anglaise pour nous taxer,' and elected to the House of Assembly almost a majority of Englishmen. But with the progress of British intrusion, they at length discovered, not only the uses of a representative system, but also that their nationality was in danger; and I have no hesitation in asserting, that of late years they have used the representative system for the single purpose of maintaining their nationality against the progressive intrusion of the British race. They have found the British pressing upon them at every turn, in the possession of land, in commerce, in the retail trade, in all kinds of industrious enterprize, in religion, in the whole administration of government, and though they are a stagnant people, easily satisfied and disinclined to exertion, they have naturally resisted an invasion which was so offensive to their national pride. The British, on the other hand, impeded in the pursuit of all their objects, partly by the ancient and barbarous civil law of the country, and partly by the systematic opposition of the Canadians to the progress of British enterprize, have naturally sought to remove those impediments, and to conquer, without much regard to the means employed, that very mischievous opposition. The actual result should have seemed inevitable. The struggle between the two races, conducted as long as possible according to the forms of the constitution, became too violent to be kept within those bounds. In order to preserve some sort of government, the public revenue was disposed of against the will of the Canadian people represented by their Assembly. The consequent rebellion, although precipitated by the British from an instinctive sense of the danger of allowing the Canadians full time for preparation, could not, perhaps, have been avoided; and the sentiment of national hostility has been aggravated to the uttermost, on both sides, by that excessive inflammation of the passions which always attends upon bloodshed for such a cause, and still more by this unusual circumstance,—that the victorious minority suffered extreme fear at the beginning of the contest, and that the now subdued majority had been led to hope every thing from an appeal to force.

There seems to me only one modification of this view of the subject. The employment by the Canadians of constitutional and popular means for their national purpose, has taught some of them, consisting chiefly of the most active and able, higher political views than such as belong to the question of nationality. These men are not at heart friendly to the barbarous institutions of their ancestors, but would readily adopt a more enlightened system, if they could do so without losing their own importance. Their necessary dependence on the prejudiced mass has alone restrained them from joining in many of the views for the improvement of the country which are entertained by the British. They have also learned to estimate the practical abuses of Government which affect all classes, and to wish for many reforms without reference to Canadian nationality. They even had, to some extent, succeeded in disseminating their opinions amongst the mass of their countrymen, and they are not unlikely to play a valuable and distinguished part under any new system of government that may put an end to the strife between hostile races.

HISTORICAL INTERPRETATIONS

3   From Fernand Ouellet, 'The Failure of the Insurrectionary Movement, 1837–1839', in *Economic and Social History of Quebec, 1760–1850: Structures and Conjunctures* (Ottawa: Gage/Institute of Canadian Studies, Carleton University, 1980), 420–47, 634–6.

The insurrection of 1837–8 has been presented in many ways. Some historians have seen it as a sudden outburst of anger and indignation, evidently without premeditation, unleashed by the resolutions of Lord Russell, which violated a constitutional principle. This view seems somewhat out of tune with the French-Canadian mentality. Spontaneous recourse to arms has never been the favoured means used by the French Canadians to realize their collective objectives or assert their demands. Lafontaine, who knew them well, said that their principal weapon was inertia and, let us add, verbal agitation. The insurrections cannot be primarily explained either as a spontaneous reaction or as a defence of principles—political or constitutional. The peasant mass was not yet living in an age of liberalism or democracy.

Other historians, sometimes the same ones, have spoken of a logical outcome to a long political and constitutional conflict, accordingly non-nationalist in its main dimensions, but ultimately of national import. Some, however, such as Filteau, are quick to postulate the nationalist character of the disturbances of 1837–8. Some have also spoken of an explosion of reform, comparing it with the English Chartist movement and with Jacksonian democracy, and, finally, have seen the insurrections of the two Canadas as part of the same reality. They have tried to show in this way that it was, in the end, a matter of overthrowing colonial oligarchies in order to promote a colonial system built on a more liberal basis. The insurrectionary phenomenon, in short, as far as its real origins, its nature, its extent, and its consequences are concerned, has been simplified in the extreme. We must not overlook either the systematic pronouncements, based on canon law and moral precepts, of which this movement has been the object for numerous historians. In this regard, Chapais is the model. He has succeeded in outclassing the clerical historians on their own ground, that is, in his moralizing fervour. That many of these interpretations are partially just, we readily admit. But what, on the whole, is most lacking is a total perspective which restores to this phenomenon its meaning and its complexity.

It seems evident that if the insurrection had only political roots, even remote ones, it would not have taken place. It is no less clear that if it had involved only abstract principles, it would

have in no way mobilized the rural masses, any more than the liberal professions. As we believe we have shown, the crisis which prepared the way for the insurrectionary upheaval was first and foremost economic and social before being political. The agricultural crisis, the demographic and social tensions, the particularly critical situation of the liberal professions were the principal foundations of the nationalist reaction, which mobilized certain elite groups and rallied a large part of the masses. Nor can the influence of ideologies other than nationalism be denied. We have already pointed out why they intruded into French-Canadian society and what functions they assumed there. French and English liberalism, British radicalism, Jeffersonian and Jacksonian democracy, in turn and in varying degrees, influenced the political elites according to their particular needs. But these ideological currents never reached the rural masses or the working-class minority. On the whole, we can say that these systems of values and thought remained dependent on the aims pursued by the dominant ideology, *nationalism*. Furthermore, because it aimed at control of the political structures to the advantage of the liberal professions and the French-Canadian nationality, the nationalist reaction asserted itself at the political level before it found expression in two successive insurrections. After 1806, political conflicts took hold at the same time as economic difficulties, demographic pressures, and social tensions. From time to time, as temporary improvements occurred in one sector or another, there was a relative reduction of the conflicts. Although the major initiator was economic, the interdependence of the different levels of activity becomes obvious at every turn. It was the same with the mental outlook and the fluctuations of collective psychology, which operated within this overall context. The time was given over to pessimism, tragic visions, and aggressiveness. [. . .]

We must not overlook either the essential role of the dominant personalities, especially that of Papineau. He was at once the reflection of the situation, one of its principal definers, and the instrument through which the nationalist reaction was expressed. His ambitions, his interests, and above all his personality made him the key figure of this reaction. Having reached the head of the nationalist movement for a variety of reasons, he managed to direct it for nearly 25 years. After 1830, he even conceived the plan of becoming the president of a French-Canadian republic, independent or attached to England by very tenuous ties. But Papineau was a man of opposition, of systematic obstruction, and of verbal agitation. He was not cut out for action. Idealistic, doctrinaire, indecisive, deeply torn between contradictory tendencies, his kingdom was the House of Assembly. He was more a symbol than the instigator of a revolutionary movement. In short, there was nothing, unless it was his ambition and faithfulness to the myth which he embodied, predisposing him to be the leader of an insurrection and to remain so in spite of everything. His political attitudes, however, were directly conducive to an armed uprising. The systematic obstruction that he practised after 1831–2 and the intransigence of his demands could have no other result unless England and the British minority of Lower Canada agreed to a number of total concessions. The latter, however, refused categorically to consider such an option. At the beginning of the year 1837, political conflicts seemed insoluble. Briefly, the insurrections of 1837–8 were the logical conclusion to a whole complex of factors, some of which had been at work since the first years of the nineteenth century. But was this enough to guarantee the success of the operation?

I. THE *CONJONCTURE* DURING THE REVOLUTIONARY PERIOD

As early as the beginning of 1837, the economic *conjoncture* was very bad, worse even than in 1834. The British economic crisis now had repercussions in the St. Lawrence Valley. It should be noted that in England this was not an ordinary contraction affecting only a few sectors of the economy, but rather a widespread crisis. There was thus a serious decline in most areas, particularly in finances. In November 1836, H. Bliss notified the president of the Quebec Chamber of Commerce of the difficult situation of the English banks.[1] In February, the crisis had taken on more serious proportions. Bliss recorded several bankruptcies. [. . .]

The rash of speculation which had prevailed in England since 1835 reached its outcome in the form of a general economic crisis complicated by poor crops. But, as usual, bad crops in Britain did not constitute a disaster for Canada, providing, of course, that they corresponded to high production in the Canadas. But in 1837, neither Lower nor Upper Canada was in a position to profit from the high prices commanded on the British market.

As the crowning misfortune, a very serious financial crisis broke out in the United States, where the *conjoncture* was to be most unfavourable until 1842. The American banks stopped cash payments in May 1837. The combined effects of these two financial panics, the English and the American, had their repercussions in Canada. The Quebec Chamber of Commerce immediately recommended the suspension of payment in cash by the banks. 'That in consequence of the suspension of specie Payments in the United States, this Committee deem it expedient that a Public Meeting of the Merchants be immediately called to adopt such measures as may be considered necessary to prevent a drain of specie in the present alarming crisis.'[2] The merchants were not content with asking the governor to permit the banks to stop cash payments, they requested permission to defray their customs duties by means of 'vouchers issued by the Banks'. To support their request, they pointed to the unusual scarcity of *specie*. Although these decisions were inspired by a desire to avoid greater evils, they did not prevent the monetary difficulties from tightening their grip. [. . .]

It was only in the month of September 1837 that Bliss was able to announce a reversal of the British situation: 'the basis on which the industry and trade of the whole country is founded and will probably lead to a further extension of every enterprise and to an improvement of prices.'³

Altogether, the year 1837 was a particularly severe one in England. When we are aware of the strict sensitivity of the Lower Canadian economy to the *conjoncture* prevailing in the mother country, we can be sure of finding similar situation in the St. Lawrence Valley. Lower Canada, moreover, was already deeply affected by an agricultural crisis.

The poor crops of 1836, which corresponded to a more or less deficient harvest in the West and an increased demand in England, had provoked a rise in agricultural prices. Thus, at the beginning of 1837, the shortage of products and money was the order of the day. [. . .]

In short, there was in 1837 an appreciable rise in agricultural prices. Table 1 illustrates the behaviour of prices during the revolutionary period.

The inflation which existed in January 1837 was not solely attributable to the factors listed above, it depended also on the speculation in produce and agricultural commodities. On 16 January 1837, an observer wrote: 'We have for a long time on various occasions spoken of the drawbacks caused by the absence of laws concerning bakers and of a tariff on bread. Again this food item has just risen in price, which can hardly be explained in view of the previous high price except by the facility with which the bakers can raise their profits to the levels which suit them. Flour in New York is a dollar more expensive than here, and yet bread costs four cents less per six pounds.'⁴

In Montreal, the crisis raged with almost as much force as in the District of Quebec. 'The ice on the river', declared one observer, 'is now furrowed with tracks crossing in all directions; and the people from the south have easy access to the city. The roads, however, are still bad, the wind fills them up as soon as people have passed by. Few people come to the market, and the price of supplies is always increasing and

money grows ever more scarce. Without the aid that the poor receive in the workhouse, there is no doubt that many of them would die of hunger and cold in the long and rigorous winter season. The distress may not be as great in our districts as in Quebec, there are none the less many who are destitute. The crops have been very mediocre in many parishes. The shortage of money is the order of the day almost everywhere in the country.'⁵

In some areas, the famine was such that there was a real fear a large part of the population would die of hunger. At Trois-Pistoles, twelve hundred people were in this tragic situation. 'A letter from Trois-Pistoles, dated the 30th of Dec.', reported one observer, 'paints a frightening picture of the misery which prevails in this area. It is so bad that several farmers are eating their horses. There have been no crops for four year and many people haven't even a potato. The most well-off barely have enough for themselves and their families, even living very sparingly. What will become of all these poor unfortunates from now until May? It is torture to think about it. It is certain that many of them will die of hunger, unless aid comes at once.'⁶

In February, nothing occurred to modify this desperate situation, apart from the intervention of private charity organizations. Moreover, since 1833, a lasting conflict had existed with the principal *Patriote* leaders, who refused to consider the social responsibilities of the State. Some asked the government to create public granaries and others demanded funds to help the unfortunate. In 1833, Papineau unwillingly agreed to some concessions, but subsequently refused to encourage, as he phrased it, a spirit of dependence among the peasants. An article in *Le Canadien* is especially indicative of these problems:

You know that for four years, almost all the parishes below Quebec have been afflicted by the destruction of their grain. Are not the great destitution of the lower, but most numerous, class, and I might add the noticeable decrease of resources among the other classes of Quebec society, the result of the distress in the country areas which form the territory around the capital and to which they should give support?[7]

This document, then, sums up the situation of the countryside of the District of Quebec since 1833. In 1834, owing to government subsidies, the farmers had been able to sow their crops. In 1835, despite pressing needs, the farmers had made no requests for help: 'They prefer to sell their animals and go into debt to the seigneurs, parish priests, and merchants. But today, these influential people can give no more without putting their own possessions in danger. . . . Should the virulent declarations of Papineau and some members from Montreal, who have always been opposed to such assistance, be able to paralyse the nerves of the chief of the Executive out of mere apprehension,

Table 1 **Average Price Increase (in *livres tournois*)**					
	1835–39	**1835–39/1830–34**	**1837/36**	**1838**	**1839**
Flour (Quebec)	21.97	61%	83%	11%	0
Wheat (Quebec)	9.66	28%	51%	8%	13%
Wheat (Montreal)	7.5	22%	38%	–5%	–5%
Moving average	6.8	3%	–	–	–
Oats (Quebec)	3.13	11%	20%	3%	5%
Moving average	2.7	–3%	–	–	–
Oats (Montreal)	–	–	26%	–	–
Beef (Quebec)	0.50	28%	53%	0	8%
Moving average	0.44	7%	–	–	–
Beef (Montreal)	–	–	high of 10% in 1836		
Butter (Quebec)	1.32	30%	39%	6%	23%
Moving average	1.17	–1%	–	–	–
Butter (Montreal)	–	–	8%	–	–
Silberling	112.4	4%	0	6%	4%
Peas (Montreal)	–	–	42%	–	–

and prevent him from doing what all his predecessors have done in similar cases?'

The harvest of 1836 had therefore been a complete failure in the Quebec region, while in the Montreal area it had scarcely been better. 'It has been part of the system', added the same analyst, 'to cultivate a little of everything and a lot of potatoes since the great scarcity of 1816; but what can they do against a climate which at times, like this year and the preceding years, despite the most favourable appearances, destroys everything in one night, even the potatoes.'[8] Thus the wheat crisis had been coupled since 1833, by reason also of bad weather conditions, with a serious crisis in alternative crops. Hence the particular seriousness of the agricultural malaise at the time of the adoption of the Russell Resolutions.

In 1837 complaints broke out everywhere. F. Papineau wrote from Petite-Nation: 'There is neither straw, nor hay, nor wheat, nor meat in the area. Animals and people are destitute.'[9] Some days later, in *Le Canadien*, the misery of the people in the Beauce was evoked:

> The distress goes on increasing in the parishes of St. François and St. Georges and even all through the Beauce. The roads, having become impassable because of the flooding rivers, have reduced the people to the most extreme want. The least afflicted, i.e., the best habitants, are themselves exhausted. They have done everything in their power to help the others and prevent them from starving by selling or lending the little bit of wheat or flour which they were setting aside for themselves, hoping to get some soon from Quebec. Our poor farmers are disconsolate, not only from enduring hunger this year, but from seeing themselves exposed to the same distress next year, since a large part of the two parishes will have to remain without crops. Most have no food at all except a little sugar which they dissolve in water. There are even those who have

no other means of avoiding death from hunger than by eating the dead animals found along the roadsides. . . . Add to this the measles and scarlet fever which have struck these unfortunate families, and imagine if you can, the state of the poor people of the Beauce.[10]

Thus, in 1837, destitution and discontent prevailed everywhere. The meagre hopes that might have been entertained regarding the next harvest were to be disappointed, so that the situation instead of improving continued to get worse. Moreover, the crisis of 1837 did not affect only agriculture; it was general. In February, Lafontaine wrote: 'Possibly the almost total distress, in business as much as in agriculture, is bringing discouragement to the peoples' hearts. I confess that in Canada the poverty is great and the misery complete.'[11]

The critical *conjoncture* of this period is revealed in the movement of exports.

The crisis thus struck all sectors, even the timber industry and shipbuilding. The agricultural crisis had repercussions in the towns, while the decline in lumbering and shipbuilding provoked unemployment. A document of 1837 very clearly illustrates the situation in the urban areas, especially among the workers of Quebec:

> St.-Roch, District of: contains from 95 to 110 widows who earn their livelihood by the day and a large part of whom very often have difficulty in finding work at this season. With them are around 200 orphans. Age, sickness, and infirmity make a large number of these poor women unable to work for part of the winter. And since these same causes stop them from entering the Work-house, which moreover can take no more people for lack of space, they will perish with their children unless the public comes to their aid. In St.-Roch, there are also 100 to 110 poor families. A certain number of them, it is true, have been brought

to poverty because of drink, whose use is so deadly and widespread among our working-classes. . . . Besides these families which suffer so much through the fault of their Head, there is a large number whose misery comes only from the contagious sicknesses which thrive almost continuously in the midst of our poor population, or, again, only from the sad results of the accidents to which the workmen who labour in the shipyards are daily exposed.[12]

Obviously, the decreased production in the sectors linked to the export trade particularly influenced imports, whether from Great Britain, the United States, or the West Indies.

On the whole, the economic crisis of 1837 was a central event which could be felt more keenly each day. It did not equally affect the whole province. It was in the District of Montreal that it reached its maximum intensity. Indeed, the Montreal region depended above all on local and western agriculture. Then the malaise spread to the district of Trois-Rivières.

Table 2

	EXPORTS 1838–42	1833–37	INCREASE 1837/36	1838/37	1839/38
Shipping: Quebec and Montreal (Tonnage)	403,048	21%	–7%	3%	9%
Shipping: Canals (Total tonnage)	265,662	4%	–21%	–3%	14%
Grain: Quebec (Barrels)	216,791	202%	–100%		
Grain: Deficit in Lower Canada (Barrels)	169,935	63%	?		
Grain: Total imports: Lower Canada	409,373	133%	–100%		
Boards and deals (Number)	2,732,645	8%	1%	3%	5%
Staves (Number)	6,083,686	1%	–7%	–11%	10%
Squared pine (Tons)	310,982	17%	–11%	6%	21%
Squared oak (Tons)	24,980	14%	stable	32%	15%
Potash, total (Barrels)	25,823	–17%	stable	–12%	–13%
Potash, Lower Canada	9,345	–12%	5%	–17%	–39%
Shipbuilding (Tonnage)	17,122	99%	–6%	–12%	80%

Table 3

	IMPORTS 1838–42	1838–42/ 1833–37	INCREASE 1837/1836	1838/1837	1839/1838
Value: Quebec and Montreal	1,943,854	35%	–26%	–6%	43%
Value: Quebec, Montreal, and St.-Jean	2,147,314	17%	–17%	–21%	50%
Value: St.-Jean	131,717	40%	–17%	2%	124%
Volume: Quebec and Montreal (Tonnage)	401,343	24%	–8%	5%	7%
Volume: Gaspé and New Carlisle	10,384	2%	–23%	–24%	97%
Molasses (Gallons)	104,265	18%	36%	–2%	27%
Sugar (Lbs.)	8,778,441	45%	–10%	28%	6%
Wine (Gallons)	335,465	–2%	–23%	67%	46%
Salt (*Minot*)	378,550	47%	–16%	28%	57%
Coffee (Lbs.)	236,207	127%	–38%	–4%	54%
Tea (Lbs.)	1,054,952	24%	–6%	62%	–6%
Rum, spirits (Gallons)	678,113	–36%	–33%	118%	–18%
Tobacco (Lbs.)	836,925	13%	38%	–23%	0.6%
Butter and Cheese (Lbs.)	450,436	10%	–13%	38%	12%
Pork and Beef (Barrels)	31,948	–6%	–15%	–24%	51%
Lard (Lbs.)	225,884	–16%	–65%	234%	–40%
Rawhides (Number)	40,870	73%	–23%	–12%	63%
Rice (Lbs.)	277,122	30%	–47%	74%	–56%
Cattle (Number)	799	–82%	–34%	–42%	–54%

Here, it was the direct result of shortages in agricultural production and overpopulation. There existed, nevertheless, in these two parts of the province some areas relatively shielded from the crisis. These were the areas, such as the Ottawa Valley, where the timber industry predominated, and partially neutralized the consequences of the difficulties which agriculture was experiencing.

This is a basic observation for the understanding of the insurrectionary movement: namely that the restlessness in men's minds and the inclination towards revolt largely reflected the agricultural context and the demographic pressures. On the other hand, despite the very marked falling off recorded in the timber sector and in shipbuilding, it seems evident that these two sectors continued to play, even in 1837, a moderating role, especially in Quebec City and in certain rural centres in this district. In June 1837, an observer noted this important phenomenon:

> Moreover, the port trade which is maintained and the employment which timber continues to supply to part of the population contributes strongly to neutralizing the effect of the seasons and other unfavourable circumstances.[13]

These are not the only factors explaining the geographical distribution of the revolutionary thrusts; but, in our opinion, they had considerable importance. We are tempted to assert without fear of error that on the eve of 1837, the rural population in almost every locality where the timber industry did not have a hold was psychologically prepared to attempt the insurrectionary venture. But certain moderating influences and other circumstances prevented them from taking part in revolutionary action.

To conclude, we can say that the year 1837, as much in England as in Quebec, was marked by a profound economic crisis, a situation eminently favourable to a pronounced aggravation of the social and political conflicts.

While the crisis in England unleashed the Chartist movement, in Canada, there occurred the conclusion of a long struggle which went back to the years around 1806. The economic crisis precipitated this denouement. [. . .]

In practice, the poor harvest of 1837 still determined the general situation. Destitution persisted in the countryside; money and supplies were scarce. Prices continued, in most cases, to rise. Speculation, the strong demand on the British market, and local poverty forced prices up. Luckily, Upper Canada had large surpluses at its disposal which it could sell either in Britain or in Quebec. But the poverty of consumers and producers, who were always in debt, was an obstacle to the satisfaction of needs. In April, Joseph Papineau mentioned the powerlessness of individuals who wished to obtain money and open up business.[14] In the autumn of 1838, extreme poverty still prevailed in the rural areas. The cities, in turn, were suffering the consequences of the agricultural disasters.

In the other sectors, moreover, despite partial improvements, circumstances were far from encouraging. Exports of squared timber (pine, 6 per cent; oak, 32 per cent) and lumber (3 per cent) increased in an appreciable fashion, but shipments of staves and potash declined by 11 and 17 per cent respectively. In shipbuilding the decline was still sharper than in 1837 (12 per cent). To complicate the situation, the banks again closed their doors after November 6. All this explains the new drop which incurred in import levels. For Quebec and Montreal, the decrease was 6 per cent, but for the ports of entry as a whole, it was 21 per cent. An itemized analysis of imports proves that the importers, stimulated by the encouraging prospects in England at the beginning of 1838, had bought excessively. This was particularly true for rum, lard, tea, rice, butter, and cheese. It should be added that the requirements of the timber industry and the troops explain these purchases.

The year 1838, in short, was also dominated by the crisis. In the timber industry, some very definite signs of recovery appeared, while the movement of grain from the West was more vigorous. But this was not enough to make up for the magnitude of the agricultural crisis, or to limit the consequences of the crisis which raged in shipbuilding.

In 1839, Lower Canadian agriculture was in a deplorable state. It was suffering from the consequences of the preceding year's failures and the plundering of the soldiers and 'Loyalists' in certain parishes of the Montreal region. [. . .]

But in 1839, Lower Canada began to feel some movement in certain sectors which had been influenced by the British economy. Aside from the potash trade which was in difficulties, all other sectors which were connected with the timber industry indicated definite progress. The most spectacular expansion occurred in shipbuilding, with an increase of 80 per cent. From then on, Quebec experienced full employment. The increase in exports of staves and lumber reached 10 and 5 per cent; the increase in squared timber was still more remarkable: pine, 21 per cent; oak, 15 per cent. It is very obvious that such a growth in foreign sales could only stimulate imports. At the ports of Quebec and Montreal, the growth in import values was 43 per cent; and 50 per cent, if we add the arrivals at the inland port of St.-Jean.

Thus, the *conjoncture* in 1839 was not comprised of solely discouraging elements. In the sector of timber and shipbuilding, the revival had been very great and coincided with the liquidation of the political crisis. The refugees in the United States little by little gave up their last plans for the invasion of Canada, and those least compromised took one by one or in small groups the road back to Lower Canada.

The insurrections of 1837–8 corresponded therefore with an economic crisis which affected not only agriculture but also the protected sectors of the economy. This crisis constituted the background to the insurrectionary venture. It suddenly sharpened the discontents and the social tensions, and hardened political attitudes. It was in this climate,

charged with hostility, that the famous Russell Resolutions appeared in March 1837. In allowing the governor to draw on the treasury, and in rejecting the principal demands of the *Patriotes*, the Resolutions forced the latter to adopt a firm position. Because of the challenge presented to them, they could only submit or rebel. Unconditional surrender was obviously impossible. Hence, from March 1837 on, they moved towards an armed uprising.

II. THE FAILURE OF THE INSURRECTIONS

The tactless resolutions of Russell were thus presented to the Imperial Parliament at a time when the atmosphere was particularly explosive in Lower Canada. That is why they marked a turning point in the political situation. From that time on, events followed one another at an increasing tempo until the day of armed confrontation. It was very clear that the *Patriotes*, although several of them had long considered the need for an armed revolt, were not immediately prepared to undertake such action. Public opinion needed further preparation and a revolutionary organization had to be set up. Spring, moreover, seemed an unfavourable time for a successful insurrection. It was better, they believed, to wait for 'the ice to set in'.

It would be wrong to suppose that all the *Patriote* leaders were sworn to armed revolution. In this regard, two distinct groups existed within the *Patriote* movement. Some, above all, believed in the efficacy of force. As for the others, they wished it only as a last resort. They advocated resistance through systematic agitation. A compromise was finally reached between the two factions. The plans drawn up in the spring of 1837 reveal that the two factions, for different motives, had united around a single solution. This plan contained two main aspects: a phase of agitation which would remain within legal limits and another, in the event that England refused to yield to *Patriote* pressures, of a revolutionary character. The

Papineau group, which believed in the intrinsic merits of verbal agitation, was convinced that Britain would give way in time. The radical elements were not so optimistic. They considered armed confrontation to be inevitable. They, therefore, looked upon the first phase as a preparatory stage for an armed uprising. We should thus not be surprised to find them working toward this final outcome. Moreover, as events unfolded, the influence of the extremist group continued to grow, until from October on these elements held the initiative in the movement.

In short, behind agitation that was 'constitutional' or within legal limits, the *Patriotes* pursued truly revolutionary ends. The series of great parish and county assemblies which began in May and culminated in the Assembly of the Six Counties responded to intentions which were not entirely peaceful. When Papineau, on 10 May 1837, made two wills in favour of his wife and children in turn, he understood perfectly the risks in the decisions taken by the *Patriote* leaders. Almost to the end, he might be deluded as to the efficacy of verbal protests, but he could not escape the exigencies of the revolutionary movement. The contradictions in his behaviour prove that he was not equal to task before him; they do not show that he acted in good faith when he claimed that no *Patriote* had thought of or wished for an armed insurrection. Likewise, the obvious lack of preparation among the *Patriote* forces in November at the outbreak of the conflict was not the infallible sign of a single-minded intention; it simply demonstrated the weakness of leadership in a movement which was under the direction of orators rather than men of action. In this regard, Wolfred Nelson was an exceptional figure.

In the evolution towards armed confrontation, the Assembly of the Six Counties marked a veritable turning point. The moderate elements were overrun by the extremists. The declaration of the rights of man issued on this occasion and modelled on the American Declaration of Independence, like the decisions adopted at this time, indicated a new direction. The unrest which had prevailed since spring in the country areas acquired a new importance. The peasants systematically blamed the British and the 'Loyalists'. Meanwhile the 'Fils de la liberté' were organized in Montreal. This society was designed not only to promote political education in a democratic and national perspective, but also to train the military forces necessary for a successful revolution. In short, starting in October 1837, the second phase of the plan outlined in the spring was set in motion. The armed uprising was to occur during the first week of December.

It is at this time that the government intervened. The government, during the second week of November, placed the principal *Patriote* leaders under arrest. This unexpected act threw the *Patriote* leaders in Montreal into disarray, and they hastened to take refuge in the countryside. Some made for St.-Denis and St.-Charles, others headed for St.-Benoit and St.-Eustache. Papineau himself, after several days of indecision and an interview with the emissaries from Upper Canada, made for St.-Denis, where a gathering of the *Patriote* forces had already commenced.

After an initial incident on the road to Longueuil between the constables and a group of *Patriotes*, the government finally decided to attack. On November 23 the battle of St.-Denis took place, and the *Patriotes* were victorious. Two days later, they were crushed at St.-Charles. Barely ten days were needed to pacify the Richelieu region. In the meantime, Colborne arrived with his troops. His orders were to put down the resistance of the *Patriote* forces billeted at St.-Eustache. Despite the fierce resistance of Chénier, the *Patriotes* were defeated.

The overthrow of this first attempt at insurrection did not discourage the *Patriote* leaders who had fled to the United States. Relying on the Americans and the Lower Canadian population, they sought to organize a new uprising. But internal dissensions, and the break between Papineau and the radicals of the revolutionary group made the task of setting up an organism capable of taking charge of a military venture particularly difficult. A first unsuccessful attempt was made in February 1838, under the direction of Robert Nelson, who managed in the end only to issue a declaration of Canada's independence. Subsequently, plans multiplied, without any consistent policy. During the summer of 1838, the *Patriotes* finally succeeded in creating and spreading the *Société des Frères-Chasseurs*. The purpose of this secret organization was to gather all the individuals capable of taking part in a revolution. The date of the uprising was fixed for the third of November. The plan of invasion contained a certain number of immediate objectives: first, to seize St.-Jean and Chambly; next, to attack Montreal and, from there, to go on to occupy Quebec. The commander-in-chief, Robert Nelson, successfully gathered together almost 5000 peasants at Napierville. But there ended the success of the insurgents. For a variety of reasons, the rebels were unable to start off, still less to display any degree of unity, energy, and readiness to fight. The suppression of the uprising by Coborne's troops was that much easier.

While the government troops were pacifying the Richelieu region, the Quebec region was the object of an organizational effort on the part of the revolutionary elements. This movement, moreover, did not seem to have any direct connection with that in Montreal. The local leaders, those that we know, were Morn, Huot, and Blanchet. But the movement also involved some Americans who acted as the principal instigators: 'Don Philippie', and Foster. This organization relied on two groups: the rural dwellers and the workers of St.-Roch. The insurrection was to begin with the establishment of a camp at Ste.-Anne de la Pocatière and another at Mont Ste.-Anne. It was here that the gathering of the peasant forces was to take place. At the same time, the *Frères-Chasseurs* of Quebec were to attempt a surprise attack, carefully prepared, on the citadel of Quebec. Unfortunately, a police agent called Hutton, who had managed to infiltrate the organization, exposed the plot. Things went no farther.

This portrayal of the revolutionary events still leaves some problems. The first concerns the geographical extent of the revolutionary agitation. How can we explain why the events affected only the Montreal region? We have already shown that in 1837 Quebec City, because of the stabilizing impact of the timber industry and shipbuilding, had formed a 'Loyalist' island in the midst of a rural region which was, however, awake to the revolutionary phenomenon. The research which we have carried out in the archives of the period prove this. Furthermore, the city of Quebec was the seat of government, so that a large part of the elite, lay and ecclesiastic, gravitated towards the Château. On the other hand, the famous Quebec–Montreal rivalry had exercised considerable influence on the relations between the political leaders of the two cities. Since 1835, a split had occurred between the two. Conflicts of interest, personal rivalries, and the opposition between the two cities explain, as much as the economic differences, the lack of solidarity among the French-Canadian political leaders in these two strategic areas. But, still in this perspective, there is another basic observation: Montreal was the centre of the *Patriote* movement. The *Patriote* party was essentially a Montreal phenomenon. Its principal leaders and its minor chiefs were Montrealers, just as its objectives were defined in terms of the realities of the rural world and the Montreal region. The party leaders had never succeeded in making the Quebeckers forget that after 1815 the direction of the nationalist movement had passed from Quebec to Montreal. Equally as important, the leadership of the group was a sort of family coterie with Papineau as the leader. In short, there was no deep unanimity between Quebec and Montreal. Since the split between Papineau and Neilson, other ruptures had occurred to break the ideological accord as well as the agreement among individuals.

Thus, when a movement that appeared insurrectionary began to take shape, there were no grounds to hope that the Quebec elements would participate. Centred too much around the Montreal region, it was almost impossible for the leaders of the *Patriote* movement to organize revolutionary action in the rural areas of Quebec and Trois-Rivières. Moreover, no serious effort was made in this direction, although these rural localities had responded well to the message delivered by the great assemblies. The concentration of the insurrectionary movement in the Montreal region ensured from this situation. But in 1838, the economic context changed. The crisis in timber and shipbuilding accentuated the difficulties in the city of Quebec, while certain political events helped to awaken part of the elite to the insurrectionary phenomenon. The Quebec leaders then organized their own plot, which woefully miscarried.

With a Montreal character, the revolutionary phenomenon united the social groups which, since the beginning of the nineteenth century, had supported, each in its turn, the *parti canadien* and the *Patriote* party. That is why we find at the head of the movement members of the groups which were most keenly attuned to the nationalist venture. First, the notaries, the lawyers, and the doctors. If, in Montreal, the lawyers played a more important role, the notaries carried more weight in the country. Then came the country merchants who, from being political organizers, became very active in the insurrections. Even here a distinction is necessary according to the financial status of these individuals. Generally, the revolutionary elements were recruited from among those who were least favoured, which was a very large number throughout this period. As for the shock forces, they were drawn from the rural setting: peasants exasperated by the agricultural crisis and the demographic pressures, day labourers in search of land and work. In Montreal, it seems clear that the small shopkeepers and the craftsmen would have been ready to take a more active part in the movement than they did.

How can we explain the rather lamentable failure of these uprisings? Some have attributed the defeat of the two insurrections to the clergy's intervention, particularly to the formidable condemnations of Mgr. Lartigue. We can be sure that the fierce opposition of a very large majority of the clergy posed a serious moral problem for the population, which in many ways found itself torn between its religious allegiance and its nationalist beliefs. The refusal of a Christian burial to those who died in the fighting was a measure designed to create very strong fears in the masses. The fear of eternal, as much as temporal, punishments had indeed a powerful influence on the peasants, and one can also say on the revolutionary leaders themselves. [. . .] Whatever may have been the influence of the clergy, which was the defender of the divine right of monarchy and of the union of Church and State, no one can, however, see it as the major reason for the revolutionary failures of 1837–8. In this context of a nationalist crisis, in which the clergy appeared as the collaborator of the English, other more decisive factors better account for the destiny of the separatist choice.

Thus, the contradictory behaviour of a man like Papineau is an important explanatory factor. The man himself was the object of a particularly vivid myth in the rural areas. Because he embodied the nationalist cause, he appeared to the peasant mass as the strong man without equal who, for more than 25 years had led a desperate battle against the conqueror. Eloquent, energetic, honest (it was thought), he raised awareness, aroused admiration, and excited the popular imagination. After the setback of 1837, the people still hoped for the triumphant return of the Messiah, whom they considered to be their eventual saviour. Witnesses of the time relate that the peasants saw him invading Lower Canada at the head of 50,000 negroes, cyclops into the bargain, armed with repeating rifles. Others, it is said, saw him flying through the air, sitting in a large bark canoe drawn by several white horses. The paradoxical fact for those impressed only by sound and fury is that this man who, they claimed, was the very person to undertake the regeneration of the French Canadians, and the one who symbolized the national struggle, did not have the qualities that they attributed to him.

When we analyze Papineau's behaviour from the spring of 1837, until his flight in disguise on the morning of the St.-Denis engagement, we cannot but be struck by the split between the individual and the demands of his role. He was constantly torn between contrary choices, he displayed chronic indecision and, in the final analysis, he showed himself incapable of truly assuming his responsibilities as leader. The task was too heavy for him, and yet, he was just as incapable of withdrawing from a movement whose direction he maintained in spite of everything. We cannot emphasize too strongly the disastrous influence of such conduct. His action, instead of stimulating and inspiring his subordinates, was rather inclined to throw the revolutionary organization into a state of anarchy. The difficulty encountered in setting up a solid cadre and a suitable organization of supply resulted in large measure from the hesitancy of the supreme leader and from the tensions which this situation encouraged. A man good for speaking but not for acting, said Robert Nelson in reference to Papineau. But it was not only Papineau in whom the propensity for endless deliberation and the disposition for passively witnessing events were to be deplored; a large number of those who gathered around him displayed the same characteristics. There were, fortunately, some exceptions to this rule: W. Nelson and Chénier are the best known. For others, heroism was to come later, namely at the time of the executions that followed the 1838 uprising. Such a patent lack of forceful *leadership* could only fall back on everyone, provoke anarchy and inefficacy, and encourage outbursts of fear. According to the documents of the period, it is obvious that fear prevailed among all the revolutionary elements and sparked the most absurd behaviour. Papineau's flight was not an isolated case; it was the expression of a much wider phenomenon.

But when we examine this failure, we are necessarily led to connect the insurrectionary movement with its objectives and origins.

The experience of 1837–8, as we have said, was of a nationalist character. Some historians, especially Mason Wade, have proclaimed that it was reformist and liberal in character, because some Anglo-Saxons had taken part in it. It must be pointed out that these elements were far too small in number ever to influence the philosophy of the movement. It would be even surprising, moreover, if the Irishman O'Callaghan had been particularly motivated by the reformist ideal. As for Brown, a small businessman in financial difficulties, the real motives at the source of his decisions are not known. There remain the Nelson brothers, who although they had been closely connected with the French-Canadian milieu, none the less pursued liberal ends. But we must say here that during the whole of the revolutionary period, the authentic liberal and democratic members of the *patriote* group had always been in conflict with those who accorded unquestionable priority to nationalist objectives. The resulting break was primarily the product of these ideological confrontations.

The major objective of the *patriotes* was Lower Canada's independence. Independence aimed at making the liberal professions the only elite in French-Canadian society, an elite which would henceforth be responsible for defining and directing the fulfillment of the common objectives of this society. Independence would allow the development or the restoration of a purely agricultural economy, of a society enclosed in the framework of the seigneurie and governed by the old French customary law. At all costs, they wished to prevent capitalism from establishing what they called inequality of conditions. We find here an unconscious quest for political and cultural isolation and for 'feudalism'. This society, furthermore, was to be democratic and liberal, to the extent, however, that no outside force threatened it. The future of individual liberties and of the secular structures was thus dependent on this fundamental need of defence. In fact, the external peril was unconsciously exaggerated in order to hide an internal danger which was much more effective. The anxiety felt in the face of the demands of progress and the fear of giving up the old securities offered by the traditional order and its taboos, formed the basis of this internal peril. The projection of the collective misfortunes onto the English served above all to hide the need for a complete recasting of the traditional social structures and outlook. When the cause of all trouble was outside, there was no need to give priority to a questioning of traditions.

Independence, in fact, was not aimed at resolving any of the important problems facing French Canada. Whereas the only solution to the agricultural crisis was through a technical revolution, the *patriotes* sought only palliatives, such as the expansion of land areas and the seigneurial territory. In this perspective, it is clear that the rapid exhaustion of the soil threatened as much the new territories of colonization as the old seigneurial lands. This was a faulty response to the demographic question. The extremely rapid growth of the French-Canadian population implied an increase in agricultural activity through improved techniques and, at least as much, the maintenance of the other economic sectors. Equally as serious, independence would mean an immediate severance of economic relations with the Empire. It implied the abandonment of the preferential system which, for other supplementary reasons, would bring about the fall of the timber industry and shipbuilding. According to the French-Canadian leaders, these activities were ladened with a whole past of immorality. Finally, independence would serve to give free reign to the real aspirations of the liberal professions towards feudalism, or at least, towards the old economic régime. On the other hand, the supremacy of agriculture, with its virtues of self-sufficiency, would be ensured by the mass of *censitaires*; on the other, the direction of society would be assumed by the landlords, the clergy, the lay seigneurs, the liberal professions. Because of their obligations in the matter of religion, education, and hospitals, the clergy would derive its revenues from tithes,

seigneurial rents, gifts, and various assessments for the construction of churches and rectories. The seigneurial system would provide for the subsistence of the lay seigneurs as it did for the ecclesiastics. There remained the liberal professionals who, in their normal activities, collected what amounted to an indirect rent, and who also could be considered rentiers in the political sphere.

A political elite protecting the nation's interests, such were the justifications given. In short, the liberal professions unconsciously saw themselves as an aristocratic elite in an hierarchical society. Despite the rationalizations based on liberal and democratic ideologies, their real intention was to preserve a society like the *Ancien Régime* on the banks of the St. Lawrence. All this was illusory, but it is partly explained by the negative reactions which the *conjoncture* of the time had engendered among the liberal professions. It was as if the event and the drama of the Conquest had belatedly invaded the collective consciousness to inhibit it, and to trigger a whole series of defensive reflexes. Thus, under the guise of democracy and liberal aspirations which had a certain authentic character, we witness the search for an impossible isolation leading to a 'feudal' and theocratic society. Under these conditions, a democracy and a liberal State were inconceivable.

The nationalist venture of 1837–8 was too tightly linked to the ambitions of specific individuals, to the immediate interests of the liberal professions, and to the particular difficulties to the period to succeed. It was not based on the elements which would have allowed the building of a better future. The economic weakness of the French Canadians was due above all to their mental outlook, their level of technical skills, their traditions, and their institutions. There certainly, for there is no need to believe that they were totally blameless, is the major reason for the failure of the insurrectionary movement.

More than anything, this lack of justification in regard to long-term interests and progressive values accounts for the behaviour of the majority of the revolutionary leaders. They were prevented from entering wholeheartedly into their venture by a sort of bad faith. This was also true of the leaders of the Banque de Peuple who, at the last moment, refused to invest in independence.

In fact, the economic crisis of 1837–8 had not seriously disrupted the structures which served to support the bourgeoisie of Lower Canada and relations with the Empire. The crisis in timber and shipbuilding was only temporary and, in 1839, expansion once again characterized the *conjoncture*. The extent of the recovery, as it appears in the averages for the years 1837–42, indicates the vigour of the sectors which helped to cushion the effects of the agricultural crisis. Nevertheless, the difficulties of those years had been great enough to make glaringly apparent an overall situation which had become intolerable. Durham, who carried out his studies during this critical period, was certainly deeply influenced by the particular events of his stay.

NOTES

1. APQ, QBT, Minute Book (1832–42), H. Bliss to the president of QBT (November 12, 1836).
2. APQ, QBT, Minute Book (1832–42). Decisions adopted from May 16 to 18, 1837.
3. Ibid. (1832–42), the same to the same (September 1, 1837).
4. *Le Canadien*, January 16, 1837.
5. Extract from *La Minerve*, idem.
6. *Le Canadien*, January 9, 1837.
7. Ibid., February 20, 1837.
8. Idem.
9. RAPQ (1951–53), pp. 288*ff.* F. Papineau to L.-J.P. (May 16, 1837).
10. *Le Canadien*, May 26, 1837.
11. APQ, P.-B., Lafontaine to Chapman (February 17, 1837).
12. *Le Canadien*, January 23, 1837.
13. Ibid., June 6, 1837.
14. RAPQ (1953–55), p. 290, J. P. to L.-L.-A. P. (April 27, 1838).

---

4   From Allan Greer, *The Patriots and the People: The Rebellion of 1837 in Rural Lower Canada* (Toronto: University of Toronto Press, 1993), 189–208.

THE QUEEN IS A WHORE!

Queen Victoria ascended the throne of England in August 1837, just as tensions in Lower Canada were reaching a boiling point. There is no indication that the 17-year-old monarch gave much immediate thought to the political squabbles wracking her North American possessions, but her coronation provided Canadians with an occasion for further reflections on sovereign authority and state forms. 'Loyal' Montreal managed to mount a parade to celebrate the happy event, and at Sorel the little garrison fired off a salute. A tavern-keeper's wife remarked to onlookers at the latter, 'There you are, celebrations for the coronation of the queen; she had better watch out or she'll be decrowned.'[1] It was the *Te Deum* ordered for the middle of August by the bishop of Montreal, the usual service on such occasions, that aroused the greatest controversy. At St. Polycarpe, where the curé dared to say a few words in praise of the new monarch, local patriots managed to stop the ceremony. 'No sooner did the *Te Deum* commence, than the people quitted the church bodily, leaving the women and *marguilliers* (churchwardens) to keep his Reverence company. The deputy beadle was beginning to ring the bell when the people got out, but the parishioners stopped him, telling him that the bell belonged to them, and not the Queen of England, and that it should not be rung.'[2] Note the language used by the *Vindicator* to describe this incident: the counterposing of 'the *people*' and 'the *women.*' Half the population of the province might well have viewed these words as ominous signals, emanating as they did from the presses of a journal dedicated to the principle of popular sovereignty!

That this was no accidental slip is underlined by the sexual references in protests against the coronation *Te Deum*. In the parish of Contrecoeur a radical merchant led an exodus from the church shouting, 'It is painful to have to sing the *Te Deum* for the damn queen, damned whore with her legs in the air.' A Patriot orator addressing the people of Nicolet from the church porch was reported to have said, 'As for the king, he is nothing but a big zero to whom Canadians pay a pension . . . The proof that kings are nothing but zeros is that we are now governed by a young queen seventeen years of age.' Later, at the time of the battles of November and December, an American patriot sympathizer got into trouble at St. Athanase by throwing 'ridicule on the person of the sovereign by saying the loyalists were governed by a little girl, that they were governed by petticoats.'[3] Such language would certainly have shocked English radicals; they were well disposed towards the young queen who seemed to them a much more sympathetic figure than her notorious uncle, William IV.[4] At the same time, it directs our attention to some important characteristics of the Patriot movement as regards both gender and concepts of legitimate political authority.

MONARCHY OR REPUBLIC?

All the abuse of poor Victoria indicates that of course the queen and the monarchy were not 'a zero' in the French Canadian countryside. For all that the habitants took for granted a certain popular sovereignty within the local community, their concept of the state and the empire was highly personalized, focusing on the reigning king or queen. There is nothing peculiar in this attitude; it is common among peasants throughout the western world. Even among the 'educated classes' the notion that a stable political structure needed to be embodied in a royal personage still enjoyed widespread support in the first half of the nineteenth century. [. . .]

Canadians of course lived far from any flesh and blood monarch, although governors under the French and British régimes did do their best to put on a display of viceregal pomp and ceremony in the colony. More generally, political authority in our period did manifest itself in personal terms that reinforced monarchical habits of thought, no doubt accentuated by the strong military presence in Canada. Moreover, the Church did its utmost to impress on the faithful their duty to the king, not only in *Te Deum* services for coronations and royal births, but also in sermons from the pulpit. Political leaders added their voices in support, including the Patriots, who until the eve of the Rebellion always protested their loyalty to the crown even as they denounced colonial Tories and wicked British ministers.[5]

A basically royalist political vocabulary does not imply a docile acceptance of authority. People who have been taught to regard the distant king as a father-figure who has the best interests of his subjects at heart, often tend to conclude, when things go badly, that exploitive officials, merchants, or aristocrats are the monarch's enemies as well as their own. In this way royalism can become a revolutionary ideology (though one with built-in limitations inhibiting the development of popular democracy), as it was indeed in countless plebeian risings, such as the one that shook rural France in the summer of 1789 when thousands of peasants attacked seigneurial chateaux, acting, so they thought, 'on orders from the king'.[6] It should be noted that the peasant class is not the only one that tends to venerate the king while blaming his advisers. The American and French revolutions were already well under way before their bourgeois leaders began to attack George III, Louis XVI, and the institution of monarchy.[7] (Tom Paine's *Common Sense* caused a sensation early in 1776 when it called for an independent American republic.) Yet the dynamic of the revolutions eventually broke the spell of royalty and led to the full development of a republican political discourse, one that had often been there all along in embryonic form. So it was in Lower Canada, where the crisis of the 1830s moved the bourgeois Patriots to an entirely republican outlook. Hence their determination to discredit the monarch as the personal symbol of government authority and metropolitan rule.

[. . .]

The spell of traditional authority, as represented by priest and bishop, governor and queen, was giving way. People of different classes and levels of education were considering new ways of constituting a state and governing a human community. Could Canadians rule themselves? Could government derive its legitimacy from the people rather than historic rights of conquest and religious sanction? Patriot leaders answered these questions in the positive, and they drove home the point explicitly in speeches and newspaper articles, while expressing the same message in symbolic forms as well, notably through the use of flags and banners. Long before he began to take the movement seriously as a military threat, the commander of British forces in Lower Canada fretted over the emblems of popular sovereignty sprouting up in the Richelieu valley. 'The tri coloured flag has been displayed at two taverns between St Denis and St Charles', wrote Sir John Colborne in October 1837. 'Many of the taverns have discontinued their signs and substituted for them an Eagle.'[8]

[. . .]

MASCULINE POLITICS

Granted that the patriots objected to the institution of monarchy and to the fact of British rule;

but why did they have to make an issue—and in such a cruel and personal way—of Queen Victoria's sex? Well, certainly their sensitivity was not unique in the international republican community of the period. Recent scholarship has demonstrated that considerations of sexual difference were of central concern to political writers and revolutionaries of the late eighteenth- early nineteenth-century period. To the degree that they challenged existing hierarchies on egalitarian grounds and insisted that 'the people' ought to rule, philosophes, Jacobins, and American patriots had to grapple with the question of what 'the people' was. It certainly was not all human beings resident in a given territory: not everyone was to participate equally and in the same way in sovereign authority. Women in particular tended to be excluded from direct political participation in the republican city. Pronouncements may have been cryptic and susceptible to multiple interpretations, with much assumed and little expressed; the effect was none the less for sex to become increasingly the primary dividing line between rulers and ruled in the age of the great bourgeois revolutions. Partly this exclusion arose by default, as older conceptions of political privilege based on birth, sacerdotal status, and so on came under attack, but also it derived from a profoundly gendered republican concept of citizenship.

Inspired by a particular reading of the history of ancient Greece and Rome, modern republicans such as Jean-Jacques Rousseau believed that men were uniquely qualified for the responsibilities of citizenship.[9] They were better suited for military combat, and, it was felt, all good citizens had to be prepared to defend their country on the battlefield. More fundamentally, Rousseau thought that males were by nature more apt to subordinate selfish and sectional interests for the good of the whole community. Women, by contrast, were necessarily associated with childbirth and nurturing; consequently, their orientation was to the family, a particularistic allegiance which they could not fully transcend without denying their nature. Thanks to their looser attachment to specific loved ones, men had the potential to develop the civic virtue—the dedication to the common good—required in any healthy republic. It is important to note, however, that Rousseau did not consider women inferior to men. On the contrary, he attached great value to the loving and nurturing domestic sphere where women found their true calling. His effusions over motherhood and conjugal bliss underline the fact that for Rousseau women's familial role was the essential complement of active male citizenship. Domestic life and public life, he implied, were equally important elements of civilized existence. In order to discharge her duty, the republican woman needed to exercise a special sort of virtue: not public-spirited courage, but 'sexual innocence and chastity' were her distinguishing characteristics, and as an outward guarantee of monogamous behaviour, she had to confine herself to the private realm.[10]

Rousseau was in no simple sense a male-supremacist; indeed his contemporary defenders insist that he accorded a great deal of legitimate power to women, though it was covert power, exercised through their sexual influence over particular men.[11] Moreover, with his emphasis on liberty and on the cultivation of the individual personality, he can plausibly be seen as the intellectual ancestor of modern women's liberation. One need only extend to females the reasoning that the philosopher applies to 'Man' and unsettling conclusions soon follow. The fact remains that Rousseau himself did not present a feminist reading of Jean-Jacques. Everywhere one turns in his writings, the needs of men take precedence, and women appear in a positive light to the degree that they are helpful to men.

I have dwelt on Rousseau, not because his works provided an instruction manual for Lower Canadian Patriots, but because he was one of the few writers of the period who gave sustained and explicit attention to the gender dimension of politics. Without denying the originality of his genius, I think it is fair to suggest that many of the essential features of Rousseau's thought in this area were characteristic of the international republican movement. Certainly echoes can be detected in the Patriot press of the notion that men and women possessed complementary but fundamentally different moral natures. An article published in *La Minerve* under the title 'The Two Republics' makes this point quite explicitly:

> The moral world is a mixture composed of men and women and it owes to this combination the greatest part of its customs, usages and ceremonies; if there were no more women in the human race, men would be unrecognizable. It is only in seeking to please the opposite sex that they manage to refine themselves . . . Women, for their part, owe everything to that other half of the human race, to which they find themselves joined . . . It is to the desire to please him [man] that they owe that gracious air, those eyes which say so many things, that modest blush which embellishes their complexion, that voice so soft and touching. This reciprocal desire is indeed a precious instinct in both sexes, one which tends towards the perfection of each of them. Thus a man with no interest in women will ordinarily become a savage; by the same token, a woman, intended by nature to get along with and to appear with man, can scarcely hate or despise him without becoming a ferocious and unbearable creature.[12]

Such sentiments were by no means limited to republican circles. Indeed, the basic notion that women belonged in a (valourized) domestic setting while men should run the state and the community became widely prevalent everywhere the bourgeoisie gained the ascendancy throughout the eighteenth century and well into the nineteenth. During the French Revolution, for example, there was some initial encouragement for the politicization of women, but it was soon followed by a policy of rigid exclusion from public life on the grounds that both the polity and the family suffered when women strayed into the male realm of active citizenship. Such treatment at the hands of the Jacobins led the feminist/royalist Olympe de Gouges to protest that 'Women are now respected and excluded, under the Old Régime they were despised and powerful.'[13] Earlier, American women had been treated similarly during 'their' revolutionary war.[14]

Women were not always 'respected' under the new order: witness the patriots' misogynous and obscene verbal assault on Queen Victoria. In this respect, too, Lower Canadian behaviour seems to reflect widespread attitudes of the period, attitudes particularly characteristic of republicanism. What one might call the 'vulgar Rousseauian' outlook venerated the virtuous woman who kept to the domestic sphere, and was profoundly suspicious of any woman who ventured into the political realm. Quite apart from the fact that women were not by nature equipped to cope with public affairs, their attempts to take part in politics posed a direct danger to the hallowed conjugal family, because public life was conceived of in republican discourse as entailing a literally *public* performance open to the gaze of the community. Whereas for men publicity was the guarantee of virtue, the opposite applied for women. Self-display was repugnant to good women because it signified sexual immorality, just as surely as female confinement to private pursuits indicated chastity. In Rousseau's words, 'A woman's audacity is the sure sign of her shame.' Thus were the two meanings of the phrase 'public woman'—that is, politically prominent individual and prostitute—elided in the republican mind of the period.[15]

Sexual disorder on the part of women, as evidenced by political self-assertion, was considered deplorable for all sorts of reasons, but it is important to note that it posed specifically *political* dangers from the republican point of view. When women forsook the family hearth,

they could not support their husbands or raise their sons as good future citizens. More fundamentally, they acted against their chaste and modest nature; the result, since women are so important and men so highly dependent on them, was to denature men, to make them effeminate and therefore susceptible to tyranny. Thus it was that republicans tended to associate political corruption among males—and this of course was the primary threat to liberty—with sexual corruption among females.[16] It is when we recognize this linkage between public roles for women, sexual disorder, and political corruption and tyranny that we begin to understand why the patriots could even conceive of accusing Victoria Regina—innocent, young, but undeniably a prominent public figure—of being a 'whore'.

A reader might well protest at this point that neither Rousseau nor the Patriots invented patriarchy. The notion that 'a woman's place is in the home' and under the authority of her husband was of course quite ancient, as Papineau made clear when he quoted Scripture to chastise his wife's 'independence'. What was new in the early nineteenth century was the peculiarly insistent emphasis on the 'cult of female domesticity', and the concomitant male monopoly over public affairs. Under an earlier tradition (what one might call, in a very loose sense, the 'ancien régime'), matters were less clear-cut, particularly where politics was concerned, and there was no justification for asserting that men should partake of the sovereign power of the state simply because they were men. Most people were regarded as *subjects* and, to that degree, men and women were politically on a par. Conversely, some women—from Madame de Pompadour in France to Madame Péan in Canada—did exercise great influence over affairs of state.[17]

[. . .]

For many years Lower Canadian women enjoyed the suffrage, at least to some extent.[18] The Constitutional Act of 1791 had accorded the vote in Legislative Assembly elections on the basis of a property qualification, with no mention of sex. Accordingly, women possessed of the requisite property (usually this meant widows) often cast their votes. Female suffrage was not universally accepted; evidence from surviving poll books indicates that, depending on the election and on the constituency, substantial numbers of women or none at all might vote.[19] Certainly there were returning officers who turned women away from the hustings 'in consequence of their sex'. In one case, this reaction provoked objections from men whose candidate stood to benefit from a sex-blind franchise. 'Property and not persons', they insisted, 'is the basis of representation in the English government', pursuing an argument for female suffrage that in the context can only be called 'conservative'.[20] (We might note in passing a fact that has escaped the attention of nationalist/feminist historians: this partial and contested female franchise was not unique to Lower Canada. It was not unheard of for women's votes to be accepted in Britain and its colonies in the eighteenth century, and there were French women who helped elect representatives to the Estates-General of 1789.)

The spectacle of women voting appeared increasingly anomalous to Lower Canadian parliamentarians, and in 1834 they passed a bill formally disenfranchising women. It is worth noting that this measure was not controversial, nor did it seem very important to its supporters. The clause in the law regulating elections that disenfranchised women in fact received less attention than matters like the appointment of returning officers and the administration of oaths. It was originally proposed by John Neilson, a moderate from Quebec City who had earlier broken with Papineau and the more radical Patriots. Nonetheless, Papineau threw his full support behind the measure, in spite of his bitter feud with Neilson. Indeed, I have been unable to find a trace of any sort of objection to the exclusion of women from the electoral process. Lower Canadian newspapers of every political stripe (needless to say, all were written by men and for men) either ignored the measure or treated it as a straightforward

housekeeping matter.[21] Even in the turbulent and fiercely partisan 1830s there were subjects on which the parties could agree!

Louis-Joseph Papineau was the only member of the Assembly to articulate a justification for an exclusion the necessity for which seemed entirely self-evident to his colleagues. Significantly, in framing his argument against females' voting, he did not allude to any sort of defect in judgment or political understanding that ought to disqualify women, although he did take it for granted that married women would vote the same way as their husbands. What concerned Papineau was rather the danger posed to the domestic sexual order by women's participating in the public exercise of the suffrage (recall that this was long before the introduction of the secret ballot). 'It is ridiculous', he declared, 'it is odious to see women dragged up to the hustings by their husbands, girls by their fathers, often against their will. The public interest, decency and the modesty of the fair sex require that these scandals cease.'[22] Never mind the fact that all this anxiety about fathers and husbands is irrelevant in a situation where almost all the female voters were widows. We might even pass over the irony of this male politician casting himself in the role of gallant protector of frail femininity as he substantially narrows the political rights of women. What seems to me impossible to ignore—and characteristically republican—about Papineau's speech is the way it associates three things: (1) 'the public interest', (2) feminine chastity and 'modesty', and (3) the withdrawal of women from the public arena. Such a linkage is of course in line with Rousseau's convictions. Thus it seems entirely fitting that, while male politicians of every persuasion were in basic agreement on gender-political issues, it should be a radical who took the strongest stand.

[. . .]

In the context of the 1830s the patriot movement certainly had no monopoly on patriarchy, and their defeat in the course of the Rebellion certainly did not signal the liberation of Lower Canada's women. Indeed, the state structure and political order instituted after 1838 was, if anything, more thoroughly masculine than anything the patriots seem to have contemplated.[23] The ideology of 'separate spheres' was gaining strength throughout the Euro-Atlantic world at this time, and influential men of virtually all shades on the political spectrum were affected. One can nevertheless see the Patriot party as the Lower Canadian spearhead of this wider shift in the politico-sexual order. It was within its ranks that the democratic conception of a 'public sphere' open to every citizen without privilege or distinction was enunciated most clearly and forcefully. Since the patriots' definition of citizenship excluded women, their discourse of liberation was as much about sex as it was about politics. Accordingly, one might well regard the Rebellion of 1837–8 as constituting, among other things, a significant moment in the process of gender formation in French Canada.

MEN AND WOMEN DURING THE REBELLION

The crisis of the summer of 1837 began, in fact, with a rather awkward attempt on the part of the Patriots to attract the active support of women. It was in the context of the campaign to boycott British imports that radical men turned to their wives and mothers for support. In both the boycott itself and the consequent mobilization of women the Patriots were following the pre-Revolutionary American experience, as Papineau and his associates were well aware.[24] Women were thought to have a critical role to play, in the first instance as consumers. Since textiles accounted for a large part of British exports to Canada, the Patriot press felt called upon to lecture the ladies of the country on the need to forgo foreign finery in favour of plain homespun.
[. . .]

The non-importation campaign entailed the mobilization of women above all in the role of domestic producers. In some parts of the province—particularly the Richelieu valley—women did take up the challenge. At St. Charles a man later recalled, 'Even the women shared the general enthusiasm . . . And they competed with one another to produce the finest cloth.'[25] Previously ignored in Patriot discourse, women began to appear repeatedly in the radical press, though usually in anonymous and stereotyped terms. At a banquet at Contrecoeur, for example, 56 men raised their glasses to toast 'Josephte, the wife of Jean-Baptiste, as patriotic as she is beautiful, no less virtuous than she is pleasant, she will make a powerful contribution to the happiness of the country by her industry and by her efforts to encourage domestic manufactures.'[26]

First they take away Josephte's vote, then they ask her to toil at the hand-loom in order to free the country! The temptation is great to treat the Patriot appeal to women with complete cynicism. Yet there was some complexity to the position of the radical men and some hints of movement in the direction of fuller citizenship for women as the crisis of 1837 deepened. A newspaper reprinted extracts from Harriet Martineau's work, 'The Political Non-existence of Women'.[27] It also gave favourable reports of the formation of patriotic women's associations in several rural parishes. Little is known about these organizations themselves, but by September 1837 they seem to have extended their attention to other matters in addition to the boycott.
[. . .]

Of course no one really expected women to shoulder arms in the coming struggle. Still, behind the condescending treatment of the 'patriotic ladies' lies a recognition of the reality of feminine patriotism and of the importance of women's contribution to the national mobilization. Like other middle-class radicals in other countries, the Patriots found themselves impelled by the revolutionary situation itself to modify their views somewhat in order to bring women into the movement. Their more democratic approach to poor men was analogous. But where women were concerned, there was perhaps a more deeply felt ambivalence about this widening process, because the relationships involved were more intimate than those of class. Thus, while it tried to stimulate and encourage women's politicization, the radical press constantly betrayed, by repeated reference to the ladies' weakness and beauty, its anxiety about the dangers of subverting the sexual hierarchy. With some misgivings, Patriot men stretched and extended the malleable concept of female domesticity in ways that allowed women to become more directly involved in the national struggle; nevertheless, they emphatically did not abandon the ideology of separate spheres.

The inescapable fact is that the Patriot movement was a fundamentally masculine phenomenon, in its style as well as in its philosophical orientation. Orators at the protest meetings held in the summer of 1837 emphasized themes of independence, honour, and manly valour in appeals clearly addressed to men. Women were certainly a presence at these meetings; in fact, Constitutionalist newspapers liked to declare that the crowds attending anti-coercion rallies were mostly composed of women and children. The response of the Patriot press was revealing: rather than challenging the assumption that a female presence detracted from the seriousness of the proceedings, the *Vindicator* would instead insist that 'the handsome and patriotic ladies' had confined their participation to waving handkerchiefs from the windows of nearby houses.[28]

[. . .]

It is hardly surprising then that women generally did not embrace the patriot cause with great enthusiasm. To say so is not to deny or to belittle the very real suffering of the hundreds of women who found their possessions stolen, their homes in ashes, and their husbands in prison in the wake of the battles of 1837 and 1838. We know, moreover, that in addition to their efforts on behalf of the non-importation campaign, women sewed banners, sheltered fugitives, and otherwise aided the insurgents; one woman even acquired a reputation in the parish of St. Benoit by composing satirical songs directed against the 'chouayen' priest of a neighbouring parish.[29] Yet aside from these auxiliary contributions, evidence of active female commitment to the patriot cause is almost non-existent. Among the 1,356 names on the official lists of political prisoners for the Rebellion period, not one can be identified as a woman.[30] The thousands of depositions and other narrative sources convey a similar impression: nowhere did women play a prominent or even a very active role, either as fighters or as spies, agitators, or journalists.[31] It is true that women have generally been slighted in the records favoured by historians, but it would be a serious mistake to attribute the resounding silence on this score merely to documentary bias.

Women do appear in the sources, but they do so principally in a stance of opposition to the patriots and their insurrection. The testimony of dozens of witnesses and prisoners mentions wives urging their husbands to stay home rather than report to a rebel camp. Of course contemporaries explained this behaviour as nothing more than the weakness of the weaker sex, but one wonders whether the women concerned might not have displayed greater firmness had they found the cause more inspiring. Certainly there is no reason to think that the women of French Canada held back from full support of the Rebellion out of any ingrained timidity or 'conservatism'. Their record of anti-government activism in the eighteenth century is sufficient refutation of that hypothesis. Obviously something had changed between 1775, when the 'Queen of Hungary' had led the peasants of the Ile d'Orléans, and 1837, when the anti-government forces could boast no heroines. One new factor on the scene was the Patriot movement which, in spite of half-hearted attempts to sponsor women's organizations, clearly stood for a masculine—indeed a masculinizing—politics in which women were not welcome. And no doubt many women had no desire to be involved in political struggle, for or against the British colonial régime in Lower Canada. After all, the evolving ideology of female domesticity was not the exclusive property of patriots, nor was it limited to men alone. As

it gained hegemonic status through the Euro-Atlantic world,[32] women themselves tended increasingly to subscribe to the notion that national affairs should be left to men.

[. . .]

NOTES

1. Bibliothèque nationale, Montreal, journal of Romuald Trudeau, 12: 25; ANQ, 1837, no. 1698, Welles to Goldie, 19 November 1838 (author's translation)

2. *Vindicator*, 1 September 1837

3. ANQ, 1837, no. 324, déposition du Baron Augustin de Diemar, 21 December 1837 (author's translation); ibid., no. 242, déposition de Joseph-Louis Pinard, 1 February 1838; ibid., deposition of Thomas Casson, 31 December 1838 (cf. ibid., no. 1483, Lacombe to Walcott, 23 August 1837). The loyalists, for their part, struck a chivalrous posture, vowing to 'make any sacrifice in maintaining the legitimate authority of our young and beauteous Queen.' Speech by the Hon. Mr McGill, Montreal, 23 October 1837, in *Assemblées publiques, résolutions et déclarations de 1837–1838*, ed. Jean-Paul Bernard (Montreal: VLB éditeur 1988), 239

4. Dorothy Thompson, personal communication

5. See, for example, Papineau's speech on the occasion of the death of George III, in *Papineau: textes choisis*, ed. Fernand Ouellet (Quebec: Presses de l'Université Laval 1970), 21–2.

6. Georges Lefebvre, *The Great Fear: Rural Panic in Revolutionary France*, trans. Joan White (Princeton: Princeton UP 1973)

7. Pauline Maier, *From Resistance to Revolution: Colonial Radicals and the Development of American Opposition to Britain, 1765–1776* (New York: Knopf 1972)

8. NA, British Military Records, C1272: 8, Colborne to Gosford, 6 October 1837

9. This point is made in several studies, but I found particularly useful Joel Schwartz, *The Sexual Politics of Jean-Jacques Rousseau* (Chicago: University of Chicago Press 1984). The basic texts are the *Discourse on the Origins of Inequality*, the *Social Contract*, *Letter to M. d'Alembert*, and *Emile*.

10. Joan B. Landes, *Women and the Public Sphere in the Age of the French Revolution* (Ithaca: Cornell UP 1988)

11. Schwartz, *Sexual Politics*

12. *La Minerve*, 28 July 1836 (author's translation)

13. Darline Gay Levy, Harriet Branson Applewhite, and Mary Durham Johnson, ed., *Women in Revolutionary Paris, 1789–1795* (Urbana: University of illinois Press 1979); Sîan Reynolds, 'Marianne's Citizens? Women, the Republic and Universal Suffrage in France', in *Women, State and Revolution: Essays on Power and Gender in Europe since 1789* (Amherst: University of Massachusetts Press 1987), 101–22; Landes, *Women and the Public Sphere*. The de Gouges quotation is from Dorinda Outram, 'Le langage mâle de la vertu: Women and the Discourse of the French Revolution', in *The Social History of Language*, ed. Peter Burke and Roy Porter (Cambridge: Cambridge UP 1987), 126.

14. Linda Kerber, *Women of the Republic: Intellect and Ideology in Revolutionary America* (Chapel Hill: University of North Carolina Press 1980)

15. Landes, *Women and the Public Sphere*. Rousseau quotation, 75

16. Outram, 'Le langage mâle.' A wonderful illustration of this outlook can be found in the work of Rousseau's English contemporary and fellow republican, Edward Gibbon. Gibbon devotes several long and salacious pages in chapter 20 of *The Decline and Fall of the Roman Empire* to the misdeeds of the sixth-century empress, Theodora, whose fond husband, Justinian, committed the fundamental error of making his wife not a consort but a co-ruler. Long before she managed to seduce Justinian, Gibbon explains, Theodora was renowned in Constantinople and beyond for her beautiful face and figure: 'But this form was degraded by the facility with which it was exposed to

the public eye, and prostituted to licentious desire. Her venal charms were abandoned to a promiscuous crowd of citizens and strangers, of every rank and of every profession: the fortunate lover who had been promised a night of enjoyment was often driven from her bed by a stronger or more wealthy favourite.' And so on.

17. 'This social system,' writes Colin Coates, referring to New France and to the tribulations of Madeleine de Verchères, seigneuresse and military heroine, 'though patriarchal, allowed certain women to wield a great deal of power.' He might have added the qualification 'overtly' to distinguish better the eighteenth century from the nineteenth, when men still expected elite women to wield power, but quietly and privately. Colin Coates, 'Authority and Illegitimacy in New France: The Burial of Bishop Saint-Vallier and Madeleine de Verchères vs. the Priest of Batiscan', *Histoire sociale—Social History* 22 (May 1989): 65–90

18. W.R. Riddell, 'Woman Franchise in Quebec, a Century Ago', Royal Society of Canada, *Proceedings and Transactions* 22 (1928), section 2, 85–99; Fernand Ouellet, *Le Bas-Canada, 1791–2840: changements structuraux et crise* (Ottawa: Editions de l'Université d'Ottawa 1976), 42–3, 350; David De Brou, 'Mass Political Behaviour in Upper-Town Quebec, 1792–1836' (Ph.D. thesis, University of Ottawa, 1989), 94–8

19. In addition to the works noted above, see NA, Lower Canada Election Records, vol. 21, poll books for: Quebec county, 1804 (no women voted); Charlesbourg county, 1817 (no women voted); borough of William Henry, 1827 (three women attempted to vote, one rejected). In the Montreal West election of 1832, on the other hand, Ouellet found 199 women among the 1,533 voters.

20. Petition of divers electors, Upper Town, Quebec, 1828, in *Documents relating to the Constitutional History of Canada, 1819–1828*, ed. A.G. Doughty and N. Story (Ottawa: King's Printer 1935), 520

21. *L'Ami du Peuple*, 27 January 1834; *Montreal Gazette*, 1 February 1834; *La Minerve*, 3 February 1834. *Le Canadien* and *L'Echo du Pays* took no notice of the disenfranchisement of women. It should be noted that the electoral

bill of 1834, after sailing through the House of Assembly, was held up at subsequent stages of the legislative process and, for reasons quite unconnected with the clause relating to female voters, it never seems to have been enacted into law. Nevertheless, women do not seem to have been admitted to the hustings after 1834. Just to be sure, the parliament of the province of Canada prohibited women from voting in 1849.

22. *La Minerve*, 3 February 1834 (author's translation). See also *Montreal Gazette*, 1 February 1834.

23. See Lykke de la Cour, Cecilia Morgan, and Mariana Valverde, 'Gender and State Formation in Nineteenth-Century Canada', in *Colonial Leviathan: State Formation in Mid-Nineteenth-Century Canada*, ed. Allan Greer and Ian Radforth (Toronto: UTP 1992), 163–91.

24. See Papineau's speech as reported in *Vindicator*, 6 June 1837. Cf. Kerber, *Women of the Republic*.

25. NA, MG24, B82, 'Quelques notes historiques sur les événements politiques de 1837 en Canada', 9

26. *La Minerve*, 17 August 1837 (author's translation)

27. *Vindicator*, 4 July 1837

28. See, for example, the accounts of the meetings at Ste Scholastique and Napierville in Vindicator, 6 Jane 1837 and 25 July 1837.

29. Marcelle Reeves-Morache, 'La canadienne pendant les troubles de 1837–1838', *RHAF* 5 (June 1951): 99–117; Micheline Dumont et al., *Quebec Women: A History*, trans. Roger Gannon and Rosalind Gill (Toronto: Women's Press 1987), 118–24

30. BPP 14: 405–25. Of course a man was more likely to be arrested than a woman, even if each committed the same political offence. Nevertheless, in spite of the obvious bias in arrest figures, the complete and absolute absence of women political prisoners is remarkable.

31. Some have attempted (see works by Reeves-Morache and Dumont et al. cited above) to make Emilie Boileau of Chambly into a patriot Madeleine de Verchères, but their case is quite unconvincing. It seems to rest on a passage in the memoirs of R.S.M. Bouchette, in which Bouchette describes a gathering of patriots at the home of Emilie and her husband, Timothée Kimber, during the crisis of 1837. Bouchette was impressed by the fact that Madame Kimber was

holding a pistol. Far from firing this weapon, or even brandishing it in any encounter with anti-patriot forces, there is no indication that she ever carried it outside her own house!

32. Among other studies suggesting a parallel tendency in various countries in the nineteenth century for women to withdraw from political activism that seemed normal in the eighteenth century, see Janet L. Polasky, 'Women in Revolutionary Belgium: From Stone Throwers to Hearth Tenders', *History Workshop* 21 (Spring 1986): 87–104.

Chapter Ten

Women in British North America

READINGS

Primary Documents

1   'To the Electors of Quebec County', *Le Canadien,* 21 May 1808

2   From *The Proper Sphere and Influence of Woman in Christian Society: Being a Lecture Delivered by Rev. Robert Sedgewick before the Young Men's Christian Association, Halifax, N.S., November 1856,* Robert Sedgewick

Historical Interpretations

3   From 'The Riddle of Peggy Mountain: Regulation of Irish Women's Sexuality on the Southern Avalon, 1750–1860', Willeen Keough

4   From 'Disenfranchised but not Quiescent: Women Petitioners in New Brunswick in the mid-19th Century', Gail Campbell

Introduction

During the first half of the nineteenth century, the British colonial presence in North America grew to the point of fostering rebellion in the Canadas. Ultimately, this growth prompted the creation of something else: a new entity called the Dominion of Canada. Along the way toward this more familiar set of political landmarks, the male-dominant farming, soldiering, and trading colonies came to include more women and families. The result was reproduction, both of the biological kind and of the social norms arising from the places from which immigrants had come. These norms meant differing rights, privileges, and expectations for men and women, both at home and in the community.

Women were not entirely without outlets for their talents, creativity, and grievances. However, these opportunities tended to be limited by the assumption that women would want to participate only in those areas of life that touched upon womanly or family welfare. Politics was one such controversial field, made even more controversial by the fact that only a small percentage of women could vote (usually widows, as heads of their families). The primary sources chosen for this topic reflect attitudes toward women in public and private life. Though the letter to voters in Quebec was probably intended to harm the election campaign of the candidate named, it tells us much about contemporary morality and expectations surrounding male–female relationships. Rev. Sedgewick's lecture, a recitation of the existing boundaries between men and women and a declaration that women were to *complement* men, is notable as well because it was pitched at young men who were supposed to be forming their own systems of belief and ethics.

Despite the official discourses, women's behaviours did not always conform to the expected norms. In her article, Willeen Keough shows that women's lives in Newfoundland during the colonial period and the first half of the nineteenth century were different from the ideal promoted by Sedgewick. Gail Campbell discusses the means of expression open to women in a society that did not grant them the right to vote: petitions and appeals to male-dominated authorities.

QUESTIONS FOR CONSIDERATION

1. What does the letter from 'The Unfortunate Jeannette' suggest about attitudes toward women's participation or non-participation in political life during the early part of the nineteenth century?

2. How does Rev. Sedgewick justify not extending various rights and privileges to women, even though he seems to be in favour of all of these benefits for men?

3. Without thinking about questions of fairness or justice, were there any practical purposes for women and men maintaining these semi-exclusive existences?

4. According to Campbell's account, what sorts of things did women create petitions about, and why?

5. Keough describes a society that is fragmented or stratified, and not only because of gender. What were the major (and minor) ways used to differentiate between people in colonial Newfoundland?

SUGGESTIONS FOR FURTHER READING

Backhouse, Constance, *Petticoats and Prejudice: Women and Law in Nineteenth-Century Canada* (Toronto: Women's Press, for the Osgoode Society, 1991)

Chambers, Lori, *Married Women and Property Law in Victorian Ontario* (Toronto: University of Toronto Press, 1997)

Gleason, Mona, Tamara Myers, and Adele Perry, eds., *Rethinking Canada: The Promise of Women's History* (Toronto: Oxford University Press, 2010)

Guildford, Janet, and Suzanne Morton, eds., *Separate Spheres: Women's Worlds in the 19th-Century Maritimes* (Fredericton: Acadiensis Press, 1994)

Keough, Willeen, *The Slender Thread: Irish Women on the Southern Avalon Peninsula of Newfoundland, 1750–1860* (New York: Columbia University Press, 2006)

Morgan, Cecilia, *Public Men and Virtuous Women: The Gendered Languages of Religion and Politics in Upper Canada 1791–1850* (Toronto: University of Toronto Press, 1996)

Noël, Françoise, *Family Life and Sociability in Upper and Lower Canada, 1780–1870: A View from Diaries and Family Correspondence* (Montreal and Kingston: McGill-Queen's University Press, 2003)

PRIMARY DOCUMENTS

1   'To the Electors of Quebec County', *Le Canadien*, 21 May 1808

TO THE ELECTORS OF QUEBEC COUNTY

Gentlemen,

Although it is not customary for women to address you at election time, I hope you will forgive the liberty of an unfortunate soul who has no other resource than to appeal to your sense of justice. To whom else could I appeal? The ungrateful wretch I complain of is the Judge himself.

You know well enough, Gentlemen, the trouble I went to in working for him during the election campaign at Charlesbourg four years ago; he had suffered badly in the election in the Upper Town; and out of pity, as many of you did, I worked as hard as I could to assure his triumph. Gentlemen, you witnessed this triumph of which he boasted so much. Yet, no sooner had he won than he forgot all I had done for him, and, coward that he is, abandoned me. He had the insolence to tell me that it was I who was harming his reputation among you. Gentlemen, will you let this kind of treachery go unpunished? Will your votes in his favour reward his betrayal? Will you elect him for having broken faith with me?

The ingrate even got married, and began to frequent the Church; this was to obtain your votes. He is inconstant I assure you; I know him, he will use any means to achieve his end.

He makes promises to you, but how many promises did he make to me? He will deceive you as he deceived me. He will deceive you as he deceived the Lower Town. How many promises did he not make to the voters on the day of his triumph four years ago?

This false man has never been able to win an election except in Three Rivers. . . . What honour will you gain in electing him? The Upper Town scorned him four years ago, Deschambault had driven him out, Nicolet had driven him out. Will it be that Charlesbourg will join Three Rivers in electing him!

What will be said of Charlesbourg? What will be said of Beauport, where he is so well known? People will say that it was because he was a Judge, that it was out of fear of losing their cases in court that voters elected him. Did the Upper Town succomb to such fears? Did Deschambault and Nicolet? What now! Canadiens who never feared enemy fire in battle will become cowards for fear of losing a court case!

What an honour for Canadiens to see *their judge* running for election, to see him profane the image of the King whom he represents so unworthily? Do English judges run in elections? . . . Only Canadiens so dishonour themselves. I am a Canadienne, Gentlemen, and I would die rather than consent to such dishonour.

The Unfortunate Jeannette

2   From Robert Sedgewick, *The Proper Sphere and Influence of Woman in Christian Society: Being a Lecture Delivered by Rev. Robert Sedgewick before the Young Men's Christian Association, Halifax, N.S., November 1856* (Halifax: J. Barnes, 1856), 3–30.

LECTURE

The errors and blunders which are interwoven with the subject of woman's rights and woman's place in modern society are, as these points now engage public attention, to be traced either to the ignoring of the fact or the omission of the fact that in the economy of nature or rather in the design of God, *woman is the complement of man*. In defining her sphere and describing her influence, this fact is fundamental. Unless this fact be admitted as an axiom in every way self-evident, no reasoning on this subject is sound, and no conclusion legitimate, and the whole theme becomes little better than a mass of mere assumption, alike illogical in its progress and unsatisfactory in its conclusions. [. . .]

If it be thus clear that woman is the complement of man, it must follow that the sphere of the one is different from that of the other. The spheres in which they severally move are concentric indeed, and thus there must be a very great similarity between them; but there is a vast difference between diversity and opposition, and hence when it is asserted that the sphere of woman is different from that of man, it is not to be understood as if it were opposed or contrary to that of man. [. . .]

It may be worth while, therefore, to enquire what, after all, is the sphere of woman; and here it may be as well to adopt the good old way of showing what it is not, and then of showing what it is, looking at the subject negatively and then positively. [. . .]

It would never do, however, from these premises, to draw the conclusion that woman behoves and is bound to exert her powers in the same direction and for the same ends as man. This were to usurp the place of man—this were to forget her position as the complement of man, and assume a place she is incompetent to fill, or rather was not designed to fill. [. . .]

Were it not that so much is said about it in the neighboring States, it would seem utterly preposterous to assert that Parliament was the proper sphere of woman, and that she is just where she ought to be when sitting on the red benches, and is engaged as she ought to be in drawing out Bills—in explaining and defending them—in standing in the arena of angry debate, and condemning and counterworking one course of policy by justifying and furthering another, and as is thought a better. Now first of all it might be asked how are women to get there? Are they to set up as candidates for the representation and come out on the hard-shell ticket or the soft-shell ticket, on the red or the blue; and are they to appear on the hustings on the day of nomination, and, unless unanimously elected, to demand a poll? One thing is certain—he would be a sheriff indeed who succeeded in keeping the peace, on the day of election, provided the contest lay between a male and a female candidate, and much more if it lay between two female candidates. And then is it to be a mixed Assembly, are the honorable man-members and woman-members to meet together and unite their wisdom in legislating for their country, [. . .] or are the women to have a separate house and to manage the public business themselves, untrammelled by the presence, unawed by the criticism of their fellow male-members? This would be a Parliament with a vengeance. This if ever would be a speaking Assembly. And what are the powers with which such a House is to be invested? Are they to be subordinate to the other House? That would never do.

Or are they to be co-ordinate with them? That would be as unsatisfactory. Or, as probably the ladies would wish it, are they to be superordinate? Why, the claim would be resented as a most presumptuous invasion of the rights of men, and as utterly intolerable as fairly beyond the limits of the Constitution. [. . .]

But seriously, that the question of investing woman with similar political rights with man, and demanding of her the discharge of similar political duties, should have arisen at this time of day, after such a world-wide and a world-long experience, is indeed one of the wonders of the age.

There is a passage in one of the Lectures of Horace Mann on the powers and duties of woman, which is every way so appropriate and withal so clear and convincing and eloquent as illustrating this point, that it deserves an acquaintanceship as extensive as possible:— '[. . .]

Nothing, as it seems to be, can account for the present clamour in behalf of women voters and women office-holders but the amazingly false notions which prevail respecting the intrinsic dignity and enduring importance of education, as compared with the ephemeral tinsel of political distinctions. Respecting the clean and beautiful work of the teacher, training up characters to empyrean height and purity, as compared with the noisome and bloody work of the politician, sometimes flaying and cauterizing, and sometimes amputating and beheading, to cure or cut away from the body politic those frightful gangrenes whose very existence would have been prevented by the intelligent and faithful performance of woman's earlier and holier service. As to the idea that woman has a self evident and inalienable right to assist in the government of the race, I reply she does assist in that government now, and would to heaven she would exercise a still larger share in its administration. But this great work, like all others, is naturally divided between the sexes, the nobler government of children belonging to women, the less noble government of adults to man.

But, if the Halls of Legislature and of Congress were opened to women, they would purify them it is said. The answer to this must recognize both hypotheses respecting the sexes. First, if woman is like man, why should she not do as man has done, only aggravating and multiplying his evil works, because then the competitors would be doubled and all restraints withdrawn. But secondly, as I contend, woman is unlike man, better when she is good and worse when she is bad. Then, at least, in the present state of society, I believe that her participation in political strifes, ambitions and cupidities, would rouse to tempestuous fury all the passions that ever swept her to swiftest perdition—Men and women are yet drawn together by too many passional affinities to allow us even to hope that husbands could leave their wives, and wives their husbands, and pass for months and months, by day and by night, through all the enforced intimacies and juxtapositions of legislative life without something more than pure platonic emotions, and she who wishes her sex to encounter these perils has forgotten the wisest prayer that was ever made, 'Lead us not into temptation.' [. . .]

In justice, however, to the other side of this question, perhaps I ought not to omit certain collateral and incidental benefits which may be claimed to accrue should woman strip off her sex and rough it with man in the turbulence and riot of the political arena. What a beautiful school for domestic debate; prolonged not merely from morn to dewy eve, but from eve to early morn, should the father be a whig, the mother a democrat, and the daughter a third party man. On the stump, at the hustings or other bear-garden, the intimate relation of husband and wife would furnish admirable facilities for mutual impeachment and recrimination, which to bachelors and marriage haters would be intensely edifying. If husband and wife were rivals for the same office, then, no matter which party might prevail, the honour and emoluments would still come into the family, or, if both were elected to Senate or House, they might pelt each other from the opposition benches, which would be a great relief from closer quarters. [. . .] As to the parents' equal right to inculcate hostile political doctrines on the minds of their children they might make a compromise, each devoting alternate lessons on alternate days to the exposure of the other's iniquities, so that the children in the end would have a good opportunity to know the weakness of them both.' [. . .]

It is now time that woman's sphere in Christian society be defined and described. [. . .] The sphere of woman is home and whatever is co-relative with home in the social economy. [. . .]

It is only at home and its co-relative situations that man finds woman to be his complement. In no other situation she can fill, in no other sphere in which she can move, will she so answer the end of her being, so far as this point goes, but at home; and this fact also, for fact it is, settles the question—what is the sphere of woman? In the camp she must either be the superior or the subordinate or the equal of man; she cannot be his complement, or, at least, she is so with multitudinous drawbacks. [. . .]

It is not the design of this lecture to treat on female education. It would seem that this point was taken for granted in the subject, and that it was admitted that, whatever the sphere, woman was qualified rightly to move in it, still the unity of the theme could not have been preserved unless some slight reference were had to this matter.

Now, there can be no doubt that the three r's, as the Irishman said, are important parts of female education, reading, writing and arithmetic. These lie at the foundation of all useful knowledge, indeed, without them the main instrumentality of acquiring knowledge is awanting, and there can be as little doubt also that the elegant accomplishments, when they can be acquired, may add very much to the usefulness of woman at home. Music and drawing, and painting and embroidery, and a smattering of French and Italian, of heavy German and clumsy Dutch, are all so many acquirements which, if once obtained, may serve to enliven a drawing room conversation and amuse and please for the nonce a drawing room party, and then they are easily retained, other things being equal, and may be exceedingly useful in various situations in life; nor can any body refuse to admit, who is willing to do woman justice, that it is quite competent and that it may be advantageous for her to dabble among the 'ologies and dive deep down into their dark regions. There is geology and ethnology and conchology and entomology, then biology and phrenology and astrology, if you will, all of them in their place somewhat instructive, all of them in their place somewhat profitable, even for a woman to know. Indeed, in certain circles of society, where these and cognate themes may happen to be the subject of conversation, a woman looks exceedingly small, if, by her silence or the irrevelancy of her remarks, she betrays her entire ignorance and the defective nature of her education; and hence the necessity and the propriety of introducing these departments of knowledge into the curriculum of our female academies and boarding-schools. But there are other 'ologies as well of which no woman, if she is to move in her sphere as she ought to, can afford to remain ignorant. There is the sublime science of washology and its sister bakeology. There is darnology and scrubology. There is mendology, and cookology in its wide comprehensiveness and its untellable utility, a science this the more profoundly it is studied it becomes the more palatable, and the more skilfully its principles are applied its professors acquire the greater popularity and are regarded with a proportionate degree of interest and complacency. Now, all this knowledge must be embraced in any system of female education that pretends to prepare woman for the duties of life.—The knowledge of housekeeping is not only not beneath her notice and regard, but is essentially necessary if she is to be at home what home expects her to be, if, in a word, she is at all to fill her place with credit to herself and comfort to those with whom she may be associated, as daughter or sister, as wife or mother, as instructress or friend, or any other relationship she may sustain to general society. And, in order that these several departments of her education may be kept in their due place and pursued according to their relative importance—that they may be purified and elevated and chastened, and thus that by their union they may subserve to the grand end of manifesting in all its varied and attractive loveliness the female character, they must be baptized, nay, permeated with the spirit and power of true religion. It has been said that man, with all his irreligion, is a religious being. The paradox, if true at all, is eminently true of woman. There is a special unnaturalness existing and manifest between the doctrines and duties and delights of evangelical Christianity and the intellectual and spiritual process of her inner nature, and hence her aptitude for piety in its principles and practices and pleasures, hence too her attainments, and hence the vast influence which godliness exerts on herself and which it enables her to exert on others. Now, to complete her education, religion must come in—not to subsidize, but to regulate and control—not as subordinate, but as principal—not as mere *addenda* to what may be regarded as otherwise complete in itself, but as that without which nothing else is or can be complete—in short, the end of true religion, the glory of God as connected with the source of true religion; the sacrifice of Christ, must be exhibited everyday as the grand object that is to be sought by all the essential and ornamental departments of her physical and mental and moral training, according as it is written. [. . .]

Having thus ascertained the sphere of woman, and adverted to the qualifications which she behoves to possess, that she may be and do what her situation demands, the way is now prepared for the consideration of the influence she exerts in Christian society.

Now, first of all the things—the qualifications just indicated being granted—this influence is extensive, nay, universal.—Where woman is she makes herself felt, but where woman is enlightened by education, and elevated and purified by piety, she makes herself felt for good through every ramification of the body-social. Like the light and heat of the sun, which diffuse themselves everywhere, so everywhere are there indications of her presence and her spirit. From the cellar to the attic there are marks of her tidy hand and her thoughtful heart. The well ordered kitchen owns her sway. The bedroom and parlour and drawing-room confess her authority. The table, and the chimney itself, are fairly within the reach of her pervasive power and must yield to the decisions of her judgment. Children smile in her approval or grieve under her frown.—Old men regard her as a ministering spirit commissioned to cheer and comfort when every other source of enjoyment has gone. She is the light of the dwelling when the dark cloud of adversity envelopes it, and when death crosses the threshhold and with ruthless hand snatches away from it the valued and the dear, it is her hand which wipes away the tear, even when her own eyes are streaming—it is her meek and quiet demeanour and calm submission which soothes and tranquillizes the bereaved mourner.

And, as has been asserted, this influence extends beyond her own proper sphere. If it be chiefly felt at home, it is nevertheless felt and acknowledged abroad. It reaches the schoolroom and college-hall. It finds its way into the workshop and the busy store. It is realized on 'Change, and even, as some of you well know, in the sweating room of the Bank. And though woman herself, as has been demonstrated, would be altogether out of her place on the red benches of the Parliament House, yet, who will deny that she makes herself felt, even in these high places of the land, and helps to modify the actings of our representatives and rulers?

And then this influence is powerful, extensive. It is mighty. It may be resisted indeed, even as the pleasant light may be excluded from some dirty room lest its filth and its disorder be made manifest. It may be resisted indeed, as the genial heat may be prevented from radiating, and thus warming all within its scope. But, let it have fair play and full action, and just as light and heat, unchecked in their operation, reveal and revive all within their reach, so will this influence affect and subdue, and enlighten and raise, and purify and etherialize and sublimate, all and every one whose nature is capable of feeling this influence, all and every thing that, as an enchantress, she touches with her wonder working wand. [. . .]

One more general statement. This influence is refining and polishing. It rubs down the hirsute coarseness of men. It frowns vulgarity into a corner, and abashes the impudent forwardness of the pert and assuming. Where it is unknown or trodden under foot, why there is savageism untamed, there is license unbridled, there is heartless cruelty and beastly debasement; but, where it is known and felt, the savage is a savage no more, licence and libertinism tremble and flee, kindness supplants cruelty and manly dignity beastly degradation. A well educated and godly woman can make, and has made, the bully quiet and the boor mannerly, and the brawler meek and gentle as a lamb. In the presence of such a woman the lips of the profane are sealed and the tongue of the obscene is locked in his jaws. Ribaldry and scurrility are frightened into propriety, and, in spite of all that is said to the contrary, it is nevertheless true that slander herself is reft of her weapons, and, if not, yet what is as good, she is shorn of her power to use them as she chooses. [. . .]

HISTORICAL INTERPRETATIONS

3   From Willeen Keough, 'The Riddle of Peggy Mountain: Regulation of Irish Women's Sexuality on the Southern Avalon, 1750–1860', *Acadiensis* 31(2) (2002): 38–70.

Feminist scholarship has argued that an important indicator of patriarchal domination is the degree to which a society seeks to regulate women's bodies in terms of marriage, sexuality and reproduction.[1] As Newfoundland was a British fishing station/colony in the period under study, hegemonic discourses on female sexuality in contemporary Britain provide context for the discussion as the extent of their infiltration into the local context is tested. By the eighteenth century, the British legal tradition was a patriarchal regime that relegated women's bodies to the control of fathers or husbands. Concerns about patrilineal inheritance and the legitimacy of heirs lent particular urgency to the protection of the chastity value of wives and daughters. At the same time, Enlightenment thought was challenging the association of sinfulness with sexuality that had been the legacy of seventeenth-century Puritanism. Yet men and women did not have equal access to the sexual freedom of the age. Uncontrolled female sexuality was seen as a threat, not only to property and legitimacy, but also to the very foundation of the social order itself. Female sexuality was, therefore, channelled into marriage and

motherhood, while the division between public (rational, active, individualist, masculine) and private (emotional, passive, dependent, feminine) domains was underscored.

These discourses grew within the context of late-eighteenth- and early-nineteenth-century evangelicalism as it shaped middle-class ideals of female domesticity, fragility, passivity and dependence. Female sexuality was further constrained as middle-class ideology fashioned a dichotomized construction of woman as either frail, asexual vessel, embodied in the respectable wife and mother, or temptress Eve, embodied in the prostitute. Separate sphere ideology intensified. Women who occupied 'public' spaces or who demonstrated a capacity for social or economic independence, even physical hardiness, were increasingly seen as deviant. Overt female sexuality was particularly problematic for it 'disturbed the public/private division of space along gender lines so essential to the male spectator's mental mapping of the civic order.'[2] As the nineteenth century unfolded, legal, medical and scientific discourses continued to embellish the construction of woman as 'the unruly body', consumed by her 'sex', problematic by her very biological nature and requiring increased monitoring and regulation.

These discourses on female sexuality and respectability were infiltrating eighteenth- and nineteenth-century Newfoundland through its British legal regime and an emerging local middle class of administrators, churchmen and merchants, many of whom maintained strong ties with Britain.[3] On the island, gender ideology was tempered by the exigencies of colonial policy as it was articulated by central authorities in St. John's. And this ideology also assumed ethnic undertones as the Irish population in Newfoundland increased. From the mid-1700s onward, as Irish servants increasingly replaced English labour in the fishery and as an Irish-Newfoundland trade in passengers and provisions expanded, Irish migration to the island swelled.[4]

British authorities in Newfoundland watched the growing number of Irish migrants with levels of concern ranging from wariness to near hysteria. Official correspondence and proclamations for the period articulated several common themes about the Irish population. The authorities claimed that the Irish were a 'disaffected', 'treacherous' people who would prove to be Britain's 'greatest Enemy' in times of war. They bred prodigiously and were already overtaking the local English-Protestant population in numbers. Officials claimed these 'Wicked & Idle People', who were prone to excessive drink and disorderly behaviour, terrorized 'His Majesty's loyal Protestant subjects' and were responsible for most of the crime that occurred over the winter. Thus, a battery of orders and regulations attempted to limit the numbers of Irish remaining on the island after the fishing season was over.[5]

Three important contextual elements framed the perspective of visiting British authorities towards the Irish in Newfoundland. First, their attitudes reflected contemporary English perceptions of difference between the Anglo-Saxon and Gaelic 'races'. Second, most of the Irish in Newfoundland were Catholics, and were therefore subject to a penal regime

similar to that which existed in Ireland and Great Britain at the time. Third, Britain was ambivalent about permanent settlement in Newfoundland until the early 1800s. For centuries, British authorities had viewed Newfoundland as a fishing station rather than a colony, and had struggled to promote the migratory fishery, at the expense of a resident sector, in order to preserve the hub of the industry in the West of England and to maintain Britain's nursery for seamen. Nonetheless, British authorities in Newfoundland expressed more concern about the Irish remaining on the island than the English, and official discourse constructed 'Irishness' as inherently feckless, intemperate, disloyal and unruly. The Irish were a 'problem' group that required constant regulation and surveillance.

Part of this official discourse focused on an image of the Irish woman immigrant as a vagrant and a whore. This fits within a broader context in which British authorities discouraged the presence of all women in Newfoundland. The very characteristics that made women essential to colonial ventures on the mainland—their stabilizing effect, their essential role in forming a permanent population—posed a threat to British enterprise in Newfoundland, as a resident fishery would weaken the migratory sector. As Capt. Francis Wheler, a naval officer in Newfoundland, reassured the home government in 1684: 'Soe longe as there comes noe women they are not fixed'.[6] While official policy discouraged women migrants in general, authorities in St. John's highlighted the undesirability of Irish women in particular. Official documents of the period portray Irish women immigrants as degenerate, unproductive and dangerous to the social and moral order. Central authorities argued that these women caused 'much disorder and Disturbance against the Peace' and inevitably became a charge on the more respectable inhabitants of the island. Many 'devious', single Irish women, they said, arrived in Newfoundland pregnant and disguised their condition until they had hired themselves out to unsuspecting employers.

Running through the records was a subtext that once Irish women were permitted to remain, all the elements for reproducing this undesirable ethnic group would be in place. The Irish woman immigrant, then, was a particular 'problem' for local authorities, requiring special regulation of her own. In particular, the single Irish female servant required monitoring, for her social and economic independence from a patriarchal family context and her potential sexual agency flouted a growing middle-class feminine ideal that embodied domesticity, economic dependence and sexual passivity. [. . .]

How did hegemonic constructions of womanhood, and particularly Irish womanhood, play out on the southern Avalon, where community formation was still in its early stages among an essentially plebeian Irish population and where gender relations were still contested terrain? [. . .] On the southern Avalon, the plebeian community was comprised primarily of fishing servants, washerwomen, seamstresses, midwives, artisans, small-scale boatkeepers and planters, and by the nineteenth century, numerous 'independent' fishing families (in as much as they could be independent from their merchant suppliers). The plebeian community shared a common consciousness and exerted political pressure on occasion—either in the form of the 'mob' in direct collective actions or as the menacing presence behind anonymous actions and threats. They were not a working class for they lacked class consciousness. But they did have a distinct and vigorous plebeian culture, with its own rituals, its own patterns of work and leisure, and its own world view. Their social superiors were the local merchants or merchants' agents, vessel owners and masters, Anglican clergy and more substantial boatkeepers and planters, who were part of an emerging middle class in Newfoundland in the late eighteenth and early nineteenth centuries. They functioned as quasi-patricians with their control of employment opportunities, relief, supply and credit, and administrative and magisterial functions. Although tied to the plebs through interdependence in the fishery,

this group maintained social distance through religious affiliation and exclusive patterns of socializing and marriage.[7] [. . .]

In Britain, the working class adopted and refashioned middle-class feminine ideals during the nineteenth century to support their own bid for respectability in the Chartist movement and to satisfy the male-centred agenda of trade unionism. Furthermore, the British middle class encouraged this development of a working-class respectability—one that imitated middle-class ideals while maintaining sufficient difference to preserve class boundaries. In rural Britain and Ireland, as well, women were impelled into domesticity by a powerful combination of proscriptive ideology and the marginalization and devaluation of women's labour in agriculture and cottage industries. But did similar processes occur on the southern Avalon? Or were there tensions between hegemonic rhetoric and the realities of Irish-Newfoundland women's lives that delayed the intrusion of such feminine ideals into plebeian culture? [. . .]

In order to answer such questions, it is necessary to examine Irish women within the context of the plebeian culture of the southern Avalon. Within this population, women acquired significant status and authority in family and community as they assumed vital social and economic roles during immigration and early settlement.[8]

With increasing numbers of women moving to the southern Avalon and elsewhere in Newfoundland, the fears of the British government were confirmed. Once women came, the population became fixed. Given the transient nature of employment in the Newfoundland fishery, male fishing servants commonly found employment in different areas from year to year, moving in and out of districts, and between harbours within a district, as work opportunities shifted. In time, the presence of women tied them to particular communities. On the southern Avalon, some Irish fishermen were joined by wives or fiancées from the home country or married women from the small, established English planter group. Increasingly, however, they found wives among single or widowed Irish immigrant women and, by the turn of the century, among an expanding group of local first- and second-generation Irish-Newfoundland women. Matrilineal bridges often factored in the clustering of families in particular coves and harbours, while matri-local/uxorilocal residence patterns played an intrinsic role in community formation, as many couples established themselves on land already occupied by the wife or apportioned from or adjacent to the family property of the wife. [. . .]

Plebeian women in the study area were an intrinsic part of the economic life of their fledgling communities. They played a vital role in subsistence production for their households. In addition, women ran public houses, looked after boarders, provided nursing services and took in paid washing and sewing—mostly catering to single, male, fishing servants. Women were 'shipped' as servants to merchant, administrative and planter families, and while the majority were recruited as domestic servants, a smaller number worked as fishing servants, heading, splitting, salting and drying fish as part of shore crews.[9] Regardless of the type of service, and whether 'shipped' by oral agreement or written contract known as a 'shipping paper', the law looked upon these arrangements as formal contracts and required both servants and employers to fulfill their obligations under the agreements.[10] The existence of this system of contractual employment, recognized by law, conjures up an image of the Irish woman servant that was far more purposeful than the impoverished, immoral woman of eighteenth-century governors' proclamations.

Some women, primarily widows, where [sic] fishing employers and operated fishing premises in their own right.[11] A greater number ran fishing plantations with their husbands or common-law partners,[12] with the responsibility for boarding fishing servants and dieters (winter servants working only for room and board) added to their other household and subsistence duties. And increasingly, plebeian women

became shore crews for the family production unit in the fishery, replacing the hired, transient, primarily male servants who had been the backbone of the traditional planter fishery.[13] On shore, they performed the crucial work of salting and drying fish, a process that required careful attention and good judgment to ensure the quality of the cure. Along the southern Avalon, the momentum for the shift to the household unit began as early as the 1780s—again, that period when the Irish were arriving in ever increasing numbers.[14] The post-war recession that followed the Napoleonic Wars saw the final demise of the older system of waged labour. War-time inflation carried over into post-war wages and provisions but fish prices plummeted. Planters, unable to offset their losses, either went bankrupt or turned increasingly to family labour to meet production needs. With the old planter fishery in its death throes and the resident fishery in crisis, women stepped into the breach and took the place of male fishing servants on the stages and flakes, producing saltfish for market. Their presence at these public sites of economic production and their vital and recognized contribution to the process was an important source of power for these women, even into the twenieth century.[15] This was terrain worth retaining, and even when fishing families hired servant girls, it was not to replace the women of the house in outdoor work, but to assume household tasks in order to 'free' their mistresses to contribute to more important family enterprises.

Further evidence of women's participation in the public, economic sphere is provided by mercantile records, which suggest that women were a vital part of the exchange economy of the area.[16] Significant numbers performed some independent form of economic activity and held accounts in their own names as *femes sole*, regardless of marital status.[17] Some were heads of households that produced saltfish and oil for market. Many more sold pigs, fowl, eggs and oakum. They earned wages haying, tending gardens or making fish on merchants' flakes. They also did washing and sewing for local single fishing servants and middle-class customers. Many combined their paid services in a package of economic coping strategies that helped families make ends meet. Women's work for a mercantile firm was credited to their accounts. Work for other people in the community was 'contra'd' against the accounts of their customers; in other words, a balancing entry was made in the merchant's ledger, giving the woman credit and her customer a debit entry. Some women had credit balances or received a small amount of cash when they 'settled up' in the fall. Some even had their profits applied towards the debts of male relatives. Many others had debit balances, but so did most men in the community—a chronic symptom of the truck system that underpinned the resident fishery. Merchants carried these debts forward and rarely wrote them off, suggesting confidence in the women's earning abilities. Of course, men's names headed the accounts more frequently than women's, for merchants would have been mindful of the repercussions of coverture[18] in relation to debt, but legal principle and accounting practice masked the full extent of women's participation in the exchange economy. Women's labour in family work units contributed to the production of fish and oil credited to accounts of fathers or husbands. Women used many of the goods appearing under the names of male household heads for household production, expending labour and producing goods that were assigned no market value and therefore were not included in formal business ledgers of the day. Furthermore, merchant books did not record female networks of informal trade— the exchange of eggs for butter, for example, or milk for wool—which helped women keep their families clothed and fed.[19]

Religion in both orthodox and informal observance was another important source of informal female power within the Irish community of the southern Avalon, particularly before the encroachment of ultramontanism and the devotional revolution of the mid- to late nineteenth century. There is evidence that Catholic women in Newfoundland performed religious rites and assumed religious authority in the century before these intrusions. Bishop Michael Fleming complained to his superiors that prior to the establishment of Catholic missions in the late eighteenth century: 'The holy Sacrament of Matrimony, debased into a sort of "civil contract", was administered by captains of boats, by police, by magistrates and frequently by women. The Sacrament of Baptism was equally profaned'.[20] Fleming was also dismayed that midwives had assumed the authority to dispense with church fasts for pregnant women. Dean Cleary's 'Notebook' refers to women at St. Mary's taking 'the sacred fire from the altar to burn a house'—perhaps a rite of exorcism of some sort, but certainly an act with ritualistic overtones.[21] According to the oral tradition, women primarily kept the faith alive before the priests' arrival by observing Catholic rituals and teaching children their prayers. [...] Furthermore, female figures were prominent in the Irish-Catholic hagiolatry of the area. To this day, the Virgin Mary, St. Brigid and 'Good St. Anne' are a powerful triumvirate. On the southern Avalon, as in Ireland, there was an alternative pre-Christian religious system operating in tandem with, and sometimes overlapping, formal Catholic practice. This melange of ancient beliefs and customary practices made up a very real part of the mental landscape of the Irish community, and women were important navigators of this terrain. Women made and blessed the bread that had special powers to keep fairies from stealing their children; the same bread could help people who were 'fairy-struck'—lost in the woods or back-meadows—find their way home. Women anointed their homes with holy water and blessed candle wax to protect their families from dangers such as thunder and lightning. Women read tea leaves and told fortunes. They ritually washed and dressed the dead, 'sat up' with corpses at wakes to guard their spirits overnight, smoked the 'God be merciful' pipes,[22] and keened at gravesides to mourn the departed and mark their passage into the next life. Certain women had special healing powers—the ability to stop blood with a prayer, for example. A widow's curse, by contrast, had the power to do great harm. The bibe, the equivalent of the Irish banshee, was a female figure, as was the 'old hag' who gave many a poor soul a sleepless night.[23] And places like Mrs. Denine's Hill, Peggy's Hollow and Old Woman's Pond (named for the women who had died there) had magical qualities that could cause horses to stop in their tracks and grown men to lose their way.[24] Thus, in both formal and informal practice, Irish women acted as mediators of the natural and supernatural worlds and, by extension, played a vital role in reinforcing the identity of the ethno-religious group in the area.

Court records for the area reveal that plebeian women also featured in numerous collective actions and individual interventions to protect personal, family and community interests during the period—deploying power through verbal threats and physical confrontations that did not fit middle-class ideals of femininity.[25] The women of the Berrigan family, for instance, were an important force in the family's struggle to hold fast to their fishing 'room'[26] on the south side of Renews harbour in the late 1830s and early 1840s. John Saunders, a local merchant and JP, made repeated attempts to take possession of their premises (likely for rent arrears or non-payment of debt), but his efforts met with persistent resistance from the family, including the Berrigan women. In 1838 and 1842, family members were charged with violently assaulting two different deputy sheriffs as the officers tried to remove them from the property. Finally, in 1843, the Berrigans were found guilty of intimidating and assaulting John Saunders, himself, as he tried to take possession of the fishing room. There were variations in terms of the family members involved in each case, but Bridget and Alice (daughters, sisters, or relatives by marriage) were involved in two of the three incidents, while the family matriarch, Anastatia, was present every time.[27] These women's participation was not unusual within the historical context of

this fishing-based economy. As essential members of their household production unit, the Berrigan women were defending a family enterprise in which they felt they had an equal stake, using compelling means to protect their source of livelihood in the face of perceived injustice at the hands of their supplying merchant and the formal legal system.

Indeed, plebeian women on the southern Avalon were not reluctant to use physical violence in sorting out their daily affairs. In assault cases brought before the southern Avalon courts during the period, women were aggressors almost as often as they were victims (by a proportion of 86:100). Of the 111 complaints involving women during the period, 50 were laid against male assailants of female victims, but 61 involved female aggressors.[28] Furthermore, these women assailants were not particular about the sex of their victims: 32 were women and 28 were men (with child victims in the remaining case). All the female aggressors were of the plebeian community. Most episodes involved the use of threatening language and/or common assault with a variety of motivations, including defence of personal or family reputation, employment disputes over wages or ill-treatment, defence of family business, enforcement of community standards and defence of individual or family property. The physical assertiveness of these women and the court's matter-of-fact handling of these cases suggest that women's violence was no more shocking to the community than men's. Gender relations within the plebeian community were fluid and these women felt they had the right to carve out territory for themselves and their families in the public sphere.[29]

Of course, there were 50 cases involving plebian women victims of male violence. These ranged from complaints of threatening language and ill treatment to more serious charges of physical and sexual assaults. In feminist scholarship, male violence against women—actual or potential—has been cited as a mechanism of patriarchal control. Yet it is evident that on the southern Avalon, the use of physical violence was not gender-specific; this was not a context characterized primarily by male aggressors and female victims. Clearly too, plebeian women felt that it was their prerogative to take their abusers to court. They perceived themselves as individuals with rights which should be protected by the legal system, and they were not deterred by notions of female respectability and self-sacrifice from asserting their claims to justice in a public forum.

Irish plebeian womanhood on the southern Avalon was not engulfed by the constraints of separate sphere ideology or constructions of passivity, fragility and dependence. Nor was it easily channeled into formal marriage— a key site for the control of female sexuality within the English common-law tradition and middle-class ideology. In marriage, a woman was accessible to male sexual needs

and could fulfill her destiny as reproducer of the race; yet her sexuality could be safely constrained within the roles of respectable wife and mother. Indeed, a woman's entire person was subsumed in the identity of her husband within marriage. As *feme covert*, she could not own property, enter into contracts without her husband's approval, sue or be sued. And her husband had a regulatory interest in her body and sole rights to her services, both domestic and sexual (the latter, again, reflecting anxiety over the legitimacy of heirs).

While formal marriage was institutionalized as the proper means of ordering society, within the predominantly Irish plebeian community of the southern Avalon, informal marriages and common-law relationships were tolerated and seen as legitimate.[30] Given the different understandings of gender that had evolved in Gaelic Ireland—one in which traditions of transhumance, communal property

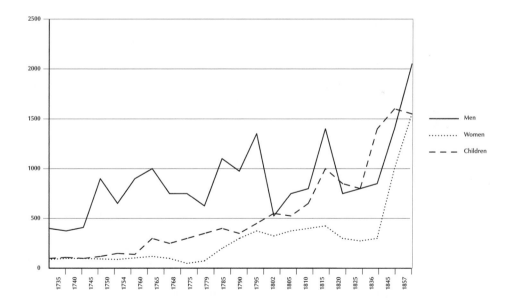

Figure 1   Over-wintering Population in Districts of Ferryland, Trepassey and St. Mary's, 1735–1857 (presented in five year intervals)

Source: Governor's Annual Returns of the Fisheries and Inhabitants at Newfoundland, 1735–1825, CO 194; Newfoundland Population Returns, 1836, 1845, 1857.

and partible inheritance contrasted with English preoccupations with private property and patrilineal inheritance—this is, perhaps, not surprising. Within the Irish tradition, the chastity requirement for wives and daughters was muted, and informal marriages and divorces, illegitimacy and close degrees of consanguineous marriage were tolerated. Irish traditions different from English norms of sexual behaviour.[31] [. . .]

Irish plebeian women who entered into formal marriages on the southern Avalon were not readily constrained either, given their vital role as co-producers in family economies. In this, they were similar to their counterparts in rural Ireland, or certainly eighteenth-century rural Ireland, where women gained status from their role as co-producers in a mixed farming and domestic textile economy.[32] Within both contexts, married women exercised considerable autonomy in running their households and also had significant influence over matters outside home. While a facade of patriarchal authority was usually maintained in both cultures, male decision-making was frequently directed by women behind the scenes. Clarkson describes this family power structure in Ireland as a 'matriarchal management behind a patriarchal exterior'.[33] The oral tradition on the southern Avalon has a more homespun equivalent: 'She made the cannonballs, and he fired them.'

In general, then, middle-class constructs of female respectability and anxieties about regulating female sexuality did not easily insinuate themselves into Irish plebeian culture on the southern Avalon. Women's essential role in community formation, powerful position in an alternative belief system, deployment of informal power in community life, and essential roles in subsistence production and the fishery mitigated against the adaptation of middle-class ideologies that did not fit local realities. Furthermore, because the southern Avalon remained a pre-industrial society into the twentieth century, plebeian women's status did not undergo the erosion experienced by their counterparts in the industrializing British Isles. In rural Ireland, the marginalization of women from agricultural work and the collapse of the domestic textile industry and the 'potato culture'[34] in the early nineteenth century led to a depreciation of women's worth, both as producers and reproducers. Similarly, in England, the masculinization of farm labour and dairying and the mechanization and industrialization of cottage industries led to the devaluation of women's labour.[35] On the southern Avalon, however, women's status as essential co-producers in the fishing economy, as well as reproducers of family work units within that economy, remained intact and forestalled any masculinist project within plebeian culture to circumscribe their lives. [. . .]

NOTES

1. The literature upon which the following discussion is based includes: Constance Backhouse, *Petticoats and Prejudice: Women and Law in Nineteenth-Century Canada* (Toronto, 1991); Linda Cullum and Maeve Baird, 'A Woman's Lot: Women and Law in Newfoundland from Early Settlement to the Twentieth Century', in Linda Kealey, ed., *Pursuing Equality: Historical Perspectives on Women in Newfoundland and Labrador* (St. John's, 1993), pp. 66–162; Joy Damousi, *Depraved and Disorderly: Female Convicts, Sexuality and Gender in Colonial Australia* (Cambridge, 1997); Anna Clark, *The Struggle for the Breeches: Gender and the Making of the British Working Class* (Berkeley, 1995); Lenore Davidoff, 'Regarding Some Old Husbands' Tales': Public and Private in Feminist History', in *Worlds Between: Historical Perspectives on Gender and Class* (Cambridge, 1995), pp. 227–76; Davidoff and Catherine Hall, *Family Fortunes: Men and Women of the English*

Middle Class, 1780–1850 (Chicago, 1987); Susan M. Edwards, *Female Sexuality and the Law: A Study of Constructs of Female Sexuality as They Inform Statute and Legal Procedure* (Oxford, 1981); Theodore Koditschek, 'The Gendering of the British Working Class', *Gender and History*, 9, 2 (August 1997), pp. 333–63; Lynda Nead, *Myths of Sexuality: Representations of Women in Victorian Britain* (Oxford and New York, 1988); Roy Porter, 'Mixed Feelings: The Enlightenment and Sexuality in Eighteenth-Century Britain', in Paul-Gabriel Bouc, ed., *Sexuality in Eighteenth-Century Britain* (Manchester, 1982), pp. 1–27; Jane Rendall, *Women in an Industrializing Society: England, 1750–1880* (Oxford, 1990); Sonya O. Rose, *Limited Livelihoods: Gender and Class in Nineteenth Century England* (Berkeley, 1992); G.S. Rousseau and Roy Porter, 'Introduction', in Rousseau and Porter, eds, *Sexual Underworlds of the Enlightenment* (Chapel Hill, 1988), pp. 1–24; Carol Smart, 'Disruptive Bodies and Unruly Sex: the Regulation of Reproduction and Sexuality in the Nineteenth Century', in Carol Smart, ed., *Regulating Womanhood: Historical Essays an Marriage, Motherhood and Sexuality* (London and New York, 1992), pp. 7–32.

2. Judith Walkowitz, *City of Dreadful Delight: Narratives of Sexual Danger in Late-Victorian London* (Chicago, 1992), p. 23.

3. Up to the early decades of the nineteenth century, most of this group were Anglo-Protestant and many returned to Britain after stays of varying lengths on the island. Those who remained kept their strong family, commercial and/or professional connections with Britain. There was a smaller Irish mercantile element in Newfoundland as well but, while this group achieved increasing prominence in St. John's in the nineteenth century, Irish merchant-planters on the southern Avalon (again, predominantly a Protestant group) had wound up their interests in the area by the late eighteenth century.

4. For information on Irish immigration to Newfoundland in general, see the scholarship of John J. Mannion, including: 'Introduction', in John J. Mannion, ed., *The Peopling of Newfoundland: Essays in Historical Geography* (St. John's, 1977), pp. 5–9; Mannion,

'Tracing the Irish: A Geographical Guide'. *The Newfoundland Ancestor* 9(1) (Spring 1993). pp. 4–18.

5. See, for example, Remarks of Naval Officer Cummins in relation to Newfoundland [c. 1705], Colonial Office [CO] 194/3/424–5. See also Capt. Van Brugh to Commissioners for Trade, 6 November 1738 (transcribed from CO 194/10/93), Subseries 04-056/01, f. 25-B-2-1; Governor Cadre Smith to Commissioners for Trade, 1742, Governor Byng to Commissioners for Trade, 1743 (from CO 194/11/41), Sub-series 04-057/02, f. 25-A-27-56, 04/058, Keith Matthews Collection, Coll. 24, box 9, Maritime History Archives [MHA]; Order, Governor Hugh Palliser, 2 June 1767, GN 2/1/A, 4/41–44/1764; Order, Palliser, 31 October 1764, GN 2/1/A, 3/272–3/1764; Order, Governor John Byron, 29 September 1769, GN 2/1/A, 4/201/1769; Order, Byron, 31 October 1770, GN 2/1/A, 4/285/1770; Order, Governor Molinoux Shuldham, 24 June 1772 GN 2/1/A, 5/60/1772; Order, Shuldham, 13 July 1772, GN 2/1/A, 5/102/1772; Order, Shuldham, 12 October 1773, GN 2/1/A, 5/143/1772; Order, Governor Robert Duff, 12 July 1775, GN 2/1/A, 6/17/1775; Orders (2), Duff, 16 October 1775, GN 2/1/A, 6/100-1/1775; Circular Letter, Governor John Montague to the Magistrates of the various districts in Newfoundland, 6 October 1777, GN 2/1/A, 7/33–35/1777; Order, Montague, 3 October 1778, GN 2/1/A, 7/70/1778; Proclamation and Public Notice, Governor Mark Milbanke, 13 October 1789, GN 2/1/A, 12/38–41/1789: Milbanke to James O Donel (Catholic Prefect-Apostolic, later Bishop, at Newfoundland), 2 November 1790, GN 2/1/A, 12/102/1790; Public Notice, Governor Richard King, 19 September 1792, GN 2/1/A, 12/157/1792; Proclamation, Governor William Waldegrave and covering correspondence to the Magistrates of Newfoundland, 27 September 1798, GN 2/1/A, 14/282–7/1798; Proclamations (2), Governor John Gambier, 18 September 1802, GN 2/1/A, 16/282–87/1802, Provincial Archives of Newfoundland and Labrador [PANL].

6. W. Gordon Handcock, '*Soe longe as there comes noe women*': *Origins of English Settlement in Newfoundland* (St. John's, 1989), p. 32.

7. I draw from E.P. Thompson's conceptualization of eighteenth-century English society in *Customs in Common* (London, 1991), chapter 2.

8. The following sections derive from a much fuller discussion by the writer in Willeen Keough, 'The Slender Thread: Irish Women on the Southern Avalon, 1750–1860', Ph.D. thesis. Memorial University, 2001. See especially chapters 2–7.

9. Numerous examples of women in these various occupations can be found in the court records for the districts of Ferryland and Trepassey-St. Mary's. See GN 5/1/C/1, 5/2/C/1–4, 8; GN 5/4/C/1, 8, PANL; 340.9 N45, Provincial Reference Library, St. John's [PRL]. Examples also appear in mercantile records for the area, particularly Sweetman Collection (records of Saunders and Sweetman, a firm operating out of Placentia with dealers in St. Mary's Bay, including portions of the study area), MG 49 and Collection of Alan F. Goodridge and Son (a firm operating out of Renews), MG 473, PANL.

10. The writer's database of court cases contains 25 employment disputes involving women of the area. In nine of these cases, formal shipping agreements were actually referenced and/or produced. See *Jane Costeloe v. Bridget Whealon*, 3 August 1795, 340.9 N45, n.f., PRL: Brigus South, 'Dwyer, Anstice', re: *Anstice Dwyer v. Cornelius Kelly*, 27 October 1797, John Mannion Name File (private collection, St. John's). See also *Frida Tobin v. Mary Bony*, 29 September 1818, St. Mary's, ff. 47–8; *Catherine Lancrop v. John Doody, Jr.*, 29 September 1818, St. Mary's f. 52, GN 5/4/C/1; *Margret Neile v. John and James Munn*, 2 November 1818, Ferryland, f. 62, GN/5/1/C/1; *Elizabeth Cullen v. James Shortall*, c. 26 September 1787, Ferryland, box 1, f. 43, GN 5/4/C/1; *Jane Austin v. Robert Brennan*, 25 September 1843, *Margaret Dunphy v. Nicholas Power*, 14 September 1846, *Ellen Leary v. John Butler*, 5 October 1848, Ferryland, Box 2, n.f., GN 5/4/C/1, PANL. The terms of all agreements, formal or informal, oral or written, were generally upheld by the court.

11. For example, in 1773, Mary Shea was granted a fishing room on the northwest side of Ferryland harbour 'to quietly and peaceably possess the same so long as you shall employ it to the advantage of the Fishery.' See Grant of a Fishing Room to Mary Shea, 15 September 1773, n.f., 340.9 N45, PRL. In 1775, Alice Thomas of Renews was sued by her fishing servants for their wages. See *Lawrence Dunn & J. Whealon v. Alice Thomas*, 5 October 1775, 340.9 N45, PRL. Catharine Clements of Renews was the proprietor of a fishing premises and fishing employer in Renews in the 1780s and 1790s. See Petition of James Rows, Renews [c. 14 August 1784], Order, Governor John Campbell, 27 August 1784, GN 2/1/A, 10/49–51/1784, PANL; *Catharine Clements v. James Rouse*, 31 August 1785, n.f., 340.9 N45, PRL. In 1794, Jane Holly was one of several boatkeepers in Ferryland district entangled in a dispute between a former and current supplier. See *Thomas Gibbs & Co. v. William Knox, John Rice, & Henry Studdy*, 11 August 1794, Ferryland, box 1, n.f., GN 5/4/C/1, PANL. In the 1820s, Ann Ryan was renting a fishing room and premises in Caplin Bay—including stages, flakes, beaches, dwelling house, gardens and lands—from Philip Tree for £6 per annum. See Philip Tree, Mortgage to John Teague, 29 November 1823, Ferryland, ff. 97–8, GN 5/1/C/1, PANL. The mercantile records of Sweetman's and Goodridge's also contain various accounts for fish and oil from households headed by women. See MG 49 and MG 473, PANL, respectively.

12. In this discussion, the term 'common-law', when applied to a relationship between a man and a woman, indicates that the couple were not married by a religious, civil, or informal ceremony, but were cohabiting and having a sexual relationship as if they were husband and wife. Common-law relationships had no legal status during the study period and were deemed a 'civil inconvenience' by central authorities because they deviated from a moral order that bolstered a patriarchal system of property inheritance. See Cullum and Baird, 'A Woman's Lot', p. 119.

13. Smaller numbers of fishing servants continued to be hired, but mostly to supplement household labour.

14. The Governors' annual returns in the CO 194 series contain a section on the personnel involved in the resident fishery. The 'momentum' referred to here is demonstrated by

dramatically declining numbers of hired servants in relation to an ever-increasing planter group (masters, mistresses and children).

15. The vital role of women in the traditional fishery has also been discussed by other writers, including Ellen Antler, 'Women's Work in Newfoundland Fishing Families', *Atlantis*, 2, 2 (1977), pp. 106–13; Sean Cadigan, *Hope and Deception in Conception Bay, Merchant-Settler Relations in Newfoundland, 1785–1855* (Toronto, 1995); Hilda Chaulk Murray, *More than Fifty Percent: Women's Life in a Newfoundland Outport, 1900–1950* (St. John's, 1979); Marilyn Porter, '"She was Skipper of the Shore Crew": Notes on the History of the Sexual Division of Labour in Newfoundland', in Carmelita McGrath, Barbara Neis and Marilyn Porter, eds., *Their Lives and Times: Women in Newfoundland and Labrador: A Collage* (St. John's, 1995), pp. 33–47.

16. See Sweetman Collection (various loose materials), boxes 2, 3, MG 49; Goodridge Collection, 1839, 1841 ledgers, MG 473, PANL. In addition, merchants' and boatkeepers' accounts, including entries involving women's services, were occasionally brought forward as evidence in court cases relating to matters such as debt and balances owing on servants' wages. See GN 5, PANL; 340.9 N45, PRL.

17. The Sweetman records are piecemeal over an extended period, but the Goodridge records are intact for 1839 and 1841 and indicate that 60 women in Renews (adult female population of approximately 150) held separate accounts in those two years. They were surely not all widowed or single women.

18. Coverture was the principle at English common law whereby a married woman's legal identity was absorbed into that of her husband.

19. For other discussions of women's participation in exchange economies, see Johanna Miller Lewis, 'Women and Economic Freedom in the North Carolina Backcountry', in Larry D. Eldridge, ed., *Women and Freedom in Early America* (New York and London, 1997), pp. 191–208; Elizabeth Mancke, 'At the Counter of the General Store: Women and the Economy in Eighteenth-Century Horton, Nova Scotia', in Margaret Conrad, ed., Intimate Relations:

Family and Community in Planter Nova Scotia, 1759–1800 (Fredericton, 1995), pp. 167–81.

20. 'Two Letters', p. 90, Fleming Papers, 103/26, Roman Catholic Archives St. John's [RCASJ], Until Governor John Campbell issued a Declaration of Liberty of Conscience in 1784, the Catholic religion operated underground, with a handful of priests travelling incognito from harbour to harbour.

21. Dean Patrick Cleary [parish priest, Witless Bay], 'A Note of Church History [1784–1850]', p. 28. Fleming Papers, 103/32, RCASJ.

22. These were communal pipes, shared by those at the wake-house. After a smoker drew in the smoke, he or she exhaled it with the invocation 'God be merciful.'

23. The 'hag' was a supernatural creature who came in the night and sat on the chest of her prey in an effort to impede or stop the victim's breathing. The visitation evoked a choking sensation and left the sufferer in a semi-conscious state from which s/he could only be wakened by calling his or her name backwards. Not all variations of the 'hag' actually involved a female apparition; sometimes she manifested herself more diffusely in the form of a bad nightmare from which the sufferer could not wake, or a feeling of paralysis that kept the victim pinned to the bed. Still, such unfortunates were said to be 'hag-rode' or 'hag-ridden'—rendered insensible by the powers of this terrifying female phantasm.

24. Information on informal religious beliefs and practices in the study area comes from the oral tradition. See Willeen Keough: 'The Old "Hag" Meets Saint Brigid: Irish Women and the Intersection of Belief Systems on the Southern Avalon, Newfoundland', *An Nasc*, 13 (Spring 2001), pp. 12–25. There is a literature on the derivative system in Ireland which includes J.S. Connolly, *Priests and People in Pre-Famine Ireland, 1780–1845* (Dublin, 1982); George Casey, 'Irish Culture in Newfoundland', in Cyril J. Byrne and Margaret Harry, eds., *Talamh An Eisc: Canadian and Irish Essays* (Halifax, 1986), pp. 203–27; W.G. Wood-Martin, *Traces of the Elder Faiths of Ireland*, vol. 2 ([1902] Port Washington and London, 1970). The oral tradition is particularly helpful in reconstructing the early spiritual life of

the community. Many of these practices survived in the area well into the twentieth century and there is no evidence to suggest that they skipped generations after migration, only to be revived later.

25. Similar incidents involving plebeian women of Conception Bay and Prince Edward Island have been reported by Sean Cadigan and Rusty Bittermann, respectively. See Cadigan, *Hope and Deception*, chapter 4; Bittermann, 'Women and the Escheat Movement: The Politics of Everyday Life on Prince Edward Island', in Janet Guildford and Suzanne Morton, eds., *Separate Spheres: Women's Worlds in the 19th-Century Maritimes* (Fredericton, 1994), pp. 23–38.

26. The term 'room' refers to fishing premises, including stages, 'flakes' (structures for drying fish), sheds, wharves and fish stores for the landing, processing and storing of fish, as well as 'cookrooms' for the accommodation of crews.

27. *John W. Saunders v. Thomas Berrigan*, 3, 5 November 1836, 1835–47 journal, ff. 62, 64–5, GN 5/2/C/3; *J.W. Saunders Esqr v. Thomas Berrigan*, Writ No. 8, Action in Ejectment, issued 25 September for return 1 November 1836, GN 5/2/C/4; *Regina v. Anastatia Berrigan & others*, 3, 20 September 1838, Ferryland, box 1, n.f., GN 5/4/C/1; *Regina v. William Berrigan, Anastatia Berrigan, Bridget Berrigan, and Alice Berrigan*, 31 December 1842, 31 January, 23 February 1843, *Regina v. James Gearing, Sr., Benjamin Wilcox, Edward Berrigan, Anastatia Berrigan, Thomas Berrigan, Sr., and Thomas Berrigan, Jr.*, 13, 14, 20, 27 June 1843, *Regina v. Thomas Berrigan, Jr.*, 5 February 1844, Ferryland, box 2, n.f., GN 5/4/C/1, PANL.

28. See Keough, 'Slender Thread', chapters 5 and 6. In gauging the significance of the number of complaints found, several factors should be kept in mind. While court records for the southern Avalon are available from 1773 onwards, these records predominantly represent post-1780s cases: references to earlier cases appear only sporadically in governors' correspondence. The court records are, themselves, incomplete as no concerted effort to preserve the records was made until the late twentieth century. As evidenced by various temporal gaps, many records have been lost due to neglect. And while a system evolved whereby matters were entered under several headings—such as causes, writs, minutes and judgments—rarely are the full set of records for any given case available. Furthermore, the cases examined here relate almost exclusively to the districts of Ferryland and Trepassey-St. Mary's. Roughly half the study area, the section from Bay Bulls to Toad's Cove, fell within the court boundaries of the central court district, and unfortunately, an examination of the records for that district (which included all cases in the capital, St. John's) was beyond the scope of this study. With the exception of occasional references from governors' correspondence, this subarea was not represented in my court case database. Finally, the number of adult women in the population of the area for which records have been examined thoroughly was quite small until the second quarter of the nineteenth century. Only by the 1830s did it exceed 400 (Figure 1). In Figure 1, data for the closest year is used when data for the five-year interval is not available. There was no 1740 census return for St. Mary's, but numbers would have been fairly low at this point. Numbers of servants were over-reported in 1836 for individual communities of the Ferryland district. There was obviously an overlap in reporting some residents as both masters/mistresses and servants, for their combined number exceeds total population figures and combined totals of religious denominations for the district. The number used here is from the Abstract at the end of the census which contains a separate total for servants that does tally with the other totals. No separate summer/winter breakdown appears in the census data for 1836, 1845 and 1847. In 1845 a total of 211 servants was reported for the Ferryland district and 141 for 1857. As these individuals are not differentiated by gender, they are not accounted for in this figure. Age categories also shifted in 1857, with the most significant change in terms of this figure being the shift from an 'under 14' category to an 'under 10' category.

29. These findings differ significantly from Judith Norton's in her examination of assault cases in the Planter townships of Nova Scotia in the first 50 years of settlement. Norton notes:

'Women were particularly vulnerable in early Nova Scotia. In the 45 recorded incidents of abuse or assault identified in the early court records, 20 of the victims and five of the assailants were females.' See Norton, 'The Dark Side of Planter Life: Reported Cases of Domestic Violence', in Conrad, ed., *Intimate Relations*, pp., 182–9, particularly p. 185.

30. This was true of plebeian and working-class communities in the British Isles as well. See, for example, Clark, *Struggle for the Breeches*; Connolly, *Priests and People*; Stephen Parker, *Informal Marriage, Cohabitation and the Law 1750–1989* (New York, 1990); Rendall, *Women in Industrializing Society*.

31. Kathleen M. Brown discusses the differences in systems of knowledge about gender between England and Gaelic Ireland in *Good Wives, Nasty Wenches, and Anxious Patriarchs: Gender, Race, and Power in Colonial Virginia* (Chapel Hill, 1994), pp. 33–7. The Irish system was eroded over time, however, by the incursions of English law and culture and an increasingly centralized and patriarchal Catholic church.

32. Rural Irish women performed domestic tasks was well as heavy agricultural work in the fields. They also gathered seaweed for fertilizer and food, carried peat for fuel, kept livestock, sold eggs and distilled and sold spirits. In addition, they generated what was often the family's only cash income through their work in cottage woollen and linen industries. For a discussion of women's status in rural Ireland and the decline in that status by the early nineteenth century, see L.A. Clarkson, 'Love, Labour and Life: Women in Carrick-on-Suir in the Late Eighteenth Century', *Irish Economic and Social History*, 20 (1993), pp. 18–34; Mary Daly, 'Women in the Irish Workforce from Pre-industrial to Modern Times', *Saothar*, 7 (1981), pp. 74–82; Hasia R. Diner, *Erin's Daughters in America: Irish Immigrant Women in the Nineteenth Century* (Baltimore, 1983); David Fitzpatrick, 'The Modernisation of the Irish Female', in Patrick O'Flanagan, Paul Ferguson and Kevin Whelan, eds., *Rural Ireland: Modernisation v. Change, 1600–1900* (Cork, 1987), pp. 162–8; Dierdre Mageean, 'To Be Matched or to Move: Irish Women's Prospects in Munster', in Christine Harzig, ed., *Peasant Maids—City Women From the European Countryside to Urban America* (Ithaca, 1997), pp. 57–97; Janet A. Nolan, *Ourselves Alone. Women's Emigration from Ireland, 1885–1920* (Lexington, Kentucky, 1989).

33. Clarkson, 'Love, Labour and Life', p. 30.

34. 'Potato culture' refers not just to horticultural practices, but a whole cycle of dependence on the potato that developed among almost half Ireland's population in the decades before the great famine—a cycle marked by early marriage, high fertility rates and subdivision of the land to accommodate growing numbers, resulting in even greater dependence on the potato to sustain following generations.

35. See, for example, Leonore Davidoff, 'The Role of Gender in the "First Industrial Nation": Farming and the Countryside in England, 1780–1850', in *Worlds Between*, pp. 180–205; Koditschek, 'Gendering of the British Working Class': Rendall, *Woman in Industrializing Society*; Deborah Valenze, *The First Industrial Woman* (New York and Oxford, 1995).

---

4   From Gail Campbell, 'Disenfranchised but Not Quiescent: Women Petitioners in New Brunswick in the Mid-19th Century', *Acadiensis* 18(2) (Spring 1989): 22–26, 35–38.*

Canadian women's participation in the political life of their society is usually dated from their struggle for and achievement of the vote.[1] Yet denial of the franchise had not prevented women from being actively involved in the political life of their communities. Indeed, from the earliest times, women had found ways to influence their government.[2] In the period prior to the introduction of manhood suffrage—a period characterized by deferential politics—distinctions between men's and women's political behaviour were often blurred. Women, as well as men, regularly participated in politics by petitioning legislatures to achieve specific political goals.[3] Women, like men, were involved in creating the political culture of their society.

Political culture, which involves much more than participation in the formal political system, is shaped by those values and attitudes that are so widely accepted they are taken for granted. Such values provide the underpinnings for the development of formal political institutions and structures.[4] The role of women both in maintaining and in shaping societal values requires further investigation. While women undoubtedly had a significant indirect impact on government and politics through their influence within their own families and as members of voluntary groups and organizations within their communities, this paper will focus on women's direct political participation by analysing the nature and extent of political lobbying by women from three New Brunswick counties, as measured by the number and content of their petitions to the Legislative Assembly during the mid-nineteenth century. In political terms, the decade selected for analysis—1846 through 1857—was a highly significant one. Political parties emerged during this period. Those great moral questions, temperance, and then prohibition, became, for a time at least, the major political issue. And it was on the moral issue that women began to petition the Legislature in numbers during the decade.

While petitions do not represent a new source for the historian, researchers have not normally attempted to identify petition signatories unless they happen to be active members of a specific organization. Often researchers have been satisfied to count the number of petitions, identify the specific sponsoring group and note the number of signatories.[5] In the past, then, petitions have been used only as supplementary evidence. Yet for those who wish to analyze the nature and significance of

women's political role in the nineteenth century, petitions provide the key. Only through the medium of petition could a woman gain official access to her government or express her views about policy to the legislators. Thus, the petition provides a useful measure of the signatory's knowledge of the way government worked, her degree of interest in the issues of the day, and her attitudes concerning those issues.

Petitions and petitioners can be divided into two discrete categories. The first category includes petitioners seeking to use the law in some way: to apply for a government subsidy to which they were legally entitled, to redress a grievance, to appeal for aid at a time of personal distress, or to request a grant from public monies to carry out a worthy public project. Individual petitioners normally fall into this first category, and while such petitions do not reveal the petitioner's opinions on the issues of the day, they do suggest the extent to which she both understood the system and was able to use it to her advantage. The second category includes petitioners seeking to change the law in some way. Through the medium of the petition, they sought to influence their government, to persuade the legislators to accept their view. Occasionally such people petitioned as individuals, but usually they petitioned in concert with others. Legislators would, after all, be more inclined to take a petition seriously if they could be persuaded that a majority of their constituents supported it. Regardless of the success or failure of the petition, such documents can provide important insights concerning societal attitudes. Whether the signatories were members of an organized group with a specific platform and goals, or a group of unorganized individuals who coalesced around a specific issue, an analysis of the demographic characteristics of the supporters of the issue can enhance our understanding of political attitudes and political culture.

The petition process was a popular political strategy used by men as well as women. During the 10-year period from 1846 through 1857, between 400 and 500 petitions to the New Brunswick Legislature were received annually. On average, between 25 per cent and 30 per cent of these were rejected and approximately 50 per cent were granted, while the remainder were tabled or sent to Committee. However, if they persisted in their petitions, even those who had initially been rejected could eventually achieve their goals. Moreover, legislators did not prove more responsive to petitions from men whose votes they might risk losing at the next election.[6] Although a minority among petitioners, women demonstrated their ability to use the strategy effectively.

This study is concerned with the women petitioners of the counties of Charlotte, Sunbury, and Albert in the mid-nineteenth century. All three counties are in the southern half of the province. Charlotte is a large, economically diverse county in the south-west corner. Sunbury is an agricultural county in the central region, just east of Fredericton; and Albert is in the south-east region between Saint John and Moncton, on the Bay of Fundy. Although originally selected because of the richness of their sources for the study of political history, Albert, Charlotte, and Sunbury proved typical in many ways. Thus, while these three counties cannot be considered a microcosm of the province as a whole, they did encompass a broad spectrum of nineteenth century anglophone New Brunswick society including areas of pre-Loyalist, Loyalist, and post-Loyalist settlement and encompassing rural communities, villages, and even large towns. Moreover, one-fifth of New Brunswick's petitioners came from one of these three counties.[7]

Together the three counties included over 30,000 people at mid-century, nearly half of them female. A large majority of those people (over 80 per cent) lived in nuclear families, although a small minority of such families (perhaps as many as 10 per cent) included one or more single or widowed relations, apprentices, boarders, or servants. Over 80 per cent of the inhabitants had been born in New Brunswick of American or British stock. Of the immigrant

population, nearly 70 per cent had been born in Ireland. Although the three counties included substantial numbers of Episcopalians, Baptists, Presbyterians, Roman Catholics, and Methodists as well as a few Universalists and Congregationalists, among others, in both Albert and Sunbury the Baptists were stronger by far than any other denomination, comprising almost 62 per cent of Albert's population and one half of Sunbury's population in 1861.[8]

In both Albert and Sunbury counties, the farm sector accounted for more than half the workers. Even in Charlotte County, which contained very little good agricultural land, over one-third of the population were engaged in agriculture, providing for the needs of the fishery and the lumbering industry. Fifteen per cent of Charlotte's families were employed in the fishery while one-quarter of that county's population depended on the lumbering industry for their livelihood. In each of the three counties 17 per cent of those whose occupation was listed were skilled artisans; a further 15 per cent listed their occupation merely as labourer; and approximately 4 per cent of all families were headed by merchants and professional men.[9] While the men were occupied in the farming, fishing, and lumbering industries, or as skilled artisans or professionals, the women were scarcely idle. Approximately one in every four women of child-bearing age actually bore a child in 1851 and, aside from running their households and caring for the needs of their 14,600 children, the 6,289 women of the three counties churned 689,363 pounds of butter and wove 94,019 yards of cloth on their hand looms.[10] Yet, despite the demands of their busy and productive lives, hundreds of women in the three counties found the time to petition their government.

A wide variety of motives persuaded these women to put their names to petitions. Many of the women in the first category of petitioners—those who sought to use the law in some way—were widows seeking financial compensation or support which they knew was their due. A cursory examination of their petitions would seem to give credence to the common notion that women were 'forever dependent' on men, and that women who lost their husbands were left destitute, dependent on their sons, family, or the charity of the public for support.[11] A more careful reading of the individual petitions leads to quite a different interpretation. Unless their husbands had been soldiers, widows did not generally petition the Legislature for support and those rare women who did appeal to their government for aid at a time of personal distress were not begging for charity or long-term support. In fact, most such petitioners were following an accepted and established formula used by men as well as women, to request compensation for the sacrifices they had made for their country and their community.

In 1848, for example, Margaret Baldwin, widow of the late Thomas Baldwin, of St. Andrews Parish in Charlotte County petitioned the Legislative Assembly for help. Her husband had been employed in the early part of the previous summer by the medical attendant at Hospital Island to help with the care of sick and destitute 'emigrants'. He proved so satisfactory in the discharge of his duties that when a second group of 'emigrants' arrived later in the year he was employed a second time. This time, however, he contracted typhus fever and died, leaving his wife destitute with no means of support for either herself or their two children.[12] Margaret Tufts faced a similar situation. Her husband, Benjamin, had also been employed on Hospital Island. He had been contracted to erect the pest house and repair the public buildings. While he was so employed, a large number of sick 'emigrants' were landed on the island and Benjamin 'devoted all his spare time in administering to the wants of the sick.' While so engaged, he was himself taken ill with typhus fever of which, in a few days, he died, leaving his wife destitute, with 'a large and helpless family' to support. In petitioning her government for help, Mrs. Tufts pointed out that she had, since her husband's death, subsisted on the meagre sum of

£10, the balance owing to him at that time. At the time when she filed her petition, she had no visible way of making a living and feared that she must, for the coming winter at least, be dependent on the sympathy of the public.[13]

Both Margaret Baldwin and Margaret Tufts received grants from a sympathetic Legislature. On the surface, these two petitions, which were the only petitions of this general nature to be submitted during the entire decade, appear to be the kind one might expect from women. However, although these petitions do point out these women's potentially destitute condition, that is not the focal point of their arguments. Margaret Baldwin and Margaret Tufts were not asking their government for charity: they were demanding, in very proper and formulaic terms, money they believed to be their just due in consideration of the services their husbands had rendered to their community. Having received their grants, neither woman saw fit to petition for money a second time. Margaret Baldwin and her family soon left the parish, while Margaret Tufts managed by sharing a house with another family and taking in a lodger.[14] [. . .]

The majority of widows who petitioned the Legislature were the widows of 'old soldiers', men who had fought in the American Revolution. The 'Act for the Relief of Old Soldiers of the Revolutionary War and their Widows', passed on 28 March 1839, entitled widows of veterans to an annual pension of £10. Despite the formulaic nature of their petitions, it would seem that the women themselves initiated their petitions, and continued to press their claims against apparently deaf officials until they were satisfied. Many such petitions referred to the women as indigent, if not destitute, and assured the Legislature that the petitioner had insufficient property to support herself and had not divested herself of any property in order to be eligible for a pension under the terms of the Act. Most of the women who applied for the widow's pension reported that their husbands had, in the past, been recipients of the pension.[15] An analysis of the content of their petitions indicates that these were not desperate and destitute women begging for charity, but, rather, capable and competent women claiming and, if necessary, persisting in claiming pensions as their right. And they needed to be persistent. Although widows' pensions were routinely granted by the Legislature, some such petitions were rejected. Seven of the women who applied for the pension received at least one rejection by the Legislature. Jerusha Black, who was living in Pennfield Parish, Charlotte County at the time of her husband's death in 1846, left that parish after his death and her first petition was filed from St. George Parish in 1848. She was granted her pension that year, but the following year, when she applied from St. David Parish, she was denied support. Back in St. George in 1850, she received her pension once more. The following year, at age 79, she returned to her childhood home, Campobello Island, where she and John Black had married in 1793. There is no record of her application in that year, but in the following year, 1852, she was receiving her pension in Campobello.[16] [. . .]

That women were aware of their rights, and counted on their government to uphold and protect those rights is nowhere more evident than in the case of the large group of young single women who fall within the first category of petitioners. Teachers, regardless of their sex, were required to petition the Legislature in order to receive the provincial school allowance. The licensing procedure was the same for both men and women, and only licensed teachers were eligible to receive the provincial subsidy. Although the criteria changed somewhat during the decade, as the Normal School was established and became generally accepted, the change was gradual and the basic requirements remained consistent until 1853, when the requirement that teachers petition the Legislature directly was dropped. Women remained at a disadvantage throughout the period. The School Act of 1837, which eliminated the previous distinction between a grant issued to a female teacher and one issued to a male, also stipulated that not more than three women teachers per parish were eligible for certification by the trustees in their semi-annual reports. Moreover, the School Act of 1852 restored the distinction between grants issued to male and female teachers. Women teachers holding a third class certificate were to receive £4 less than their male counterparts while grants to women who had attained a first class certificate were a full £10 lower than those received by men who held first class certificates. The community also had a significant responsibility in the process, for the school proprietors were required to provide a building and to match the amount paid by the province and teachers' petitions had to be certified by the local trustees.[17]

For Alice Thomson of Charlotte County, the fact that only three female teachers per parish could apply for the provincial allowance meant that although she had taught in St. Andrews for 18 months, she received the provincial allowance for only the first six. In her petition of 1847, she informed the legislators that the trustees had refused to report her for the last 12 months 'by reason of the too great number of female schools in the parish at that time.'[18] This was a not infrequent occurrence in St. Andrews, which was a large parish. In 1849, both Lydia Thomson and Mary O'Neill reported that, although they had been certified by the trustees, their petitions of the previous year could not be returned to the Legislature 'as the number of female schools allowed by law had already passed.'[19] Nor was the problem confined to large and populous parishes. Susannah Rogers of Coverdale, the smallest parish in Albert County, reported in 1850 that she could not be certified in the usual way for 1849 because the parish had exceeded its allotment of female school teachers.[20] These four young women, faced with an obstacle their male counterparts did not have to deal with, persisted in pressing their claims and all four eventually received their allowances, delayed by a full year in each case.

Nonetheless, the legal restriction did have the desired effect: significantly fewer women than men applied for the provincial subsidy each year. In Sunbury County only 2 of the 15 petitions from teachers were from women, and one of those was requesting remuneration not for her services, but rather for the services of her late husband. In Albert 4 of the 28 petitioning teachers were women. But in Charlotte County 45 of the 96 teachers who petitioned the Legislature for remuneration were women, and, although one of the female petitions was from a woman requesting the school allowance due her late husband, one of the male petitioners was requesting payment for the services of his late wife, while another was claiming the school allowance of his late daughter.

Married women did not typically petition the Legislature as individuals.[21] Nor did they sign petitions calling for the building of roads, wharfs, bridges, and other public works. They did not petition for the incorporation of either the Roman Catholic bishop or the Loyal Orange Order. Nor did they join in requests for the division of parishes or the creation of free ports. Their husbands, in contrast, did all these things. The failure of women to become involved in such lobbying campaigns can cause historians to draw misleading conclusions about women and their role within the broader society. Because nineteenth-century women were denied the vote and because they did not lobby their Legislature as part of an organized group, it has been assumed that women were not knowledgable about political issues and that they were not active politically. Politics has been regarded as an activity outside the nineteenth-century woman's 'proper sphere', as defined for her by a patriarchal society and women's political involvement is usually dated from the rise of provincial and national women's organizations in the late nineteenth century. The political awareness evinced by the women who joined such organizations is viewed as a new departure which saw women becoming active outside the domestic sphere for the first time.[22] Yet there was a far greater

degree of continuity than such interpretations would lead one to expect. At least some married women in mid-nineteenth-century New Brunswick understood the system and quickly learned to use it effectively. These women had stepped beyond the domestic sphere long before the advent of national, or even provincial women's organizations.

Take the case of John and Alice Wilson of St. Andrews Parish in Charlotte County. John was a highly successful merchant. In 1851 he was 64 years old. Alice, his American-born wife, was 58. According to the census of that year, their household also included a hired man, two female servants, and an errand boy. John and Alice had sundry relatives living in the parish including their married son Thomas, a lawyer, and John's two younger brothers who were also merchants. Between 1846 and his death in 1855, John Wilson petitioned the Legislature no less than 21 times. Some of the petitions he initiated involved lobbying for parish improvements, while others were more personal in nature. In 1847, for example, he petitioned for and received a grant of money to improve Dark Harbour, Grand Manan. In 1849 he asked to be reimbursed for the money he had expended in the care and maintenance of 'emigrants' from Ireland brought over to work for the St. Andrews and Quebec Railroad Company, of which he was president. His petition was rejected. In 1851 he requested a further grant to deepen the channel at Dark Harbour, which was, he argued, the only safe harbour in the area in the event of a storm. Once more the Legislature granted his request. In 1855 he requested yet another grant for the purpose of further improvements at Dark Harbour.[23]

During that entire decade, Alice Wilson did not sign a single petition to the Legislature. But there is every reason to assume that she understood precisely what her husband had been doing. In his will, John named his 'dear wife Alice' his sole executrix, leaving her all his 'real estate viz, land, buildings, mills, wharfs, stores' as well as all his 'personal estate of every description consisting of household furniture, all my books, debts, notes of hand, bonds, bank stock, bridge and steamboat stock, money vessels and of all description property termed personal estate'.[24] John's obvious faith in the abilities of his 'dear wife Alice' proved fully justified. Less than a year after his death, Alice petitioned the Legislature for the first time. She asked to be reimbursed the amount expended by her late husband in opening and improving Dark Harbour, Grand Manan. The following year she petitioned for the appointment of a person to look into the expenses incurred by her late husband in constructing a breakwater at Dark Harbour. That same year she requested that the government suspend the issue of debentures to the New Brunswick and Canada Railroad and Land Company until reparation had been made her for the claims of her late husband. When that request was tabled, she followed it up with a second petition.[25] Clearly Alice Wilson was a force to be reckoned with. Indeed, her immediate facility with the petition process makes one wonder if perhaps Alice had not always been the 'petitioner' in the family. Whatever her role may have been in the process while her husband was alive, after his death she quickly proved herself fully capable of handling his affairs. While Alice Wilson is undoubtedly the best example of a widow who used petitions to promote her business interests after the death of her husband, she was by no means the only example.[26]

Custom—and perhaps some husbands— prevented married women from signing more petitions dealing with individual and family affairs, but one should not assume either a lack of knowledge about or a lack of interest in the political system and the way it worked, on the part of such women. Moreover, starting in 1853, married women began to sign petitions in numbers. The petitions they signed were qualitatively different from the petitions women had signed up to that time. Such women fell into the second category of petitioners: those who sought to change the law. The issue that finally mobilized them to take up their pens was, not

surprisingly a reform issue. By the final decades of the century it would be an issue closely associated with the organized women's movement. The issue was temperance.

The temperance movement was well entrenched in New Brunswick by 1853, the first formal temperance organization having been established in 1830. Drawing inspiration and encouragement from both Great Britain and the United States, the New Brunswick movement had gained ground steadily throughout the 1830s and 1840s.[27] Temperance societies were established in Fredericton, Saint John, Dorchester, Chatham, St. Stephen, and St. Andrews and temperance *soirées* and teas were very popular.[28] During the early years, the goal had been to encourage moderation and sobriety but by the mid-1840s many temperance activists were advocating total abstinence.[29] As the depression of the late 1840s began, temperance advocates, in their search for explanations, increasingly associated drinking with the broad social problems of crime and poverty.[30] In 1847, the Sons of Temperance, the most successful of the American total-abstinence organizations, established its first division in British North America at St. Stephen, New Brunswick. The Sons of Temperance and its affiliates, the Daughters of Temperance and the Cadets of Temperance, had widespread appeal. Teas, picnics, and steamer excursions provided family diversions and attracted many to the great crusade.[31] By 1850 there were branches all over the southern part of the province.[32]

For many years temperance advocates sought to achieve their goals by moral suasion, but by the late 1840s some had become convinced that moral suasion alone was not enough. For a time, they focused their efforts on gaining control of liquor consumption within their own communities through attempts to secure limitations on the number of tavern licences issued by county and city councils.[33] But such efforts proved unsuccessful. In Maine, temperance crusaders facing a similar failure had appealed to a higher authority. By 1851 they had gained enough support in the Legislature there to achieve an effective prohibition law. The 'Maine Law', which was the first prohibitory liquor law in North America, had a significant effect on the New Brunswick temperance movement. In 1852, a so-called 'monster petition' calling for the prohibition of the importation of alcoholic beverages was presented to the House of Assembly.[34] The 9,000 signatures on the petition so impressed the province's legislators that they were persuaded to pass 'An Act to Prevent the Traffic in Intoxicating Liquors'. This act 'forbade the manufacture within New Brunswick of any alcoholic or intoxicating liquors except for religious, medicinal or chemical purposes. Beer, ale, porter and cider were excepted.'[35]

Women had, of course, been involved in the temperance cause from the time of its first appearance in New Brunswick in 1830. But men had always outnumbered women in temperance organizations and until 1853 the vast majority of temperance petitions were submitted by and signed by men.[36] Urban women were the first to take up their pens in the temperance cause: the 'Ladies' Total Abstinence Society for the City and County of Saint John' submitted the first recorded petition from women on the issue to the Legislature in 1847. Three years later Woodstock's Victoria Union No. 4 of the Daughters of Temperance submitted a petition opposing the granting of tavern licences. The following year the 'Ladies of Woodstock' went even further, calling for 'an act to prevent the sale of spiritous liquors'. In 1852, the Daughters of Temperance from Woodstock were joined in the campaign by women from Fredericton and the surrounding area.[37] Rural women, including the subjects of this article, in contrast, did not sign temperance petitions to the Legislature before 1853. Yet this cannot be taken as an indication of either a lack of knowledge or a lack of interest. Some, like the women of Albert County had, for several years, regularly signed petitions addressed to their local county councils opposing the issuance of tavern licences.[38] Such women signed petitions not as members

of any organized temperance group, but rather as members of their local community; and this pattern was to continue when they turned their attention to the Legislative Assembly in 1853. Rural women had not participated in the legislative lobbying campaign that had culminated in the drafting of the Liquor Bill. Yet they were very much in the mainstream of the temperance movement as it gathered force, attempting first to achieve sobriety through moral suasion, then seeking local solutions through no licensing campaigns. And they would soon have the opportunity to demonstrate their support for the new legislation.

The new law was to come into force on 1 June 1853. In fact, it never came into effect. No sooner had it passed into law than the lobby against it began. Petitions calling for the repeal of the new law flooded in from nearly every county in the province. And the legislators were disposed to listen. Perhaps they had, after all, been just a little too hasty. The Legislative Assembly depended mainly on customs duties for its disposable revenue and duties on rum alone represented over one-third of that revenue.[39] It was at this stage that the women of New Brunswick mobilized for action. Women who had never before signed a petition took up their pens. They begged their legislators not to repeal the new law. Men had achieved the law; the women were determined to keep it.[40]

After the election of 1854, temperance advocates, many of them women, redoubled their efforts. Through the medium of petitions, they urged their newly elected Assembly to enact yet another law 'to prevent the importation, manufacture and sale of all intoxicating liquors within this province.' [. . .]

Even though the fight was ultimately lost, the role women played in it is highly significant. The very fact that two prohibitory liquor acts were passed demonstrates the power of the petition as a political tool in mid-nineteenth-century New Brunswick. Petitions and petitioners were taken seriously. Nor was it suggested that women had less right than men to petition their Legislature. There is no evidence to suggest that women's signatures carried any less weight than men's.[41] [. . .]

Of those inhabitants who petitioned the Legislative Assembly during the 12 years covered by this study women represented only a very small minority. Thus, while female petitioners from each of the three counties numbered in the hundreds, male petitioners numbered in the thousands. Nonetheless, in Sunbury, the county for which the most complete records are available, women from over 30 per cent of the families listed in the 1851 census signed at least one petition to their Legislature during the period. Petition signatories included women of all ages, all classes, all ethnic and religious groups. But no matter what their age, ethnicity, religious denomination, or economic status, the very fact that significant numbers of women signed petitions is historically important. Women did not have the right to vote in the mid-nineteenth century. Yet, in New Brunswick, at least, women were not passive and they were not silent. Many understood the law and were determined to make it work for them. They petitioned for pensions and subsidies to which they were legally entitled and, from time to time, they petitioned for redress of personal grievances. Most were successful in achieving their ends. Many more women became politically active during the decade, seeking, through the medium of petitions, to influence their government to change the law. Working in concert with others of like mind, they effectively demonstrated their power to persuade, although ultimately they failed to achieve their goal. Whether they petitioned as individuals or in association with others, whether they were seeking to change the law or merely to use it, whether they succeeded or failed, these nineteenth-century New Brunswick women had stepped outside the domestic sphere and into the world of politics. Their lives had a political dimension and, by exercising their rights as subjects under the crown, they helped to shape the political culture of their province.

NOTES

* This paper builds on a data base that was created while I was a post-doctoral fellow at the University of New Brunswick. This particular study is part of a much broader project dealing with political culture in mid-nineteenth-century New Brunswick.

1. Although New Brunswick women were not disfranchised by statute until 1843, historians have found no record of even propertied women in the colony voting before that time. John Garner, *The Franchise and Politics in British North America, 1755–1867* (Toronto, 1969), pp. 155–6. While it is true that in debates on franchise extension in later years politicians claimed that women of the province had voted before their specific exclusion in 1843, the only evidence that has been found to support their claims is a single letter to the editor that appeared in the *Gleaner and Northumberland* *Shediasma* in 1830, cited in Elspeth Tulloch, *We, the undersigned: A Historical Overview of New Brunswick Women's Political and Legal Status, 1784–1984* (Moncton, 1985), pp. 3–4. Garner argues that exclusion by statute did not represent a new restraint on the franchise. For centuries, women in Great Britain had not exercised the franchise despite the lack of a formal legal restraint, having, as one judge argued, 'always been considered legally incapable of voting for members of Parliament.' This exclusion by convention had been accepted by the colonies as part of their legal heritage. Garner, *The Franchise and Politics*, p. 156. Indeed, evidence from extant newspapers suggests that the purpose of the 1843 statute was mainly to clarify the law in order to 'promote the public peace at elections.' By giving convention the weight of law, the revised statute provided county sheriffs with clear guidance in deciding whether a demanded scrutiny should be

carried out. The disfranchisement of women was quite incidental to the amendments and went unnoticed by the newspapers of the day and, apparently, by their readers as well. See 'The Election Law—The Loan Bill—And the Legislative Council in a Ferment', *The Standard or Frontier Gazette* (St. Andrews), 6 April 1843; 'Prorogation of the Legislature', ibid., 20 April 1843; *Weekly Chronicle* (Saint John), 31 March 1843 and 'House of Assembly', ibid., 14 April 1843; 'Provincial Legislature', *The Gleaner and Northumberland, Kent, Gloucester and Restigouche Commercial and Agricultural Journal* (Miramichi), 14 February 1843, and 'Editor's Department', ibid., 13 March 1843; 'The New Election Law', *The Loyalist* (Saint John), 23 March 1843; and 'Parliamentary', *St. John Morning News and General Advertising Newspaper*, 31 March 1843.

2.   For example, following a long-established European tradition, the women of New France took to the streets during the late 1750s to protest food shortages. Terence Crowley, 'Thunder Gusts: Popular Disturbances in Early French Canada', Canadian Historical Association, *Historical Papers* (1979), pp. 19–20. And evidence from the pre-history period strongly suggests that Iroquois women, at least, had enormous political influence in their society. See especially Judith K. Brown, 'Economic Organization and the Position of Women Among the Iroquois', *Ethnohistory*, 17 (1970), pp. 153–6.

3.   In an article discussing the role of women in American political society, Paula Baker has made this argument very effectively. Of course, the political transition which separated male and female politics occurred much earlier in the United States where the introduction of manhood suffrage (demonstrating definitively to women that their disfranchisement was based solely on sex) and the rise of mass political parties dated from the early nineteenth century. Paula Baker, 'The Domestication of Politics: Women and American Political Society, 1780–1920', *American Historical Review*, 89 (1984), pp. 620–47. For a review of the literature concerning the role of deference in male political behaviour during the antebellum period, see Ronald P. Formisano, 'Deferential-Participant Politics: The Early Republic's Political Culture',

American Political Science Review, 68 (1974), pp. 473–87.

4.   For similar definitions of political culture, see Robert R. Alford, *Party and Society: The Anglo-American Democracies* (Chicago, 1963), pp. 2–6; Gabriel A. Almond and G. Bingham Powell Jr., *Comparative Politics: System, Process, and Policy* (2nd ed., Boston, 1978), ch. II, pp. 25–30; Ronald P. Formisano, *The Transformation of Political Culture: Massachusetts Parties, 1790s–1840s* (New York, 1983), p. 4.

5.   See, for example, Carol Lee Bacchi, *Liberation Deferred? The Ideas of the English-Canadian Suffragists, 1877–1918* (Toronto, 1982), pp. 34, 38, 75, 82, 143; Catherine Cleverdon, *The Woman Suffrage Movement in Canada* (Toronto, 1970), pp. 23–110, 160–220; Wendy Mitchinson, 'The WCTU: "For God, Home and Native Land": A Study in Nineteenth Century Feminism', in Linda Kealey ed., *A Not Unreasonable Claim: Women and Reform in Canada, 1880–1920s* (Toronto, 1979), pp. 155–6.

6.   Although these figures represent the average yearly percentages, the success rate varied significantly from year to year, with legislators proving decidedly more sympathetic some years than others. But in no case did male petitioners prove more successful than their female counterparts. Even election years did not necessarily bring a greater likelihood of success than other years. Petitions to the New Brunswick Legislature are located in Record Group 4, Record Series 24, 1846–57/Petitions [RG4, RS24, 1846–57/Pe], Provincial Archives of New Brunswick [PANB]. It is also possible that the success rate of certain types of petitions varied over time. In her analysis of the WCTU and its impact, for example, Wendy Mitchinson has suggested that the petition campaign was not a particularly effective strategy and that women were naïve in their belief that they could achieve legislative change through the medium of petition. Mitchinson, 'The WCTU', p. 156. If women were naïve in this belief, however, they were certainly not alone, for the majority of petitioners were men.

7.   Of the 5,081 petitions considered, 1,029 originated in one of the three counties. This suggests that the people of Albert, Charlotte and Sunbury were slightly over-represented among the colony's petitioners, comprising 20.25 per

cent of petitioners as compared to 16.3 per cent of the total population of the province. (The discrepancy is not statistically significant, however, as differences of plus or minus five per cent could occur entirely by chance.)

8. Information on denominational affiliation is not available for 1851 and therefore the 1861 census was used in this case. See *The Census of the Province of New Brunswick, 1861* (St. John, 1862).

9. Unless otherwise noted, all information contained in the demographic profiles provided for the three counties under study is drawn from *The Census of the Province of New Brunswick, 1851* (St. John, 1852).

10. The 6,289 figure refers only to women over the age of 20. For a discussion of women's role in the dairying industry in British North America during this period, see Marjorie Griffin Cohen, 'The Decline of Women in Canadian Dairying', in Alison Prentice and Susan Mann Trofimenkoff, eds., *The Neglected Majority: Essays in Canadian Women's History*, Volume 2 (Toronto, 1985), pp. 61–70, and *Women's Work, Markets, and Economic Development in Nineteenth-Century Ontario* (Toronto, 1988), pp. 59–117. While the 1851 census does not specify who the weavers are, the manuscript census of manufacturing for 1861 indicates that virtually all of the hand loom weavers engaged in this cottage industry were women. The manuscript census of manufacturing for 1871 also supports this assumption. See Manuscript Census for Charlotte County, 1861 and 1871, PANB.

11. This view of women as forever dependent on men is argued by Rosemary Ball, '"A Perfect Farmer's Wife": Women in 19th Century Rural Ontario', *Canada: An Historical Magazine* (December 1975), pp. 2–21. And even historians like David Gagan, who recognize that 'the fact of subordination was partially, if not wholly, mitigated by environment which cast women in a central role in the farm family's struggle to improve, and endure' often conclude that 'for those women who outlived their partners, widowhood . . . was a calamity the consequence of which clearly troubled even the stoutest hearts'. David Gagan, *Hopeful Travellers: Families, Land, and Social Change in Mid-Victorian Peel County Canada West* (Toronto, 1981), pp. 89–90.

12. RG4, RS24, 1848/Pe 4, PANB.

13. RG4, RS24, 1848/Pe 5, PANB.

14. New Brunswick Manuscript Census, 1851, PANB. Not only were women less likely to petition their government for charity than were men, the Overseers of the Poor in each parish, in requesting reimbursement for monies expended on poor relief, more often listed men than women as recipients of that relief. On the rare occasions when individual men and women did petition their government for help in times of distress, they pressed their claims in very similar ways.

15. See *Acts of the General Assembly of Her Majesty's Province of New Brunswick* (Fredericton, 1839–45), 2 Victoria, Chapter 27; amended 4 Victoria, Chapter 16 and 6 Victoria, Chapter 36. Under the terms of the Act widows were eligible for the same annual pensions their husbands had received. Moreover, the eligibility clauses in the oath drew no distinction between veterans and their widows: the formulaic wording for initial applications, as set out in the 1839 Act, was the same for both.

16. RG4, RS24, 1848/Pe 152; 1849/Pe 13; 1850/Pe 56; 1852/Pe 67, PANB.

17. Katherine F.C. MacNaughton, *The Development of the Theory and Practice of Education in New Brunswick, 1784–1900* (Fredericton, 1946), pp. 89, 149.

18. RG4, RS24, 1847/Pe 471, PANB.

19. RG4, RS24, 1849/Pe 91; 1849/Pe 209, PANB.

20. RG4, RS24, 1850/Pe 21, PANB.

21. There were four exceptions to this general rule in the three counties during the 12 year period under study. They include a woman who had been named executrix of her father's estate and three married teachers. One of the latter had continued to teach after her marriage while the remaining two were applying for allowances earned prior to marriage. See RG4, RS24, 1851/Pe 239; 1852/Pe 25; 1849/Pe 84; 1850/Pe 49.

22. For a discussion of women's lack of power within the family, see Margaret Conrad, '"Sundays Always Make Me Think of Home": Time and Place in Canadian Women's History', in Veronica Strong-Boag and Anita Clair Fellman, eds., *Rethinking Canada: The Promise of Women's History* (Toronto, 1986), pp. 69, 75–7. For examples of the view that the rise of provincial and national women's organizations signalled a 'new day' for women in terms

of political activity, see Deborah Gorham, 'Flora MacDonald Denison: Canadian Feminist', in Kealey ed., *A Not Unreasonable Claim*, pp. 48, 58–64; Wendy Mitchinson, 'The WCTU', pp. 152–4, 166–7; and Veronica Strong-Boag, '"Setting the Stage": National Organization and the Women's Movement in the Late 19th Century', in Susan Mann Trofimenkoff and Alison Prentice, eds., *The Neglected Majority: Essays in Canadian Women's History* (Toronto, 1977), pp. 87–103. Historians have not altogether ignored women's political activity during this period, but in general women's participation in the petitioning process has been characterized as exceptional rather than normal. For the best discussion of women's political activity during this period, see Alison Prentice, Paula Borne, Gail Cuthbert Brandt, Beth Light, Wendy Mitchinson and Naomi Black, *Canadian Women: A History* (Toronto, 1988), pp. 105, 174–5 (for references to petitions and petitioners, pp. 70, 81, 102, 105).

23. RG4, RS24, 1846/Pe 285; 1847/Pe 67, 116, 154, 313, 402; 1848/Pe 365, 389; 1849/Pe 7, 89, 355; 1851/Pe 333, 334; 1852/Pe 320, 321; 1853/Pe 260; 1854/Pe 37, 105, 354; 1855/Pe 291, 292, PANB.

24. Charlotte County Probate Court Records, RG7, RS63B3, 1852, PANB.

25. RG4, RS24, 1856/Pe 5; 1857–58/Pe 7, 9, 164, PANB.

26. For examples of other widows who were involved in the economic life of their communities, see RG4, RS24, 1846/Pe 216; 1849/Pe 195; 1852/Pe 17, 202; 1854/Pe 215, 225, PANB.

27. For evidence of British and American influences, see J.K. Chapman, 'The Mid-Nineteenth Century Temperance Movement in New Brunswick and Maine', *Canadian Historical Review*, 35 (1954), pp. 43, 48–50 and T.W. Acheson, *Saint John: The Making of a Colonial Urban Community* (Toronto, 1985), pp. 140–50. Analysts of the nineteenth-century temperance movements in Great Britain and the United States tend to characterize the movement as an Anglo-American crusade. The American and British campaigns began at the same time and nourished each other. See, for example, Brian Harrison, *Drink and the Victorians: The Temperance Question in England, 1815–1872* (Pittsburgh, 1971), pp. 99–103;

W.R. Lambert, *Drink and Sobriety in Victorian Wales*, c. 1820–c. 1895 (Cardiff, 1983), pp. 59–61; and Ian R. Tyrell, *Sobering Up: From Temperance to Prohibition in Antebellum America, 1800–1860* (Westport CT, 1979), pp. 135, 299.

28. Chapman, 'The Mid-Nineteenth Century Temperance Movement', p. 48.

29. Acheson, *Saint John*, p. 138. The British and American movements had made this shift somewhat earlier. Teetotalism had gained popularity in Britain by the late 1830s while the 'Washingtonians' popularized teetotalism in the United States after their inception in 1840. Lambert, *Drink and Sobriety*, p. 59; Tyrell, *Sobering Up*, pp. 135–90.

30. While the prohibition advocates of a later period would focus on the effects of drinking on individual families, the women petitioners of this early period, like their male counterparts, regarded drinking as a community rather than a family problem. The petitions that went beyond a formulaic request for the enactment of 'a Law to prevent the importation, manufacture and sale of all intoxicating Liquors within this Province', generally decried intemperance as 'a great public evil'. As the authors of one 1851 petition succinctly put it, 'your petitioners are convinced that crime, pauperism and lunacy in nine cases out of ten are the direct result of drinking habits.' See RG4, RS24, 1846/Pe 45; 1848/Pe 270; 1849/Pe 87; 1849/Pe 151; 1849/Pe 363; 1851/Pe 228; 1854/Pe 220; 1854/Pe 394; 1854/Pe 395; 1854/Pe 404; 1854/Pe 465.

31. Acheson, *Saint John*, p. 149; Chapman, 'The Mid-Nineteenth Century Temperance Movement', p. 50.

32. W.S. MacNutt, *New Brunswick, A History: 1784–1867* (Toronto, 1963, 1984), p. 350.

33. Acheson, *Saint John*, p. 141. Similar attempts were made in New England to control licensing at the local level. Tyrell, *Sobering Up*, pp. 91, 242–3.

34. RG4, RS24, 1852/Pe 406, PANB. The Maine Law also had a significant impact in England and within the United States. See Harrison, *Drink and the Victorians*, p. 196; Tyrell, *Sobering Up*, p. 260.

35. Chapman, 'The Mid-Nineteenth Century Temperance Movement', p. 53.

36. New Brunswick women were by no means atypical in this regard. Barbara Epstein argues,

for example, that during this period American women in the temperance movement were generally relegated to subsidiary roles—influencing sons and husbands. Barbara Leslie Epstein, *The Politics of Domesticity: Women, Evangelism, and Temperance in Nineteenth-Century America* (Middletown CT, 1981), p. 91.

37. See RG4, RS24, 1847/Pe 465; 1850/Pe 445; 1851/Pe 431; 1852/Pe 348; 1852/Pe 402; 1852/Pe 407, PANB. The early involvement of urban women is not surprising. Harrison argues that the temperance movement in England owed much to industrialization. Led by pioneers among whom doctors, coffee traders, evangelicals, and industrialists figured prominently, the movement spread out from the towns (Harrison, *Drink and the Victorians*, pp. 92–8). Similarly, Tyrrell argues that temperance 'flourished in a society in transition from a rural to an urban industrial order', receiving its strongest support from the promoters of that change (Tyrrell, *Sobering Up*, pp. 7, 209, 241, 252). A comprehensive study of the New Brunswick temperance movement during this period remains to be done, but the pattern of petitioning is suggestive of the need for a careful comparative analysis.

38. RG18, RS146, B9 (1851), PANB.

39. Chapman, 'The Mid-Nineteenth Century Temperance Movement', p. 44.

40. Women from both Charlotte and Sunbury participated in the 1853 campaign against the repeal of the Act. See the index of the *Journal of the New Brunswick House of Assembly*, 1853, which refers to: Petition 366, Lucinda Garcelon, Clara A. McAllister, Margaret Robinson and 300 others, female inhabitants of Charlotte, and Petition 386, Israel Smith, Thomas H. Smith, Esq. and 996 others of Sunbury and York. Other petitions for Charlotte which might well have numbered women among their signatories include: Petition 318 from Charlotte County, Petition 354 from St. Andrews and Petition 355 from St. George. None of the above has survived in the PANB.

41. In discussing women signatories of the 'monster petition' of 1852, Mr. Hatheway, the Representative for York County, argued that women's signatures on petitions were 'a sufficient reason' for passing the Liquor Bill then before the House. He believed a politician needed 'the good opinion of the fair portion of the community' and declared that he 'would always rather have one lady canvasser than a dozen men'. *Reports of the Debates and Proceedings of the House of Assembly of the Province of New Brunswick* (Fredericton, 1852), p. 101. In the 1854 debates, while some members questioned the signatures of 'children in schools', the right of women to sign was generally accepted. Indeed, the majority of those who rose in the House to comment on the 1854 Bill argued that 30,000 signatures in favour of the Bill, as opposed to 4,000 against, was strong evidence of the public feeling. *Reports of the Debates and Proceedings (1854)*, pp. 70–3. Similarly, American and British legislators attacked the validity of children's signatures on temperance petitions but did not question the signatures of non-voting women for, as the women themselves argued, 'although they did not themselves vote, their husbands did, and their husbands would be heeding the advice of their spouses'. Harrison, *Drink and the Victorians*, p. 229; Tyrrell, *Sobering Up*, pp. 279–80.

Chapter Eleven

Aboriginal People in British North America

READINGS

Primary Documents

1   From 'Report on the Affairs of the Indians in Canada', (1842–44) in *Appendix to the Fourth Volume of the Journals of the Legislative Assembly of the Province of Canada 1844–45*

2   'The Robinson-Superior Treaty', in *The Treaties of Canada with the Indians of Manitoba and the North-West Territories, Including the Negotiations on which They Were Based, and Other Information Relating Thereto*, Alexander Morris

Historical Interpretations

3   From 'Empire, the Maritime Colonies, and the Supplanting of Mi'kma'ki/Wulstukwik, 1780–1820', John G. Reid

4   From 'Seeking Honest Justice in a Land of Strangers: Nahnebahwequa's Struggle for Land', Celia Haig-Brown

Introduction

Since the past few topics have focused on some compelling facets of colonial life, you might be thinking: What about the Aboriginal people? They did not flee the continent once it became clear that the uninvited newcomers were sticking around. However, the most plentiful information we have about the various First Nations during the colonial period has tended to come from documents written about them by others.

The period comprising the late eighteenth and early nineteenth centuries was one in which treaties between First Nations and colonial authorities began to institutionalize relations and to more sharply or formally segregate the two groups. In return for control over certain territories, First Nations people were to stay away from settlers taking up land for agricultural purposes. The extinguishing of Aboriginal title happened along lines set out by the Colonial Office. This dictation or shaping of the terms was the prerogative of the stronger force—a pattern that continued after Confederation.

The report from the early 1840s illustrates clearly that the British colonial authorities believed that they had continually treated an indigenous population that was prone to temptation with 'forbearance and kindness'. The second primary source is a treaty known as the Robinson-Superior Treaty. Signed in 1850, it offers lump-sum and yearly compensation to the affected bands for the loss of their lands, and grants reserves, presumably in places that the bands wanted to continue living. John Reid's reading discusses this process (which occurred earlier in the Maritimes than in Central Canada) by using the term supplanting, which is especially appropriate because it conveys a sense that one way of life was elbowed out of the way to make room for another. His view is a bit more hopeful in that he notes that Maritime First Nations experienced some success in having their grievances remedied. Perhaps this was because colonization required things to happen quickly and authorities did not want to delay the process. Clearly a story in which less success is achieved, Celia Haig-Brown's account of Nahnebahwequa's situation and the lengths to which she would go (including a trip to England to plead her case) in the years before Confederation is an early example of some of the difficulties that would arise for couples of mixed backgrounds.

QUESTIONS FOR CONSIDERATION

1. What goal does the British colonial administration seem to be moving toward? In other words, what changes do they hope to bring about in the relationship between First Nations and immigrants/settlers?

2. What did the Robinson-Superior Treaty ask of those who signed it?

3. From the perspective of First Nations people in British North America, what were the possible advantages and disadvantages of being treated as individual nations?

4. What were the strategies that Maritime First Nations used to 'negotiate' with colonial authorities?

5. What did Nahnebahwequa hope might happen after her visit to the Queen, and why didn't it happen?

SUGGESTIONS FOR FURTHER READING

Binnema, Ted, and Susan Neylan, eds., *New Histories for Old: Changing Perspectives on Canada's Native Pasts* (Vancouver: UBC Press, 2007)

Carter, Sarah, *Aboriginal People and Colonizers of Western Canada to 1900* (Toronto: University of Toronto Press, 1999)

Dickason, Olive Patricia, with David T. McNab, *Canada's First Nations: A History of Founding Peoples from Earliest Times* (Don Mills: Oxford University Press, 2009)

Miller, J.R., *Compact, Contract, Covenant: Aboriginal Treaty-Making in Canada* (Toronto: University of Toronto Press, 2009)

Miller, J.R., ed., *Sweet Promises: A Reader on Indian-White Relations in Canada* (Toronto: University of Toronto Press, 1991)

Upton, L.F.S., *Micmacs and Colonists: Indian-White Relations in the Maritimes, 1713–1867* (Vancouver: University of British Columbia Press, 1979)

PRIMARY DOCUMENTS

1 From 'Report on the Affairs of the Indians in Canada', (1842–44) in *Appendix to the Fourth Volume of the Journals of the Legislative Assembly of the Province of Canada 1844–45* (Montreal: R. Campbell, 1845), Appendix EEE.

SECTION I. HISTORY OF THE RELATIONS BETWEEN THE GOVERNMENT AND THE INDIANS.

The spirit of the British Government towards the Aborigines of this Continent, was at an early date characterized by the same forbearance and kindness which still continues to be extended to them. [. . .]

Since 1763 the Government, adhering to the Royal Proclamation of that year, have not considered themselves entitled to dispossess the Indians of their lands, without entering into an agreement with them, and rendering them some compensation. For a considerable time after the conquest of Canada, the whole of the western part of the Upper Province, with the exception of a few military posts on the frontier, and a great extent of the eastern part, was in their occupation. As the settlement of the country advanced, and the land was required for new occupants, or the predatory and revengeful habits of the Indians rendered their removal desirable, the British Government made successive agreements with them for the surrender of portions of their lands. The compensation was sometimes made in the shape of presents, consisting of clothing, ammunition, and objects adapted to gratify a savage taste; but more frequently in the shape of permanent annuities, payable to the tribe concerned, and their descendants forever, either in goods at the current price, or in money at the rate of ten dollars (£2 10s.) for each member of the tribe at the time of the arrangement. [. . .]

It has been alleged that these agreements were unjust, as dispossessing the natives of their ancient territories, and extortionate, as rendering a very inadequate compensation for the lands surrendered.

If, however, the Government had not made arrangements for the voluntary surrender of the lands, the white settlers would gradually have taken possession of them, without offering any compensation whatsoever; it would, at that time, have been as impossible to resist the natural laws of society, and to guard the Indian Territory against the encroachments of the whites, as it would have been impolitic to have attempted to check the tide of immigration. The Government, therefore, adopted the most humane and the most just course, in inducing the Indians, by offers of compensation, to remove quietly to more distant hunting grounds, or to confine themselves within more limited reserves, instead of leaving them and the white settlers exposed to the horrors of a protracted struggle for ownership. The wisdom and justice of this course is most strongly recommended by Vattel, in his Law of Nations, from which the following passage is an extract:—

There is another celebrated question to which the discovery of the new world has principally given rise. It is asked whether a nation may lawfully take possession of some part of a vast country in which there are none but erratic nations, whose scanty population is incapable of occupying the whole? We have already observed, in establishing the obligation to cultivate the earth, that these nations cannot exclusively appropriate to themselves more land than they have occasion for, or more than they are able to settle and cultivate. Their unsettled habitation in those immense regions, cannot be accounted a true and legal possession, and the people of Europe, too closely pent up at home, finding land, of which the Savages stood in no particular need, and of which they made no actual and constant use, were lawfully entitled to take possession of it and to settle it with Colonies. The earth, as we have already observed, belongs to mankind in general, and was designed to furnish them with subsistence. If each nation had from the beginning resolved to appropriate to itself a vast country, that the people might live only by hunting, fishing and wild fruits, our globe would not be sufficient to maintain a tenth part of its present inhabitants. We do not, therefore, deviate from the views of nature, in confining the Indians within narrower limits. However, we cannot help praising the moderation of the English Puritans, who first settled in New England, who, notwithstanding their being furnished with a charter from their Sovereign, purchased of the Indians the lands of which they intended to take possession. This laudable example was followed by William Penn, and the Colony of Quakers that he conducted to Pennsylvania.

Nor can the friend of the Indian claim for him a monetary compensation based on the present value of the land, which has been created solely by the presence and industry of the white settlers. Its only value to the denizen of the forest, was as a hunting ground, as the source of his supply of game and furs. Of the cultivation of the soil, he then knew nothing. The progress of settlement, and the consequent destruction of the forests, with the operations of the lumberer, and fur trader, was shortly about to destroy this value; in every case the Indians had either the opportunity of retreating to more distant hunting grounds, or they were left on part of their old possessions, with a reserve supposed at the time to be adequate to all their wants, and greatly exceeding their requirements as cultivators of the soil at the present day, to which were added the ranges of their old haunts, until they became actually occupied by settlers, and in many cases, an annuity to themselves and their descendents forever, which was equivalent at least to any benefit they derived from the possession of the lands.

If subsequent events have greatly enhanced the value of their lands, it has been in consequence of the speedy and peaceable settlement of the country, by means, chiefly, of the agreements in question, and the Indians are now in possession of advantages which far exceed those of the surrounding white population, and which afford them the means, under a proper system of mental improvement, of obtaining independence, and even opulence.

These agreements have been faithfully observed by both parties. The Indians have not disputed the title of the Crown to the lands, which they have surrendered; and the annuities have always been the first charge upon the revenue derived from the sale of Crown Lands, and have been *punctually paid up to the present time.*

From the earliest period of the connexion between the Indians and the British Government it has been customary to distribute annually certain presents, consisting chiefly of clothing and ammunition. [. . .]

The practice has continued to the present time, partly owing to a renewal of the occasions which first led to it; partly to repeated, but apparently unauthorised, declarations of officers of the Government, that the system should for ever be maintained; and partly to the apprehension that its sudden discontinuance would cause inconvenience and hardships to a large portion of the race within the Province.

The British Government have always considered the Indians to be under their special charge. In the Lower Province the tribes were early converted and collected in settlements by the Jesuits, who received large grants of land from the French Crown for this service. Upon the Conquest, the Crown took possession of these estates, and thus cut off any further benefit which the Indians might have derived from them. In the Upper Province, however, Christianity and civilization had, until a recent period, made little progress among them. They were an untaught, unwary race, among a population ready and able to take every advantage of them. Their lands, their presents and annuities, the produce of the chase, their guns and clothing, whatever they possessed of value, were objects of temptation to the needy settlers and the unprincipled trader, to whom their ignorance of commerce and of the English language, and their remarkable fondness for spirits, yielded them an easy prey. Hence it became necessary for the Government to interfere. Laws were passed to prevent or limit trading with them—to hinder the sale of spirits to them—to exclude whites from their settlements—and to restrain encroachments upon their lands. Officers were appointed at the principal Indian settlements, to enforce these laws, and to communicate between the tribes and the Government; to attend to the distribution of their presents and annuities; to prevent discussion; and, generally, to maintain the authority of the Government among the tribes.

The system of dealing with them was essentially military. For a long time they were under the head of the military department, and were considered and treated as military allies or stipendiaries.

Little was done by the Government to raise their mental and moral condition. In Lower Canada the Roman Catholic Missionaries, originally appointed by the Jesuits, were maintained. In Upper Canada, until a very late period, neither Missionary nor Schoolmaster was appointed. The omission was in later years supplied by various religious Societies, whose efforts have in many instances met with signal success, and within a still more recent period the Government has directed its attention to the same object.

As the Indian Lands were held in common, and the title to them was vested in the Crown, as their Guardian, the Indians were excluded from all political rights, the tenure of which depended upon an extent of interest, not conferred upon them by the Crown.

Their inability also to complete with their white brethren debarred them, in a great measure, from the enjoyment of civil rights, while the policy of the Government led to the belief that they did not in fact possess them.*

They were thus left in a state of tutelage, which although devised for their protection and benefit, has in the event proved very detrimental to their interests, by encouraging them to rely wholly upon the support and advice of the Government, and to neglect the opportunities which they have possessed of raising themselves from the state of dependence to the level of the surrounding population.

It is easy, at the present day, on looking back, to trace the error of the Government, and its evil consequences; but it is only just to observe that the system was in accordance with the legislation of the times. The regenerative power of religion and education was not then as now appreciated. The effects of civilization, and the necessities arising out of it, were not foreseen. The information of the Imperial Government was very imperfect. It was not easy nor safe rashly to change a mode

---

* *The records of the Courts of Justice furnish undoubted evidence that the Indians are amenable to, and enjoy the protection of, both the civil and criminal laws of the Province. That they may share in, and are entitled to, all the political privileges of the whites when individually possessed of the necessary qualifications may be inferred from the fact, that John Brant, an Indian Chief of the six nations, was elected a Member of the Legislative Assembly of Upper Canada. The subsequent loss of his seat in that body, was occasioned in consequence of his not possessing sufficient Freehold property, and not on account of his origin. Mr. Justice Macaulay's, and Mr. Attorney General Ogden's opinions on this subject are given in the Appendix, No. 98.*

of treatment to which the Indians had become accustomed, and thus the system has been allowed to continue up to the present time, long after the Government has become aware of its imperfections and inconveniences.

It must also be acknowledged that the system was never fully carried out. The protection which the Government intended to throw over the Indians was not and could not be sufficiently maintained. No supervision was adequate to guard so many detached and distant bands from the evils inflicted on them by their white neighbours, aided by their own cupidity and love of spirits. Their lands were encroached upon, frequently with their own consent, bought with a bribe to the Chief. Their complaints were often adjudicated upon by parties interested in despoiling them, or prejudiced against them; and thus a system, erroneous in itself, became more hurtful from its necessarily imperfect development. Of late years, however, the government has become sensible of the necessity for introducing some change in this policy.

2 'The Robinson-Superior Treaty' in Alexander Morris, *The Treaties of Canada with the Indians of Manitoba and the North-West Territories, Including the Negotiations on which They Were Based, and Other Information Relating Thereto* (Toronto: Belfords, Clarke, 1880), 302–4.

This Agreement, made and entered into on the seventh day of September, in the year of Our Lord one thousand eight hundred and fifty, at Sault Ste. Marie, in the Province of Canada, between the Honorable William Benjamin Robinson, of the one part, on behalf of Her Majesty the Queen, and Joseph Peandechat, John Iuinway, Mishe-Muckqua, Totomencie, Chiefs, and Jacob Warpela, Ahmutchiwagabou, Michel Shelageshick, Manitoshainse, and Chiginans, principal men of the Ojibewa Indians inhabiting the Northern Shore of Lake Superior, in the said Province of Canada, from Batchewananng Bay to Pigeon River, at the western extremity of said lake, and inland throughout the extent to the height of land which separates the territory covered by the charter of the Honorable the Hudson's Bay Company from the said tract, and also the islands in the said lake within the boundaries of the British possessions therein, of the other part, witnesseth:

That for and in consideration of the sum of two thousand pounds of good and lawful money of Upper Canada, to them in hand paid, and for the further perpetual annuity of five hundred pounds, the same to be paid and delivered to the said Chiefs and their tribes at a convenient season of each summer, not later than the first day of August at the Honorable the Hudson's Bay Company's Posts of Michipicoton and Fort William, they the said Chiefs and principal men do freely, fully and voluntarily surrender, cede, grant and convey unto Her Majesty, Her heirs and successors forever, all their right, title and interest in the whole of the territory above described, save and except the reservations set forth in the schedule hereunto annexed, which reservations shall be held and occupied by the said Chiefs and their tribes in common, for the purposes of residence and cultivation,—and should the said Chiefs and their respective tribes at any time desire to dispose of any mineral or other valuable productions upon the said reservations, the same will be at their request sold by order of the Superintendent-General of the Indian Department for the time being, for their sole use and benefit, and to the best advantage.

And the said William Benjamin Robinson of the first part, on behalf of Her Majesty and the Government of this Province, hereby promises and agrees to make the payments as before mentioned; and further to allow the said Chiefs and their tribes the full and free privilege to hunt over the territory now ceded by them, and to fish in the waters thereof as they have heretofore been in the habit of doing, saving and excepting only such portions of the said territory as may from time to time be sold or leased to individuals, or companies of individuals, and occupied by them with the consent of the Provincial Government. The parties of the second part further promise and agree that they will not sell, lease, or otherwise dispose of any portion of their reservations without the consent of the Superintendent-General of Indian Affairs being first had and obtained; nor will they at any time hinder or prevent persons from exploring or searching for minerals or other valuable productions in any part of the territory hereby ceded to Her Majesty as before mentioned. The parties of the second part also agree that in case the Government of this Province should before the date of this agreement have sold, or bargained to sell, any mining locations or other property on the portions of the territory hereby reserved for their use and benefit, then and in that case such sale, or promise of sale, shall be perfected, if the parties interested desire it, by the Government, and the amount accruing therefrom shall be paid to the tribe to whom the reservation belongs. The said William Benjamin Robinson on behalf of Her Majesty, who desires to deal liberally and justly with all her subjects, further promises and agrees that in case the territory hereby ceded by the parties of the second part shall at any future period produce an amount which will enable the Government of this Province without incurring loss to increase the annuity hereby secured to them, then, and in that case, the same shall be augmented from time to time, provided that the amount paid to each individual shall not exceed the sum of one pound provincial currency in any one year, or such further sum as Her Majesty may be graciously pleased to order; and provided further that the number of Indians entitled to the benefit of this treaty shall amount to two-thirds of their present numbers (which is twelve hundred and forty) to entitle them to claim the full benefit thereof, and should their numbers at any future period not amount to two-thirds of twelve hundred and forty, the annuity shall be diminished in proportion to their actual numbers.

Schedule of Reservations made by the above named and subscribing Chiefs and principal men.

First—Joseph Pean-de-chat and his tribe, the reserve to commence about two miles from Fort William (inland), on the right bank of the River Kiministiquia; thence westerly six miles, parallel to the shores of the lake; thence northerly five miles, thence easterly to the right bank of the said river, so as not to interfere with any acquired rights of the Honorable Hudson's Bay Company.

Second—Four miles square at Gros Cap, being a valley near the Honorable Hudson's Bay Company's post of Michipicoton, for Totominai and tribe.

Third—Four miles square on Gull River, near Lake Nipigon, on both sides of said river, for the Chief Mishimuckqua and tribe.

(Signed)	W. B. Robinson.		
	Joseph Pean-de-chat.	His x mark.	[L.S.]
	John Minway.	" x "	[L.S.]
	Mishe-Muckqua.	" x "	[L.S.]
	Totominai.	" x "	[L.S.]
	Jacob Wapela.	" x "	[L.S.]
	Ah-mutchinagalon.	" x "	[L.S.]
	Michel Shelageshick.	" x "	[L.S.]
	Manitou Shainse.	" x "	[L.S.]
	Chiginans.	" x "	[L.S.]

Signed, sealed and delivered at Sault Ste. Marie, the day and year first above written, in presence of—

(Signed)   George Ironside, S. I. Affairs.

Astley P. Cooper, Capt. Com. Rifle Brig.

H. M. Balfour, 2nd Lieut. Rifle Brig.

John Swanston, C. F. Hon. Hud. Bay Co.

George Johnston, Interpreter.

F. W. Keating.

HISTORICAL INTERPRETATIONS

3 From John G. Reid, 'Empire, the Maritime Colonies, and the Supplanting of Mi'kma'ki/Wulstukwik, 1780–1820', *Acadiensis* 38(2) (2009): 78–97.

It has become a historical truism that the effects of the Loyalist migration to the Maritime colonies, reinforced by other substantial migrations including those of the Scots, were intensely destructive for the Native populations of the territories involved. L.F.S. Upton wrote in 1979 that 'the arrival of the Loyalists completed Britain's conquest of Acadia'; the occasional 'flicker of independence' notwithstanding, wholesale dispossession followed. For Upton, it quickly became clear that, 'the Indians were no longer of account as allies, enemies, or people.'[1] In another important and influential study, Harald E.L. Prins argued in 1996 that the Loyalist influx 'overwhelmed' the Native economy, and the resulting destitution—along with the absence of support from potential diplomatic allies in France and the United States—ensured that by the 1790s, 'the Mi'kmaq and other tribal nations on the Atlantic seaboard were painfully aware that the old times were over.'[2] Depictions such as these are consistent with the more general historical narrative of an ongoing, far advanced dispossession of Native peoples in eastern North America as a whole. [. . .]

This article will suggest, however, that the supplanting of Mi'kma'ki and Wulstukwik by the Maritime colonies, while certainly entering a critical phase during the waning years of the 'long' eighteenth century, was characterized by a complex and distinctive pattern.[3] In this substantial portion of northeastern North America there were discrete though intertwined lines of development in, on the one hand, environmental and territorial matters and, on the other hand, in those connected with military and diplomatic history. That dispossession was widespread is beyond doubt, even though a review of the evidence also suggests significant spatial variations in the scale and implications of environmental change. Yet this damaging process co-existed with the continuing Native ability to represent complaints and demands based on longstanding treaty obligations, and to extract conciliatory responses from reluctant imperial officials. Owed in part to the tensions prevailing during a period of recurrent conflicts embroiling Great Britain, France, and the United States, this persistent diplomatic capacity waned after 1815. While it lasted, it had not only carried through to a later era the practice of discussing treaty-based assertions with representatives of the Crown, but it also had continued an extended narrative of Native-imperial relations through a period that had seen a profound discontinuity in the form of greatly intensified pressure imposed by colonial settlement.

In important respects, the Mi'kmaq and Wulstukwiuk shared common or analogous histories. Interaction and intermittent military cooperation with French imperial officials characterized the late seventeenth and early eighteenth centuries for both, and reached further into the eighteenth century for Mi'kmaq who maintained a relationship with Louisbourg. The Mi'kmaw experience, and to a lesser degree that of the Wulstukwiuk, also included a relationship of general though not uninterrupted peaceful co-existence with Acadian colonists while the disruptions created by the Planter migrations of the 1760s had also proved to have limited environmental consequences.[4] When it came to the history of diplomatic relations with the British, the Mi'kmaq, along with the Wulstukwiuk and Passamaquoddy, shared a process of evolution that from 1725 onwards diverged markedly from the experience of Wabanaki neighbours. It was characterized, in particular, by the negotiation of similar and closely linked treaties in 1760–1, which marked the last major phase of treaty-making even though further negotiations and more localized treaties followed during the era of the American Revolution.[5] The Mi'kmaq and Wulstukwiuk also shared an ability to meet the pressures that arose during the 1780–1820 period by drawing on two centuries of experience not only with inter-cultural trade relations but also with diplomatic engagements, including citation of treaty obligations to protect essential resource harvests and the containment of agricultural settlement. The stresses imposed by colonization during this crucial transitional era were unprecedented, with the settlement of non-Native populations characterized by land hunger and a profound sense of entitlement. The results were intensely destructive, and yet there was no military defeat, no formal land surrender, and the principle of a treaty relationship that enshrined Native-imperial peace and friendship was one that—far from weakening—continued in Native political cultures to evolve and gain strength. These are the elements that demonstrate, in this geographical and cultural context as in other areas of history, that general narratives have their place but must ultimately be disciplined according to the particularities of experience.

As Upton showed many years ago, the late eighteenth century—especially the era following the closing stages of the American Revolution—saw not only profound changes in the non-Native demographics of the Maritime colonies but also an acceleration of territorial colonization and environmental change that exerted damaging and long-lasting pressures on Mi'kmaw society and economy. Subsequent studies have elaborated and re-emphasized this characteristic of the era for the Mi'kmaq, and the evidence yields little suggestion that the Wulstukwiuk experience differed significantly.[6] For all that, within a general pattern of encroachment by Loyalist refugees, Scottish rural settlers, and others there were variations. The greatest concentration of environmental pressures came with the peninsula of mainland Mi'kma'ki, where land configuration combined with encroachment and resource depletion to create by the mid-1790s a critical juncture. In early 1794, the Nova Scotia Indian Commissioner George Henry Monk wrote from Windsor to Governor John Wentworth, enclosing a petition in the name of 'the Mickmack Indians'. Monk had been reluctant to have the Mi'kmaw concerns addressed to Wentworth, for 'their remarks and representations were such that I wished rather to discourage then [sic] to communicate them', but following a contentious meeting with Mi'kmaq from Pictou and Cape Sable and a threat that Natives would converge on Halifax to confront Wentworth directly, he finally 'reduced their Representations into the form of a Petition . . . , adhering strictly to their own Observations and remarks.'[7]

Despite the possibility that Monk may have sanitized the content as well as shaping the form of the petition, its language was uncompromising even though polite. Contrasting Nova Scotia with New Brunswick, where 'there are Countries back [i.e., back countries] for the Indians', the petitioners declared that 'all Nova Scotia is Coast and Rivers, and that the English have taken all the Coast and Rivers, and make Roads and Settlements through the

Woods every where, and leave no place for the Indians to hunt in.' As a result, they continued, 'a great many Mickmacks have died for want of Victuals and Cloaths.'[8] As the petitioners were undoubtedly aware, there was more to the dispossession of the Mi'kmaq than simply the loss of hunting territory. Fishing was another source of repeated tension. As early as in August 1784, Charles Baker of Cumberland wrote of a conversation with the Mi'kmaw leader François Argamo, who 'expressed his fears of the [Loyalist] Refugees and complained of the hardship of being drove from their hunting Grounds and fisheries.'[9] Among subsequent complaints was one directed to Wentworth from the Cape Sable Mi'kmaq in 1802, that 'white people set Nets intirely across the Brooks and small rivers, which intirely prevent any Fish running up the streams', while a correspondent of the Pictou *Colonial Patriot* recalled in 1828 that 'we have heard . . . of a white man taking a fish from the river, and an Indian taking it from him, saying it was not his.'[10] Epidemic disease was a further danger, whether smallpox and dysentery brought directly by settlers—as at Pictou in 1801—or measles, as reported at Remsheg in 1803.[11] Nevertheless, the relatively confined dimensions of the peninsula ensured that loss of territory in itself quickly became a prime threat to the Native economy and to subsistence. [. . .]

The problems in Cape Breton and on the Island of St. John—later known as Prince Edward Island—were distinct although related. Settlement in Cape Breton during the Loyalist era was initially sparse, with Sydney and surrounding communities remaining small in numbers.[12] Samuel Holland's celebrated map of Cape Breton preceded the American Revolution, but in the early years of Loyalist settlement there was little territorial encroachment that would have altered his designation of the entire northern peninsula and everything directly south of it (to a point only slightly north of the Canso Strait) as 'the Savage Country or Principal Hunting District'.[13] Change, however, was soon precipitated through overhunting

by non-Natives, although initially many of these non-Natives were not colonial residents of Cape Breton itself. While Mi'kmaw hunters responded to the earliest Loyalist settlement by selling and trading moose meat in Sydney, by March 1790 the Cape Breton Council was debating how to prevent catastrophic levels of moose kills by visiting hunters who sought hides to export to other colonies. In 1789, for instance, the council heard 'near 9,000 Moose were killed in this Island . . . merely for the sake of their Skins.'[14] A hastily mounted military expedition reached Cape North some weeks later and apprehended a few hunters, but by that time serious damage had been done to the stock. 'The Indians . . . ' reported the colony's provost-marshal, the Loyalist David Tait, in late 1792, 'complain much of the whites having destroyed their Game, which is rely [*sic*] the case, the skin and fur trade having dwindled to very Little.'[15] Less than four years later, the blame for overhunting was being put squarely on the Cape Breton settlers themselves. The colony's administrator, David Mathews, noted in the summery of 1796 that 'the Native Indians were last Winter in a most deplorable situation, the Moose Deer which were their sole dependence for a Subsistence having been almost extirpated by the new Settlers.'[16]

Worse was to come as Scottish settlement began. Increasing territorial encroachment eroded Native resource harvesting as well as raising related issues such as the desecration of sacred sites and the non-Native occupation of areas that even by colonial authorities had been designated formally or informally for Native use. By 1821 the Surveyor-General Thomas Crawley was taking aim specifically at Highland settlers as exemplifying 'those who regardless of every principle of Justice, would deprive these inoffensive Savages of their Property.'[17] In Prince Edward Island, meanwhile, the inroads made by other Scottish settlers from such tenantries as those of the former Lord Advocate for Scotland, Sir James Montgomery, led Montgomery's factor James Douglas to record in 1802 that 'the Indians complain they have not a spot of ground on all these, their ancestors and their Native Coasts to make a residence upon.'[18] In a previous letter, Douglas had obliquely revealed that overhunting was an issue there as elsewhere, commenting that 'the White people . . . alledge in times of Scarcity which is pretty frequent with them, the Indians do not scruple to kill their Cattle slyly now and then to satisfy their hunger.'[19] The heart of the matter was approached more closely in 1806, however, by the French emigré priest Jacques-Ladislas-Joseph de Calonne, who linked dispossession of the Mi'kmaq directly to the proprietary division of the Island. For 'these unhappy aborigines', Calonne informed Governor Edmund Fanning, 'the English government having divided up the entire Island among various proprietors, the result is that they cannot situate themselves anywhere without being quickly expelled.'[20] [. . .]

In New Brunswick, which represented the imperial claim to an important portion of Mi'kma'ki as well as to Wulstukwik, patterns of dispossession were similar in many respects, though again with distinct elements stemming from both historical and geographical factors. Here, Loyalist settlement assumed prime importance, as the 15,000 or so Loyalist refugees almost instantly outnumbered the pre-existing population—Native and settler combined—by a factor of perhaps three to one.[21] Dislocation of entire Native communities resulted, among the most conspicuous being the southward migration of many Passamaquoddy following the establishment of the town of St. Andrews and other encroachments.[22] By 1787, Governor Thomas Carleton felt able to offer the assurance that the Wulstukwiuk, as 'a wandering tribe', had been treated with 'civility and kindness' and that 'the plenty of fish in summer and Moose in winter has hitherto prevented the settlement of the Whites in their neighbourhood from occasioning any inconvenience.'[23] Less sanguine was the New Brunswick committee of the British-based missionary organization known as the New England Company, which in 1793

took note of a report originating in Maugerville regarding 'the great decrease of their [Natives'] hunting grounds by the Settlement of the Country.'[24] Some years later, Major-General Martin Hunter likewise informed London from Fredericton that, to the cost of Native inhabitants, 'the wild animals of the Country are become so few as to be no longer an adequate resource.' Hunter's interest, unsurprisingly, was based on military considerations, as he emphasized that the Wulstukwiuk—and, presumably, the Mi'kmaq elsewhere in New Brunswick—should be offered 'some occasional relief' because their enmity would be a severe threat 'in a Country where the settlements are made fronting on the Rivers, with a wilderness every where close upon the Rear.'[25]

Thus, in New Brunswick and in Cape Breton, unlike in Prince Edward Island and peninsular Nova Scotia, there was a back country—even though its value for subsistence was suffering continuous erosion through resource depletion and the expansion of settlement as immigration proceeded. While in New Brunswick rivers long continued to attract settlement, thus cutting off Native transportation routes as well as providing points of departure for the inland spread of settlement, elsewhere the building of roads represented a powerful thrust at the environmental integrity of Native economies. Among the earliest advocates of extensive road construction in Nova Scotia was Michael Francklin, an acting governor on a number of occasions during the 1760s and 1770s who had some command of the Mi'kmaw language and who served later in his career as the colony's superintendent of Indian affairs.[26] For Francklin, writing as early as 1766, roads would be the means by which 'the Country will become fully explored, and the most valuable of the interior parts will be soon settled . . . ; this once accomplished . . . will render abortive every effort the Indians can make, should they hereafter be inclined to give us trouble.'[27] While Francklin framed the matter in terms of projecting military force as well as economic development, a later advocate of road-building, Governor John Wentworth, was frank about its environmental consequences. 'The extended roads and Settlements', Wentworth commented of the Mi'kmaq in 1793, 'have been the means of destroying and driving off the wild beasts which formerly Supplied them with food and rayment.' Two successive mild winters, he added, had made hunting even more difficult, 'and I fear some of them perished.'[28] While this represented, in one sense, an element of the particular process by which peninsular Nova Scotia increasingly became a settler space, it also represented the more general principle that road construction could lead to rapid environmental degradation with deadly consequences.

Not that these developments went unchallenged. Remonstrances directed at Officials such as George Henry Monk were frequent. One examples was a group of mainland Mi'kmaq confronting Monk; they ended a tense conversation when 'they Instantly took up their Packs and went away without the usual acknowledgments', and Monk reported with some concern in 1794 that 'some of the more Intelligent of them make Circuitous visits to the different Tribes, and give false reasons for such long and unusual Excursions.'[29] Beyond such responses, Native strategies for offsetting the effects of settlement and environmental change included, where possible, the addition of agricultural cultivation to other sources of subsistence as well as deliberate migration. Cultivation, however, gave no protection from encroachment, as the philanthropist and would-be centralizer of Native communities Walter Bromley stated forcefully in 1822: 'You will scarcely meet an Indian, but who will tell you that he has cleared and cultivated land some time or other, but that the white men have taken it from him.'[30] Migration away from settlement sites and environmentally affected areas was reported by, among others, the surveyor and naturalist Titus Smith, who observed following a tour of northern Nova Scotia in 1801: 'I think a considerable number of them [Mi'kmaq] have left

the Province, as I have been informed at many different settlements, that there are not half so many Indians about them as there was some years ago.'[31]

As a way of turning long-established and customary mobility to advantage in the context of drastically altered environmental circumstances, migration over shorter or longer distances could enable a semblance of the traditional economy to survive in places—much to the chagrin of colonial officials such as the Nova Scotia governor the Earl of Dalhousie in 1817, who deplored in the Mi'kmaq the tenacity of 'their natural habits and inclination for a wandering life.'[32] Even in the context of the increasing creation of reserves—systematic in Nova Scotia from 1819, more haphazard elsewhere—mobility, as Natasha Simon has pointed out, was not surrendered.[33] Yet the pressures that had characterized the preceding quarter-century had taken a heavy toll and continued to do so. Unlike previous colonizing thrusts in Mi'kma'ki and Wulstukwik, the immigration of the late eighteenth and early nineteenth centuries was too strong and persistent to be decisively turned aside or accommodated by Native populations now drastically outnumbered. It had also been rapid. Although cultural and environmental pressures had not begun in 1782, but had a more extended past, retrospectives on the era of Loyalist and then Scottish immigration contrasted strikingly the previous availability of resources with the subsequent prevalence of poverty and ill-health. [. . .]

Yet the rapid change in the relationship between colonization and the Native population did not necessarily extend to Native-imperial relations. Neither the Mi'kmaq nor the Wulstukwiuk experienced military defeat or made a formal surrender of territory. And both had extended experience of diplomatic relations with French and British imperial officials based on the principle of reciprocity. In these areas, there were important elements of continuity rather than discontinuity and thus a more elongated historical narrative. It is true, of course, that the overlay of colonial settlement on Mi'kma'ki and Wulstukwik during the late eighteenth and early nineteenth centuries had its own far-reaching effect on the entire process of British-Native interaction, especially in matters affecting land use and occupancy. Most noticeably at first in those areas where back countries ceased to exist, Mi'kmaw and Wulstukwiuk access to land was narrowed and Native economies hollowed out accordingly. Varying by locality, special arrangements might be made to safeguard Native use of particular areas. These included the issuing of a series of licenses of occupation in Nova Scotia in late 1783 for eight tracts of land, such as the 2,500 acres on the Stewiacke River that also carried for local Mi'kmaq the guarantee of 'Hunting and fishing as Customary'.[34] Grants of land were made to individuals such as 'Benwa the Indian', who in 1810 received 140 acres on Boularderie Island in Cape Breton, while some grants to non-Natives contained survey references to lands designated—as at Pugwash—as 'Indian land' or—as at Chester—as 'Land Claimed by the Indians'.[35] In Cape Breton, a number of land documents referred without explanation to 'the Indian Line' or 'the Indian Boundary', or in other cases made grants that were qualified by such statements as 'if it do not interfere in the Indians Settlement.'[36] More formal was the setting aside of Chapel Island for Mi'kmaw use by the Cape Breton Council in 1792 and the ten reserves of varying size created by the Nova Scotia Council in 1820.[37] A report of the New Brunswick surveyor-general in 1803 referred to a total of some 116,000 acres 'allotted to the different Indian Tribes Throughout the Province.'[38] What all of these arrangements, formal or less formal, had in common was that they offered no immunity from further encroachment.

At a more general level, however, the legitimacy of the entire settlement project was frequently brought into question in Native-imperial dialogue, either explicitly or through diplomatic demands for reciprocity. The most direct statements were reported by imperial officials in Cape Breton. Lieutenant-Governor William Macarmick reported to London in 1790 that the Cape Breton Mi'kmaq were 'a fierce, restless and uncontrollable Tribe continually claiming an exclusive right to the possession of the whole Island', and the Cape Breton Council supported Macarmick's assessment some weeks later in declaring that 'it is well known that the native Indians have ever held up the Idea of an intrusion being made on their property by the many Settlements forming on the Island.'[39] The newspaper correspondent 'Philo Antiquarius' recalled that early settlers at Pictou 'were constrained to submit to numerous indignities from the aborigines, who viewed their operations with no very friendly eye: these considered the settlers as usurpers of their national rights, who had encroached on their undoubted property', while the Cumberland settler Edward Barron informed George Henry Monk with some dismay in 1784 that his Mi'kmaw informants had told him that colonization could in any event extend no further than the tidal limits of the rivers. 'In that case', Barron added, 'the interior of the Country can never be settled.'[40] The Native demand for reciprocity, meanwhile, raised the question of legitimacy by connecting the non-Native presence with the fulfilment of promises made in return—most often, though not exclusively, in terms of the presents that underpinned diplomatic activity.[41] From the period immediately following the 1760–61 treaties, imperial officials found this connection inescapable and directly tied to the treaties. John Cunningham declared in 1767 that the purpose of his capacity as agent in Nova Scotia for distributing presents was 'to supply the Tribes of Indians with Provisions and the Usual Presents in Virtue of Treaties of Peace', and a few months later the acting governor, Michael Francklin, wrote of the need to find a Roman Catholic priest to minister to Native groups 'Conformable to the promises made them at their first making Peace.'[42]

By the 1780s and beyond, such issues had lost none of their potency. In 1780

Lieutenant-Governor Richard Hughes of Nova Scotia noted that 'the expediency of preserving the Indians in their present Sentiments of Allegiance and Tranquility (which can only be done by these Supplies) remains still in its full Force.'[43] That Hughes chose to couch his observation in terms of 'allegiance' during a time of warfare, and to make it explicitly contingent on the supply of presents, made his statement all the more striking. Francklin, meanwhile, who was now superintendent of Indian Affairs for Nova Scotia, confirmed that presents were essential to diplomacy. 'It has ever been the Custom', Francklin reported later in 1780, 'even in times of the most Profound Peace, to Assist the Indians Occasionally with Provisions from the Kings Stores, but now it is indispensably necessary, for its is totally impossible to see, or be seen by the Indians, or can a Messenger be sent to, or from them, without an Expence of Provisions.'[44] And so it continued. The later superintendent, George Henry Monk, recorded early in 1794 a conversation with the Mi'kmaw Francis Emable, who had recently found the hunt disappointing in the Canso-Antigonish region and demanded to know what measures the Nova Scotia governor proposed to take in order to ensure a living for the Native population.[45] Cape Breton Mi'kmaq, meanwhile, exerted another form of pressure. Cape Breton's acting governor, David Mathews, complained to London in 1796 that outside of the presents more readily covered by provincial funds, 'they have cost me Privately double that sum; many families of them, during the last Winter, remained at my House for Weeks.' A year later, Mathews again reported that Mi'kmaw visitors considered his house 'a rightful home' for the leaner months of the year, or whenever they wished to visit Sydney.[46] Governor John Wentworth of Nova Scotia later reinforced the importance of reciprocity by again linking it with mutual fidelity in wartime: 'The Micmacs . . . had formerly exhibited by me some assistance for their support, from His Majesty which they considered as an obligation of Loyalty. This Gratuity I discontinued toward

the close of the late war and they, according to their savage customs, would not refuse presents form the French.'[47]

As Wentworth implied, betrayal of reciprocity—in the view of his Mi'kmaw contacts—would jeopardize any legitimacy in the British colonial presence, which existed without a formal surrender of territory and so created a reciprocal obligation. Loss of legitimacy in turn would—for them—deserve an armed response, bringing into play the absence of any military defeat inflicted on either Mi'kmaq or Wulstukwiuk. The ability of Native forces to police the relationship affirmed in the treaties of 1760–61 had thus become evident in the era immediately following the treaties.[48] In subsequent years, and notably as Scottish and Loyalist migrations gathered force, the independent military capacity of Native groups inevitably declined. Population levels, although reliable numbers are unavailable, were clearly being affected by environmental degradation and resource depletion. Poor health and the struggle for subsistence further eroded the potential for sustaining hostilities. Governor Wentworth, in 1804, was sceptical of rumours that 2,000 warriors were assembling to travel west to confront Iroquoian adversaries, 'in which case they [the Mi'kmaq] must be joined by the Marisite indians of New Brunswick, and Penobscots who inhabit in the eastern districts of Massachusetts, near to Passamaquoddy. All of these cannot, I think, send more than twelve hundred Men, of which the Micmacs cannot exceed, three hundred, very inferior Warriors, badly armed in quantity and quality—almost naked—with little ammunition.'[49] Whether or not Wentworth's estimation was accurate in its details—non-Native enumerations of a highly mobile population were notoriously arbitrary—the deterioration identified and its connection with colonial settlement were realities that could not be discounted. [. . .] Nevertheless, the later years of the 'long' eighteenth century were characterized by extended periods of imperial warfare and almost continuous tensions between, on the one hand,

Great Britain and, on the other, France and the United States. For imperial officials operating in Mi'kma'ki and Wulstukwik, who had increasing numbers of vulnerable settlements to defend as immigration accelerated, it was impossible to ignore either the localized inroads of which Native forces were capable or the potentially wider significance of such disruptions in the context of other enmities. The Cape Breton councillor and former military officer Ingram Ball, for example, worried in 1794 that in the event of war with the United States, Cape Breton might quickly find itself 'in the midst of three [fires], a French one, an American one, and an Indian one.'[50]

Such considerations figured consistently in imperial approaches to Mi'kmaw and Wulstukwiuk diplomatic representations and to demands for reciprocity. Of the four colonies, Prince Edward Island was the one in which these issues surfaced the least. The Island's acting governor Phillips Callbeck reported to London during the American Revolutionary War that 'the Indians avowed Dispositions to Rebellion in these parts' had meant that 'I am obliged to give provisions and presents.'[51] [. . .] Cape Breton, not surprisingly in view of the limited extent of initial settlement, saw much more urgently phrased assessments of the extent and the implications of shows of force by the Mi'kmaq. Macarmick, in 1790, complained of their 'frequently assembling in Bodies if four or five hundred and Boasting of the Force they could procure' and remarked on 'the impossibility in such case of enforcing the power of the civil authority and the Laws.'[52] Some two years later, the provost-marshall David Tait declared bluntly that 'the Indians talk very high' and that, in the absence of presents and the ministry of a British-supplied priest, 'at present they have in their Power to destroy the whole Colony.'[53] It was within this context, later in the 1790s, that the acting governor David Mathews—a Loyalist and a former mayor of the city of New York—found it necessary to submit to Mi'kmaw demands that they should stay at his house while in Sydney. [. . .]

In Nova Scotia, concerns on the part of Monk, Wentworth, and others regarding Mi'kmaw unrest arose frequently, and were consistently bracketed with a sense of urgency in offering presents. Late in 1793, for example, Wentworth directed Monk to the Windsor area, where a Mi'kmaw assembly had led to sheep seizures and, in Wentworth's view, 'audacious intentions'. Monk's instruction was to try to seize Mi'kmaw hostages—men, women, children—or 'on the other hand and which I should prefer, if you can attach them to our cause in such a manner that the peace of our scattered inhabitants may not be disturbed by them, and also that they will join us, in case of an invasion you may promise they shall have some provisions and cloathing for their women and children.' Monk, in turn, despatched an officer who downplayed the threat of 'any immediate hostilities', but who also confirmed that 'supplies' represented the key to resolving the situation.[54] During the ensuing winter, Monk had a series of further confrontations with Mi'kmaq who asserted, as did one group in March 1794, 'that the Governor gave [sic] the Indians Blankets, Guns, Powder and everything as much as they pleased to take.'[55] Although Monk was at a loss to satisfy the immediate demand, over the next two years Wentworth launched an increased distribution of supplies that he justified not only on humanitarian grounds but also on the ground that 'these People would probably otherwise have been disaffected and required Coercion.'[56] [. . .]

Thus, although it would be entirely wrong to portray Mi'kmaw leaders as negotiating with Nova Scotian officials from a position of strength at the turn of the eighteenth century, it remained true that they had enough remaining strengths to be able to negotiate. Recurrent periods of tension had similar results. Late in 1807 Wentworth reported that Monk had set off in an attempt to 'collect and secure the obedience of these People [Mi'kmaq], and their aid in case of necessity. Otherwise, they might prove very mischievous upon the scattering unprotected settlements.' Some weeks later, he commented again in the context of a possible United States invasion that 'the Indians having observed there are preparations making for defence, manifested a disposition to be considered of some importance' and that immediate provision of supplies 'will tend to relieve the scattering settlers from apprehensions of mischief, that might retard the Levies of Militia.'[57] Even so, by April 1808, Monk was warning that Mi'kmaq from Cape Breton and Nova Scotia were coordinating their response to the likely invasion, opting to remain neutral until they had decided who was the stronger side. Citing the threat of some to devastate Pictou, Monk cited with approval the intention of Mi'kmaq in the Cumberland area to remain neutral and perhaps even to take the British side if pressed. Since the real difficulty, in his view, lay in the undermining of the traditional economy by 'the Improvements of their Conquerors', the solution lay not only in 'management and relief' but ultimately in restricting the Native population to sedentary agricultural settlement. A by-product of Monk's report, however, was to make it clear—even though Native démarches were not necessarily united or consistent, as the Cumberland example revealed—that the 'Conquerors' still had some way to go before making 'orderly subjects' of the Indigenous population.[58]

Governor Thomas Carleton of New Brunswick, meanwhile, was initially dismissive of both the Wulstukwiuk and the Mi'kmaq. Although 1786 saw a hostile Wulstukwiuk presence at Fredericton (during the trial of two Loyalist settlers for the murder of a Wulstukwiuk man) as well as the apprehensions of upriver settlers later that year 'of being reduced to the necessity of quitting their settlement' because of Native threats, Carleton was confident of the success of forceful measures to be taken the next year 'for the removal of all future apprehensions of danger, from either the insolence or any more serious unfriendliness of the Savages.'[59] But the Loyalist and half-pay officer Daniel Lyman was not so sure:

'On the subject of the Indians, although they are not so formidable as to threaten any ruin or imminent danger to the province, yet they are sufficiently numerous to be very troublesome, particularly if they are encouraged by our enemies. . . . I would here suggest the idea, of cultivating their friendship, by the usual mode of gaining indians.'[60] Although no system of gift-giving comparable to that of Nova Scotia emerged in New Brunswick, the ensuing years saw a series of intermittent tensions that yielded equally intermittent negotiations. Carleton, finding that Wulstukwiuk interventions were capable of making communications between New Brunswick and Lower Canada 'precarious and unsafe', persuaded London to authorize an additional regiment to maintain key outposts. Yet by 1794 he was warning that, in the context of tensions with the United States that might bring about an active Wabanaki alliance, 'it is certainly requisite to guard against their disaffection.' Carleton's chosen course was to employ a French emigré priest as a missionary, although with results that were just as unreliable as those deriving from the Protestant schools and missions maintained by the New England Company.[61] Efforts by such prominent New Brunswick figures as Robert Pagan and Ward Chipman to draw on Native expertise on the geography of the disputed border with the United States yielded respectful exchanges, notably with Passamaquoddy elders, but in 1808 Major-General Martin Hunter observed 'the Indian Natives of New Brunswick', in the event of war, 'would be formidable as Enemies', and that distribution of presents was needed.[62] All in all, when the War of 1812 finally began, it seemed to be a matter for profound relief to Hunter's successor as military commander in New Brunswick, Major-General George Stracey Smyth, that not only was an agreement reached 'with the Indians in the neighbourhood of the County of Charlotte, for the purpose of securing their Neutrality', but also that—as Smyth had 'the satisfaction to state'—similar agreements had been concluded with 'the Indians of the River Saint John, Miramichi, and other parts of the Province.'[63] That the negotiation of Native neutrality was cause for celebration was an eloquent comment on the persistence of an armed capacity that was residual but still significant.

When the wars ended, changes followed. As non-Native immigration continued and accelerated, the pace of dispossession quickened with it. Walter Bromley, whose primary goal was to induce 'transient Indians' to 'become settlers' by cultivating the land, was blunt in public statements regarding the violence with which force of numbers enabled non-Natives to take control of essential Native territories. As a part of the 'gross barbarities' committed by the settlers, he reported that even a burial ground had been 'lately ploughed up'.[64] At the same time, the significance for imperial officials of any armed threat presented by Native warriors receded with the ending of any immediate external danger. [. . .]

From the early 1780s until 1815, a military and diplomatic continuity had been preserved that co-existed with the territorial and environmental discontinuity of that era. That Native leaders could readily capture the attention of imperial officials and make demands for reciprocity with conviction was a longstanding state of affairs that had persisted through many vicissitudes of both British and French assertions in both Mi'kma'ki and Wulstukwik. These demands had long depended on the threat, and sometimes the reality, that territory would be defended or reclaimed by force. Since the onset of Loyalist and other large-scale migrations, the threat of force had come to depend increasingly both on localized potential to disrupt settlements and on imperial apprehensions of invasion by French or US forces, following which Native intervention—local or more general—might prove crucial one way or the other. At the same time, as demands for reciprocity—or what might be seen on the non-Native side as 'relief'— necessarily became more urgent and insistent, officials such as Wentworth saw no alternative but to comply even at the risk of disputes

with London over budgetary excesses. As a result, the distinctive tenor of Native-imperial exchanges, far from being eroded by territorial encroachment and environmental change, was extended and entrenched. Some forms of leadership were new in style if not in substance, as in the case of the Bear River chief Andrew Meus, who spoke successfully to the Nova Scotia House of Assembly in 1821 in defence of the Mi'kmaw porpoise fishery in the Digby Gut, and subsequently journeyed to London in a less fruitful effort, according to the *Halifax Journal*, 'to solicit permanent grants of land to the Indians, in order that they may become cultivators of the soil.'[65] Other methods were tried and true, as when Joseph Howe complained in 1843 while he was Indian commissioner for Nova Scotia that his home was 'besieged, at all hours, by Indians, who had been taught to believe that unbounded wealth was at my disposal, and that they were to be fed and clothed hereafter at the expense of the Government.'[66] Rather than more general appeals to the principle of reciprocity, officials such as Howe and his successor Abraham Gesner reported more explicit references to the treaties as embodiments of the Native-imperial relationship. Gesner noted that treaty principles were 'stamped upon the minds of each succeeding generation', as he had frequently been reminded by the Mi'kmaq with whom he dealt.[67]

The era from 1780 to 1820, therefore, saw the interplay of two important though distinct processes. In a territorial and environmental sense, the Mi'kmaq and Wulstukwiuk experienced rapid, unprecedented damage and constraint. Even allowing for geographical particularities, the process was abrupt and the effects long-lasting. In terms of the ability to make diplomatic use of armed capacity, however, another process drew upon a long-established pattern of Native-imperial relations in Mik'ma'ki and Wulstukwik that extended backwards in time through the treaty-making years and beyond. The two processes were not disconnected. Although colonization would ultimately erode the threat of force that underpinned Native demands for reciprocity, the wider warfare of the era joined with the vulnerability of proliferating settlements to lend strength to these demands while the critical results of dispossession gave them added urgency. As a result, the narratives to which the two processes gave rise did not conform to any over-arching narrative of Mi'kmaw or Wulstukwiuk decline in Native-imperial affairs. Even the members of a group of Nova Scotia commissioners, which included George Henry Monk, were willing to admit in 1800 that there were moral obligations towards 'the aboriginal proprietors of this country',[68] but the claims on the Crown that were advanced from the Native side went far beyond moral obligation and with time they became more insistent and more explicitly focused on the treaties. While the realities of the nineteenth century would prove inhospitable to the realization of such claims—at least in any form that could effectively offset the depredations of land loss, economic struggle, and the social and health-related dislocations that came with them—the long version of this narrative nevertheless stretched forward into the legal evolutions of the twentieth century that would bring these issues before the Supreme Court of Canada.

That the narrative persisted was also owed in part to historical circumstances that distinguished Mi'kma'ki and Wulstukwik from other portions of North America. In particular, in contrast to most of the Aboriginal groups of eastern North America, the Mi'kmaq and the Wulstukwiuk experienced the aftermath of the American Revolution without either a forced migration or the need to deal with an entirely new imperial regime. Although the disruptions associated with colonial settlement in Mi'kma'ki and Wulstukwik were far from unusual in themselves, the long and evolutionary diplomatic response to the same Crown on the same territory was distinctive. Earlier in the eighteenth century, imperial and colonial interventions had been more complex and yet highly manageable, with both French and British regimes exerting significant but localized influences while the largely coastal and compartmentalized colonial populations of the Acadian and Planter eras had proved generally able to co-exist with Native neighbours.[69] The influx of settlers that marked the closing years of the American Revolution, an influx that only accelerated, was not manageable in the same sense. Yet the skills of those whom Wentworth referred to as 'the old men', or of younger leaders such as Andrew Meus, remained relevant. Even when, after 1815, the attention of imperial officials was harder to gain and the damage wreaked by colonization was unavoidable, the demand for reciprocity was too strongly entrenched to do otherwise than persist. That it did so spoke of a narrative of Native-imperial relations that had originated long before the period from 1780 to 1820 and would extend into a future far beyond—a narrative that this limited, 40-year era confirmed rather than muted. The colonial inroads of these years had irrevocably moved the Maritime colonies away from preceding territorial and environmental characteristics and in the direction of being colonies of settlement, with all the damage to Mi'kmaq and Wulstukwiuk subsistence that these developments implied. Yet this was no simple extension of an ineluctable, continent-wide process. In this place and in an elongated span of time, there were continuities that, for whatever they might prove to be worth, accompanied the more immediate and ruinous discontinuity.

NOTES

1. L.F.S. Upton, *Micmacs and Colonists: Indian-White Relations in the Maritimes, 1713–1867* (Vancouver: University of British Columbia Press, 1979), 78, 80, 84. An earlier version

of this article was presented at the Atlantic Canada Studies Conference at the University of Prince Edward Island in May 2009. The research was funded by the Social Sciences and Humanities Research Council of Canada. I thank my research assistants Emily Burton and Kelly Chaves as well as the three anonymous readers for *Acadiensis*.

2. Harald E.L. Prins, *The Mi'kmaq: Resistance, Accommodation, and Survival* (Fort Worth: Harcourt Brace, 1996), 161–3. Other authors who have put forward similar arguments include Daniel N. Paul, *We Were Not the Savages: A Mi'kmaq Perspective on the Collision Between European and Native American Civilizations*, 2nd ed. (Halifax: Fernwood, 2000) and, though attributing continuous dispossession to a more extended timespan rather than identifying specific turning points, Jennifer Reid, *Myth, Symbol, and Colonial Encounter: British and Mi'kmaq in Acadia, 1700–1867* (Ottawa, ON: University of Ottawa Press, 1995).

3. In this article, I have used the terms Mi'kma'ki and Wulstukwik to refer respectively to the territories of the Mi'kmaq and Wulstukwiuk (Maliseet). Following the scheme initially set out in Emerson W. Baker and John G. Reid, *The New England Knight: Sir William Phips, 1651–1695* (Toronto: University of Toronto Press, 1998), xxii. I refer separately to the Wabanaki as a broad definition of ethnicity in the portion of the later State of Maine, extending approximately from the Saco River to the Penobscot River. Also separately identified are the Passamaquoddy who, while closely related to the Wulstukwiuk in cultural terms, occupied a territory that came to straddle the Canada-United States border, and whose population centre shifted south-westwards during the 1780s following pressure from the Loyalist migration into New Brunswick. For a thorough discussion, see William Wicken, 'Passamaquoddy Identity and the Marshall Decision', in *New England and the Maritime Provinces: Connections and Comparisons*, ed. Stephen J. Hornsby and John G. Reid

(Montreal and Kingston: McGill-Queen's University Press, 2005), 53–7. [. . .] Thus, to summarize, this article will take Mi'kma'ki as extending throughout the present-day Maritime Provinces (as well as to the Gaspé and Gulf islands) with the exception of the Wulstukw Valley and territories surrounding it and to the west, while Wulstukwik is defined as including the entire Wulstukw Valley—but with the proviso in both cases that the area surrounding the mouth of that river and its lower tributaries was a borderland frequented by both Mi'kmaq and Wulstukwiuk in the relevant period. The Passamaquoddy continued to occupy territory southwest of the Wulstukwiuk, but with the primary population base now on the US side of where the still-contested boundary with British North America would eventually be drawn.

4. See John G. Reid, 'Pax Britannica or Pax Indigena? Planter, Nova Scotia (1760–1782) and Competing Strategies of Pacification', *Canadian Historical Review* 85, no. 4 (December 2004): 669–92 (esp. 687–8).

5. William C. Wicken, *Mi'kmaq Treaties on Trial: History, Land, and Donald Marshall Junior* (Toronto: University of Toronto Press, 2002); Rosalie M. Francis, 'The Mi'kmaq Nation and the Embodiment of Political Ideologies: Ni'kmaq, Protocol and Treaty Negotiations of the Eighteenth Century' (masters thesis, Saint Mary's University, 2003).

6. Upton, *Micmacs and Colonists*; Paul, *We Were Not the Savages*, 165–80; Prins, *The Mi'kmaq*, 153–66; Reid, *Myth, Symbol, and Colonial Encounter*, 31–45. Wulstukwik still awaits a detailed study of this era, But see Ann Gorman Condon, '1783–1800: Loyalist Arrival, Acadian Return, Imperial Reform', in *The Atlantic Region to Confederation: A History*, ed. Phillip A. Buckner and John G. Reid (Toronto and Fredericton: University of Toronto Press and Acadiensis Press, 1994), 201–4.

7. George Henry Monk to John Wentworth, 24 January 1794, CO 217/65/150, UKNA; on the meeting, see Report of George Monk,

12 January 1794, Monk Papers, MG 23, Letterbook, Indian Affairs, 1783–1797, pp. 1047–51. Library and Archives Canada (LAC).

8. 'Petition of the Mickmack Indians', [24 January 1794] CO 217/65/148, UKNA. See also, on Mi'kmaw exclusion from fur trapping, Julian Gwyn, 'The Mi'kmaq, Poor Settlers, and the Nova Scotia Fur Trade, 1783–1853', *Journal of the Canadian Historical Association*, new ser., 14 (2003): 65–91.

9. Charles Baker to Edward Barron, 7 August 1784. Monk Papers, MG 23, Letterbook. Indian Affairs, 1783–1797, p. 1032. LAC.

10. John Wentworth to Commissioners for Relief of Indians, 28 September 1802, RG 1, vol. 430, no. 117, NSARM; Letter of 'Philo Antiquarius', *Colonial Patriot* (Pictou), 11 January 1828.

11. William Nixon to Sir John Wentworth, 20 November 1801, RG 1, vol. 430, no. 88. NSARM; G. Oxley to Charles Morris and Michael Wallace, 4 February 1803, RG 1, vol. 430, no. 127, NSARM; see also Nova Scotia Council Minutes, 29 August 1801, RG 1, vol. 191, p. 80. NSARM.

12. See Robert J. Morgan, *Rise Again! The Story of Cape Breton Island*, Book One (Wreck Cove: Breton Books, 2008), 74–5 and Stephen J. Hornsby, *Nineteenth-Century Cape Breton: A Historical Geography* (Montreal and Kingston: McGill-Queen's University Press, 1992), 3–4, 25–8.

13. Samuel Holland, 'A Plan of the Island of Cape Breton', [1767], Additional MSS. vol. 57,701, no. 7. British Library; see also Hornsby, Nineteenth-Century Cape Breton, 19–25.

14. Minutes of Cape Breton Council, 9 March 1790, CO 217/107/138–42. UKNA: also found at RG 1, vol. 319, pp. 313–5, NSARM.

15. David Tait to Evan Nepean, 4 December 1792, CO 217/109/173, UKNA.

16. David Mathews to the Earl of Portland, 7 July 1796, CO 217/112/93, UKNA.

17. Crawley to Rupert George, 5 November 1821, RG 1, vol. 430, no. 158, NSARM. For a more focused treatment of the impact of Scottish settlement, see John G. Reid, 'Scots in Mi'kma'ki, 1760–1820', *The Nashwaak Review* 22/23, no. 1 (Spring/Summer 2009): 527–57.

18. James Douglas to Sir James Montgomery, 26 August 1802, Blackwood and Smith Papers, GD 293/2/20/4, National Archives of Scotland (NAS); see also J.M. Bumsted, 'Sir James Montgomery and Prince Edward Island, 1767–1803', *Acadiensis* VII, no. 2 (Spring 1978): 76–102.

19. Douglas to Montgomery, 24 November 1800, Blackwood and Smith Papers, GD 293/2/20/2, NAS.

20. Calonne to Fanning, 16 July 1806, CO 226/21/192, UKNA (author's translation). The original French reads as follows: 'ces malheureux aborigines'; 'le gouvernement anglois ayant distribué toute l'Isle entre divers proprietaires, il en resulte qu'ils ne peuvent se placer nulle part sans en etre bientot chassé.' See also Claude Galarneau, 'Jacques-Ladislas-Joseph de Calonne', in *Dictionary of Canadian Biography* (DCB), ed. George W. Brown et al. (15 vols. to date; Toronto: University of Toronto Press, 1966–), VI: 105–7.

21. See J.M. Bumsted, *Understanding the Loyalists* (Sackville, NB: Centre for Canadian Studies, Mount Allison University, 1986), 23–35; Condon, '1783–1800: Loyalist Arrival, Acadian Return, Imperial Reform', in *The Atlantic Region to Confederation*, 184–93; and John G. Reid, *Six Crucial Decades: Times of Change in the History of the Maritimes* (Halifax: Nimbus, 1987), 61–84.

22. Wicken, 'Passamaquoddy Identity and the Marshall Decision', 53; Vincent O. Erickson, 'Maliseet-Passamaquoddy', in *Handbook of North American Indians*: Volume 15, Northeast, ed. Bruce G. Trigger (Washington: Smithsonian Institution, 1978): 124–5.

23. Carleton to Earl of Dorchester, 31 January 1787, RS 330, A7b, Letterbook of Thomas Carleton, vol. VII, 1786–1808, no. 2, Provincial Archives of New Brunswick (PANB).

24. Minutes of New Brunswick Commissioners, 5 March 1793, New England Company MSS, vol. 07954, Guildhall Library.

25. Martin Hunter to Viscount Castlereagh, 25 May 1808, CO 188/14/27, UKNA.

26. See L.R. Fischer, 'Michael Francklin', DCB, IV: 272–6.

27. Francklin to Board of Trade, 30 September 1766, CO 217/21/357–8, UKNA.

28. Wentworth to [Henry Dundas?], 3 May 1793, CO 217/64/171–2, UKNA; see also John Parr to Viscount Sydney, 8 September 1787, CO 217/60/50–1, UKNA.

29. Report of George Monk, 12 January 1794, Monk Papers, Letterbook, Indian Affairs, 1783–1797, p. 1050, LAC.

30. Walter Bromley, *An Account of the Aborigines of Nova Scotia called the Micmac Indians* (London: Luke Hansard, 1822), 10; see also Judith Fingard, 'Walter Bromley', DCB, VII, 107–10.

31. Titus Smith, 'General Observations on the Northern Tour', 1801, RG 1, vol. 380, pp. 113–4, NSARM. For another example, see Minutes of New Brunswick Commissioners, 5 March 1793, New England Company MSS, vol. 07954, Guildhall Library.

32. Draft letter of Dalhousie, 8 March 1817, Dalhousie Papers, sect. 1, pp. 26–9, NAS.

33. Natasha Simon, 'Towards a Just Relationship: The Role of Treaty Negotiations in Mi'kmaq Reserve Formation in New Brunswick' (paper presented to Canadian Historical Association Annual Meeting, Saskatoon, SK, 2007), 1–2.

34. Licenses of Occupation, 17–18 December 1783, RG 1, vol. 430, no. 23½, NSARM.

35. Grant to Benwa the Indian, 22 January 1810, RG 20, ser. B, vol. 3, no. 550, NSARM; Pugwash Survey, n.d., RG 20, ser. C, vol. 86, no. 236, NSARM; 'Survey of the Indians Claims at Chester by William Nelson', 25 April 1791, RG 20, ser. C, vol. 90a, no. 60, NSARM.

36. See, for example, Petition of Angus MacDonald, [1806], RG 20, ser. B, vol. 2, no. 245, NSARM; Petition of Alexander and Norman MacLeod, [1822], RG 20, ser. B, vol. 13, no. 2864, NSARM; Petition of William Mathewson, 1814, and Council endorsement, 3 October 1814, RG 20, ser. B, vol. 5, no. 1067, NSARM.

37. Minutes of Cape Breton Council, 28 November 1792, CO 217/109/20–1, UKNA; Minutes of Nova Scotia Council, 8 May 1820, RG 1, vol. 193, pp. 450–6, NSARM. On equivalent measures in New Brunswick and Prince Edward Island, see Upton, *Micmacs and Colonists*, 99–101, 114–5.

38. 'State of His Majesty's Lands in the Province of New Brunswick taken from the Records in the Surveyor Generals and Auditors Office, Fredericton', 12 July 1803, CO 188/12/56, UKNA.

39. Macarmick to Lord Grenville, 30 April 1790, CO 217/107/118, UKNA; Minutes of Cape Breton Council 31 May 1790, CO 217/107/120, UKNA.

40. Letter of 'Philo Antiquarius', *Colonial Patriot* (Pictou), 11 January 1828; Edward Barron to Monk, 12 August 1784, Monk Papers, Letterbook, Indian Affairs, 1783–1797, pp. 1030–1, LAC.

41. On reciprocity as a principle, see Katherine Hermes, '"Justice Will be Done Us": Algonquian Demands for Reciprocity in the Courts of the European Settlers', in *The Many Legalities of Early America*, ed. Christopher L. Tomlins and Bruce H. Mann (Chapel Hill: University of North Carolina Press, 2001), 123–49; see also John G. Reid, 'Imperial-Aboriginal Friendship in Eastern British America, 1775–1815' (paper presented to conference on 'Loyalism and the Revolutionary Atlantic World', University of Maine, Orono, ME, 5 June 2009).

42. Memorial of John Cunningham, 14 December 1767, CO 217/45/3, UKNA; Francklin to Lord Hillsborough, 20 July 1768, CO 217/45/165–6, UKNA.

43. Richard Hughes to Lord George Germain, March 1780, CO 217/55/33–4, UKNA. For an example of the continuing significance of providing Crown-subsidized Roman Catholic clergy, see the comments of Governor Thomas Carleton of New Brunswick in Carleton to Dundas, 14 June 1794, CO 188/5/184, UKNA.

44. Francklin to Germain, 4 May 1780, CO 217/55/37, UKNA.

45. Report of George Henry Monk, 26 February 1794, Monk Papers, Letterbook, Indian Affairs, 1783–1797, pp. 1067–8, LAC.

46. David Mathews to the Earl of Portland, 7 July 1796, CO 217/112/93, UKNA; Mathews to Portland, 2 August 1797, CO 217/113/211, UKNA.

47. John Wentworth to Lord Hobart, 3 May 1804, CO 217/79/16, UKNA.

48. See Reid, 'Pax Britannica or Pax Indigena?'; for alternative interpretations, see those cited on pages 671–2 of that article as well as the more recent John Grenier, *The Far Reaches of Empire: War in Nova Scotia, 1710–1760* (Norman, OK: University of Oklahoma Press, 2008), esp. 207–15.

49. Wentworth to Hobart, 3 May 1804, CO 217/79/15, UKNA.

50. Minutes of Cape Breton Council, 30 April 1794, CO 217/110/180, UKNA. On Ball, see R.J. Morgan, 'Ingram Ball', *DCB*, V: 53–4. I thank Jim Phillips for making the point to me regarding the increasing vulnerability of proliferating settlements.

51. Callbeck to Germain, 2 September 1777, CO 226/6/188, UKNA.

52. Macarmick to Grenville, 30 April 1790, CO 217/107/118, UKNA.

53. Tait to Evan Nepean, 4 December 1792, CO 217/109/173, UKNA.

54. Wentworth to Monk, 18 October 1793, Letterbook of Wentworth, 1792–3, RG 1, vol. 50, NSARM; George Deschamps to Monk, 4 November 1793, Monk Papers, Letterbook, Indian Affairs, 1783–1797, p. 1040, LAC.

55. Report of George Monk, 7 March 1794, Monk Papers, Letterbook, Indian Affairs, 1783–1797, p. 1072, LAC.

56. Wentworth to Portland, 8 October 1796, Letterbook of Wentworth, 1793–6, RG 1, vol. 51, NSARM.

57. Wentworth to Castlereagh, 26 October 1807, Letterbook of Wentworth, 1805–7, RG 1, vol. 54, NSARM; Wentworth to Castlereagh, 3 January 1808, CO 217/82/19–20, UKNA.

58. Report of George Monk, 23 April 1808, CO 217/82/202–5, UKNA.

59. Carleton to Dorchester, 5 December 1786, RS 330, A7b, Letterbook of Thomas Carleton, vol. VII, 1786–1808, no. 1, PANB. On the Fredericton incident, see W.S. MacNutt, *New Brunswick: A History, 1784–1867* (Toronto: Macmillan, 1963), 78.

60. Memorial of Daniel Lyman, c. 1790, CO 188/4/391, UKNA; on Lyman's background, see List of MLAS, CO 188/6/141, UKNA.

61. Carleton to Dundas, 20 November 1792, RS 330 A3b, Letterbook of Thomas Carleton, vol. III, 1791–5, no. 16, PANB; Carleton to Dundas, 14 June 1794, CO 188/5/184–5, UKNA; Missionary List, 29 June 1807, CO 188/13/289, UKNA. See also Judith Fingard, 'The New England Company and the New Brunswick Indians, 1786–1826: A Comment on the Colonial Perversion of British Benevolence', *Acadiensis* I, no. 2 (Spring 1972): 29–42.

62. Chipman to Carleton, 12 August 1796, CO 188/7/211–15, UKNA; Pagan to Chipman, CO 188/10/289, UKNA; Hunter to Castlereagh, 25 May 1808, CO 188/14/27–8, UKNA.

63. Smyth to Bathurst, 31 August 1812, CO 188/18/70, UKNA. On Smyth, see D.M. Young, 'George Stracey Smyth', *DCB*, VI: 723–8; on Hunter, see D.M. Young, 'Sir Martin Hunter', *DCB*, VII: 428–30.

64. Bromley, *An Account of the Aborigines of Nova Scotia*, 7–8 (and passim).

65. *Halifax Journal*, 27 December 1824; Petition of Andrew Meus, 16 January 1821, *Journal and Proceedings of the House of Assembly of the province of Nova Scotia*, 1821, p. 36; Upton, *Micmacs and Colonists*, 88.

66. Joseph Howe, 'Report on Indian Affairs', 25 January 1843, *Journal and Proceedings of the House of Assembly of the province of Nova Scotia*, 1843, Appendix 1, p. 4.

67. Abraham Gesner, 'Report on Indian Affairs', 29 September 1847, *Journal and Proceedings of the House of Assembly of the province of Nova Scotia*, 1847, Appendix 24, p. 117.

68. 'Report of Commissioners', 15 April 1800, RG 1, vol. 430, no. 33½, NSARM.

69. See Reid, '*Pax Britannica or Pax Indigena?*' 687.

4 From Celia Haig-Brown, 'Seeking Honest Justice in a Land of Strangers: Nahnebahwequa's Struggle for Land', *Journal of Canadian Studies* 36(4) (Winter 2001): 143–70.

HISTORICAL KNOWLEDGE, SOCIAL JUSTICE AND CANADIAN NATIONAL IDENTITY

Scholars and educators committed to social justice run the risk of being labelled as biased. One does doubt, however, that many of these critics would claim to be working against justice. As Brazilian philosopher Paulo Friere suggested, knowledge *is* political: it either promotes the status quo or works to transform the world (Friere). Even those who presuppose that facts are based in 'a complete separation between subject and object' (Carr 9), often hope to put their work to use in particular arenas. This paper too has an agenda. Its point of departure is the claim that history is neither a collection of simple facts existing independent of human intervention, nor merely a creation of the human mind.[1] Rather, this paper presents a set of facts selected and organized in a way that takes a particular stance for a particular purpose. This stance is based on an *a priori* decision to seek and order some very specific information, to undermine the claim that Canadian national identity is, and/or should deserve to be, based in a history of European-driven human rights accomplishments. While there is some truth to this claim, the history of human rights in Canada demonstrates the need to move beyond Berger's 1981 call for a regime of tolerance (Berger). Our focus should instead, as Berger himself recognizes, include the places where we have failed. The paper also demonstrates the need for a more complicated view of Aboriginal missionaries and their work in early Canada amongst their own people.

The paper begins by questioning the notion that England and France are Canada's founding nations. In this, it aspires to join historian Donald B. Smith of the University of Calgary,

on a project he sometimes refers to as *The Three Canadas*.[2] While discursively and legalistically the claim to two founding nations may have been justifiable, the documentary history of the land we dwell in calls for a more nuanced view. In addition, the recent recognition of oral history and its relation to Aboriginal rights by the Supreme Court of Canada in the Delgamuukw case is a sign that even our most conservative institutions are acknowledging a more complex national past than we have been teaching ourselves and our children.[3] The paper further highlights concerns that a number of non-Aboriginal people in nineteenth-century North America and England expressed regarding the injustices perpetrated on Aboriginal peoples *even as colonization of their territories proceeded.*

These themes can be considered through an examination of the struggle of one remarkable Aboriginal woman, Nahnebahwequa, to obtain title to her land. In presenting such an examination, this paper valorizes her work and shows her deserving of a place in the histories we teach our citizens. It also challenges the separation commonly assumed to exist between missionaries and Aboriginal people, by showing Christians of Aboriginal and European ancestry working together to address the injustices of colonization. Implicitly, it demonstrates the degree to which some people of Aboriginal ancestry acted as Christian missionaries among their own people, even while they were seeking the justice that conversion to the faith had promised them.[4]

[. . .]

SETTING THE SCENE

The story that follows is one of a strong woman who stood up for her rights and those of her family at a time when too many women were constructed in history books as silent and apparently dependent on the men in their immediate context for their lives. Her story interrupts any simple understandings of the role of all women, but particularly Aboriginal women, in Canada's development as a nation. As such, hers is an exemplar of what our history books might say in schools and in the country generally about the parts women have played in Canada's history. While the focus of this paper is Nahnebahwequa's 1860 trip to London, aspects of her biography and her band's situation provide necessary context for the presentation of the trip. Most importantly, from the early 1800s on, this was a time of increasing settler encroachment on Anishinabe lands in southern Ontario.[5] Deliberately shady land deals and treaties presented to desperate people augmented the effects of a fundamental lack of understanding between the parties based in incongruous world views of the possibility of land ownership.

Nahnebahwequa was born on Credit River flats, near what is now Port Credit, Ontario, in 1824.[6] Also known as Catherine Brown Sunegoo,[7] she was the niece and adopted daughter of the Anishnabe Methodist minister Peter Jones (Kahkewayquonabee).[8] Her family, along with several other Anishnabe families, became Methodists while she was still a toddler and settled at the Credit Mission[9] located on Lake Ontario southwest of Toronto. At the age of 13, she made her first trip to England, travelling with her English-born Aunt Eliza and uncle during the year 1837–8. Peter Jones was there to meet with Queen Victoria to discuss land title for his band at Credit River.[10] Certainly this trip must have had an impact on Nahnebahwequa placing her in a more knowledgeable position from which to make the later one when subsequent land concerns emerged. While her uncle was assured of Queen Victoria's support of the recommendation to grant land titles to his people, over the years that followed, it was never achieved.[11] In 1839, at the age of 14, Nahne, as she is still

called by those close to her history,[12] married William Sutton, an English shoemaker[13] who had immigrated to Canada in 1830[14] later becoming a Methodist missionary.

When pressures to give up the last of their land at the mouth of the Credit River finally drove Chief Joseph Sawyer (Kawahjegezhegwabe) to conciliate, most of the band moved to what came to be called New Credit, on the Grand River on land that had earlier been given over by the Mississauga for the Six Nations. Although some band members considered moving north to Owen Sound, the soil quality was so poor that most changed their minds and returned to or stayed in the south.[15] By 1846, Catherine and William, along with two other families, had already commenced clearing land and decided to follow through on the original plans, to stay in Owen Sound.[16] There the Newash band allocated Catherine Sutton 200 acres, giving her written title to it.[17] They also welcomed her and her children into the band expecting that they would be entitled to the same claims and annuities as other band members.[18] Shortly thereafter, Nahnebahwequa ceased to be a member of the New Credit Mississauga, receiving a cash settlement in relation to her entitlement from that band.[19]

The move from a community of likeminded Mississauga Methodists to a remote and undeveloped wilderness must have been most difficult. In a letter written back to the Credit people where she had been the 'Leader of a Class' of young women,[20] Nahnebahwequa talks of the trials and hardships of the world and of looking forward to 'the glorious day when I shall meet you and all good Missionaries in the kingdom of our Saviour.'[21] Homesickness overwhelming her, she writes of the 'happy hours we used to spend together, while I was with you at Credit. But the happy hours are gone.'[22] Work must have occupied most of her days, with a growing family and a farm to develop in the wilderness. The couple cultivated 40 or 50 acres, 'erected thereon a commodious house, barn and stables; involving an outlay of

1,000 dollars'[23] and generally proved to be the ideal citizens that the missionaries and government of the time were purportedly looking for. Indeed, they were so successful that in 1852, William was asked by the Missionary Board to go to Garden River near Sault Ste. Marie to be the superintendent of a model farm. In light of later developments, it is interesting to speculate about possible meetings between William, Nahne, Shingwaukonse and his son Ogista, leaders in Garden River during and after this time. In addition to making a trip to London in the early 1830s, Shingwaukonse had also, before his death in 1854, 'just finished forcing the colonial crown to negotiate the Robinson Treaties (1850) by resisting forcefully an invasion of his territory by mining companies.'[24] About the time he was to leave Owen Sound, William submitted a petition to the Earl of Elgin, the Governor-General of British North America, asking to purchase the 200 acres of land encompassing the lots where they had made improvements, for protection 'should the Indians ever surrender the said land to the government, of which there is indeed too great a probability.'[25] William and Nahnebahwequa were concerned that the deed the Band had issued them might not be recognized by the Government. Nahnebahwequa and the children joined William in Garden River the following year; he had expressed concerns that the family was too far from a place of worship and from schools. Presumably Garden River promised some sense of community that they had missed in their move to Owen Sound. From Garden River, they moved again when William 'was engaged by the Rev. Shaw to asist [sic] him in making improvements on a new mission in the State of Michigan.'[26] Returning to Owen Sound in the spring of 1857,[27] they discovered that the land surrender they had feared had occurred.

In their absence, a few members of the band had met with government people and surrendered a huge portion of the band's land[28] which had subsequently been divided into farm lots and was being offered for sale by the Indian Department. At this time, Chief David Sawyer, another Credit River Mississauga who had moved to Owen Sound and become chief at the band's request, had also been away doing missionary work. The lots for sale included the Suttons' 200 acres. David Sawyer lost his 43-acre farm as well as a three-acre site that he been preparing for a wharf. Nahnebahwequa and others decided to go to the sale where she informed the Land Purchaser of her claims on her house and requested that the land be removed from the sale because she would purchase it as well as additional acreage being farmed by her sister and mother[29] at the 'upset price', in total, 491 acres.[30] As it turned out, she, David Sawyer and school-teacher, Abner Elliott, were not allowed to make the first payment which would have allowed them to exchange certificates of sale for the deeds, being told that the lots could not be sold to Indians. Conrad Van Dusen, the Methodist missionary in the area, wrote,

> They placed in my hands the certificates they had obtained from Mr. Bartlett, the agent, certifying that they had purchased the lots at a certain price, and also the money to make the payments required; and on my way to Mr. Jackson's office in another part of town, Mr. Bartlett[31] asked me to see those certificates, and retained them, informing me at the same time he had just received instructions from the Department not to sell any of those farms to Indians.[32]

In addition, Nahnebahwequa was told that she was no longer eligible for the annuity that was to be distributed to band members in partial payment for the surrendered lands because she was married to a white man.[33]

At a meeting of the General Indian Council held at Rama, in July of 1858, where the land grievances were discussed, Nahnebahwequa was appointed as the representative of the chiefs to travel to England to let the British authorities know what had happened and to seek their support to address the injustices.[34] It appears that the chiefs recognized what was continually noted as she travelled: she was an accomplished orator. In addition, they would have been aware of her earlier trip which they may have seen giving her an advantage in dealing with the English authorities. Perhaps she was seen to have some of the characteristics of a traditional Anishnabe leader described in detail in Janet Chute's study of Shingwaukonse, the chief of the Garden River Nation at the time Nahne and her family lived there. Chute argues that great Anishnabe leaders were those people who listened carefully to what the people wanted and then worked with them to get there. In addition, they were rarely those who put themselves forward as leaders: rather they worked quietly and effectively not needing fanfare to proclaim their position.[35] Although her initial leave taking was interrupted when it appeared the petition would yield results, it again became clear that such was not the case. After channels of appeal, including the Legislative Assembly of Canada, were exhausted[36] the trip to England was seen as the only remaining hope that justice would be done. Indeed, a number of Members of Parliament encouraged this line of action.[37] On the other hand, not all felt that an Aboriginal woman in this role was fitting: 'Some laughed and others, through the public journals, reproached her as an "arrant impostor,"' claiming, 'Indians could purchase land without impediment.'[38]

THE TRIP TO LONDON

When Nahnebahwequa arrived in New York where she was to embark on the boat to England, she had a letter of introduction but on approaching that person 'was disappointed'[39] by a cold reception.[40] Without any other contacts there, she did become acquainted with some friendly people whom she described as 'entire strangers'.[41] Feeling lonely and isolated, she had gone to her hotel room to pray and was interrupted by a knocking on her door.

I arose from my knees and opened it, when there stood a little girl, with a smiling countenance. She said her mother wished to see me. She said she was a little Friend. I could not think what she meant by the term 'friend'. I thought I understood what was included in the word, but now it seemed to have another application.[42]

In the dining room, Nahnebahwequa met the girl's mother and a Captain Nab who, upon hearing her mission, indicated great interest in supporting her. The two also explained to her that 'they were frequently called Quakers, but that "Friends" was their right name.'[43] The following day, she was introduced to 'another aged gentleman, Mr. H. Meriam, of Brooklyn Heights, who came on purpose to see me, and questioned me closely, and examined all my papers, and then entered into the spirit of my mission with all his heart and told me that he was a Friend.'[44]

Nahnebahwequa first was given the opportunity to address the Friends of New York at their public worship. She told them of the reasons for her travels, introducing herself as the Christian daughter of a chief of the Ojibeway tribe and focusing on the denial of land title to Indians. As a result of her speech, a committee was formed to work with her. They reviewed the papers that she carried with her, which included the following: a letter from the Indian Department; some letters from ministers of various congregations; copies of newspaper articles on the topic;[45] and most important, the Memorial addressed to the Duke of Newcastle, Principal Secretary of State for the Colonies and the Petition of David Sawyer, Catherine Sutton and Abner Elliott, which made the request that they be allowed to retain the farm lots they had purchased in the sale.[46] On 29 March, a public meeting was called on her behalf at the Friends' Meeting house on Twentieth Street. The committee presented her to a packed house outlining their informed support of her venture. She then spoke for nearly an hour,[47] 'was listened to with great interest and, many Friends shed tears'[48] and agreed to support her in her venture.[49] The New Yorkers gave her letters of introduction to many people in England and Scotland, raised approximately $500 for the passage and trip—'two young ladies, members of two opulent New York families, opened their purses to this gifted daughter of the forest'[50]—and secured a first class cabin for her on the steamship, *Persia*, which incidentally did not keep her from severe seasickness. She left New York on 25 April with enough additional money for her expenses while in England.[51]

On her arrival in Liverpool, Friends who had been informed of her mission came on board to meet her. After a few days of recovery in Liverpool at the home of Mr. and Mrs. J. Hadwin, Nahnebahwequa continued on to London and the beginning of an enduring alliance and friendship with Christine and Robert Alsop, two English Friends with whom she stayed for most of the next four months in their residence at 36 Park Road, Stoke Newington. They received her 'with warm and open hearts. . . . To their devoted and persevering labor, on her behalf, is largely to be ascribed the prosperity which attended her mission.'[52] They began by providing important connections with other members of a very significant group of British humanitarians, the Aborigines' Protection Society. In the introduction to his history of the society, Bourne writes, 'in attempting to befriend the native races in the ever growing British dominions and "spheres of influence," and as far as possible those in other parts of the world who are bound to us by the ties of our common humanity, the Aborigines Protection Society has inevitably been principally occupied in calling attention to what appeared to it errors in policy, administrative abuses, instances of wrong-doing by irresponsible adventurers, and other faults and crimes, in hopes of procuring such correction and reparation as were possible.'[53] Clearly, this group had an interest in the issue that Nahne brought to London.

She made an immediate impact on the Quaker community. A description of her in an article in the *Intelligencer*, describes her being of '"tawny skin," of pleasing aspect and most gentle manners, refined by Christianity, and gifted with the simple eloquence of nature.'[54] She caught the imaginations of her host, Robert Alsop, and Thomas Hodgkin, honorary secretary of the Friends' Society, who wrote of her thus: 'Alone and unfriended, this heroic woman left her husband and five children, her forest home still bound up in ice and snow, resigning herself to encounter unknown difficulties and perils, to prevent, if possible, the extinction of the few scattered remnants of a noble race of people.'[55] At a well-attended gathering at the Friends' Meeting house in Gracechurch Street shortly after her arrival in London, Nahnebahwequa worked her oratorical magic once more. She addressed 'the audience with such true pathos, as deeply to interest them in the story of the wrongs of the poor Indian. It was a touching appeal to those who loved and valued their homes with all their pleasing and tender associations and struck a chord that vibrated near the heart.'[56] She was careful to outline her situation in detail, bringing in the specific issues she was battling, 'When I wanted to buy my home, they took me for an Indian, and said I was an Indian: I could not buy. And when I applied as an Indian for my payment, they said I was a white woman, because I was married to a white man: and so you see they can turn the thing whichever way they have a mind to just suit their cause.'[57] She presented also her need to find a way to meet with the Queen. A number there, including John Bright, an influential Member of Parliament, took up her case. With an introductory memorial signed by many members of the Friends, she met with the Duke of Newcastle. The Court Circular of the *London Times* for 16 June 1860, indicates that she met with the Duke accompanied by the Alsops and John Bright 'on the subject of the Canadian Indians' lands'.[58] It goes on to say that, 'Private influence that had near approach to the royal family was employed and ere long she received a message through the Duke that there was an open door, and an invitation to call and see the Queen on the following day.'[59]

On 19 June 1860, Nahnebahwequa wrote excitedly to Canada in the letter also quoted above:

> My Dear Uncle and Grandfather—I have just returned from the palace. . . . The Duke [of Newcastle] went before us and he made two bows, and then I was in the presence of the Queen. She came forward to meet me, and held out her hand for me to kiss, but I forgot to kiss it and only shook hands with her. The Queen asked me many questions, and was very kind in her manners, and very friendly to me. Then my Quaker friend spoke to the Duke, and said, 'I suppose the Queen knows for what purpose my friend has come?' The Duke said, 'All my papers have been explained and laid before Her Majesty, and I have Her Majesty's commands to investigate the Indian affairs when I go to Canada with the Prince of Wales.' Then the Queen bowed to me, and said, 'I am happy to promise you my aid and protection' and asked me my name. The Queen then looked at her husband, who stood at her left side, and smiled.[60]

The Queen noted the visit in her journal;

> 19 June 1860 (Buckingham Palace) After luncheon, the Duke of Newcastle introduced . . . an Indian Chieftainess of the Ojibeways [sic], called Nahnee-bah-wee-quay, or Mrs. C. Sutton, as she is a Christian and is married to an English sailor. She is of the yellow colour of the American Indians, with black hair, and was dressed in a strange European dress with a coloured shawl and straw hat with feathers. She speaks English quite well, and is come on behalf of her Tribe to petition against some grievance as regards their land.[61]

The entry in the Court Circular for Wednesday, 20 June records, 'Her Majesty the Queen gave audience yesterday at Buckingham Palace, to Nah-ne-bah-wee-quay, Mrs. Catherine B. Sutton, of Owen Sound, Canada West accompanied by Mrs. Christine R. Alsop. Mrs. Sutton was presented by the Duke of Newcastle, Secretary of State for the Colonies.'[62] Nahnebahwequa brought with her 'some pretty articles of Indian manufacture for the Queen's children, which were presented. They were accepted and doubtless appreciated.'[63]

In a letter to E. Meriam in New York written on 7 July, Robert Alsop further described the visit confirming the Queen's promise of support to which his wife, Christine, was witness. In particular, at Her Majesty's command, the Duke of Newcastle and the Prince of Wales, who were about to leave on an official visit to Canada, were to investigate the case.[64] All felt very hopeful for a speedy resolution to the concerns. In a letter written by Nahnebahwequa herself, to a friend in New York, she acknowledged having 'dined with Mr. Rothschild in the company of thirty or forty others, and spoke of the splendour and riches of the table.'[65] But her primary connection was with the Alsops, who wrote fondly of her in a letter to a friend, 'Nah-nee-bahwe-qua has been our guest for seven weeks. We are much edified by her Christian character, and feel it is a privilege to have her under our roof.'[66]

While engaged in the serious business of seeking justice for her people, Nahnebahwequa was also engaged in another serious activity. In July, she gave birth to her sixth child, a son, whom she named Alsop Albert Edward in honour of her host and the Crown Prince. In the memoirs of both Christine and Robert Alsop, the birth is mentioned, as is the significance of the time they spent with Nahnebahwequa. Christine's includes the comment that both she and Robert 'entered warmly into the case'[67] while Robert's states 'An occurrence which took place in the year 1860 was of such an interesting character, and it engaged so much of his time and attention that we cannot pass it by. It may be remembered that an Indian lady came to this country.'[68] Robert wrote to his sister in August apologizing for not writing sooner:

'Our time has been so fully occupied that there has been no opportunity for writing. We now seem to have come to a little pause. As for our Indian guest, she is now so far recovered as not to be an object of anxiety, and her little man doing well. They call me Grandpapa, and nothing will do but he should bear the name of "Alsop," a perpetuation of the name very unlooked for.'[69] He went on to write about how busy he had been making sure that the Friends 'in the country' were getting Nahnebahwequa's case into the press and also communicating to Canada to arrange a deputation to meet the Duke of Newcastle[70] when he arrived there with the Prince of Wales. Christine also recorded these words about Nahnebahwequa's husband, William, whom the two women must have discussed as they came to know one another: he 'was an Englishman, rather older than herself, who, she used to say, "had gone over to Canada when in his teens, from a sense of duty towards the Indians, and had become an Indian that he might be useful to them."'[71]

Following the birth of her son, as August moved into the beginnings of fall, Nahnebahwequa made plans to return to Canada. The Alsops accompanied her and her son to Liverpool where, on 14 September, she made a final, stirring speech to a public meeting held under the auspices of the Aborigines' Protection Society of London. The reporter for the *Liverpool Courier* chose to include the text of her speech '*verbatim et literatim*', recognizing her oratorical prowess with an acknowledgment that 'her strong emphasis gave additional point to the words.'[72] In her speech, she began by expressing her happiness that the audience was considerably larger than she had been led to expect and went on to talk about her choice of 'simple Christian dress' as opposed to 'dress in an Indian style'.[73] Her intent, she said, was to impress upon them her Christianity and civilization; throughout her speech, she separated herself from paganism. 'I have been asked by different people, why didn't I fetch my Indian dress. I tell them I had none; this

was my dress; this is the way we dress. I tell them we are not pagans, that we try to be like white people—to be clean and decent, and do what we can to be like the civilized people.' She moved from an elaboration of this point to a focus on the real concern:

> But how can the poor Indian be civilized? As soon as he makes his land valuable then he is driven further back, and the poor Indian has to begin over again. It is said that the Indian is lazy; but he is lazy because he has alway [sic] to go further back; he is only clearing the land for the white man and making it valuable for the Indian department; and so he has to go further back. And they know that the work they put on their land, that their children won't get the benefit of it . . .[74]

She encouraged members of the audience not to lose sight of the struggle in which her people were engaged: to be able to purchase their land and ensure that this cycle would stop. 'We want people to help the poor Indian because they have been driven from one place to another, but now we are getting to the end of the peninsula, and where to go next, we dont [sic] know.' Having received a letter from her husband, saying that Indians were to be able to purchase land, she saw that this flawed proposal established a double standard:

> [We] can purchase land—but on what conditions? Why, the Indian must be civilized: he must talk English, talk French, read and write, and be well qualified for everything before he can purchase land. Why, the poor Indians, none of them can go there. Poor things, how are they to get their education? And is that the way they do with your own people? Why, I can tell you something. I have seen people in our own county that came from your country that could neither read nor write; and they came to buy Indian land! But the poor Indian

must be so well qualified before he can have a house of his own.[75]

She closed her final talk to the people of England to great applause with which the reporter comments, 'she had also been frequently interrupted in the course of her address, which she delivered with considerable force.'[76]

The next day, she boarded the vessel *Persia* once more to return to New York. The Alsops saw her and their tiny namesake off; the final parting is recorded in Christine's memoirs: 'The morning on which they left Liverpool, on their return to America, it was touching to see Christine Majolier Alsop carrying the little one in her arms on board the large steamer; evidently feeling the parting from him as from a loved and cherished object of her affection.'[77] Back in New York, Nahnebahwequa was welcomed and stayed with friends for a couple of weeks, recovered from her fatigue and took the train on 8 October, by way of Suspension Bridge and Toronto.[78] From there, she took the train to Collingwood where William met her 'with a small boat' to bring her home.[79] No doubt, she arrived with considerable hope in her heart and some sense of satisfaction with her mission.

HOME AGAIN

It soon became clear that there was only disappointing news. Although the Duke of Newcastle and his associates had met a deputation of 10 or 11 white men and three Indians on 11 September, the 'five minute' meeting was most unsatisfactory. In a memorandum presented on behalf of the Walpole Island chief, Petway Gishick, J.W. Keating outlined a summary of the major concerns. The first was land tenure; the memorandum proposed that an allotment be made for each family according to size, which 'should be made in fee . . . without the power of alienation except to transfer to the children;'[80] that reserves be secure from further dispossession; and that if

land surrenders were made, the people who have farms should be allowed to purchase those lands. Some specific requests regarding the situation of the Walpole Indians were included, as well as a reference to the mismanagement of funds that had come directly from Indian lands and the outright dishonesty of some officials of the department. The solution to these problems (ironically) was seen to lie in the transfer of Indian Administration from Britain to Canada. Finally the memorandum raised the issue of a woman being deprived of her annuity because she married a white man: '[That] a woman and her offspring should be punished, mulcted of their dues, for indulging her legitimate inclinations, seems to me, and to them, a crying injustice.'[81]

William Sutton recorded in his journal that 'the Duke remarked that he did not see how he could do anything in regard to redressing the Indians' wrongs as the Power was all-most [sic] entirely in the hands of the Provincial Authorities.'[82] Mr. Pennefeather then 'talked very rapidly for a few seconds to show that the subject of redressing Indians wrongs was beyond the Dukes [sic] jurisdiction.'[83] Indeed, the transference of the Indian Department from England to Canada had occurred in February of that year.[84] The meeting ended abruptly although the Duke did indicate that he would take the time to go over the papers he had been given and that he expected there would be another opportunity to meet before he left the country. The original petitioners waited in vain for a response to their submission.

The next year saw continuing disappointment with efforts to secure land title. On 3 March 1861, Nahnebahwequa wrote to a friend in New York, 'We ourselves do not know what to do till we hear from the Duke of Newcastle, or maybe we will not hear from him. He said he could not give an answer until he got to Portland.'[85] Another letter written on 26 March was described as one 'written after all hope of redress was given up.'[86] She refers to accusations made by the Duke that she had been engaged in land speculation when she bought more than her own farm at the sale and that she was a white woman because she had married an Englishman, pointing out that if the Duke had listened to the Indians at the meeting, instead of the government officials who surrounded him during his trip, he could have heard the truth.[87] In a letter to the Friends of New York dated 30 March, Nahnebahwequa wrote in unequivocal terms:

> [We] were sure, that if we could only have an investigation, the dark deeds of the department would be brought to light; and so we have been doomed to disappointment of a most vexatious kind. It would not be so vexing, if the Duke had been manly enough to acknowledge that he had failed in making satisfactory examination. . . . I argue that the Duke is guilty of a great wrong towards the Indians. As he has made his investigation based entirely through the parties complained of to her majesty; for he did not allow a solitary friend of the Indians to be present to plead our case.[88]

In addition, the Duke had sullied Nahnebahwequa's name by suggesting she was 'a bearer of false accusations.'[89] In her growing frustration, she writes, 'I have always heard that Canada was a free country; but it is only for some, but not for the Aborigines of America.'[90]

In the Aborigines' Protection Society Annual Report of 1861, an entry indicates that their memorial, given to the Duke as he left for Canada, had not been addressed nor had any satisfaction been secured by the supporters and complainants with whom the Duke had met in Canada. While the Aborigines' Protection Society tried to find reasons for this lack of response, the Suttons were becoming embroiled in serious questioning about the intents of those in power. In June, William Sutton again wrote to Robert Alsop about the progress to date on the land. 'We are trying to purchase our home, and expect to succeed',[91] also indicating that

they were still living on it and planting crops. Sutton disagreed with Alsop's account of the Duke's inaccessibility during the visit and the subsequent lack of response: he pointed out that the Duke had had ample time to prepare and could have arranged more time to be with the deputation about which he had been forewarned. Sutton posited that the Canadian officials had deliberately limited the time in order to conceal 'their system of wholesale Robbery and corruption.'[92] In her account of the whole situation, Nahnebahwequa railed against the Indian Department:

> The Indian Department have tried every Dodge and Quirk they could think of no matter how flimsy—at one time they have told me that I had no connection with the Owen Sound or Cape Crocker Indians— but that I allways [sic] belonged to the Credit Tribe. At another time, they have told me that I had no connection with any Band or Tribe of Indians because I had sold all right title and Claim to all Indian Benefits—and then again that I had Forfeited all my Claims because I had been living in the United States—and lastly because I was married to a White Man I could not any longer be considered as an Indian.[93]

She went on to say: 'I am charged with the unpardonable sin of marrying a White Man, I should like to know if you have a law in England, that would deprive a woman of Property left her, by her Fathers [sic] will or if you please inherited property—I ask have you a Law that would deprive that woman of her property because she got married to a Frenchman?'[94]

In 1862, there was still no result. The Aborigines' Protection Society reported:

> We regret to say that thus far these efforts have not resulted in the removal of the anomalies of which we complained; and we fear that the present state of things

will continue until the friends of the Red Man in Canada itself endeavour, by local organization and influence, to obtain for their oppressed fellow-subjects those rights which it is practically within the power of the Canadian Executive and Parliament to bestow.[95]

Nahnebahwequa, her health beginning to fail, continued to write to the Alsops, keeping them in touch with some of her news. A travelling Friend, John Ray, wrote of his visit to her and her family in the fall of 1863 in their two story log house 'standing upon the bluff shore of the Georgian Bay.' The two elder daughters played the harmonium 'performing several pieces accompanied by voice.' By this time there were eight children, 'the youngest a few days old.'[96] Ray was warmly received spending the evening listening to Nahnebahwequa reminisce about her travels and the many friends she made.[97]

Within two years, at the age of 41, Nahnebahwequa was gone. She struggled with asthma the last two years of her life and on the day of her death had seemed much better. She accompanied William in the boat to visit a neighbour and on the return home, said she felt very sick: within minutes, she was dead. Catherine Sutton never saw the deed for her land. Her mission, which had shown much promise, turned out to be only one piece in the continuing unsatisfactory efforts to secure justice for the Anishnabe people. The deed was eventually granted to her white husband, William Sutton. David Sawyer and Elliott Abner, the other two people she had represented received no land and no recompense for their land. In 1867, two years after Nahnebahwequa's death, Conrad Van Dusen wrote about David Sawyer, 'The chief was therefore dispossessed of his house and land, for which he had obtained an Indian Deed; and that part also for which he had paid the Indians in cash down the full amount agreed on before the surrender of the land; and being dispossessed of all, he was left with a large family as a pauper, without any means of support.'[98]

REFLECTIONS ON THE STORY OF NAHNE: IMPLICATIONS FOR TEACHING AND CANADIAN NATIONAL IDENTITY

Catherine Sutton, Nahnebahwequa, is a fascinating and provocative figure in Canadian history. She should be a focus in the teaching of Canadian history in that she complicates several assumptions that history texts perpetuate. She exists as a tension in the developing country—on the one hand, she complies with the stated agenda of the colonizers: she is a civilized, Christian Indian. On the other hand, her Anishnabe abilities and knowledge, her sense of justice reinforced through her Christianity, position her in a border world moving with facility, but ultimate frustration, between clashing world views and several ideologies. She faced no simple opposition between European and Aboriginal perspectives, as it is apparent that at least some of the missionaries and devoted Christians tried, albeit unsuccessfully, to fight the agenda of the profit-driven speculators who then, as now, had access to the lawmakers. As the Aborigines' Protection Society reported in England: 'Land sharks and speculators abound in Canada as they do in all countries where land is plentiful, and fortunes may be made by trading in the ignorance or weakness of its Aboriginal owners.'[99] Nahnebahwequa knew the laws and desires of the white colonizers but saw no reason to deny her Indianness because of this knowledge: 'biculturalism' (my word for her situation) became her. She steadfastly refused the choice decreed by the legislation pertaining to Indians between being a landowner and being an Indian. Racism based in a commitment to European superiority lies at the basis of this exclusionary choice. A question we as Canadians are left with is how Nahnebahwequa got as far as she did. Her upbringing in the powerful Methodist family of Kahkewaquonaby, the Reverend Peter Jones and his English wife Elizabeth, gave her knowledge of two cultures: the giving of two names, one Anishnabe and one European, exemplify this commitment to both worlds. Nahnebahwequa continued this tradition with her children.[100] She and her family were fluent in English and 'Indian'.[101] She was a strong speaker who at home and in her travels swayed audiences to her cause. Her marriage to a white man gave her added legitimacy. She and her family apparently never left their farm unattended once the difficulties began. In the end, her white husband received the title to the land which allowed the government to maintain its position in relation to Indians owning land.

What does Nahne's struggle for justice mean for Canadian national identity? [. . .] On several levels, she helps us understand the complexity of a nation built through colonization and the people who dwell therein. First she embraced European ways to a significant degree referring to her contemporaries—and herself—as 'poor Indians', and to others as pagans on occasion. In this she exemplifies the contradiction of being and becoming[102] when cultures meet and clash. Although she complied with a Christian agenda and, with her family, took up farming, she refused to deny her 'Indianness'. In this steadfastness, she serves as a model for those who would hold to two strong cultures—both recent and longer-term immigrants and settlers—not feeling the need to foster one at the expense of the other. Most Canadians seem so focused on facility in English and/or French that other languages (and cultures) including the original ones are seen as detriments rather than strengths. Not least, her story exemplifies the racist history of this land, one that we can teach in order to understand more completely who we are and how we have come to the current state of affairs.

[. . .]

POST SCRIPT[103]

Nahnebahwequa's story is not over. The foundations of her house and barn still stand near her simple grave site on Lots 28–34, Concession 3, Sarawak Township, Grey County. The land has recently been purchased by a developer from Toronto who is planning a golf course. As of 2001, the Chippewas of the Nawash and Saugeen were in negotiation to protect the grave and the land around it.

ACKNOWLEDGEMENTS

An earlier version of this paper was the basis for an invited presentation prepared for the North Atlantic Missiology Project, Centre for Advanced Religious and Theological Studies, Cambridge University, Missions Research Seminars, entitled 'Currents in World Christianity: Missions and Canadian National Identities' held at York University in 1999 and 2000. I am deeply grateful to Professor Jamie Smith of York University for the invitation. I thank James R. Miller for his very thoughtful commentary on the paper at that time. I have followed a number of his suggestions for strengthening the arguments.

I want to thank research assistant Kate Eichhorn for her thorough and thoughtful work on this project in Ottawa, Toronto and Owen Sound. Her enthusiasm and insights added immensely to the often sequestered work of the historical researcher. I also want to thank York University for the Sabbatical Leave Fellowship, which took me to London, and the Faculty of Education for the Minor Research Grant that funded parts of the work.

The librarians and archivists in the British Library, the Newspaper Library of the British Library, Friends' House in London, the United Church Archives, the Owen Sound Museum, and the Public Archives of Canada provided invaluable support and direction.

I want to thank two 'Nahnebahwequa scholars' for their generosity and openness in what feels like a real welcome to the study. Donald B. Smith, whom I yet to have the pleasure of meeting, is exemplary in his open sharing of materials and his lack of territoriality. In true collegiality, he leaves a trail of documents for those who come behind. Stephanie McMullen also welcomed me warmly to the work and immediately sent me a copy of her Masters thesis, which contextualizes Nahnebahwequa's struggle. Sincere thanks go to the two anonymous reviewers for the *Journal of Canadian Studies*, who engaged so thoughtfully with the work, giving me careful directions for strengthening it. I can only hope I have done justice to their contributions. Finally I want to thank my partner, Didi Khayatt, for taking up with me the excitement of coming to know a little of this powerful woman.

NOTES

1. Sir George Clark quoted in W.H. Carr, *What is History?* (Hammondsworth: Penguin, 1961) 8. My thanks to anthropologist, Dr. Elvi Whittaker, University of British Columbia, for the introduction to and gift of this book.

2. James Miller pointed this out in his written comments prepared as a discussant during the North Atlantic Missiology Project at York University in February 1999.

3. In this case, Chief Justice Lamer drew on the oral histories and oral tradition of the Gitxsan and Wet'suwet'en nations to make a ruling in their favour regarding the existence of Aboriginal title to lands. In the words of Maas Gaak, Chief Negotiator, Gitxsan Treaty Office, 'The Supreme Court of Canada acknowledged parts of the world view and ruled oral histories as valid evidence.' *The Supreme Court of Canada Decision of Aboriginal Title: Delgamuukw* (Vancouver: Greystone Books, 1998), v.

4. There are many people of Aboriginal ancestry who combined their cultures of origin with their developing Christianity. Nahne's uncle Peter Jones is an obvious example. Details of his life and work are available in Donald Smith's *Sacred Feathers: The Reverend Peter Jones (Kahkewaquonaby) and the Mississauga Indians* (Toronto: University of Toronto Press, 1987). Another example is Charles Pratt, a Cree catechist in Saskatchewan, who lived from 1816 to 1888. See Winona Stevenson's chapter in Jennifer Brown and Elizabeth Vibert, eds. *Reading Beyond the Words: Contexts for Native History* (Peterborough: Broadview Press, 1996) 304–29.

5. See notes 8–10 for more details.

6. Donald B. Smith. 'Nahnebahwequay.' *Dictionary of Canadian Biography. Vol. IX 1861–1870* (Toronto: University of Toronto Press, 1976) 590.

7. Catherine Sunego has a variety of spellings and there is also contradictory presentation of her second name. Smith writes in the *Dictionary of Canadian Biography* that her birth-name is Catherine Bunch Sonego presumably a derivation formed by adding her father's name to a Christian first name. However, in a later one of Smith's works, *Sacred Feathers*, he writes her name as Catherine Brown Sunegoo pointing out that she was named after 'an exemplary Cherokee Christian' (Smith, SF, 115). Giving traditional Anishnabe names, in this case Nahnebahweequa, as well as English names was one of the symbols of the melding of the two ways of life, rather than abandonment of Native ways. Again this name has many spellings but in some form or another was the name by which she was known.

8. There are a variety of spellings for the Anishnabe names of the Mississaugas in this paper. This spelling for the original name of Peter Jones is taken from the Memorial submitted by Nah-ne-bah-wee-quay [sic] to the Duke of Newcastle and reproduced in *The Colonial Intelligencer and Aborigines' Friend* (January to December 1860), compiled in *The Colonial Intelligencer and Aborigines' Friend. 1859–1866*, Vol. II. New Series (London: W. Tweedie) 149. British Library, London (BL).

9. The Mississauga is the name which British settlers used for the Anishnabe living on the north shore of Lake Ontario. 'Around 1700, they [the Mississauga] had expelled the Iroquois from their hunting territories so recently acquired from the Huron, Petun, and Neutral half a century earlier' (Robert Surtees, 'Land Cessions, 1763–1830', *Aborginal Ontario: Historical Perspectives on the First Nations*. Eds. Edward Rogers and Donald B. Smith [Toronto: Dundurn Press, 1994], 94). In 1805, William Claus, deputy superintendent of Indian affairs, negotiated the first land purchase from the Mississaugas, part of which allowed the Credit River Mississauga to keep their fishing sites at the mouths of the Credit River (20 kilometres west of York [Toronto]), Sixteen Mile [Oakville] Creek and Twelve Mile [Bronte] Creek (Surtees 110). Surtees emphasizes that it is unlikely that the Indians of Ontario understood the full implications of the land deals as 'their communal approach to land use varied so much from the Europeans attitudes' (112). In 1818, with increasing encroachment on lands and fisheries by settlers and weakened by diseases such as smallpox, the Credit people agreed to a further surrender in exchange for much needed cash annuities. This time they maintained only the Credit River site with the other two river reserves to be sold in 1820 (116–17). By 1826, working with Methodist missionaries which now included Mississauga Peter Jones and using monies from their land surrender, the people had constructed a model farming village there (Edward S. Rogers, 'The Algonquian Farmers of Southern Ontario, 1830–1945', in Rogers and Smith, 1994, 126). They had the use of nearly 4,000 acres adjacent to the reserve (Smith, SF, 121).

10. In the US when Andrew Jackson forcibly removed the Cherokee from their lands, Peter Jones feared for the Mississaugas' claim to their lands. Jackson's tactic had been to deal with three to 500 of the Cherokee to seal the fate of over 17,000. When Sir Francis Bond Head attempted relocation of the Mississaugas to Manitoulin Island, the Credit people were determined not to comply and sought the assistance of Britain to secure written title to their lands (Smith, SF, 114; 165–66).

11. In 1847, despite strong efforts to resist, the Credit River Anishnabe finally gave up their land on the river. 'The government refused to grant the band secure title to its reserve, so instead of letting the settlers take their land for nothing, the Credit River band accepted the government's offer for it and relocated to the Grand River valley.' See Arthur J. Ray, *I Have Lived Here Since the World Began: An Illustrated History of Canada's Native People* (Toronto: Key Porter Books, 1996) 159.

12. Telephone conversation with Darlene Johnston, Land Claims Co-ordinator for the Chippewas of Nawash and Saugeen. 28 September 1998.

13. William Sutton. Obituary. *Christian Guardian* (13 June 1894) 379. Copy in vertical file, William Sutton, United Church Archives, Toronto (UCA).

14. Smith, *Biography*, 590.

15. Catherine Sutton, c 1858. 'For a Reference.' Summary of her land claim attached to letter from Chiefs supporting her claim, 1. (Record Group 10, Indian Affairs, Public Archives of Canada, Ottawa [RG 10], Volume 2877, File 177, 181).

16. Letter from W.R. Bartlett, Indian Agent to R.T. Pennefeather, Supt. General of Indian Affairs. Dated 16 August 1859. (RG 10, Volume 2877, File 177, 181). Public Archives of Canada, Ottawa (PAC).

17. Deed indicating gift of 200 acres to Catherine Sutton and her heirs dated 7 November 1845. (RG 10, Volume 2877, File 177, 181). PAC.

18. Letter signed by three chiefs Peter I. Kegedonce, George. A. Tabeguon and James Newash, dated 29 June 1859. Also letter from T.G. Anderson, former Indian Agent to W.R. Bartlett, the current Indian Agent in which the former recounts from memory the admittance to the band of Catherine Sutton and her family. Dated 4 July 1859. (RG 10 Volume 2877, File 177, 181). PAC.

19. Bartlett, to Pennefeather, 16 August 1859.

20. Don Smith recounts that her work included leading a class of 10 or more female Methodists in a weekly review of 'their spiritual progress' after which Nahne was responsible for giving appropriate advice to each member. (Donald B. Smith, Nahnebahwequay (1824–1865): 'Upright Woman.' *Canadian*

Methodist Historical Society Papers. (Volume 13. Toronto, 2001) 88.

21. Letter from Mrs. Sutton quoted by S. Belton. In the Report of the Credit Mission. In *21 Annual Report of the Missionary Society of the Wesleyan Methodist Church in Canada. (1845–1846)* xiii. UCA.

22. Ibid.

23. 'Nah-ne-bah-wee-quay', *Friends' Review*, 14.1 (8 September 1860) 9. Owen Sound Museum, Grey County (OSM).

24. I am grateful to Jim Miller for pointing this out in his unpublished notes, 'Commentary on Missions and Education Seminar: Missions and Canadian National Identities': York University, 27 February 1999.

25. William Sutton, Petition to the Governor-General, the Earl of Elgin, 30 June 1852. (RG 10, Volume 2877, File 177, 181). PAC. This is the only request, I am aware of, regarding the land signed by William rather than Nahnebahwequa.

26. Sutton, 'For a Reference', 2.

27. Sutton, 'For a Reference', 1.

28. Conrad Van Dusen. [Enemikeese]. *The Indian Chief: An Account of the Labours, Losses, Sufferings, and Oppression of Ke-zig-ko-e-ne-ne (David Sawyer,) A Chief of the Ojibbeway Indians in Canada West* (London: William Nichols, 1867), (Reprinted Toronto: Canadiana House, 1969). UCA. Van Dusen writes: 'Up till 1854, this tribe owned the whole of the peninsula between Lake Huron and the Georgian Bay, from eight to eighteen miles wide and about seventy miles long.' 128.

29. Ibid.

30. Sutton, 'For a Reference', 5. (Copy of a letter from Mr. Bartlett to the Indian Office in Toronto, 9 August 1858.)

31. In a letter written by Bartlett dated 16 August 1859, he raises another issue pertaining to Van Dusen's connection to the land purchase. He writes, 'The Rev. Vandusen acted as agent for the whole of the Indians who purchased, and could probably have advanced the money to pay their installments, with the view no doubt of ultimately getting possession of the whole of the lots, which were worth much more than the upset prices' (RG 10, Volume 2877, File 177, 181). PAC.

32. *Friends' Review*, 14.1, 131.

33. Sutton, 'For a Reference', 2. See also a letter written by R. Bartlett to R.T. Pennefeather, Superintendent of Indian Affairs, 16 August 1859 which states, 'The rule of the Department is, that an Indian woman who marries a white man, follows the fortunes of her husband, becomes literally a white woman, and is deprived of her individual interest in the funds of her tribe.' (RG 10, Volume 2877, File 177, 181).

34. Authorization signed by Cape Crocker Chief, Peter Kegedonce and Rama Chief William Yellowhead. (RG 10 Volume 2877, File 177, 181). PAC. See also Van Dusen, Chief, 138.

35. See Janet E. Chute. *The Legacy of Shingwaukonse: A Century of Native Leadership* (Toronto: University of Toronto Press, 1998).

36. The various petitions, etc. are outlined in Van Dusen, *Chief*. They include a Petition to the Legislative Assembly addressed to Mr. Hogan, M.P.P. and dated 1 April 1858, a follow-up letter written by Van Dusen, dated 15 April 1858.

37. Sutton, 'For a Reference', 3.

38. Van Dusen, Chief, 138. See also Smith 2001. He points out ' . . . the *Globe* called her an impostor and claimed that Indians could purchase land in Upper Canada where they were well-treated.' 91.

39. J.G. 'Mrs. Catherine Sutton, Sarawak.' Biographical column. *Christian Guardian* (8 November 1865). In her own account 'Is there Hope for the Indians?' written in the *Christian Guardian* (28 May 1862), Nahnebahwequa does not refer to this disappointment. Photocopy OSM.

40. 'The Mission of Nah-nee-bah-wee-quay, or the Upright Woman', *Friends' Review* 11 (September 1860) 140. Photocopy, OSM.

41. Nahneebahwequa, 'Is there Hope for the Indians?' *Christian Guardian* (28 May 1862). Photocopy OSM.

42. Ibid.

43. Ibid.

44. Ibid.

45. 'Nah-nee-bah-wee-qua (The "Upright Woman.")', *Friends' Review* 13.37, 587. Photocopy OSM.

46. 'Nah-ne-bah-wee-quay', *Aborigines' Friend and Colonial Intelligencer* (January to December, 1860) 149–50.

47. 'Nah-nee-bah-wee-qua (The "Upright Woman")', *Friends' Review* 13.37 (26 May 1860). 587–8.

Photocopy at OSM. Most of the preceding account is based on this article that does not indicate an author, but which is dated New York, 4th mo. 30th, 1860.

48. Anonymous with line added *New York, 5th mo.*, 14, 1860. 'Nah-nee-bah-we-qua', *Friends' Intelligencer* (2 June 1860) 182. Photocopy OSM.

49. See Smith 2001, 103, for more details of her fund raising in New York. He cites a letter by Robert Lindley reprinted in a biography written by his wife, Ruth Murray, *Under His Wings: A Sketch of the Life of Robert Lindley Murray* (New York: Anson, D.F. Randolph and Co., 1876) 75–6.

50. E. Meriam, 'Nah-nee-Bahwe-qua presented to Queen Victoria', *Friends' Intelligencer* 17 (1861) 311. Photocopy OSM.

51. 'The Mission of Nah-nee-bah-wee-quay, or the Upright Woman', *Friends' Review* 14.9 (11 March 1860) 140. Photocopy OSM.

52. Ibid.

53. For a history of The Aborigines' Protection Society, see H.R. Fox Bourne, *The Aborigines' Protection Society: Chapters in its History* (London: P.S. King & Son, 1899). BL. This quote is taken from the introduction, 2.

54. 'Nah-ne-bah-wee-quay', Aborigines' Friend and Colonial Intelligencer (January to December 1860) 148.

55. Ibid.

56. 'The Mission of . . . ' 140.

57. Nah-ne-bah-wee-quay's speech. The Twenty-third Annual Report of the Aborigines' Protection Society (May 1860) 31. In *The Colonial Intelligencer and Aborigines' Friend, 1859–1866, Volume II. New Series* (London: W. Tweedie). James Miller points out in his discussion of the presentation version of this paper that the Indian Department was at that time moving away from their promised annuities which may have influenced this move.

58. Court Circular, *The Times* (Saturday, 16 June 1860) Second Edition, 12 column e. Newspaper Library, British Library, London (NL).

59. Ibid.

60. Robert Alsop and Thomas Hodgkin, M.D., 'Nah-ne-bah-wee-quay', *Aborigines' Friend, and the Colonial Intelligencer* (January to December 1860) 155.

61. Queen Victoria, Journal entry for 19 June 1860. Typescript at County of Grey: Owen Sound Museum. The note includes comments that there is no indication elsewhere that Mr. Sutton was a sailor. His obituary in the *Christian Guardian* (13 June 1894, typescript copy in UCA vertical file 'Win. Sutton') indicates that he worked as a shoemaker when first in Canada.

62. Court Circular, *The Times* (Wednesday, 20 June 1860) 9, column f. NL.

63. Meriam, N. presented to Queen, *Friends' Intelligencer,* 311.

64. E. Meriam, 'Nah-nee-bahwe-qua', Friends' Review (28 August 1860) 789. Photocopy in OSM.

65. E. Meriam, 'Nah-nee-bahwe-qua', *Friends' Intelligencer* 17 (1861) 343. Photocopy from OSM.

66. Meriam, *Review*, 789.

67. Martha Braithwaite, comp. *Memorials of Christine Majolier Alsop* (London: Samuel Harris, 1881) 151. FHL.

68. Author unknown. *A Tribute to the Memory of Robert Alsop* (London: West, Newman & Co., 1879). For private circulation. 30. FHL.

69. Op. cit. 31.

70. Op. cit. 32.

71. Braithwaite, *Alsop*, 152.

72. 'Aborigines' Protection Society', *Liverpool Courier* (15 September 1860) 3. BNL.

73. Talk about dress occurs in a number of places in reference to the degree of 'civilization' of the Aboriginal peoples being scrutinized—whether by self or others. For example, in a piece in the *Intelligencer* entitled 'The Prince of Wales in Canada', it is pointed out that while the Prince may have expected to find half-naked savages, in at least one village, 'the chief was dressed like an ordinary country farmer.' Further research on the trappings or signs of Christianity and/or civilization could prove revealing. *Aborigines' Friend and the Colonial Intelligencer* (January to December 1860) 157, in *The Colonial Intelligencer and Aborigines' Friend, 1859–1866, Volume II. New Series* (London: W. Tweedie).

74. Ibid.

75. Ibid.

76. Ibid.

77. Braithwaite, *Alsop*, 152.

78. 'Lo! the Poor Indian', *Friends' Review* 14.34 (27 April 1861) 538.

79. Ibid.

80. The Indians of Canada, *Aborigines' Friend and the Colonial Intelligencer* (January to December 1860) 145, in The Colonial Intelligencer and Aborigines' Friend, 1859–1866, Volume II. New Series (London: W. Tweedie).

81. Op. cit. 147.

82. William Sutton, 'Farm Journal', 112–18. Taken from typescript in Owen Sound Museum.

83. Ibid.

84. An excerpt from one of William Sutton's letters to Robert Alsop indicates an act respecting Indian lands and property was passed on 28 February 1860 at Quebec. (Robert Alsop, 'Nahnebahweequay and the Indians of the Manitoolin Islands', *The Friend*, n.s. II [1862] 4–5, photocopy from OSM.) See also Olive Dickason, *Canada's First Nations* (Toronto: Oxford University Press, 1992) 251–2. The Management of Indian Lands and Properties Act of 1860 transferred Indian administration from the Colonial Office to Canada.

85. 'Lo the Poor Indian', 538.

86. Ibid.

87. Op. cit. 539.

88. Letter to the Friends of New York from Nah-nee-bah-wee-quay, 30 March 1861. In J.C., 'Nah-nee-bah-wee-quay', Friends' Intelligencer (5 April 1861) 119. Photocopy from OSM.

89. Ibid.

90. Ibid.

91. 'Extracts from a Letter from W. Sutton, of Owen Sound, Upper Canada, husband of Nahnebahweequay, to Robert Alsop, of Stoke Newington.' *The Aborigines' Friend and Colonial Intelligencer* (January to December 1861), in *The Colonial Intelligencer and Aborigines' Friend, 1859–1866, Volume II. New Series* (London: W. Tweedie) 219.

92. Copy of letter from William Sutton to Mr. R. Alsop. 17 March 1861, typescript, OSM.

93. Sutton, 'For a Reference' 9.

94. Op. cit. 10.

95. Canada. Twenty-Fourth Annual Report of the Aborigines' Protection Society, 1862, 17. In *The Colonial Intelligencer and Aborigines' Friend, 1859–1866, Volume II. New Series* (London: W. Tweedie).

96. John Ray, 'A Visit to the Ojibway Indians', *The Friend*, Fourth Month, 1864, 79.

97. Ibid.

98. Van Dusen, *Chief*, 156. It is important to note that Van Dusen also refers to the fact that, although Sawyer had used his influence to have Nahnebahwequa become their representative to the Queen, only the Suttons had benefited from the trip. He carefully states, 'In regard to this, we have no information, only that we know that the chief, nor any other indian that we know of, ever received a cent through her agency.' Ibid. This note is disturbing for two reasons: one, it may be an indication of the divide and conquer mentality which seems to have characterized many colonial efforts (Friere, 1970) and secondly, Catherine Sutton wrote several times to Friends in England looking for help for the poor Indians. There are also several places where she accounts for the monies received. While it may be that she chose a select group to distribute the funds to, she does appear to have distributed it. This certainly raises some questions about the relationship between Van Dusen and Nahnebahwequa. A draft letter apparently written by Nahnebahwequa indicates her concerns about what she sees as an opportunist relationship Van Dusen is developing with David Sawyer. Nahnebahwequa also expressed annoyance at a visit Sawyer made to her mother, commenting, 'why does he not come to me?' (Typescript, from one of William Sutton's ledgers, Ledger 1961.27.23 [Reference could be Donald Smith's notation?] 58–62). She goes on to write a long account of Vandusen's [*sic*] dishonest claim to an invention for addressing newspapers as part of the printing process.

99. 'The Canadian Indians and the Manitoulin Islands.' *Aborigines' Friend and the Colonial Intelligencer* (January to December 1862), in *The Colonial Intelligencer and Aborigines' Friend, 1859–1866, Volume II. New Series* (London: W. Tweedie) 253.

100. At least with the first five children, Nahnebahwequa gave Anishnabe names as well as English ones. Her children included: 'Sah-gar-se-ga (rising sun,) Joseph, 18, Nah-we-ke-gee-go-quay (blue sky,) Catherine, 17, Nah-koo-quay (top buds of a tree) Sophia, 14,

Sun-e-goo-nec (little Squirrel,) Wesley, 5, Sah-sa-kah-noo-quay (little hail,) Mary Margaret, 3, Little man from over the great waters, Alsop Albert Edward.' ('Lo the Poor Indian' 539). She apparently had two more children after these ones as Ray mentions eight children during his visit in 1863, 79.

101. Ray, 'A Visit', 79.

102. See Celia Haig-Brown, 'Contradiction, Power and Control', *Taking Control: Contradiction and Power in First Nations Adult Education* (Vancouver: University of British Columbia Press, 1995) for a fuller discussion of the dialectical contradiction, especially 233–6.

103. Research assistant, Kate Eichhorn, first drew my attention to this development in a news article about the negotiations. Later a conversation with Darlene Johnston, Land Claims Co-ordinator for the Chippewas of Nawash and Saugeen, added details and a CRC interview with Stephanie McMullen on 13 January 1999 provided further elaboration.

WORKS CITED

Berger, Thomas. 'Towards the Regime of Tolerance', *Fragile Freedoms: Human Rights and Dissent in Canada*. Toronto: Clarke Irwin & Co., 1981.

Carr, W.H. *What is History?* Hammondsworth: Penguin, 1961.

Freire, Paulo. *Pedagogy of the Oppressed*. New York: Continuum 1982.

Hammersley, Martyn and Paul Atkinson. *Ethnography: Principles in Practice*. London: Tavistock, 1983.

Nock, David. *A Victorian Missionary and Canadian Indian Policy: Cultural Synthesis vs Cultural Replacement*. Waterloo: Wilfred Laurier Press, 1988.

Petrone, Penny, ed. *First People, First Voices*. Toronto: University of Toronto Press, 1985.

Tennant, Paul. *Aboriginal Peoples and Politics: The Indian Land Question in British Columbia, 1849–1989*. Vancouver: University of British Columbia Press, 1990.

The Supreme Court of Canada Decision of Aboriginal Title: Delgamuukw. Vancouver: Greystone Books, 1998.

Wilson, E.F. *Missionary Work Among the Ojebway Indians*. London: Society for Promoting Christian Knowledge, 1886.

Chapter Twelve

'Rushing' the Empire Westward

READINGS

Primary Documents

1   'Letter of Charles Major, 20 September 1859', in *Daily Globe*, Toronto, 2 January 1860

2   From *Journals, Detailed Reports and Observations Relative to the Exploration, by Captain Palliser,* John Palliser

Historical Interpretations

3   From '"A Delicate Game": The Meaning of Law on Grouse Creek', Tina Loo

4   From 'Mapping the New El Dorado: The Fraser River Gold Rush and the Appropriation of Native Space', Daniel Marshall

Introduction

Even before Canada East, Canada West, New Brunswick, and Nova Scotia signed on to Confederation, the other parts of North America further west, controlled as colonies or trading territories by the British or British North Americans, were attracting notice. The potential riches in British Columbia's gold fields and expansion of the rural settlement frontier into bison range and fur trade territory captured the imaginations of British North American colonists and colonial administrators alike. Understanding what was in these territories, and understanding how these territories and their inhabitants were defined for people who would probably never visit, is central to understanding why Great Britain (and its British North American colonies) might want to expand the imperial footprint when it seemed that maintaining the empire and international alliances was getting troublesome. (Britain had just been at war against Russia in the Black Sea region, and a rebellion was unfolding in India in 1857).

Our primary sources here represent two different kinds of reporting on the state of two separate 'frontier' areas. The letter from Charles Major paints a forbidding picture of British Columbia and is especially pessimistic about the possibility of earning a decent living. He describes a chaotic gold rush scene, one in which the authority of the empire seems restricted to Victoria and was otherwise hardly noticeable. Though it does not deal with the chase for gold, John Palliser's commentary on the vast centre of the continent captures the same sort of expansionist spirit. He mentions deserts, but raises hopes for the regions north of the 49th parallel (the border between the United States and British/Hudson's Bay Company territory) by noting that it supported trees and grasses.

The secondary sources urge us to think about what these encounters of the frontier meant, using the example of British Columbia's colonial history, which was marked by desires to settle the land and to extract wealth from it. Tina Loo reasons that even in places where the rule of law had a short history and colonial authorities desired strict enforcement, newcomers to the territory had a basic respect for the law. Daniel Marshall's article emphasizes a virtually American invasion of the territory, and shows how the task of finding gold took over the area, both crowding out the First Nations names for the local geographical features and affecting their traditional use of the Fraser River and its tributaries.

QUESTIONS FOR CONSIDERATION

1. Compare Charles Major's letter to some of the correspondence that Errington writes about in Chapter 8. Is Major trying to create the same sort of connections?
2. Judging from his report, how *scientific* do you think Palliser's expedition was?
3. How British were the inhabitants of British North America and associated territories in the late 1850s? What made them so?
4. Do you consider the informal model of miners' justice to be more suitable to areas like the BC gold fields, or were people like Governor Douglas right to push for more formal institutions?
5. When Marshall speaks of 'appropriation', what is he referring to?

SUGGESTIONS FOR FURTHER READING

Barman, Jean, *The West beyond the West: A History of British Columbia* (Toronto: University of Toronto Press, 2007)

Fisher, Robin, *Contact and Conflict: Indian-European Relations in British Columbia, 1774–1890* (Vancouver: University of British Columbia Press, 1977)

Loo, Tina, *Making Law, Order and Authority in British Columbia, 1821–1871* (Toronto: University of Toronto Press, 1994)

Owram, Doug, *Promise of Eden: The Canadian Expansionist Movement and the Idea of the West, 1856–1900* (Toronto: University of Toronto Press, 1980)

Perry, Adele, *On the Edge of Empire: Gender, Race, and the Making of British Columbia, 1849–1871* (Toronto: University of Toronto Press, 2001)

Sandwell, Ruth, ed., *Beyond the City Limits: Rural History in British Columbia* (Vancouver: UBC Press, 1999)

PRIMARY DOCUMENTS

1   'Letter of Charles Major, 20 September 1859', in *Daily Globe*, Toronto, 2 January 1860, reprinted in Robie L. Reid, 'Two Narratives of the British Gold Rush', *British Columbia Historical Quarterly* 5(3) (July 1941): 224–7.

[From *The Daily Globe*, Toronto, Canada West, January 2, 1860.]
NEWS FROM BRITISH COLUMBIA. (From the Sarnia *Observer.*)

The following letter recently received by a person in this neighborhood, from the writer who is at present in British Columbia, was handed to us for perusal. As it contains much valuable and reliable information in reference to the country, we requested permission to publish it, which was at once granted. We therefore lay the most important portions of the letter before our readers, without further apology, satisfied that it will be read with interest by all:—

Fort Hope, Frazer River
Sept. 20th, 1859
Dear Sir:—I am afraid you will think I had forgot my promise,—but I wanted to know something about the country before writing to you. In the first place, do not think that I have taken a dislike to the country because I am not making money; the dislike is general all over the country. To give you anything like a correct idea of it would take more paper than I have small change to purchase, and more time than I could spare, and then it would only be commenced.

The country is not what it was represented to be. There is no farming land in British Columbia, as far as I can learn, except a very small portion joining Washington Territory, and on Vancouver's Island, where there is one valley of 20,000 acres; but that cannot be sold until Col. Moody's friends come out from the old country, and get what they want.

It never can be a *place*, because there is nothing to support it, except the mines, and just as soon as they are done the place goes down completely, for there is absolutely nothing to keep it up; and I tell you the truth the mines are falling off very fast. There is nothing in this country but mines—and very small pay for that; they are you may say, used up. We have been making two, three and four dollars per day, but it would not last more than two or three days; and so you would spend that before you would find more. There has been great excitement about Fort Alexander, three hundred miles above this, and also about Queen Charlotte's Island. They have both turned out another humbug like this place. A party arrived here yesterday from Alexander, and they are a pitiful looking lot. They are what the Yankees call *dead broke*. They have been six hundred miles up the river. When they got down here they had no shoes to their feet. Some had pieces of shirt and trowsers, but even these were pinned together with small sharp sticks; and some had the rim of an old hat, and some the crown. They had nothing to eat for one week, and not one cent in money. This is gold mining for you!

I expect the Frazer River fever has cooled down by this time, at least I hope so; for I do pity the poor wretches that come out here to beg. They can do that at home; as for making money, that is out of the question. Since we came here (to use the miners' term,) we have been making grub; and those who can do that, think they are doing well. If there are any making arrangements to come to this place, let them take a fool's advice *and stay at home*. I would just about as soon hear that anyone belonging to me was dead, as to hear they had started to come here. They say it wants a man with capital to make money here; but a man with money in Canada will double it quicker than he will here. And if I, or any other, was to work as hard and leave [live] as meanly, I could make more money in Canada than I can here. Since we have been on the River we have worked from half-past two and three o'clock in the morning till nine and ten o'clock at night, (you can see the sun twenty hours out of the twenty-four in the summer season.)—and lived on beans! If that is not working, I don't know what it is. Besides this you go home to your shanty at night, tired and wet, and have to cook your beans before you can eat them. And what is this all for? For *gold* of course; but when you wash up at night, you may realize 50 cents, perhaps $1.

There have been some rich spots struck on this river, but they were very scarce, and they are all worked out; and the miners are leaving the river every day, satisfied there is nothing to be made. But now that I am in the country I will remain for a year or so, and if nothing better turns up by that time, I think I will be perfectly satisfied. I have met with some that I was acquainted with, and it is amusing to see those who felt themselves a little better than their neighbors at home, come here and get out of money, and have to take the pick and shovel, perhaps to drag firewood out of the woods and sell it, or make pack-mules of themselves to get a living. I do not mean to say that it is so all over the Colony, but it is from one end of Fraser River to the other. I dare anyone to contradict what I say; and I have good reason to believe it is as bad all over the country. I saw a patch of oats here the other day. They were out in head, only four inches in height, yellow as ochre, and *not thick enough on the ground to be neighbours*. Vegetables and other things are as poor in the proportion; and as for the climate, it is just as changeable as in Canada, if not more so. I can't say much about the climate on Vancouver's Island, but I think it is rather better.

I met T.G., the carpenter, from Sarnia, who left there about a year ago. He went round the Horn, and he was ten months and fifteen days in coming here. He is cutting saw logs making a little over grub. He says he is going to write to the Sarnia *Observer*, and give this place a cutting up! There are a great many Canadians here, and they would be glad to work for their board. A man could not hire out to work a day if he was starving. I have seen some parties from California; they say times are very hard there. There are just three in our party now, H.H., J.R., and myself. There were two of the H's; one was taken sick and had to leave the river; he is in Victoria, and is quite recovered again; has been there two months, and has not got a day's work yet. I was very sick myself when I just came here, but am quite healthy now, and so fat I can hardly see to write. The rest are quite well.

The Indians are not very troublesome at the mines; they are kept down pretty well. They are very numerous here and on the Island, the lowest degraded set of creatures I ever saw.

It is estimated that the number of miners who make over wages, is one in five hundred; and the number that do well in the mines is one in a thousand. So you see it is a very small proportion. If you know anyone that wants to spend money, why, this is just the place. Anyone bringing a family here would require a small fortune to support them in this horrible place, hemmed in by mountains on all sides, and these covered with snow all the year.

I have lived in a tent since I came up the river, and I have to lie on the ground before the fire and write; it gives a very poor light, so excuse the writing. It has been raining here steady one week, and the mountains are all covered with snow; for when it rains here it is snowing upon the mountains. It is a wild looking place. You will please tell our folks you hear from me, and that we are all well. I will write to some of them in about two weeks or so. I have wrote five letters already, but I have not heard from any of them; so many letters go astray in coming here and going from this place, that perhaps they do not get them at all. Give my respects to old friends, and tell them to be contented and stay at home.

I remain, yours truly
CHARLES MAJOR.

2 From John Palliser, *Journals, Detailed Reports and Observations Relative to the Exploration, by Captain Palliser* (London: Eyre & Spottiswood, 1863), 7, 10–11, 16–18.

The existence of a general law regulating the distribution of the woods in this portion of the continent suggested itself to us during our first summer's explorations, and subsequent experience during the seasons of 1858–9 fully confirmed it.

The fertile savannahs and valuable woodlands of the Atlantic United States are succeeded, as has been previously alluded to, on the west by a more or less arid desert, occupying a region on both sides of the Rocky Mountains, which presents a barrier to the continuous growth of settlements between the Mississippi Valley and the States on the Pacific coast. This central desert extends, however, but a short way into the British territory, forming a triangle, having for its base the 49th parallel from longitude 100° to 114° W., with its apex reaching to the 52nd parallel of latitude.

The northern forests, which in former times descended more nearly to the frontier of this central desert, have been greatly encroached upon and, as it were, pushed backwards to the north through the effect of frequent fires.

Thus a large portion of fertile country, denuded of timber, separates the arid region from the forest lands to the north, and the habit which the Indian tribes have of burning the vegetation has, in fact, gradually improved the country for the purpose of settlement by clearing off the heavy timber, to remove which is generally the first and most arduous labour of the colonist.

The richness of the natural pasture in many places on the prairies of the second level along the North Saskatchewan and its tributary, Battle River, can hardly be exaggerated. Its value does not consist in its being rank or in great quantity, but from its fine quality, comprising nutritious species of grasses and carices, along with natural vetches in great variety, which remain throughout the winter sound, juicy, and fit for the nourishment of stock.

Almost everywhere along the course of the North Saskatchewan are to be found simply, it would be natural to infer their existence along the whole line where the Rocky Mountains run parallel and retain their altitude; but the dry areas are evidently due to other causes primarily, and they are not found above the 47th parallel in fact. It is decisive of the general question of sufficiency of rain to find the entire surface of the upper plains either well grassed or well wooded, and recent information on these points almost warrants the assertion that there are no barren tracts of consequence after we pass the Bad Lands, and the *Coteaus* of the Missouri. Many portions of these plains are known to be peculiarly rich in grasses, and probably the finest tracts lie along the eastern base of the mountains, in positions corresponding to the most desert-like of the plains at the south. The higher latitudes certainly differ widely from the plains which stretch from the Platte southward to the Llano Estacado of Texas, and none of the references made to them by residents or travellers indicate desert characteristics. Buffalo are far more abundant on the northern plains, and they remain through the winter at their extreme border, taking shelter in the belts of woodland on the upper Athabasca and Peace rivers. Grassy savannas like these necessarily imply an adequate supply of rain, and there can be no doubt that the correspondence with the European plains in like geographical position—those of eastern Germany and Russia—is quite complete in this respect. If a difference exists it is in favor of the American plains, which have a greater proportion of surface waters, both as lakes and rivers.

HISTORICAL INTERPRETATIONS

3   From Tina Loo, '"A Delicate Game": The Meaning of Law on Grouse Creek', *BC Studies* 96 (Winter 1992–93): 41–65.

At the end of June in 1862, 100 miners returning from the Cariboo boarded the steamer *Henrietta* in Douglas for the trip to New Westminster. They refused to pay for their passage, claiming that their misadventures in the upper country gold fields had left them 'starving and broken', as well as broke. Despite the obvious illegality of the miners' actions, Douglas magistrate John Boles Gaggin advised the master of *Henrietta* to 'take the men on, and on arrival at New Westminster, apply to the proper authorities for redress.' Gaggin took this course of action believing, as he told the Colonial Secretary, that

> to attempt coercion with a force unable to command it would have weakened the apparent power of the Law; . . . [and] that the getting of these men out of Douglas was in every way desirable, . . . any attempt to arrest would have provoked a riot, perhaps bloodshed, and I believe I acted prudently in avoiding the least risk of this.[1]

In an effort to further justify his actions, Gaggin closed his report on a defiant note with this telling observation:

> Magistrates in these up country towns have a delicate game to play, and I believe we are all of opinion that to avoid provoking resistance to the Law is the manner in which we best serve the interests of His Excellency, the Governor. . . . [A]s it is the matter passed off without riot and without defiance of the Magistrate, though the Master of the steamer . . . was somewhat annoyed—I shall be very sorry if the cautious way I acted, with such quiet results, does not

meet His Excellency's approval, but I acted for the best.[2]

The colonial government chastised the magistrate for his 'want of nerve and judgment' in allowing 'the occurrence of so lawless a proceeding.'[3] 'It appears', noted Colonial Secretary W.A.G. Young,

> that you consider yourself vested with discretionary power to temporize with your duties, and that you are unaware that, while rigidly dispensing the laws for the protection of life and property, a Magistrate may act with perfect temper and discretion.[4]

This brief episode raises questions about the social meaning of the law which I am concerned to address. Gaggin considered law to be the preservation of order—'quiet results'—and told his superiors so. From his vantage point in Victoria, Governor James Douglas saw things rather differently. The law, through its rigid application, served a more particular end by securing life and property. There was yet another perspective. Both Gaggin and Douglas considered the miners' actions 'lawless', but those who boarded *Henrietta* likely did not feel the same way. Different people attached different meanings to the law, and when they used the courts to resolve their disputes these differences became apparent. As legal anthropologists argue, courts are forums in which people 'bargain for reality'; not only do they dispute the 'facts'—what happened—but they also dispute what constitutes legal and just action.[5]

From their arrival, British Columbia's miners possessed a reputation as a self-conscious and vocal interest group with a penchant for self-government which they learned in California's gold fields. Despite their impermanent character, California's gold mining camps developed an elaborate system of informal regulation centred on the Miners' Meetings.[6] These were elected tribunals of local miners who drafted the rules which governed behaviour in a specific locale. Their regulations covered a wide range of activities, from claim size, the technicalities of ditch widths and water rights to the use of alcohol and firearms in the camps.[7] This experience instilled the miners with a taste for local government and a certain degree of independence.[8] It was this independence that made those who streamed northward to British Columbia in 1858 to try their luck in the Fraser and Cariboo rushes so dangerous in the eyes of British colonial administrators like James Douglas and Supreme Court Judge Matthew Baillie Begbie.[9] These men considered the miners a lawless bunch and took steps to prevent local government from gaining a foothold on the banks of the Fraser River.

In September 1858, just a month after the mainland colony was formed, James Douglas issued the first *Gold Fields Act*.[10] It and subsequent Acts created and elaborated formal government institutions and regulations specifically designed to regulate gold mining.[11] An Assistant Gold Commissioner presided over locally based Gold Commissioner's or Mining Courts. He had jurisdiction to hear all mining or mining-related disputes and to dispose of them summarily. By doing so, the Gold Commissioner's Court allowed suitors to avoid the costly delays associated with Supreme Court actions and jury trials. A locally elected Mining Board replaced the Californian Miners' Meetings, drafting bylaws which governed behaviour. Unlike the American institution they replaced, however, the decisions of the Mining Board could be overturned by the Assistant Gold Commissioner, who also possessed the power to dissolve the board at his pleasure.

Despite the early intrusion of this formal regulatory institution into the gold fields, British Columbia's miners retained a sense of themselves and their enterprise as distinct and crucial to the development of the colony. Despite their impermanent character, gold rush communities were localistic, regardless—paradoxically—of their location.[12] Miners were particularly interested in the administration of the law, watching Mining Court decisions with an eye to their own fortunes. Though the law and the courts brought British Columbia's diverse and far-flung miners together in a common process of dispute settlement, they also were the cause of much division, for they resolved differences by creating other ones. The law defined plaintiffs and defendants, assessed guilt and innocence, and ultimately, in the eyes of those involved, determined right and wrong. The potential for conflict was thus inherent in the process of dispute settlement. As will be seen, different concepts of law stood in bold relief against this structured background of formal dispute resolution.

British Columbians understood and measured their laws with a standard that was rooted in a particular geographic, social, and cultural milieu and that was not always shared by those charged with its administration. Conflicting understandings of what constituted law underlay the disputes which culminated in the Grouse Creek War (1867) and which form the focus of the following narrative.

* * *

The three cases that lay at the centre of the controversy over the colony's judicial administration were all disputes over the ownership of mining claims.[13] Each is rather unremarkable in terms of the issues of fact involved, which consisted of the recording and re-recording of claims and the placement of stakes.[14] Once the cases were appealed to the Supreme Court, however, the issues of fact in these cases became secondary to Supreme Court Judge Matthew Baillie Begbie's actions.

The judge's behaviour in the three cases and public reaction to them neatly illustrate the problems associated with administering the law in British Columbia, and adumbrate the limits of formal, institutional dispute settlement.

The first of these, launched in 1865, pitted the Borealis Company against the Watson Company. After the Assistant Gold Commissioner's decision awarding a disputed claim to the Watson Company was upheld by Begbie, the Borealis Company took the case to the Court of Chancery.[15] There, sitting this time as Chancery Court Judge, Begbie reversed his earlier decision, and awarded the disputed ground to the Borealis Company! By all accounts, the mining community of the Cariboo was incredulous, and the colony's three main opposition newspapers wasted no time in adding their voices to the growing cries of indignation over Begbie's ruling emanating from the gold fields. Most distressing to British Columbians was the use of the Chancery Court as a court of appeal, a process that was not only expensive and protracted, but was also capricious, because decisions appeared to be unfettered by any reference to statute law. 'The late decision in the Borealis & Watson case strikes me as being the most flagrant and arbitrary stretches of power that has even been committed by an individual occupying the position of Judge', wrote 'Miner' to the *Cariboo Sentinel* in 1866:

> . . . we have mining laws containing explicit provisions as to the manner in which claims should be taken up and held, but at the same time that any parties having money enough to stand the costs of a Chancery suit may omit to comply with these provisions and set the law at defiance; it tends to create a feeling of insecurity as the value of every title, no man is secure if he strikes a good claim, as after strictly complying with the law which he supposed to be protection and spending his last dollar in prospecting, he

may find when he thinks he has reached the long hoped for goal of his ambition, that some more favoured individual had intended in taking up the same ground long previously, but had neglected . . . staking it off or recording it, a grave error certainly, but one which can be expiated by filing a bill in Equity, making a score or two of affidavits, and paying his own costs in a Chancery suit, and this is what is called 'Equity'.[16]

Less measured was the commentary of the Victoria-based *British Colonist*, which contended that the 'endless round of litigation' in British Columbia's mining districts was 'ruining claimholders, shutting up the country's wealth and causing disasters in communities hundreds of miles away from the scene of the dispute.' 'The risks of mining are a mere bagatelle', the newspaper concluded, 'it is the risks of Begbie's Chancery Court that terrify the miner.'[17]

Public indignation over Begbie's actions in the Borealis case scarcely subsided when his handling of another mining dispute again drew the attention and the wrath of British Columbians. After issuing an injunction ordering the Davis Company to cease work on disputed ground, Begbie discovered that the Supreme Court seals necessary to validate the injunction were unavailable—detained, with the rest of his luggage, on a wagon that had broken down en route to Bridge Creek. Undeterred, the judge sent a messenger to Richfield with the injunction and orders for William Cox, the Stipendiary Magistrate and Assistant Gold Commissioner there, to attach seals to the injunction in his capacity as Deputy Registrar of the Supreme Court. Cox, whose decision Begbie had overturned in issuing the injunction, declined to act as ordered, claiming that while he 'entertain[ed] high respect for Mr. Begbie as Mr. Begbie and also as Supreme Court Judge', he held no commission as Deputy Registrar. Moreover, continued the magistrate,

Finding now that it is attempted to drag me into this disagreeable quarrel, and act contrary to my own conscience, I would if I actually did hold a commission as Deputy Registrar of the Supreme Court resign the post at once.[18]

Although delayed by Cox's 'decisive stand', *Aurora v. Davis* came to trial before Matthew Baillie Begbie and a special jury on 18 June.[19] After deliberating until midnight, the jury awarded half of the disputed ground to each side, because 'the Aurora and Davis Companies have expended both time and money on said ground in dispute.'[20] According to the *Sentinel*, the jury's decision met with the general approval of the entire mining community.

> There is probably no instance on record where trial by jury has been so fully appreciated. . . . We are convinced that there is not a single miner on the creek that would not gladly submit his grievances to the decision of seven disinterested fellow citizens, and thus avoid the expensive and vexatious proceedings in Chancery.[21]

Despite the satisfaction with the jury's verdict evinced by the *Sentinel*, Begbie insisted that a decision by his court 'would not end the litigation, and the expense of actions in one or two other branches of this Court would be heavy on both parties.' Instead of accepting the jury's verdict, the judge suggested 'that the whole matter be referred to me, not in my capacity as Judge, but as an arbitrator and friend, and that whatever decision I may arrive at will be final and absolute.'[22] The two sides agreed, and the following day—19 June—Begbie rendered his decision to an 'anxious' courtroom. Perhaps hoping to forestall any criticism, the judge made it a point to downplay the irregularity of his actions and to praise the jury as an institution. 'I have always had every reason to be satisfied with the findings of juries during the whole period of my own official

experience in this colony', Begbie remarked; but if 'a jury finds a verdict contrary to the evidence, resulting from ignorance, fear, or any other cause it is [the judge's] privilege to set aside their verdict.' Noting that 'when men go to jump ground they do not see their enemies' stakes', Begbie ruled against the Davis Company and awarded all of the disputed ground to the appellant.[23]

Reaction was immediate. Five or six hundred miners and residents of Cariboo gathered in front of the Richfield Court house on a rainy Saturday night six days after Begbie's decision to discuss the administration of the colony's mining laws.[24] Amid a great many speeches lasting well into the night, the participants passed three resolutions:

> RESOLVED, 'That in the opinion of this meeting the administration of the Mining Laws by Mr. Justice Begbie in the Supreme Court is partial, dictatorial, and arbitrary, in setting aside the verdict of juries, and calculated to create a feeling of distrust in those who have to seek redress through a Court of Justice.'

> RESOLVED, 'That the meeting pledges itself to support the Government in carrying out the Laws in their integrity, and beg for an impartial administration of justice. To this end we desire the establishment of a Court of Appeal, or the immediate removal of Judge Begbie, whose acts in setting aside the Law has destroyed confidence and is driving labor, capital and enterprise out of the Colony.'

> RESOLVED, 'That a Committee of two persons be appointed to wait upon His Excellency the Administrator of the Government [Arthur Birch] with the foregoing resolutions, and earnestly impress upon him the immediate necessity of carrying out the wishes of the people.'

With three cheers for 'Judge' Cox, the *British Colonist*, the *Cariboo Sentinel* and the Queen (in that order), and three groans for Judge Begbie, the meeting adjourned.[25]

As a result of the mounting public pressure for reform, the colonial government amended the *Gold Fields Act* in April 1867, limiting appeals from the Mining Court to questions of law only.[26] [. . .]

The *Borealis v. Watson* and *Aurora v. Davis* cases set the stage for the final and, according to one magistrate, most 'humiliating' part of this mining trilogy: the Grouse Creek War.[27] Having found Chancery and arbitration wanting, and his government colleagues sensitive to public pressure, in 1867 Matthew Baillie Begbie found only one option remaining: to adhere to the newly amended *Gold Fields Act* and refuse to hear appeals from the Mining Courts. This course was not successful in restoring British Columbians' faith in the administration of the law. The fault was not Begbie's, however. A less outspoken Supreme Court judge might have succeeded in blunting the sharpest barbs, but no one could have bridged the gulf between the different meanings of law created by the colony's geography.

In late April 1864, the Grouse Creek Bedrock Flume Company, a Victoria-based joint stock company, applied to Peter O'Reilly, Richfield's Assistant Gold Commissioner, for the rights to a certain portion of land on Grouse Creek. O'Reilly granted the company title for ten years provided they fulfilled the usual conditions of occupation, licensing, and recording of the claim as outlined in the *Gold Fields Act*. During 1864 and all of 1865 the 'Flumites', as they came to be known, developed their claim, investing $20,000 to $30,000; but in late 1866 the company ran out of money, and their claim was left unoccupied from September to November. During this time—on 8 October—the Canadian Company, a locally based association of free miners, entered the Flume Company's claim, and finding it apparently abandoned, applied for rights to it. Warner Spalding, who had replaced Peter O'Reilly as

interim Assistant Gold Commissioner, duly recorded the ground in the Canadian Company's name. At the beginning of the next mining season, in March, the Flumites renegotiated their lease to the Grouse Creek claim with the crown, managing to extricate themselves from all previous conditions regulating their occupation of the ground. Inexplicably, Spalding, who had just six months earlier granted the same piece of land to the Canadian Company, presided over this renegotiation on behalf of the Crown! It was only a matter of weeks before the two companies clashed, and the dispute was taken to the district's Mining Court, again to be heard before Spalding.[28] There Spalding ruled in favour of the plaintiffs, and ordered the Canadians off the disputed ground.[29] The Canadians gave notice of appeal, but obeyed the Commissioner's order.

Though the Canadians left quietly, they were back on Grouse Creek in a month. At the end of May, Anthony Melloday and three other Canadian Company members commenced work on the Grouse Creek Flume Company's claim. This time, however, the Flumites took their complaint to the Magistrate's Court, laying criminal charges of trespass against the Canadians. The foreman, Melloday, received the heaviest sentence: one month's imprisonment The others were sentenced to seven and fourteen days.[30] [. . .]

At the beginning of July Begbie informed the two companies that he would not, in keeping with the newly amended *Gold Fields Act*, hear the appeal. [. . .] Undeterred, the Canadians regrouped, and now 30 or 40 strong, they again returned to Grouse Creek. Three constables and one surveyor were dispatched to eject the Canadians, but were prevented from doing so when the company's men 'surrounded [them] . . . without showing any hostile disposition, or making any threats of violence, but simply claiming that as they all acted as one man, if any one was liable to arrest they all were . . . '.[31] The constables left.

Local sentiment seemed to be very much on the side of the Canadians, particularly in light of Begbie's refusal to hear their appeal—a situation that was doubly ironic, given that local sentiment, and notably the pressure of the Canadian Company's principals, John MacLaren and Cornelius Booth, had led to the 1867 amendment! Writing on behalf of the members of the Canadian Company, Booth insisted they were not 'acting in opposition to the law of the land'. Since they could not appeal, they were more than willing to force a new case.[32] [. . .] Booth told the same thing to a public meeting of 500 people gathered to hear 'a full and truthful statement of the grievances and position of the Canadian Company.' The sympathetic crowd passed a resolution recording their sympathy with the Canadians and their commitment to aid the company 'by all lawful means to obtain their rights.'[33]

The good will manifested toward the Canadians made itself apparent the next day, when the district's magistrate proceeded to Grouse Creek, backed this time by 25 or 30 of 'the most prominent businessmen, and respectable citizens of this town' who had answered court summonses to act as special constables. Once there, the 'posse comitatus' exchanged 'the most friendly greetings' with the Canadians and the nearly 400 eager onlookers who had 'splashed through mud and mire, knee-deep, in haste to reach the rendezvous.' All settled in for a long and what must have been anti-climactic afternoon of negotiation by letter between the two companies. In the end, with no hope of settlement, the magistrate read a writ of injunction to the Canadian Company and asked them to leave the claim. '[A] unanimous NO was returned, whereupon Mr. Ball, along with his constables, left Williams Creek, and the crowd dispersed.'[34] The magistrate immediately telegraphed the Governor, requesting that a detachment of marines be sent to assist him.[35] The Royal Navy refused to intervene, and Seymour, 'at very considerable inconvenience to myself proceeded . . . to Cariboo.'[36]

It was this stalemate that greeted the Governor when he arrived in Richfield a few weeks later, on 7 August. Seymour, along with

the rest of the colony, had been treated to a series of alarmist reports of 'mob law' on Williams Creek from the *British Colonist* and the *British Columbian*, and no doubt expected the worst. 'In our most important gold field the arm of justice hangs powerlessly by her side, while a company of men, under the most hollow and hypocritical professions of a desire to respect the law are wantonly and openly trampling it underfoot', screamed the *Columbian*:

> It is simply a question of British Law vs. Lynch Law. . . . [with reference to Governor Seymour's visit] To go to the scene of strife unarmed with a force to *compel* submission will simply to be to toy with outlawry while the coveted treasure is being grabbed up.[37]

Calling for the imposition of 'martial law', the *Colonist* noted that 'by offering armed resistance to the mandate of a court' the Canadians were 'criminals' who 'went into court determined to obey the law if it was *with* them; [and] to break it if it was *against* them.'[38] The *Cariboo Sentinel* took issue with its competitors' treatment of the Grouse Creek 'War'. 'Victorians', the *Sentinel* speculated, 'no doubt wrought up to the highest pitch of excitement by the graphic descriptions of the warlike attitude of the Canadians, would be surprised if they were here.'

> Canadians and Flumites may be seen daily in the streets of Barkerville, habited in the usual miners' garb, saluting each other without the slightest appearance of hostility.[39]

The *Sentinel's* attempts to emphasize the peacefulness of the Cariboo were not aided by the events which followed, however.

A few days after Governor Seymour's arrival, the Canadian Company strode into Richfield, not, noted one anonymous writer 'in obedience to any order or summons', but at the suggestion of their leader, Cornelius Booth. Though Booth—the 'Talleyrand of the band'—assured his compatriots they would not be arrested, seven of their number were. Conveyed immediately to the courthouse, the seven received three-month sentences for resisting arrest (stemming from Magistrate Ball's earlier attempt to eject the Canadians from Grouse Creek); however, with the exception of one man, all refused to go to jail. Instead, they 'warned the constables not to touch any of them, and abused and blackguarded the Commissioner on the Bench!'[40] The seven told the court 'that if they had treated the Commissioner to more champagne &c. they would have won their case.'[41] Ball left the courtroom, and the Governor requested a parley with Booth. After extracting a promise from Seymour to commute the sentences to 48 hours' imprisonment, Booth *'persuaded* his comrades to walk towards the gaol, promising them that they would not be confined three days!'[42] This concession to the form of law was continued once the redoubtable Canadians arrived at the Richfield jail. There, wrote 'Crimea', 'they would not allow the doors of the jail to be locked upon them and had free access to all the Court house grounds during the term of their imprisonment.'[43] [. . .]

When Seymour left Richfield, he left behind conflicting impressions of what he accomplished. The Canadian Company believed they had secured a promise for a new trial, while the *Colonist* and the *Columbian* were convinced that Seymour had merely offered the services of Joseph Trutch, the Chief Commissioner of Lands and Works, as arbitrator. Added to this confusion was yet another round of vitriolic newspaper reports from Victoria, condemning the Governor's actions. Claiming that Governor Seymour's negotiation legitimized the actions of the Canadian 'mob', the *Colonist* predicted an end to the 'security of life and property in the country.'[44] The Canadians rejected arbitration, insisting that they would 'accept nothing less than the law allows them': a new trial.[45] [. . .]

Seymour then appointed Joseph Needham, Vancouver Island's Supreme Court

judge, as arbitrator. Needham arrived in Richfield in mid-September, prepared to try the Grouse Creek case (as well as other mining appeals) *de novo*.[46] Noting that every court had the power to suspend its rules if 'any technicality arises that might tend to defeat the ends of justice', the judge began hearing evidence in the *Canadian Company v. the Grouse Creek Flume Company* on 17 September. After two weeks of testimony, Needham awarded all of the disputed ground to the Flumites. 'I cannot be blind to the fact that much public excitement has existed with regard to this case', he told the court,

> but I do hope and believe that all will acquiesce in the decision of this court; I can only say that it has been arrived at after anxious consideration, and a simple desire to administer justice according to the law. I hope, and firmly believe, that armed alone with the authority of the law, a child may execute this judgment, and that no one will here be found whose wish is not to uphold and obey the judicial tribunals of this country—tribunals which have always been regarded by Englishmen as the fountain of justice, and the bulwark of freedom.[47]

With this plea for peace, Needham ended one of the most protracted disputes in the colony's short history, and one which was noted for the bitterness engendered between island and mainland as much as for that between the rival mining factions. It also ended Begbie's stormy tenure as mining appeal court judge. After 1867 the 'tyrant Judge' heard few mining cases, leaving them to his less controversial colleagues.[48]

* * *

These three cases have been discussed before by David Williams, who called them '*causes célèbres*'.[49] They were certainly that, and more, for *Aurora, Borealis,* and *Grouse Creek* illustrate the difficulty of, in Joseph Needham's words, 'administering justice according to the law.' The Supreme Court judge's distinction is an important one. While the Canadians and the Flumites were of one voice as to the ends of the law and the process of dispute resolution, they disagreed on how best to secure justice through the law. This was because of the variety of meanings the law in a colony as loosely organized as British Columbia. Their various definitions of the law revealed the importance of geography in determining its contours, as well as showing the limits of authority.

Despite their differences, Flumites and Canadians used the same language of laissez-faire capitalism, which linked liberty to the security of property, to frame criticisms and to justify their actions. The New Westminster *Columbian* and the Victoria *Colonist* contrasted 'British Law' with the Canadians' 'mob rule', and predicted an end to 'that security of life and property in the country which has ever been our proud boast.'

> Capital, finding its tenure insecure, will fly to countries where people are made to respect the laws, and where possession of property rests upon a more stable and secure foundation.[50]

At the same time, the Canadian Company, that 'mob' of 'footpads' and 'filibusters', used the very same language of law and property to predict the same ends if *its* demands were not met. 'There are three things the most despotic governments claim', Cornelius Booth told a crowd of 500 gathered at Fulton's saloon, 'namely the right to take property, liberty and life.'

> The first of these have already been taken from the Canadian Co., and there is but one step to the last. I repeat that these men do not wish to be looked upon as outlaws; they consider they have been unjustly shut out from having a hearing; and would be perfectly satisfied in obtaining one, even if a decision was given against them.[51]

The crowd agreed, as they had done in the wake of the *Borealis v. Watson* and the *Aurora v. Davis* cases, when they informed the colonial government that its laws and Begbie's administration of them were driving 'labor, capital and enterprise out of the Colony.'[52] To British Columbians on both sides of the Grouse Creek War, as well as the mining disputes that preceded it, just laws and legitimate authority were defined by their positive effect on economic development. Begbie's Chancery Court was viewed with contempt not only because the laws of chancery appeared capricious, but also, and perhaps more importantly, because of the costly delays associated with its proceedings. Jury trials could not guarantee satisfaction either, as *Aurora v. Davis* showed. Recourse to a jury trial was a poor alternative to Chancery because verdicts could be set aside by an 'arbitrary' judge. The 'tyranny' of Begbie's court lay in its unpredictability and inefficiency—the two enemies of capitalist enterprise.

Just as they used the same language and agreed on the ends that the law served, British Columbians on both sides of the Grouse Creek war recognized the same process of dispute resolution. The ends sought by those who opposed the government's administration were always to be achieved with the existing structures of formal dispute settlement. In *Borealis v. Watson*, Caribooites criticized the use of the Court of Chancery to resolve mining appeals because its ponderous proceedings were singularly unsuited to mining activity. But what did the miners propose as a solution? The establishment of a Court of Appeal! Similarly, in *Aurora v. Davis* arbitration was rejected in favour of trial by jury. And in the Grouse Creek war, the Canadian Company did not ask for public sanction of extralegal action (in fact, it did not consider that it was acting in an illegal manner), but for '*nothing less than the law allows us*': a full hearing of its case.[53] Indeed, as David Williams noted, both Cornelius Booth and John MacLaren visited Begbie in early July 1867 to ask for his intervention—surely an indication they had not lost faith in the legal options available.[54] Even after seven company members were arrested in August, the Canadians still demanded that the 'tyrant Judge' or his island counterpart replace Joseph Trutch as arbitrator.[55] Clearly, those who took issue with British Columbia's legal administration did not reject the structures of dispute resolution; rather it was to the official framework of English institutions that they looked for relief. In fact, the law might be seen as a kind of social cement holding colonists together.

If Caribooites agreed about the ends of the law and the institutional means of executing it, they took issue with what the law was and how to achieve justice through that law. British Columbians in other parts of the colony considered that a body of rules applied evenly and predictably ensured justice. Reflecting on the *Borealis* and *Aurora* cases, the *Colonist* pointed to Begbie's lack of legal experience as the cause of the trouble. 'Unlike Judge Needham', the newspaper reported, Begbie 'had no legal experience to recommend him, and it is by no means a matter of surprise that his decisions instead of partaking of that judicial clearness and point which are the universal characteristics of the decisions of English judges, should be generally rambling, disconnected and irrelevant.'[56] Nevertheless, both the *Sentinel* and the Canadians dismissed the Chief Commissioner of Lands and Works, Joseph Trutch, as a suitable adjudicator for the same reasons and called for the intervention of the Supreme Court: 'He [Trutch] lacks the legal acumen which is necessary to unravel those knotted points of law that are inseparably involved in the settlement of the dispute in question.' [. . .][57] 'Legal acumen' was not necessarily specialized knowledge, however. The valued acumen was a knowledge of community standards and local circumstance: what Caribooites wanted was law that was self-evident.

In the wake of *Aurora* and *Borealis*, Caribooites let it be known that 'common sense' was the chief hallmark of just laws and just administration. The *Cariboo Sentinel*

published a telling editorial emphasizing just this point by contrasting the conduct of Peter O'Reilly (the previous magistrate) with that of his predecessors and his successor, William Cox. Prior to O'Reilly's arrival, the mining court 'was virtually, if not nominally, a Court of Conscience.'

> Then the mining laws consisted of only a few proclamations issued from time to time by the Governor, and the Commissioner supplemented these with his own judgment. Since then extensive mining laws have been passed and partially consolidated. It was not until the administration of Mr. O'Reilly that this Court, by his false pretensions to legal ability, declared itself to be a Court of Equity or Law, or both combined . . . . The policy of Mr. Cox, on the other hand, was quite different: he made no pretensions to legal ability, yet his policy was at once most agreeable to the miners; he converted this Court back once again almost wholly into a Court of Conscience, and presided in it with no little success.

Cox's success, the *Sentinel* concluded, was due to the fact he was guided by 'common sense rather than a smattering of law.'[58]

As the *Sentinel's* editorial revealed, common sense was an important yardstick of the law's legitimacy. Sociologists argue that common sense occupies an important place in human interaction.[59] The strength and influence of common sense lies in its 'taken-for-granted' nature. Common sense is common knowledge; it is a body of truths that does not need explanation (and probably cannot be explained) for it is instantly recognized as self-evident.[60] According to sociologist Siegwart Lindenberg, common sense is a 'general baseline for human interaction.'[61] It is a frame of reference against which humans gauge events and understand the world as well as a 'court of appeal'.[62] 'Common sense', argue van Holthoon and Olson, 'provided the basis of appeal . . . to criticize and overthrow a more specialized and restrictive world view.'[63] By appealing to a body of self-evident truths, critics attempt to show that the status quo is unnatural and illogical. But the concept could just as easily be used to buttress the existing order of things. Just as often, notes philosopher Herman Parret, '"Use your common sense", "Behave commonsensically"—these mean "Be conventional", "Be conservative". . . . It is used to stop argument, fantasy and originality, and it is often a *deus ex machina*, a rhetorical device to express power.'[64] Given the ambiguous nature of common sense, literary critics argue that it is a powerful rhetorical device, 'part of "the formal language of ideological dispute".'[65]

Although common sense implied a commonality of experience that cut across political, social and economic divisions—indeed, this is part of its strength—it was rooted in a cultural and social matrix particular to a time and place. Concepts of common sense were tied to particular locales; they were, as anthropologist Clifford Geertz contended, part of 'local knowledge'.[66] As such, 'the law . . . is not a bounded set of norms, rules, principles and values . . . but part of a distinctive manner of imagining the real.'[67] Thus, when Caribooites appealed to common sense in criticizing the colonial legal administration, their meaning was clear only within their frame of reference. They wanted the law to be self-evident; however, what was common knowledge varied from place to place. Common sense dictated what was just, but because it was bounded by space and by local experience with the law, the concept had different meanings for different people. British Columbia's great distances, thin population and poor systems of communication accentuated the localism of the colony's mining population. The mainland lacked an internal coherence that would have narrowed the variations in common sense. Its communities were uncoupled from each other, as well as the administrative centres of New Westminster and Victoria.[68] In such a geographical context

a variety of concepts of law proliferated; the historian's task is to recreate that milieu so that others can appreciate it as 'commonsensical'.

The *Caribou Sentinel's* opposition of common sense and conscience on one hand, and law and equity on the other is important. A Court of Equity was another name for a Court of Chancery—not the miners' favourite legal institution, as Borealis showed. Initially, cases tried by equity courts had been resolved by applying the 'standards of what seems naturally just or right, as contrasted with the application . . . of a rule of law, which might not provide for such circumstances or provide for what seems unreasonable.'[69] By the early nineteenth century, however, the principles of equity had become a body of settled law rather than a personal and arbitrary assessment of fairness.[70] Ironically, though equitable jurisdiction evolved as a corrective to the inflexibility of the law, the Court of Chancery acquired a reputation as a morass of legal complexity and delay into which unwitting suitors could fall and never gain a settlement. When Caribooites equated Peter O'Reilly's tenure as Magistrate and Assistant Gold Commissioner with a 'Court of Equity or Law', and contrasted it with Cox's 'common sense', they revealed that they considered the two kinds of knowledge to be antithetical. The complexities of equity and statute law were far from self-evident truths; in fact, they were 'pretensions' that caused unnecessary delays and thwarted justice. Cox's common sense cut through all this. He circumvented legal technicalities by letting 'conscience' guide his decisions. In the eyes of Caribooites, Cox's 'court of conscience' was the surest route to justice. Yet courts of conscience were, in legal parlance, merely another name for courts of equity or chancery![71] Why was Cox's 'conscience'—his ability to apply 'standards of what seems naturally just or right'— superior to Begbie's? Why, in short, was the magistrate's common sense superior to that of the Supreme Court judge?

Caribooites recognized the magistrate's decisions and actions as expressions of common sense because he was part of their community. Common sense was bounded by locale and rooted in specific constellations of social relations. Keith Wrightson shows that magistrates, constables and jurymen were caught between 'different kinds of order' in which the execution of the law had to be balanced against the more tangible pressures of familiarity in the face-to-face communities of seventeenth-century England.[72] Nineteenth-century British Columbia demonstrates the same pattern. Because the colony's magistrates were a part of the communities they administered, they quickly became enmeshed in the politics of familiarity, a situation that both aided and limited their ability to execute the law. William Cox's knowledge of miners and mining won him the admiration and support of 490 of his neighbours, who petitioned against his removal in 1866. 'From the very long acquaintance we have had with Mr. Cox, and the intimate knowledge he has acquired of mining in Cariboo, we consider him much better qualified for the office than any other gentleman in this Colony', they wrote. 'Mr. Cox's conduct . . . has been such as to inspire the public with the utmost confidence in his integrity, . . . while his judicial decisions have had the effect of checking litigation.'[73] These judicial decisions were often unconventional: on one occasion the magistrate settled a mining court claim by making the opposing parties race from the steps of the Richfield Court House to the disputed ground—winner take all. On another occasion Cox swore in Chinese witnesses by decapitating a chicken instead of administering the usual and less spectacular oath.[74]

Cox's 'intimate knowledge' consisted of a proper understanding of community morals, and it was this empathy that underlay justice in the Cariboo. Community sentiment about what was right and wrong made it impossible to keep the Canadian Company under lock and key. Henry Maynard Ball, whose misfortune it was to preside over the Grouse Creek dispute, failed because 'he had but little experience in the mining districts'.[75] Familiarity also limited the ineffectiveness of enforcement. For the most part, policing was done by special constables, sworn in from the local population as the need arose. In the Grouse Creek case the special constables, who as men of capital and business presumably stood to lose from the unrest, were of no use in ejecting their neighbours; nor could the district's jailer incarcerate the Canadians. 'The public feeling was rather in favour of the Canadians', complained Frederick Seymour. 'At all events no one would come forward to assist the Government in an emergency.'[76]

Despite the constraints of familiarity on the execution of the law, British Columbians would have it no other way. The interventions of outsiders in their affairs were considered despotic, even when that intervention was done by a figure as magisterial as a Supreme Court judge. In this context, juries became an important bridge between law and justice. '[T]his community', reported the Richfield Grand Jury,

> owing to its isolated position, the peculiarity of its interests, and especially its national origin, has a decided preference for local trial by jury, and is extremely jealous of all verdicts by its peers. . . .[77]

The *Cariboo Sentinel* was even more direct, asserting that 'a man is wrong when almost every person in the community thinks and says he is wrong.'[78] When Begbie overturned the jury verdict in *Aurora v. Davis*, he not only breached what Caribooites perceived to be established practice, he also burned the only bridge between the law as a set of overarching rules and as a set of social and locally constructed norms. The judge's cavalier treatment of the jury in this and other cases led many colonists to conclude that Begbie did not consider them qualified to pass judgement on their peers. What these British Columbians objected to was not so much Begbie's failure to adhere to statute law and common law practice as the fact that he was not guided by the same self-evident truths as they were. He could not have been. The Supreme Court judge was outside their community: he resided in Victoria, visiting the colony's far-flung communities only once a year. His circuits were metaphors for his status as an outsider. Begbie's actions and decisions appeared arbitrary, particularly in a colony that lacked the social organization that would support the arbitrariness of paternal authority. Because his decisions were not necessarily commonsensical and because of the important role the law played in establishing some cohesion in the colony, Begbie's actions and decisions not only threatened the colonists' economic security but also eroded one of the few bonds tying them together.

Caribooites also considered the Grouse Creek Flume Company an outsider. Not only were the Flumites based in Victoria, headed by one of the city's largest merchants, but they also represented 'big capital' in a region where small, independent entrepreneurs were the norm.[79] The Canadians styled themselves a 'company', but their Victoria opponents were the real thing. The Grouse Creek Flume Company was a joint stock venture, capitalized to the tune of $50,000. The Flumites were harbingers of a different kind of resource entrepreneur in British Columbia. By the late 1860s, most of the easily accessible surface gold in the Cariboo was gone. Continued success on the upper country creeks depended on a hydraulic process which required a substantial capital investment to construct the necessary flumes. Such an investment was beyond the means of most independent miners. Part of the support for the Canadians and the wrath directed at Begbie likely stemmed from an antipathy toward this form of large corporate enterprise that would eventually dominate resource exploitation and push out the smaller upper country operations.

Conflicting concepts of law were central to the controversies surrounding the administration of British Columbia's mining laws in the colonial period. While recent writing in Canadian legal history has cast a critical eye on the law, revealing its normative nature, few studies deal with the variety of meanings the law could take on.[80] As I have discussed, despite its detached nature, the law gained much of its meaning through the very local experiences people had with it. [. . .]

The Grouse Creek War and the events leading to it demonstrate the importance of geography in creating 'local frames of awareness' that shape social meaning.[81] The law Caribooites wanted had to be self-evident; it had to be commonsensical. Because common sense was *local* knowledge, however, its meaning was spatially limited. This localism was accentuated by the colony's geography, which effectively precluded the integration of the archipelago of small settlements that was British Columbia. Geographers and sociologists have recognized that space is deeply implicated in social life.[82] Because human relations and the extension of authority are spatially as well as socially constructed, understanding what the law means involves more than contextualizing behaviour in time. Distant places like the Cariboo were uncoupled from New Westminster and Victoria, the colony's centres of authority.[83] In this spatial context, law and authority were rooted in specific and local constellations of social relations. For Caribooites, the law was more a collection of community norms than a set of hard-and-fast rules. Face-to-face relations, the politics of the personal and personality loomed large in determining authority. Being recognized as an authority conveyed more power in these localized settings than being *in* authority by virtue of some extra-community sanction.[84]

Although I have put local knowledge at the crux of understanding behaviour, local frames of reference were not the only ones that influenced the meaning of law. On Grouse Creek, common sense may have gone a long way to shape what the law meant to British Columbians, but clearly the larger framework provided by the structure, institutions, and traditions of the common law itself also played an important role.[85] Magistrate William Cox's decisions may have been commonsensical, but he and those who came before him still operated within a set of rules and procedures that at least nominally constrained action and provided a standard for measuring legality. As I discussed, British Columbians on both sides of the Grouse Creek War and the disputes that led to it never challenged the authority of the law and its institutions; instead, they took issue with their administration and looked to the existing forms of law for redress. Perhaps more important in shaping the social meaning of the law than its forms were its traditions and the expectations they created. The 'rule of law' promised freedom from the dictates of arbitrary sovereigns for all, no matter their condition. The idea of the rule of law became intimately tied to the security of life and property, and became the keystone of English liberty. For British colonists, the law was an important source of unity, particularly in the years immediately following settlement. Though differences brought them before a magistrate, the British Columbians who resorted to the law were tied together in a common adversarial process that imposed a degree of structure, organization, and predictability on social relationships in a colony where such characteristics were rare commodities. More broadly, both for those directly involved in litigation and for those who perhaps afterwards discussed and criticized its administration, the law was a link to and a symbol of a common, storied, and secure past that stood in marked contrast to the new and alien environment they found themselves in. The common law conferred citizenship to colonists whose sense of place had been eroded by the experience of migration. Much of the social meaning of the law, then, was provided by the forms and traditions of the law itself—forms and traditions which had

their genesis outside the locale that has been the focus of my analysis.

Although they were physically distant from the main centres of population, as well as from the rest of British North America, Caribooites were tied to another frame of reference through extensive webs of credit: the wider world of commercial capitalism. So dominant was economic activity in the collective experience of the colony that the language of laissez-faire infused British Columbians' discussions of the law and provided the standard with which they measured political authority. Begbie's actions and decisions provoked the reactions they did because they were the antithesis of what commercial capitalist enterprise demanded and defined as the criteria for legitimate action: efficiency, predictability, and standardization.

Though British Columbians on both sides of the mining disputes demanded these characteristics of the law and conceived of it as an instrument of economic development, there was room for a diversity of opinion because of the spatial context in which the law was administered. Divergent concepts of law became apparent only when the localism of the colony was penetrated by the annual circuits of British Columbia's Supreme Court. Begbie and the Supreme Court represented a different level of law and a different level of social interaction. To Caribooites, the Supreme Court judge was an outsider; his reasoning and decisions were not self-evident because he operated in a world outside the community of local interaction. To be effective, Begbie and his fellow magistrates had to balance the demands of colonial administration with local sentiment. With these conflicting demands, 'administering justice according to the law' was a difficult, and sometimes impossible, task. This was Gaggin's 'delicate game', and it was one that would be played over and over again amid the western mountains.

NOTES

1. Gaggin to the Colonial Secretary, Douglas, B.C., 2 July 1862. British Columbia Archives and Records Services (hereafter bcars), Colonial Correspondence, GR 1372, reel B-1330, file 621/14. For more on this episode and Gaggin see Dorothy Blakey Smith, '"Poor Gaggin": Irish Misfit in the Colonial Service', *BC Studies* 32 (Winter 1976–7) 41–63.

2. Ibid.

3. Cited in Smith, '"Poor Gaggin"', 45.

4. Ibid., 47.

5. For instance, see Clifford Geertz, 'Local Knowledge: Fact and Law in Comparative Perspective', in his *Local Knowledge: Further Essays in Interpretive Anthropology* (New York, 1983); John L. Comaroff and Simon Roberts, *Rules and Processes: the Cultural Logic of Dispute in an African Context* (Chicago, 1981) Lawrence Rosen, *Bargaining for Reality: The Construction of Social Relations in a Muslim Community* (Chicago, 1984) and his 'Islamic "Case Law" and the Logic of Consequence', in June Starr and Jane F. Collier, eds., *History and Power in the Study of Law: New Directions in Legal Anthropology* (Ithaca, N.Y., 1989), 302–19. In the latter essay, Rosen notes 'Law is . . . one domain in which a culture may reveal itself. But like politics, marriage, and exchange, it is an arena in which people must act, and in doing so they must draw on their assumptions, connections, and beliefs to make their acts effective and comprehensible. In the Islamic world, as in many other places, the world of formal courts offers a stage—as intense as ritual, as demonstrative as war— through which a society reveals itself to its own people as much as to the outside world' [318]. This essay shares Rosen's assumptions about the law and what it can reveal about society.

6. See Hubert Howe Bancroft, *Popular Tribunals* (San Francisco, 1887), v. 1, Chapter Ten; Charles Shinn, *Mining Camps: a Study in American Frontier Government*; and on California and British Columbia, David Ricardo Williams, 'The Administration of Civil and Criminal Justice in the Mining Camps and Frontier Communities of British Columbia', in Louis Knafla, ed., *Law and Justice in a New Land: Essays in Western Canadian Legal History* (Calgary, 1986).

7. Williams, 217–9.

8. See Shinn, Introduction.

9. Morley Arthur Underwood, 'Governor Douglas and the Miners, 1858–1859', University of British Columbia B.A. Essay, 1974.

10. *The Gold Fields Act, 1859* [31 August 1859]; William J. Trimble, *The Mining Advance into the Inland Empire* (Madison, Wisconsin, 1914), 187–214, 336–7.

11. Rules and Regulations for the Working of Gold Mines under the 'Gold Fields Act 1859' [7 September 1859]; Rules and Regulations for the working of Gold Mines, issued in conformity with the 'Gold Fields Act, 1859' (Bench Diggings) [6 January 1860]; Rules and Regulations under the 'Gold Fields Act, 1859' (Ditches) [29 September 1862]; Further Rules and Regulations under the 'Gold Fields Act, 1859' [24 February 1863]; Proclamation amending the 'Gold Fields Act, 1859' [25 March 1863]; The Mining District Act, 1863 [27 May 1863]; The Mining Drains Act, 1864 [1 February 1864]; An Ordinance to extend and improve the Laws relating to Gold Mining [26 February 1864] and An Ordinance to amend and consolidate the Gold Mining Laws [28 March 1865]; An Ordinance to amend the Laws relating to Gold Mining, 2 April 1867.

12. On this theme, and more generally, the idea that mining society was not as disorganized as traditionally thought, see Thomas Stone, *Miners' Justice: Migration, Law and Order on the Alaska-Yukon Frontier, 1873–1902* (New York, 1988).

13. Williams discusses them in ' . . . The Man for a New Country': Sir Matthew Baillie Begbie (Sidney, BC, 1977), 68–80.

14. Ibid.

15. A Court of Chancery is a court that has jurisdiction in equity; that is, it resolves disputes according to the rules and procedures of equity rather than the rules and procedures of common law. Though the principles of equity initially reflected the chancellor's own arbitrary and sometimes idiosyncratic ideas of justice (the Tudor Court of Star Chamber

was the repository and dispensary of equity, for instance), over the seventeenth, eighteenth and early nineteenth centuries the principles of equity evolved into a more settled body of rules. Chancery never lost its negative reputation for arbitrary, protracted, and unnecessarily complex proceedings, however (see Charles Dickens' *Bleak House* (1859), for instance). Until 1870, Matthew Baillie Begbie was British Columbia's only Supreme Court Judge. This meant that the division of labour in the colony's superior court was one in name only. Begbie acted as judge in assize, nisi prius, appeal, chancery, bankruptcy, probate, and admiralty cases, often in the same session.

16. Letter from 'Miner', *Cariboo Sentinel*, 31 May 1866.
17. 'The British Columbia Judiciary', *British Colonist*, reprinted in *Cariboo Sentinel*, 2 July 1866.
18. 'Irresponsible Deputies', *Cariboo Sentinel*, 31 May 1866.
19. Ibid.
20. 'Supreme Court', *Cariboo Sentinel*, 18 June 1866.
21. Ibid.
22. *Cariboo Sentinel*, 21 June 1866.
23. Ibid.
24. 'Mass Meeting', *Cariboo Sentinel*, 25 June 1866.
25. Ibid. Also see 'The Tyrant Judge', *British Colonist*, 28 June 1866; 'Another Verdict Set Aside', and 'From Cariboo', *British Columbian*, 27 June and 4 July 1866.
26. An Ordinance to amend the Laws relating to Gold Mining [2 April 1867].
27. Nind to O'Reilly, Yahwalpa, Pimpama, Brisbane, Queensland, 11 April 1868. O'Reilly Family Papers. BCARS. Add. MSS. 412, v. 1, file 6a.
28. *Canadian Company v. Grouse Creek Flume Co., Ltd.*, 27 September 1867. Archer Martin, *Reports of Mining Cases decided by the Courts of British Columbia and the Courts of Appeal therefrom to the 1st of October, 1902. . . .* (Toronto, 1903), 3–8.
29. 'Magistrate's Court', *Cariboo Sentinel*, 3 June 1867. Spalding heard the case on 22 April 1867, and the order ejecting the Canadian Company was issued on 24 April.
30. Ibid.
31. 'Grouse Creek Difficulty', *Cariboo Sentinel*, 15 July 1867.
32. Letter to the Editor from C. Booth, dated 13 July 1867. *Cariboo Sentinel*, 15 July 1867.
33. 'Public Meeting', Cariboo Sentinel, 15 July 1989.
34. 'Grouse Creek Troubles—Great Excitement', *Cariboo Sentinel*, 18 July 1867.
35. Seymour to Buckingham and Chandos, New Westminster, 16 August 1867. CO 60/28. NAC. MG 11, reel B-97, 333.
36. Ibid.
37. 'The Situation', *British Columbian*, 27 July 1867.
38. 'The Grouse Greek Difficulty', *British Colonist*, 24 July 1867.
39. 'The Governor and the Grouse Creek Difficulty', *Cariboo Sentinel*, 12 August 1867.
40. Anonymous letter to the Editor, dated Williams Creek, 21 August 1867, *British Colonist*, 2 September 1867.
41. Letter to the Editor from 'Crimea', dated Richfield, 20 August 1867, *British Colonist*, 9 September 1867.
42. Anonymous letter to the Editor, dated Williams Creek, 21 August 1867, *British Colonist*, 2 September 1867.
43. Letter to the Editor from 'Crimea', dated Richfield, 20 August 1867, *British Colonist*, 9 September 1867.
44. 'The Grouse Creek War', *British Colonist*, 29 July 1867; also see 'The Grouse Creek Imbroglio', 19 August 1867, and 'The Patched Up Peace on Grouse Creek', 23 August 1867.
45. Resolution passed by the Canadian Company, at Booth's Saloon, Grouse Creek, 30 August 1867. Reprinted in 'Grouse Creek Dispute Again', *Cariboo Sentinel*, 2 September 1867.
46. *Cariboo Sentinel*, 16 September 1867.
47. *Canadian Company v. Grouse Creek Flume Co., Ltd.*, 27 September 1867. Archer Martin, *Reports of Mining Cases. . . .*, 8.
48. 'Tyrant Judge' from 'The Tyrant Judge', *British Colonist*, 28 June 1866. For Begbie and mining cases after 1867, see Williams, ' . . . *The Man for a New Country*', 80.
49. Williams, ' . . . *The Man for a New Country*', 68.
50. 'The Grouse Creek "War"', *British Colonist*, 29 July 1867.

51. 'Public Meeting', *Cariboo Sentinel*, 15 July 1867.

52. 'Mass Meeting', *Cariboo Sentinel*, 25 June 1866.

53. Emphasis added. Resolution passed at a meeting of the members of the Canadian Mining Company, convened at Booth's Saloon, Grouse Greek, on the evening of the 30th August 1867. 'Grouse Creek Dispute Again', *Cariboo Sentinel*, 2 September 1867.

54. Williams, ' . . . *The Man for a New Country*', 76.

55. Letter to the Editor from Cornelius Booth, dated 31 August 1867, *Cariboo Sentinel*, 2 September 1867.

56. 'British Columbia's Judiciary', *British Colonist*, reprinted in the Cariboo Sentinel, 2 July 1866.

57. 'The Grouse Creek Dispute Again', *Cariboo Sentinel*, 2 September 1867.

58. 'The Administration of the Mining Laws', *Cariboo Sentinel*, 15 December 1866.

59. Frits van Holthoon and David R. Olson, eds., 'Introduction', *Common Sense: The Foundations for Social Sciences* (Lanham, Maryland, 1987); Thomas Luckmann, 'Some Thoughts on Common Sense and Science', in van Holthoon and Olson, eds., 179–98; Siegwart Lindenberg, 'Common Sense and Social Structure: A Sociological View', in van Holthoon and Olson, eds., 199–216.

60. Van Holthoon and Olson, 'Introduction', 3–4.

61. Lindenberg, 'Common Sense and Social Structure', 202–03.

62. Ibid.; 'court of appeal' from van Holthoon and Olson, 'Introduction', 3.

63. Van Holthoon and Olson, 'Introduction,' 3.

64. Herman Parret, 'Common Sense: From Certainty to Happiness', in van Holthoon and Olson, eds., 19.

65. Van Holthoon and Olson, eds., 'Introduction', 8.

66. Clifford Geertz, 'Local Knowledge: Fact and Law in Comparative Perspective', in his *Local Knowledge: Further Essays in Interpretive Anthropology*.

67. Ibid., 173.

68. Anthony Giddens discusses the influence of space on the integration of societies. The key to integration is the extension or the 'stretching' of experience over time and space (something he calls 'time-space distanciation'). When people do not share common understandings of time and space the communities they live in become 'uncoupled' from each other and from the central administrative state, thus posing problems for the exercise of power (i.e., the regulation of behaviour by the state). See his *A Contemporary Critique of Historical Materialism* (Oxford, 1981), 65–7.

69. David M. Walker, 'Equity', *The Oxford Companion to the Law* (Oxford, 1980), 424.

70. Ibid., 'Chancery', 204.

71. On courts of chancery and conscience, David Walker notes 'The Court of Chancery was sometimes referred to as a court of conscience because its jurisdiction was originally founded on relief granted by the Chancellor, as Keeper of the King's Conscience, in circumstances where equity and justice demanded it', See his *Oxford Companion to the Law*, 272.

72. Wrightson, 'Two Concepts of Order: justices, constables, and jurymen in seventeenth-century England'. In John Brewer and John Styles, eds., *An Ungovernable People: the English and their Law in the Seventeenth and Eighteenth Centuries* (London, 1980).

73. Petition dated Williams Creek, B.C., 3 November 1866. Colonial Correspondence. BCARS. GR 1372, reel B-1355, f 1352.

74. Both examples from Margaret Ormsby, *British Columbia: A History* (Toronto, 1958), 181.

75. Seymour to Buckingham and Chandos, New Westminster, 12 May 1868. CO 60/32. NAC. MG 11, reel B-100, 368.

76. Seymour to Buckingham and Chandos, Victoria, 4 September 1867. CO 60/29. NAC. MG 11, reel B-97, 5.

77. 'From Cariboo', *British Colonist*, 4 July 1866.

78. 'The Administration of Justice', *Cariboo Sentinel*, 30 November 866.

79. Selim Franklin was the president of the Grouse Creek Flume Company, and J.P. Cranford was its treasurer.

80. On gender bias, see Constance Backhouse's work, including 'Shifting Patterns of Nineteenth Century Canadian Custody Law', in D.H. Flaherty, ed., *Essays in the History of Canadian Law* (Toronto, 1981), v. 1, 212–48; and 'Nineteenth Century Canadian Rape Law, 1800–1892', in Flaherty, ed., *Essays in the History of Canadian Law* (Toronto, 1984), v. 2, 200–47; on class bias in enforcement, see Michael Katz *et. al.*, *The Social Organization*

of Early Industrial Capitalism (Cambridge, Massachusetts, 1982), Chapter Six and Nancy Kay Parker, 'The Capillary Level of Power: Methods and Hypotheses for the Study of Law and Society in Late-Nineteenth Century Victoria, British Columbia', University of Victoria M.A. thesis (history), 1987.

81. Geertz, *Local Knowledge*, 61; cited in Aletta Biersack, 'Local Knowledge, Local History: Geertz and Beyond', in Lynn Hunt, ed., *The New Cultural History* (Berkeley, 1988), 82.

82. According to geographers Jennifer Wolch and Michael Dear, space impinges on social practices in three generalized ways: first, social relations are *constituted* through space; they are *constrained* by space; and they are *mediated* by space. For instance, to understand law and authority we must look at how geography influences the construction of legal institutions (the constitutive role of space); how distance hinders or facilitates the imposition and articulation of law and legal institutions (the constraining role of space); and finally how space facilitates the construction of the social meanings of the law (the mediating role of space). See Michael Dear and Jennifer Wolch, 'How Territory Shapes Social Life', in Wolch and Dear, eds., *The Power of Geography: How Territory Shapes Social Life* (Boston, 1989), 9.

83. Giddens, *A Contemporary Critique of Historical Materialism*, 65–6.

84. Stephen Lukes, 'Power and Authority', in Tom Bottomore and Robert Nisbet, eds., *A History of Sociological Thought* (New York, 1978).

85. On this theme see Greg Marquis, 'Doing Justice to "British Justice": Law, Ideology and Canadian Historiography', in W. Wesley Pue and Barry Wright, eds., *Canadian Perspectives on Law and Society: Issues in Legal History* (Ottawa, 1988), 43–69.

---

4   From Daniel Marshall, 'Mapping the New El Dorado: The Fraser River Gold Rush and the Appropriation of Native Space', in Ted Binnema and Susan Neylan, eds., *New Histories for Old: Changing Perspectives on Canada's Native Pasts* (Vancouver: UBC Press, 2007), 119–44.

You can not ascend the mountains, towards the mining towns or pass from one mining camp to another, without noticing the contrast in the scenes around you to anything you ever saw before . . . Men met in groups packing their provisions; then a train of Indians . . . Anon you met throngs of Chinamen packing up the river; they pass and greet you in broken English with, 'how do you do John', . . . Next comes the Negro, with a polite 'good morning sar', or Chileano, Mexican or Kanaka, each with a heavy load.

—*Victoria Gazette* (1858)[1]

In describing the Fraser River gold rush of 1858, most academics have been content to offer the image of as many as thirty thousand miners descending upon New Caledonia, all of them 'Old Californians' of primarily Anglo-American origin. Certainly, one of the principal cultural forces that existed during this time was that of the California mining world, in addition to the fur trade and British worlds represented by the Hudson's Bay Company (HBC) and their Native allies and the neighbouring colony of Vancouver Island, respectively. These three worlds together represented the dominant political, economic, and social influences that defined the cataclysmic year of 1858, although to the exclusion of racial and ethnic minorities that had also joined the rush north. One of the most permanent indications of this racial and ethnic diversity can still be found today in the place names that continue to exist along the banks of the Fraser River—names such as China Bar, Kanaka Bar, or Nicaragua Bar—yet names that are but a mere residue of the flood tide of the California mining frontier that receded as quickly as it had risen to encompass British Columbia. These gold-rush place names that existed in 1858–9, far greater in number then, are evidence of the multiethnic and racial composition of the BC rush and, more particularly, evidence of the ethnic and racial segregation embedded in the very geography of this waterway. California mining culture appropriated the Native cultural landscape of the Fraser and brought with it the ethnic and racial tensions that marked the California goldfields. Evidence of both of these processes was present in the myriad gold-rush bar names stretching from south of Fort Hope to just north of Lillooet.

[. . .]

These landmark names are explored as the spatial-discursive forms that the gold-mining culture used to stake out its presence in the Fraser River corridor. This geographical naming is a process that Paul Carter defines as 'transforming space into place, the intentional world of the texts.'[2] It is within this theoretical context that the historical significance of gold-rush bar place names will be established. In addition, the existence of such place names today may be seen as legitimizing both the colonial presence along the Fraser River and the continued occupation of Native lands and culture.

Prior to the gold rush, Native peoples had inhabited the lands of the Fraser River corridor for millennia, and the gravel bars and bench lands renamed by the California mining frontier occurred where ancient place names had long existed. To the non-Native miner, a stream, river, or lake represented the practical power of water that would assist in washing the landscape in the pursuit of gold. A canyon wall or sheer rock cliff was considered an impediment to developing the mines. But to the First Nations of the region, the natural watercourses and pools were home to spiritual beings, while the boulders, mountains, and rock spires were markers steeped in the oral history of these peoples. Writing of the Coast Salish peoples known as the Stó:lō (who inhabit the lower

Fraser River), historian Keith Carlson points to the larger spiritual, significance of the Native world that these miners entered: 'The Rocks and other objects [known as transformer sites] bear witness to the unique and longstanding relationship between the Stó:lō and the land and resources of Stó:lō territory.' Carlson continues: 'the Stó:lō walk simultaneously through both spiritual and physical realms of this landscape, connected to the Creator through the land itself . . . transformer sites are akin to Catholic stations of the cross, each a unique and integral feature of a larger narrative, each physically embodying the Creator's existence, actions and relationship to mankind.'[3] Sonny McHalsie, a Stó:lō cultural advisor, states that these stl'áleqem sites (locations inhabited by spiritual beings known as stl'áleqem) 'are both sacred and immovable, and stl'áleqem themselves are essential to Stó:lō well-being.'[4] It was into this seemingly permanent and sacred world of longstanding that tens of thousands of goldseekers rushed, bringing not only their picks, pans, and shovels but also transplanting large-scale water companies from California that drained lakes and diverted streams, while early road builders levelled many of the natural rock monoliths that held the history of countless generations. This rapid despoiling of the Native world was not limited to the rapacious designs of Anglo-Americans, but, in this one instance, all goldseekers of varying race and ethnicity pursued a common goal in the single-minded pursuit of gold.

Many witnesses to the actual events of 1858 recorded the extent of ethnic and racial diversity. Landing at Victoria, James Bell wrote that 'every country of the world seemed to be presented.'[5] Touring Yale in June 1858, Dr. Carl Friesach, a professor of mathematics and later chief of the Observatory of Austria, believed that '[i]t would be difficult to find in one place a greater mixture of different nationalities. Americans were in the majority—California, especially had sent a large contingent. Then followed the Germans, French, and the Chinese. Next come Italians, Spaniards, Poles, etc.

The feminine population consisted of only six.'[6] Governor James Douglas was undoubtedly relieved to see such a cosmopolitan mix: 'There is no congeniality of feeling among the emigrants', he initially concluded, 'and provided there be no generally felt grievance to unite them in one common cause there will, in my opinion, always be a great majority of the population ready to support the government.'[7]

If there was little rapport found among emigrants, it can be safely assumed that such a representative sample of Californian society also embraced the racial and ethnic animosities for which California was famous. Like the Fraser River region, California represented all the nations of the world. J.S. Holliday's well-known work, *The World Rushed In*, aptly describes the similar cultural geography of California while recalling the splendid diversity of gold-rush place names of the past. 'California's dynamic intermingling', he stated, 'was colorfully reflected in the names of mining camps and towns: German Bar, Iowa Hill, Irish Creek, Cape Cod Bar, Tennessee Creek, Chinese Camp, Georgia Slide, Dutch Flat, French Corral, Michigan Bluffs, Illinois Town, Nigger Hill, Washington, Boston, Bunker Hill, Italian Bar, Dixie Valley, Vermont Bar and Kanaka Bar.'[8] Compare to this list the brief tallying of BC bar names provided by Alfred Waddington to the *Victoria Gazette* on 15 September 1858. Waddington's reconnaissance of the goldfields examined a twenty-three-kilometre stretch of claims that ran from below Fort Hope to Fort Yale. At the commencement of his trip, he related: 'I now started in my canoe [Sept. 7th] at 8 in the morning . . . and visited every bar in succession up to Fort Yale as follows: Fifty-Four Forty Bar, Union, Deadwood, Express, American, Puget Sound, Victoria, Yankee Doodle, Eagle, Alfred, Sacramento, Texas, Emory's, Rocky, Hill's, Casey, and Fort Yale.'[9] One can see by this list that many of the Fraser River names are not only as colourful as are their Californian equivalents but also reflect ethnicity. Yet they also give the impression of an American-dominated gold rush, and this is not

completely accurate.[10] There were, in fact, at least a hundred different gold-rush bar names along the full extent of the Fraser in 1858 and 1859; although only a few have found a permanent place in the toponymy of the Fraser River landscape, many of the original names were neither American nor British in origin.

If the events of 1858 are followed more closely, it becomes apparent that there were two distinct periods in the initial year of the gold rush. There were also two distinct regions, both dictated by the natural flow of the Fraser and defined by the peculiar geography found above Fort Yale: two regions, two times, and two distinctly different human geographies.

Initial cartography of the Fraser River reflected the difficult terrain that early explorations encountered. In 1808, upon descending the watercourse of Hell's Gate and the approach to Black Canyon, Simon Fraser declared, 'It is so wild that I cannot find words to describe our situation at times. We had to pass where no human being should venture.'[11] David Thompson's map of this region recorded that three separate portage sites were required before navigation would again be possible above Fort Yale.[12] All subsequent maps pinpointed Fort Yale as the head of navigation for the Fraser due to the impassable nature of the falls above, particularly once the river swelled during late spring and summer. The falls between Spuzzum and Yale also seemed to have acted as a natural dividing line for rival Native groups. A.C. Anderson, the HBC's acknowledged authority on the geography of the region, claimed that 'a ceaseless feud . . . prevail[ed] between the Couteau [Nlaka'pamux] and the lower Indians [Stó:lō], who differ from each other in many respects.'[13] Natives along the upper Fraser River and Thompson River were much more hostile than the Stó:lō towards the Americans (or 'Boston Men', as they were known) who had attempted early intrusions into their country.[14] When, as a consequence of unique geography and the potential enmity of the Nlaka'pamux, the gold rush commenced in spring of 1858, the vast majority of miners were prevented from prospecting further than the Fort Yale vicinity. Most remained within a short twenty-three-kilometre stretch of waterway below the falls. Prior to this, the earliest non-Native gold-seekers on the Fraser, mainly from neighbouring Washington and Oregon territories, had worked their placer claims before the spring thaw and consequent rise of the river.[15]

Individuals such as James Moore, one of the first miners from California, confirmed that any reconnaissance above Yale was essentially impossible until the retreat of summer flood conditions in late fall.[16] Once news of Hill's Bar and other lucrative claims had reached the outside world via newspaper reports printed in Pacific Northwest locales and reprinted by San Francisco editors, large numbers of California miners flooded into British Columbia just as the Fraser deluged its banks.[17] Then commenced a waiting game by those all too impatient to enter the Upper Country in order to stake out the unclaimed stretches of river, the richest diggings along the lower Fraser already having been claimed. By July, as many as 6,000 sojourned in Victoria ready to embark at a moment's notice once the river had fallen.[18] Moore claimed that at least twenty thousand lingered at Yale during the high-water mark.[19] California merchant James Bell described the scene: 'Close above Yale, the river cuts its way through the Cascade Mountains, causing deep foaming chasms, inaccessible either by water, or land, thus have the body of miners been shut off from the Upper Country.' Bell further lamented that 'there accumulated around Yale, an immense crowd of people. The River at the time was swelled to its greatest hight [sic], caused by the melting of snow on the mountains; The best diggings were all under water, provisions were scarce, consequently high in price. The snow covered Cascade Mountains frowned above, forbidding farther approach.'[20]

[. . .]

News of the gold discoveries had not reached California until March, and, consequently, as the water rose, a flood tide of emigration began 'at the most unpropitious moment . . . only to meet with discouragement and disappointment.'[21] With all the accessible gold-rush bars on the lower Fraser taken, the newly arrived were confronted with three choices: either return to California, wait for months until the waters receded, or attempt to push on into the upper reaches of the river. For those few who chose the last alternative, Henry De Groot related that 'all arrived so utterly impoverished, or completely broken down, as to be unfit to do anything.'[22] And yet, along with certain prospectors who climbed the river in early 1858, many goldseekers with less to lose were compelled to advance beyond Fort Yale.[23] In particular were those individuals recently persecuted in the California goldfields—individuals who undoubtedly preferred a universally applied miner's licence as instituted in New Caledonia to the California foreign miner's head tax.[24] For such people, returning south was not an attractive option as xenophobic agitation started in 1849 and, in the early 1850s, drove many 'aliens' from Californian mines.

In 1858, J.C. Bryant, a Cornish miner who travelled to British Columbia via the circuitous route of the copper mines of Lake Superior, afterwards Nicaragua, and thence to Grass Valley, California, related a scene from Fort Hope that would not have been out of character had it occurred in the Golden State. Bryant watched as a boat, captained by a white man, approached near the banks of the HBC outpost carrying a large number of Chinese miners. He recounted that 'as the boat with the Chinese crew came alongside of the bank, a crowd of Californians lined the top and declared that no Chinese would land there. The white man pleaded that he had been paid to transport these Chinese to Fort Hope . . . "Well, it doesn't matter whether you are paid or not, no Chinese will land at Fort Hope. We'll see who is going to have the say about whether Chinese come here or not. We say they shall not", said the Californian crowd.'[25] The Californians were overruled, however, as HBC chief trader Donald McLean happened to arrive on the scene,

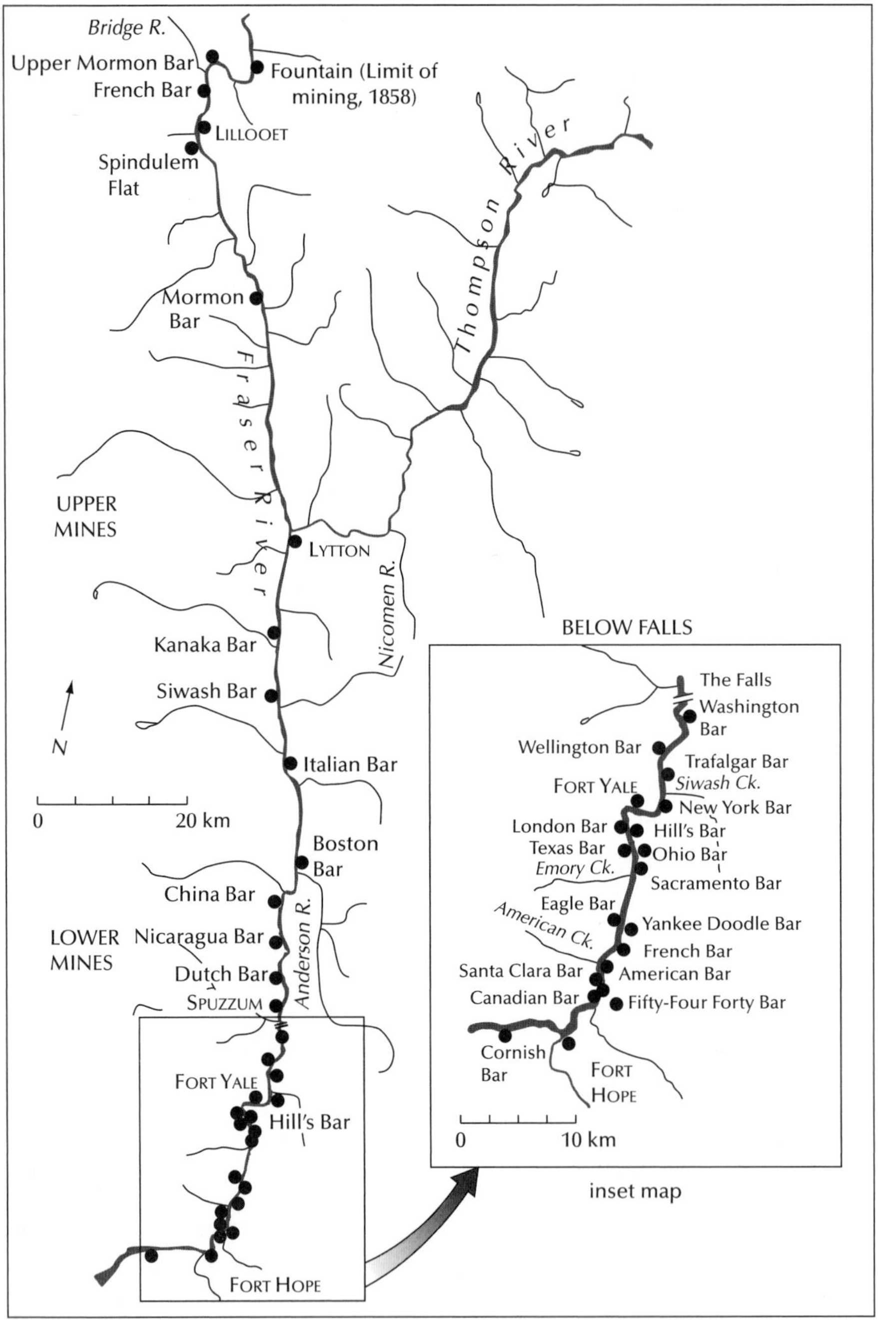

Map 1   Gold-rush bar place names reflecting race and ethnicity, Fraser River, 1858. Names of settlement are indicated with capital letters.

quickly enforcing HBC authority and inviting the Chinese to camp within the confines of the fort. Recent scholarship has drawn the conclusion that past conflict over western resources was, in fact, akin to 'race wars', and it is likely that, among those who remained on the Fraser after the exodus of Californians returning south, were those non-Anglo-Americans who undoubtedly recalled the ethnic and racial tensions that permeated the Sierra Nevada range.[26]

It was, of course, essentially Euro-Americans from Washington and Oregon territories, some early Californians, in addition to former HBC employees who secured the most profitable claims before the Fraser rose, thus pre-empting gold mining until the fall of the year. That Anglo-American influence was most dominant in the lower Fraser River mines below Yale is made plainly evident by Map 1, which illustrates the place names given to major gold-rush bars in this region.[27] To Alfred Waddington's list may be added many more that confirm the Californian, but especially British and American, control of this portion of the river. A more complete list of gold-rush bar names includes Cornish, Fifty-Four Forty, Canadian, Santa Clara, Eagle, American, Yankee Doodle, Texas, Sacramento, London, Ohio, Wellington, New York, Trafalgar, and Washington.

Anglo-Americans did not dominate the upper canyon the way they did the lower reaches. Many Californians felt that the combination of high water and high prices, poor trails and poor climate, did make the Fraser River gold rush a complete 'humbug'. The flood tide of Californians that eventually receded took with it the kind of Anglo-American dominance found in the Lower Mines but not before having forced non-Anglo-Americans out of their space. The extraordinary geography of the Fraser River canyons, unlike the expansive goldfields of California, offered only one choice to disaffected miners—only one direction for travel—and that was to continue up the river. The upper Fraser mines awaited conquest by all those who did not share in the success of

the Lower Mines; or, more particularly, those made unwelcome by California mining society, which was centred at Yale. Anxious to escape the discrimination of Fort Yale society, and driven by the commonly held notion that fine placer gold necessarily indicated the existence of an upstream mother lode, many must have felt compelled to break free from the constraints of the lower river into the higher reaches of unexplored terrain. Here, at least, might be offered prospects for gold and a certain degree of spatial autonomy. In contrast to the lack of accommodation afforded by diggings in the Lower Mines, most of the bars above Spuzzum were widely separated, offering alienated miners some peace from ethnic and, indeed, racial, intolerances.[28]

Again, if we focus solely on those place names that reflect ethnic and racial identity, we find evidence of a very different human geography above the dividing line of the Falls.[29] Gold-rush bar place names in this instance are as follows: Dutch Bar, Nicaragua Bar, China Bar, Boston Bar, Italian Bar, Siwash Bar, Kanaka Bar, Mormon Bar, Spindulem Flat, French Bar, and Upper Mormon Bar.[30] The anomalies in this decidedly non-Anglo-American list are obviously Boston Bar and the two Mormon bars. Boston Bar, still a major feature on the map today, was favourably situated across from the mouth of the Anderson River, where it enters the Fraser. It is probable that some of the earliest non-Native miners used A.C. Anderson's old HBC fur brigade trail to this point prior to the swelling of the Fraser in the summer of 1858. The Whatcom Trail from Bellingham (in its second attempt at reaching the Fraser) had connected with such HBC trails, ultimately to places above Yale like the Anderson River.[31] Even so, this name stands in stark contrast to the rest of the list. Mormon Bar and Upper Mormon Bar at the Fountain— the geographical limit of 1858 prospecting[32]— are not so unusual if one remembers that it was in 1857 and 1858 that US federal troops were ordered to invade Salt Lake City. Mormons, not generally liked by the rest of the American population, were persecuted until ultimately driven into the Utah desert.[33] It is reasonable to assume that the cultural milieu of Anglo-American dominance on the lower Fraser would have discriminated against Mormons as though they were, indeed, a race unto themselves.[34] Siwash Bar and Spindulem (Spintlum) Flat (named for a powerful Nlaka'pamux chief), represent the Native population that continued to practice placer mining.[35]

At the same time, Anglo-American culture cannot be viewed as a cohesive and homogeneous whole: Texan, Bostonian, and Ohioan Americans were undoubtedly quite divided. Charles Ferguson, a young Ohioan entering the goldfields of California, recalled how he passed several camps of his fellow countrypeople representing a variety of US regions before joining a group of unknown Ohioans who welcomed him with open arms.[36] Perhaps in this we have an explanation for the separateness of gold-rush bar names like Texas Bar, Ohio Bar, New York Bar, and Boston Bar on the Fraser. Texas had only recently been admitted to the Union, and the American Civil War would shortly divide North and South even further. These tensions must have contributed to the regional pride reflected in gold-rush place names. Still, when compared to non-Americans, there was undoubtedly more that held Americans together, in general, than kept them apart. If nothing else, there existed a consensus with regard to resource development and exploitation.

In Yale mining society, Californian ways had become well rooted. Certainly the combined forces of the Royal Engineer Corps, Royal Navy, Hudson's Bay Company, and colonial British rule ultimately tempered American enthusiasm. Yet the presence of the infamous Ned McGowan and members of the Vigilance Committee of San Francisco, along with Californian merchants, explorers, engineers, saloon-keepers, and newspaper reporters, made the lower Fraser a natural extension of the Californian world—especially with so many claiming that the Lower Mines were

inside American territory.[37] With such a secure sense of place established, even in a foreign landscape, the designation of various gold-rush bars with names like 'Fifty-Four Forty' were not only jingoistic pronouncements to the non-American mining community (that a Californian culture had arrived on the scene) but also the appropriation of the Fraser River's landscape, perhaps even an assertion of near-sovereign control. Naming legitimated the Californian presence in a British colony in the same way that earlier HBC naming of forts and landmarks authenticated the company's claim to Aboriginal lands.[38]

An examination of early maps produced before and after the 1858 Fraser River gold rush affirms this appropriation of landscape. 'Maps are never value-free images', advises J.B. Harley, but 'part of the broader family of value-laden images.'[39] A.C. Anderson's series of pre-1858 maps is decidedly different from maps produced in San Francisco during 1858 in one important regard—Anderson included Native place-naming along the Fraser, while the latter replaced such names with California-style gold camp names.[40] Anderson's explorations of 1846 through 1849 incorporated knowledge of the Thompson and Fraser rivers into a sketch map that clearly identified major Native settlements and appended Native names to these sites and all major rivers flowing into the Fraser (Map 2).[41] Many of these names were subsequently retained on an 1858 map produced in San Francisco based on Anderson's earlier work. Instead of the California-style gold-rush bar names that followed, Anderson provided names of a decidedly fur trade nature.

Once again, if we start at Fort Hope and ascend the river to the Fountain, place names function as landmarks of an HBC-controlled world that included the Native as essential in the trade relationship. Consequently, Anderson recorded: 'Fort Hope, Rapids, Upper Teet Vil[lage], Douglas Portage, Falls, lowest Couteau Vil[lage], Spuzzum, Ke-quelouse Vil & Jacobs Grave, Anderson R[iver], Tqua-yowm Vil, Tum-mulh R, Tze-wamma R, Kapath R,

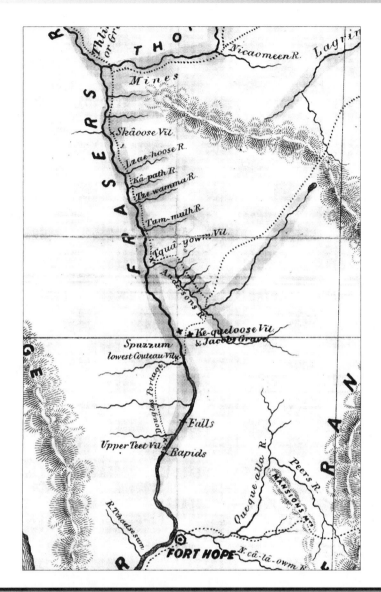

Map 2   Detail of A.C. Anderson's fur trade map. Image CM-A78 courtesy of Royal BC Museum, BC Archives.

Tzae-hoose R, Skaoose Vil, Thlikumcheen or Great Forks, Lower Fountain Vil, Bridge R., Upper Fountain Vill[age].'[42] Anderson's map is considered 'unquestionably the most accurate representation of interior British Columbia available' at this time.[43] Yet it detailed no particular gold-rush information from miners working along the Fraser, which is perhaps not surprising if one acknowledges that fur traders and gold miners viewed things quite differently from one another.

By contrast, a sketch map published by the *San Francisco Bulletin* offered a Californian depiction of the goldfields that replaced all

Native-HBC landmark names with those that were more inviting to miners (see Map 3). The ground was now made familiar to those about to embark on the long sea journey north from San Francisco. A 'New El Dorado' was invented out of the 'vacant' space of the Fraser corridor and, thus, was brought into 'cultural circulation'.[44] Arriving at Fort Langley, the Californian would ascend past Fort Hope, Hunter's Bar, Hill's Bar, Fort Yale, Rapids, Sailor's Diggings, Rapids, Mormon Bar, and Grand Falls, assuming the hopeful miner was first able to run the

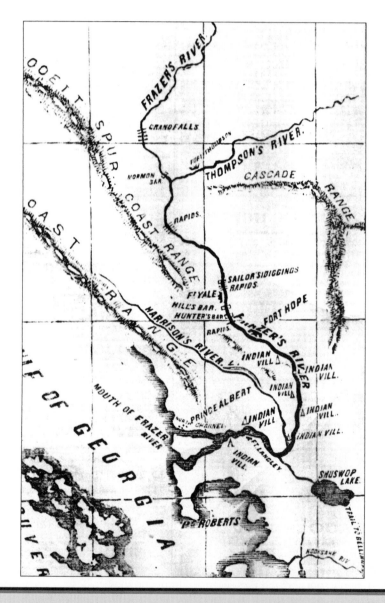

Map 3   Sketch map from the *San Francisco Bulletin* (1858), depicting the goldfields from a California perspective. Image CM-A295 courtesy of Royal BC Museum, BC Archives.

gauntlet of seven separate 'Indian Villages' that stood between the mouth of the Fraser and Fort Hope. Native names were removed from the map and, in their place, Native settlements were inscribed, not unlike warning beacons to the wary.[45]

The human geography was about to be changed dramatically by miners who had no understanding of the Native. The effects of placer mining took a considerable toll on the traditional Native landscape. At Hill's Bar, known amongst the Stó:lō as Hemhemetheqw, meaning 'good place to make sockeye salmon oil', miners stripped away the ground and overturned many boulders containing pock-marked bowls used for the collection of fish oil.[46] Throughout the Fraser and Thompson corridors, immense amounts of sand, gravel, and other natural debris were washed into the rivers and into age-old fishing and hunting grounds. Places of habitation were scarred by ditches, flumes, and test-holes preparatory to excavating entire hillsides or bench lands.[47]

Californian discourse, in representing Aboriginals as impediments to progress, encouraged a process of colonization that, in effect, not only changed the human geography but also, for Aboriginal peoples, the physical geography of boundary and space. The discourse of naming has been compared to acts of 'christening'. For example, in *Marvelous Possessions* Stephen Greenblatt argues that, under the authority of Christian imperialism, Christopher Columbus' use of place-naming was akin to christening. Greenblatt maintains that 'christening entails the cancellation of the native name—the erasure of the alien, perhaps demonic, identity—and hence a kind of making new; it is at once an exorcism, an appropriation, and a gift. Christening then is the culminating instance of the marvellous speech act: in the wonder of the proper name, the movement from ignorance to knowledge, the taking of possession, the conferral of identity are fused in a moment of pure linguistic formalism.'[48] Certainly, the myriad gold-rush bar place names along the Fraser River are

evidence of a cancellation of Native names— 'the erasure of the alien.' And befitting the kind of mass democratic society that California felt it had achieved, acts of possession were now no longer limited to a single mighty explorer but could be proclaimed by all those who 'discovered' their own version of a 'New World Bar'.[49]

These new names were the basis for an invented cultural space that enticed further discovery and the prospect of hidden gold. 'For how', as Paul Carter suggests, 'without place names, without agreed points of reference, could directions be given, information exchanged, "here" and "there" defined? . . . they embody the existential necessity the traveller feels to invent a place he can inhabit. Without them, punctuating the monotony, distinguishing this horizon from that, there would be no evidence he had travelled.'[50]

Maps are, in fact, a cultural text, and they may well tell more about the social structure of the place of origin than do the actual human and physical landscapes they describe. By 1858, the California goldfields had seen their best years, and with word of a 'new' California to the north, expectations ran high. The Fraser River fever compelled many to join the fray, only to be severely disappointed upon arrival. Gold-rush bar place names such as Humbug Bar, Poverty Bar, and perhaps even Pike's Bar are indicative of miners' expectations of a quick and easy wealth that never materialized.[51]

Indeed, it is at times more instructive to see what has been excluded from a map than what has been included. On California-produced representations of British Columbia, we may easily locate bar names of Anglo-American origin, but there is no indication of Nicaragua, China, or Kanaka bars, and virtually no Native presence. J.B. Harley, in viewing the map as a 'spatial panopticon' that produces power, wrote that 'the map maker merely omits those features of the world that lie outside the purpose of the immediate discourse.'[52] In this instance, California-based gold-rush discourse normally referred to non-Americans only when justification was required for the discriminatory practices of white society.

Once the Fraser River rush had subsided, and the remainder of the goldseekers were drawn to the Cariboo goldfields, Californian-style place names were largely dropped from colonial mapping endeavours, or rather, in keeping with a resurgent imperial discourse, they were ignored. A Royal Engineers' map for 1861 only listed Chapman's Bar and Boston Bar; John Arrowsmith's 1862 map of British Columbia contained no gold-rush names; and John Palliser's 'A general Map of the route in British North America' marked only Hope, Yale, and Lytton, as befitting a Pacific Colony that now had the institutions of British power more firmly established than had previously been the case.[53] Place names such as Hope and Yale had been bestowed prior to the gold rush by HBC authority, while Lytton honoured the pivotal role played by the British secretary of state for the colonies in 1858.[54]

Not unlike the racial blindness of gold-rush-specific cartographers, officials of Empire preferred to disregard nomenclature of a non-British sort. The mere fact that California-style place-naming could be dropped so quickly from the colonial government's lexicon further illustrates the very transient nature of gold-rush-related human geographies.

By 1870, the Fraser River rush was virtually a forgotten past.[55] The impermanence of gold-rush life meant that communities of miners devoted to the collection of gold dust soon moved on once the river sand bars had been thoroughly depleted through placer mining techniques. Of the first river-bottom bars that were prospected between Fort Hope to the Fountain, Californian historian Hubert Howe Bancroft wrote, 'Nearly all of these were wiped out of memory as the inhabitants migrated and the traces of their existence were washed away by the recurring floods of the rivers; so that only a few have found a permanent place in the geography of the country.'[56] Yet, though the presence of the goldseeker was ephemeral, the gold-rush bar names that remained had

great implications for the human geography of Native settlements in the future.

In 1871, new considerations refocused the colonial government's attention along the Fraser River corridor and rescued many gold-rush bar names from obscurity, ultimately giving them a permanence in the landscape that would perhaps have been inconceivable to earlier British cartographers. Joseph Trutch, as chief commissioner of lands and works, was responsible for gathering information on all surveyed portions of British Columbia. This information was to be included on a new map that came to be considered 'a milestone in the historical cartography of B.C.'[57] Trutch's map included, between Hope and Lytton alone, American Bar, Emory Bar, Texas Bar, Yale, Wellington Bar, Spuzzum River, Chapman's Bar, Alexandra Bridge, Big Canon, Anderson River, Boston Bar, Fargo Bar, and Mariner's Bar.[58] Perhaps it was Trutch's eight years of experience as a surveyor and farmer in the United States that gave him an affinity for California-type place names.[59] Of greater significance, though, was the emerging province's need for readily available and identifiable landmarks by which to locate the technical descriptions of the 1870–1 resurvey of Fraser River topography. Gold-rush bar place names would have provided the key for, as Carter maintains, 'Naming words were forms of spatial punctuation transforming space into an object of knowledge, something that could be explored and read.'[60] The Fraser River had already been defined by the HBC, but it was the gold rush that carved the landscape into a linear series of over a hundred points of reference.

With British Columbia's entry into Confederation, Article 13 of the Terms of Union stipulated that responsibility for Indian affairs would rest with the federal government. Under such a system, Trutch was required to furnish specific information with respect to the location and extent of 'Indian Reserves'. The act of place-naming under the earlier influences of both the HBC and the gold rush involved instances of de facto near-sovereignty over the landscape, but later colonial power enacted full sovereignty and was aided by existing place names, which explicitly defined the new ordering of life along the river.

[. . .]

The chief commissioner's use of gold-rush place names to categorize Indian reserves filled the void called wilderness and left even less room for Aboriginal peoples. The HBC's definition of place had located only the most minimal of landmarks significant for the perpetuation of their trade. Later imperial designs were primarily interested in marking the sites of colonial power and authority. By contrast, the gold rush had labelled stretches of the Fraser River so thoroughly as to suggest that this corridor was fully occupied, and, hence, Natives were confirmed only the barest minimum of land for their essential needs. The erasure of Native sovereignty through the use of California-like place names not only disconnected Natives from the physical geography of the river but also from the very soul of Native culture. As mentioned previously, place names in Native cultures such as the Stó:lō do much more than plot mere points of reference— they give oral history significance by 'spatially anchoring' it to a unique and personal geography. The place name, in this instance, offers the memory detailed pictures of the myths, sagas, and community history of centuries. A name will automatically recall a unique point in the land, and, in turn, the land invokes the wisdom of a culture. As in Stó:lō culture, so in Apache culture: geographical features 'served the people for centuries as indispensable mnemonic pegs on which to hang the moral teachings of their history.'[61] As Raymond Fogelson maintains, 'All peoples possess a sense of the past, however strange and exceptional that past may seem from our own literately conditioned perspectives.'[62] The consequences of a permanent gold-rush vocabulary have been severely underestimated as they have effectively denied an ancient and sacred worldview.[63]

It is not surprising, perhaps, that a gold rush that had refashioned the human geography of the Fraser River corridor into a series of distinct, ethnically and racially segregated mining enclaves would also compartmentalize Native peoples into a chain of racially defined reserves. Joseph Trutch's reintroduction of gold-rush landmarks naturally intertwined with Indian reserve names as they ascended the Fraser. Surveyor John Trutch used the language of the gold rush when he named the location of 'Boston Bar Indian Reserve #5', described Kop-chichen Indian Reserve #6 as 'situated on Yankee Flat', and located Shoo-ook Indian Reserve #7 'on Boothroyd's Flat'.[64] Ironically, the Fraser River gold rush not only precipitated the institution of the reserve system in Mainland British Columbia but, in certain instances, continued to define many of the limited Indian lands left behind in the wake of the events of 1858–9.

Once British Columbia joined Canada, Joseph Trutch's commemoration of the 'cult of first-comers' not only re-embedded these 'discoveries' in the geography of the canyon walls and (more permanently) on maps but also, by continuing to legitimate the colonial presence through place names, provided further justification for the curtailment of reserves.[65] Current maps covering a portion of this river feature the ironic, taunting names of 'Trafalgar Flat Indian Reserve', 'Chapman's Bar Indian Reserve', 'China Bar Indian Reserve', 'Boston Bar Indian Reserve', 'Boothroyd Indian Reserve', and 'Cameron Bar Indian Reserve'.[66] The mere juxtaposition of gold-rush bar names and Indian reserves is enough to keep alive the memory of the events that led to the appropriation of Native lands, but the incorporation of these signal acts of sovereignty into the very names of the reserves constitutes a continued occupation of the Native landscape by the miners of old. All other races that had flooded into the canyon to occupy a piece of the river ultimately receded, leaving only a name behind. But the Aboriginal, the final inheritor of a geographical corridor delineated by race, has remained within a matrix of reserves that recalls the segregated landscape of the gold rush of 1858.

NOTES

1. 'Letter from Fort Yale: Fatal Accident, Serious Trouble Anticipated with the Indians', *Victoria Gazette*, 30 July 1858, p. 2.

2. Paul Carter, *The Road to Botany Bay: An Essay in Spatial History* (London and Boston: Faber and Faber, 1987), xxiii.

3. 'Making the World Right through Transformations', plate 1, in *A Stó:lō-Coast Salish Historical Atlas*, ed. Keith Thor Carlson (Vancouver: Douglas and McIntyre, 2001), 7.

4. 'Stl'ádeqem Sites: Spiritually Potent Places in S'ólh Téméxw', plate 2, Carlson, *Stó:lō-Coast Salish Historical Atlas*, 8.

5. Letter of James Bell reprinted in Willard E. Ireland, 'Gold-Rush Days in Victoria, 1858–59', *British Columbia Historical Quarterly* 12, 3 (1948): 240.

6. Robie L. Reid, 'Two Narratives of the Fraser River Gold-Rush', *British Columbia Historical Quarterly* 5, 3 (1941): 227. Translated from Dr. Carl Friesach, *Ein Ausflug nach Britisch-Columbien im Jahre 1858* (Gratz: Drukerei Leykam-Josepfsthal, 1875).

7. British Columbia, *Papers Relative to the Affairs of British Columbia*, 29, 1 July 1858, 19–20. Douglas noted that the following 'nations' that volunteered their labour for the Harrison-Lillooet Road construction were 'British subjects, Americans, French, Germans, Danes, Africans, and Chinese'. Ibid., 34, 9 August 1858, 27–28.

8. J.S. Holliday, *The World Rushed In: The California Gold Rush Experience* (New York: Simon and Schuster, 1983), 455.

9. Alfred Waddington's letter, *Victoria Gazette*, 15 September 1858.

10. Further work is required in comparing California and British Columbia gold-rush place names as early evidence suggests that similarities found between these two regions could provide a link between emigrant miners in British Columbia and particular regions in California or the wider United States.

11. As quoted in Margaret A. Ormsby, *British Columbia: A History* (Toronto: Macmillan, 1958), 37.

12. For David Thompson's map, which includes the Fraser River, consult BCA, CM/D114.

13. Alexander C. Anderson, *Hand-book and Map of the Gold Region of Frazer's and Thompson's Rivers* (San Francisco: J.J. Le Count, 1858), 7, in British Columbia Archives (BCA).

14. This 'age old hostility' between Upper and Lower Natives is also confirmed in T.A. Rickard, 'Indian Participation in the Gold Discoveries', *British Columbia Historical Quarterly* 2, 1 (1938): 15.

15. Governor James Douglas confirmed the earlier interest of Washington and Oregon, prior to the rush from California, in Douglas to Labouchere, 8 May 1858 (no. 19), *Correspondence Relative to the Discovery of Gold In Fraser's River District* (London: 1858), 12. Bellingham Bay was to become the main stop-off point for American miners who wanted to evade the British port of Victoria and, more particularly, the miners' licence fee. See R.L. Reid, 'Whatcom Trails to the Fraser River Mines in 1858', *Washington Historical Quarterly* 18 (1927): 199–206, 271–6. For first news of this rush, which effectively closed down the Bellingham Bay Coal Company, see 'Gold Discovery Confirmed!' *Puget Sound Herald*, Steilacoom, Washington Territory, 26 March 1858.

16. Moore claimed not to have left Yale to go up-river until 17 December 1858. He and his party reached Lytton on 26 January 1859. See James Moore, 'The Discovery of Hill's Bar in 1858', *British Columbia Historical Quarterly* 3, 3 (1939): 220.

17. Army desertions in Washington Territory and the anticipated rush from California are noted in the *Puget Sound Herald*, 2 April 1858.

18. F.W. Howay, 'To the Fraser River! The Diary and Letters of Cyrus Olin Phillips, 1858–59', *California Historical Society Quarterly* 11, 2 (1932): 156. Phillips also visited Whatcom on Bellingham Bay and noted that three thousand miners were waiting there.

19. Moore, 'Discovery of Hill's Bar', 218.

20. Ireland, 'Gold-Rush Days in Victoria', 224.

21. 'Too Early—That's All', *Northern Light*, 31 July 1858.

22. Henry De Groot, *British Columbia; Its Conditions and Prospects, Soil, Climate, and Mineral Resources, Considered* (San Francisco: Alta Californian, 1859), 16–17.

23. Douglas had claimed that John K. Ledell had travelled further than anyone else up the Fraser

in the early spring of 1858, or so the prospector maintained to his wife. 'Narrative of a Miner's Trip to the Head Waters of the Gold Region', *Northern Light*, 16 March 1858. Ledell named Foster's Bar.

24. In 1850, the prohibitive Foreign Miner's Head Tax was twenty dollars a month and, although technically applied to all non-Americans, was in practice levelled primarily against Chinese and Mexicans. See William S. Greever, *Bonanza West: The Story of the Western Mining Rushes, 1848–1900* (Moscow, ID: University of Idaho Press, 1990 [1963]), 71.

25. Story of J.C. Bryant as told in 'A Sturdy Prospector', in W.W. Walkem, Stories of Early British Columbia (Vancouver: News-Advertiser, 1914), 123.

26. For the above source and a discussion of race relations in the American West, see Sarah Deutsch, 'Landscape of Enclaves: Race Relations in the West, 1865–1990', in *Under an Open Sky: Rethinking America's Western Past*, ed. William Cronon, George Miles, and Jay Gitlin (New York and London: W.W. Norton, 1992), 113.

27. See the inset in Map 1.

28. As Waddington noted, the Lower Mines comprised only twenty-three kilometres out of the approximate 230 kilometres from south of Hope to the Fountain above Lillooet.

29. See Map 1, particularly between Spuzzum and the Fountain.

30. There were two French Bars on the Fraser, one in the Lower Mines, the other in the Upper Mines. Perhaps there is a distinction to be drawn between Continental French and French Canadiens. French Canadiens, formerly employed by the HBC, undoubtedly would have been early arrivals in the Lower Mines. Gudde notes that the adjective 'French' was used more than any other ethnic description in Californian place-naming. See Erwin G. Gudde, *California Gold Camps* (Berkeley: University of California Press, 1973).

31. R.L. Reid, 'The Whatcom Trails to the Fraser River Mines in 1858', *Washington Historical Quarterly* 18 (1927): 199–206, 271–6.

32. Waddington detailed the extent of mining during the 1858 rush as follows: 'All the diggings that have been worked up to this day [1858], have been strictly speaking river diggings and lye between Murderer's [Cornish] Bar, 4 miles

below Fort Hope, and the Fountain, 6 miles above the Big Falls, stretching over a total length of 140 miles: and that the three quarters of them have been worked over a distance of 14 miles between Fort Hope and Fort Yale.' See Waddington, *Fraser Mines Vindicated*, 7.

33. In the 'Mormon War' of 1857–8, President Buchanan sent 2,500 troops, or one-sixth of the entire US army, to suppress a Mormon rebellion. See Richard White, *'It's Your Misfortune and None of My Own': A New History of the American West* (Norman and London: University of Oklahoma Press, 1991), 163–9.

34. Although of European stock, the Mormon practice of polygamy was abhorred. For a discussion of discrimination in mining camps against Mormons and other groups, see Duane A. Smith, 'Not All Were Welcome', in *Rocky Mountain Mining Camps: The Urban Frontier*, (Bloomington and London: Indiana University Press, 1967), 29–41.

35. For an examination of Native mining during the Fraser rush, see Daniel P. Marshall, 'Rickard Revisited: Native "Participation" in the Gold Discoveries of British Columbia', *Native Studies Review* 11, 1 (1997): 91–108. Further work is required to establish the multiracial flavour of the gold-rush era. Certainly church archival records may prove to be an invaluable source. A tantalizing example is found in the early Anglican Church records for Lillooet, where the marriage register for 1861 recorded the first formal exchange of vows in this locale between two Latin Americans, one from Chile and the other from San Salvador. See St. Mary's Church Register, Lillooet, 1861–1915, UBC Special Collections.

36. Charles D. Ferguson, *The Experiences of a Forty-Niner* (Cleveland: Williams, 1888).

37. Until formal surveys were finally completed in keeping with the Oregon Boundary Settlement of 1846, many Americans claimed that the Fraser—at just 23 kilometres inside the BC border—was actually in American territory.

38. The idea that naming legitimates a colonial presence is developed in Carter, *Road to-Botany Bay*, xvi.

39. J.B. Harley, 'Maps, Knowledge, and Power', in *The Iconography of Landscape: Essays on the Symbolic Representation, Design and Use of Past Environments*, ed. Denis Cosgrove and Stephen

Daniels (Cambridge: Cambridge University Press, 1988), 278.

40. For a vast dictionary-compendium of California place names comparable to those found on the Fraser, see Gudde, *California Gold Camps*.

41. A.C. Anderson's manuscript, entitled 'Original Sketch of Exploration between 1846 and 1849, c. 1850', 8000/L10, Map Division, BCA. For a detailed examination of Anderson's work, see Albert L. Farley, *Historical Cartography of British Columbia* (Madison: University of Wisconsin Press, 1961).

42. Alexander C. Anderson, comp., *Routes of Communication with the Gold Region on Frasers River* (San Francisco: J.J. Lecount, 1858), CM/A78 Map Division, BCA. This map also accompanied the guidebook *Hand-Book and Map of the Gold Region*, UBC Special Collections. This guidebook and map would have been used by the majority of miners travelling from California to British Columbia.

43. See Farley, 'The Colonial Era, 1849–1871', chap. 5, *Historical Cartography of British Columbia*, 228.

44. 'Cultural circulation' is a term coined by Carter, *Road to Botany Bay*, 28. British Columbia was often referred to as the 'New El Dorado', and at least one author made this the subject of a book. See Kinahan Cornwallis, *The New El Dorado; Or, British Columbia* (London: Thomas Cautley Newby, 1858), BCA.

45. 'Sketch of Frazer River and the New Gold Mines', *Bulletin* (1858), CM/A295: Sh. 1, Map Division, BCA. A similar map is drawn by merchant CO. Phillips, who established a store on Bridge River in November 1858. Indians are simply located and gold-rush bars are limited to the following: Sea Bird Bar, Murderer's Bar, Texas Bar, Emory's Bar, and Hill's Bar. See Howay, 'To the Fraser River!' Waddington's map of 1858 contains neither gold bar names nor Native information; rather, it simply points out where the rich diggings were located. One exception is that 'Indian Diggings' are located along the Thompson River. See A. Waddington, *A Correct Map of the Northern Coal & Gold Regions comprehending Frazer River* (San Francisco: P. de Garro, May 1858).

46. Keith Thor Carlson, ed. *You Are Asked To Witness: The Stó:lō in Canada's Pacific Coast History* (Chilliwack, BC: Stó:lō Heritage Trust, 1997), 61.

47. Elder Harold Wells of Union Bar (near Hope) was told by his grandmother how Chinese miners left a permanent scar, a 3.65 metre quarry, on their land, while they were away visiting relatives farther down the Fraser River. Carlson, *You Are Asked to Witness*, 62.

48. Stephen Greenblatt, *Marvelous Possessions: The Wonder of the New World* (Chicago: University of Chicago Press, 1991), 83.

49. Paul Carter states: 'New . . . is a name that refuses to admit the place was there before it was named.' This was typical of the gold-rush mentality that reinvented the Fraser along Californian lines. See Carter, *Road to Botany Bay*, 9.

50. In essence, naming allowed one to mark the present, possess it, and then travel onward, leaving behind beacons for future travel, landmarks for the map, and a space to enter history. See Carter, *The Road to Botany Bay*, 46–7.

51. Gudde suggests that 'Pike' was often used by gold diggers from Pike County, Missouri, and later by those unwilling to tell where they were from; finally, it was applied to rough miners or new immigrants. See Gudde, *California Gold Camps*, 265. A more pertinent explanation, perhaps, is that Pike's Peak Rush in Colorado was greatly exaggerated. It occurred in 1858–9, and it is quite possible that news of its bust would have travelled to the Fraser. Those returning from Pike's Peak to California became known as 'Pikers', or failed miners. It might be, therefore, that Pike's Bar on the Fraser is suggestive of dashed expectations. See Rodman W. Paul, *California Gold: The Beginning of Mining in the Far West, 1848–1880* (New York: Holt, Rinehart and Winston, 1963), 39, and Greever, *Bonanza West*, 158. Yet another explanation is that the bar could have been named after Zebullon Pike, who had invaded Canada during the War of 1812. Of course, Captain H.M. Snyder had commanded the 'Pike Guards' during the Fraser River War.

52. J.B. Harley, 'Deconstructing the Map', *Cartographica* 26, 2 (1989): 11.

53. Other maps consulted in the post-1858 period include: H.S. Palmer, 'Sketch of Route from Fort Hope to Fort Colville' (1859); Royal Engineer map, 'British Columbia: New

Westminster to Lillooet' (New Westminster, 1861); and John Arrowsmith, 'The Provinces of British Columbia & Vancouver Island' (South Kensington, England, 1862). All of these are located in the Map Division, BCA.

54. Fort Hope was apparently named by the HBC to commemorate the hoped-for route located along the Similkameen Trail that was to re-place the HBC's Columbia-Okanagan river route in the aftermath of the Oregon Boundary Settlement of 1846. Fort Yale was named for HBC chief trader James Murray Yale, who was stationed at Fort Langley. Lytton was named for Lord Lytton (Henry Bulwer Lytton), the then secretary of state for the colonies, who presid-ed over the creation of the Crown Colony of British Columbia.

55. See William D. Patterson, C.E., 'Map of the Cariboo & Omineca Gold Fields and the Routes there to' (1870)m CM/A123m Map Division, BCA. No such place names listed.

56. Hubert Howe Bancroft, 'Fraser River Mining and Settlement, 1858–1878' in *History of British Columbia* (San Francisco: History Company, 1890). Bancroft supplies an invalu-able list of gold-rush bar names and other landmarks compiled from a variety of sources.

57. J.W. Truch, 'Map of British Columbia', com-piled by Lands and Works Office (1871), BCA. For above quote, see Farley, *Historical Cartography of British Columbia*, BCA.

58. Ibid.

59. His time below the 49th parallel is found in Robin Fisher, 'Joseph Trutch and Indian Land Policy', *BC Studies* 12 (1971–72): 3–33. Reprinted in J. Friesen and H.K. Ralston, eds. *Historical Essays on British Columbia* (Toronto: Gage, 1980), 257.

60. Carter, *Road to Botany Bay*, 67.

61. Keith H. Basso, '"Stalking with Stories": Names, Places, and Moral Narratives among the Western Apache', *Text, Play and Story: The Construction and Reconstruction of Self and. Society*, ed. Stuart Plattner (Washington: Proceedings of the American Ethnological Society, 1984), 44–5.

62. Raymond D. Fogelson, 'The Ethnohistory of Events and Nonevents', *Ethnohistory* 36, 2 (1989): 134.

63. In addition, the building of two transcontin-ental railways on either side of the Fraser River Canyon must have resulted in the levelling of many important stone monoliths that held the ancient history of these First Nations.

64. See John Trutch's 1870 maps, which corres-pond to the A-Q schedule of reserves com-piled for the federal government in 1871. See, particularly, the sheet entitled, 'Indian Reserves situated on or near Fraser River in the Lytton District'. Copies deposited by the author at UBC Special Collections.

65. The 'cult of first-comers' is described by Carter, *Road to Botany Bay*, xviii.

66. Boothroyd Indian Reserve was named for George Washington Boothroyd, who was a member of Major Mortimer Robertson's 'Yakima Expedition', the volunteer miners' mil-itia that fought with Native peoples through the Canadian and American Okanagan in its bid to reach the Fraser River goldfields. Ironically, this Indian-fighter's name defines the space of this particular reserve. Similarly, Stout Indian Reserve is named after Edward Stout, both a '49er and a '58er, and participant in the Fraser River War. See 'A Pioneer of '58', in Walkem, *Stories of Early British Columbia*, 51–62. It should be noted that, during the writing of this chapter, many First Nations have taken steps to officially rename their reserves according to traditional Native usage. At the time of writ-ing, this reassertion of Native sovereignty and control continues.

Chapter Thirteen

Métis

READINGS

Primary Documents

1   'La chanson de la grenouillère' (1816) in *Textes poétiques du Canada français*, Pierre Falcon

2   From J. Halkett to Earl Bathurst, 3 June 1818, in *Correspondence in the Years 1817, 1818, and 1819, between Earl Bathurst and J. Halkett, Esq. on the Subject of Lord Selkirk's Settlement at the Red River, in North America*

Historical Interpretations

3   From *The Ermatingers: A 19th Century Ojibwa-Canadian Family,* W. Brian Stewart

4   From 'Prologue to the Red River Resistance: Pre-liminal Politics and the Triumph of Riel', Gerhard Ens

Introduction

The Métis in Western Canada were, initially at least, the offspring of relationships between fur trade workers and Aboriginal women. The dominant characteristic of the earliest of these relationships was that the men tended to be French-speaking, thanks to employment practices in the trade. Over time, however, this early pattern became less dominant—English-speaking men also fathered children, Métis entered into relationships with Aboriginal, European, or other Métis people—to the point that there are several possible routes to being Métis today. Biology may have defined this distinctive group at the outset, but again, over time, the economic and cultural positions of the Métis were more historically momentous and enduring.

At various times in Canadian history, especially on the prairies, 'mixed-blood' people and their interests have driven events. They found themselves between First Nations and European-origin societies, connected to each but not belonging wholly to either. To the extent that their presence served the dominant order, they were tolerated by it, but they tended to be most comfortable in communities of their own, pursuing jobs that could take advantage of their 'between-ness.' The fur trade had been their genesis, and until the middle of the nineteenth century, it had much to do with the trajectory of Métis life. Halkett's strong denunciation of the Métis as the hired thugs of the North West Company and opponents of Lord Selkirk's colonization scheme at Red River during the later 1810s shows how easily racial animosity and commercial competition could bleed together. Contrast this with Pierre Falcon's poem/song celebrating the 'Bois-Brûlés', who fought at Seven Oaks where Cuthbert Grant and his forces dealt a serious blow to the Hudson's Bay Company's control of the region. Brian Stewart reminds us that the fur trade was not the only possible career for Métis families, and that it was possible for them to move between two sharply different worlds, even inhabiting places well away from what we consider the Métis heartland. Gerhard Ens provides background to the 1869–70 Resistance, showing how divisions and doubts existed within the Métis community—divisions that were directly related to questions of identity.

QUESTIONS FOR CONSIDERATION

1. What is Halkett's attitude toward the Métis in the Red River region? Why does he hold this attitude?

2. Falcon's 'Chanson de la Grenouillière' commemorates a battle or short skirmish. How does Falcon portray the Red River colony's governor and his forces before and during the battle?

3. Why do you think people were and are so fascinated by racial or ethnic origins?

4. How does Stewart's account of the Ermatingers complicate our view of Métis people?

5. Ens presents us with a picture of Red River society on the eve of the resistance there. Compare and contrast the competing ideals of community that Ens describes.

SUGGESTIONS FOR FURTHER READING

Ens, Gerhard J., *Homeland to Hinterland: The Changing Worlds of the Red River Métis in the Nineteenth Century* (Toronto: University of Toronto Press, 1996)

Macdougall, Brenda, *One of the Family: Métis Culture in Nineteenth-Century Northwestern Saskatchewan* (Vancouver: UBC Press, 2010)

Stewart, W. Brian, *The Ermatingers: A 19th Century Ojibwa-Canadian Family* (Vancouver: UBC Press, 2008)

PRIMARY DOCUMENTS

1 Pierre Falcon, 'La chanson de la grenouillère' (1816) in *Textes poétiques du Canada français* (Montréal: Fides, 1987), vol. 2; Translation: 'The Battle of Seven Oaks' ('The Ballad of the Frog Plain') in Ken Mitchell, ed., *Horizon: Writings of the Canadian Prairie* (Toronto: Oxford University Press, 1977), 6–7.

THE BATTLE OF SEVEN OAKS
Translated by James Reaney

1816

On 19 June 1816, in a skirmish at 'Frog Plain' near the Red River Settlement (in present-day Winnipeg), Cuthbert Grant and a band of Métis (bois-brûlés) killed Robert Semple, the governor of Assiniboia, and twenty Hudson's Bay Company settlers. Falcon was present at the battle.

> Would you like to hear me sing
> Of a true and recent thing?
> was June nineteen, the band of Bois-Brûlés
>   Arrived that day,
>   Oh the brave warriors they!
>
> We took three foreigners prisoners when
> We came to the place called Frog, Frog Plain.
> They were men who'd come from Orkney,
>   Who'd come, you see,
>   To rob our country.
>
> Well we were just about to unhorse
> When we heard two of us give, give voice.
> Two of our men cried, 'Hey! Look back, look back!
>   The Anglo-Sack
>   Coming for to attack.'
>
> Right away smartly we veered about
> Galloping at them with a shout!
> You know we did trap all, all those Grenadiers!
>   They could not move
>   Those horseless cavaliers.
>
> Now we like honourable men did act,
> Sent an ambassador—yes, in fact!
> 'Monsieur Governor! Would you like to stay?

A moment spare—
There's something we'd like to say.'

Governor, Governor, full of ire.
'Soldiers!' he cries, 'Fire! Fire!'
So they fire the first and their muskets roar!
        They almost kill
        Our ambassador!

Governor thought himself a king.
He wished an iron rod to swing.
Like a lofty lord he tries to act.
        Bad luck, old chap!
        A bit too hard you whacked!

When we went galloping, galloping by
Governor thought that he would try
For to chase and frighten us Bois-Brûlés.
        Catastrophe!
        Dead on the ground he lay.

Dead on the ground lots of grenadiers too.
Plenty of grenadiers, a whole slew.
We've almost stamped out his whole army.
        Of so many
        Five or four left there be.

You should have seen those Englishmen—
Bois-Brûlés chasing them, chasing them.
From bluff to bluff they stumbled that day
        While the Bois-Brûlés
        Shouted 'Hurray!'

Tell, oh tell me who made up this song?
Why it's our own poet, Pierre Falcon.
Yes, it was written this song of praise
        For the victory
        We won this day.
Yes, it was written, this song of praise—
        Come sing the glory
        Of the Bois-Brûlés.

2 From J. Halkett to Earl Bathurst, 3 June 1818, in *Correspondence in the Years 1817, 1818, and 1819, between Earl Bathurst and J. Halkett, Esq. on the Subject of Lord Selkirk's Settlement at the Red River, in North America* (London: J. Brettell, 1819), 34–45.

Seymour Place, January 3, 1818.

MY LORD,

I take the liberty of again addressing your Lordship on the subject of the British Colonists at the Red River, in consequence of intelligence recently received from that quarter. The last accounts from the interior of North America communicate the satisfactory information that Lord Selkirk has succeeded in re-establishing the settlers upon the lands from which they had been twice driven by the North-West Company of Montreal.

Having left Fort William as early in the last summer as the state of the river navigation would admit, Lord Selkirk proceeded into the interior, and arrived at the Red River in the month of June. In the preceding winter he had taken measures to enable a small party of the settlers, who had been driven away in the summer before, to return in safety to the Settlement; and, upon his arrival there, he found that they had again begun to re-establish themselves, and to cultivate the lands which had been assigned to them. Under the circumstances in which they were placed, their agricultural operations were, of course, much circumscribed; and the horses of the Settlement having been carried away, or destroyed, by their opponents, they were prevented from putting so much land into tillage as they otherwise would have done. They had sowed, however, above sixty acres of grain. The crops of the former year had been destroyed by the persons employed by the North-West Company, who, after Mr. Semple and twenty of his people were killed,—the surviving settlers driven away,—and their habitations reduced to ashes—turned their horses loose into the fields of wheat, and other grain, for the purpose of laying them waste. The malicious satisfaction which the Company's adherents felt in thus destroying the promising crops of the Settlement, was, however, somewhat damped by the circumstance of nearly fifty of their horses having died in consequence of the surfeit. The European cattle and sheep, which had been sent to the Settlement, as a breed, were also destroyed by the persons employed by the North-West Company, whose brutality, throughout the whole of these transactions, was such as scarcely to be credited.

A few days after the 19th of June, the day when Mr. Semple and his followers were put to death without quarter by their opponents, Mr. Archibald Norman McLeod the magistrate, one of the Company's principal agents, together with several of his partners, accompanied by a considerable number of the half-breeds who had been engaged in the slaughter of the 19th, rode to the spot, and, having assured these half-breeds that they had done well, the party, with loud shouts and laughter, began to exult over, and even to kick the dead bodies which had remained upon the ground. On the side of the North-West Company, only one person, a half-breed, had fallen. His body was buried, and a paling placed round his grave; but the bodies of the settlers, (with the exception of a few who had been brought away and interred by some native Indians), were all left unburied on the spot, and were afterwards devoured by dogs. In the following spring their bones were collected, and interred by Captain D'Orsonnens, who, at

Lord Selkirk's request, had proceeded to the Red River with a party of the new colonists in the preceding winter.

Shortly after Lord Selkirk had arrived at the Settlement, he was joined by a large portion of the remaining settlers who had been driven away in the summer before. Contrary to the expectations of the North-West Company (who had exulted in the idea that these colonists must have been all compelled to go back to Hudson's Bay for the purpose of returning to Europe), they had passed the autumn and winter towards the north end of Lake Winnipic, and at the Saskatchawan. Having heard that Lord Selkirk had arrived in North America, and was proceeding into the interior, they trusted that now they would not be entirely forsaken, and that means would be found to enable them to return with safety to the Red River.

By the latest accounts from that place it appears, that these settlers, together with the new ones who had recently arrived from Canada, (including the discharged men of the De Meuron and Watteville regiments), were establishing themselves, with every reasonable prospect of success. During their route, they had invariably experienced the friendly offices of the Indian population; and the native tribes in the immediate neighbourhood of the Red River, have formally and solemnly declared their intention to support them. With respect to the miserable race termed Metifs, Half-breeds, or Bois-brulés, a band neither in the slightest degree formidable from their numbers, nor their courage, even a large portion of these have now declared that they mean to support the Red River Colony. It cannot, indeed, be expected that such banditti are to be trusted, while within the sphere of the influence and bribes of those who originally hired them to commit acts of aggression against the colony, and afterwards remunerated them for their hostility. But if the North-West Company, by whom they were so employed, can be restrained, by the interference of Government, from again instigating these ignorant and deluded people to renew the outrages against their fellow-subjects, there can be no doubt of the Settlement remaining henceforward secure and undisturbed. Without some adequate interference, however, it can scarcely be expected that the Company's partners in the interior, will be induced to relinquish their endeavours to cause it final destruction. Their rancour towards the colony has, in all probability, increased in proportion to their disappointment, in being twice baffled in their hopes to effect a permanent dispersion of the colonists.

A sufficiency of documents, I should suppose, has been submitted to your Lordship in the course of the last two or three years, fully to satisfy His Majesty's Government, that, from the commencement of the Red River Colony, there existed, on the part of the North-West Company, a determined resolution to destroy it. If that fact be admitted,—and I do not hesitate in asserting, that it is impossible for any person who will investigate the matter with attention, to entertain the slightest doubt on the subject,—every thing which ensued must appear a natural consequence of such determination. If the Company, in following up their resolution, happened not to succeed in their attempts to destroy the Settlement in one way, they were ready to try it in another. They began by endeavouring to instigate the native Indians against the colonists; but in this they completely failed. Their next proceeding—in addition to bribing and seducing a considerable portion of the settlers to desert from the colony, and break their contracts—was to hire, arm, and array their half-breed dependents, and make them, under the personal direction of partners and clerks of the Company, attack the colonists, burn their houses, and drive them by force from the Settlement. And, at the very time they were planning and executing these measures, their agents and principal partners were addressing memorials to Government, in which they boasted of their humanity and kindness towards these people, whom they were thus shamefully oppressing.

I have the honour to be,
My Lord,
Your Lordship's obedient
And humble Servant,
J. HALKETT.

Earl Bathurst,
&c. &c. &c.

HISTORICAL INTERPRETATIONS

3 From W. Brian Stewart, *The Ermatingers: A 19th Century Ojibwa-Canadian Family* (Vancouver: UBC Press, 2008), 74–81.

OJIBWA CHIEF AND MONTREAL POLICE OFFICER

In 1849, friction between Ojibwa of the Sault Ste Marie area and whites was causing the government concern. Charles saw a chance to use his influence as an Ojibwa to calm the situation. To understand his role, however, we must go back twenty years or more. In his trading days at Sault Ste Marie, Charles Sr had worked mainly on the south side of Lake Superior with the Sandy Lake and Fond du Lac Ojibwa. Among them of course were Katawabidai and his sons. Another band of Ojibwa headed by Chief Shingwaukonse lived at Garden River, close to Sault Ste Marie. Shingwaukonse became famous for his pressure on church and government to recognize Aboriginal land rights. Through intermarriage, he formed an alliance with another nearby chief, Nebenagoching, whose extended family included many of the Métis inhabitants of the Sault and surrounding areas. In time many of these Métis became de facto members of the Ojibwa band organizations.

Shingwaukonse saw the value of creating a stable and prosperous community of Ojibwa and Métis at the Sault. Charles Sr's retirement had commercially weakened the Sandy Lake Ojibwa in the Sault area, and Shingwaukonse decided to fill the vacuum. In 1842, he petitioned the governor general for the right of the local Ojibwa to take over the Ermatinger property in Sault Ste Marie. Since the general land question had never been settled between the Ojibwa and the Canadian government, the Ermatingers were legally little more than squatters. Shingwaukonse's petition apparently failed.[1]

Five years later the Ermatingers themselves submitted their own petition to the governor general's office on behalf of 'Charlotte Kattawabidé'. An accompanying letter warned the government that problems between the Ojibwa and several mining companies trying to locate near Lake Superior could result in loss of life.[2] The accuracy of this prediction suggests that the Ermatingers were maintaining links with their Ojibwa relatives. Janet Chute's biography of Chief Shingwaukonse says that the Ermatingers had their uncle Mang'osid support their claims.[3]

Charlotte's petition starts with the claim that she was the hereditary head chief of the Ojibwa.[4] Her ancestors, she maintains, had possessed the territory surrounding Lake Superior for hunting and fishing since time immemorial. According to an ancient custom, she, as the eldest child of Katawabidai, 'the late hereditary head Chief of the Chippeway', had inherited his rights and privileges. She was sending the governor general a flag, given by the French government to her 'great great ancestor' Brave Heart, then chief of the tribe. As the insignia of that chieftainship, he had handed it down to her grandfather, 'Boy-Os-wa' (Bi-aus-wah); thence to her father, Katawabidai; and then to herself.

The petition then takes a patriotic turn. In the years Charlotte had lived in Lower Canada, and after the death of her father, Ojibwa on the south shore of Superior had received compensation for ceding their land to the United States. Neither she nor her children could share in this without forswearing allegiance to Britain and becoming Americans. As loyal subjects taught 'to love and respect the flag of the Country under which they have been born and protected', they could not do so, though they 'suffered great loss' by forfeiting all claim for compensation.

The Ermatingers were here referring to an 1826 treaty between the American government and Chippewa (Ojibwa) of the American Sault Ste Marie area. Article 4 said the 'half breeds' of the area should be given permanent property and fixed residences. The Chippewa wished this because of the affection they bore to the Métis, and the interest they felt in their welfare. A schedule listed the Métis who would receive land grants, including 'the children of George Ermatinger, being of Shawnee extraction, two sections collectively.'[5] Thus the American children or grandchildren of Charles Sr's brother seem to have acquired Indian land through the treaty.

Until this point Charlotte's petition has based its land claims on the rights of Charlotte and her family. Now, the argument broadens. She has learned 'with infinite regret and pain' that the provincial government was, without her consent, disposing of lands on the Canadian shore of the lake, 'the proper inheritance of herself and her children.' The provincial government had not, she pointed out, gained the consent of the Ojibwa people for the disposal of their Canadian lands. In similar cases since the treaty of William Penn in 1682,[6] the imperial government had invariably acquired such land 'by regular and recognized principles of justice', specifically through conventions and treaties. The civilized world had sympathized with the tribes forcibly removed from their possessions by the US government, even though that was done under the cover of treaty or convention.

This was probably a reference to a treaty signed on 28 March 1836 at Washington, DC, negotiated by Henry Schoolcraft on behalf of the United States with the chiefs and delegates of the American Ottawa and Chippewa.[7] Oddly, Charles Jr had himself been a witness at the signing, presumably invited by his Ojibwa relatives and friends, not by the US government. This treaty had not worked out well for the Indians, because it forced all Chippewa to go to Sandy Lake for their annuities. They usually had to wait weeks there in highly unsanitary conditions, which lead to epidemics of measles and dysentery. Many died, many were unpaid, and others were removed to reservations in the West.[8] Andrew Blackbird, a Native historian, later wrote that the Ojibwa and Ottawa had signed under compulsion while the US government had reneged on $140,000 in payments.[9]

At this point, Charlotte appealed directly to the governor general and his 'high and well merited reputation for justice.' She wanted him to appoint a commissioner with no interest in the mining companies to investigate the claims of herself and others interested. Unlike earlier petitions from Charles Sr this one based itself on the territorial rights of the Ojibwa from 'time immemorial.' The petition in effect asserted that Charlotte and her family, as Ojibwa, should share in the territorial rights of the tribe, and hence deserved compensation.

Whatever the legal status of the claim, the Ermatingers were publicly stating that they were Ojibwa with the rights of Ojibwa. More, they asserted that Charlotte, as the eldest child of a hereditary chief, was therefore herself a chief. This is very doubtful. The Ojibwa had no tradition of women as civil chiefs and none of the ancestral chiefs whom Charlotte named were women.

The Indian Department received the petition on 8 May 1847, and the government turned it down on 24 June. In the interim, on 30 May, Charles had received a letter from Samuel Atkinson of Sault Ste Marie. Mr Ballenden, Hudson's Bay Company representative at the Sault, had approached Atkinson with a number of questions about the Ermatingers. Was Charlotte's father an Ojibwa chief? A chief of the whole nation? Did he 'adhere' to the United States? Where were Charles and Charlotte married? Where were the older children born? Atkinson felt that Ballenden 'was if anything adverse' to the Ermatingers' claim.[10]

Two years after the Ermatingers received the denial of this petition, they sent off another in the name of a very indignant Charlotte. She said she must 'earnestly protest against the opinions and proceedings of your Excellency's late advisors which, in good faith', had led him to reject the petition. The information received by the Executive Council on Matters of State 'was entirely of an ex parte nature.' She had not been not notified of the discussion, nor given the chance to testify herself and counteract the evidence. She attached Atkinson's letter and claimed that Ballenden had inquired about her under instructions from Sir George Simpson of the Hudson's Bay Company. The company was 'most hostile to the interest' of the Ermatingers, and was itself making claims to parts of the same territory. Yet, she claimed, it had been unfairly appointed arbiter of the petitioner's rights.

Even worse, some Ojibwa had apparently agreed to a treaty with a commission on land rights. Charlotte objected to any arrangements in which she and her children were not consenting parties. Proposed members of any government commission should have no interest in either the mining companies or the Hudson's Bay Company. Rather the commission should consist of an officer of the Indian Department with two others 'not in any way associated with the question', and should

be instructed to investigate the Ermatingers' claim. Charlotte also wanted the June 1847 decision reversed by the council. But on 11 August 1849, the council committee saw no reason to do so. Although both petitions failed, by arguing for Aboriginal rights, the family had supported Shingwaukonse in his fight for those rights. Later, Shingwaukonse would, in traditional Ojibwa fashion, return that support.

THE MINING COMPANIES AND THE OJIBWA

The British and the Indians had never settled the land question on the east and north shores of Lake Huron from Penetanguishene to Sault Ste Marie, nor along the north shore of Lake Superior to Batchawana Bay. With the discovery of minerals, mining companies began work and demanded the area be opened up. Local Ojibwa protested. In the summer of 1849, a group took over the buildings and property of the Quebec Mining Company at Mica Bay, Lake Superior, almost 100 kilometres from Sault Ste Marie. At a grand council, the Ojibwa decided to burn the buildings should company personnel with troops land at the bay.

Meanwhile, the government had sent a detachment of the Royal Canadian Rifle Brigade from Toronto to Sault Ste Marie via Penetanguishene. Captain A.P. Cooper had orders to take back the Mica Bay property. Rumours spread that Red River Ojibwa had agreed to send 2,000 men to help the locals in any fight. Cooper commissioned a steamship to carry the detachment to Mica Bay but violent storms drove it back to Sault Ste Marie, where the brigade wintered.[11] By now, however, the protesters at Mica Bay had returned to their homes.

In addition to troops, the government sent Commissioner William B. Robinson to negotiate treaties with the Ojibwa.[12] Canadian Ojibwa certainly knew of American Ojibwa dissatisfaction with the Washington Treaty of 1836, and perhaps that poisoned the atmosphere at the Sault. Of the Canadian negotiations, Robinson wrote that interested parties had advised the Indians 'to insist on such extravagant terms that I felt it quite impossible to grant them.' Some individuals tried hard, he said, to create dissatisfaction among the Ojibwa.[13] The discussions drew newspaper reporters from across Canada and the United States.

CHARLES GOES TO SAULT STE MARIE

When the government sent Robinson to treat with the Ojibwa, it also commissioned Charles to be magistrate at Sault Ste Marie 'should his services be required.'[14] In November 1849 Lieutenant-General Rowan ordered him to the Sault. The storm and heavy ice that had driven Captain Cooper's vessel back to Sault Ste Marie also caused Charles great difficulty. The early freeze-up prevented him from travelling by steamer to Sault Ste Marie, but the stormy weather made it 'both inconvenient and dangerous' to cross the lakes by canoe. Instead, he made a 500-kilometre journey around Lake Huron by canoe and on foot in terrible weather. He said the party, which included his brother James, endured 'great hardship and misery'. He did not exaggerate: at one point, the ice on Lake Huron destroyed two canoes in which they were travelling. The Robinson Commission later paid £2/–/– to 'Papasainse, un Sauvage' for the canoes.[15]

At this time, Charles later explained in a petition to the governor general for a position in the Indian Department, difficulties between the Ojibwa and the whites were 'imminently endangering the peace'. (This echoed the warning in the letter accompanying Charlotte's 1847 petition.) He had been 'selected on this expedition from his known influence with the tribe of Indians aforesaid, by his knowledge of their language, and by his immediate connexion with them as one of their chiefs.' He had remained with Cooper's expedition till it was withdrawn after restoring order, and 'after the conclusion of a most advantageous and

favourable treaty for his Majesty's government with the Indians.'[16]

Not long after he arrived in Sault Ste Marie, Robinson wrote in his diary that he had seen 'Mr. Ermatinger' and arranged with him to go to Garden River the next day to see the chiefs. Two days later at Garden River he explained why he had come and fixed the time of the formal meeting to be held there: 'Immediately after issue of the presents I took their agreement in writing to that effect. They all expressed themselves satisfied and promised in presence of Captain Ermatinger and others to offer no opposition to mining operations', relying on the matter being settled at the appointed time.[17] Robinson seemed to recognize that Charles had connections to, and some influence with, the Garden River Ojibwa.

The Robinson-Huron and Robinson-Superior Treaties were signed with 'the principal men of the OJIBEWA INDIANS, inhabiting and claiming the Eastern and Northern Shores of Lake Huron, from Penetanguishine to Sault Ste Marie, and thence to Batchewanaung Bay on the Northern Shore of Lake Superior; together with the Islands in the said Lakes, opposite to the Shores thereof, and inland to the Height of land which separates the Territory covered by the charter of the Honorable Hudson Bay Company from Canada; as well as all unconceded lands within the limits of Canada West to which they have any just claim.' The Ojibwa ceded this huge area for £4,000 cash, plus £1,100 in annual payments. They received 'full and free privilege' to hunt and fish on unoccupied Crown lands and they retained reserves that they could sell only to the Crown.[18]

Commissioner Robinson later wrote that the 'half-breeds' of the area might seek to be recognized by the government in future payments. To forestall this, the commissioner had told them he came to treat with the chiefs. When the chiefs received compensation they could give as much or as little to the Métis as they pleased. This, he said, silenced the critics. He also advised non-Indian residents at Sault Ste Marie who were anxious to obtain title to their land to memorialize the government in the usual way. He recommended that the government deal liberally with those who could show a fair claim.[19]

Following Robinson's recommendation, the name C.O. Ermatinger headed a list of 55 inhabitants of Sault Ste Marie petitioning the government. All but five or six, said the petition, were 'of mixed Indian blood and had been born upon the soil.' They had all held and cultivated the land where they had resided for years. Many had inherited the land from their Indian mothers, or had bought it from Métis. But the land they lived on had been ceded by the recent treaty. If the properties came on the market in the usual way, the petitioners would lack the means to buy them and would be dispossessed. They prayed that they 'would not be disturbed in their possessions . . . or in any way molested' and that the lands would be confirmed to them by a free grant from the Crown.[20]

Four leading Ojibwa chiefs backed this petition. The chiefs said that the petitioners had settled and cultivated the land for upwards of 40 years 'by and with the consent of ourselves and peoples.' With scarcely an exception, all had married Indian women and had families with them. They were 'the children of the sisters and the daughters of your Memorialists, thus having an inheritance in the country equal to our own, and bound to it by as strong and heart felt ties as we ourselves.' The chiefs also asked that 100 acres of land be granted freely to Métis scattered throughout the ceded territories. Included among the Sault residents listed by the chiefs for a free grant is Charles Jr, with four acres of land. Curiously the three witnesses to the chiefs' petition were C.O. Ermatinger, his brother James Ermatinger, and Allan MacDonnell.[21]

The four chiefs also signed another petition specifically regarding the Ermatingers. They had asked Robinson to provide in the treaty itself 'for those of their kindred who had claims upon them for past benefits and services.' By this, they had 'hoped to repay, in some measure, the benefits and services received by them at the hands of the late Charles Oakes Ermatinger and his wife, Charlotte Maun-nun-once Caw-daw-be-tai.' Because Robinson had not done this, the petition asked that each of the Ermatinger children be granted a mining location of their choice in the ceded land. An accompanying document referred to the Ermatinger family and 'their uniform kindness while they were living amongst us.'[22]

The chiefs signing the petitions of 1850 were Shingwaukonse himself, Nebenagoching (Joseph Sayers), Piabetassung, and Kabaosa (John). The last two were Shingwaukonse's sons-in-law. None seem to be direct relatives of Charlotte, but the phrases 'for those of their kindred' and 'children of the sisters' demonstrate the closeness of the relationship.

Following the treaty, the commissioner of Crown land, John Rolph, recommended a grant of 50 acres of land to each Métis applicant at a nominal rate of one shilling per acre, provided applicants settled there within the next year.[23] Presumably for that reason Charles did not apply since he was now living permanently in Montreal. In July 1852, he leased the old stone house to Mr and Mrs D. Pim, who began a hotel business. The following year he quit deeded the place to the Pims for $3,000.[24] Not only were the Ermatingers no longer resident in the house but they were not, after all, granted mining rights.

The chiefs' petitions, made no doubt at the behest of Charles, show he was no disinterested observer at the treaty negotiations; rather, he had three conflicting interests. As magistrate, he had a duty to support Robinson in keeping the peace. As a claimant for land in Sault Ste Marie and as one seeking mining rights, he had self-interest. And as one of the 'children of the sisters' and an Ojibwa 'chief', he had a moral obligation towards his relatives and friends. Yet we find him later pleading for personal compensation from the government for helping in 'the conclusion of a most *advantageous and favourable treaty for his Majesty's government* with the Indians.' The italicized phrase strikes a disturbing note: just where did his loyalties lie?

Charles was not alone in this conflict of interest. Métis had long participated in treaty making between Indians and government. In doing so, they were protecting their own interests, as were the federal government and the Indian representatives involved in the negotiations.[25] All the Ermatingers' many petitions aimed at securing their Sault Ste Marie land, including the petitions based on their claim to be Ojibwa. This did not prove insincerity. In Ojibwa culture the exchange of material gifts was itself part of the bonding process. The chiefs' request that land and mining rights be granted the Ermatingers in repayment of earlier 'kindness' confirms their kinship with the Ojibwa.

Nor can Charles be faulted for supporting the treaties. In 1850 they were not, on their face, unjust. In particular, one clause promised the Ojibwa that the government would in the future increase the annuity if the lands proved sufficiently productive to do so 'without Government loss'. The annuities were increased in 1878, bringing the annual grant from 96 cents to $4 per head, or a total of $14,000.[26] That $14,000 was little enough considering the billions of dollars in minerals later extracted from the lands, however, and it was the only adjustment ever made. The Crown used the phrase 'without Government loss' to avoid future increases.

According to the recent Royal Commission on Aboriginal Peoples, Robinson cannot be blamed for failing to predict either the scale of resource development in the area, or that the Ojibwa would lose their rights under the treaties due to the actions of both private interests and government. Despite the treaties' clause guaranteeing access to Crown lands, the Ojibwa were 'denied even the same terms of access as non-Aboriginal people.' For instance, one Ojibwa, after staking a gold mining claim, found his stakes pulled out and replaced by those of a white man. The authorities took no corrective action. Government officials took control even of Aboriginal lands, the commission found, with a stewardship that was 'abysmal' and employment policies that were mostly failures. Government violations of treaty rights forced increasing numbers of Aboriginal people onto public assistance. Neither Robinson nor Charles Ermatinger could have foreseen that the treaties, seemingly fair in 1850, would largely fail to protect Ojibwa rights against encroachment by both government and private enterprise. But fail they did.[27] [. . .]

NOTES

1. Janet Chute, *The Legacy of Shingwaukonse.* Toronto: University of Toronto Press, 1998, 72–3, 81, 99–100.
2. Library and Archives Canada (LAC), RG 10, vol. 163 (reel C-11501), no. 94932, William to T.E. Campbell, 7 May 1847.
3. Chute, *Legacy of Shingwaukonse*, 99–100.
4. LAC, RG 1, L-3, vol. 279, Canada Land Petitions, K bundle 5, 1848–50, no. 13½, Petitions of Charlotte, 1847 and 1849.
5. 'Treaty with the Chippewa, 5 August 1826', in *Indian Affairs: Laws and Treaties*, ed. Charles Joseph Kappler, Washington, DC: Government Printing Office, 273.
6. William Penn (1644–1718), a Quaker, founded what became the state of Pennsylvania. Whether in fact he signed a Great Treaty at the village of Shackamaxon in 1682 is open to doubt, as the treaty has never been found. But he and his agents bought land from the Delaware, whom he saw as its rightful 'owners'.
7. 'Treaty with the Ottawas, etc., 28 March 1836', in *Indian Affairs*, ed., Kappler, 455.
8. Victor Barnouw, *Acculturation and Personality among the Wisconsin Chippewa.* American Anthropological Association, 1950. Reprint, Millwood, NY: Kraus, 37.

9. Andrew J. Blackbird, *History of the Ottawa and Chippewa Indians of Michigan*. Ypsilanti, MI: Ypsilanti Printing House, 1887, 51–52.

10. LAC, RG 1, L-3, vol. 279, Canada Land Petitions, K bundle 5, 1848–50, no. 13½i.

11. LAC, MG 13, WO1, vol. 563, nos. 51–54 and 69, Reports by Capt. A.P. Cooper, 3 and 16 December 1849.

12. William B. Robinson (1797–1873) was a Tory politician and member for Simcoe. He had trading posts in the Muskoka district, which gave him much influence with the Indians there.

13. W.B. Robinson, 'Report to Indian Affairs, 24 September 1850.' In *Treaties of Canada with the Indians of Manitoba and the North-West Territories, Including the Negotiations on Which They Were Based, and Other Information Relating Thereto, 1826–1889*, ed. Alexander Morris, 17–20. Toronto: Belfords, Clarke, 1880. These individuals possibly included Allan MacDonell (1808–88), a lawyer who helped the Ojibwa pressure the government for compensation. Donald Swainson, 'MacDonell, Allan', in *Dictionary of Canadian Biography*. Vol. 11, 553. Toronto: University of Toronto Press, 1982.

14. LAC, RG 8 (C series), 1A, vol. 80, no. 94, Certificate as magistrate to the Rifle Brigade at Sault Ste Marie.

15. Province of Canada, LAJA, 1851, vol. 10, app. II, 'Réponse à une addresse distribué aux sauvages du Lac Superior.' Papasainse was a signatory to the Lake Huron Treaty.

16. LAC, RG 8 (C series), 1A, vol. 163 (reel C-11501), no. 94932, William to T.E. Campbell, 7 May 1847; RG 8 (C series), 1A, vol. 500, nos. 92–95, Charles Jr. 'Memorial to Lord Elgin', 8 November 1850.

17. Archives Ontario (AO), MS 4, W.B. Robinson, Transcription of Diaries, Sault Ste Marie, 29 April and 1 May 1850.

18. W.B. Robinson, *Copy of the Robinson Treaty: Made in the Year 1850 With the Ojibwa Indians of Lake Huron Converying Certain Lands to the Crown*. Reprinted from the Edition of 1939 by Roger Duhamel, F.R.S.C. Queen's Preinter and Controller of Stationery Ottawa, 1964. Cat. No. Ci 72-1264, 3–8. See also William B. Henderson, 'Indian Treaties', in *The Canadian Encyclopedia*, vol. 2, 873–4. Edmonton: Hurtig Publishing, 1985.

19. Robinson, 'Report to Indian Affairs', 20.

20. LAC, RG 1, L3, 182B, e-bundle 6, no. 21, Petition of the Undersigned Inhabitants, n.d., 21e–21f.

21. Ibid., Petition of 16 [four] Undersigned Chiefs, 21h–21i.

22. LAC, RG 1, L3, 182B, e-bundle 6, no. 3, Memorial of the Undersigned Chiefs, 10 September 1850, 3a–3b.

23. LAC, RG 1, L3 182B, e-bundle 6, no. 21, Commissioner of Crown Lands, John Rabb to the Governor-General, 29 November 1850, 21, 21a, 21b.

24. Heather Ingram, *Views of the Sault*. Burnstown, ON: General Store Publishing House, 1995, 101; Sneakers, 'Pim Family.' http://www3.sympatico.ca/sneakers/Pimfamily.htm.

25. David T. McNab, 'Métis Participation in the Treaty Making Process', *Native Studies Review* 1, 2 (1985): 74.

26. Alexander Morris, *The Treaties of Canada with the Indians of Manitoba and the North-West Territories, Including the Negotiations on Which They Were Based, and Other Information Relating Thereto, 1826–1889*. Toronto: Belfords, Clarke, 1880, 18 and note.

27. Royal Commission on Aboriginal Peoples, *Final Report*, vol. 2, 4.3 'Failure of Alternative Economic Options', Opening Statement, 486–87, 491–92.

4   From Gerhard Ens, 'Prologue to the Red River Resistance: Pre-liminal Politics and the Triumph of Riel', *Journal of the Canadian Historical Association* 5(1) (1994): 111–23.

The Red River Resistance of 1869–70 is usually thought to have begun in October of 1869 with the stopping of the Canadian survey, the formation of the Métis 'National Committee' led by Louis Riel, and the blockade of the road to Pembina. As well, most historians credit Riel with taking the initiative in formulating a Métis response to the Canadian plan to acquire Rupert's Land. What these accounts miss is the vibrant debate and conflict within the Métis community about what their response to Confederation should be. The first coherent plan of assuring Métis rights was formulated in July 1869 and was opposed by Riel. It was not until Riel had defeated this first plan and its leaders that he assumed leadership of the movement against annexation.

It is this early 'pre-liminal'[1] phase of the Red River Resistance—July through October 1869—that this paper proposes to examine in some detail. During this period, two Métis groups, one led by William Dease and the other by Louis Riel, were locked in a power struggle. It was a struggle on a symbolic level in which the two sides offered different paradigms of Métis 'communitas'[2] as the basis on which to present their case to the Canadian government. The struggle occurred at the grass roots level involving such tactics as negotiation and coalition formation. It was not until Riel had defeated William Dease for the leadership of the Resistance and consolidated his basis of support among the French Métis that he felt strong enough to initiate the breach of October 1869. The analysis offered here concentrates on the activities of individuals vying for power within very limited political settings, and is interested in how those who achieved power carried out the consciously held goals of the group.

It is my contention that the initial Métis conflict between Dease and Riel not only set the tone for the larger Resistance to come but determined, to a large extent, the problems Riel and his faction would have in building a consensus in the Colony. To this end, the paper will explain the nature of this power struggle, the opposing paradigms of Métis communitas, the tactics Riel used to defeat his rivals, and the implications that this power struggle had for Métis unity in the Colony after October 1869.

The few historians who have examined this early period of the Red River Resistance in any detail have tended to denigrate the Métis that opposed Riel. W.L. Morton, in his extended introduction to Alexander Begg's journal, tried to show that the true nature of the Resistance was revealed in the conflict between the Métis 'half-articulated demand for corporate rights . . . and the intention of the Canadian authorities to grant individual rights in due course.'[3] In his view, it was the 'new nation' of the Métis which was 'the central and dynamic protagonist of the Red River Resistance.'[4] To make this argument Morton downplayed the role the Catholic clergy had in championing Riel's leadership,[5] and implied that those Métis opposed to Riel were dupes of the Canadians in Red River.[6] To have accorded the Métis opponents of Riel some volition and legitimacy would have undercut his argument that Riel was the undisputed leader of the French Métis in Red River.

Philippe Mailhot's account of the same period provides a much more accurate account of the role the Catholic clergy, especially that of Father Ritchot. Based on a detailed reconstruction of Ritchot's journal, Mailhot details the active part he played in directing Riel's Resistance.[7] Mailhot's account, however, closely follows Ritchot's partisan perspective. While Mailhot does not completely endorse Ritchot's argument that Dease's actions were directed by John Christian Schultz,[8] he does note that Dease's proposals mirrored those of the Canadian Party,[9] and that Dease and his party were not up to the task of directing the Resistance to annexation.[10] What both Morton and Mailhot overlook are the antecedents to the Dease proposals, and the active role the Catholic clergy had in discrediting the Dease party.

The first major Métis response to the news of the impending transfer of Rupert's Land to Canada came during the summer of 1869. In response to the vitriolic demonstrations of the Canadians in the Colony,[11] and in order to protect their land rights, a number of Métis called a large public meeting. This group included some of the traditional Métis leadership in the Colony such as William Dease, Pascal Breland, and William Hallet. Dease was the son of John W. Dease and Jenny Beignoit, and had been born in 1827 at Calling Lake. He settled at Red River and married Marguerite Genthon. The couple and their large family lived and farmed in both St. Vital and St. Norbert. By 1869 Dease was a prominent French-Métis trader and farmer, and member of the Council of Assiniboia. An indication of Dease's close connection to the various native communities around Red River was his fluency in French, English, Ojibwa, and Sioux.[12] Pascal Breland, a son-in-law of Cuthbert Grant, was a hunt and trading chief of numerous hivernant villages, the patriarch of St. François Xavier, and was also a member of the Council of Assiniboia in 1869. William Hallet was the most prominent English-Métis chief of the annual buffalo hunt with close family ties to numerous French-Métis families.[13]

These men placed an advertisement in the *Nor'Wester* inviting all Métis to meet at the Court House on 29 July 1869 to discuss what the Métis response should be to the proposed transfer of Rupert's Land to Canada.[14] At this meeting, William Dease quickly took the initiative and advanced what might be termed an 'Aboriginal Rights' paradigm for Métis rights.[15] Dease called on the Métis to defend their rights to land in the Settlement, and disputed the

validity of the Earl of Selkirk's purchase of the same from the Indians. The Métis, he said, should demand the £300,000 that Canada was about to pay to the Hudson's Bay Company. To this end the Métis should form a new government in the Colony to displace the HBC, and make their case to the Canadian government. While the first proposal elicited considerable support, the call to form a new government did not and the meeting broke up with no clear plan of action decided.

Historians have generally regarded this first initiative as a failure and attributed its lack of success to the notion that Dease and Hallet were dupes of John Christian Schultz and that their program too closely resembled that of the Canadians in the Settlement—perceptions which apparently put the Métis on guard and restrained them from supporting Dease and his proposals.[16] However, this view is based on an entirely uncritical acceptance of the comments of Fathers Dugast and Ritchot,[17] both of whom were themselves not only steadfast partisans in the conflict but had also been the first to draw attention to the similarity between Dease's proposal and the Canadians' plans in order to undermine the former. The meeting of July 29, consequently, was not a failure, but merely the opening round of a debate that would continue until early October.

Looking at the history of the Red River Settlement in a little longer perspective, it is also clear that the Dease proposal, far from being inspired by Schultz's Canadian faction in Red River, was an aboriginal rights position designed by the traditional leadership of the Métis. Indeed, the Métis position as presented by Dease had been worked out nearly a decade earlier, in 1860, when it seemed likely that Red River would become a Crown Colony, a possibility which raised questions about Indian title, Hudson's Bay Company jurisdiction, and individual land rights in Red River.[18]

Debate over who had title began in 1860 when Peguis, the Saulteaux Chief, challenged the HBC claim to land in the Red River Settlement with the simple argument that the

Indians had never sold it to Lord Selkirk and the Hudson's Bay Company.[19] That prompted the Métis, under the chairmanship of Pascal Breland, to hold a large meeting at the Royal Hotel near Fort Garry to discuss their position. The most eminent Métis traders and hunters—William Dease, Urbain Delorme, Pierre Falcon, William Hallet, George Flett, and William McGillis—all spoke, and all agreed that, the treaty being one of friendship, not sale, the HBC had not received title to the Red River Settlement by treaty with Peguis in 1817. Indeed, it was their view that the Métis had a legitimate claim to the land and, moreover, that their claim should have priority; they were descendants of the Cree, the first residents of the area, while the Saulteaux had arrived in the Red River region only shortly before 1817. Accordingly, the meeting concluded with an agreement by all present that since no proper arrangements had been made with the Native tribes of the region and since the Métis were now on the land and the immediate representatives of the first tribes in the region, the Métis should use every legitimate means to advance their claim for consideration in any arrangement which the Imperial Government might see fit to make. The meeting then adjourned until May, when the various Indian chiefs and wintering Métis would be in the Colony.[20]

This second gathering confirmed the conclusions of the first, and a statement was taken from André Trottier, one of three witnesses to the 1817 Selkirk Treaty, who swore that the Chiefs had not sold the land but only rented it to Selkirk for 20 years.[21] The controversy died down when it became clear that Crown Colony status was not forthcoming, but it subsequently flared up again in 1861 when the HBC decided to exact payment for all lands occupied in the Colony at the rate of 7s 6d per acre. If this payment was not received, the HBC warned, these lands would be sold to the first purchaser, in which case all improvements would be lost to the present occupiers. While the threat was soon withdrawn, it provoked an indignant reaction in several parishes where the Métis

reaffirmed that no monies would be paid, that the HBC had no right to the land (never having purchased it in the first place), and that it was the Métis themselves who had a very palpable right to it, being the 'descendants of the original lords of the soil.'[22] While arguably minor incidents, these indignation meetings illustrate that the traditional Métis leadership had worked out a theory of aboriginal rights as early as 1861 and were already using it to defend their land claims in Red River. It was a position that owed nothing to the Canadians in Red River, and it was this theory that Dease reiterated in July 1869.

Given Riel's opposition to Dease and his party, it is important to delineate Riel's paradigm of Métis communitas and the sources for it. That Riel should have assumed leadership of the Métis in 1869 is somewhat surprising. His father, who had been a leader of the free trade movement in 1849, was fondly remembered in Red River, but Louis Riel Jr. had no natural constituency among the Métis. He had left the Settlement at the age of thirteen in 1858 to attend school in Montreal and had only returned to the Colony in the summer of 1868. He did not farm; he did not participate in the buffalo hunt; he did not trade; and, on his return to Red River, he refused his friend Louis Schmidt's suggestion to begin freighting to St. Paul. Indeed, from his return to Red River until he assumed leadership of the Resistance, it is not clear that Riel did very much of anything. The one report of his activities, albeit from an unsympathetic observer, George R. Winship, gives the impression that he was just an ordinary town loafer who lived entirely off his mother. Winship, who had arrived in Red River about the same time as Riel, also noted that Riel was never known to earn anything himself by manual labour, preferring to hang around saloons a good deal 'waiting for something to turn up for him to do suitable to his tastes.'[23] Those historians who even bother to question why Riel rose to the leadership of the Métis usually point to his education as putting him naturally in the forefront. While this reasoning is plausible, it would not have carried much weight with the Métis buffalo hunters, merchant traders, or Métis councillors of Assiniboia.[24]

In fact, Riel's true constituency in 1869 was the Catholic Church, and it was through the Church that most of his influence would come. The most recent study of the Catholic Church's role in the Resistance leaves off deciding whether Riel or Catholic priests directed the Resistance, but clearly proves that Father Dugast (the main teacher at the St. Boniface College) and Father Ritchot (the parish priest of St. Norbert) were close partners with Riel in deciding Métis strategy in 1869–70.[25] With Archbishop Taché out of the Settlement, Dugast and Ritchot took the lead in guiding their Métis flock. Both men were secular priests who had been born in Quebec and shared a French-Canadian nationalism that saw the French Métis sharing a common history, language and culture with the *canadiens*. Ritchot in particular felt very threatened by the recent arrivals from Canada and feared for the religious rights of the Métis.[26] Furthermore, both men condemned the traditional buffalo-hunting economy of the Métis, hoping to win them over to a settled agricultural way of life.[27] It is therefore not surprising that the two men distrusted the traditional Métis leadership and their aboriginal-rights justification for Resistance in 1869. For his part, Ritchot personally disliked William Dease (though Dease was a Catholic) and regarded him as a man 'sans princippe et aussi hignorant qu'orgueilleux.'[28] Father Dugast, meanwhile, criticized Dease's aboriginal-rights justification of Resistance in a report to Taché, calling Dease a fool and adding that if the details of the assembly of July 29 were heard in Canada, the Métis would all be taken for a band of lunatics.[29]

For Dugast and Ritchot, then, Riel most closely represented their ideal for the Métis of Red River. Attending the College of Montreal, he had been educated by the Sulpician fathers (who trained their students 'as a Catholic and French-Canadian elite, proud of their difference

from the English majority of North America'[30]) and so was steeped in the twin tenets of patriotism and religion. As Riel wrote in 1874, 'The French-Canadian Métis of the North (West) are a branch of the French-Canadian tree. They want to grow like that tree, with that tree; they never want to be separated from it, they want to suffer and rejoice with it.'[31] Accordingly, it is easy to understand why Ritchot viewed Riel as a 'jeune homme du pays (et de talent)'.[32]

With this paradigm of Métis communitas in mind, the events during and after the Assembly of July 29 become more explicable. Following Dease's speech, John Bruce, who would later become the first president of Riel's 'National Committee', took the floor and castigated Dease for advocating revolt. As a magistrate and member of the Council of Assiniboia, Dease should be the first to defend the government of the country, Bruce contended, and all such intrigues should be opposed. Apparently Bruce's arguments found their mark and the assembly broke up without endorsing Dease's plan of action. Father Dugast's lengthy report of this meeting makes it clear that Bruce had been carefully coached in his address.[33] Most of the evidence suggests that Ritchot, Dugast, and possibly Riel, had done the coaching and, indeed, Ritchot later admitted that he had advised his parishioners to be on their guard, and that he considered the object of the meeting to be of a dangerous character.[34] As well, both Ritchot and Dugast went out of their way to paint the Dease initiative as being inspired by John Christian Schultz.

Further meetings followed in August as the Métis continued to debate the position they should take to protect their rights considering the proposed transfer to Canada.[35] The Dease initiative, however, had collapsed by early October and with it the aboriginal-rights paradigm of Métis communitas. Writing later, Ritchot attributed the collapse of this early movement to a failure of leadership (the leaders being bought off by Canadian transportation contracts), to the Protestant clergy's interceding with the English Métis to accept the transfer, and to the greed of some French Métis merchants who saw Confederation as an economic opportunity.[36] While there was some truth to Ritchot's assessment, more important was the determined opposition of Riel, Ritchot, and Dugast, and their elaboration of another paradigm of Métis communitas that carried more emotional weight with the French Métis.

By the end of August, the French Métis had increasingly come to see Confederation as the annexation of Red River by Protestant Orange Ontario and, consequently, as a threat to their religious rights.[37] News that William McDougall would be the new governor of the territory only raised the fears of the French-Catholic clergy and the many French Métis who viewed him as one with the other Canadians in the Colony (John Schultz, Charles Mair, John Snow and J.S. Dennis), all of whom were widely distrusted.[38] Moreover, by this time there were also rumours circulating that McDougall was a 'priest murderer'.[39]

Dugast, writing to Taché, recounted a conversation between the Métis and John Snow that clearly showed the mindset of the time. Snow, who had been sent from Canada to build a road from Fort Garry to Lake of the Woods, tried to calm the fears of the Métis of Pointe-de-Chêne, but they would have none of it. They replied that he was friendly now that he was weak, but that they knew how the English had treated the Catholics of Upper Canada. 'You are orangemen and you are all alike.'[40]

How these sentiments and rumours were spread remains unclear, but these sentiments were undoubtedly shared by the Catholic clergy who, by October 1869, increasingly justified resistance to Canada in terms of protecting French and Catholic rights in Red River and who closely supported Riel, clearly the ascendent Métis leader. Thirty-five years later Dugast was to write:

> In reality he [Ritchot] was the soul of the movement. It was he who launched it and without him the movement would not have taken place. . . .

> It was M. Ritchot and I who not only guided but who drove on that opposition to the Canadian government—this is the real truth. I did not say it in my book because all truth is not suitable for publication. I say it to you. The ignorant métis would never have thought of vindicating their constitutional rights if M. Ritchot and I had not made them aware of them. Without M. Ritchot and me the movement remains inexplicable.[41]

With Dease's initiative in disarray, and with the active support and encouragement of Ritchot and Dugast, Riel moved to take the lead. Along with Baptiste Tourond and a few other Métis, he stopped the Canadian survey on 11 October as it approached the river lots of the Parish of St. Vital, an action which, given the increasing fears and paranoia of the French Métis, won him considerable support. Then, when news arrived of the imminent arrival of McDougall in Pembina, Riel and his faction—which by this time included many of the younger and more militant boatmen of the Colony—took steps that would breach the established order, and initiate a period of crisis in the Red River Settlement. On October 20, Riel and his men met in the home of John Bruce where they organized a 'National Committee' and made plans to stop McDougall from entering the Settlement. All was planned with the approval and knowledge of Ritchot.[42] The next day 'la barrière' was erected across the Pembina trail at St. Norbert, and all incoming and outgoing traffic was stopped and searched.

This act overturned the status quo, directly challenged the Council of Assiniboia's legitimacy, and threw the Colony into an uproar. Already humiliated by the combined efforts of Riel, Ritchot, and Dugast, and aware that most Métis still did not agree with the precipitous and resolute action Riel and his men had taken, William Dease now took an uncompromising stand against Riel, arguing that McDougall should be permitted to enter the territory and hear the Métis complaints. Sensing that support for Riel's course of action was slipping, Ritchot called for an assembly of Métis to meet in St. Norbert on October 24 to resolve the divisions among the people. At this meeting, Dease and his supporters threatened to dismantle the barricade across the Pembina trail and only the intercession of Ritchot quieted the following uproar. Ritchot calmed the assembly by asking if they did not agree that Canada had treated the Colony with a lack of respect, and if it was not proper that some resistance be made. Even Dease's men could not disagree with this, and Ritchot eventually persuaded the majority of the Métis at the assembly to agree to back the path taken by Riel. Most of the rest agreed to stay neutral.[43] Dease, however, was not satisfied and continued his opposition.

The following day Riel was summoned before the Council of Assiniboia and asked to abandon his plans to prevent McDougall from entering the Colony. When Riel refused, the Council approached Dease and asked if he could raise enough French Métis to overturn the decision taken on October 24 and force Riel's men to disperse.[44] Dease moved quickly to raise a group of men to attend another meeting at St. Norbert on October 27, at which both sides repeated their arguments for or against Riel's strategy. While Ritchot later claimed that he had not taken a leading role, another account, almost surely based on intelligence supplied by Dease, noted that Ritchot had declared 'in favour of the stand taken, and called upon the insurgents to maintain their ground.'[45] Still another of Dease's party testified that Ritchot had 'raved and tore his gown addressing the assemblage in the most frantic and excited manner.'[46] The appeals of Ritchot and Riel together convinced even 20 of Dease's 80 supporters that Riel was right, Ritchot observing later (with an almost palpable disdain) that Dease had been supported by only George Racette, six Indians, and a handful of others.[47] Defeated, Dease and his supporters left the ground to Riel.

Riel had won. While Dease would continue to oppose Riel throughout the winter and spring of 1869–70, and other prominent French Métis would slide back and forth between neutrality and opposition, Riel never again lost the support of most of the French Métis. The Council of Assiniboia met for the last time on October 30, agreeing there was nothing more they could do.

Usually treated as a minor and almost inconsequential interlude, the Dease/Riel conflict played a major role in defining the nature of the Métis Resistance in 1869–70. On a symbolic level, it was a battle over whether the Resistance would be grounded broadly on a concept of Métis aboriginal rights and led by the traditional Métis leadership, or whether the Resistance would be more narrowly a defence of French and Catholic rights in the settlement and led by the young Riel. To be sure, the Resistance had many other facets not touched upon here, and there were other reasons (class, economic, familial, and generational) why many French Métis opposed Riel;[48] however, unless one understands the symbolic nature of the Dease/Riel conflict, one cannot understand how key participants understood the events in which they were involved. Those Métis leaders who had been upstaged by Riel, and sometimes badly mistreated,[49] were never able to accept his leadership.

Later in the Resistance, Riel tried to bridge the chasm that had developed between his followers and those of Dease, who continued to enjoy a good deal of support among the Métis in both Red River and in St. Joseph[50] and whose help Riel needed if he hoped to build a consensus around his leadership. Writing to Dease in St. Joseph, where he had sought refuge from Riel's men after they had surrounded his house, Riel pleaded with his opponent to join forces:

> We have been in hostility till now, but I am certain it was not our intent to have bloodshed, among friends and relatives, or to strike terror or mourning in the lives of the Métis along the R.R. . . .
> Mr. Dease when have I ever done you any harm. If just recently our soldiers

surrounded your home, it was with the intention of bringing you here to accept our word of honour and assuring us that you would do all in your power to restore peace & public safety. . . . I beg you this favour, let us re-unite and join hands. . . . Mr. Dease, I beg of you, why are you so opposed to us, after we have already discussed and aired these problems. My personal ambition is a thing not in my heart, and if I am capable of doing something it will be for the good of all. I do not ask for a reward, but only for that support and sustenance before all Métis.[51]

Dease, however, remained unmoved.

Riel also tried to broaden the scope of the Resistance after October 1869 to win over the support of the English Métis, but it never lost the French and Catholic tinge it had acquired in the period from July through September. This made it extremely difficult for Riel to build any settlement-wide consensus. After Riel and his men seized Upper Fort Garry in November of 1869, they raised a flag adorned with the fleur-de-lis and the Irish Shamrock. This ceremony was carried out by a Catholic priest who was attended by 60 of the scholars of the Roman Catholic seminary in St. Boniface.[52] This symbolism was not lost on the English Métis. By allying himself so clearly with the Catholic clergy to defeat the Dease faction, Riel would never be acceptable as a leader to anything more than a small minority of English-Protestant Métis.

The Riel/Dease conflict also has some implications for the question of whether the Métis of 1869 were concerned with their aboriginal rights. Thomas Flanagan, in a useful study of the political thought of Louis Riel, has argued that the question of aboriginal rights played no role in the public debates of the 1869–70 Resistance. Riel's strategy in 1869, he argued, was to present the Métis as civilized men with rights equal to those of any British subject.[53]

> Riel wanted the Colony to enter Confederation as a Province with institutions modelled on those of Quebec: local control of land and natural resources, responsible government, a bilingual Governor, bilingualism in the legislature and courts, and a tax-supported system of Protestant and Catholic schools.[54]

This is an accurate assessment of Riel's paradigm of Métis communitas in 1869. It does not, however, accurately describe competing paradigms that were part of the public debates on resistance before October 1869.

This paper has argued that the idea of Métis Resistance in 1869 did not spring from the brow of Riel alone and that, as early as July 1869, other Métis leaders such as William Dease had proposed another paradigm of resistance that was based on a theory of aboriginal rights. This aboriginal-rights paradigm, however, was opposed by Riel and his clerical advisors, Fathers Ritchot and Dugast, in their struggle to gain the leadership of the Métis Resistance. Their strategy consisted of stressing a defence of French and Catholic rights threatened by the Canadians in the Colony. With the triumph of Riel and defeat of Dease in the Assembly of October 27, the Aboriginal-rights paradigm disappeared from public view in Red River. It is interesting to note, however, that once Riel was in control of the Resistance in Red River, Father Ritchot utilized an aboriginal rights argument to rationalize the Métis Children's land grant (section 31 of the Manitoba Act) in his negotiations with the Canadian Government in Ottawa in 1870.[55]

NOTES

The author would like to acknowledge and thank John Foster, Tom Flanagan, Gerald Friesen, Paul Chartrand, and Allen Ronaghan, who read an earlier draft of this paper and made a number of useful comments and suggestions.

1. This term is borrowed from the anthropologist Victor Turner who pioneered a processual approach to studying political conflict as social drama. From his study of symbol and ritual, Turner outlined a three or four stage process by which social dramas unfold. In this process, the first phase of a social drama was a period of 'separation' or 'breach' that Turner refers to as a pre-liminal phase. This phase is comprised of symbolic behaviour signifying the detachment of the individual (or group) from either an earlier fixed point in the social structure or from an established set of cultural conditions. This is a period when the norms that govern social relations between persons or groups within the same social system (village, chiefdom, university department) break down. Such a breach is signalled by an overt or deliberate non-fulfillment of some crucial norm governing the intercourse of the parties. See Victor Turner, *Dramas, Fields, and Metaphors: Symbolic Action in Human Society* (Ithaca, 1974), 13–42.

2. This is a term that Turner uses to describe the bond uniting a people over and above any formal social bond.

3. W.L. Morton, Introduction to *Alexander Begg's Red River Journal and other papers relative to the Red River Resistance of 1869–70* (Toronto, 1956), 3. Morton's introduction runs from page 1 to 148. The section dealing with the events from June through October 1869 are found on pages 31 to 55.

4. Ibid, 3

5. Ibid, 50–1. Morton argues that some of clergy approved of Riel's aims, but only followed the Métis and did not instigate or lead the Resistance. It is interesting to note that while Morton included one of Father Dugast's letters of 1869 (29 August 1869) in his collection of documents, he left out the more interesting ones (those of 14, 24, and 31 August 1869) which deeply implicated Dugast and Ritchot in the actual planning of Riel's campaign for the leadership of the Métis.

6. Ibid, 33

7. See Philippe R. Mailhot, 'Ritchot's Resistance: Abbé Noël Joseph Ritchot and the Creation and Transformation of Manitoba', (Ph.D. Dissertation, University of Manitoba, 1986), 14–62.

8. Schultz had arrived in the Red River Settlement in 1861, and was the acknowledged leader of the Canadian faction openly advocating annexation to Canada.

9. Philippe R. Mailhot, 'Ritchot's Resistance', 21–2, 48

10. Ibid, 29–30, 47

11. Among other activities that were alarming the Métis, the Canadians were staking out land, they freely denounced the Americans, Fenians, and Métis in the Colony, they ran up the Canadian flag as if a symbol of conquest, and the Métis were openly and contemptuously spoken of as cowards. Hudson's Bay Company Archives (HBCA), A12/45, William McTavish to W.G. Smith, 24 July 1869, fo. 269–70. HBCA, RG 1, Series 4/8, William McTavish to Joseph Howe, 14 May 1870, 2

12. State Historical Society of North Dakota, A26, Albert E. Dease Papers.

13. Two of William Hallet's sisters married French Métis and converted to Catholicism.

14. *Nor'Wester*, 24 July 1869. It was later reported that Pascal Breland had not given permission to use his name on the invitation.

15. While no minutes exist for this meeting it can be reconstructed using the various accounts that do exist. See Archives de l'archevêché, Saint-Boniface (AASB), Dugast to Taché, 29 juillet 1869, T6695–6698; HBCA, A12/45, William McTavish to W.G. Smith, 10 August 1869, fos. 282–283; and Provincial Archives of Manitoba (PAM), MG3 B14, M151, Ritchot's Narrative of the Resistance, volume 1.

16. George F.G. Stanley, *Louis Riel* (Toronto, 1963), 56–57. W.L. Morton, 'Introduction', to *Alexander Begg's Red River Journal*, 32–34

17. AASB, Dugast to Taché, 29 juillet 1869, T6695–6698; PAM, MG3 B14, M151, Ritchot's Narrative of the Resistance, volume 1.

18. See 'Red River a Crown Colony', *Nor'Wester*, 28 February 1860.

19. This debate can be followed in the pages of the *Nor'Wester*. See 'Native Title to Indian Lands', 14 February 1860; 'Peguis Refuted', 28 February 1860; 'The Land Question', 14 March 1860; 'The Political Condition of the Country', 28 April 1860; 'Peguis Vindicated', 28 April 1860; 'The Peguis Land Controversy', 14 May 1860; 'The Land Question', 14 June 1860; 'The Halfbreed Meeting', 28 June 1860; 'Paketay-Hoond on the Land Question', 28 June 1860; 'The Land Controversy', 28 June 1860; 'The Last Half-Breed Meeting', 28 September 1860.

20. 'The Land Question', *Nor'Wester*, 14 March 1860

21. 'The Land Question', *Nor'Wester*, 14 June 1860

22. 'Indignation Meetings', *Nor'Wester*, 15 June 1861

23. PAM, MG 3 B15, George B. Winship Account of 1869–70 (typescript)

24. See for example Philippe Mailhot, 'Ritchot's Resistance', 30.

25. Ibid, 31

26. A.G. Morice, *History of the Catholic Church in Western Canada*, Vol II (Toronto, 1910), 10

27. Philippe R. Mailhot, 'Ritchot's Resistance', 9–10

28. PAM, Ritchot's Narrative of the Resistance, volume 1, 16

29. ASSB, Dugast to Taché, 29 juillet 1869, T6695

30. Thomas Flanagan, *Louis 'David' Riel: Prophet of the New World* (Toronto, 1979), 7

31. Louis Riel writing to the President of the Saint Jean-Baptiste Society of Montreal, 24 June 1874. Quoted in Thomas Flanagan, 'The Political Thought of Louis Riel', in A.S. Lussier (ed.) *Riel and the Métis: Riel Mini-Conference Papers* (Winnipeg, 1979), 140.

32. PAM, Ritchot's Narrative of the Resistance, volume 1

33. AASB, Dugast to Taché, 29 juillet 1869, T6697

34. Canada. Parliament, House of Commons, *Sessional Papers*, 1874, No. VII, 'Report of the Select Committee on the Causes of the Difficulties in the North West Territories in 1869–70', Appendix No. 6, Testimony of Noël Joseph Ritchot, 20 April 1874.

35. AASB, Dugast to Taché, 31 aout 1869, T6778–6780

36. PAM, Ritchot's narrative, Vol. 1

37. HBCA, A12/45, W. McTavish to W.G. Smith, 2 November 1869, fo. 313–314

38. This sentiment is clearly visible in the letters written by Father Dugast to Taché in the AASB. See his letters of 14 Aout 1869, T6734–37; 24 Aout 1869, T6764–67; and 31 Aout 1869, T6778–80.

39. HBCA, RG 1, Series 4/8, W. McTavish to Joseph Howe, 14 May 1870, 13. The basis of this rumour had to do with McDougall's role in the Manitoulin Island Incident of 1862–3 in Canada. For an explanation of this incident and its bearing on McDougall's reputation among the Métis see Neil Edgar Allen Ronaghan, 'The Archibald Administration in Manitoba, 1870–1872' (Ph.D. Dissertation, University of Manitoba, 1987), 61–85.

40. AASB, Dugast to Taché, 31 Aout 1869, T6781

41. Archives du Collège Sainte-Marie, Fonds-Immaculée-Conception, Dugast to Fr. Joseph Grenier, 15 April 1905. Quoted in W.L. Morton (ed.) *Alexander Begg's Red River Journal*, 51n. Morton quotes this letter only to dismiss it as inaccurate citing as reasons that it was written 35 years after the fact, that Dugast possessed a flair for inaccuracy, and that Dugast was a vain and garrulous man. A close reading of Dugast's correspondence written in 1869, along with Ritchot's Narrative, suggests exactly the opposite.

42. See Ritchot's narrative, Vol. 1. These events and Ritchot's influence on them is described in some detail in Philippe Mailhot, 'Ritchot's Resistance', 31–39.

43. PAM, Ritchot's narrative, Vol. 1, 22–25

44. PAM, Minutes of the Council of Assiniboia, 25 October 1869

45. Canada. Parliament, House of Commons, *Sessional Papers* 1870, No. 12, 'Correspondence

and Papers Connected with Recent Occurrences in the North West Territories.' Letter of J.S. Dennis to William McDougall, 27 October 1869. That Ritchot took an active role at this meeting is also backed up by Ritchot's subsequent actions during the Resistance. In December of 1869, after Riel and his men had seized Fort Garry, they began to run low on supplies and approached the Hudson's Bay Company for an advance. William McTavish, the presiding HBC officer, refused the request and told the Métis to leave the Fort. This caused a dilemma for the Métis Council and Riel. Their choices at this point were to either abandon the Resistance or forcibly seize HBC property. In the meeting held to decide their course of action, Ritchot took a prominent role advising the Métis to continue their course. Their case was already before the Canadian government, he argued, and soon the present ministry would fall and the demands of the Métis would be secured. With this encouragement the Métis decided not to disperse and the HBC stores and safe were broken into. See HBCA, A12/45, William McTavish to W.G. Smith, 11 December 1869, fos. 328–329.

46. Canada. Parliament, House of Commons, *Sessional Papers* 1870, No. 12, 'Correspondence and Papers Connected with Recent Occurrences in the North West Territories.'

47. PAM, Ritchot's Narrative, Vol. 1

48. See chapter five of Gerhard J. Ens, 'Kinship, Ethnicity, Class and the Red River Métis', (Ph.D. dissertation, University of Alberta, 1989).

49. Many of the Métis who opposed Riel were later imprisoned by Riel including: William Dease, Baptiste Charette, William Gaddy, William Hallet, and Gabriel Lafournaise. Hallet was kept in chains in an unheated room through the worst of the winter.

50. St. Joseph was a Métis community just across the US border near the present-day town of Walhalla, North Dakota.

51. Louis Riel to William Dease, 15 February 1870. Reprinted in G.F.G. Stanley (general editor) *The Collected Writings of Louis Riel/ Les Ecrits Complets de Louis Riel, Vol. 1* (Edmonton, 1985), 52.

52. HBCA, A12/45, William McTavish to W.G. Smith, 11 December 1869, fos. 328–329.

53. Thomas Flanagan, 'The Political Thought of Louis Riel', 150–2. See also his 'Political Theory of the Red River Resistance: The Declaration of December 8, 1869', *Canadian Journal of Political Science* XI: 1 (March 1978): 153–64; and 'The Case Against Métis Aboriginal Rights', *Canadian Public Policy* IX: 3 (September 1983): 316–7.

54. Ibid, 139

55. For Ritchot's use of this argument see his Ottawa journal published in W.L. Morton (ed.) *Manitoba: The Birth of a Province* (Winnipeg, 1965), 140–2.

Chapter Fourteen

Confederation and Anti-Confederation

READINGS

Primary Documents

1   From a speech by Joseph Howe at Dartmouth, Nova Scotia, 22 May 1867

2   From *Parliamentary Debates on the Subject of the Confederation of the British North American Provinces*, A.A. Dorion

Historical Interpretations

3   From 'The Case Against Canadian Confederation', in *The Causes of Confederation*, Ged Martin

4   From 'Who's Afraid of the Fenians? The Fenian Scare on Prince Edward Island, 1865–1867', Edward MacDonald

Introduction

Confederation is the worst-kept secret in Canadian history. We've referred to it in earlier topic intro-ductions, and students frequently foreshadow it in essays focusing on the 1840s or even earlier. We know the outcome, and want to dissect the past so that we can better explain how predictable (or perhaps shocking) the result was. We do this regardless of how important the constitutional changes brought about in 1867 actually were for people living in the newly confederated colonies. For some, like those who got access to a railway as part of the package, Confederation was life-changing. It affected their livelihoods, their prospects, and their sense of being linked to the rest of the world. For others, such as those who remained relatively isolated from the reconfigured state's gifts or demands, life went on much as it had before.

To contend that everything changed for everyone in the middle of 1867 (and at intervals through the next few years as territories and new provinces were added) would be to simplify the picture too much. We have become so accustomed to Canada as a single entity that it is difficult for us to acknowledge the independent spirit of people about a century and a half ago, some of whom conceived of nations as smaller, more ethnically and religiously uniform, more manageable. The voices of Joseph Howe and A.A. Dorion were the voices of educated males, members of the political class, and wary of what might happen if the ambitious scheme to unite British North America could not deliver on its promises. Dorion, especially, mentions several reasons why the arrangements for Confederation seemed to be rather too hastily made.

We should acknowledge, as Ged Martin does, that opposition to Confederation was not based on a lack of vision, but on different *kinds* of visions. 'Progress' was one of the most powerful watchwords of the age. Devotion to a certain kind of progress had already determined that First Nations would play only a marginal role (as 'obstacles') in the arrangements. This devotion to progress also disadvantaged Confederation's opponents, who, like the landlords on Prince Edward Island who managed to delay the Island's entry until 1873, were preaching caution and complaining that their rights were being violated by the massively popular policy of ending their reign over their tenants. The threat of large-scale invasion from the Fenian Brotherhood, as Edward MacDonald shows, was a phantom force, but effective. Confederation, because it was so strongly linked to progress and a sense of destiny for British North America, acquired a momentum of its own, fed also by factors including a British desire to spend less money and effort protecting British North America, and a wariness of American ambitions.

QUESTIONS FOR CONSIDERATION

1. Based on his pronouncements here, what seems to be Howe's conception of the right size for a nation?
2. Dorion's speech introduces us to some of the potential problems associated with the creation of a new nation from the provinces of British North America. What were some of these?
3. What are the advantages and disadvantages of being linked politically (e.g., as part of a federation like Canada) with distant places that might not share the value systems that predominate in your community?
4. Ged Martin outlines some of the case against Confederation. Where would you have stood on the issue? Would it have mattered where you lived?
5. According to MacDonald, how did the Fenian threat to Prince Edward Island affect support for Confederation?

SUGGESTIONS FOR FURTHER READING

Buckner, Philip, 'The Maritimes and Confederation: A Reassessment', *Canadian Historical Review* 71(1) (1990): 1–30

Martin, Ged, *Britain and the Origins of Canadian Confederation, 1837–67* (Vancouver: UBC Press, 1995)

Martin, Ged, ed., *The Causes of Canadian Confederation* (Fredericton: Acadiensis Press, 1990)

Morton, W.L., *The Critical Years: The Union of British North America 1857–1873* (Toronto: McClelland and Stewart, 1964)

Romney, Paul, *Getting It Wrong: How Canadians Forgot their Past and Imperilled Confederation* (Toronto: University of Toronto Press, 1999)

Silver, I.A., *The French-Canadian Idea of Confederation, 1864–1900* (Toronto: University of Toronto Press, 1997)

Smith, Andrew, *British Businessmen and Canadian Confederation: Constitution-Making in an Era of Anglo-Globalization* (Montreal and Kingston: McGill-Queen's University Press, 2008)

Waite, Peter B., *The Life and Times of Confederation, 1864–1867: Politics, Newspapers, and the Union of British North America* (Toronto: Robin Brass Studio, 2001)

PRIMARY DOCUMENTS

1 From a speech by Joseph Howe at Dartmouth, Nova Scotia, 22 May 1867, in Joseph Andrew Chisholm, ed., *The Speeches and Public Letters of Joseph Howe*, vol. 2 (Halifax: Chronicle Publishing Company, 1909), 510–13.

The old men who sit around me, and the men of middle age who hear my voice, know that thirty years ago we engaged in a series of struggles which the growth of population, wealth and intelligence rendered inevitable. For what did we contend? Chiefly for the right of self-government. We won it from Downing Street after many a manly struggle, and we exercised and never abused it for a quarter of a century. Where is it now? Gone from us, and certain persons in Canada are now to exercise over us powers more arbitrary and excessive than any the Colonial Secretaries ever claimed. Our Executive and Legislative Councillors were formerly selected in Downing Street. For more than twenty years we have appointed them ourselves. But the right has been bartered away by those who have betrayed us, and now we must be content with those our Canadian masters give. The batch already announced shows the principles which are to govern the selection.

For many years the Colonial Secretary dispensed our casual and territorial revenues. The sum rarely exceeded £12,000 sterling, but the money was ours, and yielding at last to common sense and rational argument, our claims were allowed. But what do we see now? Almost all our revenues—not twelve thousand but hundreds of thousands—are to be swept away and handed over to the custody and the administration of strangers.

The old men here remember when we had no control over our trade, and when Halifax was the only free port. By slow degrees we pressed for a better system, till, under the enlightened commercial policy of England, we were left untrammelled to levy what duties we pleased and to regulate our trade. Its marvellous development under our independent action astonishes ourselves and is the wonder of strangers. We have fifty seaports carrying on foreign trade. Our shipyards are full of life and our flag floats on every sea. All this is changed: we can regulate our own trade no longer. We must submit to the dictation of those who live above the tide, and who will know little of and care less for our interests or our experience.

The right of self-taxation, the power of the purse, is in every country the true security for freedom. We had it. It is gone, and the Canadians have been invested by this precious batch of worthies, who are now seeking your suffrages, with the right to strip us 'by any and every mode or system of taxation.'

We struggled for years for the control of our Post Office. At that time rates were high, the system contracted; offices had only been established in the shire towns and in the more populous settlements. We gained the control, the rates were lowered and rendered uniform over the Provinces, newspapers were carried free, offices were established in all the thriving settlements and way offices on every road, but now all this comes to an end. Our Post Offices are to be regulated by a distant authority. Every post-master and every way office keeper is to be appointed and controlled by the Canadians.

Since the necessity for a better organization of the militia became apparent, our young men have shown a laudable spirit of emulation and have volunteered cheerfully, formed naval brigades, and shown a desire to acquire discipline and the use of arms. I have viewed these efforts with special interest. There is no period in the history of England when the great body of the people were better fed, better treated, or enjoyed more of the substantial comforts of life, than when every man was trained to the use of arms, and had his long-bow or his cross-bow in his house. The rifle is the modern weapon, and our people have not been slow to learn the use of it. Organized by their own Government, commanded by their friends and neighbours, 50,000 men have been embodied and partially drilled for self-defence. But now strangers are to control this force—to appoint the officers and to direct its movements; and while our own shores may be undefended, the artillery company that trains upon the hills before us may be ordered away to any point of the Canadian frontier.

By the precious instrument by which we are hereafter to be bound, the Canadians are to fix the 'salaries' of our principal public officers. We are to pay, but they can fix the amount, and who doubts but that our money will be squandered to reward the traitors who have betrayed us? Our 'navigation and shipping' pass from our control, and the Canadians, who have not one ship to our three, are already boasting that they are the third maritime power in the world. Our 'sea-coast and inland fisheries' are no longer ours. The shore fisheries have been handed over to the Yankees, and the Canadians can sell or lease to-morrow the fisheries of the Margaree, the Musquodoboit or the La Have.

Our 'currency,' also, is to be regulated by the Canadians, and how they will regulate it we shrewdly suspect. Many of us remember when Nova Scotia was flooded with irresponsible paper, and have not forgotten the commercial crisis that ensued. In one summer thousands of people fled from the country, half the shops in Water Street, Halifax, were closed, and the grass almost grew in the Market Square. The paper was driven in. The banks were restricted to five-pound notes. All paper, under severe penalties, was made convertible. British coins were adopted as the standard of value, and silver has been ever since paid from hand to hand in all the smaller transactions of life. For a quarter of a century we have had free trade in banking, and the soundest currency in the world. Last spring Mr. Galt could not meet the obligations of Canada, and he could only borrow money at ruinous rates of interest. He seized upon the circulation, and partially adopted the greenback system of the United States. The country is now flooded with paper; only, if I am rightly informed, convertible in two places—Toronto and Montreal. The system will soon be extended to Nova Scotia, and the country will presently be flooded with 'shin-plasters,' and the sound specie currency we now use will be driven out.

Our 'savings banks' are also to be handed over. Hitherto the confidence of the people in these banks has been universal. We had the security of our own Government, watched by our own vigilance, and controlled by our own votes, for the sacred care of deposits. What are we to have now? Nobody knows, but we do know that the savings of the poor and the industrious are to be handed over to the Canadians. They also are to regulate the interest of money. The usury laws have never been repealed in Nova Scotia, and yet capital could always be commanded here at six, and often at five per cent. In Canada the rate of interest ranges from eight to ten per cent., and is often much higher. With confederation will come these higher rates of interest, grinding the faces of the poor.

But it is said, why should we complain? we are still to manage our local affairs. I have shown you that self-government, in all that gives dignity and security to a free state, is to be swept away.

The Canadians are to appoint our governors, judges and senators. They are to 'tax us by any and every mode' and spend the money. They are to regulate our trade, control our Post Offices, command the militia, fix the salaries, do what they like with our shipping and navigation, with our sea-coast and river fisheries, regulate the currency and the rate of interest, and seize upon our savings banks. What remains? Listen and be comforted. You are to have the privilege of 'imposing direct taxation, within the Province, in order to the raising of revenue for Provincial purposes.' Why do you not go down on your knees and be thankful for this crowning mercy when fifty per cent. has been added to your *ad valorem* duties, and the money has been all swept away to dig canals or fortify Montreal. You are to be kindly permitted to keep up your spirits and internal improvements by direct taxation.

Who does not remember, some years ago, when I proposed to pledge the public revenues of the Province to build our railroads, how Tupper went screaming all over the Province that we should be ruined by the expenditure, and that 'direct taxation' would be the result. He threw me out of my seat in Cumberland by this and other unprincipled warcries. Well, the roads have been built, and not only were we never compelled to resort to direct taxation, but so great has been the prosperity resulting from those public works that, with the lowest tariff in the world, we have trebled our revenue in ten years, and with a hundred and fifty miles of railroad completed, and nearly as much more under contract, we have had an overflowing treasury, and money enough to meet all our obligations, without having been compelled, like the Canadians, to borrow money at eight per cent. and to manufacture greenbacks.

But if we had been compelled to pay direct taxes for a few years to create a railroad system that by-and-by would be self-sustaining, and that would have been a great blessing in the meantime, the object would have been worth the sacrifice. But we never paid a farthing. What then? The falsehood did its work. Tupper won the seat, and now, after giving our railroads away, and all our general revenues besides, the doctor, after being rejected by Halifax, is trying to make the people of Cumberland believe that to pay 'direct taxes' for all sorts of services is a pleasant and profitable pastime. Cumberland may believe and trust him again, but if it does, the people are not so shrewd or so patriotic as I think they are.

2   From A.A. Dorion, in *Parliamentary Debates on the Subject of the Confederation of the British North American Provinces* (Quebec: Hunter, Rose and Co., 1865), 245–69, 690–5.

HON. MR. DORION—But, sir, I may be asked, granting all this, granting that the scheme brought down is not the scheme promised to us, what difference our bringing in the provinces at once can make? This I will endeavor to explain. When they went into the Conference, honorable gentlemen opposite submitted to have the votes taken by provinces. Well, they have now brought us in, as was natural under the circumstances, the most conservative measure ever laid before a Parliament. The members of the Upper House are no longer to be elected, but nominated, and nominated by whom? By a Tory or Conservative Government for Canada, by a Conservative Government in Nova Scotia, by a Conservative Government in Prince Edward Island, by a Conservative Government in Newfoundland, the only Liberal Government concerned in the nomination being that which is controlled by the Liberal party in New Brunswick, whose fate depends on the result of the elections that are now going on in that province. Such a scheme would never have been adopted if submitted to the liberal people of Upper Canada. When the

Government went into that Conference they were bound by the majority, especially since they voted by provinces, and the 1,400,000 of Upper Canada with the 1,100,000 of Lower Canada—together 2,500,000 people—were over-ridden by 900,000 people of the Maritime Provinces. Were we not expressly told that it was the Lower Provinces who would not hear of our having an elective Legislative Council? If, instead of going into Conference with the people of the Lower Provinces, our Government had done what they pledged themselves to do, that is, to prepare a Constitution themselves, they would never have dared to bring in such a proposition as this which is now imposed upon us by the Lower Colonies—to have a Legislative Council, with a fixed number of members, nominated by four Tory governments. Why, taking the average time each councillor will be in the Council to be fifteen to twenty years, it will take a century before its complexion can be changed. For all time to come, so far as this generation and the next are concerned, you will find the Legislative Council controlled by the influence of the present Government.

HON. MR. DORION—The honorable member for Lambton says that makes no difference. It makes just the difference that we are to be bound by the scheme or by a Constitution enabling the Council to stop all measures of reform, such as would be desired by the Liberal party; if the honorable member for Lambton thinks that makes no difference, I beg to differ from him, and I believe the Liberal party generally will. The Government say they had to introduce certain provisions, not to please themselves, but to please the provinces below, and they have pledged themselves to those provinces that this House will carry out the scheme without amendment. Does not the honorable member see the difference now? If the two Canadas were alone interested, the majority would have its own way—would look into the Constitution closely—would scan its every doubtful provision, and such a proposal as this about the Legislative Council would have no chance of being carried, for it is not very long since the House, by an overwhelming majority, voted for the substitution of an elected for a nominated Upper Chamber. In fact, the nominated Chamber had fallen so low in public estimation—I do not say it was from the fault of the men who were there, but the fact is, nevertheless, as I state it—that it commanded no influence. There was even a difficulty in getting a quorum of it together. So a change became absolutely necessary, and up to the present moment the new system has worked well; the elected members are equal in every respect to the nominated ones, and it is just when we see an interest beginning to be felt in the proceedings of the Upper House that its Constitution is to be changed, to return back again to the one so recently condemned. Back again, did I say? No, sir, a Constitution is to be substituted, much worse than the old one, and such as is nowhere else to be found. Why, even the British house of Lords, conservative as it is, is altogether beyond the influence of the popular sentiment of the country. Their number may be increased on the recommendation of the responsible advisers of the Crown, if required to secure united action or to prevent a conflict between the two Houses. From the position its members occupy, it is a sort of compromise between the popular element and the influence or control of the Crown. But the new House for the Confederation is to be a perfectly independent body—these gentlemen are to be named for life—and there is to be no power to increase their number. How long will the system work without producing a collision between the two branches of the Legislature? Suppose the Lower House turns out to be chiefly Liberal, how long will it submit to the Upper House, named by Conservative administrations which have taken advantage of their temporary numerical strength to bring about such a change as is now proposed? [. . .] I venture to prophesy, sir, that before a very short time has elapsed a dead-lock may arise, and such an excitement be created as has never yet been seen in this country. (Hear, hear.) Now, if this Constitution had been framed by the members of our Government, we could change some of its provisions. [. . .] But no, the Constitution is in the nature of a compact, a treaty, and cannot be changed. (Hear.)

I now come to another point. It is said that this Confederation is necessary for the purpose of providing a better mode of defence for this country. There may be people who think that by adding two and two together you make five. I am not of that opinion. I cannot see how by adding the 700,000 or 800,000 people, the inhabitants of the Lower Provinces, to the 2,500,000 inhabitants of Canada, you can multiply them so as to make a much larger force to defend the country than you have at present. Of course the connection with the British Empire is the link of communication by which the whole force of the Empire can be brought together for defence. (Hear, hear.) But the position of this country under the proposed scheme is very evident. You add to the frontier four or five hundred more miles than you now have, and an extent of country immeasurably greater in proportion than the additional population you have gained; and if there is an advantage at all for the defence of the country, it will be on the part of the Lower Provinces and not for us. And as we find that we are about to enter into a very large expenditure for this purpose of defence—this having been formally announced in a speech delivered by the President of the Council at Toronto—and as Canada is to contribute to that expenditure to the extent of ten-twelfths of the whole, the other provinces paying only two-twelfths, it follows that Canada will pay ten-twelfths also of the cost of defence, which, to defend the largely extended country we will have to defend, will be much larger than if we remained alone.

[. . .]

This I contend, then, that if the military and naval defences of all the provinces are to be provided for by the General Government, and if you have to increase the militia for this purpose, the Lower Provinces will pay only their proportion of two-twelfths, and Canada, while obtaining no greater defensive force than at present, will have to pay five times as much as we are now paying. (Hear, hear.) Why, sir, take the line dividing New Brunswick from Maine and you find it separates on the one side 250,000, thinly scattered over a vast territory, from 750,000 on the other, compact and powerful. These 250,000 Canada will have to defend, and it will have to pledge its resources for the purpose of providing means of defence along that extended line. (Hear, hear.) And, if rumor be true, the Intercolonial Railway, this so-called great defensive work, is not to pass along Major ROBINSON'S line. The statement has been made—I have seen it in newspapers usually well informed—that a new route has been found that will satisfy everybody or nobody at all; and while I am on this point I must say that it is most singular that we are called upon to vote these resolutions, and to pledge ourselves to pay ten-twelfths of the cost of that railway, without knowing whether there will be ten miles or one hundred miles of it in Lower Canada, or whether it will cost $10,000,000 or $20,000,000.

HON. MR. DORION—In 1862, when the question of the construction of this road was before the country, what was the cry raised by honorable gentlemen opposite? Why, that the MACDONALD-SICOTTE Government had pledged itself to build a railway at whatever cost it might come to; and those who were loudest in these denunciations, were the very gentlemen who have now undertaken to build the road without knowing or even enquiring what the cost of it will be. (Hear, hear.) This, if I remember right, was the purport of a speech made by the Hon. Attorney General West at Otterville. (Hear, hear.) I was satisfied, sir, at that time, to press my objections to the scheme and retire from the Government; but my colleagues were denounced without stint for having undertaken to build the railway and pay seven-twelfths of its cost, and now the House is asked by the very men who denounced them to pay ten-twelfths of it, without even knowing whether the work is practicable or not. (Hear, hear.) [. . .] It is folly to suppose that this Intercolonial Railway will in the least degree be conducive to the defence of the country. We have expended a large sum of money—and none voted it more cordially and heartily than myself—for the purpose of opening a military highway from Gaspé to Rimouski; and that road, in case of hostilities with our neighbors, would be found of far greater service for the transport of troops, cannon and all kinds of munitions of war, than any railway following the same or a more southern route possibly can be. That road cannot be effectually destroyed; but a railway lying in some places not more than fifteen or twenty miles from the frontier, will be of no use whatever, because of the readiness with which it may be attacked and seized. An enemy could destroy miles of it before it would be possible to resist him, and in time of difficulty it would be a mere trap for the troops passing along it, unless we had almost an army to keep it open. [. . .] Sir, I say it here candidly and honestly, that we are bound to do everything we can to protect the country—(hear, hear,)—but we are not bound to ruin ourselves in anticipation of a supposed invasion which we could not repel, even with the assistance of England. [. . .] The best thing that Canada can do is to keep quiet, and to give no cause for war. (Hear, hear.) Let the public opinion of this country compel the press to cease the attacks it is every day making upon the Government and people of the United States; and then if war does come between England and the States—even if from no fault of ours—we will cast our lot with England and help her to fight the battle; but in the meantime it is no use whatever to raise or keep up anything like a standing army.

[. . .]

Now, sir, when I look into the provisions of this scheme, I find another most objectionable one. It is that which gives the General Government control over all the acts of the local legislatures. What difficulties may not arise under this system? Now, knowing that the General Government will be party in its character, may it not for party purposes reject laws passed by the local legislatures and demanded by a majority of the people of that locality. This power conferred upon the General Government has been compared to the veto power that exists in England in respect to our legislation; but we know that the statesmen of England are not actuated by the local feelings and prejudices, and do not partake of the local jealousies, that prevail in the colonies. The local governments have therefore confidence in them, and respect for their decisions; and generally, when a law adopted by a colonial legislature is sent to them, if it does not clash with the policy of the Empire at large, it is not disallowed, and more especially of late has it been the policy of the Imperial Government to do whatever the colonies desire in this respect, when their wishes are constitutionally expressed. The axiom on which they seem to act is that the less they hear of the colonies the better. (Hear, hear.) But how different will be the result in this case, when the General Government exercises the veto power over the acts of local legislatures. Do you not see that it is quite possible for a majority in a local government to be opposed to the General Government; and in such a case the minority would call upon the General Government to disallow the laws enacted by the majority? The men who shall compose the General Government will be dependent for their support upon their political friends in the local legislatures, and it may so happen that, in order to secure this support, or in order to serve their own purposes or that of their supporters, they will veto laws which the majority of a local legislature find necessary and good. (Hear, hear.) We know how high party feeling runs sometimes upon local matters even of trivial importance, and we may find parties so hotly opposed to each other in the local legislatures, that the whole power of the minority may be brought to bear upon their friends who have a majority in the General Legislature, for the purpose of preventing the passage of some law objectionable to them but desired by the majority of their own section. What will be the result of such a state of things but bitterness of feeling, strong political acrimony and dangerous agitation? (Hear, hear.) [. . .] But, sir, respecting the defences of the country, I should have said at an earlier stage of my remarks that this scheme proposes a union not only with Nova Scotia, New Brunswick, Prince Edward Island, and Newfoundland, but also with British Columbia and Vancouver's Island. Although I have not been able to get the information from the Government—for they do not seem to be very ready to give information—yet I understand that there are despatches to hand, stating that resolutions have been adopted in the Legislature of British Columbia asking for admission into the Confederation at once. I must confess, Mr. SPEAKER, that it looks like a burlesque to speak as a means of defence of a scheme of Confederation to unite the whole country extending from Newfoundland to Vancouver's Island, thousands of miles intervening without any communication, except through the United States or around Cape Horn. (Oh!) [. . .]

So far as Lower Canada is concerned, I need hardly stop to point out the objections to the scheme. It is evident, from what has transpired, that it is intended eventually to form a legislative union of all the provinces. The local governments, in addition to the General Government, will be found so burdensome, that a majority of the people will appeal to the Imperial Government for the formation of a legislative union. (Hear, hear.) I may well ask if there is any member from Lower Canada, of French extraction, who is ready to vote for a legislative union. What do I find in connection with the agitation of this scheme? The honorable member for Sherbrooke stated at the dinner to the delegates given at Toronto, after endorsing everything that had been said by the Honorable President of the Council:—

> We may hope that, at no far distant day, we may become willing to enter into a Legislative Union instead of a federal union, as now proposed. We would have all have desired a legislative union, and to see the power concentrated in the Central Government as it exists in England, spreading the aegis of its protection over all the institutions of the land, but we found it was impossible to do that at first. We found that there were difficulties in the way which could not be overcome.

Honorable members from Lower Canada are made aware that the delegates all desired a legislative union, but it could not be accomplished at once. This Confederation is the first necessary step towards it. The British Government is ready to grant a Federal union at once, and when that is accomplished the French element will be completely overwhelmed by the majority of British representatives. What then would prevent the Federal Government from passing a set of resolutions in a similar way to those we are called upon to pass, without submitting them to the people, calling upon the Imperial Government to set aside the Federal form of government and give a legislative union instead of it? (Hear, hear.) Perhaps the people of Upper Canada think a legislative union a most desirable thing. I can tell those gentlemen that the people of Lower Canada are attached to their institutions in a manner that defies any attempt to change them in that way. They will not change their religious institutions, their laws and their language, for any consideration whatever. A million of inhabitants may seem a small affair to the mind of a philosopher who sits down to write out a constitution. He may think it would be better that there should be but one religion, one language and one system of laws, and he goes to work to frame institutions that will bring all to that desirable state; but I can tell honorable gentlemen that the history of every country goes to show that not even by the power of the sword can such changes be accomplished. I am astonished to see the honorable member for Montreal West helping a scheme designed to end in a legislative union, the object of which can only be to assimilate the whole people to the dominant population. In that honorable gentleman's own country the system has produced nothing but a dissatisfied and rebellious people. Is it desirable that in this country then we should pass a measure calculated to give dissatisfaction to a million of people? You may ascertain what the cost of keeping down a million of dissatisfied people is by the scenes that have been and are now transpiring on the other side of the line, where a fifth of the people of the United States has risen and has caused more misery and misfortune to be heaped upon that country than could have been wrought in centuries of peaceful compromising legislation. Sir, if a legislative union of the British American Provinces is attempted, there will be such an agitation in this portion of the province as was never witnessed before—you will see the whole people of Lower Canada clinging together to resist by all legal and constitutional means, such an attempt at wresting from them those institutions that they now enjoy. They would go as a body to the Legislature, voting as one man, and caring for nothing else but for the protection of their beloved institutions and law, and making government all but impossible. The ninety Irish members in the British House of Commons, composed as it is of nearly seven hundred members, by voting together have caused their influence to be felt, as in the grants to the Maynooth College and some other questions. It would be the same way with the people of Lower Canada, and a more deplorable state of things would be the inevitable result. The majority would be forced by the minority to do things they would not, under the circumstances, think of doing. This is a state so undesirable that, although I am strongly opposed to the proposed Federal union, I am still more strongly opposed to a legislative union. Those who desire a legislative union may see from this what discordant elements they would have to deal with in undertaking the task, and what misery they would bring upon the country by such a step. (Hear, hear.) I know there is an apprehension among the British population in Lower Canada that, with even the small power that the Local Government will possess, their rights will not be respected. How, then, can it be expected that the French population can anticipate any more favorable result from the General Government, when it is to possess such enormous powers over the destinies of their section of the country? Experience shows that majorities are always aggressive, and it cannot well be otherwise in this instance. It therefore need not be wondered at that the people of Lower Canada, of British origin, are ready to make use of every means to prevent their being placed at the mercy of a preponderating population of a different origin. I agree with them in thinking that they ought to take nothing on trust in this matter of entering upon a new state of political existence, and neither ought we of French origin to do so, in relation to the General Government, however happy our relations to each other may be at present.

[. . .]

I contend that the local constitutions are as much an essential part of the whole as the general Constitution, and that they both should have been laid at the same time before the House. (Hear, hear.) We ought, besides, to have a clear statement of what are the liabilities specially assigned to Upper and Lower Canada. (Hear, hear.) It is well that Upper Canada should know if she has to pay the indebtedness of Port Hope, Cobourg, Brockville, Niagara, and other municipalities which have borrowed from the municipal loan fund, and what these liabilities are; and it is important for Lower Canada to be told what are the amounts they will be required to tax themselves for. We ought, besides, to obtain some kind of information upon the subject of the Intercolonial Railway, what is the proposed cost, and what route is to be followed; and before these facts are before the House, we ought not to take it upon ourselves to legislate on the subject. Still further, the people of the country do not understand the scheme. (Hear, hear.) Many members of this House, before hearing the explanations which have been offered, were, and others are still, in doubt as to the bearing of many of these resolutions. [. . .] I owe an apology to the House for having offered such lengthened remarks on this question, and I have to thank honorable members for having so kindly listened to them. (Cries of 'go on'.) I will simply content myself with saying that for these reasons which I have so imperfectly exposed, I strongly fear it would be a dark day for Canada when she adopted such a scheme as this. (Cheers.) It would be one marked in the history of this country as having had a most depressing and crushing influence on the energies of the people in both Upper and Lower Canada—(hear, hear)—for I consider it one of the worst schemes that could be brought under the consideration of the House; and if it should be adopted without the sanction of the people, the country would never cease to regret it. (Hear, hear.) What is the necessity for all this haste? The longer this Constitution is expected to last, the greater the necessity for the fullest consideration and deliberation. [. . .] There are three modes of obtaining the views of the people upon the question now under discussion. The most direct one would be, after debating it in this House, to submit it to the people for their verdict, yea or nay. The second is to dissolve the House and appeal to the people. The third is to discuss and pass the resolutions or address to a second reading, and afterwards leave it open to the public to judge of its merits, by meeting and discussing it, and sending in petitions and instructing their representatives how to vote upon it when they came to Parliament at the next session. Any one of these methods would elicit the views of the people. But to say that the opinions of the people have been ascertained on the question, I say it is no such thing. (Hear, hear.) We have heard one side of the question discussed, but we have heard none of the views on the other side; and yet the feeling, as exhibited in some parts of the country, has been unmistakeably in favor of an appeal to the people. Some fifteen counties in Lower Canada have held meetings and declared for an appeal before the scheme is allowed to pass; and when honorable gentlemen on the other side have held second meetings, they have been condemned more conclusively than at first. (Hear, Hear.) [. . .]

There is no hurry in regard to the scheme. We are now legislating for the future as well as for the present, and feeling that we ought to make a Constitution as perfect as possible, and as far as possible in harmony with the views of the people, I maintain that we ought not to pass this measure now, but leave it to another year, in order to ascertain in the meantime what the views and sentiments of the people actually are. (The honorable gentleman was loudly cheered on resuming his seat.)

HISTORICAL INTERPRETATIONS

3 From Ged Martin, 'The Case Against Canadian Confederation', in Gen. Martin, ed., *The Causes of Confederation* (Fredericton: Acadiensis Press, 1990), 19–49.

The men who met at Charlottetown and Quebec in 1864 to design the Dominion of Canada live in legend as the 'Fathers of Confederation'. They gaze at us, from sombre photographs and dignified portraits, with a grave demeanour which makes it hard to believe that any of them could ever have called an opponent a liar or promised to build a bridge to win an election. We need not begrudge them their mythic status in Canadian history, for our real difficulty lies in reconciling the claim for their far-sighted wisdom with the equally patriotic efforts of Canada's historians, who have related the saga of the coming of Confederation as if it were the inevitable outcome of the problems of the 1860s.[1] 'Only a general union, balanced with all the care and precision of a cantilever, was practical in 1864', wrote W.L. Morton a century later. If Confederation was indeed the inescapable solution in 1864, how can we attribute such superior wisdom to the Fathers? Surely they were no more than the unconscious instruments of historical inevitability? Morton implicitly confronted the issue by describing the cabinet headed by John Sandfield Macdonald, which immediately preceded the Confederation Coalition in the province of Canada, as 'provincial politicians who had failed to sense the new currents which had begun to flow in Canadian politics since 1857.'[2] Confederation, then, was inevitable, but perspicacity and vision were needed to grasp this evident fact. By implication, those who failed to see the necessity for Confederation got it wrong.

Such an approach can hardly encourage an unprejudiced analysis of the arguments advanced between 1864 and 1867 by those who opposed the new constitutional system.[3] The scheme drawn up at Quebec in 1864 was rejected by the voters in New Brunswick in 1865, would probably have been decisively rejected had there been an election in Nova Scotia, and might even have failed to win a majority in Lower Canada. Indeed, it is at least possible that Confederation was ultimately accepted in spite of the case against it rather than because of the arguments in its favour. Consideration of the objections raised by opponents may enable us to decide whether Confederation really was the logical deduction from interlocking circumstances, or whether we should look to other explanations for its adoption. [. . .]

The two major sources on which this paper is based are the *Confederation Debates* of 1865 in the province of Canada, and the Nova Scotia petitions of 1866 in the *British Parliamentary Papers*. The Canadian parliament had not previously printed its debates, and we may echo the lament of Dr. Joseph Blanchet, four weeks and 545 pages after discussion began on 3 February 1865, that the decision 'to have the speeches of this House printed in official form certainly did no good service to the country.' Yet vast as was the eventual volume, it does not necessarily do justice to the opposition case. In the early phases of the debate, there was a tendency to demand further information, for the Quebec plan required much fleshing-out of practical details on which the ministers were unforthcoming—and it was tempting to debunk the visionary orations of Macdonald and McGee by trumpeting that there was no case to answer. Luther Holton replied to the first great onslaught of explanations with the flourish that if the government's speeches 'contain all that can be said in favour of this scheme, we have no fear of letting them go unanswered.' As the Canadian debate was getting into its

stride, so news arrived of Tilley's defeat in New Brunswick which, A-A. Dorion claimed, caused the issue 'to lose much of its interest'.[4] Much of the debate was taken up with members taunting each other with inconsistency, which often provoked elaborate apologetics. Some speeches were intended to drag matters out while petitions were circulated:[5] Cartier embarrassed Eric Dorion, by reading into the record a circular letter he had sent to supporters requesting them to have anti-Confederation petitions 'signed as soon as possible by men, women and children.'[6] Similar devices were used to produce petitions in Nova Scotia, as the governor-general, Lord Monck, and a former lieutenant-governor, the Marquess of Normanby, assured the House of Lords in 1867.[7] It is certainly hard to believe that the 210 inhabitants of the district of Port Medway who signed their names to a massive, 2,000-word petition against Confederation were entirely unprompted,[8] and it may be doubted if any of the petitions emerged from the sober atmosphere of a political science seminar. [. . .]

'I do not know of any one opposed to union in the abstract', said New Brunswick's Timothy Warren Anglin. 'But my impression is that the time has not arrived for any kind of union, and I will oppose it to the last.'[9] This was a common theme among the critics: intercolonial union in principle, union one day, but not this union, not now.[10] As Edward Whelan put it, the critics accepted the principle of ploughing the field, but objected to destroying the daisies and field mice.[11] How sincere were these protestations—by some, but by no means all the critics of Confederation—in favour of an eventual British North American union? Perhaps they were gestures of open-mindedness merely to win over waverers. David Reesor found it 'extraordinary' that so many members of the Canadian Legislative Council spoke 'strongly and emphatically against many of the resolutions' while declaring their reluctant intention to vote for the package.[12] Yet even A-A. Dorion, who went to some lengths to clear his name of the slander of having ever spoken favourably of the idea, could leave open a faint and distant possibility: 'Population may extend over the wilderness that now lies between the Maritime Provinces and ourselves, and commercial intercourse may increase sufficiently to render Confederation desirable.'[13] As late as August 1864, admittedly at a social occasion, Joseph Howe proclaimed: 'I have always been in favour of uniting any two, three, four, or the whole five of the provinces.'[14] [. . .]

If some of the opponents subscribed to the idea of an eventual intercolonial union, most of the critics in the province of Canada argued that Confederation was not a solution to present difficulties, and it would itself require a far greater degree of political wisdom than was necessary to rescue the existing system. Henri Joly felt that the various provinces would meet in a confederated parliament 'as on a field of battle'. Christopher Dunkin referred to the airy dismissals of such warnings by ministerial supporters: 'Oh! there won't be any trouble; men are in the main sensible, and won't try to make trouble.' If public men were so reasonable as to be able to work the new system, why then had the province of Canada had 'four crises in two years'? In any case, even if it were accepted that Upper and Lower Canada were not living together in harmony, the answer was surely for them to work out a new system of government and not to claim that only through a wider union could they get along.[15] [. . .]

While some critics of Confederation admitted that the Canadian Union had its problems, others felt them to have been exaggerated. Henri Joly contrasted Taché's claim that 'the country was bordering on civil strife' with the ministry's throne speech, which thanked 'a beneficent Providence for the general contentment of the people of this province.'[16] Joseph Perrault asked 'have we not reason to be proud of our growth since 1840, and of the fact that within the past twenty-five years, our progress, both social and material, has kept pace with that of the first nations in the world'?[17] [. . .]

The core of the case against Confederation was that there was no crisis sufficient to justify so large a change. Consequently, critics largely refused to enter the trap of offering alternative solutions. 'We are asked, "what are you going to do? You must do something. Are you going to fall back to our old state of dead-lock?"', Dunkin reported, adding that whenever he heard the argument 'that something must be done, I suspect that there is a plan on foot to get something very bad done.' Henri Joly took the same line. 'I am asked: "If you have nothing to do with Confederation, what will you have?" I answer, we would remain as we are.'[18] 'Now my proposition is very simple', Joseph Howe told the people of Nova Scotia. 'It is to let well enough alone.'[19] Not surprisingly, the opponents of Confederation indignantly rejected the argument that they were—wittingly or otherwise—working for annexation to the United States. They replied that the campaign for Confederation itself contained the germ of an annexationist threat. Matthew Cameron, one of the few prominent Upper Canada Conservatives to oppose the scheme, warned that the delusive arguments of material gain from Confederation with the tiny Maritimes 'are arguments ten-fold stronger in favour of union with the United States.'[20] [. . .] Joseph Howe similarly predicted that the imposition of Confederation on unwilling provinces would lead to 'undying hatreds and ultimate annexation'.[21]

[. . .]

Coupled with resentment at the rejection of any possibility of amendment was anger at the total refusal of a popular vote on so major a constitutional change. An exasperated Hamilton paper exclaimed that if there was to be no general election on Confederation, the polling booths 'may as well be turned into pig-pens, and the voters lists cut up into pipe-lighters.'[22] In Nova Scotia, where petition after petition dwelt on the province's long tradition of representative and responsible government, the people of Shelburne put the issue in more fundamental and sober terms: 'whilst Your Majesty's petitioners freely admit the right of their representatives in Provincial Parliament to legislate for them within reasonable limits, they cannot admit the right of such representatives to effect sudden changes, amounting to an entire subversion of the constitution, without the deliberate sanction of the people expressed at the polls'. As Joseph Howe put it in more succinct and homely terms, the local legislature had 'no right to violate a trust only reposed in them for four years, or in fact to sell the fee simple of a mansion of which they have but a limited lease'. Even if the scheme were beneficial, which the people of Queen's County flatly doubted, 'the means employed to force it upon the country without an appeal to the people, and with full knowledge of their intense dislike of the measure' were enough to discredit it.[23]

Both in Canada and the Atlantic provinces, opponents of Confederation attacked the scheme as 'very costly, for the money is scattered on all sides in handfuls.'[24] Simply listing the promised commitments left critics breathless with horror. Joseph Howe recounted that with a debt of $75 million, 'the public men of Canada propose to purchase the territories of the Hudson's Bay Company, larger than half Europe', take over British Columbia and Vancouver Island, 'provinces divided from them by an interminable wilderness', as well as absorb the Atlantic provinces, 'countries severally as large as Switzerland, Sardinia, Greece, and Great Britain.'[25] Dunkin similarly warned that with 'a promise of everything for everybody', the scheme could only 'be ambiguous, unsubstantial and unreal'.[26] Others feared not disappointment but jobbery. 'The proposed Constitution framed by arch jobbers is so devised as to provide for the very maximum of jobbing and corruption', Arthur Gordon assured Gladstone.[27] Unfortunately, responses to the threat of corruption depended on assessments by individuals of whether they would be victims or gainers from it. [. . .] Christopher Dunkin warned that the representatives of each province would seek popularity back home by inching up federal subsidies or by taking special arrangements for one province as a benchmark and precedent for comparable concessions. They would prove to be 'pretty

good daughters of the horse-leech, and their cry will be found to be pretty often and pretty successfully—"Give, give give!"'[28] His warning can hardly be dismissed as inaccurate.

Related to the general question of cost were various predictions about the effect of Confederation on tariffs. James Currie predicted that Canada's tariff would have to rise by 50 per cent to produce the necessary revenue to pay for Confederation. Other Canadian critics recognized that the province's existing tariff, which leaned towards protectionism, would have to be cut in order to meet the free-trading Maritimers half-way. This would reduce revenue at a time when more, not less, money was needed to meet increased costs. Letellier de St. Just predicted that 'the deficit which that reduction of our revenue will produce will have to be filled up by the agriculture and industry of Canada' and Dunkin thought it 'rather strange' that a government should propose to cut its tariff income and 'at the same time, so to change our whole system as to involve ourselves in the enormous extravagances here contemplated.' Dunkin felt that no plan of direct taxation could possibly meet the cost, and that the only alternative was a reckless policy of borrowing, except that 'we cannot even borrow to any large amount unless under false pretences.'[29] The argument that Confederation would create a larger credit base and make it easier to attract investment evidently did not convince everybody.

If Canadian critics feared the consequences of lowering the tariff at the dictation of the lower provinces, Maritimers feared even the compromise increase that Confederation seemed to imply. 'Unless Canada consents to economize and curtail its expenses to a very considerable degree, which is not likely to happen', explained the Fredericton *Headquarters*, 'the Lower provinces will have to raise their tariffs to that standard, as they will require a greater revenue to meet the expenses of government under the new confederation.'[30] Whereas the Canadian tariff was intended to protect industry, Nova Scotia's commercial policy was aimed at fostering the province's worldwide carrying trade.[31] Thus raising the tariff would destroy trade rather than increase revenue—pointing to direct taxation which, Ambrose Shea warned, was 'a point on which it is easy to alarm the masses everywhere.' It certainly had that effect on Prince Edward Island, where the despairing Edward Whelan reported that it scared 'the asses of country people, who can't see an inch beyond their noses.'[32] A British journalist who visited Charlottetown in 1865 reported that taxation was regarded as 'an evil which not only the Prince Edward Islanders, but the British colonies generally throughout North America, seem to consider as the greatest which can befall a community.'[33] [. . .]

Textbook explanations of the coming of Confederation assume that it was necessary for the construction of the Intercolonial Railway, and that the Intercolonial was necessary both for defence and to give Canada a winter outlet, freeing its trade from the twin strangleholds of a frozen St Lawrence and a capriciously hostile United States. Opponents accepted neither argument and indeed found much to object to in the whole scheme. First, to reassure Maritimers who had not forgotten the Canadian bad faith of 1862, the railway project was actually written into the Quebec Resolutions, and would thus form part of the British legislation and the constitution of the Confederation—'a novelty, perhaps, that might not be found in the constitution of any country.'[34] It certainly gave an unusual status to a mere railway line, the more so as its route had yet to be agreed. [. . .]

Canadian critics were less concerned by the constitutional impropriety of giving a railway the same status as peace, order and good government as by the fact that the Intercolonial would gain an advantage over their own preferred projects, especially hopes for improved communications to the Red River.[35] Suspicions were further fuelled by ministerial reluctance to say where the Intercolonial would run or how much it would cost, thus prompting the prediction that 'it will be a piece of

corruption from the time of the turning of the first shovelful of earth'.[36] It was widely appreciated that the reason for vagueness lay in the local politics of New Brunswick, where military security pointed to a route along the thinly populated North Shore, but political expediency required a vote-pulling line up the Saint John valley, never far from the American border. [. . .] The question of the cost of the Intercolonial was a sore point to Upper Canada critics of Confederation. In 1862, the Sandfield Macdonald-Sicotte ministry had withdrawn, abruptly and in an unedifying manner, from an interprovincial agreement backed by an imperial loan guarantee, by which the province of Canada undertook to pay five-twelfths of the cost of the line—which, as Henri Joly pointed out, meant that the railway could be built if required without an accompanying political union. Now Canada, with three-quarters of the population, was accepting a *pro rata* obligation to shoulder double the share envisaged in 1862. 'This will involve five to seven millions of dollars of an expense more than we had any occasion for incurring', complained David Reesor, 'for the other provinces were all [sic] willing to have been responsible for the rest, and there is very good reason why they should.'[37] Indeed, Gall had assured Maritimers at a banquet in Halifax in September 1864, 'you will get the best of the bargain.' Yet, ironically, Canada's sudden outburst of generosity aroused counter-suspicions. In New Brunswick, Albert J. Smith hinted darkly that Canada must have some hidden motive for increasing the very offer it had so recently dishonoured.[38]

Fundamentally, opponents argued that the Intercolonial was no more attractive a project in 1865 than it had been when rejected in 1862. 'I have not heard any reason why we should pledge our credit and resources to the construction of the Intercolonial Railway, even previous to any estimate of its cost being made, that was not urged in 1862 when the question was before the country', A-A. Dorion asserted. [. . .] Henri Joly also doubted whether the Intercolonial could be used to send flour to the

Maritimes, for 'the cost of transport over five hundred miles of railway would be too great.'[39]

The critics did not simply doubt whether trade could profitably flow along the Intercolonial; they also wondered whether Canada and the Maritimes were likely to have any trade at all. 'Let us not . . . be lulled with fallacies of the great commercial advantages we shall derive from a Confederation of these provinces', intoned Eric Dorion. 'We have wood, they produce it; we produce potash, and so do they.'[40] 'With regard to timber', said Henri Joly, 'the Gulf Provinces have no more need of ours than we of theirs.' Canada imported its coal direct from Britain, as ballast on returning timber ships. If that supply should ever fail, 'Upper Canada will probably get its coal from the Pennsylvania mines, which are in direct communication with Lake Erie.'[41] Yet, at the same time, Canadian critics could argue that free trade with the Maritimes could be achieved without 'this mock Federal union', just as the provinces had enjoyed a decade of closer economic relations with the United States through the Reciprocity Treaty.[42] [. . .]

The critics were no more convinced by the argument that the Intercolonial was necessary for the defence of the provinces. A-A. Dorion argued that 'a railway lying in some places not more than fifteen or twenty miles from the frontier, will be of no use whatever. . . . An enemy could destroy miles of it before it would be possible to resist him, and in time of difficulty it would be a mere trap for the troops passing along it, unless we had almost an army to keep it open.' However far the Intercolonial snaked away from the American border, there was an existing stretch of the Grand Trunk 'at places within twenty-six miles of the boundary of Maine', and thus easily vulnerable to American attack. Far from transporting large numbers of troops, the Intercolonial would need large forces simply to guard it. 'Unless with a strong force to defend it, in a military point of view, it would be of just no use at all.' In summary, the Intercolonial, centrepiece of so many textbook explanations of the causes of Confederation,

was comprehensively dismissed by James L. Biggar: 'Looking at it from a military point of view, it is well known that part of the proposed line would run within twenty-six miles of the American frontier, and that communication could be cut off at any moment by an American army; and that as a commercial undertaking it could never compete with the water route during the season of navigation; and in winter it would be comparatively useless on account of the depth of snow.'[43]

The opponents of Confederation were unconvinced that the political union of the provinces would strengthen their defences in any way. 'We do not need Confederation to give us that unity which is indispensable in all military operations—unity of headship. A commander-in-chief will direct the defence of all our provinces', argued Henri Joly. Defence had remained outside the orbit of colonial self-government until very recent times, and Canada's record on militia reform was hardly impressive. Consequently, the argument that unity meant strength is one which appeals more to the twentieth century observer than it did to contemporaries, especially when the unity proposed involved such tiny provinces. John S. Sanborn was simply bewildered. 'How the people of New Brunswick could be expected to come up to Canada to defend us, and leave their own frontier unprotected, he could not comprehend.' Conversely, Matthew Cameron asked why Canada should be taxed to build fortifications in the Maritimes: 'Fortifications in St. John, New Brunswick, would not protect us from the foe, if the foe were to come here.'[44] [. . .]

In the Atlantic colonies, the arguments were inverted. Petitioners from Nova Scotia's Digby County were ready to rally to 'the defence of their country and their flag' but were 'not disposed to adopt, as a means of ensuring their more efficient defence, a union with a Province which in 1862 refused to sanction a measure involving increased outlay for the better and more elaborate organisation of their militia.'[45] Joseph Howe deftly alluded to Canadian complicity in border raids by Southern sympathizers, and the resulting threats of Northern retaliation, proclaiming: 'let those who provoke these controversies fight them out.'[46] He objected to a system under which Nova Scotia's militia 'may be ordered away to any point of the Canadian frontier.'[47] Prince Edward Islanders feared that they would be 'marched away to the frontiers of Upper Canada' or, as John Hamilton Gray put it with vivid bitterness, 'drafted for slaughter'.[48] [. . .]

In three of the four Atlantic provinces, insularity was a physical as well as a mental factor. 'We are surrounded by the sea', proclaimed Joseph Howe and—what was more to the point—'within ten days' sail of the fleets and armies of England.'[49] J.C. Pope of Prince Edward Island echoed Canadian critics in predicting that an American attack would make it 'necessary to retain all available strength in each of the provinces for the defence of their respective territories.' His emphasis differed in his confidence that local efforts would be powerfully seconded by the British navy and army.[50] Many critics argued that Confederation would actually make the defence of British North America more difficult. Henri Joly argued that there was 'no need' of political union to warn 'our neighbours' not to pick on a single province.[51] [. . .]

'With Confederation, neither the number of men in the several provinces, nor the pecuniary resources now at their disposal, will be increased.' The kernel of the Canadian opposition case on defence was that Confederation involved too much territory and no additional manpower. 'Can you alter the geographical position of the country?', asked Benjamin Seymour. 'Will you have any more people or means?' 'If nature were to make the necessary effort and move their territory up alongside of us, and thus make a compact mass of people, I would at once agree that it would strengthen us in a military point of view', Philip Moore ironically conceded. In reality, however, Confederation 'will weaken instead of strengthen us', since 'the union will give an extension of territory

far greater in proportion to the number of the population than [sic] now exists in Canada.' The planned massive extension into empty and inaccessible territory westward to the Pacific struck A-A. Dorion as 'a burlesque' in terms of defence. In short, critics found the defence argument literally laughable: 'If we could attach the territory possessed by the moon to these provinces, and obtain the assistance for our joint defence of the man who is popularly supposed to inhabit that luminary, we might derive strength from Confederation.'[52]

Critics were equally unimpressed by ringing talk of a 'new nationality' in British North America. 'I cannot see that the Federation of these provinces has anything of a national phase in it', commented Thomas Scatcherd. 'When you speak of national existence, you speak of independence; and so long as we are colonists of Great Britain we can have no national existence.'[53] Some Nova Scotian petitions protested that British North America was 'incapable of forming a new nationality',[54] but the loyal people of Barrington township had an each-way bet in wanting no part of 'new nationalities too feeble to stand alone, yet difficult to be controlled.'[55] [. . .]

In fact, critics feared that Confederation would actually provoke Americans into hostilities. Howe warned: 'let this guy of "new nationality" be set up . . . and every young fellow who has had a taste of the license of camp life in the United States will be tempted to have a fling at it.'[56] Christopher Dunkin even expressed alarm at the tone of the Confederation debates, asking 'how is the temper of the United States going to be affected . . . by the policy here urged on us, of what I may call hostile independent effort—effort made on our part, with the avowed object of setting ourselves up as a formidable power against them[?].' The Northern States, A-A. Dorion pointed out, had put into the field an army of 2,300,000, 'as many armed men as we have men, women and children in the two Canadas.' Military expenditure on any large scale would be useless and 'we are not bound to ruin ourselves in anticipation of a supposed invasion which we could not repel.' Public opinion should force the Canadian press to cease its anti-American outbursts: 'The best thing that Canada can do is to keep quiet, and to give no cause for war.'[57] [. . .]

Given their overwhelming rejection of the case for Confederation as a defence measure, it is hardly surprising that this aspect of the scheme produced some of the most colourful imagery among critics. Joining with the Maritimes, said James Currie, 'was like tying a small twine at the end of a long rope and saying it strengthened the whole line.' Incorporating the vast Hudson's Bay Territories, said Henri Joly, would create 'the outward form of a giant, but with the strength of a child.'[58] John Macdonald, member for Toronto West, thought 'the casting of the burden of defence upon this country is like investing a sovereign with all the outward semblance of royalty, and giving him a dollar per day to keep up the dignity of his court.' Macdonald has been overshadowed by his namesake to the point of invisibility, but he had a homely touch in his comments, telling the legislators as they met for the last year in Quebec City that Confederation was like taking the engine from the Lévis ferry and using it 'to propel the *Great Eastern* across the Atlantic.'[59] In a far smaller town, an angry young Rouge editor denounced Confederation in less whimsical imagery. As a defence against the United States it was like being 'armed with an eggshell to stop a bullet . . . a wisp of straw in the way of a giant.'[60] The writer's name was Wilfrid Laurier. [. . .]

There was little direct contact between Canada and Maritimes prior to Confederation: during a visit to Montreal in 1860, T. Heath Haviland of Prince Edward Island had encountered 'the utmost difficulty' in finding 'so much as a newspaper from the Lower Provinces.'[61] It is therefore surprising to discover the extent of their mutual antipathy. The 'plain meaning' of the Canadian ministry's desire to force through the Quebec Resolutions without amendment was 'that the Lower Provinces have made out a Constitution for us and we are to adopt it', said

A-A. Dorion. Voting at the Quebec Conference had been by provinces, which 'made Prince Edward Island equal to Upper Canada.' Dorion complained of 'the humiliation of seeing the Government going on its knees and begging the little island of Prince Edward to come into this union.'[62] Only by appreciating the existence of this sentiment of disdain for the Maritimes among Canadian critics can we understand why Macdonald and his colleagues had no alternative but to outface and outmanoeuvre opposition in Nova Scotia and New Brunswick. Maritimers returned the hostility. James Dingwell of Prince Edward Island thought 'Canadians had not been able to manage the business of their country as we have been to manage ours; and why should we trust the management of our own affairs to people who have never been able to manage their own with satisfaction?'[63] With colourful exaggeration, Joseph Howe claimed that Canadians were 'always in trouble of some sort, and two or three times in open rebellion.'[64]

Despite Howe's suspicions that Lower Canadian solidarity in the federal parliament would entrench French power, hostility to Confederation in the Atlantic colonies seems to have been directed against the whole of what later became the monster of 'central Canada' and was relatively free of explicit francophobia. There was a hint of it an open letter to the British Colonial Secretary in January 1867, when a recitation of Nova Scotia's loyal service to the Empire in wars against France was followed by the waspish comment: 'We are now asked to surrender it to Monsieur Cartier.'[65] Although francophobia was so endemic that it was not necessary to articulate it, inter-communal flashpoints in the mid-nineteenth century were more likely to concern sectarian schooling than the politics of language. Memories of their homeland's forced unification with Britain led many Irish Catholics to oppose Confederation. If anti-Confederates had warned of the danger of French power, Irish Catholics might have concluded that Confederation could bring benefits for their Church. In any case, Acadians were as suspicious of Confederation as their anglophone neighbours, and it suited Howe to portray them as one of the contented minorities—along with Micmacs and Blacks—who had flourished under the benign institutions of an autonomous Nova Scotia.[66] [. . .]

Behind these mutual suspicions, there surely lay something deeper than the cussedness which we normally dismiss as parochialism. Even in the superheated provincial politics of the mid-nineteenth century, it seems exaggerated that Cartier could have been accused of 'la lâchéte la plus insigne dans la trahison la plus noire', merely for forming a coalition with George Brown, or that Prince Edward Island representatives at the Charlottetown conference were pointed out in the street as 'the men who would sell their country.'[67] The fact that such remarks were made suggests that the different provinces felt themselves to possess distinct social and political cultures. This was most obvious in predominantly French-speaking and Catholic Lower Canada. [. . .] The complication in Lower Canada was the existence of a minority-within-a-minority, equally suspicious of those aspects of the new constitution which guaranteed provincial autonomy under a local francophone majority. Principal Dawson of McGill thought that 'scarcely anyone among the English of Lower Canada desires Confederation, except perhaps as an alternative to simple dissolution of the Union.'[68] This was a case where clashing objections had a reinforcing effect, for every reassurance offered to the Lower Canada English was a confirmation of French Canadian fears.[69]

The separate identity of French Canadian society on an Anglo-Saxon continent was obvious enough. What may be less obvious is that in the Maritimes—and especially in Nova Scotia—there was as great a sense of being different from the province of Canada as modern Canadians would today feel separates themselves from their neighbours in the United States. True, Joseph Howe could welcome a party of Canadian visitors to Halifax in August 1864 with the sentiment: 'I am not one of

those who thank God that I am a Nova Scotian merely, for I am a Canadian as well.'[70] Yet the picture which emerges from his subsequent anti-Confederation campaign is of a province not simply resentful of losing its autonomy, but fearful of being subordinated to the capricious and unattractive values of 'those who live above the tide', 'the administration of strangers'.[71] A recurrent theme of Nova Scotian opposition was loss of its historic self-government. Behind the issue of high principle, there lay practical and local fears. The petitioners of Digby County pointed out that 'while that portion of this county which borders on the sea is thickly inhabited and rapidly increasing in population and wealth, there are still considerable districts but lately reclaimed from the primaeval forest', which required grants of public money for the development of roads and bridges. They regarded 'with dismay' the transfer of control over public expenditure 'to a Government by which they would necessarily all be expended for widely different purposes.'[72] Canada was as distant from Nova Scotia as Austria from Britain.[73] 'You cannot . . . invest a village on the Ottawa with the historic interest and associations that cluster around London', wrote Joseph Howe—and he emphatically preferred 'London under the dominion of John Bull to Ottawa under the dominion of Jack Frost.'[74] [. . .]

Another theme common to the critics, whatever their regional loyalty, was rejection of both the proposed provincial governments and the confederate upper house as safeguards for their rights. [. . .] George Coles predicted that under Confederation, the legislature of Prince Edward Island 'would be the laughing stock of the world', left 'to legislate about dog taxes, and the running at large of swine.'[75] While some critics concluded that the whole plan of union should be abandoned, others argued from similar premises that the union should be strengthened. The Halifax *Citizen* agreed that the Quebec scheme 'has given these local legislatures very little to do', and predicted that they would occupy themselves in mischief, preserving local loyalties which would prevent 'the fusion of the British American population in one actual indivisible nationality.'[76] 'One of the worst features of the Union plan proposed by Canada is, that it will leave our local legislature still in existence', lamented the Saint John *Globe*, which would have preferred to see outright unification.[77] Even the fervent anti-Confederate, T.W. Anglin, writing in the rival *Freeman*, agreed that if they had to have Confederation, 'it would be better to abolish the local Legislatures at once in appearance as well as in reality.'[78]

The critics were not reassured by the fact that both lieutenant-governors and members of the upper house were to be appointed by the central government. The prospect of lieutenant-governors drawn from provincial politics aroused little enthusiasm. 'Let any one of our dozen or twenty most prominent Canadian politicians be named Lieutenant-Governor of Upper or of Lower Canada, would not a large and powerful class of the community . . . be very likely to resent the nomination as an insult?', asked Christopher Dunkin.[79] In Canada, where the legislative Council had become elective in 1856—with life members retaining their seats—there was resentment at the reintroduction of nomination, 'because the Maritime Provinces are opposed to an elective Chamber, and hence we in Canada—the largest community and the most influential—must give way to them.'[80] There was also resentment at the provision in the Quebec Resolutions by which the first Confederate legislative councillors would be appointed from the existing Legislative Councils (except in Prince Edward Island)—a transparent bribe to curb the opposition in the upper houses. Worse still, the first Confederate upper house was to be appointed for life, on the nomination of the existing provincial governments—with the central government not even possessing a veto. A-A. Dorion's objection was not to the principle but to the unlucky fact that most British North American governments were Conservative. 'For all time to come, as far as this generation and the next are concerned,

you will find the Legislative Council controlled by the influence of the present government.'[81] Future appointment by the central government aroused no more enthusiasm, since as Dunkin suggested, a government might be formed in which an entire province 'either is not represented, or is represented otherwise than it would wish to be.'[82] [. . .]

The arguments of the critics of Confederation must be conceded to have been at least plausible. Why then did they fail to prevent the passage of the British North America Act in 1867? First, of course, their arguments did not pass unchallenged. Just as conventional studies of the causes of Confederation tend to underplay the opposition case, so a study of the critics necessarily distorts the debate in their favour. Indeed, arguments which high-minded posterity may find irrefutable could perhaps have produced diametrically opposite responses among contemporaries: Upper Canadian critics, in damning the Intercolonial as an irresponsible waste of money, might have convinced some Lower Canadians of its pork-barrel value.[83] Even if the opposition case against the Intercolonial Railway had been overwhelming, Confederation might still have been supported on general grounds as the most practicable solution to a range of problems. The Confederation package mattered more than the interlocking detail, and not everybody bothered with those details. [. . .] In any case, even if the argument were won inside the provinces, there remained that 'atmosphere of crisis' over the North American continent. 'Look around you to the valley of Virginia', McGee challenged those who wanted to know why Confederation was necessary, 'look around you to the mountains of Georgia, and you will find reasons as thick as blackberries.'[84] Perhaps the fundamental mistake of the opponents of Confederation was to ask people to react logically to the activities of Macdonald and Cartier in the conference chamber rather than to the operations of Grant and Sherman on the battlefield. The question for explanation then becomes why it should have been intercolonial union—rather than, say, neutrality or annexation—which met the psychological need for a dramatic response to continental crisis. One explanation may be that the idea had been around for a long time, answer looking for a question. 'Everybody admits that Union must take place sometime', said John A. Macdonald, 'I say now is the time.'[85] In seeking to account for the adoption of so vast a scheme as Canadian Confederation, historians have naturally turned to the arguments of its supporters, and have been tempted to conclude that the arguments put forward *for* Canadian Confederation equal the reasons *why* Canadian Confederation came about. Certainly hindsight finds it easy to draw neat lines of causation linking argument to outcome: the lines may be straight, but the process itself is circular, since it identifies the winners of history as—in Morton's terms—those who sensed the currents of events. Yet we should not forget that the case against Confederation was argued as tenaciously, as eloquently and—we must

assume—as sincerely as the arguments in its favour. However much historians may admire the 'Fathers of Confederation', only by recognizing not just the strength of opposition to Confederation but also the plausibility of some of the arguments put forward, can we begin to see that the outcome was by no means inevitable. Of course, some historians believe that posterity is not entitled to second-guess past controversies, that a century later we cannot award points to individual arguments, for or against, since we cannot make ourselves fully part of the atmosphere of the time. Yet such an attitude is tantamount to an uncritical abdication of our own judgement to each and every claim made by those who were on the winning side perhaps for reasons other than the simply intellectual. 'La raison do plus fort, c'est toujours la meuilleure', is not the most appropriate explanatory strategy for the historian to adopt. Hindsight may yet conclude that while the Antis lost the battle, they won at least some of the arguments.

NOTES

1. The major accounts of the coming of Confederation remain D.G. Creighton, *The Road to Confederation: The Emergence of Canada 1863–1867* (Toronto, 1964); W.L. Morton, *The Critical Years: The Union of British North America 1857–1873* (Toronto, 1964) and P.B. Waite, *The Life and Times of Confederation 1864–1867: Newspapers, and the Union of British North America* (Toronto, 1962). My debt to Waite's study of press sources is obvious from the footnotes below, in which the book is cited as *Life and Times*.

2. W.L. Morton, *The Kingdom of Canada: A General History from Earliest Times* (2nd ed., Toronto, 1969), pp. 317, 314–5.

3. Paradoxically, given the relative lack of general overviews, opposition to Confederation in individual provinces and sections has been widely studied, conveying the impression that parochialism predominated. For bibliographies, see D.A. Muise, ed., *A Reader's Guide to Canadian History: I, Beginnings to Confederation* (Toronto, 1982), pp. 237–48 and *Life and Times*, pp. 342–52.

4. Christopher Dunkin, *Parliamentary Debates on the Subject of the Confederation of the British North American Provinces* (3rd Session, 8th Provincial Parliament of Canada, Quebec 1865) [hereafter cited as CD], pp. 545 (Blanchet); 147 (Holton); 682 (Dorion).

5. *Life and Times*, p. 154.

6. Not reported in CD, but see Waite ed., *The Confederation Debates in the Province of Canada 1865* (Torono, 1963), pp. xv–xvi.

7. *Hansard's Parliamentary Debates* (3rd series), CLXXXV, 19 February 1867, cols. 579–80, 577.

8. *British Parliamentary Papers* [cited as BPP], 1867, XLVIII, *Correspondence Respecting the Proposed Union of the British North American Provinces*, pp. 75–77.

9. Speech of 7 April 1866, quoted in William M. Baker, *Timothy Warren Anglin 1822–1896:*

Irish Catholic Canadian (Toronto, 1977), p. 103, and see also p. 58. Anglin was editor of the Saint John *Morning Freeman*. According to Creighton, Anglin was 'an unsubdued ex-rebel' who 'flung the full force of his abusive and mendacious journalism against Confederation' (*Road to Confederation*, p. 251, and see also p. 247). It is unlikely that Anglin took part in the Irish rising of 1848 and there is no reason to think that his journalism was unusually abusive or mendacious by contemporary standards, which were admittedly low. Thus have critics of Confederation been dismissed.

10. Similar views were expressed in the Canadian Legislative Council by James G. Currie, Bill Flint and David Reesor and in the Assembly by Christopher Dunkin, Joseph Perrault, Thomas Scatcherd and T.C. Wallbridge. CD, pp. 46, 164, 319, 483, 585, 749, 660.

11. Charlottetown *Examiner*, 30 January 1865, quoted in *Life and Times*, p. 186.

12. CD, p. 328.

13. CD, p. 248. In May 1860, Dorion had said that he regarded a federation of the two Canada as 'le noyau de la grande confédération des provinces de l'Amérique du nord que j'appelle de mes voeux.' Quoted by Joseph Cauchon, *L'Union des Provinces de l'Amérique Britannique du Nord* (Quebec, 1865), p. 7.

14. Speech in Halifax, 13 August 1864, in J.A. Chisholm, ed., *The Speeches and Public Letters of Joseph Howe* (2 vols, Halifax, 1909), II, p. 433.

15. CD, pp. 352 (Joly); 508, 485 (Dunkin).

16. CD, p. 357.

17. CD, p. 586.

18. CD, pp. 543 (Dunkin); 356–57 (Joly).

19. Open letter, 10 April 1866, in Chisholm, ed., *Speeches and Public Letters of Joseph Howe*, 11, p. 463.

20. CD, p. 456.

21. Howe to Isaac Buchanan, 20 June 1866, in Chisholm, ed., *op. cit.*, II, p. 464. In his 1866 pamphlet, *Confederation Considered in Relation to the Interests of the Empire*, Howe complained that in the New Brunswick election that year, 'one half of an entirely loyal population were taught to brand the other half as disloyal.' Quoted in ibid., II, p. 484.

22. Hamilton *Times*, November 1864, quoted in *Life and Times*, p. 122. See also Bruce W. Hodgins, 'Democracy and the Ontario Fathers of Confederation', in Bruce Hodgins and Robert Page, eds, *Canadian History Since Confederation: Essays and Interpretations* (2nd ed., Georgetown, Ontario, 1979), pp. 19–28.

23. BPP, 1867, XLVIII, *Correspondence*, pp. 70, 75; Howe *et al.* to Carnarvon, 19 January 1867, p. 18.

24. CD, p. 179 (L.A. Olivier, MLC for the Lanaudière).

25. Quoted in Chisholm, ed., *op. cit.*, II, p. 473.

26. CD, p. 490.

27. Gordon to Gladstone, private, 27 February 1865, in Paul Knaplund, ed., *Gladstone-Gordon Correspondence*, 1851–1896 (Transactions of the American Philosophical Society, n.s., LI, Pt 4, 1961), p. 46.

28. CD, p. 520.

29. CD, pp. 50 (Currie); 188 (Letellier); 524 (Dunkin).

30. Fredericton *Headquarters*, 19 October 1864, quoted in A.G. Bailey, 'The Basis and Persistence of Opposition to Confederation in New Brunswick', *Canadian Historical Review*, XXIII (1942), p. 375.

31. 'We have the trade of the world now open to us on nearly equal terms, and why should we allow Canada to hamper us?', Yarmouth *Herald*, 15 December 1864, quoted in *Life and Times*, p. 202.

32. Shea to Galt, 15 December 1864 and Whelan to Galt, 17 December 1864, in W.G. Ormsby, 'Letters to Galt Concerning the Maritime Provinces and Confederation', *Canadian Historical Review*, XXXIV (1953), pp. 167, 168.

33. Charles Mackay, 'A Week in Prince Edward Island', *Fortnightly Review*, V (1865), p. 147.

34. CD, p. 17 (Holton).

35. Article 69 of the Quebec Resolutions offered only that improved communications to the Red River 'shall be prosecuted at the earliest possible period that the state of the Finances will permit'. According to T.C. Wallbridge, this meant 'that the North-West is hermetically sealed.' CD, p. 453 and cf. Matthew Cameron, pp. 452–3.

36. CD, p. 759 (Scatcherd).

37. CD, pp. 356 (Joly); 164 (Reesor). The 1862 agreement involved only the two provinces of New Brunswick and Nova Scotia.

38. C. Wallace, 'Albert Smith, Confederation and Reaction in New Brunswick, 1852–1882',

Canadian Historical Review, XLIV (1963), p. 289. The Nova Scotian deputation to London in 1867 could 'scarcely bring themselves to discuss' the Intercolonial, 'so selfish and unfair at all times has been the conduct of the public men of Canada in regard to it.' BPP, 1867, XLVIII, Howe et al. to Carnarvon, 19 January 1867, p. 8. For Galt's Halifax speech, see Edward Whelan, comp., *The Union of the British Provinces* (Charlottetown, 1865), p. 48.

39. CD, pp. 263 (Dorion); 356 (Joly).
40. CD, p. 863, Canada took 1.11 per cent of its imports from the other British North American territories, and sent them 2.2 per cent of its exports. New Brunswick took 2.3 per cent of its imports from Canada, to which it sent 0.87 per cent of its exports. Prince Edward Island took 2.1 per cent of its imports from Canada, to which it sent 0.6 per cent of its exports. Newfoundland took 3.9 per cent of its imports from Canada, to which it sent 0.68 per cent of its exports. (Calculated from BPP, 1866, LXIII, *Colonial Trade Statistics*, pp. 132, 152, 170, 177.) Nova Scotia figures are less helpful, but in 1866 the province took 5.5 per cent of its imports from Canada, and sent 7.15 per cent of its exports (1865 figures being 3.5 per cent and 4.96 per cent). (Calculated from BPP, 1867–68, LXXI, *Colonial Trade Statistics*, p. 144.)
41. CD, p. 355.
42. CD, pp. 356 (Joly) and 528 (Dorion).
43. CD, pp. 257 (Dorion); 750 (Scatcherd); 521 (Dorion); 883 (Biggar).
44. CD, pp. 355 (Joly); 123 (Sanborn); 456 (Cameron).
45. BPP, 1867, XLVIII, *Correspondence*, pp. 69–70.
46. Halifax *Morning Chronicle*, 11 January 1865, quoted in Chisholm, ed., *op. cit.*, II, p. 435 (the first of the celebrated 'Botheration Scheme' letters).
47. Speech at Dartmouth, 22 May 1867, quoted in ibid., II, p. 512.
48. Islander, 6 January 1865 and J.H. Gray to Tupper, 7 January 1865, quoted in Life and Times, pp. 186, 183.
49. Quoted in Chisholm, ed., op. cit., II, pp. 435–36.
50. Quoted in Bolger, ed., *Canada's Smallest Province*, pp. 175–76.

51. CD, pp. 354 (Joly).
52. CD, pp. 176 (Olivier); 203 (Seymour); 229 (Moore); 263 (Dorion); 234 (John Simpson, MLC for Queen's). The Halifax *Citizen* alleged that Tupper was perfectly capable of campaigning for federation with the Moon if he thought it would divert public attention. Quoted in *Life and Times*, p. 200.
53. CD, p. 748. Critics dismissed appeals to Italian and German unity as proving that the spirit of the times pointed to wider unions. Henri Joly gave a list of federations which had failed (CD, pp. 346–48), while the imperially minded Howe likened Confederation to a handful of small states withdrawing from the North German Confederation, or 'a few offshoots from Italian unity' attempting to form 'an inferior confederation'. BPP, 1867, XLVIII, Howe et al. to Carnarvon, 19 January 1867, p. 21.
54. E.g. Petition from King's, BPP, 1867, XLVIII, *Correspondence*, p. 67.
55. Ibid., p. 71.
56. Quoted in Chisholm, ed., *op. cit.*, II, p. 487.
57. CD, pp. 529 (Dunkin); 257 (Brome).
58. CD, pp. 46 (Currie); 353 (Joly). Henri Joly doubted comparisons between the Hudson's Bay Territories and European Russia, doubting that the West could ever support a large population. It may be noted that he ended his public career by serving as lieutenant-governor of British Columbia, 1900–1906. John A. Macdonald believed in 1865 that the prairies were 'of no present value to Canada' which had 'unoccupied land enough to absorb the immigration for many years.' To open Saskatchewan would be to 'drain away our youth and strength.' Macdonald to E.W. Watkin, 27 March 1865, in J. Pope, *Memoirs of the Right Honourable Sir John Alexander Macdonald* (Toronto, 1894), pp. 397–8.
59. CD, p. 753.
60. Quoted in J. Schull, *Laurier: The First Canadian* (Toronto, 1966), p. 57.
61. Speech at Montreal, 28 October 1864, in Whelan, comp., *Union*, p. 115.
62. CD, pp. 252, 47, 656.
63. Quoted in Bolger, ed., *Canada's Smallest Province*, II, p. 177.
64. Howe to Earl Russell, 19 January 1865, quoted in Chisholm, ed., *op. cit.*, II, p. 437.

65. BPP, 1867, XLVIII, *Howe et al. to Carnarvon*, 19 January 1867, p. 16. See also ibid., p. 12 for an unsubtle reference to the Hundred Years War.

66. Ibid., p. 17. Cf. Leon Thériault, 'L'Acadie, 1763–1978: Synthèse Historique' in Jean Daigle, éd., *Les Acadiens des Maritimes: Etudes Thématiques* (Moncton, 1980), pp. 63–8.

67. *Le Pays*, 27 June 1864, quoted in Creighton, *Road to Confederation*, p. 78, and ibid., p. 122.

68. Dawson to Howe, 15 November 1866, quoted in *Life and Times*, p. 135.

69. CD, p. 351 (Joly).

70. Speech, 13 August 1864, in Chisholm, ed., *op. cit.*, II, p. 433. Howe rose to speak at ten minutes to midnight. 'Who ever heard of a public man being bound by a speech on such an occasion as that?', he asked three years later. J.M. Beck, *Joseph Howe: II, The Briton Becomes Canadian 1848–1873* (Kingston, 1983), p. 182. In fact, Howe spoke before the Charlottetown conference.

71. Speech at Dartmouth, 22 May 1867, in Chisholm, ed., *op. cit.*, II, p. 511.

72. BPP 1867, XLVIII, Correspondence, pp. 69–70.

73. Port Medway petition, BPP, 1867, XLVIII, *Correspondence*, p. 76; Howe et al. to Carnarvon, 19 January 1867, p. 7.

74. BPP, 1867, XLVIII, Howe et al. to Carnarvon, 19 January 1867, p. 15. J.W. Longley, *Joseph Howe* (Toronto, 1906), p. 202, and cf. Beck, op. cit., II, p. 202. The reference to 'a village' was, of course, unfair, but Dunkin was concerned that the federal capital was to remain 'within the jurisdiction of a subordinate province.' CD, p. 507.

75. Quoted in Bolger, ed., *op. cit.*, p. 174.

76. Halifax *Citizen*, 19 November 1864, quoted in *Life and Times*, p. 203. The lieutenant-governor, Sir Richard MacDonnell, used the same argument a few days later in a despatch: 'I do not believe that so long as the boundaries of the different Provinces are maintained and Local Legislatures and petty politics fostered, the Confederation can rise to that status, and that dignity of national feeling, which creates and maintains a national military spirit and self-reliance.' PRO, CO 217/235, MacDonnell to Cardwell, 22 November 1864, fos 187–212.

77. Saint John *Daily Evening Globe*, 17 October 1864, quoted in *Life and Times*, p. 136.

78. Saint John *Freeman*, 3 November 1864, quoted in Baker, *Anglin*, p. 65. Joseph Howe also condemned the duplication of legislatures as 'cumbrous and expensive'. Howe to Earl Russell, 19 January 1865, in Chisholm, ed., *op. cit.*, II, p. 437.

79. CD, p. 504. Perrault alleged that some politicians were influenced by hopes of 'being governor of one of the Federated Provinces', as did Letellier, who subsequently became a lieutenant-governor himself. CD, pp. 626, 188.

80. CD, p. 157 (James Aikins).

81. CD, p. 253. Dorion chose to overlook the provision in Article 14 of the Quebec Resolutions that 'in such nomination due regard shall be had to the claims of the Members of Legislative Council in Opposition in each Province, so that all political panties may as nearly as possible be fairly represented.'

82. CD, pp. 494–5.

83. Support for the Intercolonial might not translate into support for Confederation, as in the case of J.B. Pouliot, MPP for Témiscouata.

84. Speech at Montreal, 29 October 1864, in Whelan, comp., *op. cit.*, pp. 122–23.

85. Speech at Halifax, 12 September 1864, in ibid., p. 46.

4   From Edward MacDonald, 'Who's Afraid of the Fenians? The Fenian Scare on Prince Edward Island, 1865–1867', *Acadiensis* 38(1) (Winter/Spring2009): 33–51.

It is easy, from where we sit, to scoff at the Fenians. First there is the implausible conceit—at least to us—of the Fenian strategy in the 1860s. The American offshoot of the Irish Republican Brotherhood intended to seize part of British North America and hold it hostage to help liberate Ireland from British rule or, if conquest proved impractical, draw off British forces to improve the odds for an insurrection in Ireland itself. Then there is the undertone of buffoonery beneath the surface bluster of the Irish-American cause: a secret society that could not keep its secrets, a brotherhood in arms consumed with sibling rivalries, and invaders who barely got beyond gunshot of the British North American-American border. But few people were laughing in the winter of 1866, when Fenianism's giant shadow obscured the real magnitude of the threat it posed, and rumour multiplied what British North Americans thought they saw: thousands of well-armed, battle-hardened veterans of the American Civil War, backed by the willing alms of millions of anglophobe Irish-Americans, controlled by scheming demagogues in league with Irish revolutionaries back in the 'Old Sod', and condoned by an American government willing to countenance a 'Fenian republic' on British North American soil. But then came a puff of wind, and the Fenian shadow blew away like smoke.

Within living memory of the event, the Fenian interlude commanded a modicum of respect, but over time perceptions of it have descended into the realm of absurdity.[1] Historians of Confederation have noted the Fenians' role in pushing New Brunswickers towards Confederation.[2] The military defence argument for union, after all, got much of its traction after 1865 from the Fenian menace, and, in New Brunswick particularly, pro-Confederates used the spectre of fifth-column Fenian sympathizers within the colony to mobilize anti-Irish and anti-Roman Catholic sentiment in support of their cause during the crucial election of 1866.[3] In the more recent past, time and historiographical trends have shifted the focus to other dimensions of Fenianism in Canada. Military historians have measured the militia response to the invasion threat while religious historians have provided a more nuanced treatment of the position of the Roman Catholic hierarchy in North America with respect to the Fenian

issue. At the same time, social historians have explored the sectarian and ethnic attitudes the Fenian interlude exposed in British North America.[4]

But the Fenian scare on Prince Edward Island has failed to attract much attention.[5] And why should it? No Fenian army ever postured along its borders. No Fenian 'navy' descended on its coastline. And yet, even in this little colony, the Fenians provoked an intense spasm of fear and panic that, in turn, provoked draconian legislative reaction. But was the provincial government as afraid of the Fenians as many Islanders evidently were? Beneath the brittle shell of popular hysteria ran a strong current of political calculation. As in New Brunswick, it had more to do with domestic politics than Irish insurrectionists but, unlike the New Brunswick case, the Fenian issue on Prince Edward Island had much less to do with the politics of Confederation than the electoral implications of two enduring, treacherous, and divisive issues: the century-old Land Question and the genie of sectarian discord. These helped define how the Fenian issue was perceived and then dealt with in the little island colony.

I

It was Leland H. Stumbles—'Rufus' to the street urchins around Charlottetown—who played the role of Chicken Little to the falling sky of the Fenian uprising. Later disparaged as 'a half-witted schoolteacher', he was a long way from his little school in the frontier community of Mount Pleasant when he brought the news to Charlottetown in early March 1866.[6] 'One thousand Fenians', Stumbles told anyone who would listen, 'were organizing in some back-settlement, and were preparing to march on Charlottetown for the purpose of sacking and burning it.'[7] The uprising was to take place on Saturday, 17 March (St. Patrick's Day). On his way to Government House with these tidings, Stumbles encountered George D. Atkinson, private secretary to Lieutenant Governor George Dundas.

Unacquainted with Stumbles's reputation, Atkinson quickly brought news of the conspiracy to T.H. Haviland, Jr., solicitor general in the Conservative government of James Colledge Pope. The secretary and solicitor general conferred while Stumbles stood by expectantly. When Haviland discovered Atkinson's source, he allegedly burst out laughing.[8] And yet 'deeming an ounce of prevention better than a pound of cure', as the Conservative *Islander* explained, his government took a number of precautions that either reassured a jittery populace (according to the ruling Tories) or inflamed the public mood by dignifying ridiculous rumours (according to the opposition Liberals). At the government's suggestion, officials at Charlottetown City Hall called out a hundred or more special constables to keep the peace on St. Patrick's Day. Meanwhile, the volunteer militia's rifles were removed from the Charlottetown Armoury to the military barracks for safekeeping; the government argued that this was 'necessary, and becoming prudence' while the opposition charged that it was 'the most unjust and foul imputation of disloyalty.'[9] Meanwhile, the two companies of British regulars temporarily stationed in the city were confined to barracks 'at unusually early hours' in the nights leading up to St. Patrick's Day.

Although it was politically expedient for critics of the government to blame 'a man of phrensied mind and over-heated imagination' for the Fenian scare, since it made the administration look either gullible or duplicitous, Leland Stumbles was only parroting a rumour that had already swept the countryside around Charlottetown. And that rumour, in turn, was a local variant of a larger, more distant portent, rooted in dark mutterings from Fenian spokesmen in the United States, that St. Patrick's Day would somehow be a day of reckoning in the British colonies.[10]

The grafting of local fears onto a foreign threat was both typical and suggestive. Fed by stories in the gossip-mongering American press, the Fenian menace had been steadily growing in British North America since late 1865. Founded in 1858 by a fugitive rebel, John O'Mahony, the Fenian Brotherhood was an American counterpart to the Ireland-based Irish Republican Brotherhood. Support for the Fenians blossomed at the close of the American Civil War when thousands of Irish-American soldiers were demobilized, which swelled the Fenian ranks. O'Mahony's strategy had concentrated on using the American organization to support an insurrection in Ireland, but during 1865 his leadership had gradually been usurped by William Randall Roberts, chief executive of the newly created Fenian 'senate' and an outspoken advocate of invading British North America as a lever to loosen the British hold on Ireland.[11] Well-armed, well-funded, and (ostensibly) well-trained, the Fenian 'army' turned its attention in the closing months of 1865 to the long, lightly defended borders of British North America.

By February 1866, the swirl of conflicting rumours had made it almost impossible to distinguish between Fenian fact and fiction in the British colonies. News-hungry newspapers scornfully reprinted mainland stories about the 'Finnegans', but their editorial mockery concealed a spreading anxiety. Thus, when the Catholic Young Men's Literary Institute staged a one-sided debate on Fenianism before a packed house at Charlottetown's St. Andrew's Hall on 28 February, and when the principal speaker, Father Angus Macdonald—generally regarded as the Bishop of Charlottetown's mouthpiece on political matters—roundly condemned Fenianism and exhorted Irish Catholics to have nothing to do with it, the denunciations merely convinced many people that Fenianism must be widespread in the colony.[12]

By early March, concern was turning to fear in some quarters. The alarm was so great in several parts of Queen's County that Liberal leader George Coles later claimed 'Many men brought their wives and children to town for safety; and others barricaded their homes, and prepared for a midnight attack, by arming themselves with pitchforks and other implements of husbandry.'[13] Charlottetown, where more than 40 per cent of the population was Irish in origin, hardly felt more secure.[14] 'Firearms of all kinds were in great demand', the Liberal, Catholic *Examiner* jeered. 'Guns which had lain on merchants' shelves for years, now found eager purchasers; and, in short, every preparation was made just as if the Town had been on the eve of a terrific massacre'.[15]

Unlike the Orange Order in other parts of British North America, Prince Edward Island's Orange lodges were largely Scots Presbyterians rather than Irish Protestants and their condemnation of popery was by no means restricted to Irish Catholicism. But Fenianism played heavily on their fears.[16] Galvanized by the rumoured uprising, the local Orange lodges were 'in full blast' that March. A mass meeting of Orangemen was convened, and night watches were organized across the town to ferret out conspiracies.[17] Even allowing for rhetorical hyperbole, it is clear that many people in central Prince Edward Island were panicking.

St. Patrick's Day dawned mild and fair. Down at the barracks, according to partisan accounts that were neither denied nor admitted, 50 soldiers were called out and issued with 60 rounds of ball cartridge each and a cannon was set up on the Barrack Square to disperse any potential attackers.[18] Down at the Police Court, the special constables, Roman Catholics as well as Protestants, reported for duty. Much of the authorities' attention focused on the day's most prominent celebrants, the Benevolent Irish Society (BIS). Founded in 1825 as a non-sectarian charitable organization, the BIS had gradually grown more Catholic in its membership and by the 1860s was generally perceived as a sectarian, overtly Roman Catholic society.[19]

In view of the public mood, the officers of the Benevolent Irish Society decided to forego the traditional St. Patrick's Day march, but the rank-and-file were either ignorant of the decision or ignored it.[20] Preceded by the City Amateur Band (and shadowed by a few Orangemen wearing yellow badges), they marched from St. Andrew's Hall on Pownal Street to morning mass at St. Dunstan's Basilica, where Father William Phelan preached on the manifest virtues of Ireland's saint. They then marched back to the hall, where Father Patrick Doyle proposed three cheers for the Queen and three more for Lieutenant Governor Dundas before they quietly dispersed. That night there was 'miscellaneous entertainment', which ended with a rendition of 'God Save the Queen.'[21] It had all been, the *Examiner* editorialized, 'tame beyond precedent—indeed, it was ridiculously un-Irish.'[22]

II

In the fortnight following the phantom uprising, relief was tempered by political embarrassment in the inevitable backwash of partisan recrimination. The Catholic Liberal press, in particular, paraded the alleged insult to Irish Catholics before its readers. 'Oh what a silly farce was played,/ And met with fitting scorn', rhymed 'Anti-Fenian' in the *Examiner*:

> When Special Constables were made
> To quell a bugbear Fenian raid
> The last St. Patrick's morn.
> Schemers and Terrorists combined,
> With visionary seers,
> To agitate the public mind,
> Which satisfaction seems to find,
> In fabricated fears.[23]

There was nothing for the government to gain by acting sheepish, and in the newspaper exchanges of late March, knee-deep in ridicule, it clung to its dignity. 'As might have been anticipated', the Tory *Islander* began its first report of the incident, 'a wave of Fenian excitement has passed over our Island.' Distinguishing between passive Fenian sympathizers and active supporters, it commented on the 'excitement, at once intense and alarming' that had pervaded the country districts. 'Reason seemed powerless against the alarm which had seized the minds of many of the inhabitants.

. . . Some at least in the city, and many in the country, did, and do believe that Fenian Circles have been organized in our midst.' But while those about them were losing their heads, the editorial concluded, government had maintained a steady approach—choosing prudence over panic.[24]

The newspaper controversy quickly spilled over into the colony's legislature once the spring session opened on 9 April, and speakers there predictably echoed the debating points already rehearsed in the local press. In many ways, the Fenian scare on Prince Edward Island resembled those in neighbouring colonies. On St. Patrick's Day, a rumour had swept Halifax that three Fenian ironclads had left New York to attack the Nova Scotian capital while New Brunswick, which had lived through several panics since December 1865, endured another on the 17th.[25] But timing and geography were crucial. By land and sea, New Brunswick and Nova Scotia were well within the supposed Fenian reach. Prince Edward Island in March, however, was surrounded by 'an almost impassable barrier of ice', so exactly how were these Fenian raiders supposed to get there? And once having pillaged Charlottetown, exactly how were they supposed to escape with their booty?[26] If the Fenians could not come from outside, then Protestants and the all-Protestant government they had elected in the bitter 'no-popery' election of 1863 must fear Fenians from inside the colony. And that meant, as Catholic Liberal George Howlan blustered, that the government suspected Irish Catholics in general, and the Benevolent Irish Society in particular, of wholesale treason. But, he continued, if the government did not really suspect its Irish Catholic citizens of Fenianism, why did it seem willing to let the public believe that they were involved? The handling of the Fenian scare, Howlan charged, was 'a slander on the character of the Irish Roman Catholics of this Colony.'[27]

Not so, protested Conservative assemblymen. The government had neither created nor promoted the Fenian panic. And its anti-Fenian precautions intended no slur against Catholics. 'Surely', said Conservative Frederick de St. Croix Brecken, 'there was no member of the House who would dare, for one moment, to say that there was one single respectable Roman Catholic in the Island connected with such a society, or tinctured with their abominable principles.' Nor, insisted Solicitor General T.H. Haviland, did the government harbour

> suspicions injurious to the loyal or peaceable character of the Irish Society; but they had good reason to believe that there were many in the Island, both Town and country, who strongly sympathized with the Finnegans, and who, in the event of any disturbance arising, would not, had they been provided with arms and ammunition have been slow to avail themselves of an opportunity for violence and rapine. Is it to be supposed that, in a population of 80,000, there are not many of these restless, discontented, and rapacious spirits to be found, as well as in Ireland, America, and England?

It was this element, he continued, and not rank-and-file Catholics, that posed the threat:

> The Government were far from apprehending any concerted or organized outbreak on the part of any portion of the people of that day; but they were very well aware that, besides a few Irish Yankees, there were many idle, loafing vagabonds, loungers at the corners of streets, who, conscious of the prevailing excitement of the day, and, through drunkenness rendered careless of consequences even to themselves, would be on the watch for any opportunity of joining in a row and creating a riot.[28]

And what evidence did the government have of Fenian sympathizers among such 'loose, debauched, and altogether ruffianly characters'?[29] Fenian ballads and Fenian buttons were being openly sold in the capital, which was 'undeniable evidence', charged Brecken, 'that the leven [sic] of treason and disloyalty was too largely diffused amongst us.'[30] It was left to a correspondent in the Liberal *Examiner*, however, to remark on the suspicious resemblances between the typeface used for the Fenian broadsides and the typefaces employed in the printing shop of the *Examiner's* bitter rival, the *Herald*—an insinuation *Herald* officials quickly and angrily denied.[31]

By now, the campaign of exaggerated indignation at supposed aspersion had been overtaken by events in New Brunswick, where the Fenian phantasm at last seemed to be acquiring substance. Stung into action by a factional struggle within the Fenian hierarchy, and in an attempt to regain power within this hierarchy, the O'Mahony wing of the movement ostentatiously massed a modest force along the Maine-New Brunswick border near St. Stephen with the poorly concealed objective of seizing Campobello Island as a bargaining chip and base of operations in British territory. These dramatic developments, which moved the Fenian threat from abstract to actual, provided both the pretext and the context for the extraordinary series of security measures enacted during the following weeks on Prince Edward Island.

On 18 April, Solicitor General Haviland moved that, 'in consequence of the threatened invasion of British North American colonies by bands of Fenian marauders', the House of Assembly place the whole of the colony's public revenues at the disposal of the Executive for purposes of defence. In the debate that followed, members on both sides of the House of Assembly competed in flights of patriotic rhetoric. Prince County member Colin McLennan flew highest: 'I would sooner cover the ground on which I now stand with my dead body', he declared, 'than allow one Fenian to pass by me, in his murderous and sacrilegious career.'[32] Setting aside for the moment the matter of the St. Patrick's Day panic, members focused on the danger ahead once the navigation

season opened and the American mackerel fleet returned to the Gulf of St. Lawrence. As in the other Maritime colonies, the Island's defences were decayed to the point of uselessness, its militia flourished mainly on paper, and only a handful of British soldiers stood between the Island and any Fenian attack. With the Confederate irregulars' 1865 raid on St. Alban's, Vermont, in mind (and, perhaps, the American privateering raid on Charlottetown during the Revolutionary War), Liberal Joseph Hensley warned that 30 to 40 Fenians on a single fishing vessel mounting a 20-pound gun could essentially hold Charlottetown for ransom, rob all the banks, and pillage the town at will. Conservative John Longworth thought this was not only possible, but 'very probable.'[33] Even lush-born Edward Whelan, who for months had been mocking the Fenians and the threat they posed, was caught up in the moment: 'It appears to me that the alarm has taken possession of nearly all the members of the House, and, I must confess, of myself among the number.'[34]

As the debate ended, Premier James C. Pope stood to read a telegram from New Brunswick: an American revenue cutter had just seized a Fenian-chartered schooner, laden with arms, between Portland and Eastport, Maine. Solicitor General Haviland's resolution was then put, and it passed unanimously amid the cheers of a packed visitors' gallery.[35] A few days later, in a much less bellicose mood, the House of Assembly quietly voted the usual sums for the usual purposes.

But the explicitly anti-Fenian measures were only just beginning. At the urging of the lieutenant governor, the House of Assembly followed New Brunswick's lead in over-hauling its militia structure. The nominal roll was divided into the Active Militia (males between the ages of 16 and 45) and the Sedentary Militia (those between 45 and 60). The Active Militia was itself broken down into the Regular Militia and the Volunteer Militia.[36] While three 32-pounder cannon were requisitioned to protect Charlottetown Harbour, the government contracted with a regular army officer to drill the volunteers into a semblance of martial efficiency.[37] Sixty-three years later, George Fall of Crapaud could still remember the weekly military drill that filled the summer of the Fenians in his community.[38]

The likely threat from local and not foreign Fenians inspired the next three bills. On 12 March, Lieutenant Governor Dundas had queried the attorney general about the legal grounds for suppressing seditious literature and secret military drill.[39] The apparent result was An Act to prevent the Concealment of Arms or Munitions of War, intended for unlawful purposes; An Act to prevent the clandestine training of persons to the use of Arms, and to the practice of Military Evolutions; and an Act for the better security of the Crown and Government of the United Kingdom, within this Island.[40] The first two bills were largely self-explanatory, and carried a penalty of two years of imprisonment with or without hard labour.[41] The third embraced those committing, planning, speaking, writing, publishing, advocating, assisting, or contemplating sedition. Conviction carried a sentence of seven years with or without hard labour. Anyone involved in unauthorized military drill—from organizers to those drilling—was liable to prosecution. When it came to the concealment of arms, British legal process was reversed: the burden of proof lay with the accused, who was guilty until proven innocent.

Some might feel such measures were unnecessary on Prince Edward Island conceded Solicitor General Haviland when he introduced the first two acts in the House of Assembly on 30 April, 'but when it would be remembered that a band of Fenians had recently made enquiry in a town in Maine, U.S. to know if they could ship, in fishing schooners, fire-arms, in order to land them on our shores, he thought no objections would be offered to the Bill.'[42] None were, despite the acts' rough trespass on basic legal rights. The House of Assembly meekly endorsed them without recorded debate and they passed into law.[43] Having rallied the house

to defend against a Fenian invasion, the government adjourned the legislative session—the last before the next general election.

On the face of it, what had just happened seems straightforward: infected with the same fear that was sweeping British North America, many Prince Edward Islanders had panicked in March 1866 because they were convinced that a Fenian insurrection was at hand that involved either foreign raiders or local Irish Catholic insurgents or both. The government's reaction had temporarily inflamed sectarian animosities. Then, with Fenians massing on the New Brunswick border, the legislature had armed itself with bills designed to suppress both Fenian raiders and local sympathizers. Yet without denying the potency of the Fenian scare, which had so easily leap-frogged the ice-floes of the Northumberland Strait, another reading of the issue on Prince Edward Island is possible. It is considerably more cynical and is necessarily speculative. It is rooted in the local context of politics in the mid-1860s, and is aimed directly at the general election of February 1867.

III

If, behind the panic and patriotism, the Fenian threat to Prince Edward Island remained stubbornly insubstantial, the civil authorities already faced a genuine and serious challenge to peace and good government in 1866. Launched early in 1864, the Tenant League was a frustrated response to successive governments' failure to legislate a solution to the colony's intractable and by then infamous Land Question. Nearly a century after the British government had divided up almost the entire landmass of Prince Edward Island among less than a hundred 'absentee' proprietors, over half of the colony's lands remained part of large-scale, leasehold estates—a situation that stirred deep resentment among tenants and squatters as well as frustration among the many who considered the anachronistic leasehold system a severe brake on the little colony's development.[44] Both of the colony's two main political parties in the responsible government era had struggled to find politically satisfying solutions that would eliminate leasehold tenure without trespassing unduly on the rights of property. Under George Coles, the Reformers *cum* Liberals passed the Land Purchase Act of 1853—enabling legislation to allow government to purchase estates from consenting proprietors—but it could neither force proprietors to sell nor dictate price. Britain's subsequent refusal to guarantee a £100,000 loan to finance the transactions greatly slowed progress in buying out even those proprietors who might be convinced to sell. The hard kernel of the colony's Conservative party might have been the Island's old Family Compact, but the party had successfully broadened its appeal during the 1850s. When it came to power in 1859 by exploiting sectarian divisions between the Protestant majority and the sizeable Roman Catholic minority, it confronted the leasehold question by appointing a land commission to investigate. But, the commission's recommendation, that the Britain government finance the liquidation of leasehold tenure in the colony, was set aside by the Colonial Office. In the wake of political failure, the popular mood turned away from legislated solutions to the Land Question.[45]

Rejecting both politicians and the political process, the Tenant League's members pledged themselves to withhold their rents until the remaining proprietors consented to sell farms to their tenants at League-defined 'fair' prices— and to support each other's non-compliance. By 1865, the Tenant League had an alleged membership of some 11,000 people in a population of only 80,000. When land agents, supported by the colony's legal apparatus (sheriffs and their deputies), attempted to enforce the rights of property against delinquent tenants, passive resistance turned inexorably towards violence. That August, unable to trust a militia riddled with Tenant Leaguers to enforce

civil law and unwilling to coerce one set of citizens with another, the Conservative government reluctantly called for British troops from Halifax. When their mere presence in Charlottetown failed to quiet discontent in the countryside, the government, even more reluctantly, used them.[46] As British redcoats escorted legal writs into Tenant League strongholds in early October 1865, defiance abruptly lapsed into an 'angry and hostile' acquiescence to the rule of law.[47] On 7 November, making strategy mimic what was already happening, the Tenant League's Central Board resolved that

on account of the high-handed acts of the present Government, in collecting rents at the bayonet's point, and reviving an obsolete law relating to the service of Legal Process, the Central Board permit all tenants belonging to the union to satisfy their landlords' claims for the present, if they are disposed to do so. Rather than witness the scenes of misery, cruelty and bloodshed that would probably follow from collecting rents by a military force, they recommend tenants to commit no breach of the law.[48]

In January 1866, those arrested during the Tenant League disturbances of the previous summer were tried and sentenced without incident.[49]

But was the Tenant League crushed or merely cowed? Lacking any concrete evidence either way, the government thought it best to retain the two companies of British infantry sent to Charlottetown the previous July. But while it craved British troops to help smother any 'smouldering embers of discontent', the government did not want to pay for it, and in 1865–66 a furious row, couched in the polite language of diplomatic discourse, raged with the Colonial Office over who should bear the expense of transporting, quartering, and employing the soldiers. The Prince Edward Island government was willing to pay for transporting the troops to the colony and for sending them out into the countryside (and for the barracks that had to be built to house them), but not for ordinary wages and maintenance. The Colonial Office maintained that if the colony wished to use British troops as a police force, it should bear all expenses.[50]

And so, with a general election less than a year away, the Conservative government found itself in a political quandary. Using British infantry to help serve writs and collect rent may have reassured proprietors and British officials but, in a colony where the vast majority of voters were tenants, squatters, or small freeholders, it was electoral suicide. Yet further coercion, legal as well as military, might still be necessary to smash the Tenant League. Then along came the Fenians. Not only did the Fenian scare provide an external threat to justify Britain keeping—and, perhaps, paying for—troops on Prince Edward Island, but it also provided a convenient justification for the sweeping security measures passed during the spring legislative session. Thus, Colonial Office officials might wish they could recall the two companies stationed in Charlottetown to help ward off potential Fenian raids in New Brunswick, 'but, on the other hand, there may be Fenians, who want keeping in order, on P. E. Isld.'[51] And when Lieutenant Governor Dundas forwarded to London the text of the act outlawing 'clandestine training and drilling', someone at the Colonial Office scribbled in the margin, 'The Act is available agt. Fenians or agt. the Tenant League.'[52]

While British authorities might make such observations, for obvious political reasons these were not publicly made on Prince Edward Island. The ruling Conservatives had everything to lose and the Liberals nothing to gain by publicizing a link between anti-Fenian measures and the campaign against the Tenant League. Both parties had officially denounced the Tenant League's challenge to civil government, but it was the government that stood to pay the heaviest price at the polls for calling in the troops. That realization probably prevented the Conservatives from trying to exploit

the known divisions within the Liberal camp when it came to the Tenant League movement. For their part, Liberal leaders may have denounced the Tenant League's *modus operandi*, but the Liberal Party stood to gain Tenant League votes. Better for the Conservatives if they could set some distance between their dealings with the Tenant League and the next election. Better for the Liberals to hammer away at the government's mishandling of the Land Question, which had driven tenants to such dangerous and deluded misconduct, rather than confronting the league directly.[53] And better for both parties if the various security measures introduced in the spring of 1866 focused on the Fenians and not the members of the Tenant League. Admittedly, identifying the political advantage of exploiting the transient Fenian threat as something that might also prove useful in suppressing the Tenant League does not prove that this was the underlying reason. Since it did not serve the interests of the opposition Liberals to press the point, since there was little to be gained by emphasizing it to the Colonial Office, and since private papers, the most likely place to raise such considerations, are scant for the principals involved, hard evidence is lacking and the connection must therefore remain speculative.

Of course, it was also possible that the Fenian movement might have infiltrated the Tenant League. While the league's leadership was predominantly English in ethnic origin, many among the rank-and-file were Irish Catholics, and some of these were first-generation immigrants who might be expected to sympathize with the Fenian agenda. Certainly, 'A Native of P. E. Island' thought so. Writing 15 years after the fact in a virulently anti-Irish pamphlet entitled *Fenianism, Irish land Leagueism, and Communism*, he freely mixed land reform with Irish insurrection: 'And so inherent was the spirit of rebellion and agrarianism in [Irish emigrants], that at one time in the Island old settlers had reason to suspect that a general uprising of the Irish Catholic malcontents was in contemplation to carry out

Irish land league principles, when a division of farms and other property was to have been made among the aggressive victors. This also would have been an act of patriotism for the redress of Ireland's wrongs!'[54]

Yet no one was publicly making that connection in 1866. It is significant that in the contentious exchanges over the Fenian insurrection that was to have occurred during the annual St. Patrick's Day procession, no one in either the press or the House of Assembly ever mentioned the obvious parallel to events of the previous St. Patrick's Day when several hundred Tenant Leaguers had paraded through Charlottetown with banners flying and music blaring. When Deputy Sheriff James Curtis tried to arrest one of the marchers, Sam Fletcher, for arrears of debt, the Tenant Leaguers set upon Curtis, knocked him down, and rescued Fletcher.[55] A year later, the silence was deafening. If anyone was equating Fenianism with Tenant League extremism, they were not saying so; political debate carefully compartmentalized the two issues.

The Conservatives were less wary of harnessing the Fenian menace to another of the era's great questions. Religion, specifically, the place of religion in the colony's public education system, had engendered a vicious cycle of sectarian conflict on mid-century Prince Edward Island. Three times in the previous eight years, the Tory party had successfully exploited fears of Catholic domination to rally a solid bloc of Protestant support at the hustings.[56] It was a dangerous and socially divisive strategy in such a small and physically integrated community, since sectarian emotions were difficult to control once aroused, but it had worked. Would it work again?

The Liberals, who traditionally relied on the Irish Catholic tenant vote, professed to see in the Conservative response to the Fenian scare another appeal to denominational prejudice. Stripping the militia of its arms, mobilizing the garrison, mounting a citizens' guard over the Benevolent Irish Society, and generally giving credence to the St. Patrick's Day panic: all were portrayed as a studied insult, inviting Protestants to suspect their Irish Catholic neighbours. In the press and the legislature, the Liberals employed a strategy of exposing subterfuge. 'The whole', wrote John Roberts to the *Examiner,* 'was a political dodge to revive the religious bitterness which has so lately disgraced the Christianity of the Colony.'[57] Editorials in the Tory *Islander* subtly seconded the Liberal accusation even while denying it. The disaffection in Ireland that had fostered the Fenian movement, it observed in an editorial dismissing the St. Patrick's Day panic, 'is really not Celt against Saxon, but of Roman Catholic against Protestant.'[58]

But if Conservative strategists on Prince Edward Island really were contemplating another appeal to entrenched sectarianism, the Fenian scare proved too flimsy a pretext. In New Brunswick, the pro-Confederation faction had successfully equated Catholic New Brunswickers with Fenianism.[59] But the situation was fundamentally different on Prince Edward Island. While 44 per cent of the colonists were Roman Catholics, Irish Catholics were neither the most numerous nor the most influential. Not counting a sizable Acadian Catholic minority, as many Catholics were Highland Scots as Irish,[60] and the clerical leadership within the Diocese of Charlottetown was both solidly Scottish and publicly anti-Fenian. In New Brunswick, the leading Catholic politician, Timothy Anglin, was tarred with accusations of being a Fenian sympathizer, but Prince Edward Island's most prominent Catholic public man, Edward Whelan, had repeatedly condemned the Fenian movement in the pages of his newspaper, *The Examiner.*[61] Even if the Conservatives could convince public opinion that many among the Irish Catholics were Fenian sympathizers, it would be difficult to smear the larger Catholic community with the Fenian brush. In balancing political risk, the certainty of alienating Catholic voters might well outweigh the possibility of enlisting Protestant ones.

It was even more unlikely that the Fenian threat might be used to persuade the population of the benefits of Confederation. In New Brunswick, where Confederation already had a reasonable base of support, the issue had considerable traction and certainly contributed to the breakdown of Albert Smith's anti-Confederation coalition in the spring of 1866.[62] In the same climate of fear and uncertainty, Charles Tupper would slip a quasi-endorsement of Confederation through the Nova Scotia legislature.[63] But on Prince Edward Island almost no one favoured union, which offered the colony so little but would cost so much in terms of lost power and resources. It would take more than a fleeting Fenian scare to shake Islanders out of their anti-Confederate convictions. Nor was the Conservative government inclined to try. It was already badly divided on the Confederation issue. Ex-premier John Hamilton Gray, who had hosted the Charlottetown Conference in 1864, had been forced out of office over his support for union in a dispute that had also driven anti-Confederate Edward Palmer out of the Executive Council, leaving anti-Confederate James Colledge Pope as premier. From the fringes of his party, Gray discounted the Fenian menace but warned of a post-Reciprocity falling out with the Americans.[64] Of the other executive councillors, only T.H. Haviland, Jr., the solicitor general, and W.H. Pope, the colonial secretary and brother of the premier, were ardent Confederates. They were clearly out of temper with the mood of their party. Responding to pro-union pressure from the British Colonial Office, the 1866 session defiantly endorsed the famous 'No Terms' resolutions, declaring that nothing could persuade Islanders to contemplate Confederation.[65]

In the end, W.H. Pope was the only Conservative to use the Fenian threat as a pro-union lever. During the 'No Terms' debate, Edward Whelan, one of the only Liberal Confederates, had justified Confederation as a means to help defend the colony against Fenian or American aggression. It was more likely, rebutted other members, that local militiamen would be sacrificed to fend off attacks on more vulnerable colonies.[66] Pope, who had been absent on a trade mission to Latin America during the session, took up Whelan's argument. In a passionate letter to the Charlottetown *Patriot* (which he forwarded to the Colonial Office), he decried the defenceless state of the colony. Despite the extravagant patriotism of the spring session, he claimed, practically nothing had been done to protect the colony in the intervening period. Echoing the debates of April, Pope stated: 'If a pinnace, carrying armed Fenians, and provided with a couple of guns, were seen approaching our harbor, could we, without the assistance of the regular troops, prevent the Fenians from landing and plundering the capital? I assert that we could not.'[67]

But by this time Pope was in no position to influence policy. Citing irreconcilable differences with his party on the Confederation issue, Pope resigned from the government in the aftermath of the 'No Terms' resolution—further weakening an already divided administration.[68] In any case, his Confederation-for-defence arguments found more favour with the Colonial Office than with readers of the *Patriot*, who remained resolutely anti-union. The Fenian Scare could no more further Confederation than it could unite Protestants or make tenants forget that their government had used soldiers against them.

IV

In June 1866, when the Fenian sword finally fell—in Canada West and then East—excited crowds gathered outside the telegraph office in Charlottetown to learn the latest news about the defence of Canada. 'That there were no sympathizers with the Fenians among the crowds which surrounded these offices, it is impossible to say', *The Islander* editorialized.[69] But there was no sudden relapse into panic on Prince Edward Island, no public appeals for Royal Navy protection against Fenian raiders disguised as American mackerel schooners, and no exhortations to the volunteer militia that had been dutifully drilling in the colony's defence. Even as the Fenian moment climaxed in British North America, it had already passed on Prince Edward Island. It was not that the long-expected blow had fallen elsewhere or even that the 'invasion' had turned out to be a pair of bungled raids. Instead, it may be argued, the Fenian Scare had always been less an external threat than a domestic phenomenon, sustained in the loud echo of a non-event by the short-term electoral needs of a deeply unpopular and fatally divided Conservative government as well as the necessity of trying to crush the Tenant League's challenge to the prevailing social order.

One by one, the trial balloons the Tories had floated with the hot air of the Fenian conspiracy popped. And, by late 1866, it was apparent to all observers that the Tenant League movement had truly collapsed. The three Tenant Leaguers sentenced to prison in January were released that August. Shortly afterwards, the league's Central Board, which had continued to meet monthly through the summer, quietly lapsed. Although there was no more resistance to rent collection, special pleading and ever more specious arguments from the provincial government kept the British regulars on the Island for another winter until after the following general election; local officials argued the troops were needed to prevent a resurgence of Tenant League sympathy at the hustings.[70] Confirmation of the Tenant League's collapse made the homeland security measures seem less urgent as well. They remained on the books, but were not employed.

In October 1866 a guest editorial in the *Islander* asked, 'Is There Any Danger of a Roman Catholic Ascendancy on This Island?'[71] The editorialist 'G. S.' thought there was, but neither Protestant nor Roman Catholic readers rose to the bait. It was left up to the grand secretary of the Orange Order's Provincial Grand Lodge to lament the devotional declension

from the Orange cause since 'the morbid state of excitement of last year, when Fenianism and incendiarism were keeping all awake and at their posts.'[72] In the tangle of overlapping, often conflicting loyalties that defined the Island community, the 'religious card' failed to trump residual Tenant League sympathies. Sectarian loyalties would play little role in the forthcoming elections.

The Legislative Council elections in December 1866 went badly for the Conservatives, and in the general election that followed in February 1867 they were badly beaten by George Coles's Liberals.[73] In reporting the results, Lieutenant Governor Dundas offered two main reasons: internal divisions within the Conservative party over Confederation and the government's suppression of the Tenant League.[74] By the time fresh sectarian discord destroyed the Liberal ascendancy in 1870, the Fenians were planning their last, desperate forays into British America (brief incursions into Quebec and Manitoba). Already, on Prince Edward Island, they were well on their way to historical oblivion. Distance would reduce them to absurdity and then obscurity.

In parsing the 'Fenian Scare' on Prince Edward Island, it is important to distinguish between the genuine panic of March 1866 and the manner in which politicians then sought to exploit it. In the spring of 1866, the ruling Conservatives were a fragile party desperately in search of a platform. Several of its leaders tested the Fenian issue, but motivating fear of an actual insurrection quickly evaporated, and none of the various local applications of Fenianism—sectarian loyalties, camouflage for suppression of the Tenant League, support for Confederation—offered much political traction. The Fenian Scare faded, then, not just because Islanders had regained their nerve but because the Fenian issue had little political utility. That Islanders had panicked at all is a needful reminder that communal fear is only tangentially tied to measurable reality. That the government would try to exploit the panic is a reminder that political strategy is less often grand design than intelligent improvization. And that the Fenian menace mutated as it did in the Island milieu is a salutary reminder of the unique ways in which transnational issues collide with local ones, imparting energy and direction to both.

NOTES

1. See, for example, militia veteran John A. Macdonald's sober account, *Troublous Tunes in Canada: A History of the Fenian Raids of 1866 and 1870* (Toronto: W.S. Johnston, 1910).

2. The argument is made most forcibly, perhaps, in P.B. Waite. *The Life and Times of Confederation, 1864–1867: Politics. Newspapers, and the Union of British North America* (Toronto: University of Toronto Press, 1962), 263–76; but see also W.L. Morton, *The Critical Years: The Union of British North America, 1857–1873* (Toronto: McClelland & Stewart, 1964), 190–2. Even revisionist accounts of Confederation, such as Christopher Moore, *1867: How the Fathers Made a Deal* (Toronto: McClelland & Stewart, 1997), 183–84 and Ged Martin, ed., *The Causes of Canadian Confederation* (Fredericton: Acadiensis Press, 1990), follow the same line (although they are not much concerned with the Fenians' role).

3. In the expedient logic of pro-Confederation propaganda in New Brunswick, for a Catholic voter to be anti-Confederate was to be pro-Fenian. See Harold A. Davis, 'The Fenian Raid in New Brunswick', *Canadian Historical Review* 36, no. 4 (1955): 316–34 and especially William M. Baker, 'Squelching the Disloyal, Fenian-Sympathizing Brood: T.W. Anglin and Confederation in New Brunswick, 1865–66', *Canadian Historical Review* 55, no. 2 (1974): 141–58. During the Centennial era, especially, when the über-topic of Confederation resonated through Canadian historiography, academics took the Fenian issue more seriously. See, for example, the following classic nationalist school histories: W.L. Morton, *The Critical Years: The Union of British North America, 1857–1874, Canadian Centenary Series* (Toronto: McClelland & Stewart, 1964); P.B. Waite, *The Life and Time of Confederation, 1864–67: Politics, Newspapers, and the Union of British North America* (Toronto: University of Toronto Press, 1962); and Donald Creighton,

The Road to Confederation: The Emergence of Canada, 1863–1967 (Boston: Houghton Mifflin, 1964). For a useful, if superficial, overview of the Fenian scare in Nova Scotia, see James M. Cameron 'Fenian Times in Nova Scotia', *Nova Scotia Historical Society Collections* 37 (1970): 103–52. Hereward Senior addresses Quebec's attitudes in 'Quebec and the Fenians', *Canadian Historical Review* 48, no. 1 (1967): 26–44. More comprehensive Fenian narratives followed, and prominent among them are Hereward Senior, *The Fenians and Canada* (Toronto: Macmillan of Canada, 1978) and W.S. Neidhardt, *Fenianism in North America* (University Park and London: Pennsylvania State University Press, 1975). For a contemporary popular rendering of the Fenian issue, see the exhibit at Founders' Hall, the packaged version of Confederation on display in Charlottetown, Prince Edward Island. In an attraction that is admittedly 'history lite', the Fenian threat is treated in comic fashion.

4. For the military dimension see, for example, Robert L. Dallison, *Turning Back the Fenians: New Brunswick's Last Colonial Campaign* (Fredericton: Goose Lane Editions and New Brunswick Military Heritage Project, 2006) and Hereward Senior, *The Last Invasion of Canada: The Fenian Raids, 1866–1870* (Toronto: Dundurn Press and Canadian War Museum, 1991). On the religious front, see Oliver Rafferty, 'Fenianism in North America in the 1860s: The Problems for Church and State', *America: History and Life* 84, no. 274 (April 1999): 257–77. An Irish-Canadian preoccupation underpins the traditional interpretive line in Peter Berresford Ellis, 'Ridgeway, the Fenian Raids and the Making of Canada', in *The Untold Story: The Irish in Canada,* ed. Robert O'Driscoll and Lorna Reynolds, vol. 1 (Toronto: Celtic Arts of Canada, 1988), 537–53.

5. In fact, it is probably safe to say that most historians remain unaware that there even was a Fenian scare on Prince Edward Island. Even

in Island historiography the Fenians hardly merit mention. In his *Prince Edward Island and Confederation* (Charlottetown: St. Dunstan's University Press, 1964), F.W.P. Bolger concentrates on how the generic Fenian threat was used in the Confederation debate in the Island legislature. Brendan O'Grady downplays the Island dimensions in *Exiles and Islanders: The Irish Settlers of Prince Edward Island* (Montreal and Kingston: McGill-Queen's University Press, 2004), 182–3. Otherwise, aside from David Webber, *A Thousand Young Men: The Colonial Volunteer Militia of Prince Edward Island, 1775–1874* (Charlottetown: Prince Edward Island Museum and Heritage Foundation, 1990), the only references that come within historical hailing distance of the incident are the following: J.H. Meacham & Co.'s *Illustrated Historical Atlas of Prince Edward Island* (1880) contains a brief 'Historical Sketch' by an anonymous author that gives a whole paragraph to the Fenians, but only one sentence to the 'extraordinary apprehensions of disturbance' that swept the Island in the late winter of 1866; J.B. Pollard's *Historical Sketch of the Eastern Regions of New France . . .* (Charlottetown: 1898) makes a bare mention of it; and 'A Native of P. E. Island', *Fenianism, Irish Land Leagueism, and Communism* (Halifax, 1881), references the Fenian scare but not by name.

6. This account is a composite of the congruent versions given in 'How Fenian Scares Originate', (Charlottetown) *Herald*, 4 April 1866, which supplied the nickname, and the *Debates and Proceedings of the House of Assembly of Prince Edward Island, 1866*, 56–61, which surnames him 'Stumbles' and describes him variously as a 'half-witted schoolmaster' and 'the crazed domine.' *The Journal of the House of Assembly of Prince Edward Island for 1867*, Appendix C (Warrant Book), supplied his full name and most recent school, but records only one quarterly salary payment for 1866 (in January).

7. 'How Fenian Scares Originate', *Herald*, 4 April 1866.

8. Haviland did not deny this. His version of the episode, delivered in the House of Assembly, did not differ significantly from the *Herald's* account, except in tone. See *Debates and Proceedings, 1866*, 60–1. He also offered the alternate explanation of intemperance for Stumbles' condition.

9. *Debates and Proceedings, 1867*, 56, 60. The government had in mind, perhaps, one particular militia unit—Charlottetown's Irish Rifles.

10. As observed by T.H. Haviland, Jr., see the summary of transactions in *Debates and Proceedings, 1866*, 14.

11. For a précis of the internal split in the Fenian Brotherhood, see Ellis, 'Ridgeway, the Fenian Raids and the Making of Canada', *The Untold Story,* 540.

12. 'Fenianism', (Charlottetown) *Examiner,* 5 March 1866. This was the second denunciation in two weeks. Father Angus, rector of St. Dunstan's College and president of the institute, had kicked off the institute's lecture season on 14 February with 'Ireland and the Fenians'; see 'Catholic Young Men's Literary Institute', *Examiner,* 19 February 1866. The larger position of the North American episcopacy was a little more ambivalent. Although Archbishop Thomas Connolly of Halifax had publicly condemned the Fenians, American bishops were wary of antagonizing the United States government, which seemed pro-Fenian. See Rafferty, 'Fenianism in North America in the 1860s', 259–60. For the claim that Macdonald's denunciation only made matters worse, see 'The Fenian Alarm', (Charlottetown) *Islander,* 23 March 1866 as well as *Herald,* 7 March 1866.

13. *Debates and Proceedings, 1867,* 60. Similarly, David Ross, who farmed on the Hillsborough River near Charlottetown, tersely noted in an undated entry within his 1866 diary: 'Fenian excitement. Fear of an invasion.' See David Ross Diary, transcript, PEI Collection, Robertson Library, University of PEI.

14. O'Grady, *Exiles and Islanders*, 195.

15. 'The Latest Fenian Scare', *Examiner*, 19 March 1866.

16. Although founded in 1851, the Orange Lodge expanded rapidly during the sectarian quarrels of 1856–63. See Ian Ross Robertson, 'Party Politics and Religious Controversialism in Prince Edward Island from 1860 to 1863', *Acadiensis* VII, no, 2 (Spring 1978): 29–59.

17. 'The Latest Fenian Scare', *Examiner*, 21 March 1866. In his remarks in the House of Assembly, George Coles used much the same language. See *Debates and Proceedings, 1866,* 50.

18. The allegations about the mobilization of British regulars appear in 'The Latest Fenian Scare', *Examiner*, 19 March 1866.

19. Brendan O'Grady, *Exiles and Islanders: The Irish Settlers of Prince Edward Island* (Montreal: McGill-Queen's University Press, 2004), 177–8.

20. 'The Latest Fenian Scare', *Examiner*, 19 March 1866.

21. 'St. Patrick's Day', *Herald*, 21 March 1866.

22. 'The Latest Fenian Scare', *Examiner*, 19 March 1866.

23. 'Impromptu on Reading "The Examiner" of the 19th', *Examiner*, 26 March 1866.

24. 'The Fenian Alarm', *Islander*, 23 March 1866.

25. As cited in James M. Cameron, 'Fenian Times in Nova Scotia', *Collections of the Nova Scotia Historical Society* 37 (1970): 120–4 and Dallison, *Turning Back the Fenians*, 26–9.

26. See, for example, 'St. Patrick's Day', *Herald*, 21 March 1866 and speeches by Liberals Joseph Hensley and Edward Whelan, *Debates and Proceedings, 1866*, 69–70.

27. *Debates and Proceedings, 1866*, 14, 56–7. The minutiae of the debates in the House of Assembly betray the gradations of position within the colony's still-fragile party system. In seconding the insult offered Irish Catholics, more moderate (and less 'Catholic') Liberals chose to dwell on the effect rather than the intent. See, for example, comments by George Coles and Edward Whelan, *Debates and Proceedings, 1866*, 60, 70.

28. *Debates and Proceedings, 1866*, 70, 60.

29. The quote is excerpted from remarks by Executive Councillor John Longworth, *Debates and Proceedings, 1866*, 68. Longworth essentially reiterated Haviland's defence.

30. *Debates and Proceedings, 1866*, 70. The Examiner ('Hop-and-Go-Fetch-It', 26 March 1866) identified the seller as 'the keeper of a small Variety Shop on the East side of Queen Street (who is supposed to be Irish Catholic).' This may have been James McCraith, an Irish Catholic immigrant who had a grocery on Queen Street near Sydney Street. McCraith is listed on the census return for Charlottetown, Ward 5, in 1861, and appears in *Hutchinson's Prince Edward Island Directory*, 1864, 102. On St. Patrick's Day, according to James Warburton (*Debates and Proceedings, 1866*, 58) 'three or four young men', none of them Catholics, had broken his windows. See as well Aggie-Rose Reddin,

comp. 'The Reddins of Prince Edward Island' (unpublished typescript, 2005), 210–11.

31. See 'Fenian Treason', a letter from 'A Briton' in Examiner, 19 March 1866; *Herald*, 21 March 1866; and, again, 'A Briton' to editor, *Examiner*, 26 March 1866 as well as the editorial squib, 'Hop-and-Go-Fetch-It', *Examiner*, 26 March 1866. The *Herald* claimed that Whelan was, in fact, 'A Briton', an allegation Whelan ridiculed but did not deny. It is instructive here to distinguish between Edward Whelan's *Examiner*, and Edward Reilly's *Herald* vis-à-vis Fenianism. Both were Liberal newspapers, but Reilly had emerged as Whelan's undeclared rival for the colony's Irish-Catholic vote. Reilly walked a fine line editorially. Since he wished to curry favour with Peter MacIntyre, the Bishop of Charlottetown, he repeatedly disassociated Fenianism from Catholicism, but, in deliberate contrast to Whelan, was generally non-committal about Fenianism itself to avoid alienating potential sympathizers among Irish Islanders. See Ian Ross Robertson's profiles of Whelan and Reilly in the *Dictionary of Canadian Biography* Online: Whelan at http://www.biographi.ca/EN/Show Bio.asp?BioId=38892&query=Edward%20 AND%20Whelan and Reilly at http://www. biographi.ca/EN/ShowBio.asp?BioId.39346& query=Edward%2AND%20Reilly as well as Edward MacDonald, '"My Dear Clark": Edward Whelan and the Elections of 1867', *The Island Magazine*, 52 (Fall/Winter 2002): 19–28.

32. *Debates and Proceedings, 1866*, 16, 94.

33. *Debates and Proceedings, 1866*, 98 (for Hensley's statement) and 93 (for Longworth's). Other speakers concurred, including Col. J.H. Gray, the House of Assembly's ranking military expert. See *Debates and Proceedings, 1866*, 94. The same point is made in W.H. Pope to Earl of Carnarvon, 14 August 1866, The National Archives (TNA): Public Record Office (PRO) Colonial Office (CO) 226/102/294.

34. *Debates and Proceedings, 1866*, 95.

35. *Debates and Proceedings, 1866*, 17.

36. Address of Lt. Gov. George Dundas at Opening of Legislature, 9 April 1866, TNA: PRO CO 226/102/118; 29 Vict., c. 32. See, too, David Webber, *A Thousand Young Men*, 101–3.

37. Dundas to Edward Cardwell, 5 June 1866. TNA: PRO CO 226/102/221.

38. 'Gene Autumn' [George Fall], 'My Life in Crapaud', *Morning Guardian*, 9 November 1929, 14. Fall is identified, and his article re-printed, in Crapaud Women's Institute, comp., *History of Crapaud* (n.p.: n.p., 1955).

39. George D. Atkinson to Attorney General, 12 March 1866, RG 1, series 4, subseries 1, vol. 6, Letterbooks, 1859–1869, Provincial Archives and Records Office of Prince Edward Island (PARO). Atkinson wrote at the direction of Governor Dundas, following up on a conversation held on 7 March.

40. *Acts of the Legislature of Prince Edward Island, 1866*, 39 Vict., c. 3; 39 Vict., c. 8; and 39 Vict., c. 9. The act dealing with the concealment of weapons was introduced in the Legislative Council while the other two bills originated in the House of Assembly.

41. Those guilty of clandestine military training were also subject to a fine.

42. *Debates and Proceedings, 1866*, 39. In remarks attached to the 'better security' act, Attorney-General Edward Palmer justified it to the British Colonial Office by citing 'circumstances which have recently transpired in the neighbouring Provinces', See 'Remarks of the Attorney-General of Prince Edward Island on the Acts of the said Island passed on the 20th April and 11 May 1866', TNA: PRO CO 226/102/401.

43. See *Debates and Proceedings, 1866*, 39–40, 51 as well as *Assembly Journals, 1866*, 77, 94, 109. No formal division is recorded.

44. The historical literature on the Land Question is voluminous but still capable of new insights. The most recent contributions to the literature include Rusty Bittermann, *Rural Protest on Prince Edward Island from British Colonization to the Escheat Movement* (Toronto: University of Toronto Press, 2006), which emphasizes the depth and breadth of rural protest but stops well short of the 1860s and Rusty Bittermann and Margaret McCallum, *Lady Landlords of Prince Edward Island: Imperial Dreams and the Defence of Property* (Montreal: McGill-Queen's University Press, 2008), which canvasses the Tenant League era, but from a British proprietorial point of view.

45. The best short summary is probably the introduction in Ian Ross Robertson, ed., *Prince Edward Island Land Commission of 1860* (Fredericton: Acadiensis Press, 1988).

46. The most meticulous and comprehensive treatment of the Tenant League is Ian Ross Robertson, *The Tenant League of Prince Edward Island, 1864–67* (Toronto: University of Toronto Press, 1996). See also Robertson, 'The *Posse Comitatus* Incident of 1865', *The Island Magazine* 24 (Fall/Winter 1988): 3–10 and Peter McGuigan, 'Tenants and Troopers: The Hazel Grove Road, 1865–68', *The Island Magazine* 32 (Fall/Winter 1992): 22–8. The argument against using the militia to enforce property rights appears in Robert Hodgson, Administrator, to Edward Cardwell, 2 August 1865. *Journal of the House of Assembly*, 1866, Appendix G.

47. The use of troops and the tenants' reaction is described in Robert Hodgson to Edward Cardwell, 25 October 1865, TNA: PRO CO 226/101/489.

48. 'Tenant League Literature', *Examiner*, 27 November 1865.

49. See, for example. *Islander*, 2 February 1866.

50. The Island government's position is laid out in a memorandum from Executive Council to Edward Cardwell, 17 October 1865, TNA: PRO CO 226/101/496. The Colonial Office hoped to use the prospect of heavy military expenditure to soften the Island government's opposition to Confederation. See Lieutenant Governor George Dundas to Edward Cardwell (confidential), 25 August 1865, TNA: PRO CO 226/101/664. Dispatches pertaining to the issue were tabled in the legislature; see *Journals of the House of Assembly*, 1867, Appendix K. Lieutenant Governor Dundas's reference to 'smouldering embers of discontent' can be found there in a letter to the Duke of Buckingham and Chandos, dated 2 April 1867. Appendix K.

51. The comment, initialled and dated 29 March 1866, is appended to a letter from the Undersecretary of State for War Office to the Under Secretary of State, Colonial Office, dated 27 March 1866, about who should incur the cost of the troops while in the field. See TNA: PRO CO 226/102/537.

52. TNA: PRO CO 226/102/405.

53. The Liberal strategy is evidenced in *Debates and Proceedings, 1866*, 11–4, 23–6.

54. 'A Native of P. E. Island', *Fenianism, Irish Land Leagueism, and Communism* (1881), 14. It is hard to know how representative such arch-conservative opinions might have been.

55. The event is recounted in Robertson, 'The *Posse Comitatus* Incident of 1865', 5–6.

56. This situation is dissected in Ian Ross Robertson, 'The Bible Question in Prince Edward Island from 1856 to 1860', *Acadiensis* V. no. 2 (Spring 1976): 3–25 and Robertson, 'Party Politics and Religious Controversialism in Prince Edward Island from 1860 to 1863', *Acadiensis* VII, no. 2 (Spring 1978): 29–59.

57. John Roberts to Editor. *Examiner*, 26 March 1866. A similar accusation is articulated in 'St. Patrick's Day', *Herald*, 21 March 1866.

58. 'The Fenian Alarm', *Islander*, 23 March 1866. Government spokesmen in the House of Assembly repeatedly denied any imputation of Irish Catholic disloyalty; see remarks by Premier J.C. Pope. Solicitor General T.H. Haviland, Jr., J.H. Gray, John Longworth, and John Brecken in *Debates and Proceedings, 1866*, 14, 56, 60–1, 63, 68, 70.

59. William M. Baker, '"Squelching the Disloyal, Fenian-Sympathizing Brood"', *Canadian Historical Review* 55, no. 2 (June 1972): 141–58.

60. G. Edward MacDonald, *The History of St. Dunstan's University, 1855–1956* (Charlottetown: Board of Governors of St. Dunstan's University and Prince Edward Island Museum and Heritage Foundation, 1989): 53, 67(n. 16). There were about 7,000 Acadians, while the Irish and Scots communities totalled roughly 12,000–12,500 people.

61. For New Brunswick and Anglin, see Baker, '"Squelching the Disloyal, Fenian-Sympathizing Brood"', 146–7; for Whelan, see Robertson's profile in the *Dictionary of Canadian Biography Online*, http://www.biographi.ca/EN/ShowBio. asp?BioId=38892&query=Edward%20 AND%20Whelan.

62. The coalition was already weakened by the failure of its 'western extension' railway policy, meant to link Saint John to the American railway network and the loss of reciprocity with the United States. See A.G. Bailey, 'The Basis and Persistence of Opposition to Confederation in New Brunswick', in *Culture and Nationality: Essays by A.G. Bailey* (Toronto: McClelland & Stewart, 1972), 93–118.

63. Waite, *Life and Times of Confederation*, 269–71.

64. *Assembly Debates, 1866*, 63, 111–2.

65. The best summary of the Island debate on Confederation remains Bolger, *Prince Edward Island and Confederation*. The debates in the 1866 session are summarized on pages 138–47. The vote in the House of Assembly was 21–7; in the Legislative Council it was unanimous.

66. As summarized in Bolger, *Prince Edward Island and Confederation*, 142–3.

67. W.H. Pope to Earl of Carnarvon, 14 August 1866, TNA: PRO CO 226/102/294–97. He attached an off-print of his letter to the *Patriot*, 'The Military Defences of Prince Edward Island.'

68. Ian Ross Robertson, 'Pope, William Henry', *Dictionary of Canadian Biography Online*, http://www.biographi.ca/009004-119.01-e.php?&id_ nbr=5212&&PHPSESSID=jch0a10vfb37bi5 3bf17c21rl1; W.H. Pope to George Dundas, 26 May 1866, TNA: PRO CO 226/102/215. No issues of the *Patriot* for this period are extant. Pope first resigned in September 1865, but had been persuaded to stay on. See Robert Hodgson, Administrator, to W.H. Pope, 5 September 1865, and Pope to Hodgson, 5 September 1865, both in W.H. Pope Papers, reel 3078, PARO.

69. See, for example, 'The Fenian Invasion of British Territory at Last!' *Examiner*, 4 June 1866; 'The Fenian Raid', *Examiner*, 11 June 1866; and 'The Fenian Invasion of Canada', *Islander*, 8 June 1866.

70. Dundas to Carnarvon, 7 September 1866, TNA: PRO CO 226/102/306.

71. 'G. S.', 'Is There Any Danger of a Roman Catholic Ascendancy on This Island?' Islander, 12 October 1866.

72. *Report of the Sixth Annual Session of the Provincial Grand Lodge, Loyal Orange Institution of Prince Edward Island* (Charlottetown: n.p., 1867). The date given for the meeting is 14 February 1866, but this appears to be an error, since the reprinted speeches reference Fenian raids that took place in June 1866.

73. Ian Ross Robertson notes the Tories' loss of rural Queen's County over the Land Question was the tipping point in the election. That the Fenian scare was deepest there may help explain Conservative interest in exploiting the issue. See Robertson, 'Political Realignment in Pre-Confederation Prince Edward Island, 1863–1870', *Acadiensis* XV, no. 1 (Autumn 1985): 41–3.

74. Dundas to Earl of Carnarvon, 5 March 1867, TNA: PRO CO 226/103/35. In many ridings, electors forced all candidates to pledge not to vote for Confederation in the future without first going to the polls.